Fieldwork in the Library

A Guide to Research in Anthropology and Related Area Studies

R. C. Westerman

American Library Association

Chicago and London

1994

Cover and text design by Dianne M. Rooney

Composed by Publishing Services, Inc.
in Times and Avant Garde
on Xyvision/Linotype L330

Printed on 50-pound Glatfelter, a pH-neutral
stock, and bound in 10-point C1S cover
stock by Braun-Brumfield, Inc.

The paper used in this publication meets the minimum requirements of American National Standard for Information Sciences—Permanence of Paper for Printed Library Materials, ANSI Z39.48–1984.∞

Library of Congress Cataloging-in-Publication Data

Westerman, R. C. (Robert C.)
Fieldwork in the library : a guide to research in anthropology and related area studies / by R. C. Westerman.
p. cm.
Includes index.
ISBN 0-8389-0632-X (acid-free paper)
1. Reference books—Anthropology—Bibliography. 2. Anthropology—Research. 3. Anthropology—Bibliography. I. Title. II. Title: Field Work in the library.
Z5111.W47 1994
[GN42] 94-5684
016.301—dc20

Printed in the United States of America.

98 97 96 95 94 5 4 3 2 1

For Leadership in My Profession:
Millicent Abell
John Haak
Dorothy Gregor
Melvin Voigt

CONTENTS

Part II
Access by Area Studies: With an Emphasis on Empirical Investigations

ACKNOWLEDGMENTS

Professor Adam Kuper, when he was editor of *Current Anthropology,* once asked me why I did not prepare a bibliography of reference works for anthropology. At the time it seemed a frightful responsibility. None of the traditional conceptual systems used to organize bibliographic guides could give meaning to the mountainous output.

It is hardly five years since that suggestion, and the day of reckoning has arrived. A work of this scope cannot be completed without the help of a lot of people in many institutional settings. Some of the most important support was hardly visible. It is buried in the context of my life. There are the years of support for any scholarly effort by the librarians to whom this book is dedicated. There was an apprenticeship in the skills of bibliography under that master of the art, William Webb. There was the experience of doctoral work at UCLA, where Walter Goldschmidt insisted that all graduate students be thoroughly grounded in each of the major subdisciplines of anthropology. And there was the wondrous excitement generated by the remarkable professors there who transmitted so powerfully the grammar of anthropological thinking.

It was important that the book develop within a tradition of scholarly publishing, with editors who take an active role in establishing standards of treatment and content. Without the help of Herbert Bloom and Mary Huchting at ALA Editions, this book in its finished form would not have been possible. They had an enormous influence by insisting on structural clarity. To work with these scholars was instructive and enjoyable. Then there was the can-do attitude of Kathy Marzec, who put the first draft into WordPerfect. Her having to cope with my chaotic handwritten notes devastated my naïvete.

In the United States I owe special thanks to the professional skill of the reference librarians at the Library of Congress, the University of Washington, and UCLA. My thanks go to the most-energetic Linda Lorano for special guidance at the University of Texas libraries and to Ray Jones for his gracious and unfailing assistance in the libraries of the University of Florida. From experienced bibliographers came always-generous communications. I am especially indebted to Marilyn Haas, Janet Stanley, Paula Covington, and Josephine Kibbee.

In the United Kingdom, I am grateful for the kind assistance of Angela Sabin at the School of Oriental and African Studies Library. T. A. Barringer, librarian for the Royal Commonwealth Collection, with the effective energy for which she is noted, found time to be helpful even as that great collection was being moved from its London location to Cambridge University. Important resources became available when W. G. Simpson provided access to the enormous community of scholarly librarians serving the patrons of the libraries of the University of London with such steady competence. In London, Alan Biggins at the Institute of Latin American Studies reawakened my preference in taking on the task at hand in a workmanlike way; it gave me pleasure to observe this careful scholar at work. At the Museum of Mankind, the whole staff was consistently helpful; among these skilled professionals, Anne Alexander most consistently demonstrated the kind of invaluable insight that only a seasoned bibliographer can bring to a manuscript. With great generosity she took the time to review some sections of the manuscript in draft form, and her comments were penetrating. For example, she suggested that resources about indigenous peoples as they lived before contact with the modern nation-state could be called "tribal." But for resources about indigenous peoples living in a modern nation-state, she suggested as more appropriate the terms "peoples" or "ethnic groups." While the description of titles must preserve the language of a work's author, in narrative discussion this distinction can be maintained.

Anyone noting errors or omissions, or who can suggest inclusions for a subsequent edition, should correspond with R. C. Westerman, P.O. Box 4774, Seattle, WA 92104.

INTRODUCTION

Fieldwork in the Library organizes the extensive reference literature of anthropology. It is divided into two major parts. Part I, "Access by Discipline and Subdiscipline," focuses on the theoretical advances of anthropology and its major subdisciplines. In part II, "Access by Area Studies," five chapters focus on empirical advances of anthropology and its subdisciplines. Each chapter is divided by a set of headings describing search strategies. For a display of the structure of *Fieldwork in the Library,* see the distribution of these strategic headings across all chapters in the table of contents. These strategic headings reflect a shared understanding among librarians that the resources needed to process the dynamics of problem-solving activities such as "Searching for Current Materials" can be different from the resources needed for retrospective searches and that in retrospective searches bibliographies of bibliographies are useful. Most search strategies make use of reference sources in the reference collection to identify materials shelved outside the reference collection. In contrast "Informational Reference Searches" can often be completed in the reference section by consulting encyclopedias and handbooks that contain all of the information needed to answer an inquiry.

It is the purpose of *Fieldwork in the Library* to ease the search for anthropological material by librarians who are without anthropological training and to provide helpful guidance to students of anthropology who are without library training. It is structured to encourage a comfortable movement back and forth between the same strategic heading in different chapters. The heading, "Searching Bibliographic Guides," for example, refers not to the bibliographic guide as a form but rather to a strategy for identifying reference works that lead to the selection of other reference works and relate the chapter to the book as a whole. The compact structure of *Fieldwork in the Library* would have been impossible without the support of the bibliographic guides listed in the first section of each chapter. The entries listed under "Searching Bibliographic Guides" in all chapters collectively identify a bibliographic base from which *Fieldwork in the Library* is constructed. Each chapter is developed on the assumption that the annotations to defining guides from all relevant chapters have been inspected. Nearly any search will profit from a movement back and forth between guides listed under the same strategic heading in each of several chapters. Thus a comprehensive search of African archaeology would begin with the annotations describing the content of the guides for chapters 1, 2, 3, and 7. A comprehensive search of Mesoamerican linguistics would begin first with the annotations describing the content of the guides for chapters 1, 2, 5, and 8.

The particular organization of each chapter is intended to provide a complementary companion to the bibliographic guides selected to define that chapter. This approach often makes it possible to emphasize research issues that have been less fully developed in previously published guides. For example, in chapter 4, "Ethnology/Cultural Anthropology," *Fieldwork in the Library* elaborates on reference sources that display, by their arrangement, the historical development of anthropological concepts. The chapter as a whole is structured to increase opportunities for entry by the names of tribal or indigenous ethnic groups. This consideration influenced the selection of reference sources in that particular chapter and informed the content of annotations. The possibility of making tribal entry so central to the development of chapter 4 emerges from the solid coverage by Kibbee's *Cultural anthropology* **(D01),** of reference sources available for literature searches on other topics.

Strategic headings common among chapters make it possible to quickly scan the reference works listed under them. As a structural feature, these headings are of the first importance. In terms of the currently fashionable "chaos theory," they encourage patterns of search in contrast to linear arrangements. This is a conscious effort to slightly expand an organizational tradition among librarians that uses form, such as a guide or bibliography, to organize the commonality between resources. In a complementary process, cross-references guide the reader to particular works listed under different strategic headings in any chapter of the book. Cross-references make it possible to reveal the multiple value of a reference source. For example, in chapter 7, "Africa South of the Sahara," a cross-reference in the headnote to "Searching Bibliographic Guides" brings into this search Scheven's *Bibliographies for African studies* **(G24),** for the entries found under the heading "Retrospective Bibliographies" within the search strategy "Retrospective Searches." Because of its excellent coverage, organization, and annotation, Scheven's work is often used by anthropologists as a guide.

But to proceed with our argument, another cross-reference in the same headnote draws attention to Porgès's *Sources d'information sur l'Afrique noire* **(G75),** which is fully described as a resource for "Informational Reference Searches" under the subheading "Directories." The value of this work extends far beyond the values usually assigned to directories. In fact, it provides masterly guidance into reference sources for Africa studies in all scholarly languages. In a strategic search, the form of a publication can be a secondary interest.

Since the dynamics of searching styles dominate the development of *Fieldwork in the Library,* attention is frequently drawn to Scheven's *Bibliography for African studies* **(G24),** even though it lacks coverage of informational reference sources usually found in a bibliographic guide. Indeed, if other bibliographic guides with a broad scope did not exist, it would be appropriate to list Scheven under the heading "Searching Bibliographic Guides" instead of placing it under "Retrospective Bibliographies—Bibliographies of Bibliographies." In that case, a cross-reference would have guided the reader from "Retrospective Searches" to the full bibliographic description listed under "Searching Bibliographic Guides." Even in the company of excellent bibliographic guides, Scheven's published bibliography provides the best resource with which to conduct searches for material on indigenous ethnic groups.

Computer Files

When the contents of computer files are subject-specific, they are described in appropriate chapters. On the other hand, descriptions of broad-scope computer files from selected related academic disciplines tend to be collected into chapter 2. Because computer databases are undergoing rapid expansion, descriptions related to hard copy counterparts indicate only that some portion of the published source is available for online or CD-ROM searching. Only at the point of use can an accurate assessment of coverage be determined consistently.

Throughout the text, descriptions of printed indexes include some indication of the availability of complementary computer files if the files are widely available. For example, there is an indication of the availability of related computer files in the description of the printed edition of the American Geological Institute's *Bibliography and index of geology* **(F23),** in chapter 6, "Physical and Biological Anthropology." The computer files to this resource are not listed in chapter 2. The lucid system of classed arrangement that informs the printed version of this continuing reference source is not visible when entry is made through the computer file. A preliminary search in the hard-copy version will greatly increase the effectiveness of later entry in the computer files. The descriptive choice is intended to guide the reader to the form of the resource that is most useful in searches for anthropological material and to note the availability of computer files.

Main-entry Forms

The author/title entry forms used here were selected for their relevance to the activities of librarians and library users. In the past, major publications of the American Library Association such as Balay's *Guide to reference books* **(B02),** have used bibliographic styles influenced by cataloging traditions. It was useful to have main entries in books published for librarians match those main-entry descriptions in research collections. This tradition is no longer completely satisfactory, but cataloging rules continue to identify useful innovations in bibliographic style. Following Balay's *Guide to reference books* **(B02),** the main entries for computer files used in *Fieldwork in the Library* are based on cataloging practices. Recently, a system of main entries for cataloging has been devised on the basis of abstract principles, without regard to usage. This system, often labeled "A-2" in professional library literature, introduced new rules for main entries into the cataloging practices of American libraries. As a result, the holdings records of most American research libraries include descriptions created by two contradictory sets of rules. The date at which cataloging was undertaken determined which set of rules was used to establish the main entry of a particular book, the only thing that determined which form of heading was used. As a result, description standards for the main entry in bibliographies published by ALA Editions have sometimes attempted a compromise to formal bibliographic consistency in the interest of using entries that were most effective in library usage. The traditional link between bibliographic styles used at ALA and the styles used in Library of Congress cataloging has been disturbed. It can be argued that cataloging and bibliographic forms are of a different order. It can also be argued that it is useful in a book about library usage to have entries that match the entries found in records of holdings in a research library. Sheehy in "Archaeology and ancient history" **(C01)** has successfully increased the chances that main-entry descriptions will match descriptions found in the catalog files of American libraries even in the present somewhat chaotic transition period. Sheehy embraced a clearly defined compromise to internal consistency. According to the "Introduction" in Sheehy's "Archaeology and ancient history" **(C01),** entries for older materials used the "pre A-2" main-entry cataloging forms, but "A-2" forms were followed in the description of recent materials. The first draft of *Fieldwork in the Library* followed this practice. All entries followed the form established by Library of Congress cataloging, so that some entries were in "pre A-2" and some in "A-2" form depending on the date of cataloging. When this draft was circulated for comment, even some librarians found the graphics of this variation in entry form disturbing.

When usage in *Fieldwork in the Library* departs from the usage found in Sheehy's "Archaeology and ancient history" **(C01)** and from my earlier work on "Anthropology" in Webb's *Sources of information in the social sciences* **(D03),** the standard of style b, as established in the *Chicago manual of style,* 13th ed. (Chicago and London: University of Chicago Press, 1982 [738p.]), has been used to establish bibliographic form for main entries. Consider our treatment of references that support the arguments of the book but do not contribute as reference books to the structure of *Fieldwork in the Library.* We simply refuse the option of style b found in rule 7.130 which states that "Obviously, a title mentioned in the text need not be complete there where it is cited in a note or a list of references." This rule is permissive rather than mandatory. In *Fieldwork in the Library,* since discursive articles appear only once and are fully described in the text when introduced, there is no need for a list of references. This treatment of references follows Webb's *Sources of information in the social sciences* **(D03)** and is closely related to the most usual bibliographic treatment of individual titles listed in the annotation of a monographic series.

Arrangement of Entries

Fieldwork in the Library is arranged in a classed system in which chapters are assigned one or more alphabetical values (A, B, C . . .) with each entry an alphabetic letter for a prefix, followed by a number. Within this order **(A01, A02, A03** . . .) works judged to be of the first importance are alphabetized by main entry under subheadings in the text. These entries are indented with the prefixed item number placed at the edge of the left-hand margin. Some entries are given secondary status. These entries are always described in primary-entry annotations or in narrative paragraphs specifying a subordinate relationship to the indented and alphabetized entry under which they are placed. The prefixed item number for these subordinate entries is set with bold type in parentheses at the end of the reference. This assigned item number retains its serial order (**A01, A02, A03** . . .) but cannot be entered into the alphabetic list because the secondary relationship of the entry to the more important alphabetized entry determines its place in the text. When the index refers to entry **(A10),** and entries alphabetized at the left-hand margin skip from **(A09)** to **(A11),** then the reader must infer that **(A10)** is embedded either in the annotation of **(A09)** or in a discursive paragraph somewhere between **(A09)** and **(A11).** This arrangement follows usage in Webb's *Sources of information in the social sciences* **(D03).** Both primary and secondary entries may be cited as cross-references in the same annotations. These cross-references are given paragraphs of their own that continue the annotations.

It is important to remember that the assignment of primary or secondary values applies only to the relationship between these resources in the structure in which they are used. Again these are not absolute values. In chapter 2, Balay's *Guide to reference books* **(B02)** is assigned a secondary value to Haas's "Anthropology" **(B01).** This does not mean that Balay's *Guide to reference books* **(B02)** is less valuable as a reference source than Haas's "Anthropology" **(B01).** It means Haas's "Anthropology" **(B01)** provides the best guide to continuing indexing services from other disciplines for use in anthropological searches. Balay's *Guide to reference works* **(B02)** in this structured arrangement can be used to identify well-annotated descriptions of the computer file editions of these indexing services and as a selective introduction to other computer files that might be useful. Thus the ranking of primary and secondary must be related to the whole structure of *Fieldwork in the Library.* The features held in common between these resources are as important as the features that make them different. This follows the example of biology, where an affinity between species is dependent on the whole plan or structure of each group of individuals.

Explication of this arrangement

The primary or secondary value of a work can be determined only by reference to its arrangement in the single list in which it is given full bibliographic description. The cross-reference is meant only to point to this full description and to the annotated notes that accompany the description.

Full bibliographic description of entries with primary reference value

The assigned bibliographic number of these entries is *always* placed at the left-hand margin and *before* the bibliographic description. This bibliographic code number is *always* followed by an indented bibliographic description of a reference source. These entries are listed alphabetically under strategic headings. *Only* the bibliographic descriptions of primary entries are listed in alphabetic order by author or title when no author is provided.

Full bibliographic descriptions of entries with secondary reference value

These entries *never* appear in the alphabetic list of entries. The identifying bibliographic number for these entries is *always* located in the space just *after* the bibliographic description and within the body of an annotation or discursive text. Nevertheless, secondary entries are *always* assigned that chapter's next bibliographic code number in the serial order (1, 2, 3 . . .). This serial number placement in the body of text provides additional visual signal of their status.

Secondary entries support and extend the coverage of the alphabetized primary entry and are useful but not essential instruments for an effective use of the search strategy as it is structured. To better understand the relationship between primary and secondary descriptions, inspect entries described at **(I20)**, **(I21)**, and **(I22)**. Entries Haywood's *Bibliography of North American folklore and folksong* **(I20)** and Clements's *Native American folklore, 1879–1979* **(I22)** both have primary reference value for anthropology and are numbered at the margin *in front of* the bibliographic descriptions to visually dramatize by the indented form their importance to the search strategy under review. Haywood's *Bibliography of North American folklore and folksong* **(I20)** has a broad scope of topical coverage that makes it uniquely useful as a primary reference source. It covers an enormous range of ethnographic possibilities. On the other hand, Walls's *Bibliography of Washington State folklore and folklife* **(I21)** updates for one geographic area the coverage of indigenous peoples, with a scope very much like that of Haywood's *Bibliography of North American folklore and folksong* **(I20)**, but because of its limited geographic coverage the Walls volume is of secondary value, providing, as it does, an extremely limited expansion of the information contained in Haywood. Therefore Walls's *Bibliography of Washington State folklore and folklife* **(I21)** is given a prefixed bibliographic code number which is placed after the bibliographic description and annotated internally as part of the annotation to Haywood's *Bibliography of North American folklore and folksong* **(I20)**. The fact that indented numbers at the margin skip from **(I20)** to **(I22)** alerts the reader to the presence of **(I21)** in the text of the annotation to **(I20)**.

Full bibliographic description of entries with tertiary reference value

Entries with tertiary value are *never* given bibliographic enumeration, are *never* alphabetized, and are not indexed. They appear in running text of paragraphs and annotations only to illustrate or slightly expand the reference sources being discussed for their primary and secondary reference value. If the individual volumes of a fully described series are not of the first importance, they would be treated as tertiary entries. Between Haywood, *A bibliography of North American folklore and folksong* **(I20)** and Walls, *A bibliography of Washington State folklore and folklife* **(I21)**, find Richard M. Dorson's *Handbook of American folklore*, which is an example of a tertiary entry.

Abbreviated descriptions used with cross-reference notations

Cross-references are used only to point to a single additional source either to support or illustrate an argument or to expand a topical search. They appear in the text with brief name author entry without a period and to a short title of the work followed by the bibliographic code number assigned to the fully described entry to which they refer. Since this number violates the serial order of the surrounding entries and since it is so clearly incomplete, it is visibly different from any other form of entry. When the bibliographic item number is in the narrative text with the cross-reference notation form, it does not at that point identify the entry as either primary or secondary. It is a neutral signal to the position in the text where it is fully described and where its rank in a reference search can be more fully understood. As a visual signal, when it expands the search past an annotation, it is usually, but not always, placed in narrative text that has been indented to form a new paragraph. All cross-reference occurs in narrative content and can be identified by unique descriptive features. Given the organization of *Fieldwork in the Library* around problem-solving search strategies, this separation invites an inspection of other entries listed near the description of the cross-reference.

All bibliographic code numbers placed in the running text of an annotation or in a discursive paragraph are printed in bold. This is done to increase their visibility while scanning. Descriptions of secondary entries can be distinguished from cross-references because secondary entries have the author's full name/title and subtitle, and full bibliographic descriptive information including place of publication, publisher, date of publication, pagination, and series information. For cross-references *only* the most abbreviated information precedes the bibliographic code number. By its nature, a cross-reference is *always* out of serial order wherever it appears.

Even the best bibliographic work can only support and expand the recommendations of other scholars with related interests. The reading list prepared by Professor David Jordan for students of Chinese ethnology is detailed, expansive, and probably publishable. Most directories prepared by anthropologists include indexes that identify the interests of other scholars. These directories, perhaps because they are prepared under the close supervision of anthropologists, often include new features of great value. The directory of the European Association of Social Anthropologists, which has recently set a new standard for excellence, can be used as an example. Edited by Rolf Husmann and Gaby Husmann, the *EASA register, 1992* (Göttengen, Germany: EASA, 1992 [514p.]), under the heading MARITIME ANTHROPOLOGY, lists the last names of four anthropologists. Under "Country/individual index," CHINA has the name of one anthropologist. This is direct to-the-point indexing. But, in a remarkable innovation, the "Ethnic groups/populations index," under the subject head of AZTECS/MEXICO, has the last names of two anthropologists. One anthropologist is listed under HERERO/NAMIBIA. It is hoped that indexes identifying scholars with experience with a particular tribe will become standard in anthropological directories.

Still, directories are not widely cataloged or even distributed. A bibliography of anthropological directories, newsletters, and Internet addresses might be interesting. Anyone knowing a candidate for entry into such a work is invited to send details to the author by Internet to filgrp@halcyon.com or filgrp.seanews.akita.com or ALA Editions.

The cut-off of *Fieldwork in the Library* is March 1993.

Part One

Access by Discipline and Subdiscipline: With an Emphasis on Theory

1

What Every Anthropologist Needs to Know

Chapter 1 provides entry only into reference materials covering more than one subdiscipline of anthropology. Here one finds the resources that every anthropologist needs to know. Within the chapter, strategic headings divide cited resources by different search objectives. Guided by these headings, a strategic search moves across chapters to stretch coverage of related subjects and culture areas. A search can follow any one of the several strategies. Each strategic search is patterned to move across other chapters to resources listed under a common heading. Cross-references bring into the search process resources with more than one possible strategic value.

The lament of anthropologists that indexing systems based on the Library of Congress (LC) classification system fail to address anthropological needs has some basis in fact. It is worth knowing some of the ways the LC system violates the natural direction of an anthropological literature search. In the LC classification system, entries by culture area for topical searches such as those for works on KINSHIP range from erratic to nonexistent in coverage of many culture areas. Even in archaeology, which is better served than ethnology, an LC entry requires conceptual adjustments for anthropological entry. For example, in many libraries that follow LC cataloging practices, resources on Mesoamerican archaeology will be treated as ANTIQUITIES and distributed over four or five countries representing current political divisions that share location for Mesoamerican materials. To improve understanding of how the system works, consult Charles Frantz's *The student anthropologist's handbook* **(A15),** for one chapter devoted to a discussion of this valuable system of classification. A discussion of recent modifications of the LC classification system that are relevant to anthropological searches can be found in John M. Weeks's *Introduction to library research in anthropology* **(A71).** Another, more general source, Knapp's *Contemporary thesaurus of social science terms and synonyms: A guide to natural language computer searching* **(B06),** can be useful in adjusting natural language searches to the variations in controlled vocabularies encountered as a social science search moves from database to database or from card catalog to card catalog.

In cultural anthropology a concept of commonality dependent on resemblance to a whole plan of structure is called "pattern." The classed arrangement of *Fieldwork in the Library* can be understood in terms of this tradition. As a result, the commonalities shared by resources take on more importance than the differences between resources. Strategic headings in each chapter describe a commonality across chapters that relates the whole plan of searching activity to listed resources. The movement of these searches between chapters is two-directional. A search moves back and forth. In anthropological terms, the movement of a search back and forth across strategic headings is mandatory rather than permissive. The most fruitful uses of this guide will always inspect resources from more than one chapter and will always make use of both the headnote and cited resources of chapter 1.

Only this chapter expands each strategic search headnote with detailed discussions of search strategies. Since any reference book listed in this chapter can be vital to some search that starts in any chapter, all searches are referred back to this chapter and to the discussions under the search strategy headings. Since organization by form is subordinated to organization by search strategy, the same reference books may be useful to more than one search strategy; and cross-references can be used to encourage movement between strategic headings within a chapter. For example, a cross-reference cited under any headnote in this chapter can be used in all of the chapters devoted to area studies and most of the chapters devoted to subdisciplines. For example, "Searching for Current Materials" brings into the current search the Royal Anthropological Institute's *Anthropological index,* described at **(A35)** under the subheading "Retrospective Bibliographies—Continuing Bibliographies." This cross-reference invited the reader to inspect the latest quarterly issues of that indexing publication as a scanning list of manageable size. Since searches in all chapters refer back to chapter 1, the organization of *Fieldwork in the Library* makes it possible for the reader to move a search from any chapter to the subject heading "Searching for Current Materials" in chapter 1 and to integrate this cross-reference into searches for current information about biological anthropology, anthropological linguistics, ethnology and cultural anthropology, archaeology, or area studies defined in terms of geographic regions.

In much the same way, most searches for retrospective materials in any chapter can profitably start with Tozzer Library's *Author and subject catalogues of the Tozzer Library* [microfiche] **(A26)** and the Museum of Mankind's *Museum of Mankind Library catalogues* **(A25).** Add to these resources *Abstracts in anthropology* **(A32)** and *Anthropological literature* **(A36)** and the minimum core of absolutely essential anthropological reference sources has been identified.

Searching Bibliographic Guides

Searching a well-structured and carefully annotated guide can swiftly establish a basic survey of available resources. While no search need be specific only to chapter 1, "What Every Anthropologist Needs to Know," Auckland's "Getting into the literature" **(A01)** is relevant to all searches of anthropological literature. Since the framework of a search is often defined by subdiscipline (archaeology and material culture, ethnology and cultural anthropology, anthropological linguistics, or physical and biological anthropology) or by the culture area context of an investigation, searching the guides specific to subdisciplines or geographic context can be helpful to a strategic search.

The development of each chapter is defined by the bibliographic guides cited there under "Searching Bibliographic Guides." For this reason, the development of a chapter does not duplicate the advances achieved by that guide. From this bibliographic base, each chapter attempts only to answer the question, "What else can be done when this guide has been exhausted?" Thus in chapter 7, "Africa South of the Sahara," Scheven's *Bibliographies for African studies* **(G24)** and McIlwaine's *Africa* **(G96)** are extensive and sensitive to anthropological issues. For this reason, in *Fieldwork in the Library* we can turn our focus almost entirely on resources recently published or on the earlier works that were published before the starting date of Scheven's contribution. This makes possible a concise chapter to cover a vast literature. In much the same way, the reference literature supporting studies of the North American Indian can be compressed into one chapter only because of the groundbreaking contributions of Haas's *Indians of North America* **(I02)** and Corley's *Resources for native peoples studies* **(I01).** The focus on entry to ethnic groups undertaken in chapter 4, "Ethnology/Cultural Anthropology," would not have been possible without the lucid coverage of topical approaches to this literature by Kibbee's *Cultural anthropology* **(D01).** In chapter 3, "Archaeology and Material Culture" relies completely on references provided by Woodhead, *Keyguide to information sources in museum studies* **(C03)** which are so complete that the topic is excluded from coverage in *Fieldwork in the Library.* The inspection below of Auckland's "Getting into the literature" **(A01)** should be part of searches for bibliographic guides that start in other chapters, and the guides of relevant chapters should be consulted when a search starts in chapter 1. The table of contents in *Fieldwork in the Library* provides graphic visibility to the commonality of guides listed under the heading "Searching Bibliographic Guides."

Bibliographic guides

A01

Auckland, Mary. "Getting into the literature." In *Ethnographic research: A guide to general conduct,* p.159–70. Ed. by R. F. Ellen. London: Academic, 1984. 403p. (ASA Research methods in social anthropology, no.1)

Concentrates on large, recurrent bibliographic tools. These resources provide entry to all of the subdivisions of anthropology. For each source, find here a precise identification of the most useful features and a clear discussion of its strengths and weaknesses in relation to other available resources. This concise and accurate analysis of the essential reference sources reflects the distilled experience of a skilled librarian who has worked closely with anthropologists for an extended period of time. The basic volume is widely available as a desk reference book and is used by teaching anthropologists all over the world. The extensive distribution of this work provides us with a widely held bibliographic base from which this chapter is developed. The coverage closely parallels that of Haas's "Anthropology" **(B01),** which was published in a serial publication that is widely held in reference collections. Haas also includes continuing indexing services from closely related disciplines, which makes her work equally useful as a guide to chapter 2.

Searching for Current Materials

Exploratory searches for current materials often take place in the current periodical sections of research libraries. These searches follow highly individualistic patterns because each scholar has a different research agenda. In time, most scholars place individual subscriptions with the most important sources. Attempted here is the identification of those major published sources that have something for almost everyone in the profession. In addition, on inspection these periodicals may identify titles for recent specialized research reports. See also the Royal Anthropological Institute's *Reference list to current periodicals* **(A14)** for a carefully selected list of the most useful journals for coverage of international anthropology. For navigating the Internet workshop list use listserver mailing lists available at navigate@UBVM.cc.buffalo.edu, the science FAQ list scifaq.1@YALEVM.cis.yale.edu, and research methodology at methods@vm.ecs.rpi.edu.

There are no hard and fast rules of inclusion or exclusion under a particular strategic heading such as "Retrospective Searches." If a resource has value in several types of searches, it is listed in only one place with cross-references to suggest its alternate value. Throughout this book the quarterly issues of abstracting services—such as *Abstracts in anthropology* **(A32),** *Abstracts in German anthropology* **(A33),** and *Francis bulletin signalétique* **(A34)** as well as indexing publications like *Anthropological index* **(A35),** *Anthropological literature* **(A36),** *MLA international bibliography of books and articles on the modern languages and litera-*

tures **(A37),** and the various continuing indexing services described in Ruble's *A scholar's guide to humanities and social sciences in the Soviet Union* **(A38)**—are listed as instrumentalities of a retrospective search and are placed under the subheading "Retrospective Bibliographies—Continuing Bibliographies."

In much the same way, for "Retrospective Searches," newsletters that maintain current awareness can have retrospective value. Most newsletters from professional associations are circulated to all members and are available to others by subscription. They provide a compact source of current information on a broad band of professional interests and activities. Examples of newsletters with a discipline-wide focus and an international perspective would include *Anthropology newsletter,* v.1– , 1974– (Washington, D.C.: American Anthropological Assn.) **(A02),** which appears ten times a year as a continuation of the American Anthropological Association's *Newsletter* (1947–73) and continues to be an outstanding source of information about grants, conferences, and research and teaching opportunities. *Anthropology today* v.1– , 1985– (London: Royal Anthropological Institute) **(A03),** is a continuation of *RAIN: Royal Anthropological Institute news,* v.1–65, 1974–84 (London: Royal Anthropological Institute), and has such excellent coverage of upcoming conferences, grant opportunities, and recent news from all parts of the Commonwealth that American scholars of Commonwealth countries such as Kenya find it indispensable. On Internet, use Gopher to access current contents of anthropological journals at usc.library.cc.anthropology. Internet listserver can be used to access General Anthropology Bulletin Board at anthrol@UBVM.cc.buffalo.edu.

The British Museum's Museum of Mankind Library (London) has long retained all copies of newsletters, which are kept in the reference reading room because retrospective issues are frequently used for bibliographic purposes. In effect, the library has come to serve (by the default of other libraries) as library of record for more than 100 newsletters of value to anthropologists. Yet the collection would probably have to be expanded fivefold to approach comprehensive coverage of newsletters of value to every aspect of the discipline of anthropology. Fortunately, cataloging practices in research libraries are slowly adopting a policy of retaining copies of bibliographically significant newsletters. As studies of the history of anthropology become more frequent, the policy of retention will become even more appropriate.

The well-known problems encountered in the retention of and access to the bibliographic services of newsletters might be countered by republishing current contents of bibliographic features in newsletters in continuing hardcover volumes that can be bound and placed on the shelves without any special handling. Because the need for information in anthropology is so narrowly focused, this material could be usefully added to publications such as the British Library of Political and Economic Science, comp., *Anthropology and related disciplines* v.1– , 1990– (London: International Current Awareness Service) **(A04),** with its monthly coverage of current materials on developmental anthropology. In some chapters of *Fieldwork in the Library,* newsletters are identified for their continuing assumption of bibliographic responsibilities. This function is part of an effort to provide a valued forum for current issues between members. Annual reports from foundations, professional societies, and governmental institutions are another source of information about current research activities and can sometimes generate elusive but valuable reference publications. An annual report from any institution listed in Cantrell's *Funding for anthropological research* **(A54)** can identify both these elusive publications and help define the current parameters of financial support from listed organizations for specific research efforts in anthropology.

Select Sources of Review in Scholarly Publications

Various levels of review are possible according to the needs of the search. It is possible to scan the content of the articles to find out what kinds of issues are finding publication in a particular journal. For more profound review, the "State-of-the-Art Reviews" section identifies excellent reviewing journals that attempt to consolidate results in research agendas that have recently benefited from a surge of activity. Often the notes and news sections provide information about conferences or grant opportunities. Book reviews provide a concise view of the ideas developed in a recent and select sample of monographs.

Consult "Retrospective Bibliographies—Continuing Bibliographies" and examine the printed quarterly issues of the *Anthropological index* **(A35)** as a current classified survey of the contents of periodical titles adjusted completely to the way the anthropologist organizes a search for information. When a title appears frequently under a subject heading that guides a search, the journal itself might be inspected even if none of the cited articles are relevant to the immediate search.

REPRESENTATIVE SAMPLE OF REVIEW JOURNALS

A05

American anthropologist. v.1– , 1888– . Washington, D.C.: American Anthropological Assn. 6/yr.

Outstanding for coverage of the discipline with substantive interest on significant research findings and theoretical analysis in the full range of anthropological topics. This journal has increased the number of books and films reviewed each year to about 300, only to find the output climbing higher. "Current book review" normally leads off with a lengthy review article that attempts a synthesis of work in some strategic area. The main section consists of book reviews under broad headings, such as general and theoretical, ethnology, political anthropology, linguistics, archaeology, and physical anthropology. Other sections include film reviews. Also useful in each issue, a list of publications received for review.

Other publications of the association include the American Anthropological Association's *Annual report and directory,* v.1– , 1969– (Washington, D.C.: American Anthropological Assn.) **(A06),** which sets forth the structure for the association, and the *Directory of practicing anthropologists* (Washington, D.C.: American Anthropological Assn., 1985 [89p.]) (NAPA Bulletin, 1) **(A07),** which identifies an increasing number of American anthropologists working for the government and for other non-teaching institutions.

A08

Anthropos: Revue internationale d'ethnologie et de linguistique. v.1– , 1906– . Fribourg, Switzerland: Editions St. Paul. 3/yr.

The "Rezension" section contains 175–250 critical reviews per year (100–1,300 words). These reviews are indexed by author, subject, and geographical areas.

A09

Current anthropology: A world journal of the sciences of man. v.1– , 1960– . Chicago: Univ. of Chicago Pr. 5/yr.

Book reviews cover the entire range of anthropological interest from an international perspective and are a hallmark of this publication. Focuses on archaeology, biological anthropology, folklore, physical anthropology, and social and cultural anthropology. Long, evaluative reviews with comments that place a work in the matrix of other scholarly advances. "Recent Publications" provides a list of books received for review. Irregular inclusion of reports from departments like "Institutions," which reports on the emergence of new anthropological associations and foundations, establishes this journal as the informal publication of record for anthropological associations worldwide.

A10

L'Homme: Revue française d'anthropologie. v.1– , 1961– . Paris: Mouton for École pratique des hautes études. Quarterly.

Six to twenty articles per issue cover studies in physical anthropology, cultural anthropology, ethnology, and linguistics. Some double issues. Author index.

A11

Man: The journal of the Royal Anthropological Institute. n.s. v.1– , 1966– . London: The Royal Anthropological Institute. Quarterly.

Inherits a tradition of high standards. Reviews 200–250 books and films per year. Recent issues included articles on myth, floral analysis, sex roles. There is an emphasis on the theoretical aspects of all dimensions of anthropology. Annual index of authors and reviewers.

A12

Mundus: A quarterly review of German research contributions on Asia, Africa and Latin

America. v.1– , 1965– . Stuttgart: Wissenschaftliche Verlagsgesellschaft. Quarterly.

More than 400 analytic reviews a year. Includes geography, prehistory, and scholarly application of natural science methodologies to social science problems (population studies). Reflects the context of German anthropology, which is closely tied to the natural sciences, including geography, and the humanities, including history and folklore.

A13

Wenner-Gren Foundation for Anthropological Research, New York. *Report on the foundation's activities,* 1941– . New York: The Foundation. Annual.

Title of the report varies. In early years called Viking Fund. This foundation dedicates itself solely to the advancement of anthropology. An excellent review of the conferences, publications, and research support that have made this institution an important leader in establishing which of the many research possibilities are currently most likely to secure widespread institutional support. The report is often the first to identify major shifts in the research focus among opinion makers in the discipline.

Selective Lists of Scholarly Journals in Anthropology

While journals do cumulate into great retrospective sources, only published bibliographies and annual periodical indexes provide reasonable entry into the older volumes. Many journals have regular departments and even special editors for maintaining an even flow of book reviews focusing on the special interests of the particular journal. Almost all scholarly journals have special features ranging from extensive continuing bibliographies to brief reports on current research activities. Developing an intimate familiarity with most frequently cited journals relevant to a specialized research interest can greatly ease the difficulty of keeping abreast of narrowly defined areas of research.

There are several ways to identify a journal that may be useful for a particular research focus. Once the name of a journal with relevant subject coverage is identified, it can be inspected to determine just what special features it regularly maintains. If it is frequently cited for a relevant topic in respected anthropological bibliographies and indexes, then its special features may also be useful. Inspect Anthropological Index's *Reference list of current periodicals* **(A14)** and the Peabody Museum of Archaeology and Ethnology Library's "List of serials" **(A17).** Another approach to the identification of useful journal titles relies on specialized guides such as Frantz's *A student anthropologist's handbook* **(A15)** and Williams's *Anthropology journals and serials* **(A20).**

The list of journals covered by any indexing service is selected by some methodology. It is possible to send out questionnaires to a large group of scholars. It is also possible to establish a selection committee of scholars. Since the selection for inclusion in the *Anthropological index* is the result of an intimate and continuing interaction between anthropologists and librarians in literature searches for current research, inclusion becomes a kind of certification of value to the profession.

A14

Anthropological index. *Reference list of current periodicals.* London: Royal Anthropological Institute, 1992. 38p.

An alphabetic list of abbreviations paralleled by full bibliographic descriptions of the serial publications indexed by the Royal Anthropological Institute. Since the indexing service is arranged by culture area, it is possible to quickly identify which journals in this select list are most frequently cited in a particular culture area. This list is indispensable when the index is consulted and can be purchased separately so that, as a desk reference, it places at hand a select but hardly sparing list of anthropologically significant journals. No other available list so completely covers all aspects of anthropology in all culture areas. With fewer than 500 titles, the task of serving all members of a large and active society has been met within the constraints of a limited budget. Selection is a continuing process. No individual or committee could compile such a list with complete authority.

Brought up to date each quarter by the department, "List of abbreviations," in *Anthropological index* **(A35).** This resource provides an update of new editions, discontinued titles, as well as titles held but not indexed, providing a continuing correction of the original list. These listings and corrections should be treated as supplementary to the Anthropological Index's *Reference list of current periodicals* **(A14).** This can be treated as a supplement to the original publication **(A14),** which is not duplicated in each issue of the published index. This alphabetic list of the abbreviations can be used to identify journals indexed in *Anthropological index* **(A35)** and provides complete bibliographic information for those journals. Yet because it is less than 100 pages, many libraries will not provide separate cataloging for this item. It is sometimes found bound with one of the volumes near its date of publication. All of the original file cards used to establish each author entry listed in the Royal Anthropological Institute, *Anthropological index* **(A35)** are now housed at the British Museum, Museum of Mankind Library. They are alphabetically listed and preserved in a closed file for the years 1962–89. In 1989, when computer technology was introduced to the construction of the printed index, this card file was discontinued. See British Museum, Museum of Mankind Library, *Museum of Mankind Library catalogues* **(A25).**

A15

Frantz, Charles. *A student anthropologist's handbook: A guide to research, training, and career.* Cambridge, Mass.: Schenkman, 1972. 228p.

Select lists of anthropological serials in all Western scholarly languages. There are lists in all scholarly languages of journals appropriate to each subdiscipline and to every culture area: General (p.145–47); Social anthropology and ethnology (p.152–55); Archaeology and prehistory (p.157); Biological anthropology (p.159–60); Linguistics and folklore (p.162–63); The Americas (p.171–72); North America (p.174); Latin America and the Caribbean (p.178); Europe and CIS (p.188–89); North Africa and Southwest Asia (p.191–92); Asia general and South Asia (p.195); Southeast and East Asia (p.199–200); and Oceania (p.202–203).

A16

Library-Anthropology Resource Group. *Serial publications in anthropology.* 2d ed. South Salem, N.Y.: Redgrave, 1982. 177p.

An alphabetic list by title, with subject index for 4,387 entries given in a Library of Congress form at the time of publication. Includes some cross-references. Subject index by broad terms. Since entries are in numbered order classed by geographic area, journals covering the subject KINSHIP, for example, can be identified within a numeric range covered by items about that culture area. The corporate index is useful for identifying centers of learning for a special topic.

A17

Peabody Museum of Archaeology and Ethnology. Library. "List of serials." In v.1, Peabody Museum of Archaeology and Ethnology. Library. *Catalogue: Subjects. Second supplement,* p.xi–xxv. Boston: Hall, 1971. 4v.

Provides a list of serials indexed at that library.

Consult also "Supplement to the list of serials" v.1, Peabody Museum of Archaeology and Ethnology, Library, *Catalogue: Subjects, Third supplement,* p.ix–xvi (Boston: Hall, 1975 [4v.]) **(A18),** again followed by "Supplement to the list of serials" in v.1, Tozzer Library, *Catalogue: Subjects, Fourth supplement,* p.ix–xvi (Boston: Hall, 1979 [v.4–7]) **(A19).**

The descriptive entries in this publication do not conform to those found in Library-Anthropology Resource Group's *Serial publications in anthropology* **(A16),** and neither of these sources has entry forms that conform to the current cataloging standards of the Library of Congress. Since so many libraries list journals with LC cataloging, a title listed in these resources at a research library may fail to identify holdings in a research library. It is always appropriate to expect titles listed in these resources to be in a collection under another entry form. However, the contents of any journal listed have been made more accessible by indexing available in the published Tozzer Library's *Author and subject catalogues of the Tozzer Library* [microfiche] **(A26)** and Peabody Museum Library's *Catalogue: Subjects* **(A29).** Even scanning a section of older hardbound editions of the Peabody Museum's *Catalogue: Subjects* **(A29)** will often identify several frequently cited journal titles in coverage of a particular topic or culture area. These journals can in turn be expected to have book reviews published and special features. Since almost any literature search in anthropology will benefit from use of these catalogs, the act of scanning a section for a frequency count of journals relevant to a culture area can be undertaken as part of an essential first step in searching anthropological topics in the context of a culture area.

A20

Williams, John T. *Anthropology journals and serials: An analytical guide.* Westport: Greenwood, 1986. 182p. (Annotated bibliographies of serials: A subject approach; no.10)

English-language publications worldwide are given full entries and long annotations. Identifies many special features. The book's organization makes it possible to identify journals in terms of the subdisciplines of anthropology. Skillfully and knowledgeably annotated, it is well served with adequate indexes. One of the most useful reference tools available in the discipline of anthropology.

Some English-language journals of the first importance, such as *Reviews in anthropology* **(A58),** are not included. Also excluded are many journals that report anthropological advances in a specific technical tradition, such as the *Bulletin of the Historical Metallurgy Group* **(C09).**

Retrospective Searches

Most retrospective searches make use of resources in the reference collection to identify bibliographic descriptions of other resources located either in other departments of the library or in the libraries of an interlibrary loan network. Bibliographies of bibliographies most concisely consolidate a record of bibliographic work completed and published. When no published bibliography can be quickly identified, it is often useful to search the retrospective bibliographies specific to the subdisciplines or to relevant culture areas. These resources often have coverage of the literature in its broadest definition with the greatest time depth.

Yet, in some scholarly activities like European anthropology (where Europe is the object of ethnographic studies), the lists of publications after the names in a biographical directory may be almost comprehensive for the identification of contributions that have been made by trained anthropologists. At the same time, some out-of-date bibliography on a specialized topic can be brought up to date by using the continuing volumes of annual indexing or abstracting services. Often even the latest topical bibliography needs to be supplemented by coverage for the latest years with these annual continuing sources. When no bibliography relevant to a research interest can be found, the search can start with the broad-based retrospective sources and proceed in the continuing sources.

Additionally, the subject matter and methodology of the physical sciences especially lend themselves to productive use of citation indexes since so much research in these disciplines expands on a development reported in a seminal article. Citation indexes are multidisciplinary and more general than most resources cited in this book. However, since they are so clearly representative of the new search technology made possible by the computerization of bibliographic files, their specialized use for anthropology is discussed more fully in chapter 2.

Human Relations Area Files's *HRAF source bibliography* **(D16)** and the UNESCO *International bibliography of social and cultural anthropology* **(D20)** cover all aspects of anthropology but most powerfully a search strategy in "Ethnology/Cultural Anthropology." Each of these resources has entry by name of indigenous people. Once a specialist for any area of study has been identified, consult the author entry to the Tozzer Library's *Author and subject catalogues of the Tozzer Library* [microfiche] **(A26)** and the author indexes of the British Museum, Museum of Mankind Library's *Museum of Mankind Library catalogues* [microfiche] **(A25).**

Consult also Bonnie R. Nelson's "Anthropological research and printed library catalogs," *RQ* 19 (1979): 159–70, for a detailed introduction to other published library catalogs and for a discussion of the unique classification schedules used for specialized entry. Many bibliographies of an individual anthropologist can be identified in Winters and the Library-Anthropology Resource Group's *International directory of anthropology* **(A22)** and Mann and the Library-Anthropology Resource Group's *Biographical directory of anthropologists born before 1920* **(A23).**

Retrospective Bibliographies—Bibliographies of Bibliographies

Any bibliography of bibliographies requires careful and knowledgeable use. Typically, many items of variable reference value are entered with equal weight into lengthy lists under broad subject headings. Yet for a specialized topic within a particular bibliography of bibliographies, each bibliographic item listed can provide something close to an exhaustive coverage of a selected topic. Sometimes the focus is so specialized that a listing of fifty items is exhaustive. The very next citation in the long list of bibliographies may be to a continuing source that over the years manages, by tiny increments, to cumulate into definitive coverage of even a vast field of scholarly effort. The scholar who discovers a bibliography in an article or a book that provides a respectable base for a literature search has greatly reduced the difficulty of constructing a comprehensive bibliographic search. Bibliographies of bibliographies also can be used to identify definitive reviews in periodicals. These can serve as a basis for productive searches with the citation indexes described as *Arts and humanities search* [computer file] **(B10)** for ethnohistory, linguistics, and archaeology; the *Social scisearch* [computer file] **(B37)** for cultural and social anthropology. Use the *Scisearch* [computer file] **(B35)** for archaeology and physical anthropology.

For bibliographies of bibliographies specific to whole culture areas, a reader should be prepared to consult the masterpieces because coverage achieved in these older efforts is not repeated in this new work. Instead, users are nearly always expected to consult earlier resources, which are carefully identified in the introductions of newer and additive works. Sometimes, in anthropology, the only information available on a tribe was published fifty years ago. Many earlier reference works still retain great value. For example, inspect the superb list of 290 bibliographies found in Gibson's "A bibliography of anthropological bibliographies: The Americas" **(H01)** and an equally powerful list of 978 bibliographies in his "A bibliography of anthropological bibliographies: Africa" **(G23).**

A21

Library-Anthropology Resource Group, comp. *Anthropological bibliographies: A selected guide.* Under the direction of Margo L. Smith and Yvonne M. Damien. South Salem, N.Y.: Redgrave, 1981. 307p.

A new edition is in preparation and scheduled for publication in 1994. Of the first importance. Includes bibliographic essays in collections, bibliographies in journal articles, and separately published monographs. Coverage extends to bibliographies of filmographies and discographies. More than 3,200 items are arranged first into six major geographic areas. Each area is subdivided, followed by topical bibliographies on those items with no identifiable geographical focus. Deserves careful study. Worldwide coverage for all aspects of anthropology in all scholarly languages. An "open entry" (v.1–) identifies continuing sources but sometimes fails to provide closing information on discontinued series.

The index by geographic area, ethnic group, language, and subject may seem to need expansion; but since all entries are listed in numbered order, a reference to forty items under KINSHIP is not formidable since the user can easily identify the sequence of numbers that are appropriate to the culture area under investigation.

Can be informally expanded for recent material by consulting the *Bibliographic index: A cumulative bibliography of bibliographies,* v.1– , 1938– , fully described as item 11 in the annotation to Haas's "Anthropology" **(B01)** and available as *Bibliographic index* [computer file] **(B11).**

Retrospective Bibliographies—Biographical Directories

In making a retrospective search of a culture area with a very narrow focus, it is extremely useful to be able to identify all of the work of anthropologists who have labored in that area. For any tribe or ethnic group, the number of professionally trained observers is severely limited. The bibliographic features in a biographical directory become, with the passage of time, quite as valuable as information about the birth and death dates, place of birth, and professional affiliations of listed scholars.

A22

Winters, Christopher, ed., and Library-Anthropology Resource Group (Chicago). *International directory of anthropology.* New York: Garland, 1991. 823p. (Garland reference library of social science, v.638)

Each entry is supported by a select bibliography of the published work of the cited professional and often includes reference to an obituary which attempts an exhaustive bibliography of the scholar's work. This bibliographic coverage, in conjunction with the biographical essays on more than 500 anthropologists from fifty countries, establishes a much needed coverage of both American and foreign anthropological traditions.

OTHER BIOGRAPHICAL SOURCES

A companion volume by Thomas L. Mann, ed. (and the Library-Anthropology Resource Group), *Biographical directory of anthropologists born before 1920* (New York: Garland, 1988 [245p.]) (Garland reference library of the humanities, v.439) **(A23),** provides a selective list of each scholar's contributions to anthropology and often includes an exhaustive bibliography of published work by and about the cited scholar. Other narrowly focused biographical directories continue to appear, and they often provide unique opportunities to gain access to important retrospective material. For example, Ute Gacs's *Women anthropologists: A biographical directory* (Westport, Conn.: Greenwood, 1988 [428p.]) **(A24),** reissued under a variant title as Ute Gacs's *Women anthropologists: Selected bibliography* (Urbana: Univ. of Illinois Pr., 1989 [428p.]). Each of the entries includes date of birth and death, birthplace, major publications, and sources for published biographical information. The extensive biographies in this resource reveal something of the special nature of being a woman in a fieldwork situation. Also provides valuable paths into published results about fieldwork situations from a woman's perspective. When the observer and the informant are of the same sex, discussion of child care might differ from discussion between investigators and informants of a different sex.

Separately published bibliographies for the individual anthropologist also continue to appear. A recent example is *Edmund Leach: A bibliography* (London: Royal Anthropological Institute, 1990 [79p.]) (Occasional paper. Royal Anthropological Institute of Great Britain and Ireland, no.42). In *Fieldwork in the Library,* the contributions of particular scholars are included only if they pioneered a unique approach to anthropological questions. When this is true, the bibliography of their work is included in topical bibliographies of the appropriate chapter. It is included not for their work alone but rather to mark a milestone in a particular methodology of anthropology. Examples of this treatment include the groundbreaking validation of the early use of psychological methodology in anthropological questions recorded in the publications cited in Joan Gordan's *Margaret Mead: The complete bibliography* (The Hague: Mouton, 1976 [206p.]). It is cited here, in chapter 1, for its historical record of this individual's continuing influence on the range of questions asked by American anthropologists.

Retrospective Bibliographies—Broad Scope

Often the best broad-based entry into a discipline or a culture area is through the published catalog of a great specialized library. Typically, an anthropologist will scan fifty titles on Melanesia to discover two titles on Melanesian kinship among other titles on research in Melanesia.

Alternatively, few anthropologists may feel a compelling need to scan a list of fifty titles on kinship on the chance that the list includes one title relevant to the specialized focus of Melanesian kinship and less of enduring interest in Melanesian studies. The value of carefully constructed vocabularies specific to anthropological problems can best be understood when they are contrasted with the controlled vocabularies developed for use by scholars from other disciplines as they are described in chapter 2. The impact of anthropologists on the classification schedules in both the Tozzer Library's *Author and subject catalogues of the Tozzer Library* [microfiche] **(A26)** and of the British Museum, Museum of Mankind Library's *Museum of Mankind Library catalogues* [microfiche] **(A25)** subordinates topical interest to geographic (or culture area) headings. Both libraries are of the first importance among reference sources in almost all retrospective searches of anthropological results in any of the subdivisions (archaeology, ethnology, cultural anthropology, linguistics, physical anthropology) not only because of the strength of their collections but also because their collections have been organized to provide reasonable entry into the kind of information anthropologists think is important.

Anthropology is doubly blessed with published editions of the cataloging achieved by the Tozzer Library's *Author and subject catalogues of the Tozzer Library* [microfiche] **(A26)** for books, periodical articles, and essays in collection, and the British Museum, Museum of Mankind Library's *Museum of Mankind Library catalogues* [microfiche] **(A25),** which for monographs only parallels the Tozzer Library in covering all aspects of anthropology worldwide. In the cataloging practices of these two institutions, the whole structure of classification contradicts the notions about the appropriate direction of hierarchy used by the Library of Congress system. The impact on search techniques is concisely stated by the Peabody Museum—"The optimal search strategy is to identify an area or group associated with the subject and then identify the specific topic"—in the "Introduction" to the Peabody Museum's *Third Supplement,* 1: vii **(A18).** Any search of anthropological subjects under culture areas or indigenous peoples is central to an understanding of the organization of many of the resources discussed in this chapter and to the structure of *Fieldwork in the Library.* The organizations of knowledge that are implicit in these two classification systems are remarkably compatible.

Coverage includes files for each of the several collections housed together at the British Museum, Museum of Mankind Library, since several related libraries were merged into the British Museum Library system. These collections are often the strongest in areas most unevenly covered by Tozzer Library's published *Catalogues* **(A26).** These two libraries can be viewed as complementary. Neither is comprehensive for all aspects of anthropology. For retrospective biblical classical cultures, consult also l'École Biblique et Archaéologique's *Catalogue* **(C19).** For Greek and Roman cultures, consult the Deutsches Archäologisches Institut's *Kataloge* **(C16).**

AUTHOR AND CLASSIFIED SUBJECT COVERAGE OF MONOGRAPHS

A25

British Museum. Museum of Mankind Library. *Museum of Mankind Library catalogues* [microfiche]. Bath, England: Mindata, 1989. 763 microfiche.

This cover title identifies for the publisher two subsets of microfiche and a number of collections and card catalogs housed at the Museum of Mankind (London). It serves to identify the two microfiche sets published together as a record of the holdings of several card catalogs housed at the British Museum, Museum of Mankind, through 1988, at which time the card catalogs were closed and machine-readable files were put in place. Within this microfiche set, each of two subsets can be purchased separately from the publisher. These are treated descriptively as volumes in a set. Each of the publisher's subsets includes a number of named and separate catalogs and indexes. These are treated as titled internal contents (or articles) in a subset volume. We describe two microfiche subset titles used by the publisher for the two subsets of microfiche contained in British Museum, Museum of Mankind's *Catalogues* **(A25).** Those titled internal contents, which are profoundly useful in a strategic search for anthropological literature, are described separately.

The Museum of Mankind's "Tribal index" is found in the publisher's subset Museum of Mankind's *Museum of Mankind books and pamphlets, author/subject and tribal catalogues: The Sir Eric Thompson Library* **(D13).** The Bliss classified subject cataloging applied across the monographic collection places a worldwide output of anthropological literature about every culture area in clusters easily accessed for anthropological interests. The second subset title of the microfiche publisher contains, along with other files, a microfiche reproduction of the Royal Anthropological Institute card catalog file of author entries as they appeared in the hardcover serial publication *Anthropological index* **(A35).** The publisher's description of this valuable title is included in the publisher's subset Museum of Mankind's *Periodical catalogues* **(A31).** This publisher's set also reproduces the record of the merged periodical series held in the collections housed at the British Museum, Museum of Mankind.

The retrospective cataloging of monographs in the British Museum, Museum of Mankind, which in 1976 merged the collections of the library collections held by the British Museum, Department of Ethnology, and the Royal Anthropological Institute Library, makes available to the larger scholarly community even the tribal indexing classed by the Bliss schedules to one of the world's most comprehensive anthropological collections.

Now that the Tozzer Library has converted to the LC cataloging system, the British Museum, Museum of Mankind, has become the only specialized library collecting anthropological materials worldwide that even attempts to maintain specialized cataloging that was created to accommodate anthropological patterns of thought. This is an enormous undertaking that deserves international support of future efforts. It takes a massive effort to ready a working file for published distribution to an international audience. Few institutions allow distribution to their working files. One exception would be the Library of Congress, African Section, General Reference and Bibliography Division, Reference Department's *Africa south of the Sahara* **(G21)** inclusion of cutouts from foreign-language abstracting services (including French and Russian) and arrangement of these entries into a single classified list. Some librarians at the Library of Congress objected to the resulting variability in the abbreviations for journal titles in the text, and this service was discontinued. With the introduction of Internet as described by Krol's *The whole Internet* **(B04),** some Australian anthropological research centers released their working files to international access through this computer network. It is possible that descriptive standards for entries to machine-readable information networks can be more relaxed and that more institutions will be willing to provide entry to their working files in this context. The conversion to machine-readable cataloging by this institution creates opportunities to share the resources with the worldwide community. Only the passage of time will tell whether one institution alone can carry the burden of original cataloging for classified subject entry.

AUTHOR, AND CLASSIFIED SUBJECT ENTRY INTO BOOKS, PERIODICAL ARTICLES, AND THE CONTENTS OF ESSAYS IN COLLECTIONS

A26

Harvard University. Peabody Museum. Tozzer Library. *Author and subject catalogues of the Tozzer Library* [microfiche]. 2d ed. Boston: Hall, 1988. 1,122 fiche in 8 binders.

Title varies. Separately published vocabularies for the classifications system developed at the Peabody Museum (Harvard) in close consultation with all members of the anthropological faculty provided detailed analytic entry into monographs, Festschriften, articles from 1,000 periodicals, and the proceedings of congresses. These vocabularies were organized with a classification system that often subordinates topical entry to geographic classes. The system is well suited to anthropological searches and provides retrospective coverage arranged alphabetically. The catalog is divided into two parts with classified subject entries in one part and author/title entries in the other part. In these single alphabets, monographs received by Tozzer are entered through June 1986 and selected periodical articles are classified through June 1983. No discipline in the social sciences has a published source of retrospective coverage that even approaches the range and depth established over the years by this great cataloging effort.

As its editors have pointed out, even Tozzer's cataloging efforts by no means present international anthropology in all its dimensions. The catalog appropriately reflects the broad research interests of Harvard University. It is weak in its coverage of the Middle East but exhaustive in its coverage of Middle America. It is strong in its coverage of Slavic language materials. Coverage for some periodicals is extensive, while for others only one article may have been analyzed. Prehistoric and historic [but not Greek and Roman] archaeology, ethnology, biological anthropology, cultural anthropology, and linguistics (especially Western hemisphere) are covered. In the earliest years, the historical archaeology of Europe, Asia, and Africa was excluded. Only recently have African linguistics, some Near Eastern archaeology, and sociolinguistic studies of Europe been included.

It is possible to consult Tozzer's classification system, introduced in 1977 and explicated in the Tozzer Library's *Index to anthropological subject headings,* 2d rev. ed. (Boston: Hall, 1981 [177p.]) **(A27),** in which the emphasis for superordinate categories is on the ethnic groups, languages, and major archaeological sites and in which classification schedules add nine new subject subdisciplines of anthropology not covered in the older edition. The earlier Peabody Museum of Archaeology and Ethnology Library's *Catalogue: Subjects: Index to subject headings,* rev. (Boston: Hall, 1971 [237p.]) **(A28),** must also be used to capture material published before 1977. What was in reality two catalogs with two classification systems were merged in the microfiche edition under a single alphabetic arrangement without cross-references, even though the two systems are structured on different superordinate categories. Therefore, two searches are necessary in any comprehensive subject entry (one with each of the two subject headings lists). Many scholars make a first entry by using the earlier classification schedules to guide entry into the graphically inviting forty-three hard-copy volumes of the Peabody Museum of Archaeology and Ethnology Library's *Catalogue: Subjects* (Boston: Hall, 1963 [27v.]) **(A29),** with *Supplements* 1–4, and then proceed to make a second entry into the Tozzer Library's *Author and subject catalogues of the Tozzer Library* [microfiche] **(A26).**

To master the use of this classification system, start the search using Peabody's *Catalogue* **(A29).** Consider a few sample entries for the identification of published investigations of the Navajo dance. The search must first find ATHABASCAN and move to NAVAJO thereunder. Once the Navajo section of the ATHABASCAN (spelled "Athapaskan" by the Library of Congress) bibliography has been located, specific entry into Navajo dance can be identified only by reference first into ATHABASCAN—NAVAJO—TECHNOLOGY with DANCING as a subordinate category under TECHNOLOGY. The classification system used in this great resource starts from the conceptual viewpoint that the activity of dancing is a social technology and that the Navajo are best identified as a tribe speaking an Athabascan language. While this system is difficult to use, as a cataloging activity, the simplicity of the organization made it possible for the work to be done by part-time graduate students of anthropology. This in turn made it possible for Harvard University for many years to carry the burden of providing subject cataloging to the contents of books and periodical articles without support from the larger community with which they so generously shared their labors.

Beginning in 1983, periodical indexing was transferred from the Tozzer Library subject catalog to its new annual publication *Anthropological literature* **(A36).** In this resource, entry by culture area is laborious and unsatisfactory. More significantly, Tozzer at this time abandoned the tradition of providing cumulated supplements of a card catalog, which brought all forms of anthropological publications into a single index organized with subject heading list and classification system that either made culture areas, ethnic groups, or archaeological site units superordinate to topical terms. However, for some years monographic cataloging was continued with the specialized classification scheme developed at that library. Beginning in 1987, monographs entering the collection at Tozzer Library were no longer cataloged with the LC list of subject headings. Instead, LC subject headings and the LC classification system are found in the *Bibliographic guide to anthropology and archaeology* **(A30).**

PLANNED AS A PUBLISHED CONTINUATION OF TOZZER LIBRARY'S ACCESSIONS

A30

Bibliographic guide to anthropology and archaeology, v.1– , 1987– . Boston: Hall. Annual.

Excludes periodical articles. Provides a dictionary arrangement of monographs of anthropological interest by author, title, and subjects. Includes books cataloged at Tozzer Library during the year of record. Many monographs from earlier years find their way into each edition. Compiled from OCLC [computer file], the entries include full cataloging information for books and other materials on topics related to cultural anthropology, physical anthropology, archaeology, and linguistics. LC and Dewey classification numbers are given. Subject searches for a particular culture area in these volumes are often extremely difficult. It is not user-friendly, but it does act as a holding record for a comprehensive monograph collection.

Retrospective Bibliographies—Continuing Bibliographies

CUMULATED AUTHOR INDEXES

A31

Royal Anthropological Society. Anthropological index. "Author index (1963–1989)" [microfiche]. In Museum of Mankind's *Periodical catalogues* (Bath, England: Mindata, 1989). 335 microfiche.

An author index covering the years 1963–89. This microfiche cumulation is included in the contents of the microfiche subset titled Museum of Mankind *Periodical catalogues* from the British Museum, Museum of Mankind's *Museum of Mankind Library catalogues* [microfiche] **(A25)** and is a reproduction of the hardcopy index housed at the British Museum, Museum of Mankind. The subset (*Periodical catalogues*) records the merged periodicals holdings of several collections now housed at the British Museum, Museum of Mankind Library, which cover all aspects of anthropology on a worldwide basis. They record many rarely held journals and newsletters. There is much more strength in the cataloging of periodical articles by Tozzer Library's *Catalogues* [microfiche] **(A26),** which provides both author and classified subject entry to journal output for a time span of more than 100 years, ending in 1982.

RUNS OF ANNUAL RETROSPECTIVE VOLUMES OF CLASSIFIED INDEXING SERVICES

Cumulated volumes in "Continuing Bibliographies" fall into two groups: "Indexing Services" and "Abstracting Services." The abstracting services display the contrast between scholarly traditions by contrasting the results identified in the abstracting services published in the English, French, and German languages. The most significant characteristic of the annual cumulated volume rests in its capacity to make available in a series of retrospective volumes bibliographic entries to complete the coverage between the cutoff date of the best selective bibliography available and the date of the literature search. Sometimes this can mean a laborious search through many quarterly issues covering ten or fifteen years. Fortunately, advances in computerized typesetting may in the future lead to the construction of machine-readable databases that can be used to search a file of all issues of these indexes. When the full texts of abstracts are included in a database, the power of keyword searches gives abstracting services a special significance. Ethnic group, tribal, and site name entries become more reliable; in anthropology, inclusion of this kind of information constitutes a significant advance.

Indexes specific to anthropology do not always include sources from other disciplines, even though there may be a shared topical interest. *Anthropological literature,* described in **(A36),** indexes just over 1,000 journals; yet the reference source *Serial publications in anthropology,* described in **(A16)** and which attempts to list all journals relevant to anthropological studies, identifies 4,837 relevant titles. There are numerous ways to search the contents of journals that are excluded from *Anthropological literature.* Some indexing services of related disciplines are available in computer files and are described in chapter 2.

CONTINUING ABSTRACTING SERVICES

A32

Abstracts in anthropology. v.1– , 1970– . Westport, Conn.: Greenwood. Quarterly.

Divided into archaeology, cultural anthropology, linguistics, and physical anthropology, and subdivided as appropriate. Includes some submitted but unpublished conference papers. Provides the only indexing into a number of significant publications. Annual cumulated author and subject indexes.

A33

Abstracts in German anthropology. v.1– , 1980– . Göttingen, Germany: Edition Herodot for the Arbeitskreis für Internationale Wissenschaftskommunikation. 2/yr.

Each issue of about 150 pages contains concise abstracts in English for all anthropological publications appearing in German and publications by German, Austrian, and Swiss authors in languages other than German. Includes dissertations. To facilitate use, there is a subject and an author index. Includes all subdisciplines and all geographic areas with unique strength in the ethnography of Eastern Europe.

A34

Francis bulletin signalétique. v.45– , 1991– . Paris: Centre Nationale de la Recherche Scientifique. Institut de l'Information Scientific et Technique. Sciences Humaine et Sociales. Quarterly.

Continues *Bulletin signalétique,* which continues *Bulletin analytique.* Sections 19–24; *Sciences humaines, philosophie.* Sections 19–24 also issued separately. Many of value to anthropologists. Split into: 519: *Philosophie, sciences religieuses;* 520: *Pédagogie;* 521: *Sociologie, ethnologie, préhistoire et archéologie;* 522: *Histoire des sciences et des techniques;* 523: *Histoire et science de la literature, arts du spectacle;* 524: *Sciences du language;* 525: *Préhistoire and protohistoire;* and 526: *Art and archéology;* 529: *Ethnologie.*

Coverage is international in scope for all research published in Western languages. To a remarkable degree, strongest in exactly those culture and subject areas most weakly covered in the indexing achieved by catalogers at Peabody Museum Library and Tozzer Library. The arrangement has subsections slightly different from the usual orientation of American scholars (fossils under "Préhistoire"). Broad subject headings and the fact that quarterly listings did not cumulate even annually have long made this a clumsy source for retrospective searches. Computerized technology has changed that. Since 1972, this resource has been available online from *FRANCIS* [computer file] **(B19).** Book reviews are indicated by the abbreviation "C.R." Includes references to conference proceedings, dissertations, essays in collected works, and periodical articles. Ethnic-groups indexing has been a sustained objective.

CONTINUING INDEXES

A35

Anthropological index. v.1– , 1963– . London: Royal Anthropological Institute. Quarterly.

Title varies. Coverage includes ethnography (with the only sustained coverage of European ethnology), ethnomusicology, biological anthropology, archaeology, linguistics, and cultural anthropology. Absence of any subject index at present reduces the ease with which the bound version of this valuable reference tool can be used for retrospective searches. A high standard of accuracy. Annual author index eases some searches.

A separate publication, *Reference list of current periodicals,* described at **(A14),** arranges alphabetically the list of abbreviations to journal titles indexed and provides up-to-date bibliographic descriptions for each journal placed next to its indicated abbreviation. The Royal Anthropological Institute's cumulated author index of *Anthropological index* (1963–88) was housed in the British Museum, Museum of Mankind when Mandata's staff photographed and published this resource. For that reason, this card file was included in the Museum of Mankind, *Museum of Mankind Library catalogues* [microfiche] **(A25).**

A36

Anthropological literature: An index to periodical literature and essays. v.11– , 1989– . Cambridge, Mass.: Tozzer Library. Quarterly.

Continues the index issued in microfiche, *Anthropological literature: An index to periodical literature and essays* [microfiche], v.6–10, 1984–88, which continues publication with the same title issued in a paper format (v.1–5, 1978–83). This publication brings the periodical indexing of Tozzer Library to the research community in conventional form. Organized by subdiscipline as superordinate category (in contrast to older arrangements of subject headings at Peabody [now Tozzer]). Five sections include cultural and social anthropology, archaeology, biological/physical anthropology, linguistics, and general/method/theory. In the geographic index, some subject headings in a single quarterly issue may have as many as twenty-three item numbers. Useful cumulations will be impossible without some indexing expansion, which might make possible Boolean searches in computer files. Journals are selectively indexed, yet a serious attempt has been made to provide worldwide coverage of all of the subdisciplines of anthropology. Invaluable for physical anthropology and archaeology, and especially strong on Indians of North, Central, and South America. Improved organization is achieved by the inclusion of an ethnic/linguistic index; an archaeological site/culture index; and a joint author index.

A37

MLA international bibliography of books and articles on the modern languages and literatures. v.1– , 1921– . New York: Modern Language Association. Annual.

Title has varied. Volumes 1969–80 organized by classified listings and author index. Volumes from 1981 forward are organized by classified listing, and author and subject indexes. Since 1970 this resource has covered folklore studies. Provides reliable international coverage of linguistics. Each department is the responsibility of a recognized authority. For example, William Bright was long responsible for the coverage of North American Indian languages. Each year three volumes are bound as one. Includes periodical articles, books, and the contents of essays collected in monographs. A reliable record of what has been achieved, including even some dissertations.

The online version, *MLA international* **(B29),** available from DIALOG (1964–80). Since 1980 available on CD-ROM for the years 1980 forward, with searching modes Browse, Wilsearch, and online Wilsonline. A companion volume published biennially, *MLA directory of periodicals: A guide to journals and series in language and linguistics* **(E09),** provides extensive information about the special features in all journals and series in the master list of *MLA international bibliography.* For Third World countries, where the array of specialized journals is more limited and the scholarly journals are less narrowly focused on a single subject discipline, this directory is valuable far beyond its stated purpose.

A38

Ruble, Blair A., and Mark H. Teeter. *A scholar's guide to humanities and social sciences in the Soviet Union.* Armonk, N.Y.: M. E. Sharpe, 1985. 310p.

Arranged as a directory of institutions. After a discussion of the services of each institute, a list of continuing services and other publications are itemized. The continuing indexes for anthropology and related disciplines are easily identified in this resource, which also discusses access to the extensive computer files. Altogether the institutes index 250,000 books, articles, and reviews published in all languages of the Soviet Union and in thirty-five foreign languages from 115 countries around the world. One-half of the indexing is based on foreign-language titles. See especially the list of publications for the "Institute of Scientific Information in the Social Sciences" (p.14–17), "Institute of Archaeology" (p.19–23), the "Institute of Ethnology" (p.23–28), and the "Institute of Linguistics" (p.72–76). Also included are the many separate institutes for area studies. The detailed subject index greatly expands the utility of this valuable resource.

Some readers with a strong interest in Russian-language materials may want to consult another more general resource introduced since the cutoff date of Ruble and Teeter's *A scholar's guide to humanities and social sciences in the Soviet Union* **(A38).** For that purpose inspect *Social sciences in the USSR: An annotated bibliography,* v.1– , 1989– (Moscow: INION)

(A39), an annual publication in a classed arrangement with authors listed under each heading. The 1989 issue included under the heading "Archaeology" items 89–95; "Ethnology" items 235–62; "Oriental studies" items 353–400; "African studies" items 398–417. There is an author index. The continuity of this resource cannot be predicted with confidence. It is mentioned here only because it is a recent and promising resource.

Retrospective Bibliographies—Topical Bibliographies

A40

"Classification of articles." In v.17, *Index in International encyclopedia of the social sciences,* p.83–108. New York: Macmillan and Free Pr., 1968. 17v.

To identify articles relevant to anthropology, examine volume 17. Consult "Anthropology" (p.84–85) for the 132 topics and seventy-four biographies, and "Archeology" (p.85–86) for the fourteen topics and ten biographies. Cross-references from these topics lead to other lists of articles in this classified list. In the *Biographical supplement,* v.18 (New York: Free Pr., 1979 [820p.]), find additional biographical entries for anthropologists who can be identified in the "Classification of Biographies" (p.xxxv–xxxviii). For more current topical bibliographies, consult another classified list of encyclopedia articles under the terms "Anthropology" (p.xxi), "Biology" (p.xxi–xxii), and "Linguistics" (p.xxiv), which are found in Adam Kuper and Jessica Kuper's *The social science encyclopedia* (London: Routledge, 1985) [916p.] **(A41).** Adam Kuper has served as the editor of *Current anthropology,* and experience gained in that position has influenced the content and organization of this encyclopedia. His command of the broad issues and his careful selection of authorities give this resource special value for anthropological searches. The articles are signed and supported by selective bibliographies.

A42

Erickson, Paul A. *History of anthropology bibliography.* Halifax, Nova Scotia: Department of Anthropology, Saint Mary's Univ., 1984. 142p. (Occasional papers in anthropology [Halifax, N.S.], no.1)

Supplements no.1 (1985), no.2 (1985), no.3 (1987). The base volume had 2,036 English-language entries, excluding reference sources. A list of indexes (p.v–vii) attempts to guide the reader. The use of this resource requires detailed scanning of a great number of entries. For example, under FRANZ BOAS there are fifty-three items without subject expansion.

A43

Kemper, Robert V., and John F. S. Phinney. *The history of anthropology: A research bibliography.* New York: Garland, 1977. 212p. (Garland reference library of the social sciences, v.31)

Classes 2,400 entries under general sources, background, modern anthropology, related disciplines, biographical sources. Each section is subdivided as appropriate by subject, geographic area, and personality. Author index.

Informational Reference Searches

Bibliographies in the reference section often are used to identify bibliographic descriptions of monographs, periodicals, and dissertations that must be located outside the reference collection. The reference works cited from chapter to chapter under the heading "Informational Searches" provide within themselves the information sought.

Encyclopedias, Dictionaries, and Compendiums

Articles in encyclopedias and compendiums attempt an orderly presentation of statements that are believed to be durable truths. Encyclopedia articles written by anthropologists in the 1930s on topics such as "Culture" and "Language" command attention and respect even today. In addition to content review, these articles provide select bibliographic review in references gathered to support the arguments of the articles. Therefore, when an encyclopedia includes a classified synopsis of its articles, it can be used as a survey of anthropological knowledge. Collectively, the authors of the articles have constructed in their list of references a select bibliography.

Searches for informational reference sources across other chapters of *Fieldwork in the Library* expand coverage. As always in anthropological searches, a comprehensive search requires a movement back and forth between resources every anthropologist needs to know and resources specific to a subdiscipline or culture area. To confirm this point, turn to "Informational Reference Searches" in chapter 5, "Anthropological Linguistics," and find the several multivolume sets published in the last three years. There has been in this discipline a surge of scholarly activity centering on the consolidation of the dramatic gains made by students of language since 1960.

One of the advantages of placing structural emphasis on commonalities between reference books is that it allows us to enjoy the organizational possibilities that come from the definition of form, without submitting us to the tyranny of definitions that do not reflect current usage by the community of scholars. Contribution to a search can be used to measure the value of a reference source. The scholarly community is constantly struggling to transmit and consolidate larger and larger amounts of information. It is innovative. In several instances, we exploit a recent trend in anthropology to publish monographic series devoted to a specific culture area. This development can be seen as an attempt to control and consolidate results. This possibility is discussed in some detail in chapter 7, "Africa South of the Sahara," with Crammer and Streak's *Sudanesische Marginalien* **(G116)** as an example. For the area specialist, some monographic series can be used as a handbook in searches. This is especially true when a series starts with a burst of five or six volumes with contributions from the leading authorities. This method of organizing results usually points to intense efforts in an area of research that is either new or long neglected. For example, consult the historical perspectives in the monographic series *History of anthropology* **(A48)** to gauge the collective results and emerging boundaries of an increasingly vigorous research focus in anthropology.

An encyclopedia contains a summary of knowledge or of a branch of knowledge. There are purists who contend that the term *encyclopedia* must be limited to works covering the whole of human knowledge and that the term *dictionary* must be applied when only a branch of learning is covered. The term *dictionary,* as it is commonly used, refers to a lexicon in which the words of a system of knowledge are entered alphabetically and briefly defined. Most students would expect a book such as Johnston's *Dictionary of human geography* **(A44),** to be called a "desk encyclopedia." Usage is far from uniform. *Fieldwork in the Library* describes a resource from the title page. In the classified arrangement, works used as a concise record of established truth tend to be listed as encyclopedias or handbooks under the heading "Searching Informational Reference Material." Inspect also *L'Anthropologie* **(A51).** Like many dictionaries published in Europe, it is constructed as an alphabetized collection of essays with an index to specific terms. For our purposes, the publisher announced this resource as a "dictionary." It can be used in a library as a dictionary. Most bibliographic guides describe it as "dictionary." But it could also be used as a desk encyclopedia of French-language anthropology.

Find in Ronald John Johnston and Associates, *Dictionary of human geography,* 2d ed. (Oxford, England: Blackwell, 1986. 600p.) **(A44)** an alphabetic arrangement of signed articles with suggested readings. There are 42 pages of index. For an older but still valuable consolidation of the results of study in this tradition, consult Renato Biasutti's *Le razze e i popoli della terra,* 4th ed. (Turino: Unione Tipografico-editrice Torinese, 1967 [4v.]), which provides a comprehensive account of the physical and cultural anthropology of the world, arranged on regional basis. Each chapter has a good bibliography. Many illustrations, photographs, and maps. Truly a compendium for the use of geographic variables as an organizing principle, and one of the best general and not overly condensed surveys available. Major divisions include coverage of race, population, and culture in a classed arrangement that includes Europe, Asia, Africa,

Oceania, and the Americas. There is an index volume. For informal updating of research completed with this organizing principle.

Consult also chapter 2 for a description of *Geobase* [computer file] **(B20)** for its coverage of human geography.

A45

Hunter, David E., and Phillip Whitten, eds. *Encyclopedia of anthropology.* New York: Harper, 1976. 411p.

Lists 1,400 entries. Many articles signed by the 100 contributors can be identified by disciplines. The articles tend to be brief, and the organization is a forthright alphabetic arrangement.

Concentrates on concepts, theories, and leading figures in anthropology. Range of coverage can be extended by reference to the ethnic and ethnic group entries available in Roger Pearson's *Anthropological glossary* (Malabar, Fla.: Krieger, 1985 [282p.]) **(A46),** which adds 5,000 recent terms identified in studies from the subdisciplines of cultural anthropology, physical anthropology, linguistics, and archaeology. Includes descriptions of archaeological sites. Older terms find better treatment in the Royal Anthropological Institute's *Notes and queries on anthropology,* 6th ed. rev. (London: Routledge, 1951 [403p.]), valuable for its inclusion of physical anthropology and material culture as those disciplines were conceptually organized at the date of publication. Encyclopedia arrangement with subject index to terms. For Marxist terms, consult Charlotte Seymour-Smith's *Dictionary of anthropology* (Boston: Hall, 1986 [305p.]) **(A47).** Includes biographies of some leading anthropologists and selected lists of their works. The bibliography at the end of the volume (p.293–305) is selected for Marxist anthropology. Dictionaries from all of the subdisciplines of anthropology as they are distributed under "Informational Reference Searches" should be consulted. For example, Winthrop's *Dictionary of concepts in cultural anthropology* **(D47)** has a list of concepts (p.viii–xiv) that guides the reader to brief but accurate and well-documented discussions of these ideas. The name index under BOAS has been enlarged with twenty-one expansions. Culture is subdivided with five terms. The index makes this an unusually valuable source. Also in chapter 4, use Murdock's *Atlas of world cultures* (1981) **(D12)** to identify monographic summaries of ethnic cultures.

The encyclopedic coverage of the various research traditions in anthropology has not yet been accomplished. However, an understanding of the impact of these traditions on the works of individual scholars can be of great importance. In a field of specialty that is active but still fluid, it is not unusual for a monographic series to serve in an encyclopedic tradition of regular consolidation of advances. Consult the historical perspectives in the monographic series *History of anthropology,* v.1– , 1983– (Madison: University of Wisconsin Pr.) **(A48).** The pragmatic flexibility of George W. Stocking in his definitions of history and of anthropology increases the utility of this series. For example, contributors feel free to discuss the literary activities of Franz Boas and Ruth Benedict, which helped establish the tradition of readability so widely characteristic of the early investigators. Volumes to date: *Observers and observed: Essays on ethnographic fieldwork* (1983); *Functionalist historicized: Essays on British social anthropology* (1984); *Malinowski, Rivers, Benedict, and others: Essays on culture and personality* (1986); *Bones, bodies, behavior: Essays on biological anthropology* (1988); *Romantic motives: On anthropological sensibility* (1989).

A49

International Symposium on Anthropology, New York, 1952. *Anthropology today: An encyclopedic inventory.* Prepared under the chairmanship of Alfred L. Kroeber. Chicago: Univ. of Chicago Pr., 1953. 966p.

This major postwar professional assessment is divided into six parts, each consisting of essays by specialists, with bibliographies for each. This work effectively established what is still the rationale for anthropology as a separate university department in the United States. A companion to Wenner-Gren Foundation's *Yearbook of anthropology, 1955* (New York: Wenner-Gren Foundation for Anthropological Research, 1955 [836p.]) **(A50),** which was launched as the first of an annual series that failed to materialize, it forms a consolidation of anthropological knowledge to the date of publication. Elaboration can be found in nineteen essays selected by William L. Thomas, Jr., and reprinted under the title *Current anthropology: A supplement to Anthropology today* (Chicago: Univ. of Chicago Pr., 1956 [377p.]). The record of consolidated worldwide research efforts in anthropology can be supplemented by consulting the published sources cited for each institution listed in the *International directory of anthropological institutions* **(A56).** An assessment of the traditions of French anthropology, *L'Anthropologie* (Verviers, France: Marabout, 1974 [690p.]) **(A51)** provides maps, 400 brief articles, and bibliographic notes.

Directories

Directories of institutions often list individuals affiliated with each institution. If those persons are listed under the institutional entry, then a personal name index provides an institutional address for all affiliated scholars. For example, inspect the annual *AAA Guide* **(A53).** Some directories with a narrow range of coverage will be described in the more specialized chapters to which they are appropriate. When biographic directories such as Winters' *International directory of anthropology* **(A22)** and Mann's *Biographical directory of anthropologists born before 1920* **(A23)**—which include reliable bibliographies of the first importance—are used, the permanent reference value transcends current address information. Some directories include selective bibliographies of each listed scholar. If the directory has a limited topical or geographic scope, then this bibliographic information has continuing and historical value in defining the scholarly traditions and progress of that community for the decade it covers. In such cases when this possibility has been fully developed by the editors, a directory may be given full description in the section devoted to retrospective bibliographies or the consolidation of results. For example, the *Directory of Europeanist anthropologists in North America* **(O18),** described in chapter 10, "CIS and Europe," is the best available entry into the study of European cultures by scholars based in North America and trained in anthropology.

Most professional associations publish membership directories like the *AAA guide* **(A53).** Some of these have great specialized bibliographic value. For example, the American Anthropological Association has published a number of these, which are of considerable importance. Inspect, for example, Herman Blakely and Pamela A. R. Blakely's *Directory of visual anthropology* (Washington, D.C.: Society for Visual Anthropology, a unit of the American Anthropological Association, 1989 [177p.]) **(A52),** which provides a historical review of North American institutional support for visual anthropology, followed by an alphabetic listing by scholar. Each entry provides relevant personal and address information and a bibliography of that scholar's film work. There is an alphabetic-by-author bibliography of printed scholarly works by these individuals. Recently there has been a trend toward national directories of ethnographic workers.

A53

AAA guide v.1– , 1989/90– . Washington, D.C.: American Anthropological Assn. Annual.

Includes a name index to individuals that identifies the most recent institutional home of 4,869 individuals holding positions in anthropology in the listed departments. Contains five divisions, each filled with useful information: (1) Lists institutions in four categories: "Colleges and Universities," "Museums," "Research Institutions," and "Government." Arranged alphabetically under each category, there is detailed information under the entry for each institution. (2) Provides directories first of "AAA membership" and then of "AAA unit members." (3) Provides statistics in seven categories: "Sources of Degree," "Degrees Held," "Breakdown of Individual and Positions," "Location of Academic Departments," "Students Enrolled," "Total Degrees Granted," and "Ph.D. Dissertations." (4) Recent listing for Ph.D. dissertations in anthropology gives name, title, university, and area of current specialized focus. An alphabetic list without subject entry. (5) Index of "Individuals" and "Index of Departments."

A54

Cantrell, Karen, and Denise Wallen, eds. *Funding for anthropological research.* Phoenix: Oryx Pr., 1986. 308p.

Seven hundred and four programs that support research in anthropology. Listed by sponsor with a subject index. Includes a list of sponsors by type. The annotated bibliography includes printed sources and online databases useful in funding.

A55

Fifth international directory of anthropologists. Pref. by Sol Tax. Chicago: Univ. of Chicago Pr., 1975. 496p.

First to third editions published under the title *International directory of anthropologists.* Includes both bibliographic and detailed biographical information. While not nearly comprehensive as a worldwide directory for anthropologists (this is a resource that depends on the participation of scholars), it has international coverage and lists 4,300 scholars qualified (by election and dues) as "associates" in *Current anthropology.* Associates of *Current Anthropology* who did not respond to the questionnaire are listed by name and address only in a separate section. Its considerable reference value centers on the detailed Geographical, Chronological, and Subject/ Methodological indexes.

Informally updated by *Current anthropology* **(A09).**

A56

"International directory of anthropological institutions." 4th ed. *Current anthropology* 8 (1967): 647–751.

Acts as a compendium of anthropological work in the context of institutional support. For each institution includes a detailed record of the research focus, facilities available, publications (both continuing and recent). Does not supersede earlier editions such as the 3d edition in *Current anthropology* 6 (1965): 485–568, and William L. Thomas, Jr., and Anna M. Pikelis, eds., *International directory of anthropological institutions* (New York: Wenner-Gren Foundation for Anthropological Research, 1953 [468p.]). Arranged geographically with an outline of history and scope for regional development of the discipline. This description of the theoretical and methodical emphasis of each region is followed by detailed information on individual institutions. Indexes by institution and city.

Informally kept up to date by the department "Institutions" in *Current anthropology* **(A09).**

State-of-the-Art Reviews

State-of-the-art reviews often contain a valuable retrospective bibliographic record. They are most often consulted for a consolidation and appraisal of current research issues and are expected to reveal in their text something of the relationships between various contemporary contributions. They rarely retain their value for more than twenty years. Review articles as found in *Current anthropology* **(A09)** and the *Annual review of anthropology* **(A57)** have been especially alert in identifying unexpected activity in a new direction and providing both a bibliographic and conceptual synthesis of emerging research perspectives. *Reviews in anthropology* **(A58)** provides comparable but more sharply specialized reviews of recent significant monographs dealing with a common research focus.

A57

Annual review of anthropology. v.1– , 1972– . Palo Alto, Calif.: Annual Reviews. Annual.

Except for frequency of issue, this series continues the tradition of excellence established in *Biennial review of anthropology,* v.1–13, 1959–71 (Stanford, Calif.: Stanford Univ. Pr.; London: Oxford Univ. Pr.). Does provide timely evaluations of current research on carefully delimited problems. All subdisciplines of anthropology are touched, but continuity or complete coverage of specific problems or geographic areas does not seem to be an editorial objective. The "Literature cited" listed at the end of each review forms a succession of retrospective bibliographies of serious work in anthropology. In terms of improved bibliographic control over English-language research work, the cumulative benefits to anthropological scholarship are very considerable. An editorial flaw has been the erratic use of abbreviations in the bibliographies, which vary even between articles in the same volume. A five-year cumulative author and subject index covering volumes 3 to 7 is bound in volume 7, with five-year cumulations in each volume thereafter.

For a more international focus of editorial viewpoint, consult *Current anthropology* **(A09)**, sponsored by the Wenner-Gren Foundation. *Current anthropology* embodies some of the features of an organ of general review. The review article has been its hallmark.

A58

Reviews in anthropology. v.1– , 1974– . Pleasantville, N.Y.: Redgrave. Bimonthly.

Became bimonthly in 1976. Has sustained a record of publishing quality, in-depth reviews of about 100 books a year in a format that leads to evaluative comparison of various contributions and to extensive bibliographies. The "Commentary" section gives authors an opportunity to reply. Again, coverage includes all subdisciplines in anthropology.

Searching Graphic Materials

While some standard reference sources are identified here, any search for visual aids can benefit from contact with trained professionals. The map librarian, the art librarian, and the audiovisual librarian all have contributions to make. This section should be used as a preliminary survey that can inform your consultation with these specialists. Holdings of these materials often require special handling, and the specialized help of library personnel is sometimes useful in locating them in the space of a research library.

A59

American Geographical Society of New York. Map Department. *Index to maps in books and periodicals.* Boston: Hall, 1968. 10v.

Supplemented by American Geographical Society of New York, Map Department, *Index to maps in books and periodicals, Supplement* (Boston: Hall, 1971 [603p.]), by *Second supplement* (Boston: Hall, 1976 [568p.]), and by *Third supplement* (Boston: Hall, 1987 [668p.]). Look under the headings ETHNOLOGY and LANGUAGES. On Internet [computer network] Listserver mailing lists try images-1@csearn.bitnet for image processing of remotely sensed data and maps-1@UGA.cc.uga.edu for mailing lists of Maps and Air Photo Systems Forum.

A60

Clarke, Lawrence, and others, eds. *Atlas of mankind.* Chicago: Rand McNally, 1982. 191p.

The first section covers migration and race, languages, environment and survival, the search for food, kinship systems, marriage, death, religions, and health and nutrition. The second section describes eleven geographic areas. Provides thematic background through world maps, diagrams, and photographs. Cross-referenced to ethnographic groups described in "Peoples of the world" (p.56–191), which divides the world into eleven regions: the Arctic, Europe, Africa, the Middle East, all four parts of Asia, Oceania, North America, and Latin America. The length of each section varies from six pages (the Arctic and Central Asia) to seventeen pages (Latin America). For each region there are maps of language distribution and a history time bar providing key dates.

A61

Collier, John, Jr., and Malcolm Collier. *Visual anthropology: Photography as a research method.* Albuquerque: Univ. of New Mexico Pr., 1986. 248p.

The definitive handbook on data gathering and analysis with photographic records. Includes detailed and knowledgeable summaries of everything now known about the use of photography as a research tool, including methodologies for tightly controlled sequential photography to record and study processes such as ceremonies and stages of social interaction. Discusses photographers as "participant observers" and techniques like surveying, mapping, and technology. Makes precise the grammar for photographing social interaction and the process of interviewing with photographs.

A62

Garrett, Wilbur E., ed. *National geographic index, 1888–1988.* Washington, D.C.: National Geographic Society, 1989. 1,215p.

An earlier index covered 1888 through December 1946. This volume has 5,000 subject entries to 47,000 color pictures made for a society that has supported anthropological research and exploration since 1890.

A63

Heider, Karl G. *Films for anthropological teaching.* 7th ed. Washington, D.C.: American Anthropological Assn., 1983. 312p. (American Anthropological Association, Special publication, no.16)

Arranged by film title. Indexed by geographic area, subject, distributor, and persons involved. A select list of distributors. Consult also Blakely and Blakely's *Directory of visual anthropology* **(A52).**

A64

Root, Nina J. *Catalog of the American Museum of Natural History film archives.* New York: Garland for American Museum of Natural History Library, Department of Library Services, New York, 1987. 410p.

Describes 291 films listed by film title, with some bibliographic references. Alphabetized genre list, chronological list, and index by subject personal names, expedition names, corporate names, film title, and geographic location.

A65

Spencer, Robert F., and Eldon Johnson. *Atlas for anthropology.* 2d ed. Dubuque, Iowa: W. C. Brown, 1968. 61p.

Five maps of culture areas and ethnic groups in North America, South America, Africa, Eurasia, and Oceania. Five maps of language families in the same areas. Four maps of Old World and New World prehistory.

Searching Unpublished Materials

Unpublished materials tend to be housed in special locations where specialized assistance can be given. While some archival material can be found only at one location, much of it can be reproduced in microfilm for interested scholars. Some archival material is widely distributed in this form. This section is devoted to guides that can be used to identify archival materials that are widely available. It is equally devoted to the identification of records that assist in locating anthropologically significant dissertations. Once again, the scholarly use of either archival materials or unpublished dissertations often requires special assistance from library staff. It is important to remember that in some research libraries holdings of these materials are not recorded in the regular cataloging services as individual items.

Archives

A66

Guide to the microfilm collection of the professional papers of Franz Boas. Wilmington, Del.: Scholarly Resources, 1972. 2v.

Organized alphabetically by the name of the person with whom the correspondence was undertaken. Under this name there is a listing of both the correspondence of that person and the letters of Boas.

A67

Institut d'ethnologie. *Archives et documents, micro-édition. Sciences humaines.* 1979– . Paris: Institut d'Ethnologie, Musée de l'Homme. Irregular.

The archives of the Institut d'Ethnologie (Musée de l'Homme) are all available in a micro-edition. French contact as a colonial power generated unpublished reports and ethnographic and linguistic studies that poured into this archive. Especially strong for material on French West Africa, Indochina, and the Pacific. Well-organized schedules, with summaries in English.

A68

Kenworthy, Mary Ann, and others. *Preserving field records: Archival techniques for archaeologists and anthropologists.* Philadelphia: University Museum, University of Pennsylvania, 1985. 102p.

"List of archival suppliers, 1985" ([4]p.) inserted in pocket. "Bibliography" (p.96–102). A massive body of literature on this topic is consolidated and organized into a select list with concise annotations in the chapter titled "Archaeology."

A69

National Anthropological Archives. *Catalog to manuscripts at the National Anthropological Archives.* Department of Anthropology. National Museum of Natural History. Smithsonian Institution, Washington, D.C. and Boston: Hall, 1975. 4v.

Photographic reproductions of catalog cards for documents collected to 1965 in three divisions: (1) Indians North of Mexico; (2) Geographical file on Mexico, Central America, and non-North American areas; (3) Numerical file indicating subject under which cards have been filed. Subject approach by tribe and linguistic group. The resources of the archive continue to grow. The National Archives has a worldwide interest that guides its collection development. Among the private papers are correspondence series, vocabularies, grammatical data and texts of rarely spoken languages, ethnographic and archaeological field notes and drafts of reports, and transcripts of oral history and of music. Many important early maps.

Some finding aids have been published for holdings of this library. For example, James R. Glenn's *Register to papers of Neil Merton Judd* (Washington, D.C.: The Archives, 1982 [23p.]) (Finding guide to the National Anthropological Archive) **(A70),** which includes records of American Bureau of Ethnology expeditions between 1915 and 1920, describes cartographic materials resulting from these expeditions, and identifies seven and one-half feet of photographs collected between 1874 and 1964.

A71

Weeks, John M. *Introduction to library research in anthropology.* Boulder, Colo.: Westview, 1991. 281p.

Provides an inviting introduction to library research appropriate to the needs of an undergraduate; includes a chapter on how to use the card catalog. Some chapters appear to be exhaustive for the topic covered and can be inspected with profit by even the most seasoned librarian. The chapter "Anthropological Films and Photography" (p.210–19), even without annotation, effectively consolidates a list of reference sources useful for entry in this difficult field.

The chapter, "Guides to Archives and Manuscripts Collections" (p.53–60), introduces the reader to many national bibliographies that are beyond the scope of *Fieldwork in the Library,* even though they provide useful support for some anthropological searches. Weeks has identified bibliographic guides to archives of Colonial Latin America. He also includes a more general classified list of fifty-three sources for entry into archival materials arranged by geographical area, and then by subject, with some very brief annotations.

Fieldwork in the Library relies on Weeks to introduce descriptions of entry into the more general national archives. Our lists, in each chapter, focus on resources that are more specifically designed to meet the needs of anthropological research.

The following guides, under the heading "Archives" in "Access by Discipline: What Every Anthropologist Needs to Know," are resources of the first importance to anthropology that are not included in the list prepared by Weeks: (1) the *Guide to the microfilm collection of the professional papers of Franz Boas* **(A66),** (2) *Archives et documents, micro-édition* **(A67),** and (3) Pacific archival material. Weeks neglects bibliographic resources describing the vast and easily obtainable microform collections of Pacific materials: the National Library of Australia, *Australian joint copying project handbook* **(N22)** and the equally important Pacific Manuscript Bureau's *PMB DOC 1–1000* **(N23).** Unpublished fieldwork and doctoral dissertations can be found in the Melanesian Archive's *Melanesian newsletter and accessions list* **(N84).**

Data Processing by Computerization

The International Union of Anthropological and Ethnological Sciences, through its world congresses, international congresses, and commissions, brings together individuals with interests in anthropology, archaeology, and related matters. Its Commission on Documentation includes the computerization of anthropological data and data retrieval as appropriate activity for that organization and issues a newsletter (three times a year). It also served as a sponsor to the *International bibliography of social and cultural anthropology* during the early developmental years. See also the electronic journal *World cultures* [computer file] (La Jolla, Calif.: World Cultures) **(A72),** with a variable title, *Journal of comparative and cross cultural research* [computer disc] (La Jolla, Calif.: World Cultures). Included on disc are text and numerical data, codebooks, sampling frames, bibliographies, descriptions of societal focuses, and programs. Some volume numbers are issued in parts.

Some volume numbers are accompanied with a supplement disc. Examples of coverage: The data from the 1,267 societies coded on 152 variables identified in Murdock's *Ethnographic atlas,* described at **(D73),** is converted to machine-readable form in disc, *World cultures* [computer file]: file 2#4. Also available, a Hominid fossil database by Beals and Smith, *World cultures* (file: 3#2); and an anthropometric database on living populations, *World cultures* (file 3#3). System requirements are IBM or compatible microcomputer with 256K. Not user-friendly.

Dissertations

For many culture areas, the work completed at institutions in Australia, Great Britain, or India can be useful. The anthropological work completed as dissertations by scholars outside the United States is often most easily identified in bibliographic guides to dissertations of a defined culture area. Several of these guides are described in the appropriate chapters of *Fieldwork in the Library.*

A73

Anthropology: A dissertation bibliography. Ann Arbor, Mich.: University Microfilms International, 1978. 65p.

Supplements appear irregularly. Classed arrangement of 3,400 American doctoral dissertations. The broad classifications are subdivided by topical and regional fields. Can be updated and expanded by the more comprehensive database *Dissertations abstracts* [computer file] **(B14),** which contains records not found in DAI. Consult also *Abstracts in German anthropology* **(A33);** and *Francis bulletin signalétique* **(A34).**

A74

McDonald, David R. *Masters' theses in anthropology: A bibliography of theses from United States colleges and universities.* New Haven, Conn.: HRAF Press, 1977. 453p.

Lists 3,835 theses completed in 109 institutions from 1898 to 1975. Subject, ethnic, national, cross-cultural, and institutional indexes greatly increase the value of this reference work. Subject index has multiple entries.

A75

"Ph.D. dissertations in anthropology." In *AAA Guide.* v.1– , 1963– . Washington, D.C.: The American Anthropological Association. Annual.

A special feature. Each edition includes some older titles from institutions new to the directory. This is an author list with no subject or title entry that serves as a much needed journal of record.

2

Related Disciplines

Disciplines such as sociology and psychology often achieve advances relevant to questions of anthropological importance. The relationship between these disciplines and anthropology is different from that between anthropology and its subdisciplines: archaeology, ethnology, linguistics, and physical anthropology. Results from related disciplines are sometimes distant from the agenda of anthropological concern. They are committed to an entirely different set of theory and methodology. Traditional anthropology in all of its subdisciplines shares a common set of theory and methodology. The hallmark of anthropological inquiry is, of course, its intense interest in local-level activities as they are revealed at archaeological sites, in the behavior of the genus *Homo*. The methodology is firmly grounded in the importance of a comparative analysis of evidence recorded from direct observation. The related disciplines are more firmly committed to the use of statistical distributions as a method of guiding research, and often implicitly assume that results stated in terms of statistical continuum embody the only method of making scientific statements about human behavior. Nevertheless, the massive bibliographic computer files of related disciplines include coverage of important anthropological journals. The technology for reading machine-readable databases makes possible entirely new kinds of subject search. Among many library users, available computer files are the first-choice reference strategy.

The selection of bibliographic databases from other disciplines for inclusion in this chapter is anchored in the pioneering work of Haas's "Anthropology" **(B01)** because her work benefits from years of reference experience with anthropologists and with anthropological questions. Only four entries of computer files extend past the selection of printed indexes recorded in our annotation to that excellent guide. These additions represent a sample of the computer files with a more limited usefulness which are described in the chapters defined by the subdisciplines of anthropology and geographic regions. Following our usual practice, we select guides listed under "Searching Bibliographic Guides" to define the parameters of this chapter. Haas's "Anthropology" **(B01),** as updated with more recent resources identified in Balay's *Guide to reference books* **(B02),** establishes the bibliographic base upon which this chapter is constructed. Even though it is hardly seventeen years since the Haas guide was published, parts of each listed indexing service now have corresponding computer file editions. These files are described in this chapter as new databases for the old. This chapter is about updating and expanding on the contribution of Haas's "Anthropology" **(B01).**

If these computer files had not been invented, discussion of resources from related disciplines would have been covered in the annotation to Haas's "Anthropology" **(B01),** as one of the guides to chapter 1, and chapter 2 would not exist. For retrospective searches, machine-readable databases turn what was once a laborious search through numerous retrospective volumes into a much simpler task. Even skimpy coverage of a research issue scattered through many volumes can be accessed with a reasonable effort. The older volumes of printed indexing services have thus been transformed into a viable resource for retrospective searches. Additionally, machine-readable databases greatly increase the possibility of entry by keyword and citation searches.

The universe of computer files changes so rapidly that standards for their bibliographic description have not been firmly established. How is the reader best served when a database is available in several editions? Descriptions of databases often vary in content or time span covered. We attempt to list a database as one computer file, and to describe variant versions in the annotation. For descriptive standards, we follow library tradition and apply cataloging rules to the main entry description. In this we follow Balay's *Guide to reference books* **(B02),** which can be used to identify recent general reference sources.

Consult *Ulrich's international periodicals directory* **(B42)** for extensive lists of computer databases, for classified lists of printed anthropological journals, and for information about the availability of a machine-readable edition. An excellent organization guides searches through serial publications and their related machine-readable editions.

Searching Bibliographic Guides

Balay's *Guide to reference books* **(B02)** is selective for recent general reference sources, including the most useful machine-readable databases. Accepting printed indexing services selected by Haas's "Anthropology" **(B01),** as a bibliographic base of useful resources from related disciplines, sets a standard that invites inclusion of recently issued computer files that correspond to parts of these older printed publications. To understand just what is possible in the use of computer files, inspect the pioneering effort of Jeffrey G. Reed and Pam M. Baxter's *Library use: A handbook for psychology* (Washington, D.C.: American Psychological Assn., 1992 [129p.]) for its lucid attempt to address the problems and opportunities of using many computer files which in anthropology have value only as resources from a related discipline.

Bibliographic Guides

B01

Haas, Marilyn. "Anthropology: A guide to basic sources." *RSR: Reference services review* 5, no.4 (1977): 45–57.

Based on her solid experience in libraries, the author adds a practical dimension to the discussion of how reference sources can be used for anthropological topics. After providing a valuable discussion of many of the basic anthropological reference works, Haas identifies additional printed periodical indexes from related disciplines. These printed editions of continuing indexing and abstracting services described in Haas include: (1) *America: History and life, A guide to periodical literature,* v.1– , 1964– . (Santa Barbara, Calif.: American Bibliographic Center, Clio Pr.), quarterly; (2) *Comprehensive dissertation index, 1861–1972* (Ann Arbor, Mich.: University Microfilms, 1973), and *Supplement,* v.1– , 1973– , annual; (3) *Historical abstracts: A bibliography of the world's periodical literature,* v.1– , 1955– (Santa Barbara, Calif.: American Bibliographic Center, Clio Pr.), quarterly; (4) *Humanities index,* v.1– , 1974– (Bronx, N.Y.: Wilson), quarterly with annual cumulations; (5) *Social sciences index,* v.1– , 1974– (Bronx, N.Y.: Wilson); (6) *Social sciences citation index,* v.1– , 1969– (Philadelphia, Pa.: Institute for Scientific Information), quarterly with annual cumulations; (7) *Sociological abstracts,* v.1– , 1953– (San Diego: Sociological Abstracts), quarterly with annual cumulations; (8) Modern Language Association of America's *MLA international bibliography of books and articles on modern languages and literatures* **(A37);** (9) *Psychological abstracts,* v.1– , 1927– (Lancaster, Pa.: The American Psychological Assn.), monthly with annual cumulations; (10) *Ulrich's international periodicals directory,* described at **(B42);** (11) *Bibliographic index,* v.1– , 1937– (Bronx, N.Y.: Wilson), quarterly with annual cumulations.

Haas relates these printed abstracting and indexing services from other disciplines to anthropology with great skill. She prepares the reader for author/subject entry in indexes prepared with the vocabulary of other disciplines. This makes it possible for us to emphasize the specialized use of citation indexes as they link seminal investigations to bodies of published research with common conceptual standards. For more general reference sources not covered in Haas **(B01),** consult Robert Balay's *Guide to reference books: Covering materials from 1985–1990: Supplement to the tenth edition* (Chicago and London: American Library Assn., 1992 [613p.]) **(B02),** which provides accurate descriptions and knowledgeable annotations to the latest handbooks and bibliographic guides to related academic disciplines and to the geographic divisions of area of nation states. This contrasts with an anthropological preference for using culture areas to define geographic limits. Balay serves as an indispensable guide to all academic disciplines. Selective entry for the best computer files and comprehensive for continuing indexing and abstracting services in all disciplines. Guides to the related disciplines discussed in this chapter need not be listed unless they have been published in the last year.

Searching for Current Materials

Many scholars maintain personal contact by telephone and correspondence with other investigators working with the same kind of research interest. These communications make it possible to obtain copies of conference papers and preliminary reports that contain results and information that may not get into print for years. Some investigators find it is useful to keep abreast with who is working on what problems where. Bibliographic computer files have a limited ability to address these issues. There is a serious publication lag even between the time research is completed and the time it is entered into a printed record. These facts limit the usefulness of *Current contents on diskette: Social and behavioral sciences* [computer file] (Philadelphia: Institute for Scientific Information) **(B03),** which provides a table of contents to approximately 1,300 journals in the social and behavior sciences. In recent years, scholarly and scientific information has increasingly been discussed on computer networks.

B04

Krol, Ed. *The whole Internet: User's guide and catalog.* Sebastopol, Calif.: O'Reilly and Associates, 1992. 376p.

For those who would like to access a span of information that ranges from a list of the U.S. Library of Congress holdings to the computerized databases of other agencies of the U.S. government such as ERIC that can be accessed from personal computers. For example, scholars who would like to access a collection of records from the Aboriginal Studies Electronic Data Archives of the Australian Institute of Aboriginal Studies and the Australian National University can do so through Internet. The National Science Foundation can be reached with the symbol NET. Does not require exotic operating systems. Can use the PC/DOS command "A: Telnet." Krol's *Whole Internet* tells how to connect to Internet. Designed for those who want to use Internet as a tool. Discusses basic utilities that are used in Internet. Another Internet source for current information and an excellent source for announcements about U.S. Government machine-readable data files is the U.S. National Technical Information Service, *NTIS* [computer file], 1980– (Springfield, Va.: U.S. National Technical Information Service) **(B05).** Updated quarterly. Available on CD-ROM as *NTIS* on *SilverPlatter* [computer file] from SilverPlatter, and from DIALOG Information Services as *NTIS on disc* [computer file]. Available online from DIALOG. Replaces the now discontinued Smithsonian Science Information Exchange *SSIE Current Research* [computer file], 1972–78 (Washington, D.C.: Smithsonian Science Information Exchange). This new resource lists both government and privately funded research projects either currently in progress or initiated and completed during the most recent two years. Includes project descriptions from more than 1,300 private and governmental agencies. Includes work in progress in the biological and the social sciences, including anthropology. Canada's University of Western Ontario's *Register of research and researches in the social sciences* [computer file] (Ontario: University of Western Ontario) has a subbase *Can Register* [computer file] available online (CISTI), which tracks 5,000 projects by 8,000 social scientists.

The Sante Fe Institute publishes a printout: Una Smith, *A biologist's guide to Internet resources* (Santa Fe, N.M.: Santa Fe Institute, 1993, [33p.]) (Version 1.4, 24 May 1992) and provides the Internet address of Una Smith at the Department of Biology, Yale University, New Haven, Connecticut (06511)) as smith-una@yale.edu for which the conditions of use suggest as a citation: Smith, Una R. (1993) "A biologist's guide to Internet resources," usenet sci.answers. Available via anonymous FTP and e-mail from rtfm.mit.edu as file pub/usenet/news.answers/biology/guide (30p.). This resource can be downloaded by scholars with Internet access. It contains detailed guidance to many sources of strictly anthropological news groups, archival resources, and bibliographic information available on specific Internet addresses. For example, from p. 29 of the appendix, "Assorted Listserver Mailing Lists":

anct-ne@vm.byu.edu	Ancient Near Eastern Studies
anthro-1@UBVM.cc.buffalo.edu	General Anthropology Bulletin Board
arch-1@TAMVM1.tamu.edu	Archaeology List
humevo@GWUVM.gwu.edu	Human Evolutionary Research Discussion
native-1@TAMVM1.tamu.edu	Issues Pertaining to Aboriginal Peoples
pacarc-1@WSUVM1.csc.wsu.edu	Pacific Rim Archaeology Interest List
pan@GWUVM.gwu.edu	Physical Anthropology News List

Retrospective Searches

Anthropologists have found many other computer files useful. Some descriptions of especially valuable resources are scattered through the chapters devoted to disciplines and geographic areas. Printed indexing services for which computer files are available are sometimes listed in both editions. Cross-references guide the reader back and forth between these two forms. This is done when a more general approach would suggest the use of *Linguistics and language behavior abstracts* [computer file] **(B25),** while a more specialized search could benefit from an inspection of the printed *Linguistics and language behavior abstracts* described at **(E20).**

Sometimes the printed index is listed in a chapter when the structure of the index is so elaborate that some use of the printed index may be mandatory. Some printed indexes and their corresponding computer file editions are useful in more than one discipline. For example, in establishing records of studies of geologically defined time, the same databases are equally useful to archaeology and to physical anthropology. For this purpose inspect *Zoological record* **(F26),** and the American Geological Institute's *Bibliography and index of geology* **(F23).** Find below a discussion of the use of keyword, citation, and controlled vocabulary subject searches. These subject entries made practical the use of subject searches by keyword-in-context and an accurate method of tracing the influence of groundbreaking contributions as they are cited to support conclusions of more current research. These two techniques have reduced the constraints on subject entry found in printed indexing and abstracting services. The manuals for these classification systems and the specialized vocabulary of listed resources are also discussed. The manuals must be consulted to realize the maximum potential for subject entry through these resources. Even the much less demanding entry from keyword-in-context searches can often be effective in the massive databases.

How to Conduct a Citation Search

Citation indexes are especially useful in anthropological literature searches of research defined by rigorous operational definitions. A dated reference in hand, and known to be seminal for the topic of a literature search, can be used as a point of entry into citation indexes. Consulting these indexes, it is possible to identify who in a given year, if anyone, has cited the work in hand. If any publication cites an article known to be seminal, then it may also discuss the issues defined by the seminal article. The search has identified a likely source of information relative to a bibliography under construction. By using the items identified in each newly identified citation and by discovering where each of these new sources has been cited, a bibliography can be created based on published reports that share a common conceptual control. This method of work yields best results for research conceived in an operationally defined paradigm. *Arts and humanities search* [computer file] **(B10),** *Social scisearch* [computer file] **(B37),** and *Scisearch* [computer file] **(B35)** have been constructed to support this kind of literature search. In addition to citation searches, all of these citation indexes permit author and keyword searches. The introductions to the paper editions of printed citation indexes provide extensive discussions of a wide range of specialized uses made possible by these indexes.

Subject Entry by Controlled Vocabulary

Vocabularies developed for use by other disciplines have to be carefully studied for methods of entry into anthropologically significant material. It is unlikely that any term that comes easily to mind for the anthropologist will appear on the list of subject terms developed for sociology. However, by consulting *Sociological abstracts: Thesaurus of sociological indexing terms* (San Diego: Sociological Abstracts, 1992 [330p.]), useful alternatives can be found for some terms. For example, FAMILY is a better term of use when searching for articles on kinship in *Sociological abstracts* [computer file] than the term KINSHIP. For this reason, the annotations of some of the computer files listed below include published subject heading lists. If the subject commands other than keyword searches are to be used, these controlled vocabularies are of critical importance. They can reach content of cited material that may not be included in the title words. Certainly, if professional assistance is requested for online searches, there is a widespread and reasonable expectation that a patron will select the terms of the search. This process can be eased by consulting Sara D. Knapp's *Contemporary thesaurus of social science terms and synonyms: A guide to natural language computer searching* (Phoenix: Oryx Pr., 1993 [400p.]) **(B06),** which can be studied to identify the scientific vocabulary most useful for a particular database and for the possibility that a word in mind can be replaced by a better natural language subject in keyword searches, or in the technical language of a related discipline.

B07

America: History and life: Articles, abstracts and citations of reviews and dissertations covering the United States and Canada [computer file]. 1964– . Santa Barbara, Calif.: ABC-Clio Information Services. Available online (DIALOG: 38).

Both the online service and the CD-ROM utilize portions of the printed version, *America: History and life,* described as item 1 in the annotation of Haas's "Anthropology" **(B01).** The computer file has more than 200,000 records and adds 12,000 a year.

Variant CD-ROM title: *American history and life on disc* [computer file], with variant time span of 1982– . Includes research on the American Indian and on American and Indian folklore. Abstracts and annotates articles from 2,000 journals and publishes appropriate user manuals. Includes dissertations and selected monographs. Primary strength is in U.S. and Canadian history defined to include prehistory, area studies, and topics related to history from other disciplines in the social sciences and humanities. Includes citations to book reviews and, since 1988, film reviews from about 150 journals.

B08

Arctic and Antarctic regions (AAR) [computer file]. 1972– . Calgary, Alberta: Arctic Institute of North America (AIN). Available online (QL Systems: AST). Available on CD-ROM (AIN).

Includes eight files. Time span varies by file. The file *Arctic science and technology information service (ASTIS)* [computer file], with variant time span 1978– , has included coverage of native peoples, art, and archaeology of northern Scandinavia, northern USSR, Canadian Arctic, Alaska, and Greenland. In the more comprehensive anthropological bibliographies, the Arctic is sometimes treated not as a unified culture area but rather as part of culture areas in North America, Europe, and the USSR. This reflects the fact that the concept "culture area" serves as a descriptive convenience that varies according to the defining culture traits selected for study.

B09

Art and archaeology technical abstracts [computer file]. 1955– . Marina del Rey, Calif.: Getty Conservation Institute. Available online (CHIN [Canadian Heritage Network]).

Utilizes portions of the published *Art and archaeology technical abstracts (AATA)* **(C24),** and available online through the Getty Conservation Institute Information Network.

Comprehensive indexing and abstracting of the international literature on the conservation of cultural property, including advances in techniques of restoration and preservation and the technical aspects of artifact documentation. Includes archaeological methods, the history of technology, and the treatment of works of art. The Canadian Heritage Information Network is part of the Getty Conservation Information Network [computer file], which has a file for conservation materials and a products/supplier directory of sources of conservation and preservation materials.

B10

Arts and humanities search [computer file]. 1980– . Philadelphia: Institute for Scientific Information. Available online (BRS:AHCI, DIALOG: 439). Available on CD-ROM (ISI).

CD-ROM has a variant title, *Art and history citation index: Compact disc edition* [computer file], with a variant time span 1990– . All editions utilize portions of the printed edition *Arts and humanities citation index.*

Covers archaeology, expressive culture, films, folklore, history, linguistics, and religious studies in 1,300 journals comprehensively. Selects appropriate items appearing in another 5,600 journals indexed by other reference sources and published by the Institute for Scientific Information. All of the references in articles selected for inclusion are manipulated, and the range of the coverage is vast. Inclusion of book reviews provides entry to those monographs selected for review by the scholarly journals and included in the source index. Available on CD-ROM since 1990.

B11

Bibliographic index [computer file]. Bronx, N.Y.: Wilson. Available online (Wilsonline: BIB). Available on magnetic tape (Wilson: BIB).

Utilizes portions of the printed edition *Bibliographic index,* described as item 11 in the annotation to Haas's "Anthropology" **(B01).** Other vendors that have announced plans to add this database to their resources include OCLC ERIC, OCLC FirstSearch, and BRS.

Author-title-subject index to bibliographies of at least fifty items in books, essays in collection, and periodical articles. Monitors 2,600 periodicals and about 50,000 monographs a year for materials in the English, German, and the Romance languages. Identifies bibliographic reviews that can productively facilitate entry into a particular subject through citation indexes. Index by the names of indigenous peoples.

B12

BIOSIS previews [computer file]. 1969– . Philadelphia: Bio Sciences Information Services. Available online (DIALOG: 5, 55, BRS: Biol). Available on disc, CD-ROM, and magnetic tape from BIOSIS. Available on CD-ROM (SilverPlatter).

Records of more than 6 million citations. Database may be ordered together with *Biological abstracts* as *Biological abstracts on tape* [computer file]. Utilizes portions of the printed *Biological abstracts,* described at **(F24).** Adds about 270,000 abstracts and citations a year. Among the CD-ROMs, *Biological abstracts: A* *compact disc* [computer file], 1985 (SilverPlatter) corresponds to *Biological abstracts* and parts of *BIOSIS previews* [computer file] and *Biological abstracts RRM* [computer file].

The physical anthropologists working in technical areas such as blood types or the systematics of taxonomies will find this computer file especially useful. Indexed by author, broad taxonomic category, genus species, and specific subject. Searches can be made more effective by consulting BioSciences Information Service of Biological Abstracts, *BIOSIS search guide: BIOSIS previews edition* (Philadelphia: BioSciences Information Service, 1983 [loose-leaf]).

B13

Cumulative book index [computer file]. 1982– . New York: Wilson.

Utilizes portions of the printed *Cumulative book index*, v.1– , 1898– (New York: Wilson). Available online (Wilsonline). Available on CD-ROM (Wilsondisc and SilverPlatter).

Adds 50,000 records a year. Excellent subject entry. Includes any book published in English. Can be used to identify the series notation for individual monographs from English-language monographic series.

B14

Dissertations abstracts ondisc [computer file]. 1980– . Ann Arbor, Mich.: University Microfilms International. Available online (DIALOG File 35, BRS[DSS]; BRS/Saunders Colleague). Available on CD-ROM (University Microfilms).

The CD-ROM has variant title: *Dissertations abstracts international on disc.* Contains portions of the printed *International dissertations abstracts* described as item 2 in the annotation to Haas's "Anthropology" **(B01),** and records from *American doctoral dissertations.* Records of more than 1 million citations, including nearly 30,000 master's theses not listed in *DAI.* Especially valuable for the identification of ethnographies by American scholars and for American linguistics research, including dissertations supervised by Chomsky at MIT, which does not contribute to *DAI.*

B15

EMbase plus [computer file]. 1980– . Amsterdam: Excerpta Medica. Available online (BRS [EMEZ], Data Star, DIALOG: 72, 73, and 172, DIMDI: UTOPIA). Available on diskette and magnetic tape (Excerpta Medica).

Utilizes portions of forty-three abstracting journals. Includes access to special coverage for anthropology detailed in the paperbound editions of *Excerpta Medica* as section 1, *Anthropology.* Find also the subfile, EMFORENSIC, which is available online (DIMDI). Another subfile, EVOC, is available online (Data Star). Computer tape services are available for the *MALIMET thesaurus* [computer file] (Excerpta Medica) and the *EMCLAS classification* [computer file] (Excerpta Medica).

The subfile EVOC provides access to the master list of medical indexing terms, MALIMET. The subfile EMFORENSIC provides access to research in forensic sciences. The basic file contains citations of articles from more than 3,500 biomedical journals published throughout the world. Physical, psychological, and medical anthropology are covered. For study of the controlled vocabulary, inspect Excerpta Medica's *Guide to the classification and indexing system* (Amsterdam: Excerpta Medica, 1984 [280p.]), organized by classifications for each section. Use this index to identify 3,500 concepts. There is a list of 200 secondary concepts. The database *Excerpta medica vocabulary (EVOC)* [computer file] (Amsterdam: Elsevier) contains the full text of the EMBASE's *Guide to EMTRE and indexing system,* the master list of medical indexing terms (MALET), the item index, and the EMBASE list of journals with English-language abstracts issued as an annual available through the vendor Data Star (EVOC).

B16

ERIC [computer file]. 1966– . Rockville, Md.: ERIC Processing and Reference Facility, Portions of this file are printed as *Current index to journals in education,* v.1– , 1966– (Phoenix: Oryx Pr.), and as *Resources in education,* v.1– , 1966– (Phoenix: Oryx Pr.). Available online (BRS, BRS

Saunders Colleague, DIALOG on File 1, and OCLC). Available on CD-ROM (DIALOG on disc, SilverPlatter, Cambridge Scientific Abstracts).

Corresponds to *Current index to journals in education (CIJE).* Report literature corresponds to *Resources in education (RIE).*

Variant title for CD-ROM is *ERIC on SilverPlatter* [computer file], 1966– (SilverPlatter). All versions record 750,000 citations. Valuable for bibliographic information about linguistics, the social anthropology of North American Indians, and the ethnology of American ethnic groups. A thesaurus of ERIC descriptors available from Oryx provides a list of subject headings for indexing and retrieval. Most of the described entries are available only on microfiche collections at research libraries. However, *ERIC: Catalog of ERIC Clearing House publications 1993* (Washington, D.C.: National Institute of Education, 1993 [149p.]) identifies ERIC Clearing House publications in print and available.

B17

Foundation grants index [computer file]. 1980– . New York: Foundation Center. Bimonthly. Available online (DIALOG file 26, Life Sciences Network).

Contains portions of *Foundation directory.* Searchable for information included in the abstracts by descriptors, foundation name, limitation, and recipient type. Free text searching is the best entry. Includes a "grants awarded" feature. Limited to 400 American foundations and to grants of more than $5,000.

Many institutions have an alternative for undergraduates called *Sponsored Program Network SPIN* [computer file] (Albany: State University of New York); available online (DIALOG file 62). Any search for funding should also consult the printed reference source Cantrell's *Funding for anthropological research* **(A54),** which offers guidance beyond the scope of these databases. Additionally, descriptions of directories that list individuals serving on grant review committees of the NIH can be found in *Medical documents (MEDOC)* [computer file] (Salt Lake City: Eccles Health Sciences Library, Building 89) **(B18).** Available online (BRS File MDOC).

B19

FRANCIS [computer file]. 1984–90. Nancy, France: Institut de l'Information Scientifique et Technique, Sciences Humaines et Sociales. Available online (Télésystemes-Questel, FRANCIS). Available on magnetic tape and CD-ROM (INIST).

Time span varies on subfiles. Utilizes twenty files, including portions of the printed *Francis bulletin signalétique,* described at **(A34),** and *Repertoire d'art et archéologie.* Contains 1.2 million records dating from 1972. Adds 76,000 records a year. Available on magnetic tape and CD-ROM in twenty files from publisher as *FRANCIS CD-ROM* [computer file], 1984–90 (INIST), of which the file "Ethnologie" contains more than 60,000 citations corresponding to the printed *Francis bulletin signalétique,* Section 529, "Ethnologie." File "Prehistoire et Protohistoire" corresponded to the printed *Francis bulletin signalétique,* Section 525; "Prehistoire et Protohistoire." File "Sciences du Language" contains 74,000 citations and corresponds to *Francis bulletin signalétique,* Section 524, "Science du Language." File "Archaeology," with 43,000 citations, corresponds to the printed *Francis bulletin signalétique,* Section 526, "Art et Archaeologie."

A list of subject areas in which non-French descriptors have been entered along with their entry date is available from Centre de Documentation, Sciences Humaines.

B20

Geobase [computer file]. 1986– . Norwick: Elsevier/GeoAbstracts. Available online (DIALOG; 292).

Title varies. Utilizes portions of the computer files that are published in five printed indexes. Of these *Geographical abstracts: Human geography* is the most useful for ethnographic searches. Contains 260,000 records.

Maps and theses are excluded. Includes coverage of topics such as human geography and paleontology, and techniques such as remote sensing.

B21

GPO monthly catalog [computer file]. 1976– . Washington, D.C.: GPO. Available online

(BRS:GPOM, OCLC FirstSearch Catalog (GPO), DIALOG File 66, Wilsonline). Available on CD-ROM (Wilsondisc, SilverPlatter, Auto-graphics, Information Access Company, Marcive).

Some of the CD-ROMs have title variations: *Government disc* (Auto-graphics), *Government publications index* (Information Access Company), *GPOCAT/PAC* (Marcive). *GPO on SilverPlatter* (SilverPlatter). Utilizes portions of the printed *Monthly catalog of United States government publications,* v.1– , 1895– (Washington, D.C.: U.S. Government Printing Office). Records 200,000 citations.

Environmental impact studies of archaeological sites that have been mandated by federal law can be identified in this resource, which provides a sometimes neglected entry into anthropological reports. In the eyes of government agencies, many federally funded archaeological studies are environmental impact studies of departments of the government which can be identified in this list of publications. The departments can be consulted not only for publications produced by the Government Printing Office but also for publications sponsored by them but processed by other printers.

B22

Historical abstracts [computer file]. 1980– . Santa Barbara, Calif.: ABC-Clio. Available online (DIALOG file 39). Available on magnetic tape (ABC-CLIO). Available on CD-ROM (ABC-CLIO).

CD-ROM variant title is *Historical abstracts on disc,* and the time span is 1982– . Utilizes portions of the printed *Historical abstracts* described as item 3 in the annotation of Haas's "Anthropology" **(B01).** Corresponds to parts of *Historical abstracts: Part A, Modern history abstracts (1450–1914); Part B, Twentieth-century abstracts (1944–).*

Worldwide coverage of history defined to include archaeology, 1450 to the present. Includes archaeology and colonial history of the Third World countries. Abstracts and annotates more than 2,000 journals published in ninety countries in some forty languages. Includes book citations derived from book reviews.

B23

Humanities index [computer file]. 1984– . Bronx, N.Y.: Wilson. Available online (Wilsonline). Available on CD-ROM (Wilsondisc).

Utilizes portions of the printed *Humanities index.* This indexing service is described as item 4 in the annotation to Haas's "Anthropology" **(B01).**

Especially useful for its select multidisciplinary entry into English-language periodicals covering archaeology, prehistory, area studies, and folklore. Most of the 345 journals covered are sponsored by important professional associations. A final section in each issue identifies current book reviews and provides a source index.

B24

Life sciences collection [computer file]. Bethesda, Md.: Cambridge Scientific Abstracts. Available online (BRS, DIALOG: 76, Knowledge index:BIOL1, Life Sciences Network). Available on CD-ROM (Compact Cambridge).

The CD-ROM has variant titles, *CSA Life sciences collection* and *IRL Life sciences collection,* both with a time span variant of 1982– . Each of these CD-ROMs utilizes portions of seventeen printed abstracting journals, including *Genetics abstracts* and *Animal behavior abstracts.* Records nearly 1 million citations.

Citations and abstracts from about five thousand serial titles provide international literature in life sciences subjects. Consult the printed Cambridge Scientific Abstracts on Line File's *User's manual* (Bethesda, Md.: Cambridge Scientific Abstracts, 1985 [loose-leaf]).

B25

Linguistics and language behavior abstracts LLBA [computer file]. 1974– . San Diego: Sociological Abstracts. Available online (BRS:LLBA, BRS/Saunders Colleague, DIALOG: 36, Knowledge Index). Available on CD-ROM (SilverPlatter). Available on magnetic tape (Sociological Abstracts).

Utilizes portions of the printed *Linguistics and language behavior abstracts.* This abstracting service is described in chapter 5, "Linguistics," at **(E20).**

Indexes articles on speech, phonology, lexicography, syntax, semantics, nonverbal communication, psychopathology, interpersonal behavior. These topics are approached from the perspective of anthropological, descriptive and structural studies. An excellent user's manual is available from the publisher.

B26

Medline [computer file]. 1966– . Bethesda, Md.: National Library of Medicine. Available online (BRS:ESB [MESH], DIALOG: 152, 153, 154, 155). Available on CD-ROM (SilverPlatter, Compact Cambridge, and DIALOG ondisc manager).

Variant title for CD-ROM is *Medline: Standard.* Utilizes portions of the printed *Index medicus* and of *EMbase plus* [computer file], described at **(B15).** Records 6 million citations. Adds 300,000 records a year.

Worldwide coverage of 3,400 journals in medicine and related disciplines. Since 1975 author abstracts for more than 40 percent of records. For study of the controlled vocabulary, consult National Library of Medicine's *Medical subject headings: Annotated alphabetical list* (Bethesda, Md.: National Library of Medicine, 1993 [922p.]). *Medical subject headings* is available online (DIALOG). The use of this list has been discussed in detail in *DIALOG chronology* 10, no.5 (1985): 92–94 **(B27).**

B28

Mental health abstracts [computer file]. Alexandria, Va.: IFI/Plenum Data Company, 1983– . Available online (DIALOG on File 86, Life Sciences Network, Knowledge Index).

Valuable supplement to *PsycINFO* [computer file] **(B32).** Source material from 1,500 journals in English, French, German, Hungarian, Italian, Japanese, and other languages. Includes entries on child psychology, genetics, motivation, personality, psychopharmacology, and sexology. Books, periodicals, research reports.

B29

MLA international [computer file]. 1981– . Bronx, N.Y.: Wilson for the Modern Language Association of America. Quarterly. Available online (DIALOG, BRS, Wilsonline). Available on CD-ROM (Wilson and SilverPlatter).

Utilizes portions of *MLA international bibliography of books and articles on the modern languages and literatures.* This indexing service is described at **(A37)** and is included in the list of continuing bibliographies from other disciplines listed by Haas **(B01).** Records nearly 900,000 citations.

Database of articles, parts of books, and dissertations on folklore, language, and literature of America, Europe, Asia, Africa, and Latin America. Nearly half of the citations are in languages other than English. Input from 3,500 journals.

B30

PAIS international [computer file]. 1972– . New York: Public Affairs Information Service. Available online (BRS, BRS/Saunders Colleague, DATA STAR, DIALOG File 49/PAIS International). Available on CD-ROM (SilverPlatter).

Variant CD-ROM title: *PAIS on SilverPlatter,* which utilizes portions of the printed *PAIS bulletin.*

Useful for anthropological searches centered on ethnic groups residing in Third World countries. Excellent area entry for periodical articles, government documents, monographs, pamphlets, festschriften. Foreign-language coverage in French, German, Italian, Portuguese, and Spanish. For a subject vocabulary that makes use of 50,000 headings and subheadings, consult Lawrence J. Woods and Associates, *PAIS subject headings* (New York: Public Affairs, Information Service, 1984 [319p.]), which includes a thirty-page list of subheadings. Consult also Lawrence J. Woods, *PAIS on CD-ROM: User manual* (New York: Public Affairs Information Service, 1988 [67p.]).

B31

PASCAL [computer file]. 1973– . Nancy, France: CNRS. Institute of Scientific and Technical Information (INIST). Available online (DIALOG: Subfile PASCAL; INIST). Available on CD-ROM (INIST).

Utilizes the PASCAL online databases in science and technology. Includes PASCAL: Biological sciences (2.46 million citations) and PASCAL: Medicine (70,000 citations), with titles and keywords in English, German, and French.

Comprehensive for French-language publications that are relevant to the study of anthropological issues.

B32

PsycINFO [computer file]. 1967– . Washington, D.C.: Psychological Abstracts for American Psychological Association. Available on CD-ROM (SilverPlatter format as *PsycLIT*). Available online (BRS, DIALOG File 11, OCLC EPIC, BRS online, BRS After Dark, Life Sciences Network).

The CD-ROM has a variant title, *PsycLIT,* and a variant date, 1974– , with books from 1987– . Utilizes portions of *Psychological abstracts,* described as item 9 in the annotation to Haas's "Anthropology" **(B01).** Records more than 550,000 citations.

Indexes more than 4,000 terms. Records are selectively gathered from 1,300 periodicals. Psychology in the broadest possible definition of scope. Records of anthropological research are organized in terms of their psychological content by the classification system. Includes technical reports, journal articles, conference proceedings, and symposia. Coverage is 90 percent English language. For a study of the controlled vocabulary used with this resource, consult *Thesaurus of psychological index terms,* 5th ed. (Washington, D.C.: American Psychological Assn., 1988 [291p.]), which contains user's guide in two parts: Relational section and Rotated alphabetical terms section.

Psychoanalysis has had as much influence on American anthropology as it has had on academic psychology. For bibliographic coverage, consult the CD-ROM *Psyndex* (1977– , SilverPlatter) **(B33),** which has bibliographic descriptions and abstracts in English or German. Corresponds to *Psychologischer index* and is remarkable for its universal coverage. The inclusion of social variables also tends to be more inclusive here than is usual in American indexing services.

B34

Religion index [computer file]. 1949– . Chicago: American Theological Library Assn. Available online (BRS RELI). Available on CD-ROM (Wilsondisc).

Utilizes portions of the printed versions of *Religion index one: Periodicals* (1949–59 and 1975–); *Religion index two: Multi-author works* (1970–); *Religion index: Festschriften* (1960–69).

Especially useful for entry through national subject headings such as CHINA. Excellent coverage of ethnology. Attempts universal coverage and contributes a controlled vocabulary to its indexing.

B35

Scisearch [computer file]. Philadelphia, Pa.: Institute for Scientific Information.

Utilizes portions of the printed *Science citation index,* v.1– , 1961– (Philadelphia: Institute for Scientific Information). Available online (DIMI, DATA STAR, DIALOG SciSearch Files 34, 94, 186, 187, and 188). Also available on CD-ROM from the publisher.

Allows keyword-in-context and citation searches. The CD-ROM comes in two editions, one with entries without abstracts: *Science citation index: Compact disc* and *Science citation index: Compact disc edition with abstracts,* which provides both bibliographic descriptions of entry and English-language author abstracts. The introductions to printed volumes provide detailed discussions on how to use this index, which functions without a controlled vocabulary. Especially valuable for citation searches in narrowly defined paradigms. Anthropology shares with other sciences a pragmatic use of definitions. If the same concept has two different definitions, it is useful to be able to identify research completed in terms of only one of these definitions. A journal article that establishes a particular definition will be cited when that definition is used. Therefore, it is possible to use a citation index to identify other work based on that pragmatic definition. Inspect the annotation to Dulbecco's *Encyclopedia of human biology* **(F39).** The index of that work integrates the reality of variable science constructs. When a construct is listed in the index, alternate definitions in the running text are identified. The indexer understood how scientific workers think.

B36

Social sciences index [computer file]. 1983– . Bronx, N.Y.: Wilson. Available online (*Wilsonline*). Available on CD-ROM (Wilsondisc, SilverPlatter).

Utilizes portions of printed *Social sciences index,* described as item 5 in the annotation to Haas's "Anthropology" **(B01).**

For social and cultural anthropology and the related disciplines of sociology and psychology, this resource provides a superb and sometimes neglected entry into multidisciplinary sources. It is severely selective for English-language contributions, often the publications of professional associations. Author and subject indexes. Book reviews are under the name of the author of the monograph.

B37

Social scisearch [computer file]. 1986– . Philadelphia: Institute for Scientific Information. (DIMDI, DIALOG on File 7)

The CD-ROM is published in two versions with the variant time span 1986 and the variant titles *Social sciences citation index: Compact disc edition* and *Social sciences citation index: Compact disc edition with abstracts,* which provide English-language author abstracts from 1,400 important journals. All of these databases utilize a portion of *Social sciences citation index (SSCI),* described in item 6 as a printed index in the annotation to Haas's "Anthropology" **(B01).**

Covers 1,400 journals, with selective coverage of more than 4,100 other titles included in the indexing of the publisher's other citation indexes. Since the database manipulates all references identified in the articles included in the *Social sciences citation index: Source index,* v.1– , 1969– (Philadelphia: Institute for Scientific Information) the final range of coverage is vast. For guidance in searches for ethnographic material using this index, consult Bernard's guide **(D02).**

B38

Sociological abstracts [computer file]. 1963– . San Diego: Sociological Abstracts. Available online (BRS: SOCA, DIALOG: 37, OCLC Epic, OCLC FirstSearch, Life Sciences Network). Available on CD-ROM (SilverPlatter, CSA).

Utilizes portions of the printed *Sociological abstracts,* described as item 7 in the annotation to Haas's "Anthropology" **(B01).** The title variants for the CD-ROM are *SocioFile* (SilverPlatter) and *Sociological abstracts: The complete collections* (formerly *Compact sociodisc*) (Cambridge Scientific Abstracts). Both of these CD-ROMs have a variant date: 1974– . Records more than 200,000 citations.

Records are collected from 1,500 journals, monographs, conference and symposia proceedings, and dissertations.

Included indexing terms for social psychology, culture, group interaction, sociology of the arts, social change, demography, and social control. These terms illustrate the body of information in which sociology and anthropology have a shared interest.

B39

The zoological record [computer file]. 1978– . London: The Zoological Society of London. Available online (BRS: ZREC, BRS/Saunders Colleague, DIALOG:185 on magnetic tape from BIOSIS). Available on CD-ROM (SilverPlatter).

Utilizes portions of the printed *Zoological record,* described at **(F26).**

Aside from its value in paleontology in establishing time frame in dating fossil remains, it provides systematic and taxonomic information for twenty-seven animal groups, since students of animal behavior are usually interested in specific species. Also includes information on ecology, genetics, behavior, biometrics, communication, habitat, life cycle and development, nomenclature, techniques, and zoogeography. Geographical, paleontological, and systematic indexes. The biological and behavioral relationship between humans and other species clearly drives some primate studies. But the influence of biological methodology is everywhere to be seen in anthropology, which is remarkable for its ability to integrate notions of commonality. This is usually done within the framework of biological classification systems, which avoid some of the more usual problems of analogous thinking. There is widespread use of biological terms such as AFFINITY. In biology a relation between species or higher groups dependent on the whole plan of structure indicates community of origin. In kinship studies the term AFFINITY denotes a relationship by marriage to the whole structure of kinship relationships. In *Fieldwork in the Library,* the commonalities of the classed system are often defined in terms of search strategies and the relationship of these strategies to the whole book. This makes possible a patterned or nonlinear approach. Thus the more traditional commonalities of form are subordinated to the more dynamic commonalities of a search routine. This is also true of the American Geological Institute's *Bibliography and index of geology* [computer file], 1969– (Washington, D.C.: Geological Society of America) **(B40).** Available online (DIALOG). Available on CD-ROM (SilverPlatter). Corresponds in part to the printed American Geological Institute's *Bibliography and index of geology,* described at **(F23).** Includes listing of journal articles on fossil humans and includes book reviews of monographs about early humans. Again, paleobotany is covered comprehensively as one of the technical specialties that contribute to investigation of issues in paleontology.

Informational Reference Searches

Telephone communication with the vendors of databases and software systems is the only way to be assured of absolute accuracy in statements about the coverage of databases because this technology is changing constantly and rapidly. For most purposes, the information provided by directories is adequate.

Directories

There are many directories of databases. Since they vary in content and quality, Beverly Feldman's "Data base directories: Review and recent developments" (*RSR: Reference services review* 12, no.2 (1985): 17–19) **(B41)** can be consulted for additional guidance.

B42

Ulrich's international periodicals directory, v.1– , 1932– . New York: Bowker. Quarterly with annual cumulations. Available as *Ulrich's periodicals* [computer file] on CD-ROM (Bowker) and online (Bowker).

The classed arrangement of this resource expands searches from one identified source to a list of the several related titles in the class section "Anthropology." Inspection of volume 3 of the 1989–90 edition shows a listing of "Serials Available Online" (p.3681–3730) and a directory of "Online Vendors" (p.3733–43). The description for each entry includes a record of availability for that database either through some edition using CD-ROM laser technology or through online databases from established vendors.

Monographic Series

This chapter has been devoted to reference sources with an emphasis on machine-readable databases, which were organized to meet the needs of several disciplines that share with anthropology some research interests. Other chapters of *Fieldwork in the Library* assume that Balay's *Guide to reference books* **(B02)** has been consulted to secure coverage of more general reference works with value to anthropology. Occasionally, in *Fieldwork in the Library* individual volumes of more general bibliographic series are identified. These entries can be treated as illustrative and may encourage an inspection of other titles available in the series. An example of a bibliographic series with worldwide coverage of specialized geographic areas can be found in the *World bibliographical series* **(B43).**

Another example of a more general resource listed in *Fieldwork in the Library* might be Hanifi's *Historical and cultural dictionary of Afghanistan* **(M52),** with the series notation Historical and cultural dictionaries of Asia, no.5. Other volumes in this series cover other nations in the area. They all follow a common format and devote almost half of their contents to an extensive bibliography. Many of these volumes are sensitive to anthropological interests. Other volumes in the series can be identified when the user consults Balay's *Guide to reference books: Covering materials from 1985–1990: Supplement to the tenth edition* **(B02)** for more general resources about a specific culture area.

At its most useful level, *Fieldwork in the Library* is designed to assist the development of a search strategy that can pattern bibliographic entry into the literature of a particular interest as it develops. A discovery process for reference works establishes sources of information about a particular subject. This discovery process can be laborious in its first development. When a reference book is in a series, it is sometimes useful to identify the other volumes in the series, which can be done under the series entry in most research libraries.

Establishing familiarity with an inventory of useful resources can require an inspection of many reference books before it is possible to wisely select a few for regular usage by a particular scholar. But once the apparatus of reference works is clearly structured, it can greatly increase the economy of future searches. At that point in time, the process of bibliographic discovery is replaced by a process of regular use, which provides continuing access to information about a specific topic.

Part of this process leads to journals publishing recent results in referred articles. Another part of the process leads to the identification of monographic series that are editorially friendly to a special culture area or a special theoretical position. The main thing is to guide the search by a sense of process rather than by a knowledge of forms. Directories can include excellent retrospective bibliographies. Monographic series can provide encyclopedic coverage of developments in an area. In some cases a series comes close to being a handbook or a set. These divisions by form are not in the real world very firmly established. How else can you explain the fact that two great research libraries would catalog a massive and continuing series both as a series and as a set? *Australian joint copying project handbook* **(N20)** and Pacific Manuscripts Bureau's *Short title and index to microfilms PMB DOC 1–1000* (Printed documents series) **(N21)** clearly describe each entry in an enormous series. The University of Hawaii cataloged these resources as a serial. Much of that cataloging went directly to the shared cataloging database of OCLC. Yet the University of California, San Diego, chose to reject that cataloging and absorb the expense of cataloging all of the individual volumes as a set. Clearly two well-qualified groups of cataloging specialists place a lot of importance on correct form of entry. It is equally clear that they disagree about which definition applies where.

In truth, a series can often function as a set in a search. For example, a series devoted to recording research developed as a result of activities by the Berlin Sudan Research Project has been announced. The first volume—Fritz W. Kramer and Bernhard Streck, eds., *Sudanesische marginalien—ein ethnographisches programm* **(G116)**—has articles that introduce the program, written by the authors whose monographs will appear in later volumes in the series. The product of this effort promises to consolidate what is known about the tribes of the Sudan. Still, it does not have the organizational constraints of an editorially controlled set and apparently leaves open the possibility that additional volumes will be published not as a supplement but as a set.

On the other hand, the encyclopedic Wauchope, *Handbook of Middle American Indians* **(KA62),** has recently issued supplements only loosely related to the structure of the set. The set is being used by scholars in a new dimension that has some of the features of a series. In fact, Tulane University has a monographic series that is dominated by Middle American archaeology. Most of the early ethnographies were published in four- or five-monographic series. Students of the North American Indian would be well served to know the contents of these series.

More recently the University of California Press has announced a new series devoted entirely to Melanesian materials.

B43

World bibliographical series, v.1– , 1978– . Santa Barbara, Calif.: Clio Pr. Irregular.

A series of national bibliographies planned to cover every country in the world. By editorial policy the resources listed are almost always English-language materials. A uniform format is flexibly applied to increase comparability across various volumes. Some of the topical coverage of interest to anthropologists includes listings for the country and its people, population and social structure, customs and folklore, language and literature, art, and music as well as bibliographies and other reference works. Some of these resources have considerable anthropological value. Fry's *Pacific basin and Oceania,* described at **(N03),** and Biggins's *Argentina* **(KB85)** are among those listed in various chapters.

Reference librarians consult this series with confidence. As a successful publishing venture, it has attracted duplicate efforts in volumes such as Tania Kona's *Soviet studies guide: Critical references to the political, economic, and social sciences literature* (London: Bowker-Saur, 1992 [237p.]) (Area studies guides, no. 1) **(B44).** This first volume of an announced series also follows a format of entries selective for English-language publications arranged under broad subject headings. On the other hand, Sanford R. Silverburg's *Middle East bibliography* (Metuchen, N.J.: Scarecrow, 1992 [564p.]) (Scarecrow area bibliography series, 1) **(B45)** provides 4,435 entries (mostly English-language) under broad topics with few annotations. In this first volume, an excellent introduction lists other bibliographies and identifies research material on microfiche and microfilm. Most of the resources identified can be identified in the standard reference sources for this region. As a model for areas studies guides, it needs some comment on the quality of entries—if not in annotations, then in bibliographic essays or through the expanded use of appropriate headnotes.

3

Archaeology and Material Culture

This chapter assumes that the reader has exhausted the reference sources cited in chapter 1, "What Every Anthropologist Needs to Know," in Sheehy's "Archaeology and ancient history" **(C01),** Woodhead's *Keyguide to information sources in archaeology* **(C02),** and Balay's *Guide to reference books* **(B02).** Even though these basic works are recent, an astonishing flood of recent publications from Cambridge University Press dates not only the summary literature but also most of the manuals cited in Woodhead. Nevertheless, Woodhead's *Keyguide* **(C02)** liberates us from coverage of many retrospective volumes, provides generous directory information, and permits us to focus on recent coverage. The closely related Woodhead and Stansfield's *Keyguide to information sources in museum studies* **(C03)** makes it possible to almost completely omit reference to this important subject field with its extensive specialized literature. Sheehy's "Archaeology and ancient history" **(C01),** on the other hand, provides detailed entry into the literate traditions in the Near East and the Western world. Only works that are significant enough to interest and influence scholars from outside the classical traditions are retained for these areas. This does not end the challenge of finding entry into a vast and highly specialized literature worldwide. Of all anthropological subdisciplines, archaeology is the most local in focus; so despite the bulk of this chapter on archaeology, its focus has been limited to entry into theoretical issues. From the bibliographic base provided by Woodhead, our discussion of archaeological reference sources can proceed to concentrate comfortably on selected reference works. This chapter can expand the range of coverage of archaeological sources beyond the resources identified under the various strategic headings in chapter 1.

For an international coverage of current book reviews in archaeology, consult the journals annotated in **(C04)** through **(C11).** To identify the titles of journals with substantive content and institutional news about specific culture areas or narrow topical interests, consult the journal lists in the reference sources *History periodicals directory* **(C12)** and *World museum publications* **(C14)** for candidates for current features on a specialized topic. Find also Frantz's *A student anthropologist's handbook* **(A15)** for a select international list.

For retrospective searches, the sources annotated in **(C16)** through **(C20)** can be used to complement sources identified in chapter 1, "What Every Anthropologist Needs to Know," for descriptions of the Tozzer Library's *Catalogues* [microfiche] **(A26)** and the continuing indexing services *Anthropological literature* **(A36)** and *Anthropological index* **(A35).** These can be used after searching for archaeological bibliographies annotated in **(C22)** through **(C27),** which can also be used to update the consolidations of specialized bodies of knowledge found in the retrospective topical bibliographies annotated in **(C28)** and **(C29)** and in the encyclopedic surveys identified in entries **(C38)** through **(C41).** State-of-the-art reviews are listed in **(C42)** through **(C50),** and the consolidation of technical information can be found in the manuals and handbooks identified in entries **(C51)** through **(C90).** Graphic materials are described in the items **(C91)** to **(C94),** and the identification of useful archival materials finds some explication in *Archives of archaeology* [microform] **(C95).**

All searches should start with the reference sources identified in chapter 1. Refer to the discussion there of the reference strategies signaled by headings such as "Searching for Current Materials" and "Retrospective Searches," which do not greatly change from chapter to chapter. However, most discussion of archaeological literature must focus on extremely limited geographical ranges. Even in as small an area as the United States, there are several technical systems developed primarily for investigations of a single small geographic range. The distribution of entries establishes a hierarchy so that only the most important resources are alphabetized after a key reference identification number that is made clearly visible by its placement in the left-hand column. A discussion of this arrangement can be found in the introduction to this book. Archaeological reference works that are specific to a single culture area are covered in the geographically defined chapters of *Fieldwork in the Library,* where guides to the literature of many culture areas are identified. It is here that the reader is alerted to any bibliographic coverage of archaeological reference sources specific to a particular geographic area.

Searching Bibliographic Guides

The resources identified in Auckland's "Getting into the literature" **(A01),** and resources listed under the various search strategies in chapter 1, should be exhausted before the specialized resources listed in this chapter are inspected.

Bibliographic Guides

Most of the resources listed in Auckland's "Getting into the literature" **(A01)** cover all aspects of anthropology. To better conduct literature searches of material culture as it is related to ancient history rather than to ethnology, consult "Archaeology and ancient history" **(C01)** in Eugene Paul Sheehy's *Guide to reference books,* p.980–86, 10th ed. (Chicago: American Library Assn., 1986 [1,560p.]). It provides brief, knowledgeable annotations to reference books on prehistory placed at the beginning of some of the many area divisions that are used as historical subdivisions. Only the most important reference works of "Prehistory" described in this most basic of resources will be repeated here, since our emphasis will be on archaeology as it has been influenced by ethnology and linguistics.

For regional bibliographies of archaeology, consult the various chapters of *Fieldwork in the Library* that are geographically defined. Selection of regional guides for these chapters assumes that Woodhead's *Keyguide to information sources in archaeology* **(C02)** and other reference works identified in this chapter have been exhausted.

C02

Woodhead, Peter. *Keyguide to information sources in archaeology.* London: Mansell, 1985. 219p.

Superb selection and organization provide entry to all aspects of archaeology on an international level. Part 1 is a bibliographic essay that makes reference to entries found in part 2, an annotated list of 759 reference sources. Part 3 is a worldwide list of organizations that can be contacted for additional information about newsletters and other sources developed for specialized focus on a geographic area or topical interest. Thirty pages of professionally structured indexing establishes this work as a standard source.

In a companion volume, Peter Woodhead and Geoffrey Stansfield's *Keyguide to information sources in museum studies* (London and New York: Mansell, 1989 [p.194]) **(C03)** develops three sections: part 1, "Overview of museum studies"; part 2, "Bibliographical listing of sources of information"; and part 3, "List of selected organizations." This work includes 420 annotated entries, including descriptions of machine-readable databases such as *Conservation bibliographic database* [computer file] (1955–); *Artbibliographies modern* [computer file] (1974–); and *Architecture database* [computer file] (1978–). Loaded with useful value judgments, such as a comment that establishes *Curator,* v.1– , 1955– (New York: American Museum of Natural History), as the best single source for current information about anthropological museums.

Searching for Current Materials

The journals listed below were selected for their more general coverage. But for most, work journals with highly localized coverage are an essential resource and the lists can be usefully consulted to identify the more specialized anthropological journals. Consult also the lists of periodicals identified in chapter 1 and in the geographically defined chapters of *Fieldwork in the Library* under the headings "Select Reviews in Scholarly Journals" and "Select Lists in Scholarly Journals." For identifying especially useful current awareness features in scholarly journals, inspect first the Royal Anthropological Institute's *Reference list of current periodicals* **(A14),** which is arranged so that listings in any issue will identify a select list of articles from journals relevant to a specialized topic in a particular culture area. These journals may have special features of continuing value even when the contents make no substantive contribution to a single literature search. To reach an Internet [computer network] resource in archaeology, consult Krol's *The whole Internet* **(B04).** Users may Gopher to Archnet at: Gopher spirit.lib.uconn.edu. The Archnet files are located in the /Academic Services/Social Sciences and History/Anthropology/Archnet directory. Users can join *ARCH-L* by sending e-mail message to LISTSERV@DGOGWDG1.BITNET, which maintains a record of discussions, conferences, job announcements, calls for papers, publications, and bibliographies and serves as a central depository for public domain or shareware software related to archaeological studies. Use listserver (Unix-based) to reach arch-l@TAMVM1.tamu.ed on Internet. There is also a usenet address, sci.archaeology, for archaeological discussion.

Select Reviews in Scholarly Journals

C04

American antiquity. v.1– , 1935– . Washington, D.C.: Society for American Archaeology. Quarterly.

"Reviews and books notes" provides between twenty and twenty-five signed reviews per issue. There are usually five or six articles which focus on theoretical issues, and five or six reports which focus on data collection and interpretation. The trendsetting functions of this journal can appear in any department. Consider this recent example: Peter R. Schmidt's "An alternative to a strictly materialistic perspective: A review of historical archaeology, ethnoarchaeology, and symbolic approaches in African archaeology" 48 (1983): 62–79, with about 120 references, mostly later than 1970.

"Current research" is a regular feature rotating coverage each quarter over the range of North American, South American, and Siberian research in progress. For example, the February issue covers the Greater Southwest, Mesoamerica, and Central America. The May issue in turn covers the Caribbean, the Amazon, eastern Brazil, the Orinoco River, Andean South America, and the Southern Cone. A style guide, "Editorial policy and style guide for American antiquity" 48 (1983): 429–42, explains the policies and format used, and includes a list of references to other style guides.

C05

American journal of archaeology, second series: The journal of the Archaeological Institute of America. v.1– , 1895– . Boston: Archaeological Institute of America. Quarterly.

Fifteen to twenty book reviews per issue and valuative reviews. Special features have been institutionalized. One department lists books received, another obituaries, and another compiles an annual list of North American theses. Covers the Mediterranean and the Near East on topics like art, artifacts, excavation reports, floral and faunal remains, settlement patterns, site analyses, social life and customs, rituals, and myths.

C06

Antiquity: A periodical review of archaeology. v.1– , 1927– . Oxford, England: Antiquity Publications. 3/yr.

As many as thirty lengthy book reviews per issue are not unusual. "Book chronicle" provides bibliographic information on about twenty-five titles. The department "Notes and news" provides a regular source of institutional news worldwide. Cumulative indexes: v.1–25 (1927–52) and v.26–50 (1951–72). From Neolithic to Iron Age, all aspects of material culture are covered. A vigorous interest in both historic and prehistoric studies of agriculture and grazing, in art forms and artifacts and in floral and faunal remains. The editorials combine lively wit with considered comment on topics of current interest, and regularly denounce humbuggery and quackery.

C07

Archaeology. v.1, 1948– . New York: Archaeological Institute of New York. Bimonthly.

The department "Archaeology news and features" reviews ongoing archaeological investigations. The departments "About photography" and "Archaeology films" provide current reviews of productive advances in these specialized technologies. Substantive interest in art and art forms, artifacts, excavations, religions, rituals, myths. Noteworthy for production of drawings and maps.

C08

Journal of field archaeology. v.1– , 1974– . Boston: Boston University for the Association for Field Archaeology. Quarterly.

"Special studies" reviews new methodologies. Regularly alerts the reader to available grants and forthcoming conferences. The department "Publications" presents analytic review articles of up to twenty-one pages about a monograph or set of monographs that achieve some critical synthesis of advances to the date of publication. "Books received" gives bibliographic information on several dozen titles. Especially valuable for its continuing focus on the recovery, restoration, and protection of antiquities. Substantive interest in art, artifacts, religions, rituals, myths.

Archaeologists often publish research results in specialized technical and historical journals. For example, inspect *Bulletin of the Historical Metallurgy Group,* v.1– , 1963– (Oxford, England: Historical Metallurgy Group, Ltd.) **(C09),** issued twice a year with a cumulated index for v.1–7 (1963–73). It covers the history of metallurgy, foraging, and production and includes book reviews and abstracts of publications in the field. Keeping in mind the importance of local archaeological traditions, inspect the retrospective bibliography in Spande's *Historical perspective on metallurgy in Africa: A bibliography* **(G66).**

Inspect *Tools and tillage: A journal on the history of the implements of cultivation and other agricultural processes,* v.1– , 1968– (Copenhagen: National Museum) **(C10),** an annual covering the history of agriculture from the beginning of cultivation to the industrial period. It publishes infrequent but long, discursive and signed book reviews. The continuing expansion of findings on the domestication of animals and the identification of bones from wild specimens in excavations at archaeological sites is recorded in *Bibliographie zur archaeozoologie und geschichte der haustiere,* v.1– , 1971– (Berlin: Akademie der Wissenschaften der DDR, Zentralinstitut für Alte Geschichte und Archaeologie for International Council for Archaeozoology) **(C11),** an annual that publishes contributions of archaeozoology to the understanding of the history of domesticated animals in three sections: "Archaeo-Zoologie," "Archaeologie," "Rezent-Zoologie." Any serious investigation of serial publications in archaeology can benefit from an inspection of M. H. Hasso, who found 1,649 archaeological titles by consolidating several lists in his *Bibliometric study of the literature of archaeology* (London: City University (London) M. Phil. Thesis, 1978 [193p.]).

Select Lists in Scholarly Journals

In chapter 1, "What Every Anthropologist Needs to Know," consult the excellent, select international list of serials for archaeology and prehistory found in Frantz's *A student anthropologist's handbook* **(A15)** before consulting the more specialized *Acta praehistorica et archaeologica,* v.10 **(C22),** for an extensive list of journals with an emphasis on Eastern Europe. For many purposes, a careful use of the following resources can be productive:

C12

Boehm, Eric H., Barbara H. Pope and Marie S. Ensign. *Historical periodicals directory.* Santa Barbara, Calif.: ABC-Clio, 1981– . 5v.

A brief summary of subject scope is given for each entry. This makes it possible to scan for appropriate titles in long lists in which archaeology and history are interfiled. Arranged alphabetically by title within the country of publication. Title index to each volume. Title and subject/geographic index.

C13

Woodhead, Peter, and Geoffrey Stansfield. "Museums by area/country." In *Keyguide to information sources in museum studies,* 125–32. London and New York: Mansell, 1989. 194p.

Directories are listed alphabetically by country or continent, with each entry carefully annotated. In research libraries the card catalog can be inspected for new editions of even the most recent publication. The basic volumes in which this directory appears are comprehensive worldwide in their coverage of this discipline. It maintains excellence in organization and indexing.

Areas that have not had a directory for decades will suddenly have a flood of candidates for the best entry, each with some special feature. For example, the listing in Woodhead and Stansfield's *Keyguide* identifies France P. Cabanne's *Guide des musées de France,* 3d ed. (Paris: Bordas, 1987 [567p.]), which lists 1,700 museums. It may be less useful for anthropological purposes than the even more recent Brigitte Lequex, Monique Mainjonet-Brun, and Suzanne Roseian's *Les collections archéologiques dans les musées de France* (Paris: Editions du CNRS, 1989 [304p.) (CNRS, Dossier de Documentation Archéologique, v.12), which lists alphabetically every museum in France with a description of any archaeological collection. Includes address, phone number, a description of the collections, and details of publications and catalogs. Indexed alphabetically by personal name, subject, types of collection, area of origin, and names of collections.

C14

World museum publications: A directory of art and cultural museums, their publications and audio-visual materials. New York: Bowker, affiliated with Reed Pub. Co. U.S.A., 1982. 731p.

More than 25,000 entries to publications and audiovisual items. The "Geographic guide to museums" lists institutions by country, with publications itemized thereunder. Author and title indexes.

Retrospective Searches

Inspect first Tozzer Library's *Author and subject catalogues of the Tozzer Library* [microfiche] **(A26)** and Peabody Museum Library's *Catalogue: Subjects* **(A29)** for classified entry into journal articles, internal contents of books, and monographs on all aspects of anthropology. Inspect also the British Museum, Museum of Mankind Library's *Museum of Mankind Library catalogues* [microfiche] **(A25),** which provides author and classified subject entry into monographs about all aspects of anthropology. Find additional entry through the Human Relations Area Files, *HRAF source bibliography* **(D16),** and the *International bibliography of social and* *cultural anthropology* **(D20),** which provide some author and classified subject entry into all aspects of anthropology.

Retrospective Bibliographies—Bibliographies of Bibliographies

C15

Heizer, Robert F., Thomas R. Hester, and Carol Graves. "Sources of primary data." In *Archaeology: A bibliographical guide to the basic literature.* By Robert F. Heizer, Thomas R. Hester, and Carol Graves, p.393–99. New York: Garland, 1980. 434p. (Garland reference library of social science, v.54)

Notice the use of "primary source material" as a heading by a scholar from the archaeological traditions to identify the seventy-four bibliographies of bibliographies on which this work was based. To the archaeologist untutored in the established jargon of librarianship, this is a perfectly logical title. The classified arrangement of 4,818 items identifies broad class subject entry into English-language sources. Additional sections, "The purpose . . .," "The history . . .," and "The work of the archaeologist," are central to the development of Heizer, Hester, and Graves's *Archaeology* **(C15)** which has a heavy emphasis on the problems encountered in active excavation. Author index. No subject index.

For an expanded bibliography of bibliographies that includes worldwide results reported in other Western languages and also a much more useful subject index, consult Library-Anthropology Resource Group's *Anthropological bibliographies* **(A21).**

Retrospective Bibliographies—Broad Scope

Anthropological archaeology is doubly blessed with the published editions of the Peabody Museum, Tozzer Library's *Author and subject catalogues of the Tozzer Library* [microfiche] **(A26),** and the British Museum, Museum of Mankind Library's *Museum of Mankind Library catalogues* [microfiche] **(A25).** Indexing resources listed in this chapter are narrow in scope and highly specialized in focus. The continuing indexes listed in chapters 1 and 2 of *Fieldwork in the Library* must be consulted.

C16

Deutsches Archäologisches Institut. Romische Abteilung. Bibliothek. *Kataloge der Bibliothek des Deutschen Archäologischen Instituts.* Boston: Hall, 1969. 13 v.

Autoren- und Periodica Kataloge (7 vols.) *Systematischer Katalog* (3 vols.) Since 1957, this library has classified into 1,200 subject headings monographs, periodical articles, and internal contents of Festschriften. *Zeitschriften-Autorenkatalog* (3 vols.) lists authors of articles on classical archaeology and epigraphy as published. Covers all areas of European prehistory and Near Eastern and Egyptian archaeology, and includes Near Eastern philology from the prehistoric to the Byzantine periods; also includes Christian archaeology.

Like the earlier *Katalog der Bibliothek des Kaiserlich Deutschen Archäologischer Instituts in Romische Abteilung. Bibliothek* (Berlin: W. de Gruyter, 1913–32. [2 vols. in 4] and *Supplement* (1930, 516p.), this has strong retrospective coverage in areas for which the Tozzer Library was less elaborately developed. Therefore, a complementary companion to Tozzer Library's *Catalogues* described in chapter 1, "What Every Anthropologist Needs to Know," at **(A26).** Can be informally updated for Greek and Roman remains with *Archäologische bibliographie* **(C23)** and *Fasti archaeologici* **(C25),** and for Eastern Europe with *Acta praehistorica et archaeologica* **(C22).** Find summaries of the literature in *Enciclopedia dell' arte antica, classica e orientale* **(C36),** Müller-Karpe's *Handbuch der vorgeschichte* **(C41),** and Ebert's *Reallexikon der vorgeschichte* **(C94).**

C17

Nelson, Bonnie R. *A guide to published library catalogs.* Metuchen, N.J.: Scarecrow, 1982. 342p.

Describes published catalogs of twenty-nine library collections with coverage in archaeology. Identifies most collections with culture area focus.

Of the collections with a topical focus, consult especially (New York) Metropolitan Museum of Art's *Library catalog of the Metro-*

politan Museum of Art, New York, 2d ed. revised and enlarged (Boston: Hall, 1980 [48 vols.]) **(C18).** More than 220,000 citations are recorded in this dictionary catalog, with published supplements to 1989. Five thousand years of art and archaeology. For a dense display of excellent photographs, consult *Encyclopedia of world art* **(C35).**

Consult also Jerusalem, *Catalogue de la Bibliothéque de l'École Biblique et Archaéologique Française* (Catalog of the Library of the French Biblical and Archaeological School, Jerusalem, Israel) (Boston: Hall, 1975 [13v.]) **(C19),** which is strong in scripture studies, archaeology, papyrology, and linguistics. Books and articles are covered. Subject headings in French. For reference sources from disciplines that relate archaeological findings to biblical texts, find sensitive, accurate coverage in Balay's *Guide to reference books* **(B02).** For news of ongoing historical research and archaeological discovery, consult *Biblical archaeologist,* v.1– , 1938– (Cambridge, Mass.: American School of Oriental Research) **(C20).** In a typical issue, this quarterly contains five to seven articles and several signed book reviews. "Miscellany" annotates an additional fifteen to twenty titles. Establishes communication between biblical and classical scholars on the subjects of biblical interpretation and developments relating to the Dead Sea Scrolls and other ancient documents. Weeds out humbuggery. For a more technical orientation, examine the *Palestine exploration quarterly,* v.1– , 1869– (London: Palestine Exploration Fund) **(C21).** Also publishes semiannual reports on the excavation by the British School of Archaeology in Jerusalem at Jericho (1952–) and in Jerusalem (1960–).

Retrospective Bibliographies—Continuing

First, in chapter 1, "What Every Anthropologist Needs to Know," consult *Anthropological literature* **(A36)** and *Abstracts in anthropology* **(A32),** then consult *Acta praehistorica et archaeologica* **(C22).**

C22

Acta praehistorica et archaeologica, v.1– , 1970– . Berlin: Bruno Hessling Verlag Berliner Gesellschaft für Anthropologie, Ethnologie und Urgeschichte. Annual.

Worldwide coverage in English, French, and German, with emphasis on investigations of Eastern Europe. For an international list of title abbreviations of periodicals, series, monographic sets, and dictionaries of European and Oriental archaeology, consult v.9, no.10.

C23

Archäologische bibliographie. Beilage zum jahrbuch des Deutscher Archäologischen Instituts, v.1– , 1899– . Berlin: W. de Gruyter. Annual.

International in scope. Covers books and articles for the whole Mediterranean, from prehistory to late antiquity. 1,000 periodicals are scanned. Arrangement into three sections: "General," "Greek and Roman Culture," "Other Cultures." Author index. Book review index. Subject index.

C24

Art and archaeology technical abstracts, v.1– , 1955– . Marino del Rey, Calif.: The Getty Conservation Institute; London: International Institute for Conservation of Historic and Artistic Works, London. 2/yr.

Approximately 1,000 references per year to cover books, conferences, articles from museum bulletins, and scholarly journals. Classified subject arrangement to include microscopy, photography, radiography, archaeozoology, and dating. Bibliographical supplements on special topics are frequent. Includes a directory of publishers of journals, monographs, and audiovisual materials listed. Annual subject index.

For online entry to *Art and archaeology technical abstracts (AATA),* see **(B09).** Public access to an archive on paleoclimatology is possible under the Internet [computer network] code name ngdcl.ng.dcnoaa.gov (USA) and can be accessed through anonymous FTP. For additional information use name info@mail.ngdc.noaa.gov.

C25

Fasti archaeologici: Annual bulletin of classical archaeology, v.1– , 1946– . Firenze: Sansoni Editore for the International Association for Classical Archaeology. Annual.

Lists 14,000 references a year. A classified list that contains references to books, reports, conference proceedings, and articles from about 140 scholarly journals. Covers all aspects of classical archaeology. Contains: (1) general (by country), (2) prehistoric and classical Greece, (3) Italy before the Roman empire, (4) Hellenistic world and Eastern provinces of the Roman empire, (5) Roman West, and (6) Christianity and late antiquity. Indexed by authors (ancient and modern); by geographic name, subject, lexically; and by epigraphical sources.

C26

Francis bulletin signalétique. 525: Préhistoire et protohistoire. v.34– , 1980– . Nancy, France: Institut de l'Information Scientifique. Quarterly with annual index.

Continues: *Bulletin signalétique, 525: Préhistoire et protohistoire,* which continues France, Centre National de la Recherche Scientifique's *Bulletin signalétique 525: Préhistoire,* v.24– , 1970– . Worldwide coverage as published in periodical articles, essays in collections, books, and dissertations. Four hundred fifty archaeological and 200 multidisciplinary journals are covered. General, then subdivided by geographic area. Indexed by culture, geographic area, site and region, subject, and author.

C27

Francis bulletin signalétique. 526: Art et archéologie: Proche-Orient, Asie, Amérique. v.45– , 1991– . Nancy, France: Institut de l'Information Scientifique et Technique. Quarterly.

Continues: *Bulletin signalétique, 526: Art et archéologie: Proche-Orient, Asie, Amérique,* which supersedes, in part: *Bulletin signalétique, 521: Sociologie, ethnologie, préhistoire et archéologie,* and continues its volume numbering v.1– , 1910– . Worldwide coverage of periodicals, essays in collections, books, and dissertations. Broad subject headings in the printed quarterly edition provide some current review of periodical production. Annual index.

All records of the *Bulletin signalétique* series since 1972 have been entered into one of two machine-readable databases. Use *PASCAL* [computer file] **(B31)** through DIALOG for biological anthropology. Use *FRANCIS* [computer file] **(B19)** through Télésystemes Questel for social sciences and humanities. Consult also chapter 2.

Retrospective Bibliographies—Topical

C28

Ellis, Linda, comp. *Laboratory techniques in archaeology: A guide to the literature, 1920–1980.* New York: Garland, 1982. 419p. Index. (Garland reference library of social science, v.110).

Thoroughly indexed by subject terms such as remote sensing, data management. International in scope in all languages. Also indexed by geographic location, method of analysis, type of material, and author. A recent attempt to briefly summarize the massive results recorded in this literature can be found in Patricia Phillips's *The archaeologist and the laboratory* (London: Council for British Archaeology, 1985 [70p.]).

C29

Polach, Dilette. *Radiocarbon dating literature: The first 21 years, 1947–1968: An annotated bibliography.* London: San Diego: Academic, 1988. 370p.

Detailed annotations. Comprehensive. Can be informally updated by *Radiocarbon,* v.1– , 1959– (New Haven, Conn.: American Journal of Science), three times a year. A recent effort to summarize the most important features of this vast body of literature can be found in Sheridan Bowman's *Radiocarbon dating* (Berkeley: University of California; London: Trustees of the British Museum by British Museum Publications, 1990 [64p.]).

Informational Reference Searches

Among available informational reference sources in American anthropology, consult first the *AAA guide* **(A53)** for directory information. The best international directory is still the "International directory of anthropological institutions" **(A56),** which could usefully be reissued in a new edition.

Dictionaries

C30

Bray, Warwick, and David Trump. *The Penguin dictionary of archaeology.* Drawings by Judith Newcomer. 2d ed. Harmondsworth, Middlesex, England; New York: Penguin, 1982. 283p.

German and Italian editions give this volume special value when translation is a consideration. Many entries have bibliographies, which makes this the best nontechnical dictionary. Excludes classical, medieval, and industrial archaeology. Includes the sites, cultures, and peoples of prehistory worldwide. Covers cities, periods, techniques, terms, and personalities. Some maps. Regional index. Cross-references among 1,600 entries in an alphabetical list. For references on subjects such as aerial photography, consult also Sara Champion's *A dictionary of terms and techniques in archaeology* (New York: Facts on File, 1980 [144p.]), now available from University Microfilms. For technical terms introduced during the last decade, consult *The Facts on File dictionary of archaeology.* **(C31).**

C31

Whitehouse, Ruth D., ed. *The Facts on File dictionary of archaeology.* rev. ed. New York: Facts on File, 1983, 1988. 597p.

Published in England under the title *The Macmillan dictionary of archaeology.* Technical and concise. Sensitive to the enormous number of technical terms introduced in the last decade. Therefore, helpful with individuated definitions of terms that have recently appeared in scholarly journals. Topical subject index with nine pages for Europe and Africa, and five pages for the rest of the world.

A useful companion to the Bray's less-technical *Penguin dictionary of archaeology* **(C30),** for some descriptions of sites, and the Whitehouses' *Archaeological atlas of the world* **(C92)** for location of 5,000 sites. Dictionaries intended to ease the task of specialized translation abound. The complexity of these needs can best be surmised by an inspection of Mary L. Apelt's *English-German dictionary: Art history–archaeology (English-Deutsches wörterbuch für kunstgeschichte und archäologie)* (Berlin: E. W. Schmidt, 1987 [253p.]) **(C32)** and her *German-English dictionary, art history, archaeology (Deutsch-englisches wörterbuch für kunstgeschichte und archäologie)* (Berlin: E. W. Schmidt, 1990 [277p.]) **(C33);** both volumes are arranged alphabetically. Not limited to specialized terms. Includes shapes, colors, materials, articles of clothing, dyestuffs, pigments, and mythological animals. For their intended use, they set a standard of excellence.

Directories

Woodhead's *Keyguide to information sources in archaeology* **(C02)** and Woodhead and Stansfield's *Keyguide to information sources in museum studies* **(C03)** include worldwide lists of organizations supporting archaeological and museum activities. *World museum publications* **(C14)** acts as a select directory of museums and their publications. Once an institution with a research interest in a particular area has been identified, associates of that institution can be identified in the *AAA guide* **(A53)** and the more general directories identified either in Sheehy's *Guide to reference books* or in Webb's *Sources of information in the social sciences* **(D03).** Consult also Sease's *Conservation manual for the field archaeologist* **(C88)** for a directory of manufacturers and distributors of conservation supplies in appendix 3, and a list of conservation organizations and their publications in appendix 4. More general sources, such as Balay's *Guide to reference books* **(B02),** offer resources beyond the scope of *Fieldwork in the Library.* As an example, see Bettina Bartz's *Museums of the world,* 4th ed. (New York: Saur, 1992), with its detailed index.

Encyclopedias, Handbooks, Manuals, Summaries

C34

Cambridge ancient history. 3d ed. London: Cambridge Univ. Pr., 1970– .

Many individual chapters of this newest edition have already appeared as fascicles. Each chapter includes bibliographies. Chapters in hardcover: v.1, pt.1, *Prolegomena and prehistory,* 1970 [758p.]; v.1, pt.2, *Early history of the*

Middle East, 1971 [1,058p.]; v.2, pt.2, *History of the Middle East and the Aegean region, c. 1380–1000 B.C.,* 1975 [1,128p.]; v.3, pt.1, *The prehistory of the Balkans; and the Middle East and the Aegean World, tenth to eighth centuries, B.C.;* v.3, pt.2, *Assyrian and Babylonian empires and other states of the Near East, from the eighth to the sixth centuries B.C.,* 2d ed., 1992 [906p.]; v.3, pt.3, *Expansion of the Greek world, eighth to sixth centuries B.C.;* v.4, *Persia, Greece and the Western Mediterranean, c. 525 to 479 B.C.;* v.5, *The fifth century B.C.;* v.7, pt.1, *The Hellenistic world;* v.7, pt.2, *The rise of Rome to 220 B.C.;* v.8, *Rome and the Mediterranean to 133 B.C.*

C35

Encyclopedia of world art. New York: McGraw-Hill, 1959–68. 15v.

In addition to the basic set, there are two supplements (1983 and 1987). Approximately half of each volume consists of excellent plates selected to illustrate the topics of the other half. These plates, when added to those of Ebert's *Reallexikon der vorgeschichte* **(C94),** provide an enormous inventory of printed plates as visual aids. The original articles in the *Encyclopedia of world art* were written in several languages and translated into English from the Italian edition. Each article has a short bibliography of recommendations for additional information. While these bibliographies represent an effort by acknowledged experts to identify the best sources of information for the subject in which they have the greatest expertise, the contributions from English-language sources are underrepresented. Suggested for its generous sample of articles on primitive art and architecture which are sometimes approached in terms of cultural traditions. An example of this treatment can be found under the heading "Melanesian Culture."

There are two supplements: *World art in our time* (Palatine, Ill.: Jack Heraty & Associates, 1983 [278p.]) and David Eggenberger and Susan Carroll, eds., *New discoveries and perspectives in the world of art* (Palatine, Ill.: Under the auspices of the Fondazione Giorrgio Cini in cooperation with Jack Heraty and Associates, 1987 [649p.]). For classical studies this set can be supplemented by *Enciclopedia dell' arte antica, classica e orientale* (Roma: Instituto della Enciclopedia Italiana, 1958–66 [7v.]) **(C36),** which has signed articles and bibliographies for classical antiquity in Asia, Northern Africa, and Europe for the period following the prehistory of these regions to about A.D. 500.

C37

Sherratt, Andrew, ed. *Cambridge encyclopedia of archaeology.* New York: Crown/Cambridge Univ. Pr., 1980. 495p.

Covers origin, growth, and revolution in archaeological thinking in the late 1960s and 1970s. Discusses process in economic and social change, various applications for systems theory, relations between early populations and their resources, historical archaeology that is supported by documentary evidence, and technical advances. Contains a concise synthesis of archaeological knowledge from earliest man to the European conquest of the Americas. Sixty-four chapters on separate topics signed by fifty-five contributors. Primarily chronological in arrangement, with chronological tables and an excellent selection of maps and plans. Analytical index.

Omits industrial archaeology. For this subject, consult Hudson's *World industrial archaeology* **(C75).**

ENCYCLOPEDIC SURVEYS

Many of the archaeological surveys are listed in the geographically defined chapters of *Fieldwork in the Library.*

C38

Daniel, Glyn E., ed. *Ancient peoples and places.* v.1– , 1956– . New York; London: Thames & Hudson. Irregular.

Most volumes in this series examine the artifacts and summarize studies that focus on one segment of the civilizations of antiquity. Written by distinguished archaeologists and historians with editorial control that effectively achieves a consistent style that is understandable to any literate reader. Each volume contains a detailed bibliography and a generous selection of plates and maps. Some volumes have lists of sites.

For a list of the titles published in this series, consult Alan Edwin Day's *Archaeology: A reference handbook,* p.21–22 (Hamden, Conn.:

Linnet Books, 1978 [319p.]) **(C39);** also useful for its review of British archaeological publications and institutions. Notice especially Glyn E. Daniel's *Hundred and fifty years of archaeology* (Cambridge, Mass.: Harvard Univ. Pr., 1975 [410p.]) (Ancient peoples and places, v.100) **(C40),** which provides an excellent and concise study of the origins and development of the discipline.

C41

Müller-Karpe, Hermann. *Handbuch der vorgeschichte.* Munich: Beck, 1966– . 5v.

This worldwide survey includes many hundreds of plates and an abundance of helpful maps. For each volume there is a list of abbreviations for sources cited as well as subject, name, locality indexes. For example, inspect v.2, p.396–550 for a list of 655 sites. Consult an older summary survey, Ebert's *Reallexikon der vorgeschichte* **(C94),** which provides an alphabetical arrangement and many plates.

STATE-OF-THE-ART REVIEWS

C42

Advances in world archaeology. v.1–5, 1982–86. New York: Academic. Annual.

Critical reviews of progress in methodological and theoretical advances. Synthesis of knowledge worldwide. Each chapter covers a particular part of the world. References provided are often definitive to the date of review.

These reviews are not afraid of the hard questions. Consider: the comprehensive review of difficult time sequences in Africa in John Parkington's "Changing views of the late Stone Age of South Africa," *Advances in world archaeology* 3 (1984): 89–142 **(C43).**

C44

Archaeological method and theory. v.1– , 1989– . Tucson: Univ. of Arizona Pr. Annual.

Sponsored by the same Michael B. Schiffer who edited the previous *Advances in archaeological method and theory,* vols. 1–11, 1978–1987, published in association with Academic Press. This series provides an overview of important theoretical issues, recent findings in important areas of research, and the most recent developments in method. Each issue contains a range of topics for which recent research has achieved advances. There seems to be no special effort to maintain continuing coverage of research on any specific topic until productive research again produces advances that invite evaluative review. As this knowledge cumulates, it provides an almost encyclopedic coverage of theoretical and methodological issues in anthropology with many useful extensive bibliographies that collectively achieve a retrospective record of research in the area of coverage.

C45

Archaeoastronomy. v.1– , 1978– . College Park, Md.: Center for Archaeoastronomy, University of Maryland. Quarterly.

Prehistoric astronomy. Consult also *Archaeoastronomy: Supplement to Journal for the history of astronomy.* v.1– , 1979– (Chalfont St. Giles, England: Science History Publications) **(C46),** an annual that includes state-of-the-art surveys for Mesoamerican studies, megalithic studies, etc., and signed book reviews.

C47

Archaeometry. v.1– , 1958– . Oxford, England: Oxford University, Research Laboratory for Archaeology and the History of Art. 2/yr.

Includes review articles on the physical sciences as they relate to archaeology. Bibliographic information on new monographic titles relevant to archaeological chemistry and physics. Cumulative index: v.1–15 (1958–73).

C48

New directions in archaeology. v.1– , 1969– , Cambridge, England, and New York: Cambridge Univ. Pr. Irregular.

Edited collections of papers on sharply focused topics which concentrate on research advances to the date of publication. The following titles from this unnumbered series are given full author description, the date of publication, and pagination: *The archaeology of prehistoric coastlines,* ed. by Geoff Bailey and John Parkington (1988 [154p.]); *Documentary archaeology in the New World,* ed. by Mary C. Beaudry (1988 [218p.]); *Specialization, exchange and complex societies,* ed. by Elizabeth M. Brumfiel and Timothy K. Earle (1987 [150p.]); *The archaeology of death,* ed. by Robert Chapman, Ian Kinnes, and Klavs Randsborg (1981 [159p.]);

Approaches to the archaeological heritage: A comparative study of world cultural resource management systems, ed. by Henry Cleere (1984 [138p.]); *The uses of style in archaeology,* ed. by Margaret Wright Conkey and Christine Ann Hastorf (1990 [124p.]); *Prehistoric quarries and lithic production,* ed. by Jonathon E. Ericson and Barbara A. Purdy (1984 [149p.]); *Origins and development of the Andean state,* ed. by Jonathan Haas, Sheila Pozorski, and Thomas Pozorski (1987 [188p.]); *Bad year economics: Cultural responses to risk and uncertainty,* ed. by Paul Halstead and John O'Shea (1989 [145p.]); *Intrasite spatial analysis in archaeology,* ed. by Harold J. Hietala with editorial contributions by Paul A. Larson, Jr. (1984 [284p.]); *Simulation studies in archaeology,* ed. by Ian Hodder (1978 [139p.]); *Symbolic and structural archaeology,* ed. by Ian Hodder for the Cambridge Seminar on Symbolic and Structural Anthropology (1982 [188p.]); *Archaeology as long term history,* ed. by Ian Hodder (1987 [145p.]); *The archaeology of contextual meanings,* ed. by Ian Hodder (1987 [144p.]); *The transition to statehood in the New World,* ed. by Grant D. Jones and Robert R. Kautz (1981 [254p.]); *Domestic architecture and the use of space: An interdisciplinary cross-cultural study,* ed. by Susan Kent (1990 [192p.]); *Farmers as hunters: The implications of sedentism,* ed. by Susan Kent (1989 [152p.]); *Island societies: Archaeological approaches to evolution and transformation,* ed. by Patrick Vinton Kirch (1986 [98p.]); *Quantifying diversity in archaeology,* ed. by Robert D. Leonard and George T. Jones (1989 [160p.]); *Ideology, power, and prehistory,* ed. by Daniel Miller and Christopher Tilley (1984 [157p.]); *Time, energy and stone tools,* ed. by Robin Torrence (1989 [124p.]).

C49

One world archaeology. v.1– , 1986– . London: Unwin Hyman for the World Archaeology Congress. Irregular.

Peter Ucko has edited some twenty-two titles. Each volume is a collection of papers and is strengthened by remarkably astute editorial control; each is also prefaced by the editor's introductory remarks and by the comments of the general editor. To emphasize just how recent these volumes are, date of publication and pagination are included in the descriptions that follow: v.4, *State and society* (published as two volumes with subtitles, as *The emergence and development of social hierarchy and political centralization* (1988–89 [347p.]) and *Domination and resistance* (1989 [332p.]); v.6, *The meaning of things: Material culture and symbolic expression* (1989 [265p.]); v.7, *Animals into art* (1989 [265p.]); v.8, *Conflict in the archaeology of living traditions* (1989 [243p.]); v.9, *Archaeological heritage management in the modern world* (1989 [318p.]); v.11, *Centre and periphery: Comparative studies in archaeology* (1989 [240p.]); v.12, *Politics of the past* (1990 [319p.]); v.13, *Foraging and farming: The evolution of plant exploitation* (1989 [733p.]); v.14, *What's new: A closer look at the process of innovation* (1989 [353p.]); v.15, *Hunters of the recent past* (1990 [415p.]); v.16, *Signifying animals: Human meaning in the natural world* (1990 [258p.]); v.17, *The excluded past: Archaeology in education* (1990 [314p.]); v.18, *From the Baltic to the Black Sea: Studies in medieval archaeology* (1990 [322p.]); v.19, *The origins of human behavior* (1991 [119p.]); v.20, *Who needs the past? Indigenous values and archaeology* (1989 [215p.]).

C50

World archaeology. v.1– , 1969– . London: Routledge. Irregular.

Each issue focuses on a topic and attempts a summary survey of that topic. Collectively issues can be treated as an encyclopedia of contemporary archaeology. To date: v.1, no.1, *Recent work and new approaches;* v.1, no.2, *Techniques of chronology and excavation;* v.1, no.3, *Analysis (includes computer analysis);* v.2, no.1, *Early man;* v.2, no.2, *Urban Anthropology;* v.2, no.3, *Subsistence;* v.3, no.1, *Technological innovations;* v.3, no.2, *Archaeology and ethnology;* v.3, no.3, *Art and design;* v.4, no.1, *Population;* v.4, no.2, *Nomads;* v.4, no.3, *Theories and assumptions;* v.5, no.1, *Colonization;* v.5, no.2, *Trade;* v.5, no.3, *Stone Age studies;* v.6, no.1, *Political systems;* v.6, no.2, *Miscellany;* v.6, no.3, *Currency;* v.7, no.1, *Burial;* v.7, no.2, *Dating;* v.7, no.3, *Archaeology and history;* v.8, no.1, *Archaeology and linguistics;* v.8, no.2, *Climate change;* v.8, no.3, *Human biogeography;* v.9, no.1, *Island archaeology;* v.9, no.2, *Architecture and archaeology;* v.9, no.3, *Landscape archaeology;* v.10, no.1, *Field techniques and research design;* v.10, no.2, *Archaeology and religion;* v.11, no.1, *Early chemical technology;* v.11, no.2, *Food and nutrition;* v.11, no.3, *Water management;* v.12, no.1, *Classical archaeology;* v.12, no.2, *Early man, some precise moments in the remote past;* v.12, no.3, *Archaeology and musical instruments;* v.13, no.1, *Miscellany;* v.13, no.2, *Regional traditions of archaeological research I;* v.13, no.3, *Regional traditions of archaeological research II;* v.14, no.1, *Quantitative methods;* v.14, no.2, *Photometry/Miscellany;* v.14, no.3, *Islamic archaeology;* v.15, no.1, *Transhumance and pastoralism;* v.15, no.2, *Industrial archaeology;* v.15, no.3, *Ceramics;* v.16, no.1, *Coastal archaeology;* v.16, no.2, *Mines and quarries;* v.16, no.3, *Watercraft and water transport;* v.17, no.1, *Studying stones;* v.17, no.2, *Ethnoarchaeology;* v.17, no.3, *Early writing systems;* v.18, no.1, *Perspectives in world archaeology;* v.18, no.2, *Weapons and warfare;* v.18, no.3, *Archaeology and the Christian Church;* v.19, no.1, *Urbanization;* v.19, no.2, *Rock art;* v.19, no.3, *New direction in paleolithic research;* v.20, no.1, *Archaeology in Africa;* v.20, no.2, *Hoards and hoarding;* v.20, no.3, *Archaeo metallurgy;* v.21, no.1, *Ceramic technology;* v.21, no.2, *The archaeology of public health;* v.21, no.3, *Architectural innovation;* v.22, no.1, *Soils and early agriculture.* In preparation: *Archaeology and arid environments; Craft production and specialization; Chronologies; Archaeology of empires.*

MANUALS, HANDBOOKS

Many technical manuals are valid regardless of the culture area in which they are applied. Sometimes the resources are specific to a culture area; when this is true, the preferred organization places the resource in a specific culture area. A reasonable example of this kind of thing would be several surveys of laws that protect archaeological artifacts in the United States. In Hester's *Field methods in archaeology* **(C72),** there is a discussion of the laws of the United States and of the various states as applied to archaeological sites. To identify reference sources on the laws applied by Mexico and the countries of Central America, consult Block's "Anthropology" **(J01).** For an additional review of the laws regulating archaeology in Peru, consult Ravines's *Introducción a una bibliografía general de la arqueología del Perú, 1860–1988* **(KB28).**

C51

Adkins, Lesley, and Roy A. Adkins. *Archaeological illustration.* Cambridge, England, and New York: Cambridge Univ. Pr., 1989. 259p. (Cambridge manuals in archaeology)

After an introduction, there are chapters devoted to equipment, techniques, drawing in the field, drawing in the office, drawing buildings, drawing reconstructions, drawing finds, and drawing for reproduction. Computer graphics are thoroughly introduced (p.215–37). An extensive bibliography (p.238–47) guides the reader to other sources.

For many archaeological purposes the essentials can be found in Brian D. Dillon's *The student's guide to archaeological illustrating,* 2d rev. ed. (Los Angeles: Institute of Archaeology, UCLA, 1985 [185p.]) (Archaeological research tools, v.1) **(C52).** Especially useful for basic techniques and tools used in rendering maps, floor plans, relief monuments, reconstructions, stratigraphic sections, ceramics and figurines, burials, and artifacts of shell, bone, and lithics. For more detailed coverage of lithic illustration, consult International Flint Symposium, 4th: 1983: Brighton Polytechnic's *The scientific study of flint and chert* **(C76),** Bordes's *Typologie du paléolithique ancien et moyen* **(C77),** and Addington's *Lithic illustration* **(C78).**

C53

Allen, Ralph, ed. *Archaeological chemistry 4.* Developed from a symposium sponsored by the Division of History of Chemistry at the 193rd meeting of the American Chemical Society, Denver, Colorado, April 5–10, 1987. Washington, D.C.: American Chemical Society, 1989. 508p. (Advances in chemistry, 220)

A systematic and highly technical overview of the application of methods and concepts of chemistry to archaeology which is a continuation of earlier published (about every six years) symposia with the same title *(Archaeological chemistry)* in *Advances in chemistry* 138 (1974); 171 (1978); and 205 (1984). Collectively, these volumes are encyclopedic for the topic covered.

C54

Amorosi, Thomas. *Postcranial guide to domestic neo-natal and juvenile mammals: The identification and aging of Old World species.* Oxford, England: Oxford Univ. Pr., 1989. 380p. (BAR International series S533)

Delineates the aging of domestic animals. Tables of fusion and dental data are presented: (1) Detailed table of contents guides the reader through a general section; (2) Relative methods and incremental methods; (3) Age determinants based on bone, teeth, and horn; (4) Juvenile morphology with twenty plates and contour drawings of bone elements to scale (p.315–48). Includes a generous list of references (p.349–80).

The line drawings of morphology found here are intended to complement the illustrations of adult domesticated species found in Elisabeth Schmid's *Atlas of animal bones: For prehistorians, archaeologists, and quaternary geologists* (Amsterdam and New York: Elsevier, 1972 [159p.]) **(C55),** which organizes drawings of the descriptive changes brought by the domestication of a wide range of animal species.

C56

Bettess, F. *Surveying for archaeologists.* Durham, England: Univ. of Durham, Excavation Committee, 1984. 116p.

Basic manual on how to make an intelligent survey. Concise and completely accurate, it applies robust common sense to the problems of establishing a survey and recording the results.

A useful and recently published companion volume to the more dated but lucid organization of Hester, Heizer, and Graham's standard *Field methods in archaeology* **(C72).**

C57

Bradley, Raymond S. *Quaternary paleoclimatology: Methods of paleoclimatic reconstruction.* Boston: Allen & Unwin, 1985. 472 p.

An extensive index and a massive bibliography lead to entries that answer questions about the increasingly wide span of dating techniques and methods available to research centering on climatic reconstruction. Some of the dating methods covered: radiocarbon, potassium-argon, uranium-series, thermoluminescence, obsidian hydration, tephrochronology, lichenometry, and dendrochronology—all with a review discussion of research topics and a list of primary references. Use itrdbfor@asuvm.inre.asu.edu for Dendrochronology Forum. The Internet [computer network] makes e-mail subscriptions to Climate/Ecosystem Dynamics available from Daniel Pommert, daniel@ecsuc.ctstateu.edu; gopher access available via Internet.edu.

For dendrochronology, current research is often published in the journal *Tree-ring bulletin,* v.1– , 1935 (Tucson: Tree-ring Society) **(C58),** a quarterly that cumulates into a fundamental resource for southwestern archaeology. For additional sources, consult *World archaeology* **(C50),** especially v.7, no.2, *Dating,* and v.8, no.2, *Climate change.* For expansion of a literature search, consult Polach's *Radiocarbon dating literature* **(C29);** Ralph Allen's *Archaeological chemistry* **(C53);** Clement W. Meighan et al., *Obsidian date IV: A compendium of obsidian hydration determinations made at the UCLA obsidian hydration laboratory* (Los Angeles: Institute of Archaeology, 1988 [511p.]) (Monograph 29) **(C59),** with twenty-three discussion papers and three lists of reference bibliographies; and *Art and archaeology technical abstracts* [computer file] **(B09).**

C60

Cambridge manuals in anthropology. v.1– , 1986– . Cambridge, England: Cambridge Univ. Pr. Irregular.

A numbered series which provides comprehensive handbooks for technical aspects of archaeology. Most of these volumes are marked by a readability that is rare when the focus is so clearly technical. The organization and indexing of these volumes are uniformly excellent.

Described in this section, find Adkins and Adkins, *Archaeological illustrations* **(C51);** Courty, Goldberg, and Macphail's *Soils and micromorphology in archaeology* **(C61);** Dorrell's *Photography in archaeology and conservation* **(C63);** Hillson's *Teeth* **(C73);** and Wheeler and Jones's *Fishes* **(C89).**

C61

Courty, Marie Agnes, Paul Goldberg, and Richard Macphail. *Soils and micromorphology in archaeology.* Cambridge, England: Cambridge Univ. Pr., 1989. 344p. (Cambridge manuals in archaeology)

Basic to environmental archaeology. Pt.1, "The basic principles," includes a discussion of the basic concepts and methods, field strategies, the microscopic approach, the thin-sector approach, sediments, anthropogenic features, and post-depositional processes. Pt.2, "Case studies," provides ten detailed case studies. Packed with examples. Focus is on information from micromorphology on human behavior, including organic occupation remains, agriculture, buildings, and fire.

C62

Dillon, Brian D., ed. *Practical archaeology: Field and laboratory techniques and archaeological logistics.* Los Angeles: Institute of Archaeology, UCLA, 1982. 125p. (Archaeological research tools, v.2)

Papers on chemical reduction of clay matrices, methods of establishing precise provenance, surface collecting using transits, simplified mapping techniques, computerizing the archaeological laboratory, use of X-rays in artifact analysis, archaeological surveying from muleback, choosing and maintaining an archaeological field vehicle, and the use of small boats in archaeological investigations.

C63

Dorrell, Peter R. *Photography in archaeology and conservation.* Cambridge, England: Cambridge Univ. Pr., 1989. 262p. (Cambridge manuals in archaeology, no.3)

Select bibliography (p.253–55). Ninety-nine illustrations. Pt.1, "Technical and theoretical knowledge"; pt.2, "Applications to archaeology and conservation." Chapters are concisely defined and can stand alone as a single area of study. Covers the use of photography at excavation and for recording data, analyzing discoveries, and communicating results.

See also the journal *Archaeology* **(C07)** and Grinsell, Rahtz, and Williams's *Preparation of archaeological reports* **(C71).** To update, informally consult *Art and archaeology technical abstracts* [computer file] **(B09);** and for updating other technical issues such as remote sensing, consult *Geobase* [computer file] **(B20).** Inspect also Rahtz and Richards's *Computer applications and quantitative methods in archaeology* **(C83)** for coverage of such issues as digital enhancement of photographs.

C64

Driesch, Angela von den. *Guide to the measurement of animal bones from archaeological sites: As developed by the Institut für Palaeoanatomie.* Cambridge, Mass.: Peabody Museum of Archaeology and Ethnology, Harvard University, 1976. 136p. (Peabody Museum Bulletin, no.1)

Prepared in the tradition that advances in science are made from the unexpected observations arising from careful and detailed measurements. Pt.1 covers theory and method. Pt.2 covers instructions for measurement for ten species of mammalia (cranium) and for measurement for eight species of (postcranial) skeleton (p.65–101). Pt.3 covers instructions for the measurement of bird bones. A brief but useful source by Ann Stirland, *Human bones in archaeology* (Aylesbury, Bucks., England: Shire, 1986 [64p.]) **(C65),** has ten drawings and eighteen plates. It discusses not only measurements but also identification, dating and treatment for preservation, pathology, and cremations. Includes a useful list of references.

C66

Gaines, Sylvia W., ed. *Data bank applications in archaeology.* With contributors Louis Bourrelly et al. Tucson: Univ. of Arizona Pr., 1981. 142p.

Discusses successful applications of computer to archaeological data worldwide. Articles by twelve experts on topics ranging from data management to analysis and graphics. Includes articles on applications and results of several computerized systems, including Azsit, Sarg, Oracle, and Sofia.

For more current information, consult *Science and archaeology,* v.1– , 1970– (Strafford, England: Research centre for computer archaeology) **(C67);** annual. Each issue has five or six articles and publishes information about relevant conferences and meetings. See Rahtz and Richards's *Computer applications and quantitative methods in archaeology 1989* **(C83)** for recent use of the computer in solving problems of quantitative methodology. Consult Roberts's *Planning the documentation of museum collections* **(C86)** and Woodhead and Stansfield's *Keyguide to information sources in museum studies* **(C03)** for more generous coverage of the problems encountered in museum documentation.

C68

Gilbert, Robert I., Jr., and James H. Mielke, eds. *Analysis of prehistoric diets.* Orlando, Fla.: Academic, 1985. 436p.

Articles summarize the status of dietary reconstruction with archaeological food remains and skeletal analysis. A concise sourcebook of paleoethnobiology.

C69

Green, Jeremy. *Maritime archaeology: A technical handbook.* San Diego: Academic, 1990. 282p.

Techniques and procedures are given detailed development. Divided into five areas: "Searching for sites"; "Excavation and management of collections"; "Study"; "Research"; and "Publication."

More recently, Jordon E. Kerber's *Coastal and maritime archaeology: A bibliography* (Metuchen, N.J., and London: Scarecrow, 1991 [400p.]) **(C70)** has organized books, articles and conferences under four broad topics. In the ethnohistoric/ethnographic section, nearly 50 percent of the 2,800 entries are for the Northeast United States, with some coverage of Andean, Austronesian, Caribbean, and European regions. Excellent coverage of coastal subsistence strategies. Author index. Many closely related problems are discussed in Purdy's *Wet site archaeology* **(C81).**

C71

Grinsell, Leslie Valentine, Philip Rahtz, and David P. Williams. *Preparation of archaeological reports.* 2d ed. New York: St. Martin's, 1974. 105p.

Practical manual on preparation of excavation and nonexcavation reports. Includes distribution maps with a useful bibliography.

C72

Hester, Thomas R., R. F. Heizer, and J. A. Graham. *Field methods in archaeology.* 6th ed. Palo Alto, Calif.: Mayfield, 1975. 408p.

Appendixes include information on state and federal regulations in the United States as they concern archaeological sites. The standard manual on surveying, recording data, stratigraphy, and photography.

For American archaeology, this work can be a companion volume to the more recent and equally concise Bettess, *Surveying for archaeologists* **(C56),** and Dillon, *Practical archaeology* **(C62).**

C73

Hillson, Simon. *Teeth.* Cambridge, England, and New York: Cambridge Univ. Pr., 1986. 376p. (Cambridge manuals in archaeology, no.2)

Nineteen plates, 110 drawings, and 38 tables facilitate the identification of teeth from more than 150 genera. Covers tooth form, dental microstructure, teeth and age, size and shape, dental diseases. Summary information on the importance of teeth in identification of genera. The extensive bibliography (p.341–67) establishes this resource as a bibliographic review of the evidence provided by teeth in the investigations of archaeology and physical anthropology.

C74

Hole, Frank, and Robert F. Heizer. *Prehistoric archaeology: A brief introduction.* New York: Holt, 1977. 477p.

Sixty-two pages of bibliographic guidance makes this a favored desk reference book among professional archaeologists. Includes a detailed narrative overview of studies of surveying and excavating, methods of analysis, and ways of interpreting results.

C75

Hudson, Kenneth. *World industrial archaeology.* Cambridge, England, and New York: Cambridge Univ. Pr., 1979. 247p.

An introductory section discusses the aims and techniques of industrial archaeology. Topical chapters follow on extractive industries, food and drink, construction, metal processing, transport, textiles, clothing and footwear, power, and chemicals.

This subject is excluded from Sherratt's *Cambridge encyclopedia of archaeology* **(C37).**

C76

International Flint Symposium, 4th: 1983: Brighton Polytechnic. *The scientific study of flint and chert: The proceedings of the fourth International Flint Symposium held at Brighton Polytechnic, 10–15 April, 1983.* Edited by Gale de G. Sieveking and M. B. Hart. Cambridge, England: Cambridge Univ. Pr., 1987. 290p.

Covers flint tools, microware, and texture analysis. There is a discussion of replication of tool making sequences, spatial analysis, flint mining, and flint technology. Some of the articles include historical reviews of the literature, with extensive bibliographies.

As a model of excellence in the investigation of flint, consult François Bordes's *Typologie du paléolithique ancien et moyen,* 4th ed. (Paris: CNRS, 1988 [102p.]) **(C77)**—descriptions and illustrations of Paleolithic struck flints as classified by Bordes on the basis of their form, probable use, and method of manufacture. Consult also Lucile R. Addington's *Lithic illustration: Drawing flaked stone artifacts for publication* (Chicago: Univ. of Chicago Pr., 1986 [139p.]) **(C78),** which relates definitions and the topology of artifacts to the problems of graphic illustration and production. Devices for the illustration of texture, flake direction, and cleavage surface are discussed and illustrated. Written for the professional illustrator. Deals with all aspects of the substantive issues, processes, and preparations for publication. Detailed index. Consult also Adkins and Adkins's *Archaeological illustrations* **(C51)** and Dillon's *The student's guide to archaeological illustrating* **(C52).**

C79

Kent, Bretton W. *Making dead oysters talk: Techniques for analyzing oysters from archaeological sites.* Annapolis: Maryland Historical Trust, 1988. 107p.

The narrative is forthright. The illustrations are adequate. Includes an appendix of useful chemical solutions discussed in the running text. Thirty-five drawings illustrate possibilities for measurement and observation.

C80

Koch, Christopher P. *Taphonomy: A bibliographic guide to the literature.* Orono, Maine: Center for the Study of First Americans at the University of Maine, 1989. 67p. (Peopling of the Americas publications. Bibliographic series)

More than 1,200 entries. International in scope. Covers a wide range of subtopics included in the larger field of taphonomy. Many cross-references.

C81

Purdy, Barbara, A., ed. *Wet site archaeology.* Caldwell, N.J.: Telford Pr., 1988. 338p.

Twenty articles by specialists on such topics as the location and assessment of underwater sites (including the use of remote sensing) and problems and responsibilities of excavation.

John M. Coles and Andrew J. Lawson have written a companion volume, *European wetlands in prehistory* (Oxford, England: Clarendon Pr.; New York: Oxford Univ. Pr., 1987 [299p.]) **(C82);** a detailed table of contents leads to discussions of research (including archival research), search and survey (including electron and aerial survey), predisturbance survey, field photography, excavation, recording, conservation, artifact drawing, computers, and post-excavation research.

C83

Rahtz, Sebastian P. Q., and Julian Richards, eds. *Computer applications and quantitative methods in archaeology,* 1989. Oxford, England: Oxford Univ. Pr. 385p. (BAR International series S548)

Earlier volumes in this special subset in the BAR international series include Rahtz, S. P. Q., ed., *Computer and quantitative methods,* 1988 (Oxford, England: BAR, 1988 [2v.]) (BAR S446(i) and BAR 446(ii)); and G. L. Ruggles and S. P. Q. Rahtz, eds., *Computer and quantitative methods, 1987 (CAA87)* (Oxford, England: BAR, 1988 [299p.]) (BAR 393).

Widely distributed in the *BAR International monographic series.* In the 1989 volume thirty-four papers, including nine on surface and solid modeling and on image enhancement (patterning of distributions, image processing, rectification of air photos); seven papers on statistical methods of data analysis and interpretation; three papers on recording systems; four papers on expert systems and artifact classification. Production of the volume is used to illustrate some of the latest methods in text and graphic handling.

Consult also *World archaeology,* v.1, no.3, *Analysis (includes computer analysis)* **(C50);** Gaines's *Data bank applications in archaeology* **(C66);** and Roberts's *Planning the documentation of museum collections* **(C86).** The best, concise hands-on treatment can be found in Gary Lock and John Wilcoc's *Computer archaeology* (Prinees Risborough, England: Shire, 1987 [64p.]), which, after discursive chapters on computers and data, there includes chapters on different archaeological situations, on descriptive statistics, graphics, and on complex statistics. Glossary and index. The bibliography is organized to identify continuing sources, including the *Archaeological computing newsletter* (Britain), v.1– , 1984– (Stafford, North Staffordshire, United Kingdom: Department of Computing, North Staffordshire Polytechnic), quarterly. A sensible introduction to computing can be found in J. D. Richards and N. S. Ryan's *Data processing in archaeology* (Cambridge, England: Cambridge Univ. Pr., 1985 [232p.]) (Cambridge manuals in archaeology) **(C84).**

C85

Rice, Prudence M. *Pottery analysis: A source book.* Chicago: Univ. of Chicago Pr., 1987. 559p.

Extensive documentation. First there are definitions of terms and a history of ceramic technology, followed by coverage for Near East, Far East, Europe, Mediterranean, and New World. Pt.2, "Clays," explains their origin and discusses their properties and behavior under firing. Pt.3, "Process of manufacturing," and pt.4, "Studies and research designs." Many cross-references. Regional reference works on pottery are located in the appropriate geographically defined chapters of *Fieldwork in the Library.*

C86

Roberts, David Andrew. *Planning the documentation of museum collections.* Duxford, England: Museum Documentation Association, 1985. 568p.

Attempts to standardize concepts for management of data. Four appendixes form two-thirds of the monograph: first, a thesaurus of museum activities and documentation terms; second, detailed guidelines for documentation practices; third, a review of computer hardware and software for use at museums; and finally a summary of documentation practices in thirty-five museums in the United Kingdom.

Consult *World archaeology* **(C50),** v.4, no.1, and Gaines's *Data bank applications in archaeology* **(C66).** These works can be informally updated in the issues of *Science and archaeology* described at **(C67).** Consult also appropriate sections of Woodhead and Stansfield's *Keyguide to information sources in museum studies* **(C03),** and for computer graphics, Adkins and Adkins's *Archaeological illustrations* **(C51).**

C87

Schlereth, Thomas J., ed. *Material culture: A research guide.* With contributions from Kenneth L. Ames et al. Lawrence: Univ. of Kansas Pr., 1985. 224p.

A collection of bibliographic essays by specialists in the field, who bring folk art and Western traditions into the mainstream of modern archaeological and ethnographic analysis. Especially strong on everyday life, architecture, and technology. Excellent chapter bibliographies, which are more or less independent. "Select listing of serials literature in material culture research" (p.200–205) is useful in identifying the literature of a kind of archaeology that combines archaeology with European ethnography as well as American decorative arts, costume, folklore, art, and geography.

C88

Sease, Catherine. *Conservation manual for the field archaeologist.* Los Angeles: Institute of Archaeology, UCLA, 1987. 169p. (Archaeological research tools, v.4)

The first section deals with the basic concepts, while the second deals with technical issues such as transport, storage, and the use and disposal of chemicals. The third chapter is devoted to sources of supplies and materials, while the fourth deals with general treatment techniques. The fifth chapter deals with specific materials and treatments, arranged alphabetically from "Amber" to "Wood" (thirty-six classes of items). Appendix 1, "Making impressions"; Appendix 2: "Making up solutions"; Appendix 4, "Conservation organizations and their publications." Plates one through forty-six (p.141–69). Subject index. Bibliography (p.137–40), which seems skimpy when compared to the mass of the available literature.

Contrast this bibliography, with its reduced range of subject focus, to the rich bibliography available for a small segment topic in M. Bogle's "A bibliography of textile conservation," *ICCM Bulletin* 8 (1982): 33–58. For expansion, consult Woodhead and Stansfield's *Keyguide to information sources in museum studies* **(C03).**

C89

Wheeler, Alwyne C. and Andrew K. G. Jones. *Fishes.* With illustrations by Rosalind Wheeler. Cambridge, England, and New York: Cambridge Univ. Pr., 1989. 210p. (Cambridge manuals in archaeology, no.9)

Consolidates research that establishes the reciprocal relationships between archaeology, paleontology, and ichthyology. Provides a handbook on solutions to the problems of observation, recovery, and analysis. Some of this research depends on the osteological and squamatological (scale) collections needed for the identification of fossils. Covers otoliths, scales, and vertebrae of fish in archaeological investigations. Bibliography (p.189–200).

C90

Zohary, Daniel, and Maria Hopf. *Domestication of plants in the Old World: The origin and the spread of cultivated plants in west Asia, Europe, and the Nile Valley.* Oxford, England: Clarendon, 1988. 249p.

Distillation of primary data on plants from west Asia, Europe, and Africa north of the Equator. Nearly twenty pages of bibliography (p.223–42). Consolidates research results of genetic, taxonomic, and ecological studies, and the plant remains from archaeological sites.

Recent advances in the study of domestication are reported in *Tools and tillage* **(C10).**

Searching Graphic Materials

Searches for maps should consult first American Geographical Society of New York, Map Department, *Index to maps in books and periodicals* **(A59).** For ethnographic films, Heider's *Films for anthropological teaching* **(A63)** is especially valuable for its selectivity.

Atlases

C91

Scarre, Christopher, ed. *Past worlds: The Times atlas of archaeology.* London: Times Books, 1988. 319p.

Arranged chronologically in thirteen spreads for an overview of humankind's earliest attempts at social, geographic, cultural, technical, and religious unity. Covers "Human origins," "The agricultural revolution," "Empires of the Old World," and "Empires of the New World." Adequate glossary, useful gazetteer, and brief bibliography. This information is distributed over eighteen time periods in Chris Scarre, *Smithsonian timelines of the ancient world: A visual chronology from the origins of life to AD 1500* (New York: Dorling Kindersley, 1993 [256p.]).

C92

Whitehouse, David, and Ruth Whitehouse. *Archaeological atlas of the world.* Paris: Tallandier, 1978. 290p.

Masses of information, consolidated into 103 maps drawn by John Woodcock and Shalom Schotten, provide a synthesis of archaeological knowledge. Identifies 5,000 sites.

C93

The world atlas of archaeology. Foreword by Michael Wood. Boston: Hall, 1985. 423p.

Twenty-five geographical or topical chapters, each with subsections. World coverage. Most references in French and German. Integrates ethnographic information into archaeological inferences.

Useful companion to Sherratt's more scholarly *Cambridge encyclopedia of archaeology* **(C37).**

Photographs and Films

Nearly half of each volume of McGraw-Hill's *Encyclopedia of world art* **(C35)** is devoted to plates. An adequate index leads to relevant articles, and plates are identified in the running text. This resource is widely available, and the selections have been made by experts. Consult also *World museum publications* **(C14),** which lists sources for many audiovisual items. "Archaeology films," a department in *Archaeology* **(C07),** reviews current releases of film productions.

C94

Ebert, Max, ed. *Reallexikon der vorgeschichte.* Berlin: W. de Gruyter, 1924–32. 15v. in 16.

Most volumes have about 150 plates each. Each article is prepared by a specialist and includes references in the running text to these plates. Many excellent maps. Important articles carry lengthy bibliographies. Shorter entries have selected references. The general index has 60,000 entries.

Searching Unpublished Materials

Searches for unpublished materials often benefit from an inspection of National Anthropological Archives, *Catalog to manuscripts at the National Anthropological Archives* **(A69).**

Archives

C95

Archives of archaeology [microform]. v.1– , 1960– . Madison: Published jointly by the Society for American Archaeology and Univ. of Wisconsin Pr. Irregular.

A series on microcard of occasional publications of primary documentation of archaeological investigations and related materials. Hopes to make available the primary data (includes line drawings and photographs as well as textual material) from archaeological sites that are rarely published in any form.

A list of publications available from this project, and purchasing information, can be found in *American antiquities* 34 (1969): 364.

C96

Pickin, Frances R. *Worldwide archaeological sample.* New Haven, Conn.: Human Relations Area Files, 1983. 2v. (HRAFlex Books, W6-009 Bibliography series)

Worldwide bibliography of site data from twenty-nine prehistoric sequences (seven in Europe; five in western Asia; seven in Americas; six in eastern Asia; four in Africa). Indexing by site is also a feature described in chapter 1, "What Every Anthropologist Needs to Know," *Anthropological literature* **(A36),** and *FRANCIS* [computer file] **(B19).** Consult also the various geographically defined chapters in *Fieldwork in the Library* for regional site indexes. Regional machine-readable databases and archaeological networks can be identified on Internet, for which consult Krol's *The whole Internet* **(B04).**

Dissertations

The quarterly issues of the hard-copy *Francis bulletin signalétique* **(C26** and **C27)** include some coverage of dissertations. For machine-readable searches, consult French and international coverage in *FRANCIS* [computer file] **(B19)** and some international and most American dissertations and theses in *Dissertations abstracts ondisc* [computer file] **(B14).** For German-language dissertations consult chapter 1, "What Every Anthropologist Needs to Know," to identify issues of *Abstracts in German anthropology* **(A33).** Reference sources about a specific culture area can be identified in chapters of *Fieldwork in the Library* that are defined by geographic regions. For current coverage of North American dissertations, consult *American journal of archaeology* **(C05).**

4

Ethnology/Cultural Anthropology

This chapter proceeds on the assumption that the reader has mastered the topical entries of both Kibbee's *Cultural anthropology* **(D01),** Bernard's "Literature search" **(D02),** and Balay's *Guide to reference books* **(B02),** especially for more general resources with powerful anthropological content.

For current substantive contributions to innovative methodologies, consult *Ethnology,* v.1– , 1962 (Pittsburgh: Univ. of Pittsburgh Pr.), a quarterly with international influence on the development of a wide range of topics in ethnology and cultural and social anthropology.

When retrospective searches include searches for descriptions of indigenous peoples, consult Human Relations Area Files, *HRAF source bibliography* **(D16)** and the Museum of Mankind Library's "Tribal index" [microfiche] **(D13).** For continuing coverage of the international output of periodical articles, consult *Anthropological literature* **(A36),** *Anthropological index* **(A35),** and *Abstracts in anthropology* **(A32).** The annual *International bibliography of social and cultural anthropology* **(D20)** succeeds in maintaining some ethnic group entry in its indexing.

The anthropologist cannot always depend on reference librarians to identify printed indexes of the Human Relations Area File's *HRAF source bibliography* **(D16),** exactly because their potential to identify works in the general collection are not widely appreciated. Many research libraries collect comprehensively materials about some large region outside the United States. Their collection in that area will include paper editions of the journal articles and monographs made available in microfiche by Human Relations Area Files, Inc. Libraries with the microfiche files have two copies of many monographs. The paperbound copy is in the stacks. The microfiche copy of a monograph can be found in the HRAF's *Human relations area files* **(D69).** Murdock's *Outline of cultural materials* **(D48)** and Murdock's *Outline of world cultures* **(D49)**—both HRAF manuals—provide entry to the printed looseleaf *HRAF source bibliography* **(D16)** and are also used to provide entry into HRAF's *Human relations area files* **(D69).**

Kibbee classes the separately published *HRAF source bibliography* **(D16)** under the subject heading "HRAF" to encourage use of the microfiche files. *Fieldwork in the Library* encourages a more general use for ethnic group entry into the collections of research libraries that do not even have the HRAF's *Human relations area files* **(D69).** The importance of using HRAF printed indexes as published in the

HRAF source bibliography **(D16)** to identify the journal titles and monographs located in research library collections cannot be overemphasized. Libraries that do not have the archival files can have the indexes as well as most of the resources to which the indexes refer. However, the HRAF printed indexes can be used to access hardcover monographs and journal titles held as hard copy in the book stacks of research libraries. They have a unique organization and cannot be approached casually. They are not graphically attractive. Many reference librarians have not encountered and do not fully understand the organization of these resources. But the structure of the printed indexes mirrors the structure of the HRAF's *Human relations area files* **(D69).** Most students of anthropology will want to master the organizational complexities of both resources. Using the printed indexes provides excellent preparation in using the microfiche files for the archival material and the many unique translations they contain.

In contrast to resources that attempt detailed retrospective coverage, some resources are designed to provide selective entry to ethnic group material. Inspect Murdock's widely available *Atlas of world cultures* **(D12)** for an example of this resource. For a different select list, it is possible to use Price's *Atlas of world cultures* **(D64).** It identifies, on a map, the location of tribes in close or contiguous contact. For each tribe, Price provides a select list of published ethnographic descriptions. This arrangement encourages studies of the distribution of culture traits with a methodology of controlled comparison.

Some topical bibliographies are described in entries starting with Divale's *Warfare in primitive societies* **(D22).** However, topical coverage does not attempt to duplicate the lucid coverage found in Kibbee's *Cultural anthropology* **(D01).** Our emphasis can be on bibliographies that record by arrangement the developmental history of conceptional categories or topics across time. Entries in these developmental bibliographies are arranged on the basis of the date of publication. The first published records are followed by the second published record, with the most recent published record listed last. Some of Kibbee's entries for dictionaries and encyclopedias have also been repeated to illustrate the differences between encyclopedias developed in the ethnographic, the ethnological, and the structural traditions. This discussion is distributed across the list of encyclopedias and dictionaries spread from **(D34)** through **(D47).** Useful handbooks are included in items **(D48)** through **(D56).** Find among the handbooks the helpful list of ethnic names in UNESCO's *Thematic list of descriptors,* p.489–514 **(D56),** developed to standardize entry into *International bibliography of social and cultural anthropology* **(D20).** Another frequently cited list of ethnic names can be found in Murdock's *Outline of world cultures* **(D49).** When a bibliography identified in Kibbee **(D01)** is duplicated here, there will often be in the annotation an emphasis on its provision for indigenous ethnic group entry.

The graphic materials between **(D62)** and **(D66)** are followed by sources for unpublished ethnographic information. Many anthropological resources with entry by name of indigenous people find listing in part 2 "Access by Geographic Area," and under appropriate geographic subheadings, in *Fieldwork in the Library.* If the geographic area for a tribe is known, then the table of contents of *Fieldwork in the Library* can be used to identify additional valuable regional bibliographies. The basic organization of all chapters mirrors the organization established in chapter 1. Reference works are assigned to broad categories of search strategies signaled by headings such as "Searching for Current Materials" or "Retrospective Searches."

Searching Bibliographic Guides

Collectively the guides to all chapters form the bibliographic base upon which *Fieldwork in the Library* is constructed. Guides to culture areas of interest are indispensable to many searches. Consult first the resources listed in Auckland's "Getting into the literature" **(A01).**

Bibliographic Guides

D01

Kibbee, Josephine Z. *Cultural anthropology: A guide to reference and information sources.*

Englewood, Colo.: Libraries Unlimited, 1991. 205p. (Reference sources in the social sciences, no.5)

Annotates 668 entries arranged in six major divisions with many subdivisions including topics such as economic, political, and urban anthropology. Excellent topical classification of the major anthropological reference sources. She also identifies for each category of her classed system more general reference sources available for specialized searches. Detailed and accurate bibliographic descriptions and lucid annotations guide the reader. Kibbee is uniquely useful for her citations of bibliographic reviews published in the *Annual review of anthropology.* She often identifies the summary texts that consolidate results for a particular topic. The headnote to this chapter defines how profoundly Kibbee's work limits what is attempted here. The index is adequate; the table of contents introduces a vast span of research interest.

Consult also Russell H. Bernard's "Literature search" in *Research methods in cultural anthropology,* p.126–44 (Newbury Park, Calif.: Sage, 1988 [520p.]) **(D02),** to find a solid discussion of how to use reference sources in ethnographic searches. Bernard includes a series of detailed sample searches to demonstrate successful strategies. He concisely records the process of specific literature searches that are used to illustrate these productive strategies. Some special attention is given to the information requirements of urban and political anthropologists. By cross-reference, Bernard's "Literature search" **(D02)** includes one more discussion on the best use of the HRAF's *Human relations area files* **(D69)** archival holdings and uniquely discusses the use of special coding combinations to organize entry into the files.

D03

Webb, William H. *Sources of information in the social sciences: A guide to the literature.* 3d ed. Chicago: American Library Assn., 1986. 777p.

Revised edition of *Sources of information in the social sciences,* by Carl M. White and associates, 2d ed., 1973. Includes Robert Westerman's "Anthropology—Survey of the reference works" (p.352–402). This essay centers on ethnology, linguistics, and folklore in keeping with the editorial parameters of the larger work. The context of the whole volume, including related disciplines such as the exceptionally lucid chapter on "Geography," contributes to the anthropological importance of the work. Author, title, and subject indexes of 189 pages are an important feature. The anthropology section concentrates on recent sources, with a strong emphasis on the social sciences, and only marginally develops archaeology and physical anthropology.

Searching for Current Materials

For special current awareness features of scholarly journals, inspect first the Royal Anthropological Institute's *Reference list of current periodicals* **(A14),** which is arranged so that listings in any issue will identify a select list of articles from journals relevant to a specialized topic in a particular culture area.

For the ethnologist, current awareness about research activities in progress often comes from newsletters devoted to area studies. Several are discussed in *Fieldwork in the Library,* "Access by Geographic Area," including: *ASA news: For African Studies Association members,* v.14– , 1981– , described in chapter 7, "Africa South of the Sahara," at **(G10).** Consult also *Asian studies newsletter,* v.1– , 1971– , chapter 9, "Asia and the Pacific," at **(L12).** The International Work Group for Indigenous Affairs (IWGIA) has published the *IWGIA yearbook, 1990* (Copenhagen, 1991 [292p.] **(D04),** which identifies organizational protection of ethnic groups as minority populations. Pt.1, "Annual report of the International Work Group for Indigenous Affairs"; pt.2, "Geographic distribution of activities and addresses for action groups in each of these areas"; pt.3, "Agencies of the U.N. that are working among indigenous people."

Select Reviews in Scholarly Publications

D05

American ethnologist: The journal of the American Ethnological Society, v.1– , 1974– .

Washington, D.C.: American Ethnological Society, a division of the American Anthropological Assn. Quarterly.

Book reviews. Some issues include signed reviews of five or ten pages devoted to titles clustered around a topical interest, plus brief reviews of an additional twenty to forty titles. "Critical commentary" includes critical responses to articles and the replies of their authors. Recent articles have included research on class and occupational roles, social life and customs, kinship groups, symbolism, and sex roles. Coverage of comparative ethnology remains a continuing interest.

D06

Anthropos: Revue international d'ethnologie et de linguistique. v.1– , 1906– . Fribourg, Switzerland: Editions Saint-Paul. 3/yr.

The "Rezensionen" section contains about 175 to 250 critical reviews per year. "Notes on books and articles" itemizes signed reviews of books and articles selected from more than 100 journals of anthropological interest. Twenty to forty critical reviews plus bibliographical information on several hundred other titles. The "Review of reviews" lists content information of current serial titles. Book reviews are indexed by author, subject, and geographical area. Substantive interests include social power, social class, social structure, myth and ritual, and ethnographic linguistics. Includes the broadest possible range for inclusion of ethnological topics as they are developed internationally.

D07

Ethnos, v.1– , 1936– . Stockholm: Ethnographical Museum of Sweden.

Valuable for "Publications received." Book reviews reflect an interest in the application of ethnographic techniques to modern complex societies. Publishes articles on social process in egalitarian societies, class, rituals, and myths. Remarkable for its regular inclusion of innovative studies.

D08

Human organization: Journal of the Society for Applied Anthropology. v.1– , 1941– . Washington, D.C.: Society for Applied Anthropology. Quarterly.

Book reviews reflect the interest of this journal in subdivisions of applied anthropology to include studies of government and industry, health and medical care, and anthropology.

D09

Social anthropology. v.1– , 1993– . Cambridge, England: Cambridge University Pr. 3/yr.

Sponsored by the European Association of Social Anthropologists. An issue usually contains three articles in European languages. "Reviews" includes fifteen to twenty-five lengthy and signed reviews, often with cited references to older material. "Notebook" provides half-page reviews to additional volumes. "Publications received" lists the current European published output alphabetically.

Selective Lists of Scholarly Journals

For a selective list of journals that actively publish research results in social and cultural anthropology, consult Frantz's *Student anthropologist's handbook* (p.152–55) **(A15).** For a more exhaustive selection, consult the list of periodicals indexed in each annual volume of the *International bibliography of social and cultural anthropology* **(D20).**

D10

Burt, Eugene C., comp. *Serials guide to ethnoart: A guide to serial publications on visual arts of Africa, Oceania, and the Americas.* New York: Greenwood, 1990. 368p. (Art reference collection, no.11)

Identifies ethnographic journals worldwide. Includes information on publisher, editorial focus, content features, and a relevancy rating. A preface is followed by the serial title database arranged in alphabetical order with annotations. Appendix A, "General serial titles ratings"; appendix B, "Ethnoart (General) serials recommendations"; appendix C, "African art serials recommendations"; appendix D, "Latin American art serials recommendations"; appendix E, "Native American art serials recommendations"; appendix G, "Serials with indexing, bibliographic and abstracting services"; appendix H, "Ceased serials"; appendix I, "Serial titles by country of publication." Rotated title keyword index.

Retrospective Searches

This section deals with retrospective searches for published studies of ethnic groups. There is no attempt to cover all entries to the vast literature of ethnicity in its modern nation state. For that purpose start with Cartu C. Bentley's *Ethnicity and nationality: A bibliographic guide* (Seattle: Univ. of Washington Pr., 1981 [455p.]), which includes about 90 anthropological reports in the 308 entries that are annotated, and provides an additional list of 2,030 unannotated entries. Tozzer Library's *Author and subject catalogues of the Tozzer Library* [microfiche] **(A26),** Peabody Library's *Catalogue: Subjects* **(A29),** and the British Museum, Museum of Mankind Library's *Museum of Mankind Library catalogues* [microfiche] **(A25)** provide entry into all aspects of anthropology worldwide in retrospective depth.

Find listed in this chapter other resources such as Human Relations Area Files, *HRAF source bibliography* **(D16),** and the *International bibliography of social and cultural anthropology* **(D20).** Each of these resources provides entry by name of indigenous peoples. The cross-references used in other chapters to bring attention to these resources are placed in the headnote to indicate their equal importance with entries that are fully described in these chapters.

Retrospective Bibliographies—Bibliography of Bibliographies

D11

Burt, Eugene C. *Bibliography of ethnoarts bibliographies.* Seattle: Data Arts, P.O. Box 30789, Seattle, WA 98101, 1990 [40p.]. (Ethnoarts index supplements bulletin, no.5)

The best and most up-to-date single source for the identification of bibliographies of bibliographies of indigenous peoples worldwide. A classed arrangement with excellent identification of local and regional bibliographies with ethnic group entry. Includes all available ethnographic bibliographies.

Can be used as a companion to the invaluable area and topical coverage of Library-Anthropology Resource Group's *Anthropological bibliographies* **(A21).** The wide distribution of this publication makes it possible for us to proceed with a more manageable emphasis on recent materials, continuing sources, and encyclopedic reviews and handbooks.

Retrospective Bibliographies—Broad Scope

D12

Murdock, George Peter. *Atlas of world cultures.* Pittsburgh: Univ. of Pittsburgh Pr., 1981. 151p.

Not an atlas in the usual sense. For the ethnologist, this sample identifies ethnic groups for which there is a developed body of published findings. H* indicates that the society was selected by HRAF for its so-called Probability Sample and is included in Human Relations Area Files, *HRAF source bibliography* **(D16).** After the classification of each of these peoples, there is a bibliography of the most nearly definitive ethnographic reports for that group. For an elaboration on this kind of list, consult Raoul Naroll et al., "A standard ethnographic sample: Preliminary edition," *Current anthropology* 11 (1970): 235–48, for a list of published reports that record the work of investigators who stayed in the field for at least twelve months and learned the indigenous language. Arranged first by region and then by tribe.

There has been limited expansion of this kind of bibliographic study. Frank A. Salamone has applied the standards and coding system developed by Naroll to all of the entries in Salamone and McCain's two-volume *The Hausa people: A bibliography* **(G64).**

D13

Museum of Mankind Library. "Tribal index." In Museum of Mankind Library. *Museum of Mankind Library books and pamphlets, author/subject and tribal catalogues. Old Department of Ethnography author and subject book catalogues; the Sir Eric Thompson library* [microfiche]. Bath, England: Mindata, 1989. 428 fiche.

The "tribal" headings are arranged alphabetically under each of the geographical headings used in the Museum of Mankind classification schedules. These schedules also define the absolutely magnificent structure of the main subject catalog, where these geographic schedules are used to subsume other anthropological resources as they are cataloged and arranged in the collection. The tribal index provides 17,000 entries to resources in the collections at the Museum of Mankind Library. This feature could be separately published as a hard-copy set. The collection from which this feature was drawn is arranged by the Bliss classified system for subject entry into all aspects of anthropology. Topical entry according to a different schedule provides entry to generalized resources and is used for subdivisions under these geographical topics. The collection also provides entry by author. The time span and depth of monographic coverage are equal to the coverage of Tozzer Library's *Catalogues* [microfiche] **(A26).** The classification system is sensitive to anthropological issues establishing a hierarchy in which topical terms can be subsumed by geographic terms. Thus the organizational interest is focused on the identification of local-level materials.

The geographic classification schedules are useful guides to any monographs with ethnology/cultural coverage as they are located in the British Museum, Museum of Mankind Library's *Museum of Mankind Library catalogues* **(A25),** which also provide author entry to monographs and pamphlets. The schedule has the advantage of simplicity and is much more forthright than the system used by Tozzer Library. The several collections from which these catalogs have been constructed parallel the Tozzer Library in coverage of all aspects of anthropology worldwide. This cumulated author catalog to journal articles in *Anthropological index* **(A35)** (1963–88) is housed by the Royal Anthropological Institute in the Museum of Mankind Library and published in British Museum, Museum of Mankind Library's *Museum of Mankind Library catalogues* **(A25).**

Retrospective Bibliographies—Continuing Bibliographies

D14

Demos: Internationale ethnographische und folkloristische informationen. v.1– , 1960– . Berlin: Akademie Verlag for the Institut für Deutsche Volkskunde. Quarterly.

A bulletin that classifies and fully annotates books, articles, and pamphlets in ethnography and folklore that originate in the cooperating countries. Prepared under the auspices of Institut für Deutsche Volkskunde an der Deutschen Akademie der Wissenschaft zu Berlin in cooperation with learned societies and ministries of culture in the C.I.S., Czechoslovakia, Poland, Albania, Bulgaria, Romania, and Hungary. One section devoted to bibliography. Author index.

D15

Geo abstracts. v.1– , 1966– . Norwich, England: Geo Abstracts at the University of East Anglia. 7 ser., each 2/yr.

Title varies. Published 1966–71 as Geographical abstracts. D. *Social and historical geography.* G. *Remote sensing, photogrammetry, and cartography.* 1974– . Included in series D, "Social and historical geography," find coverage of population distribution, population change, population migration, population fertility, man and environment, natural hazards, perception, medical, regional, cultural, historical, field evidence, historical and documentary evidence. *Annual index,* v.1– , 1986. Indexes for 1973–85 issued as one volume in 1986.

Consult also the machine-readable database *Geobase* [computer file] **(B20).**

D16

Human Relations Area Files, Inc. *HRAF source bibliography: Cumulative.* New Haven, Conn.: HRAF, 1972– . Loose-leaf.

Regular supplements; last in 1979. Can be used to gain control of the complicated methodology of entry before proceeding to the *Index to the Human relations area files* [microform]. A new edition prepared by the National Museum of Ethnology in Osaka, Japan (New Haven, Conn.: Human relations area files, 1988) [microfiche] **(D17).** Title on eye-readable header: HRAF "Subject index . . . to the Human Relations Area Files . . . through December, 1986" (Intro., p.i). *Supplement* (1979) contains most of the resources made available in microfiche for the files. It supplies scholars with full bibliographic descriptions for all sources of information held in the files. Most of these resources are held in research library collections with the hard-copy resources.

The organization of both the printed and the microfiche editions is by area and then by tribe or ethnic group, with extensive bibliographic listings of ethnographic, linguistic, archaeological, and biological materials thereunder. By editorial choice, only those tribes covered by a substantial body of research are included. The powerful and detailed controlled vocabularies used in these publications are published and are regularly updated. Inspect Murdock's *Outline of world cultures* **(D49)** for the symbols used to identify tribes in the arrangement of Human Relations Area Files, *HRAF source bibliography* **(D16)** and of *Human relations area files* **(D69).** Additionally, the companion volume, Murdock's *Outline of cultural materials* **(D48),** can be consulted for symbols used to identify research about cultural artifacts such as marriage ceremonies or dancing. Each of these thesauri depends on the complementary support of the others. Follow the cross-references in Bernard's "Literature search" **(D02)** to his detailed discussion on using the archival *Human relations area files* [microfiche] **(D69).** This discussion can be applied in part to both the archival files themselves and Human Relations Area Files, *HRAF source bibliography* **(D16).** In a more recent innovation by HRAF, the selected subject entry can be obtained from a database published on CD-ROM (SilverPlatter) in a five-year project starting in 1989. SilverPlatter, under the title *Cross cultural info* [computer file] (New Haven, Conn.: Human Relations Area Files) **(D18)** (alternate title *Cross-cultural CD*) publishes full-text databases to about 1,000 periodical articles and monographs in a set of computer files on broad topics such as human sexuality, marriage, and family. Use of the various resources produced by Human Relations Area Files benefit from conceptual and technical preparation by the user. A recent guide to this resource can be found in Ellen D. Sutton's "The Human Relations Area Files and cross-cultural CD: Enhanced access to selected subjects," *RSR: Reference services review* 19 (1991): 57–70 **(D19).**

D20

International bibliography of social and cultural anthropology. v.1– , 1955– . London: Tavistock; Chicago: Aldine. Annual. (International bibliography of the social sciences)

Prepared by the International Committee for Social Sciences Documentation. The early issues were published in cooperation with the International Union of Anthropological and Ethnological Sciences. One of four current bibliographies that originated with an early UNESCO policy decision to help strengthen bibliographic control over social science literature. Arranged according to a detailed classification scheme under ten major categories, which are further divided by topic and geographical area. Book reviews are indicated by the abbreviation "CR." A three-year lag is not unusual, but the only studies of some tribes can be decades old. For the vast majority of this information, a three-year lag is irrelevant. This index attempts to identify and organize work significant enough to be considered part of the global record of scholarship in the field. Experience has somewhat reduced the gap between the goal and the accomplishment. Selective list. French and English titles are entered in the language of publication. For other entries, a translation of the title into English follows the language of publication. There is an author index and an alphabetic subject index first in French and then in English.

For a published edition of the controlled vocabulary used, consult UNESCO's *Thematic list of descriptors* **(D56).** For ethnographic searches, this controlled vocabulary provides standardized spelling of tribal names established in the indexes of the *International bibliography of social and cultural anthropology* **(D20).**

D21

Internationale volkskundliche bibliographie= Bibliographie internationale des arts et traditions populaires=International folklore and folklife bibliography. v.1– , 1939–41– .

Bonn: Rudolph Habelt Verlag for Commission internationale des arts et traditions populaire. Irregular.

A best source for identifying the literature of European ethnology and ethnographic folklore. Maintains a worldwide span of interest, although its special strength is in the Spanish and Portuguese countries of Europe and Latin America. A broad range of subject and geographic coverage.

Retrospective Bibliographies—Topical Bibliographies

There follows several entries that are either newer editions published since the Kibbee cutoff date or which fell outside the range of resources development in the structure of that important book. Kibbee's *Cultural anthropology* **(D01)** develops topical entry under headings such as "Art and material culture," "Cognitive anthropology," "Medical anthropology," "Religion and mythology," and "Research methods and fieldwork." Topical bibliographies will be included here only when ethnic group entry can be made the focus of the annotation, or when they are arranged chronologically to reveal the development of a conceptual technology, or when these entries support integration of resources described in other works, such as Harrison and Cosminsky's *Traditional medicine* **(D25)** and **(D26),** which are referred to as a complementary source for resources listed in chapter 6, "Physical and Biological Anthropology," such as Johnson and Sargent's *Medical anthropology* **(F50).**

The references to articles in Borgatta and Borgatta's *Encyclopedia of sociology* **(D39)** in their totality can be seen as a bibliographic review of recent contributions to the issues, theories, and research findings in a number of areas of interest to social anthropologists. The careful indexing and the many cross-references make entry to these bibliographic resources available even from the most specialized focus. In this function, the encyclopedia serves as a selective guide to recent literature for the many research interests shared between sociologists and anthropologists.

D22

Divale, William T. *Warfare in primitive societies: A bibliography.* Rev. ed. Santa Barbara, Calif.: ABC-Clio, 1973. 123p.

Ethnic group and author index to entries ordered in a topical arrangement with headings that range from concepts to descriptive terms like "Scalping." Distributes a bibliography across sixteen sections. More interesting, as a support for anthropological research, are the maps of seven geographical regions and lists of sources for the investigation of warfare between the various peoples of these regions.

A more general source for locating tribes in geographic spaces can be found in Price's *Atlas of world cultures* **(D64).**

D23

Driver, Edwin D. *The sociology and anthropology of mental illness: A reference guide.* Rev. and enlarged ed. Amherst: Univ. of Massachusetts Pr., 1972. 487p.

Often excluded as superseded, this work is included here because so many of the concepts examined and methods used in recent investigations duplicate exactly the methods and reported results found in earlier publications like this. For entries with significant interest in the cultural and social aspects of mental illness worldwide. Comprehensive coverage to the date of publications.

D24

Ethnoart index, v.1– , 1984– . Seattle: Data Arts. Irregular.

Many of the local art sources are defined by an ethnic group. Identifies most bibliographies of indigenous groups. Classifies about 800 articles, books, and dissertations per issue from all Western languages in each issue.

Consult also the *EthnoArt index, Supplemental publication,* v.1– , 1988– (Seattle: Data Arts). No.1, A five-year cumulation, 1983–88; no.2, *Oceanic art* (1988 [55p.]); no.4, *Native American art* (1990 [157p.]); no.5, Burt's *Bibliography of ethnoarts bibliographies* **(D11).**

D25

Harrison, Ira E., and Sheila Cosminsky. *Traditional medicine: Implications for ethno-*

medicine, ethno-pharmacology, maternal and child health, mental health, and public health: An annotated bibliography of Africa, Latin America, and the Caribbean. New York: Garland, 1976. 229p. (Garland reference library of social science, v.19)

D26

Harrison, Ira E., and Sheila Cosminsky. *Traditional medicine, 1976–1981: Current research: An annotated bibliography.* New York: Garland, 1984. 327p. (Garland reference library of social science, v.147)

Grouped by region with subsections. Lists 2,526 entries. Some entries have long abstracts. A general section is followed by sections on Africa and the Latin America/Caribbean area. Each section is subdivided by topics such as health-care delivery, mental health, and ethnomedicine. An author index at the end of each section and a country index at the end of the volume.

Consult also Johnson and Sargent's *Medical anthropology* **(F50).** Consult also *EMbase plus* [computer file] **(B15),** *Geobase* [computer file] **(B20),** *Life sciences collection* [computer file] **(B24),** and *Medline* [computer file] **(B26).**

D27

Jacob, Jean-Pierre, Riccardo Bocco, and David Brokensha. *Bibliographie sélective et commentée d'anthropologie du dévelopment.* Genéve: Institut Universitaire d'Études du Dévelopment, 1989. 74p. (Itineraires. Notes et Travaux, no.37)

General development is arranged into two sections—one for French titles and one for English titles. There is an additional section with specific themes which intermixes the languages. All 260 entries have annotations in French.

D28

Rosenstiel, Annette. *Education and anthropology: An annotated bibliography.* New York: Garland, 1977. 646p. (Garland reference library of social science, no.20)

International coverage of books, periodical articles, reports, dissertations, prints, papers. Arranges 3,435 items by author, with subject and name indexes. Includes theoretical issues and the problems of interfaces between disciplines. Foreign-language titles are given English translations. Kibbee expands this subject with eight other entries but does not include *Anthropology & education quarterly,* v.7– , 1976– (Washington, D.C.: Council on Anthropology and Education). First published as *Quarterly newsletter* (v.1–6, 1969–76), which acts as a forum for this subject.

RETROSPECTIVE BIBLIOGRAPHIES—TOPICAL BIBLIOGRAPHIES—ORGANIZED AS TIME-ORDERED CONTRIBUTIONS

Anthropologists have an enduring interest in the historical development of conceptual systems. This has been institutionalized in time-ordered entries in the bibliographic notation. This arrangement of bibliographic entries is more common in the physical sciences than in the social sciences. Inspect the following applications of this method toward full-length bibliographies. The results display the resources needed to understand the movement across time of these concepts, and the oscillation back and forth between favored points of interest.

D29

Favazza, Armando R. *Anthropological and cross-cultural themes in mental health: An annotated bibliography, 1925–1974.* Columbia: Univ. of Missouri Pr., 1977. 386p. (University of Missouri studies: 65)

Lists 3,600 English-language entries in chronological arrangement, with brief descriptive abstracts. Victor Barnouw reviews the anthropological themes and constructs tables of the distribution of these themes across cultural areas. There is a subject index in broad categories and an author index. The expansion in Armando Favazza and Ahmed D. Faheem's *Themes in cultural psychiatry: An annotated bibliography, 1975–1980* (Columbia: Univ. of Missouri Pr., 1982 [195p.]), includes non-English-language resources.

Find related topical entries in Kibbee's *Cultural anthropology* **(D01)** under the heading "Medical anthropology."

D30

Feldforschung: Bibliographie 1967–1981: Methoden und erfahrungen=Enquête sur le terrain:

Approches et expériences. Fribourg, Switzerland: Universitätsverlag, 1982. 111p. (Studia Ethnographica friburgensia, bd.9)

Lists 325 bibliographic descriptions without annotation; items distributed in a classed arrangement by date of publication and with authors entered alphabetically thereunder. Followed by three essays (p.59–109) on approaching ethnographic knowledge through the analysis of proverbs, on the problems encountered in an investigation of women in society, and on the use of cognitive studies. German and French index.

Find related topical development in Kibbee's *Cultural anthropology* **(D01)** under the heading "Research methods and fieldwork."

D31

Kessing, Felix M. *Culture change: An analysis and bibliography of anthropological sources to 1952.* Stanford, Calif.: Stanford Univ. Pr., 1953. 242p. [Stanford anthropological series, no.1]

Pt.1, Chronological analysis of the progress of anthropological thought on this topic and a critique of research and the literature; pt.2, Chronological listing of 4,212 bibliographic descriptions of works discussed in this analysis. Most items are post-1865; all essential elaborations of the conceptual framework for the investigation of culture change had been established by 1952.

D32

Pas, H. T. Van der, comp. *Economic anthropology, 1940–1972: An annotated bibliography.* Oosterhout, Netherlands: Anthropological Publications; New York: Dist. by Humanities, 1973. 221p.

Long annotations. Organized by date and then by author with an author index. Since 1978 there has been a regular consolidation of significant work in *Research in economic anthropology,* v.1– , 1978– (Greenwich, Conn.: JAI Pr.). Annual.

D33

Van Willigen, John. *Anthropology in use: A bibliographic chronology of the development of applied anthropology.* Boulder, Colo.: Westview, 1991. 254p.

Detailed introduction to each of the 530 entries. Organized by time period. Identifies and evaluates an elusive body of research. Does not systematically include fugitive literature. With great generosity this work shares the accessions lists to the important Applied Anthropology Documentation Project. The annotations provide insightful entry into the body of literature covered. Provides annotated author and geographical indexes. Since entries are listed only once under broad categories without cross-references, care must be taken to use several terms for the same concept in searching for a topic. The author's textbook *Applied anthropology* (South Hadley, Mass.: Bergin and Garvey, 1986 [277p.]) provides a rare and useful assessment of this material, and his *Anthropology in use: A source book on anthropological practice* (Boulder, Colo.: Westview, 1991 [254p.]) describes and annotates published reports on the activities of non-academic anthropologists classed under broad topics.

For a directory of American non-academic anthropologists, consult the American Anthropological Association's *Directory of practicing anthropologists* **(A07).**

Informational Reference Searches

For American anthropology, consult first the *AAA guide* **(A53)** for directory information. The best international directory is still the "International directory of anthropological institutions" **(A56),** which could usefully be reissued in a new edition.

For summaries and records of the myths in the ethnographic tradition, see Gray and Moore's *Mythology of all races* **(D44).** For an attempt to identify universal and unifying archetypes, consult Campbell's *Historical atlas of world mythology* **(D40).** For a more comprehensive inclusion of folk traditions, including even "dance" and "music," and of English-language resources constructed in an ethnological framework, consult Leach and Fried's *Funk and Wagnalls standard dictionary of folklore, mythology and legend* **(D45).** For a consolidation of results achieved in the structuralist tradition, consult Bonnefoy's *Mythologies* **(D36).**

Encyclopedias and Dictionaries—Ethnology

D34

Levinson, David, general editor. *Encyclopedia of world cultures.* Boston: Hall, 1991– .

Issued to date: v.1, *North America,* edited by David Levinson and Timothy O'Leary; v.2, *Oceania,* edited by Terence Hays; v.3, *South Asia,* edited by Paul Hocking; v.4, *Europe,* edited by Linda A. Bennett. A ready reference that makes available in conventional form the information in Murdock's *Ethnographic atlas* **(D73)** and the Human Relations Area Files, *HRAF source bibliography* **(D16).** Projected as a ten-volume set with additional coverage to include: South Asia; Europe and the Middle East; Africa; East and Southeast Asia; the C.I.S. and China; and South America, Middle America, and the Caribbean.

Each regional volume contains maps that pinpoint the current location of living ethnic groups described in that volume, a filmography of select films, an ethnonym index, and a glossary. The tenth volume will contain a cumulative list of cultures of the world and their alternative names, with select bibliographies. The descriptions of ethnic groups in each volume are arranged alphabetically under major geographic headings. The information on each group follows a severely limited but standardized outline including subsistence activities, land tenure, kinship, marriage and family, and sociopolitical organization. The supporting bibliographies, usually of two items, seem to exclude comprehensive ethnic group bibliographies even when they are available. This encyclopedia does not attempt to cover the theoretical issues beyond the implicit assumption that the selected variables describe "lifeways."

D35

Poirier, Jean. *Ethnologie regionale.* Paris: Gallimard, 1972–78. 2v. (Encyclopedie de la Pleiade, 33, 42)

For anthropology, the same editor in the same set is responsible for: v.24, *Ethnologie, generale* (1968 [1,909p.]) in which the article on the ethnology of Europe is especially useful, and v.47, *Histoire des moeurs* (1990 [2v.: 1,658p., 1,738p.]), with many topics, including cannibalism and the aesthetics of ethnology. These volumes use a small but readable type and collectively form the most elaborate summary of ethnology in any language. Use the volume editor entry when searching for this book in American research libraries. Most libraries follow LC cataloging and treat each volume of the encyclopedia (but not volumes within an encyclopedic volume) as a monograph. They are scattered throughout stacks. In libraries with computer files, the name of the general encyclopedia can sometimes identify all available volumes with keyword searches. Brilliantly edited with signed articles arranged under broad topics with selective bibliographies (predominantly French-language). The indexing is a model of excellence and is sensitive to any conceivable scholarly interest.

Encyclopedias and Dictionaries—Folklore, Mythology, and Religion

An explication of the variations among reference sources dealing with mythology and religion can be found in the annotation given to Bonnefoy's *Mythologies* **(D36),** which is shaped by a theoretical interest in structuralism. This is in contrast to the factual, direct reporting of the myths themselves in Gray and Moore's *Mythology of all races* **(D44)** and the more ethnographic (ethnic group) orientation of Leach and Fried's *Funk and Wagnalls standard dictionary of folklore, mythology and legend* **(D45).**

D36

Bonnefoy, Yves, comp. *Mythologies.* Prepared under the direction of Wendy Doniger. Chicago: Univ. of Chicago Pr., 1991. 2v.

A translation of *Dictionnaire des mythologies et des religions des societes traditionnelles et du monde antique,* under the direction of Yves Bonnefoy. (Paris: Flammarion, 1981 [2v.]). Articles in the English translation are organized by geographic region and cultural tradition. Signed articles on mythologies and religions from societies without a written language. Excludes the mystery religions Judaism, Christianity, Islam, Gnosticism, Taoism, and the legacies of Buddha, for which see Eliade and Adams's *Encyclopedia of religion* **(D43).**

Contributors provide worldwide coverage from Africa to Scandinavia, England to the Americas, the Middle East to the Far East, and the Mediterranean to the South Pacific. Unified by the use of the methods of structuralism to interpret cultural traditions. Assumes that "primitive" and "modern" modes of thought, belief, and conduct have no substantive difference. Most bibliographic entries are in the French language, although the English-language classics are included. The territorial coverage is more representative of the range of French than of English scholarship. It consolidates the advances achieved by building on the perspective developed by Claude Lévi-Strauss and Georges Dumézil, and provides a thoroughly modern reference source for searches in the areas of mythology, primitive religion, and the analysis of folklore that identify work in the forefront of new theories and methods.

For a guide to the work of the structuralists for anthropology, consult especially Joan Nordquist's *Claude Lévi-Strauss: A bibliography* (Santa Cruz, Calif.: Reference and Research Services, 1987 [60p.]) (Social theory: A bibliographic series, no.6) **(D37),** which first lists books by Lévi-Strauss with relevant reviews of his contributions before listing essays by the author. Nordquist then lists books about the author and in a final section lists articles about his work. The format allows quick access to critical works on particular publications and relevant sections of Joan M. Miller, comp., *French structuralism: A multidisciplinary bibliography: With a checklist of sources for Louis Althusser, Roland Barthes, Jacques Derrida, Michel Foucault, Lucien Goldmann, Jacques Lacan and an update of works on Claude Lévi-Strauss* (New York: Garland, 1981 [553p.]) (Garland reference library of the humanities, v.160) **(D38).** After a survey of the general literature, individual authors are covered. A third section applies bibliographic citations to specific academic disciplines, including anthropology and folklore.

D39

Borgatta, Edgar F., and Marie L. Borgatta. *Encyclopedia of sociology.* New York: Maxwell, Macmillan International, 1992. 4v.

Comprehensive summaries of the issues, theories, and recent research on all issues in which there is a shared interest between sociology and anthropology. The many citations to anthropological advances reveal a sensitivity to the anthropological viewpoint. The bibliographies are selective for the best recent work, and resources cited here can be referred to with confidence. There are 339 contributors. There are a number of area studies covered as well as ethnic studies under such headings as "African-American studies" and "American Indian studies." Strong editorial leadership is visible in the readability of the text and the selective bibliographies, which are notable for their uniform excellence. Both the articles and the index are arranged letter by letter.

D40

Campbell, Joseph. *Historical atlas of world mythology.* v.1– , 1983– . New York: A. van der Marck Editions; San Francisco: dist. by Harper.

The first two volumes—*The way of the animal powers*—cover hunting and gathering tribes and the earliest planting societies in a treatment that attempts to isolate archetypes that provide meaning to individuals. V.3, *The way of the celestial lights,* when published, will cover the sky mythologies of the great ancient cities; v.4, *The way of man,* is an exercise in dynamic insight and discusses the transformation of mythological structures in the post-Renaissance world. Encyclopedic for this type of analysis. Indexed by subject, place, and myth motif.

Consult also Kenneth L. Golden's *Uses of comparative mythology: Essays on the work of Joseph Campbell* (New York: Garland, 1992 [278p.]) (Garland reference library of the humanities, v.138) **(D41).** It acts as a comprehensive survey of the methodology, with strong bibliographical references and a useful index. For concise summaries of myths, consult Hans Wilhelm Haussig's *Wörterbuch der Mythologie* (Stuttgart: Ernst Klett, 1961 [5v.]) **(D42).** For international coverage see Cotterell's *A dictionary of world mythology,* new ed., rev. and expanded (New York: Oxford Univ. Pr., 1986 [314p.]), which is divided into seven geographic areas defined in terms of cultural traditions, with a comprehensive index. Consult Bonnefoy's *Mythologies* **(D36)** for an encyclopedic application of structural analysis, and Gray and Moore's *Mythology of all races* **(D44)** for its detailed text.

D43

Eliade, Mircea, and Charles J. Adams, eds. *The encyclopedia of religion.* New York: Macmillan, 1987. 16v.

Rich bibliographies follow articles which are listed alphabetically. Provides topical and geographic entry. Valuable for folklore and all of the world's religious traditions. Sensitive to anthropological contributions throughout. For example, the article on "Play" lists in its bibliography nine anthropological publications.

D44

Gray, Louis Herbert, and George Foot Moore, eds. *Mythology of all races.* Boston: For Archaeological Institute of America by Marshall Jones Co., 1916–32. 13v.

J. A. Macculloch and George Foot Moore edited v.2, 4–5, 7–8, 13. Contents of this set include collections of mythology for: v.1, W. S. Fox's *Greek and Roman;* v.2, J. A. Macculloch's *Eddic;* v.3, J. A. Macculloch's *Celtic;* Jan Machal's *Slavic;* v.4, Uno Holmberg's *Finno-Ugric, Siberian;* v.5, S. H. Langdon's *Semitic;* v.6, A. Berriedale Keith's *Indian;* Albert J. Carny's *Iranian;* v.7, Mardiros H. Ananikian's *Armenian* and A. Werner's *African;* v.8, J. C. Ferguson's *Chinese;* U. Hattor and Masaharu Anesak's *Japanese;* v.9, Roland B. Dixon's *Oceanic;* v.10, Hartley B. Alexander's *North American;* v.11, Hartley B. Alexander's *Latin-American;* v.12, W. Max Müller's *Egyptian;* James George Scott's *Indo-Chinese;* v.13, *Complete index.* Basic resource. Several of these contributors were distinguished anthropologists.

D45

Leach, Maria, and Jerome Fried, eds. *Funk and Wagnalls standard dictionary of folklore, mythology and legend.* New York: Funk & Wagnalls, 1972, 1,236p.

International in coverage. Includes fifty-five survey articles on subjects such as "Dance," "Folk and primitive," "Primitive and folk art." Includes an international directory of museums. Key to the identification of 2,035 culture areas and tribes.

Consult the *Neues wörtbuch der völkerkunde,* edited by Walter Hirschberg and Marianne Fries (Berlin: Reimer Verlag, 1988 [536p.]) **(D46),** for references, biographical entries, and a directory of folk museums. For the integration of the developments of the 1970s and 1980s, this valuable resource can be supplemented by reference to Bonnefoy's *Mythologies* **(D36)** and chapter 5, "Linguistics," for the impact of linguistics on folklore studies, noting especially the *Journal of folklore research* **(E94).**

D47

Winthrop, Robert H. *Dictionary of concepts in cultural anthropology.* Westport, Conn.: Greenwood, 1991. 347p. (Reference sources for the social sciences and humanities, no.11)

The list of concepts (p.viii–xiv) guides the reader to brief but accurate and well-documented discussions of these ideas. The name index under BOAS has been detailed to twenty-one expansions. "Culture" is subdivided with five terms. This detailed indexing makes this resource especially useful in tracing the conceptual technology of anthropological investigations.

Handbooks, Manuals, and Scholarly Compendiums

For the most part, more general handbooks can be identified in Balay's *Guide to reference books* **(B02),** although in the geographically arranged section of *Fieldwork in the Library,* some more general handbooks influenced by anthropologists are included. It might be useful to inspect the entry for *African historical dictionaries* **(G77),** in which a basic format provides a general introduction and chronology; tables consolidate numeric information; alphabetical listing of topics; organizations and people; and bibliographies that nearly always come to half of the volume. Many of these monographs were prepared by anthropologists. For some countries covered, a quality bibliography of any size is difficult to identify. Many volumes rely heavily on English-language sources, but they frequently do include entries in other European languages where necessary for adequate coverage. The series shows unusually loose editorial control. Quality is uneven but frequently marked by a sensitivity to anthropological resources. A serious effort is being made by the publisher to bring out new editions of these important sources before they become completely out-of-date.

D48

Murdock, George Peter, ed. *Outline of cultural materials.* 5th ed. rev. with modifications. New Haven, Conn.: Human Relations Area Files, 1987. 247p.

Used as one of the controlled vocabularies for entry into the printed edition of the HRAF archive described as *Human relations area files* **(D69)** and the Human Relations Area Files, *HRAF source bibliography* **(D16).** Divides all cultural and background information into seventy-nine major and 619 minor divisions. Following the number and title of each category is a descriptive statement of the type of information included, with cross-references to other categories.

D49

Murdock, George Peter, ed. *Outline of world cultures.* 6th rev. ed. New Haven, Conn.: Human Relations Area Files, 1983. 259p.

A reprint was published by the University of Chicago Press in 1973. Used as one of the controlled vocabularies for entry into the *Human relations area files* **(D69)** and the *HRAF source bibliography* **(D16).** Cultures selected for inclusion are all found in the *Human relations area files* **(D69).** There is an allocation into eight major regions. Tribes are assigned code names to facilitate identification. An alphabetical list provides appropriate codes for all areas, continents, geographic regions, historical and prehistoric periods, nations, and ethnic groups included in the outline.

D50

Naroll, Raoul, and Ronald Cohen, eds. *A handbook of method in cultural anthropology.* Garden City, N.Y.: Published by Natural History Pr. for the American Museum of Natural History, 1970. 1,017p.

Its dual objective is an assessment of the position of anthropology and a synthesis of critical insight into scientific inquiry that will inform and guide the young anthropologist. Linguistic analysis, which has been a major influence during the past decade, is ignored. In chapter 5, "Linguistics," find extensive reference to the influence of formal linguistics models on anthropology. Also consult the bibliographies in the annotation to Bonnefoy's *Mythologies* **(D36),** which trace the influence of the linguistics of structuralism on structural anthropology. Consult also Nordquist's *Claude Lévi-Strauss* **(D37)** and Miller's *French structuralism* **(D38).**

Nonverbal communication is also ignored by Naroll and Cohen. Studied explication can be found in Mary Ritchie Key's *Nonverbal communication: A research guide and bibliography* (Metuchen, N.J.: Scarecrow, 1977 [439p.]) **(D51).** In the review section (p.139), Key identifies all of the research strategies for approaching this research problem; that section is followed by a list of references (p.142–428) arranged alphabetically by author. Can be informally updated by reference to the database *Linguistics and language behavior abstracts* [computer file] **(B25).**

For entry into the literature of folklore, consult F. A. De Caro's *Women and folklore: A bibliographic survey* (Westport, Conn.: Greenwood, 1983 [170p.]) **(D52),** which leads the reader through many of the agendas and topics in which anthropology and folklore studies have a shared interest. The most useful discussion of purely reference works is found in Jan Harold Brunvand's *Folklore: A study and research guide* (New York: St. Martin's, 1976 [144p.]) which covers in a more general way scholarly works of folklore in several languages. The first chapter attempts a synthesis of leading theories and the identification of definitive works. The second chapter evaluates the standard reference works, with an overwhelming emphasis on English-language sources. An author index is included, and the table of contents provides a helpful subject outline. Inspect also the bibliographic headnotes in Susan Steinfirst's *Folklore and folklife: A guide to English-language reference sources* (Hamden, Conn.: Garland, 1992 [2v.]) (Garland reference library in the humanities, v.1429), which provides selective annotated entry to English-language reference sources arranged by broad subject with chapters devoted to ritual and rites, material culture, folklife and folklife societies, and journals. Indexed by author, title, and subject.

D53

Nettl, Bruno, and Philip V. Bohlman, eds. *Comparative musicology and anthropology of music: Essays on the history of ethnomusicology.* Chicago: Univ. of Chicago Pr., 1991. 378p. (Chicago studies in ethnomusicology)

Introduction and epilogue identify the underlying theses of contributions by nineteen scholars from five countries who examine the methodological and theoretical foundations and provide a critique of the discipline. Organized in clusters: (1) The world musical diversity, (2) Major issues of interpretation and analysis, (3) Contributors who have influenced the present course of ethnomusicology, and (4) The interdisciplinary nature of research in ethnomusicology.

See also Ann Briegleb Schuursma's *Ethnomusicology research: A select annotated bibliography* (New York: Garland, 1992, 173p.) (Garland library of music ethnology, no.1) **(D54),** which lists 468 entries on the study of music in culture for emphasis on methods, theories, and approaches to research. Author and subject indexes.

D55

Triandis, Harry C., ed. *Handbook of cross-cultural psychology.* Boston: Allyn and Bacon, 1980–81. 6v.

Includes several articles of reference value. See especially Herbert Barry's "Description and uses of the Human Relations Area File" (p.445–78). Long articles intended to summarize progress in cross-cultural psychological topics. The volume titled *Perspectives* has six major topics, each with seven or eight subheadings. Each article has a standard format that includes a list of contents, an abstract, an introduction, and the main body of the work, with supporting bibliography. Recognized authorities have contributed; v.2, *Methodology;* v.3, *Processes;* v.4, *Developmental psychology;* v.5, *Social psychology;* and v.6, *Psychopathology.* These volumes should be used in conjunction with Raymond J. Corsini's *Encyclopedia of psychology* (New York: Wiley, 1984 [4v.]), which contains brief signed articles and selective bibliographies for highly technical aspects of psychology.

D56

UNESCO. International Committee for Social Science Information and Documentation. *Thematic list of descriptors: Anthropology.* London: Routledge, 1989. 522p.

A controlled language for indexing social and cultural anthropology. Includes thematic list, list of descriptors, list of geographic names, list of ethnic names, list of languages, list of nationalities.

These descriptors provide reliable spelling for entry to UNESCO's *International bibliography of social and cultural anthropology* **(D20).** Sometimes used as an authority file for names of indigenous peoples.

Directories

The directories listed in chapter 1, "What Every Anthropologist Needs to Know," and chapters devoted to subdisciplines of anthropology (see part 2 under "Access by discipline") can be consulted both for address and biographic information and for their inclusion of selective bibliographic reference to the work of the listed individuals.

Recently there has been a trend toward national directories of ethnographic filmmakers. For example, *Catálogo de filmes etnológicos: v.1, Encyclopaedia cinaematographica* (San Paulo: University of San Paulo, School of Communications and Arts, Bibliographic and documents service, Film Section, 1987 [43p.]) **(D57),** which relies heavily on the list of films about Brazilian Indians in the German collection as described in the 1952 edition of *Handbuch der deutschsprachigen ethnologie (A guide to German-speaking anthropology),* ed. by Godegard Baeck and Rolf Husmann (Göttingen, Germany: Edition Re, 1990 [270p.]) **(D58),** which lists German ethnologists (and records recent publications of each individual), institutions, and associations with a regional index; topical index in which English meaning is given for each topical term. For American scholars, consult *AAA Guide* **(A53).** For directories of scholars in residence throughout the world, consult the "Directories" section in other chapters of *Fieldwork in the Library* and *Annals of the Association of Social Anthropologists of the Commonwealth and directory of members,* v.1– , 1979– (Canterbury, Kent, England: Assn. of Social Anthropologists of the Commonwealth) **(D59),** which has focused on institutions of Great Britain and the Commonwealth but lists all affiliated members. An anthropologist teaching in a university in Turkey, for example, may be a member of the association.

State-of-the-Art Reviews

The *Annual review of anthropology* **(A57)** provides a continuing update on ethnographic topics as soon as cumulated research warrants a new review. Periodically there are extensive reviews of the literature of culture areas in which a burst of activity is in evidence. Ethnographic work in Third World countries can often be found in *Urban anthropology and studies of cultural systems and world economic development* **(D60).**

D60

Urban anthropology and studies of cultural systems and world economic development. v.14– , 1985– . Brockport, N.Y.: Institute for the Study of Man. Semiannual.

Continues *Urban anthropology,* v.1–13, 1972–84 (New York: Plenum). Most issues are organized around a theme, with an overview by a guest editor. The collective bibliographies of these articles can provide either some selective entry into current work in specific areas or contributions from some smaller community of scholars. Examples: v.12, no.1, *Israeli anthropologists and sociologists* (1984), five articles; v.15, no.2, *The anthropology of the Middle East* (1987), five articles. Other recent volume topics: *Anthropological research in Bangladesh: Studies of households, land, and subsistence in the countryside and city; Polish ethnographers and sociologists.*

Occasionally there is bibliographic integration such as John Gulick's "The essence of urban anthropology: Integration of micro and macro perspectives" 13 (2–3) (1984): 295–306 **(D61).**

Searching Graphic Materials

Searches for nonprint materials should first consult American Geographical Society of New York, Map Department, *Index to maps in books and periodicals* **(A59).** Ethnographic resources in this index are often identified under the heading "Linguistic maps"; and since the internal contents of books and journals are cited, the identified resources often have ethnographic significance to match their graphic value. For a select list of widely held ethnographic films, see Heider's *Films for anthropological teaching* **(A63).**

Maps

In anthropology enormous amounts of information are consolidated into an atlas. Gordon W. Hewes's "World map of culture-areas for about 1500 A.D." in his *A conspectus of the world's cultures in 1500 A.D.* (Boulder: Univ. of Colorado Pr., 1954) (University of Colorado Studies, Series in anthropology, no.4) **(D62)** provides a summary of the results of research in cartographic form. Answers questions about distribution of cultures before European contact. Another recent addition to this type of investigation would be Jacquetta Hawkes and David Trump's *Atlas of early man* (New York: St. Martin's, 1976 [255p.]) **(D63),** containing an overview of eight "time-steps" between 5000 B.C. and A.D. 500. Charts summarize economy, events, religion, technology, and inventions. A useful summary of the evidence for independent inventions, with implications for any hypothesis of a universal mentality.

D64

Price, David H. *Atlas of world cultures: A geographic guide to ethnographic literature.* Newbury Park, Calif.: Sage, 1989. 156p.

The maps in this work locate ethnic group information in space. The bibliography on p.99–125 is a numbered list, by author, in alphabetic order of 1,237 published sources for ethnographic information. A culture index to 3,500 ethnic groups assigns up to two of these descriptive ethnographies to each ethnic group. Identification of appropriate map (from a set of forty-one) and of ethnic group numbers on each map makes it possible to work the other way and identify ethnographies about contiguous tribes. For each tribe, the HRAF number and ethnic group symbol assigned to that ethnic group in Murdock's *Atlas of world cultures* **(D12)** are also indicated if they have been coded in these sources.

For distribution maps with ethnic group location of information on warfare, consult Divale's *Warfare in primitive societies* **(D22).**

Photographs and Films

First, consult Blakely and Blakely's *Directory of visual anthropology* **(A52)** for a list of the film and hardcover print publications of many American scholars and the references under "Searching Graphic Materials" in chapter 1, "What Every Anthropologist Needs to Know," and the appropriate chapters in *Fieldwork in the Library*'s "Access by Area Studies."

Consult also *Catálogo de filmes etnológicos: v.1, Encyclopaedia cinaematographica* **(D57)** and Weeks's *Introduction to library research in anthropology* **(A71)** for the chapter "Anthropological films and photography" (p.216–19), which discusses the LC subject headings for this topic and provides a valuable classified list of nineteen reference sources with value for students of ethnographic film. For example, the term ANTHROPOLOGY identifies ten entries; under various geographic subheadings, another fourteen items are identified.

D65

Carlisle, Richard, ed. *The illustrated encyclopedia of mankind.* New ed. New York: M. Cavendish, 1990. 22v.

Rich with color ethnographic photography inserted in the running text. Fifteen volumes, alphabetic for 508 tribes and regions. Five volumes devoted to conceptual issues such as the role of trade and technology. V.21, Time progression of civilization; v.22, Thematic indexes, population charts, geographic guide, and glossary. Articles are unsigned but accurate. One brief bibliography.

D66

Royal Anthropological Institute. *Film Library catalogue.* London: The Film Committee, Royal Anthropological Institute in association with the Scottish Central Film Library (distributor). v.1, ed. by James Woodburn (1982 [86p.]); v.2, ed. by Margaret Willson (1990 [92p.]).

The reference features of this resource make it a preferred entry to ethnographic films. Booking procedures are followed by an alphabetical list of films with running time and name of director. A bibliography provides readings to expand understanding of the ethnographic content of the films. Indexed by ethnic group names, by director, and by topic and geographic area (subdivided by ethnic group). For example, the term COLUMBIA is subdivided for five ethnic groups and one topic, and the term GENDER ROLES is subdivided for fifteen ethnic group entries. In the second volume, the index continues to be notable for its generous expansion of indexing terms from ethnic group names and topic and geographic area subdivided for ethnic group names with expansions.

Searching Unpublished Materials

Searches for unpublished materials often benefit from an inspection of the National Anthropological Archives, *Catalog to manuscripts at the National Anthropological Archives, Department of Anthropology, National Museum of Natural History, Smithsonian Institution* **(A69).** The unpublished material contained in archival collections of either the professional papers of anthropologists or the field notes of contact period observers are sometimes available in microform. Find under "Archives" in chapter 1, "What Every Anthropologist Needs to Know," a description of the contents of a microform edition of the papers of Franz Boas **(A66)** and in the North American section of chapter 8, "The Americas," descriptions of the microfilm edition of John Peabody Harrington's extensive unpublished field notes **(I169).**

Archives

For many collections not available on microform, libraries have prepared at least preliminary lists of manuscript collections as they were received. The location and availability of archival resources are frequently reported in professional newsletters. For example, "Margaret Mead papers," *History of anthropology newsletter* 8:1 (1981): 3–4 **(D67),** describes the installments received by the U.S. Library of Congress during 1980: "ac. 17,788 (ca. 350,000 items); ac. 18046 (ca. 275,000 items); and ac. 18,060 (ca. 300 items)." The Mead material has been described in a typescript finding list available at the Library of Congress. Labeled as a preliminary list of Margaret Mead papers, that typescript is remarkably complete, including even entries for the records of the work by other anthropologists but collected by Mead during her lifetime. This includes many papers and field notes by people like Ruth Benedict and Gregory Bateson.

The *Melanesian newsletter and accessions list* **(N84)** is fully described in chapter 9, "Asia and the Pacific," and is devoted almost entirely to the description of anthropological materials gathered into an archival conservation program at the University of California at San Diego. In that program, if the author permits, all papers are reproduced on microfiche. Copies are then made available on a fee basis to any interested scholar but are distributed without cost to academic libraries and research facilities in the Melanesian area. This reflects a growing concern among anthropologists that indigenous populations have fuller access to the products of anthropological research about them.

D68

California. University. Berkeley. Department of Anthropology. *Guide to ethnological documents (1–203) of the Dept. and Museum of Anthropology, University of California, Berkeley, now in the University Archives.* Comp. by Dale Valory, Berkeley, Calif.: Dept. of Anthropology, Archaeological Research Facility, 1971. Ethnic group index.

Identifies field notes held by the department. An index provides ethnic-group entry.

D69

Human relations area files. v.1– , 1968– . Ann Arbor, Mich.: University Microfilms International.

A microfiche edition is widely available. Social scientists are devising new research tools to aid in exploiting the data accumulating in data storage files. HRAF is an older, growing file of data on different societies that organizes the data according to a universal topical classification; it is the hub of a research consortium. It has data on primitive and nonprimitive societies, classified according to more than 700 categories of human behavior. Complete sets of files are located in more than twenty-eight research centers. This database contains 700,000 pages of ethnographic information and often duplicates hard copy holdings of research libraries.

One brief introduction that explains the nature of the files and how to use them can be found on p.453–579 in Bernard's "Literature search" **(D02).** Consult also the machine-readable journal called *World cultures* [computer file] (P.O. Box 12524, La Jolla, CA 92039) **(D70),** which makes available not only new data in the format of this file but also new mathematics to manipulate the data. Includes a machine-readable version of the codes found in Herbert Barry and Alice Schlegel's *Cross-cultural samples and codes* (Pittsburgh: Univ. of Pittsburgh Pr., 1980 [458p.]) **(D71),** which is also valuable for its extensive bibliography. More formally, *Behavior science research,* v.1– , 1966– (New York: HRAF) **(D72)** (titled *Behavior science notes* from 1967 to 1974), publishes bibliographies, comparative studies, essays describing sampling procedures, coding, and estimates of reliability. Reports societies added to HRAF's *Human relations area files* **(D69).** For one consolidation of statistical research based on the codes of this resource, inspect George P. Murdock's *Ethnographic atlas* (Pittsburgh: Univ. of Pittsburgh Pr.: HRAF Pr., 1967 [128p.]) **(D73),** in which societies are analyzed under twenty-six characteristics, and *A cross-cultural summary,* compiled by Robert B. Textor (New Haven, Conn.: HRAF Pr., 1967 [204p.]) **(D74),** a 400-culture sample. Lengthy tables are used to display for a given cultural characteristic what series of other characteristics may be expected to occur with a specified degree of probability. Some of this archival material has recently been restructured as *Cross-cultural CD* [computer file], available from SilverPlatter **(D18)** in a set of ten units. Provides specialized topical entry to information recorded in the *Human relations area files* **(D69)** and in the Human Relations Area Files, *HRAF source bibliography* **(D16).** Also of interest is Human Relations Area Files' *HRAF research series on quantitative cross cultural data* [floppy disc], available from HRAF for use with IBM personal computers in three volumes, with information on a wide range of topics, including religion, social organization, social problems, cultural complexity, social change, birth, marriage, and death.

D75

Kaplan, Bert, ed. *Primary records in culture and personality.* v.1– , 1956– . Madison, Wis.: Microcard Foundation, 1956– .

The purpose of this microcard series is to make hitherto unpublished source material and field data collected by anthropologists and psychologists available for interpretation and further research. The materials pertain primarily to individuals living outside the mainstream of Western culture. Each volume consists of a number of separate contributions and contains a set of data from a single culture. These data are of several types: Rorschach tests, thematic apperception tests (TATS), dreams, and life histories. In addition, each contribution has an explanatory introduction by the contributor, describing the nature of the study being conducted at the time the material was collected, the locale and characteristics of the culture group, the methods used, and the conditions under which the samples were taken. Classified according to controlled vocabularies found in Murdock's *Outline of cultural materials* **(D48)** and Murdock's *Outline of world cultures* **(D49).**

D76

Streit, Robert, ed. *Bibliotheca missionum: 1895–1936.* Fribourg, Switzerland: Herder for Institute für Missionwissenschaftliche Forschung, 1916–1954. 30v.

V.4–14 deal with different regions in Asia, and v.15–20 deal with Africa. Of the recent supplementary volumes, twenty-seven deal with India, twenty-nine with Southeast Asia, and thirty-eight with Japan and Korea. Annotated. Some items extensively annotated. Indexes by author; personal names; and subject (includes ethnology, folklore, history), places, lands and peoples, and languages. Consult also *Bibliografia missionaria,* v.1–49, 1934–85 (Vatican City: l'Unione missionaria del clero, Pontifical Urban University [48v.]) **(D77),** an annual that provided entry into an enormous store of ethnographic material produced by missionaries.

D78

Van Keuren, David K. *The proper study of mankind: An annotated bibliography of manuscript sources on anthropology & archaeology in the Library of the American Philosophical Society.* Philadelphia: American Philosophical Society, 1986. 79p. (Publication. American Philosophical Society. Library, no.10)

Starts with a discussion of the relationship between the society and the development of American archaeology and ethnology. Next introduces a user's guide to the entries, which are alphabetic by name of anthropologists.

Dissertations

Recent German-language dissertations can be identified in *Abstracts in German anthropology* **(A33).** Subject entry to many dissertations in the English is provided by the machine-readable databases *Dissertation abstracts ondisc* **(B14)** and for French-language materials in *Francis bulletin signalétique,* described in the annotation to **(B19).** Some specialized entry can be found in the sources below.

Journals and newsletters often contain, as continuing features, some record of dissertations. For example, "Abstracts of theses in social anthropology for which high degrees were awarded by the University of Oxford in 1988," *Journal of the Anthropology Society of Oxford* 20 (1989): 3: 260–72 **(D79),** an author list with long annotations, or J. E. Laferriére and K. Hays's "Recent doctoral dissertations of interest to [ethnobiologists]: Fall 1985–Fall 1989," *Journal of ethnobiology* 9 (2) (1989): 265–71 **(D80),** a list arranged alphabetically by author, or "Recent Ph.D. dissertations in medical anthropology," *Medical anthropology newsletter* 10 (3): 6–8 **(D81),** an author list.

D82

Burt, Eugene, comp. *Ethnoart: Africa, Oceania, and the Americas: A bibliography of theses and dissertations.* New York: Garland, 1988. 191p.

By country and by ethnic group thereunder which includes many ethnographies. Lists 323 records arranged alphabetically by author without annotation. Subject index is not professionally structured. For example, under CERAMICS find forty-nine items without any subdivisions. Indexed by author, by date of completion, and by institution.

D83

Webber, Jonathan, comp. *Research in social anthropology, 1975–1980: Register of theses accepted for higher degrees at British universities 1975–1980.* London: Royal Anthropological Institute, 1983. 425p.

An alphabetic list with abstracts by author when these are available. Lists 255 doctoral dissertations and 149 master's papers. Index by university, by subject country, and by peoples and cultures, and a professionally structured subject index. Under FOLKLIFE, four doctorates and three master's papers are distributed across six subordinate topical terms. Especially useful for African anthropology.

5

Anthropological Linguistics

For a science of linguistics based on the spoken word, find in DeMiller's *Linguistics* **(E01)** guidance to bibliographies of bibliographies, topical bibliographies, and bibliographic guides and manuals published before 1989. Bibliographic control of the more philological traditions can be identified in Walford, Mullay, and Schlicke's 1988 "Language" **(E03).** Relying on this superb pair of recent linguistic guides, *Fieldwork in the Library* concentrates on the flood of publications that have recently consolidated the work of a revolutionary decade. Older works are included when they deal with the less frequently spoken languages of special interest in anthropological research.

In a search for current materials, consult book reviews, lists of publications received, and news of professional meetings in the journals listed from **(E04)** through **(E12).** The vast majority of linguistic research is published in serials. Therefore, the carefully selected and annotated list of series published in DeMiller's *Linguistics* **(E01)** and Wawrzyszko's "Linguistics and series" **(E11)** provides inviting introductions into these resources.

For "Retrospective Searches" entries under the subtopic "Retrospective Bibliographies—Topical" **(E22)** through **(E33),** though generous and including work that is central to anthropological concerns, is superseded by DeMiller's *Linguistics* **(E01)** for depth of coverage. Many searches can profitably start with reference sources identified in chapter 1, "What Every Anthropologist Needs to Know." Consult especially the entries under "Retrospective Bibliographies—Continuing" and "Bibliographies—Broad-based." For example, the Tozzer Library's *Catalogues* [microfiche] **(A26)** and two published catalogs of the British Museum, Museum of Mankind, entitled *Museum of Mankind Library catalogues* [microfiche] **(A25).** For additional retrospective resources, consult the rich and carefully annotated coverage found in DeMiller's *Linguistics* **(E01).** Much linguistic work by anthropologists has been conducted in the context of an interest in a specific culture or culture area. For this reason, it is important to point searchers toward the vast empirical resources found in those chapters devoted to geographic areas in *Fieldwork in the Library.*

In "Informational Reference Searches" the "Dictionaries" subheading identifies entries **(E34)** through **(E39),** the subheading "Encyclopedias" **(E43)** through **(E49).** "Handbooks and Manuals," which are in plentiful supply, are listed in **(E50)** through **(E93).** "State-of-the-Art

Reviews" are listed in the reference sources described in **(E94)** through **(E97).** Rich sources of archival material are described at **(E98)** and **(E99).** Additional sources can be found under the heading "Searching for Unpublished Materials" in the culture area chapters of *Fieldwork in the Library.*

From the resources described in this chapter, the best entry into basic resources available for material on the spoken languages of anthropological interest can be found in Ruhlen's *A guide to the world's languages* **(E73)** and Bright's *International encyclopedia of linguistics* **(E43).** The best companion for fieldwork can be found in Shopen's *Language typology and syntactic description* **(E92).** For theory that treats language as an innate mental module, consult Newmeyer's *Linguistics* **(E49).** It includes articles on the sociocultural context of linguistics and has generous indexes and extensive bibliographies. The twenty-eight references at the beginning of Crystal's *Dictionary of linguistics and phonetics* **(E36)** can be used as a select list of fundamental works in linguistics.

Searching Bibliographic Guides

Most of the resources listed in Auckland's "Getting into the literature" **(A01)** cover all aspects of anthropology, including anthropological linguistics. For anthropological linguistics, Ruhlen's *A guide to the world's languages* **(E73)** provides a resource of first importance.

E01

DeMiller, Anna L. *Linguistics: A guide to the reference literature.* Englewood, Colo.: Libraries Unlimited, 1991. 256p.

Informed by an intimate understanding of specialized ways a linguist approaches information. Masterly identification of special features. Extensive coverage of linguistic reference works published between 1956 and 1989. The emphasis is on English-language sources, but important works in German, French, and Russian are well represented. Pt.1, Theoretical linguistics; pt.2, Topical coverage; pt.3, Individual languages. The coverage of online databases and CD-ROM resources is lucid and well informed, with adequate breadth, precise organization, and lucid annotations. In every chapter this resource maintains a consistent excellence that reflects knowledge of both the discipline of linguistics and the discipline of library science. The list of "Core periodicals" (p.73–84) and the attention given to "Directories" (p.58–61) and to "Professional associations and societies" (p.62–68) make it possible to extend coverage here more surely into the anthropological significance of reference sources in linguistics.

For a desk reference, Harold Byron Allen's *Linguistics and English linguistics,* 2d ed. (Arlington Heights, Ill.: AHM, 1977 [184p.]), still retains value for its selection of 3,000 English-language books and articles published up to 1975. For recent English-language publications consult Rosemarie Ostler's *Theoretical syntax 1980–1990: An annotated and classified bibliography* (Philadelphia: John Benjamins, 1992 [192p.]) (Amsterdam studies in the theory and history of linguistic science. Series V: Library and information sources in linguistics, v.21). There is an index by languages studied.

For a German-language guide to English, Russian, and German reference materials, consult Peter Schmitter's *Bibliographien zur linguistik: Nach themenkreisen unter mitwirkung einer arbeitsgruppe zusammengestellt und vershen mit einem anhang: Zur technik der titelaufnahme* (Muenster, Germany: Institut für Allgemeine Sprachwissenschaft der Westfälischen Wilhelms-Universität, 1984 [91p.]) (Studium Sprachwissenschaft, bd.2) **(E02),** especially for its list of bibliographies on individual linguists and linguistic schools.

E03

Walford, Albert J., Anthony Chalcraft, Ray Prytherch, and Stephen Willis, eds. "Language and literature." In *Walford's Guide to reference materials,* v.3, *Generalia, language and literature, the arts,* p.482–571. 5th ed. London: The Library Association, 1991. 1035p.

Reference books on linguistics, with an emphasis on the philological tradition, are annotated. Equally valuable for the anthropologist, the next chapter, "Oriental, African, etc. languages" (p.572–597) includes dictionaries of rarely spoken languages and some bibliographies of unwritten languages. All descriptive entries are followed by brief extracts from cited reviews which serve as annotations and give some information about the quality and scope of each entry.

Searching for Current Materials

To identify special current awareness features in scholarly journals, inspect first the Anthropological Index's *Reference list of current periodicals* **(A14),** which is arranged so that listings in any issue will identify a select list of articles from journals relevant to a specialized topic in a particular culture area. These journals can be individually inspected for reoccurring departments that act as a forum for scholarly issues.

Select Reviews in Scholarly Journals

Although it is dated, William Orr Dingwall's *Bibliography of linguistic esoterica: 1970* (Edmonton: Linguistic Research, 1971 [161p.]) (Linguistic bibliography series, no.1) has a list of sources for identifying unpublished and projected papers which review research reports, master's theses, doctoral dissertations, and clandestine conferences. An enormous amount of excellent work in linguistics is never published. Scholars need to get on mailing lists for activity in the areas of their interest. The indexing by languages and language families makes this resource especially helpful.

E04

Anthropological linguistics, v.1– , 1959– . Bloomington: Archives of Languages of the World, Anthropology Department, University of Indiana. 9/yr.

Indexed every ten years. Includes five to eight book reviews per issue. Includes lexical lists and analyzed texts, charts, and diagrams. Contains theoretical and methodological articles related to special problems in phonetics, morphemics, syntax, and comparative grammar. The department "Announcements" acts as a forum for information on organizations, institutes, courses, and new publications. Primary focus is on languages that are still spoken but not usually written. Provides immediate publication of data from the tape recordings. These are available on a fee basis in reproduction of the depository copies through a procedure described in Urciuoli's *A catalog of the C. F. and F. M. Voegelin archives of the languages of the world* **(E98).**

E05

Language. v.1– , 1925– . Washington, D.C.: Linguistic Society of America. Quarterly.

"Review articles" devote up to fifteen pages to one or several books in a cluster. Shorter reviews are found in the departments "Reviews" and "Book notes." These reflect an interest in a broad spectrum of languages and specialized topics such as phonetics, phonology, morphology, syntax, semantics and discourse, synchronic and diachronic linguistics, dialectology, ethnolinguistics, neurolinguistics, mathematical and computational linguistics, and linguistic theory and methodology. Includes news of organizational activities.

E06

LSA bulletin. v.1– , 1970– . Washington, D.C.: Linguistics Society of America. Quarterly.

A continuation of the *Bulletin* (Linguistic Society of America, 1926–69). Publishes news and notes about linguistic activities, including awards, conferences, exhibits, grants, and seminars. Provides a calendar of meetings scheduled by scholarly organizations working in linguistics, which identifies contact person and meeting places. The December issue lists members and includes addresses.

E07

Word. v.1– , 1945– . South Orange, N.J.: International Linguistic Association. 3/yr.

Publishes articles on structure and function of languages, including psycholinguistics and ethnolinguistics. Reviews about ten books in each issue and regularly reports on the organizational activities of the International Linguistic Association. There is an occasional double issue devoted to a topic such as "National languages" or "Systemic linguistics."

E08

Zeitschrift für phonetik, sprachwissenschaft und kommunikationsforschung. v.14– , 1961– . Berlin: Akademie-Verlag. Quarterly.

Publishes in all scholarly languages and covers a broad range of topics, including semantics, grammar, linguistic methodology, and historical linguistics. Especially valuable for the anthropological linguist working with the languages of Africa and Asia.

Selective Lists of Scholarly Journals

For a select and international list of serials, consult chapter 1, "What Every Anthropologist Needs to Know," for a description of Frantz's *A student anthropologist's handbook* **(A15),** which contains "Linguistics and folklore" (p.162–63). Also useful is DeMiller's *Linguistics* **(E01).** For more detailed entry consult:

E09

Modern Language Association of America. *MLA directory of periodicals: A guide to journals and series in language and linguistics.* v.1– , 1978–79. New York: Modern Language Assn. of America. Annual.

Sets a standard of excellence in arrangement, descriptive relevance, and quality of indexing. Truly international in scope. Each entry provides a description of special features, substantive content, and the presence or absence of book reviews and review articles.

For a more specialized and selective focus, consult a numbered list of 693 periodicals related to semeiotic studies defined broadly to include pragmatics, semantics, and syntactics in Eschbach and Eschbach-Szabo's *Bibliography of semeiotics, 1975–1985* **(E24).**

E10

Wares, Alan Campbell. "Directory of books and periodicals and list of abbreviations." In v.1, *Bibliography of Summer Institute of Linguistics,* xv–xxvi. Dallas: Summer Institute of Linguistics, 1985. 2v.

This basic set—v.1, 1935–75, and v.2, 1976–82—has been supplemented by Alan Campbell Wares's *Supplement to the bibliography of the Summer Institute of Linguistics (to December 1985)* (Dallas: Summer Institute of Linguistics, 1986 [100p.]) **(E11).** This institution devotes itself almost exclusively to establishing a written tradition for spoken languages shared by a small number of speakers. Because of this orientation toward fieldwork, many of the publications in the list of abbreviations hold potential interest as either fundamental or continuing sources of information relevant to fieldwork preparation.

Section 1, "Technical works," lists alphabetically by author (p.5–125) useful publications supporting work with rarely spoken languages; section 2, "Vernacular works," is classed by country and arranged alphabetically (Australia . . . Vietnam), with individual peoples listed under the country in which they are most numerous. Dense documentation for each ethnic group includes the literacy materials when available. The output of SIL publications has now passed the 11,000 mark.

E12

Wawrzyszko, Aleksandra K. "Linguistics and series." In *Bibliography of general linguistics: English & American,* p.101–13. Hamden, Conn.: Archon Books, 1971. 120p.

Covers linguistic periodicals and series, and includes all aspects of the discipline. Serves as a bibliographic guide for scholars working in linguistics beyond the university level. The coverage of reference books includes 344 sources. This resource retains reference value for a knowledgeable discussion of abstracting and indexing services in linguistic studies. The institutional index and a list of important monographic series are useful features.

Retrospective Searches

The Tozzer Library's *Author and subject catalogues of the Tozzer Library* [microfiche] **(A26)** and Peabody Library's *Catalogue: Subjects* **(A29)** provide author and classified subject entry to books, periodical articles, and the internal contents of books for anthropological linguistics through 1982. The British Museum, Museum of

Mankind's *Museum of Mankind Library catalogues* [microfiche] **(A25)** provides author and classified subject entry monographs through 1988. Both of these libraries cover all aspects of anthropology and have complementary strengths. The Human Relations Area Files, *HRAF source bibliography* **(D16)** identifies books and journal articles. Many of these resources are available in hard copy in university library collections. The bibliography, which is ongoing, provides entry by name of indigenous peoples and a large number of topical issues.

Retrospective Bibliographies—Bibliographies of Bibliographies

E13

Kukushkina, E. I., A. G. Stepanova, and E. S. Kubriakova. *Bibliografiya bibliografii po iazykoznaniiu.* Moscow: Publichnaiza Biblioteka. Otdel. Spravochn-bibliograficheskoi i informatsionoi raboty, 1963. 411p.

Arranged by language and language groups. Sometimes cataloged under Institut Iazyka. Includes bibliographies published as periodical articles, and separately published monographs.

More recent coverage elaborates on this basic source and can be identified under the term *bibliography* in the machine-readable database described as *MLA international* [computer file] **(B29).** Updating can also be achieved by consulting Ruble and Teeter's *A scholar's guide to humanities and social sciences in the Soviet Union* **(A38)** for the identification of continuing bibliographic serials.

E14

Smith, Margo L. "Language, linguistics and communication." Chapter in *Anthropological bibliographies: A selected guide.* Library-Anthropology Resource Group, Margo L. Smith, and Yvonne M. Damien, eds., p.260–62. South Salem, N.Y.: Redgrave. 307p.

Lists bibliographies basic to anthropological linguistics. Inspect also chapters organized by culture area, which include many linguistic resources. At first glance the indexing seems to need expansion. However, this organization by culture areas for most of the entries makes it possible to select from forty items the six or seven entries that refer to the serial order that spans a particular culture area.

Find additional regional coverage in Library-Anthropology Resource Group's *Anthropological bibliographies* **(A21),** with chapters organized by geographic area and with extensive coverage of indigenous languages. These chapters appropriately provide useful empirical elaboration on the theoretical emphasis of this chapter.

Retrospective Bibliography—Broad Topic

E15

Ashnin, F. D., et al. *Obshchee iazykoznanie: Bibliograficheskii ukazatel' literatury izdannoi v SSSR s 1918 po 1962 god.* v.1– , 1950– . Moscow: Izd Nauka, 1965. 276p.

Sometimes cataloged under Institut Iazykoznaniia. A bibliographic guide to linguistic works published by Russian authors through 1962. Lists 4,328 books and articles in a classified scheme with an author index.

For more recent coverage use the term BIBLIOGRAPHY in the machine-readable database described as *MLA international* [computer file] **(B29)** and in B. A. Malinskaia and M. T. Shabat's *Obshchee i prikladnoe iazykoznanie: Ukazatel litertury, izdannoi v USSR x 1963 po 1967 god* (Moscow: Izd Nauka, 1972 [295p.]) **(E16),** which uses the same system of classification as Ashnin's and carries the record through 1967. These two items were selected for entry here because they carry the Russian record forward to the beginning for selective coverage found in Permanent International Committee of Linguists, *Bibliographie linguistique de l'année (Linguistic bibliography, for the year . . . and supplement for previous years)* **(E21).** Other sources for continuous and more comprehensive updating of Russian-language sources can be found by consulting Ruble and Teeter's *A scholar's guide to humanities and social sciences in the Soviet Union* **(A38),** described in chapter 1, "What Every Anthropologist Needs to Know." Consult DeMiller's *Linguistics* **(E01)** for the identification of the most important five- and ten-year cumulations and the titles of Russian-language continuing indexing publications.

E17

Center for Applied Linguistics, Washington, D.C. *Dictionary catalog of the Library of the Center for Applied Linguistics.* Boston: Hall, 1974. 4v.

Reproduces approximately 53,100 catalog cards. Includes unpublished material. Gives annotations for grammars, dictionaries, readers, and teaching aids. Assumes the teacher will also be a student of the language. Pt.1, *Languages of Western Europe: Pidgin and Creoles (European based);* pt.2, *Languages of Eastern Europe and the Soviet Union;* pt.3, *Languages of the Middle East and North Africa;* pt.4, *Languages of South Asia;* pt.5, *Languages of Eastern Asia;* pt.6, *Languages of Sub-Sahara Africa;* pt.7, *Languages of Southeast Asia and the Pacific;* pt.8, *Languages of North, Central, and South America.*

Retrospective Bibliographies—Continuing

The most useful single source is described in chapter 1, "What Every Anthropologist Needs to Know," as *MLA international bibliography of books and articles on the modern languages and literatures* **(A37),** an annual. The machine-readable edition for portions of this serial publication is described as *MLA international* [computer file] **(B29).** Worldwide coverage of linguistics in all scholarly languages. This machine-readable database provides entry through the search term BIBLIOGRAPHY into a variety of specialized topics, including recent consolidations of studies in Arabic linguistics, modern linguistic works on Turkish, and many Russian bibliographies on specialized topics.

E18

Francis bulletin signalétique. 524: Sciences du language. v.1– , 1991– . Nancy, France: Institut de l'information scientifique et technique. Centre de Documentation: Sciences humaines. Quarterly.

Portions of this resource are available online as a section of *Francis bulletin signalétique* [computer file] in the annotation to *FRANCIS* [computer file] **(B19).**

Continues *Bulletin signalétique. 524* (1961–90). Classified arrangement in twelve categories. In 1968 changed from an abstracting service to a bibliography. Book reviews are indicated by the abbreviation "C.A." Quarterly author and subject indexes cumulate annually and include languages, conceptual terms, and personal names.

E19

Frankfurt am Main. Stadt- und Universitätsbibliothek. *Bibliographie linguistischer literatur.* Frankfurt am Main: V. Klostermann, 1976– . v.1– , 1977.

Available as *Bibliography of linguistic literature data base (BLLDB)* [computer file] (Frankfurt am Main: Stadt- und Universitätsbibliothek), which corresponds to the printed edition. Vendor (STN international BLLDB).

A set with five-year cumulations of quarterly and annual supplements. Basic set titled *Bibliographie unselbstandiger Literatur-Linguistik.* Titles of supplements vary. Lists nonmonographic work only. Well organized and international in scope for the languages covered. Useful beyond the scope of languages covered for its inclusion of theoretical issues in the "General" section. Cumulative annual and five-year indexes for author and subject.

Contains records of 135,000 citations. Adds about 10,000 new entries each year. Provides keyword entry from titles in original language. Especially useful for coverage of theoretical issues and for coverage of biolinguistics, psycholinguistics, and neurolinguistics, all of which have interest to linguists with an anthropological interest. Does not attempt coverage of spoken languages. Includes journals, books, theses, reports, and conference proceedings.

E20

LLBA: Linguistics and language behavior abstracts. v.1– , 1967– . La Jolla, Calif.: Sociological Abstracts. Quarterly.

Publisher varies. Title varies. Screens 1,000 publications from twenty-five disciplines for language-related research. Subject and author indexes. Portions of this serial are available as the machine-readable edition described as *Linguistics and language behavior abstracts*

(LLBA) [computer file] **(B25).** Especially valuable for concise annotations and for coverage of material in related disciplines.

E21

Permanent International Committee of Linguists. *Bibliographie linguistique de l'annee = Linguistic bibliography, for the year... and supplement for previous years.* Published by the Permanent International Committee of Linguists under the auspices of the International Council for Philosophy and Humanistic Studies. Utrecht: Spectrum, 1948– . Annual.

Publication lag of about two years. Absence of indexing makes skillful and multiple entry into the classed arrangement a survival skill. Each volume covers general linguistics and related branches of study under topical headings such as "Interrelations between families of languages," "Indo-European languages," "Asiatic and Mediterranean languages," "Languages of Eurasia and Northern Asia," "Dravidian languages," "Languages of South-east Asia," "Languages of Australasia and Oceania," "Languages of Negro Africa," "American languages," and "Creolized languages." Author index.

Retrospective Bibliographies—Topical

The comprehensive coverage found in DeMiller's *Linguistics* **(E01)** of twenty-nine topical bibliographies greatly reduces the need for an expansive development of this section.

E22

Beard, Robert, and Bogdan Szymanek, comps. *Bibliography of morphology 1960–1985.* Philadelphia: John Benjamins, 1988. 193p. (Amsterdam studies in the theory and history of linguistic science. Series 5: Library & information sources in linguistics, v.18)

For researchers seeking to expand a theoretical interest, this is a valuable source covering influential works published since 1960. Arranged alphabetically by name of author, it excludes dissertations, but includes working papers, conference proceedings, periodical articles, monographs, and the internal contents of books. Extremely selective in its coverage of less well-known languages for which theoretical issues are seldom the focus of publication. Indexed by language and subject. The language index covers more than 250 languages with reference to the authors who discuss the morphology of that particular language in the text. Transliteration of nonroman names does not follow the Library of Congress.

E23

Center for Applied Linguistics. *A survey of materials for the study of the uncommonly taught languages.* Dora E. Johnson [et al.], comps. Arlington, Va.: Center for Applied Linguistics, 1976. 8v.

Annotates grammars, dictionaries, readers, and teaching aids. Assumes that the teacher acts also as a student of the language. V.1, *Languages of Western Europe: Pidgin and Creoles (European based);* v.2, *Languages of Eastern Europe and the Soviet Union;* v.3, *Languages of the Middle East and North Africa;* v.4, *Languages of South Asia;* v.5, *Languages of Eastern Asia;* v.6, *Languages of Sub-Sahara Africa;* v.7, *Languages of Southeast Asia and the Pacific;* v.8, *Language of North, Central, and South America.*

E24

Eschbach, Achim, Viktoria Eschbach-Szabo, and Gabi Willenberg, comps. *Bibliography of semeiotics, 1975–1985.* Philadelphia: John Benjamins, 1986. 2v. (Amsterdam studies in the theory and history of linguistic science, Series 5. Library & information sources in linguistics, v.16).

Covers pragmatics, semantics, and syntactics. Pt.1, Lists of 693 periodicals related to semiotic studies. Pt.2, Entries for 10,831 periodical articles, books, conference proceedings, dissertations, Festschriften, and reviews (five pages). Reference value is greatly increased by the 165-page dictionary index of subjects and names.

E25

Gazdar, Gerald, et al. *Natural language processing in the 1980's: A bibliography.* Stanford, Calif.: Center for the Study of Language and Information, 1987. 240p. (CSLI Lecture Notes, no.12)

In this printed edition, 1,764 items are listed alphabetically by author with cross-references for multiple authors. Keyword subject index supports the printed edition. A disc edition containing a machine-readable copy of the file can also be purchased. Plans to continuously update this machine-readable database.

E26

Gordon, W. Terrence. *Semantics: A bibliography, 1986–1991.* Metuchen, N.J.: Scarecrow, 1992. 280p.

Covers books, periodical articles, and conference papers in English, French, German, Italian, Spanish, and Portuguese. Twenty-three sections covering topics in semantics. History of semantics, semiotics, discourse analysis, lexicology, and logical semantics are excluded. Includes anthropological treatments of kinship and color terms. Definitions, models of meaning, semantics and syntax, and semantics and child language are other topics of interest to anthropologists. Arrangement is by topic and by author thereunder for books, periodical articles, and doctoral dissertations. Earlier volumes by the same author include *Semantics, 1965–1978* (Metuchen, N.J.: Scarecrow, 1980 [307p.]) **(E27),** which lists 3,326 entries, and *Semantics: A bibliography, 1979–1985* (Metuchen, N.J.: Scarecrow, 1987 [292p.]) **(E28).**

Another entrance to child language can be found in Adele A. Abrahamsen's *Child language: An interdisciplinary guide to theory and research* (Baltimore: Univ. Park Pr., 1977 [381p.]) **(E29),** which lists 1,500 annotated entries in a classified arrangement, with author and subject indexes.

E30

Koerner, E. F. K., Matsuji Tajima, and Carlos P. Otero, comps. *Noam Chomsky: A personal bibliography 1951–1986.* Amsterdam and Philadelphia: John Benjamins, 1986. 217p. (Amsterdam studies in the theory and history of linguistic science, Series 5. Library & information sources in linguistics, v.11)

Reflects Chomsky's influence in linguistics, language acquisition theory, psycholinguistics, anthropology, and cognitive psychology.

Consult also Ambrose-Grillet's *Glossary of transformational grammar* **(E34).**

E31

Mackey, William Francis. *Bibliographie internationale sur le bilinguisme: Avec index analytique = international bibliography on bilingualism.* Québec: Presses de l'Université Laval, 1982. 575p. 14 microfiche. (Travaux du Centre international de recherche sur le bilinguisme, F-3)

Provide entries into sociocultural and developmental studies, with index on microfiche.

E32

Spiller, Bernd. *Error analysis: A comprehensive bibliography.* Philadelphia: John Benjamins, 1991. 552p. (Amsterdam studies in the theory and history of linguistic sciences. Series 5: Library and information sources in linguistics, v.12)

Multidisciplinary, with the first 5,398 entries listed by author and numbered. A second list is by title. There is an addendum. Especially useful for its chronological index, which enables a scholar to place an article or book in the context of the historical development of a construct. The index by languages meets the specialized needs of linguists to work in the full context of a language system. There is an author/title index.

E33

Van Noppen, Jean-Pierre, and Edith Hols, comps. *Metaphor II: A classified bibliography of publications 1985–1990.* Philadelphia: John Benjamins, 1990. 342p. (Amsterdam studies in the theory and history of linguistic science, Series 5. Library and information sources in linguistics, v.20)

Alphabetic by author list of 3,500 entries for books, book reviews, articles, conference papers, unpublished manuscripts, and theses published between 1984 and May 1990. A basic volume published in 1971 (with a continuation published in 1985) is given complete description and lucid, detailed, and knowledgeable annotations by DeMiller's *Linguistics* **(E01),** which this chapter assumes the reader has consulted. The four indexes refer the reader back by author and year to the bibliographic list, which is alphabetical by author. There is an index of disciplines which is helpful in identifying a preliminary reading list. There is an index of tenors, vehicles, and semantic fields; an index of theoretical constructs; and an index of the names of persons who are the subject of study or whose publication is being reviewed.

Informational Reference Searches

DeMiller's *Linguistics* **(E01)** has an extended section devoted to the description and annotation of dictionaries and encyclopedias (p.3–23) and to the description and annotation of dictionaries (p.58–61). The most complete entry to a definition developed with some awareness of the variations between linguistics schools can usually be found in Bright's *International encyclopedia of linguistics* **(E43).** Other resources can be more valuable as a desk copy or for a selective theoretical focus. For directory information about American anthropology, consult first the *AAA guide* **(A53),** and for international coverage, the "International directory of anthropological institutions" **(A56)** still identifies the more established centers of anthropological linguistic research.

Dictionaries

See especially the 1,800-term glossary in Bright's *International encyclopedia of linguistics* **(E43).** The terminological complexíties introduced into linguistics during the Chomskyian revolution are integrated into the works of Ambrose-Grillet, *Glossary of tranformational grammar* **(E34),** and Crystal, *A dictionary of linguistics and phonetics* **(E36).** Access into the broad core of linguistic work is better served by Hartmann and Stork's *Dictionary of language and linguistics* **(E39)** and Dubois et al.'s *Dictionnaire de linguistique* **(E40).** Ducrot and Todorov's *Encyclopedic dictionary of the sciences of language* **(E37)** is available in translation in most Western languages that have an established linguistic tradition and provides a multilingual frame of reference for a work that is encyclopedic in its approach. In the search for a dictionary of some less widely spoken languages, some assistance can be found in Wolfram Zaunmüller's *Bibliographisches Hanbuch der Sprachwörterbücher. Ein internationales Verzeichnis von 5600 Wörterbüchern der Jahre 1460–1958 für mehr als 500 Sprachen und Dialekte (An annotated bibliography of language dictionaries)* (Stuttgart: A. Hiersemann, 1958 [496 col.]), which provides a critical bibliography of 5,603 dictionaries arranged alphabetically by language. Three hundred and eighty-seven languages, more than 180 dialects, and several extinct languages are covered. European languages account for about one-half of the entries. Infrequently spoken languages such as Bini, Nuer, Tiv, and Yoruba are included. For many languages, the only dictionary was published before the turn of the century. Author and language indexes.

E34

Ambrose-Grillet, Jeanne. *Glossary of transformational grammar.* Rowley, Mass.: Newbury House, 1978. 166p.

Terms selected are taken from the standard theory of Noam Chomsky and are direct quotes from Chomsky. Provides exact definitions for some of the more specialized terminology likely to be encountered by students influenced by this scholar. The index can be used for exact entry into relevant works by Chomsky.

For in-depth treatment of the specialized conceptual system, consult Koerner, Tajima, and Otero, comps., *Noam Chomsky* **(E30),** which reflects his influence on linguistics, language acquisition theory, psycholinguistics, anthropology, and cognitive psychology. Consult "Quibs and discussion" section of *Linguistic inquiry,* v.1– , 1970– (Cambridge, Mass.: MIT Pr.) **(E35).** The substantive content of this quarterly reflects the active contribution both of Noam Chomsky and of Roam Jakobson, who serve on the editorial advisory board. It has achieved an outstanding record of encouraging the exchange of ideas among related disciplines, such as anthropology, biology, psychology, and linguistics.

E36

Crystal, David. *A dictionary of linguistics and phonetics.* 3d ed. Oxford, England: Blackwell in association with A. Deutsche, 1991. 389p.

The second edition adds 125 new main entry terms from the vocabulary of discourse analysis, pragmatics, and text linguistics, and more than 100 secondary terms within the main entries. Many of the 2,000 definitions carried in the first editions have been expanded and reformulated. Straightforward definitions set the terms in the context of current usage. Captures the recent proliferation of idiosyncratic terminology in linguistics. The twenty-eight references listed at the beginning of the book can be used as a basic list of fundamental works in linguistics.

E37

Ducrot, Oswald, and Tzvetan Todorov. *Encyclopedic dictionary of the sciences of language.* Baltimore: Johns Hopkins Univ. Pr., 1979. 380p.

Organized in a classified subject arrangement in which single autonomous paragraphs are entered alphabetically. An eleven-page index. Critically compares the various methodological approaches: the transformational, the functional approach of French structuralism, and more traditional approaches. The bibliography is reliable. The translation is solid. The anthropologists working with linguistic concepts from several traditions will find this a valuable reference source.

More recently, Werner Abraham's *Terminologie zur neurern linguistik* (Tübingen: Niemeyer, 1988 [2v.]) (Germanistische Arbeitshefte, no.1) **(E38)** provides German and English entry and has more extensive support in its bibliographic references (p.xiii–cx). Generous use of illustrations and cross-references.

E39

Hartmann, R. R. K., and F. C. Stork. *Dictionary of language and linguistics.* New York: Wiley, 1972. 302p.

Still an excellent general dictionary of linguistics. Covers terminology from all branches of linguistic scholarship. For a companion volume that specifically reflects usage in the European tradition, consult Jean Dubois et al., *Dictionnaire de linguistique* (Paris: Larousse, 1973 [516p.]) **(E40),** organized encyclopedically to draw a wide range of concepts into related context. Indexed for expanded subject entry.

Directories

E41

Directory of programs in linguistics in the United States and Canada. 5th ed. Washington, D.C.: The Linguistic Society of America, 1987. 181p.

Divided into five sections: (1) Geographic guides to programs; (2) Institutions in the United States (programs, chairs, degrees, special facilities, uncommonly taught languages, staff); (3) Institutions in Canada (programs, chairs, degrees, special facilities, uncommonly taught languages, staff); (4) Other institutions offering courses in linguistics and uncommonly taught languages; (5) Research institutes, linguistic societies (papers, meetings, publications, special programs). Name index for staff. Index of uncommonly taught languages.

Consult DeMiller's *Linguistics* **(E01)** for other directories such as the *Guide to grants and fellowships in linguistics, 1988–1990* (Washington, D.C.: Linguistic Society of America, 1988 [78p.]) **(E42),** which is loaded with essential information about grants and fellowships sponsored by institutions, associations, foundations, and governments, and issue no.4 (directory issue) of *PMLA: Publications of the Modern Language Association of America* (New York: Modern Language Assn. of America), which includes a list of current members.

Encyclopedias

E43

Bright, William, ed. *International encyclopedia of linguistics.* London: Oxford Univ. Pr., 1992. 4v.

The planning and organizing of 750 articles by 400 scholars into a work that is internally consistent and stylistically readable is an editorial achievement of the first importance. Attempts to cover all major branches of linguistics and to describe all languages (living or extinct). The entry "Languages of the world" provides cross-reference to the language articles. The synoptic outline and the index of the *International encyclopedia of linguistics* have been detailed with professionally structured expansions. The illustrations truly support the text.

There is a 1,800-term glossary. Each essay has a bibliography and a list of recommended readings that identify the seminal contributions to the subject under discussion. All contributions are signed. This set will be a standard reference source for the next decade.

For some topics, more extensive recent coverage can be found in Newmeyer's *Linguistics* **(E49).** For anthropological investigations, this section can be expanded by the still-useful bibliographic guidance found in Ruhlen's *Guide to the world's languages* **(E73).**

E44

Collinge, N. E., ed. *An encyclopedia of language.* London and New York: Routledge, 1990. 1,011p.

The broad subject arrangement is supported by detailed topical and name indexes. Twenty-six signed articles with extensive bibliographies from distinguished contributors. Topics include "The inner nature of language," "The larger province of language," and the "Special aspects of language." There is coverage for phonetics and phonology, grammatical organization, neurological and psychological aspects of language, speech pathology, and the prehistory and history of language. In some sections, items with outstanding value or relevance are marked with an (*). The bibliographies are highly selective for excellence. For example: from the section "Language in society," John Joseph Gumperz's *Discourse strategies* (Cambridge, England: Cambridge Univ. Pr., 1982 [225p.]) **(E45)** is included to provide a handbook in intercultural communication and conversation. From the section on "Language as form and pattern," find *Studies in relational grammar,* ed. by David Perlmutter (Stanford, Calif.: Stanford Univ. Pr., 1983–86 [3v.]) **(E46),** which brings into one definitive work a recent and remarkably vigorous surge of theoretical innovation.

E47

Crystal, David, ed. *The Cambridge encyclopedia of language.* Cambridge, England, and New York: Cambridge Univ. Pr., 1987. 472p.

Sixty-five thematic sections integrate comprehensively the modern multidisciplinary nature of linguistics. The appendix provides a useful glossary of about 1,000 terms. The indexes by author, by language, and by topic are constructed with great care to provide adequate expansion of terms.

E48

Malmkjaer, Kirsten, and James M. Anderson. *Linguistic encyclopedia.* London: Routledge, 1991. 575p.

Covers about 150 topics from traditional and current areas of research, with special strength in applied linguistics. There is a list of references and a well-designed index. A handy size for a desk reference, this work lacks the coverage of languages—so important to ethnologists and anthropological linguists—found in Bright's *International encyclopedia of linguistics* **(E43).**

To a limited extent, the *Linguistic encyclopedia* can be supplemented by the companion volume, Campbell's *Compendium of the world's languages* **(E59),** or by the even more useful Ruhlen's *Guide to the world's languages* **(E73).** Other recent desk encyclopedias would include Crystal's *Cambridge encyclopedia of language* **(E47)** and for bibliographic excellence, the superior coverage of Collinge's *Encyclopedia of language* **(E44).**

E49

Newmeyer, Frederick J., ed. *Linguistics: The Cambridge survey.* Cambridge, England: Cambridge Univ. Pr., 1988. 4v.

V.1, *Linguistic theory: Foundations,* contains articles on language structure, syntax, lexical categorization, semantics, pragmatics, morphology, phonology, phonetics, topology, the philosophy of language, and the mathematical aspects of language. Interface articles include those on syntax = semantics, syntax = phonology, and phonology = phonetics. Diachronic articles include those on syntactic change, morphological change, and phonological change. An appendix publishes "A history of linguistics," by R. H. Robins. V.2, *Linguistic theory: Extensions and implications,* includes coverage of psycholinguistic topics like language processing, first language acquisition, second language acquisition, abnormal language acquisition, brain structure, and speech errors. On pragmatics, there are articles on conversational principles and discourse analysis. Two authors exchange comments on the study of Creole languages. Coverage extends to speech acts, the use of metrics, the use of computer applications, and the study of sign languages. V.3, *Language: Psychological and biological aspects,* begins with an overview of psycholinguistics and continues with articles on language processing, lower-level word recognition, word recognition and the structure of lexicon, production, structure children give to speech, human evolution, animal communication, and second language acquisition. A review article on neurolinguistics is followed by articles on aphasia and a discussion of the absence of any connection between linguistic theory and the study of speech pathology in the U.S. V.4, Frederick J. Newmeyer, *Language: The sociocultural context* (Cambridge, England: Cambridge Univ. Pr., 1988 [292p.]) **(E50),** includes articles on social class, gender, culture, dialectology, syntactic variation, bilingualism, language planning, the emergence of pidgin and Creole, language death, discourse conversational analysis, and a survey of the ethnography of speaking.

Handbooks and Manuals

E51

Allen, W. Sidney, ed. *Cambridge language surveys.* Cambridge, England: Cambridge Univ. Pr., 1980– .

This series is still in process. All surveys attempt to establish both the relationships between the languages described and the morphological features that individuate them. Among the titles published to date, find: Comrie, Bernard, *The languages of the Soviet Union* (1981 [317p.]) **(E52);** Dixon, Robert M. W., *The languages of Australia* (1980 [547p.]) **(E53);** Foley, William A., *The Papuan languages of New Guinea* (1986 [305p.]) **(N82);** Holm, John A. *Pidgins and Creoles* (1988–89 [2v.]) **(E54);** Masica, Colin P., *Indo-Aryan* (1991 [539p.]) **(E55);** Norman, Jerry, *Chinese* (1988 [292p.]) **(E56);** Shibatani, Masayoshi, *The languages of Japan* (1990 [411p.]) **(E57);** Suárez, Jorge A., *Mesoamerican Indian languages* **(KA59);** Maucalay, D., et al., *Celtic* (1992 [466p.]) **(E58).** Among the volumes announced for publication: *Austronesian,* by R. Blust; *Balkans,* by J. Ellis; *Dravidian,* by R. E. Asher; *German,* by P. Lass; *Korean,* by M. Shibatani and Ho-Min Sohn; *North American Indian,* by W. Shafe; *Slavonic,* by R. Sussex; *South-east Asia,* by J. A. Matisoff.

E59

Campbell, George L. *Compendium of the world's languages.* London: Routledge, 1991. 2v.

Covers 370 languages with a standardized structure for each article to provide historical and sociolinguistic information, a description of script, phonology, morphology, and syntax. References are listed at the end of volume 2. There is an appendix with forty scripts. There is a liberal use of headers to guide the reader. However, even with this extensive coverage, anthropologists may find more material on the languages they are interested in by consulting the bibliographies in Ruhlen's *A guide to the world's languages* **(E73)** and Bright's *International encyclopedia of linguistics* **(E43).**

E60

Comrie, Bernard, ed. *The world's major languages.* New York: Oxford Univ. Pr., 1987. 1,025p.

Title accurately reflects the scope of this work. Many anthropologists will be more interested in what's left out, including all of New Guinea and North and South America. There is detailed information on the structure of the languages covered, with bibliographic guides at the end of each essay. Contributions from forty-four scholars deal with a broad spectrum of the world's languages. Organized by language families, with contents as follows:

There is detailed coverage of "IndoEuropean languages." A general essay precedes treatment of the Germanic languages: English, German, Dutch, Danish; then the Latin and Italic languages; followed by treatments for the Romance languages: French, Spanish, Portuguese, Italian, Rumanian; followed by treatment of the Slavonic languages: Russian, Polish, Czech and Slovak, Serbo-Croat; then Greek; followed by treatment of the Indo-Aryan languages: Sanskrit, Hindu-Urdu, Bengali; and the Iranian languages: Persian, Pashto.

There is less elaboration in the section on "Uralic language," which includes Hungarian,

Finnish, Turkish, and the Turkic languages; or in the section on "Afroasiatic languages," which includes only Semitic, Hausa, and Chadic; still less elaboration in "Tamil and Dravidian languages" or "Tai languages" or "Vietnamese languages." "Sino-tibetan languages" include only Chinese and Burmese; "Japanese language"; "Korean language"; "Austronesian" languages cover only Malay and Tagalog; "Niger-Kordofanian languages" cover only Yoruba, Swahili, and Bantu. A language index makes it possible to extract some information about a large number of less frequently used languages mentioned in the basic essays.

Anthropologists will usually find more material on the languages they are interested in by consulting the bibliographies in Ruhlen's *Guide to the world's languages* **(E73)** and Bright's *International encyclopedia of linguistics* **(E43).**

E61

Decsy, Gyula. *Statistical report on the languages of the world as of 1985.* Bloomington, Ind.: Eurolingua for the Transworld Linguistic Assn., 1986–88. 5v. (Bibliotheca nostratica, v.6/1–6/4)

V.1, Lists of languages of the world in decreasing order of the speaker numbers with phyletic and geographic identifications, 1986 [136p.]; v.2, Lists of languages of the world arranged according to linguistic phyla and speaker number data, 1986 [112p.]; v.3, Lists of languages of the world arranged according to continents and countries, 1988 [224p.]; v.4, Alphabetical lists of languages of the world arranged according to continents, 1988 [200p.]; v.5, Includes a cumulative alphabetical list of languages of the world.

The introduction discusses the difficulties of collecting reliable information on less widely spoken languages and their speakers. Identifies 2,800 languages. A handy consolidation that can be expanded by reference to Bright's *International encyclopedia of linguistics* **(E43),** Campbell's *Compendium of the world's languages* **(E59),** Comrie's *World's major languages* **(E60),** Grimes's *Ethnologue index* **(E66)** for 33,000 names of languages, Ruhlen's *A Guide to the world's languages* **(E73),** and Voeglin and Voegelin's *Classification and index of the world's languages* **(E93).**

E62

Fischer, Susan D., and Patricia Siple, eds. *Theoretical issues in sign language research.* v.1– , 1990– . Chicago: Univ. of Chicago Pr. Irregular.

State-of-the-art essays review sign language behavior. Investigates the theory of language acquisition, comprehension, and production across various modes of communication. Surveys findings on the relative contributions of biology and teaching on language acquisition and use.

Consult also Leonard G. Lane's *The Gallaudet survival guide to signing,* rev. ed. (Washington, D.C.: Gallaudet Univ. Pr., 1990 [203p.]) **(E63),** which illustrates with charts basic handshapes for the manual alphabet and numbers. Some frequently used concepts are included. Still useful, Tom Federlin's *A comprehensive bibliography on American sign language: A resource manual* (New York: Federlin, 1979 [84p.]) **(E64).**

E65

Grimes, Barbara F., ed. *Ethnologue: Languages of the world.* 11th ed. Dallas: Wycliffe Bible Translators for Summer Institute of Linguistics, 1984. 748p.

More than 26,000 names of languages arranged by country for each language. Information includes variant names, number of speakers, location, dialects, linguistic affiliation, and bilingualism of the speakers. Detailed maps are scattered throughout the work to graphically illustrate distribution of linguistic groups. Includes separate index to ten continent maps (p.735) and to thirty-six country maps (p.735–36). All known names for a language are entered under the main name and given a number code. The bibliography (p.717–29) gathers an enormous inventory for identifying variant regional descriptions of rarely spoken languages.

A separate publication, *Ethnologue index,* 11th ed. (Dallas: Summer Institute of Linguistics, 1988 [403p.]) **(E66),** leads the scholar from entries for variant forms to an established main form in a list of 33,000 names. Identifies countries in which these languages are spoken.

E67

Katzner, Kenneth. *The languages of the world.* Rev. ed. London: Routledge and Paul, 1986. 376p.

Divided into three parts: pt.1, Language families of the world; pt.2, Individual languages (p.41–333); pt.3, Country-by-country survey. Index (*ca.* 750 entries). For each language a passage, in original characters, is given, plus English translation and linguistic notes.

Consult also Université Laval, Centre international de recherche sur bilinguisme, *Linguistic composition of the nations of the world (Composition linguistique des nations du monde),* edited by Heinz Kloss and Grant D. McConnell (Québec: Centre internationale de recherche sur bilinguisme, Les Presses de l'Université Laval, 1974 [5v.]) (Publications of the International Center for Research on Bilingualism, no.1) **(E68),** for the special feature in each volume of a directory to statistical offices for each country.

E69

Perrot, Jean, ed. *Les langues dans le monde ancien et modern.* Paris: Édition du Centre Nationale de la Recherche Scientifique, 1981. 691p. 12 maps.

Includes maps of 12 linguistic areas. The first 615 pages cover languages in sub-Saharan Africa. The remainder of volume 1 is devoted to Creoles. There are twenty-seven contributors. For each entry there is information on the morphology, phonology, and grammar. There is an index of languages and a bibliography. This is the beginning of a new edition of the older Antoine Meillet and Marcel Cohen, eds., *Les langues du monde* (Paris: Centre Nationale de la Recherche Scientifique, 1952 [1,294p.]) **(E70),** which contains information on 10,000 languages and dialects. Under each language group, there is a discussion of classification, features, syntax, and the various dialects as well as a detailed bibliography. Includes a still-valuable linguistic map. For individual languages there is a description of phonology, grammar, phraseology, and morphology.

E71

Paulston, Christina Bratt, ed. *International handbook of bilingualism and bilingual education.* New York: Greenwood, 1988. 603p.

Records the relentless progress of the major languages as they integrate larger and ever more diverse population groups. Since the eleven case studies are each followed by a bibliographic essay, the documentation becomes a consolidated bibliographic source on the major languages of the world.

E72

Pullum, Geoffrey K., and William A. Ladusaw. *Phonetic symbol guide.* Chicago: Univ. of Chicago Pr., 1986. 266p.

Entries are arranged according to the shape of the symbol. Forty-nine diacritic marks follow the character series. Includes information on International Phonetic Association usage, Block and Trager's vowel symbols, American usage vowel symbols, and the Chomsky/Halle vowel system, with many cross-references inserted to reduce confusion.

Also useful is International Phonetic Association, London, *The principles of the International Phonetic Association: being a description of the international phonetic alphabet and the manner of using it, illustrated by texts in 51 languages* (London: International Phonetic Assn., 1949 [53p.]), for its examples of transcriptions and charts.

E73

Ruhlen, Merritt. *A guide to the world's languages.* v.1, *Classification.* Stanford, Calif.: Stanford Univ. Pr., 1987. 3v.

This first volume discusses the history and present status of the genetic classification of the world's languages, organized to present a complete classification. This monograph is based on itemized language lists and includes 5,000 languages distributed over the classification system given with cross-references to common variants. In chapter 1, there is an introduction to genetic classification. Chapter 2 includes a discussion of historical context and linguistic background, and precedes sections devoted to descriptions of Indo-Hittite, Uralic-Yukaghir, and Caucasian languages. Chapter 3 classifies African languages before developing the sections devoted to Afro-Asiatic, Niger-Kordofanian, Nilo-Saharan, and Khoisan languages, and includes a criticism of Greenberg's methodology in its final paragraphs. Chapter 4 is organized to discuss Altaic, Chukchi-Kamchatkan, Dravidian, Sino-Tibetan, Austric:Miao-Yao, Austroasiatic, and Daic languages. Chapter 5 has sections on Austric, Austronesian, Indo-Pacific, and Australian. Chapter 6, "North and South America," is developed to cover Eskimo-Aleut, Na-Dene, and Amerind. Chapter 7 discusses prospects for research; chapter 8 introduces a list of language names to develop a discussion of taxonomic conventions and provide an overview of language phyla, an index of classification, and an identification of major language groups that ends in a complete classification (p.301–81) followed by a language group index and a language index.

Twenty-one maps illustrate global language distribution. Ten tables bring great masses of information into a concise statement. Twelve figures illustrate key concepts. Bibliographies follow each class section and each subsection. There are extensive references to linguistic atlases when available. There are maps to illustrate many clusters of bibliographies as they are attached to the organizational structure of the book. Consider this example as typical: after twenty-one bibliographic items that follow the discussion of OCEANIC PACIFIC, AUSTRONESIAN is described, and this description in turn is supported with a twenty-nine item bibliography, followed by FORMOSA with eight items, including a monograph on Taiwan aboriginal groups devoted to problems of cultural and linguistic classification on that island, followed by a description of languages in the PHILIPPINES supported by twenty-one bibliographic items, including a linguistic atlas and articles with titles like "A subgrouping of 100 Philippine languages," followed by a discussion of OCEANIC languages with an extensive bibliography, followed by descriptions of POLYNESIAN language with ten bibliographic items, including three monographs. All of this before reaching the discussion of the INDO-PACIFIC languages, including the 1,000 distinct languages spoken in New Guinea.

In effect, everything is included for which there is more than the skimpiest literature, but it is not exhaustive and the reader can consult also the lists of Grimes's *Ethnologue* **(E65)** and Voegelin and Voegelin's *Classification and index of the world's languages* **(E93).**

E74

Sebeok, Thomas A., ed. *Current trends in linguistics.* The Hague and Paris: Mouton, 1961–73. 14v.

Consult DeMiller's *Linguistics* **(E01)** for more detailed coverage of this series, described in the context of related volumes. Each volume has an editorial board. Volumes devoted to geographical areas have an index of languages, and an index of authors and coauthors. Theoretical volumes have an index of names and other features, some of which are mentioned in the brief annotations that follow: v.1, Sebeok, Thomas A., ed., *Soviet and East European linguistics* (1961 [606p.]) **(E75),** includes nine chapters on languages and language families; v.2, Sebeok, Thomas A., ed., *Linguistics in East Asia and South East Asia* (1967 [979p.]) **(E76),** includes a bibliography of Chinese linguistics and articles about each national group *(China; Japan; Korea, Mongolia, Tibet, Burma, Thailand and Laos, Vietnam, Indonesia and Malaysia)* and a comparative table of transliteration for Chinese, which compares Pinyin, Yale, Wade-Giles, Zhuyin Zimu, and Gwoyen Romatzyh; v.3, Sebeok, Thomas A., ed., *Theoretical foundations* (1966 [537p.]) **(E77),** with contributions from Noam Chomsky, Joseph H. Greenberg, Charles F. Hockett, Kenneth L. Pike, and others; v.4, Sebeok, Thomas A., ed., *Ibero-American and Caribbean linguistics* (1965 [659p.]) **(E78);** v.5, Sebeok, Thomas A., ed., *Linguistics in South Asia* (1969 [814p.]) **(E79),** after covering topics on several language groups, specialized articles cover semantics of kinship in South India and Ceylon; v.6, Sebeok, Thomas A., ed., *Linguistics in South West Asia and North Africa* (1970 [802p.]) **(E80),** Indo-European (Iranian and Armenian), Altaic (Turkish and Mongolian), and Afroasiatic (Semitic, Egyptian, Coptic, Cushtic, and the Berber languages); v.7, Sebeok, Thomas A., ed., *Linguistics in Sub-Saharan Africa* (1971, [814p.]) **(E81),** with articles on some languages and language families, on click languages, and on surrogate languages; v.8, Sebeok, Thomas A., ed., *Linguistics in Oceania* (1971 [2v.] **(E82),** after articles on indigenous languages of the area, articles examine such topics as the Indo-Pacific hypothesis, pre-contact period writing, and a checklist of

Oceanic language and dialect names; v.9, Sebeok, Thomas A., ed., *Linguistics in Western Europe* (1972 [2v.]) **(E83),** includes articles on the various areas of general linguistics and on the study of selected languages. One appendix surveys country by country the organizations devoted to linguistic research and teaching, which is out of date but still useful. Another appendix surveys periodical publications devoted to Western European languages and published in Western Europe. The index of names is bound separately from the two-volume set. V.10, Sebeok, Thomas A., ed., *Linguistics in North America,* 2d ed. (1973 [2v.]) **(E84),** describes the major European languages spoken in this region as well as the native languages. Pt.3 of v.2, "Checklist," by H. L. Lander (pp.205–527), lists ethnic groups and languages and maps of ethnic groups in the Americas **(E85);** v.11, Sebeok, Thomas A., ed., *Diachronic, areal and topological linguistics* (1973 [604p.]) **(E86),** designed to present a survey of methodological issues with a case study that exemplifies that mode of inquiry; there is a history of language classification and an index of languages and of writing systems; v.12, Sebeok, Thomas A., ed., *Linguistics and adjacent arts and sciences* (1974 [4v.]) **(E87),** which argues against the overspecialization of linguistics; v.13, Sebeok, Thomas A., ed., *Historiography of linguistics* (1975 [2v.]) **(E88),** which is especially useful for the discussions of area studies and for its coverage of European and American structuralism, its annotated bibliography of the history of phonetics, a select bibliography of the history of linguistics from 1945 through the early 1970s, with an index of names and an index of languages; v.14, Sebeok, Thomas A., ed., *Indexes* (1976 [952p.]) **(E89),** with contents of volumes 1–13 listed alphabetically by author's name; index of languages, subject index, index of names, and biographical notes on editors and contributors. Cumulated index.

E90

Sebeok, Thomas A., ed. *Encyclopedic dictionary of semiotics.* Berlin: Mouton, 1986. 3v. (Approaches to semiotics, v.73)

Two hundred thirty-six contributors for 426 signed articles. Extensive cross-references. Many articles relate the methodology of linguistics to anthropological problems. See, for example, J. H. McDowell's "Semeiotics in folkloristics." Supplemented annually by volumes in the series *Approaches to semiotics* entitled *The semiotic web:* Thomas A. Sebeok and Jean Umiker-Sebeok's *The semiotic web 1987* (Berlin: Mouton, 1988 [853p.]) (Approaches to semiotics, no.81); *The semiotic web 1988* (Berlin: Mouton, 1989 [430p.]) (Approaches in semiotics, no.85); *The semiotic web,* 1989 (Berlin: Mouton, 1990 [797p.]) (Advances in semiotics, no.92); and most recently, Thomas A. Sebeok and Jean Umiker-Sebeok, eds., *Recent developments in theory and history: The semiotic web* (Berlin: Mouton, 1990 [554p.]) (Advances in semiotics, no.100) **(E91).**

E92

Shopen, Timothy. *Language typology and syntactic description.* Cambridge, England: Cambridge Univ. Pr., 1985. 3v.

This manual guides field workers into techniques of discovery that have been sharpened by a more complete understanding of what to look for. Each chapter is written by a recognized authority. Relevant topics, detailed explanations, and ease of entry to specific questions through an appropriately expanded index all make this a useful companion in the field. In each volume extensive bibliographies are arranged alphabetically by author. Thus: in v.1, *Clause structure,* the bibliographies (p.365–80) are followed by an extensive index (p.381–99) that is professionally structured to greatly enhance the value of the volume. In v.2, *Complex combinations,* the bibliography (p.287–98) is followed by a detailed index (p.299–317). In v.3, *Grammatical categories and the lexicon,* the brief bibliography is supported by a superb index (408–27).

E93

Voegelin, Charles Frederick, and F. M. Voegelin. *Classification and index of the world's languages.* New York: Elsevier, 1977. 658p.

Arranged alphabetically by the names of language groups. Bibliographic references are included at organization breaks in the discussion. Indexed by name of language group and subgroup, language, dialect, and ethnic group with cross-references to related names. Biographic references (p.359–834) are densely cited in the discussion. Index should be consulted only after reading the "Introduction to the index" (p.385–86).

Consult also Grimes's *Ethnologue* **(E65),** which includes a much more exhaustive list of language names.

State-of-the-Art Reviews

E94

Journal of folklore research. v.1– , 1964– . Bloomington: Folklore Institute, Indiana University. 3/yr.

Title varies. Guest editors for special issues provide topical reviews. For example: (1) Longbois, Janet, ed., *Folklore and semeiotics* 22 (2/3) (1985): 77–195 **(E95),** an introduction is followed by articles applying semiotics to traditional lore, rites of conversion, verbal performance, and festivals; (2) Dégh, Linda, ed., *Comparative method in folklore* 22 (2/3) (1985): 77–195 **(E96),** in which various articles discuss methods of application, including a contrast between structural (in the linguistic sense of that word) and thematic applications.

E97

Lingua. v.1– , 1947. Amsterdam: North-Holland. Monthly.

In the hallmark "Review articles," discussions of a related group of monographic titles can run to thirty-five pages in length. Covers the full range of linguistic interest from dialectology to semiotics. Includes linguistic studies in a cultural setting. Provides a forum for organizational news.

Searching Graphic Materials

Searches for graphic materials should consult American Geographical Society of New York, Map Department, *Index to maps in books and periodicals* **(A59).**

Searching Unpublished Materials

Searches for unpublished materials often benefit from an inspection of the National Anthropological Archives, *Catalog to manuscripts at the National Anthropological Archives. Department of Anthropology. National Museum of Natural History. Smithsonian Institution* **(A69).**

Archives

The Archives of the Languages of the World project are administered by the Archives of Traditional Music (ATM) at Indiana University. A major phase of its preservation project has been completed, and 2,300 reels of linguistic audiotape and 300 discs can, for a fee, be copied from several hundred hours of recordings retained in master copies by the ATM. The entire collection has been organized and described in Bonnie Urciuoli, comp., *A catalog of the C. F. and F. M. Voegelin archives of the languages of the world* (Bloomington: Archives of the Languages of the World, ATM, Morrison Hall 117, Indiana University, 1988 [8v.]) **(E98),** a photocopy edition that is cross-indexed by language, language family, and phylum for each specific collection. Collectors, participants [informers], and language are indexed in volume 8. For each transcription, availability is specified in a descriptive annotation that includes a record of sites and dates of the recording and of the contents and duration of each recording, identifies who the speakers are and where they are from, and provides a collection accession number and bibliographic references related to the transcription. Nearly one-third of these resources are of North American Indians. The catalog has been prepared in seven sections: North American Indian languages, South American Indian languages, African languages, Asian and Middle Eastern languages, Australian languages, Oceanic languages, and European languages, including European languages in the Americas.

E99

Voegelin, Charles Fredrick, and Z. S. Harris. *Index to the Franz Boas collection of materials for American linguistics.* Baltimore,

Md.: Linguistic Society of America, 1945. 43p. (Language monograph, no.22)

Manuscripts gathered by Franz Boas, as authors submitted manuscripts to him for publication. Each entry describes the physical item(s) and gives a short description of its contents and its relationship to subsequent publication. Arranged by language studies. Indexed by manuscript number and by author.

Dissertations

For detailed coverage, consult DeMiller's *Linguistics* **(E01).** Some topical bibliographies include dissertations in their coverage. Examples would include Eschbach, Eschbach-Szabo, and Willenberg's *Bibliography of semeiotics* **(E24),** Gordon's *Semantics* **(E26),** and Beard and Szymanek's *Bibliography of morphology* **(E22).** A recently completed German-language work is listed in chapter 1, "What Every Anthropologist Needs to Know," as *Abstracts in German anthropology* **(A33).** Useful machine-readable databases are described at *Dissertations abstracts ondisc* [computer file] **(B14)** for emphasis on American dissertations and theses, and at *Francis bulletin signalétique* [computer file], described in the annotation to *FRANCIS* **(B19),** which provides subject access to many French-language dissertations.

6

Physical and Biological Anthropology

Many useful and recent reference sources listed in Balay's *Guide to reference books* are not duplicated here. This frees us to concentrate on the best strategic searches for specifically anthropological materials.

Some idea of the range of scientific interest in physical anthropology can be achieved by inspecting Levine's *A topical guide to vols. 1–21 (new series) of the American journal of physical anthropology* **(F06).** At the most general level, it studies the relationship of humans to other species and the variations between population groups and individuals. The ultimate interest of these studies rests in a conviction that human behavior has a biological basis. It is widely assumed that behavior shared with other primates is more fundamental to survival than behaviors specific to man. This has given vigor to studies of primate behavior. The study of the evolutionary process sends the anthropologist into studies of classification systems and geological time. Any facet of human anatomy that can be described becomes potentially a useful index to one of these problems. The measurement of differences between individuals leads into such interests as the identification of specific individuals from skeletal remains. Variations in blood types establish differences between population groups. The reference resources for some specialized aspects of physical anthropology can be identified in the available bibliographic guides. Inspect Day's *A guide to fossil man* **(F01)** and Wolfe's *Field primatology* **(F02).** Journals for reviews of current materials and research activities are listed **(F03)** through **(F15).** Retrospective searches can start with the bibliographies **(F16)** through **(F36).** A bibliographic base that can be expanded by searching retrospective volumes of continuing sources **(F23)** through **(F26).** Topical retrospective bibliographies are listed **(F27)** through **(F36).** Encyclopedias, dictionaries, and manuals are listed **(F39)** through **(F80).** To identify a useful atlas of anatomy, inspect **(F81)** through **(F83).**

Entry into biological and physical anthropology has been greatly eased by the invention of the citation indexes, such as *Scisearch* [computer file] **(B35)** for which the printed edition is fully described in the annotation to Haas's "Anthropology" **(B01).** Since most science progresses incrementally within narrowly defined paradigms, a knowledge of the seminal publications in these paradigms makes it possible to use the citation indexes described in *Fieldwork in the Library,* chapter 2. These resources help the investigator develop bibliographies of research conducted with internally consistent definitions. The variable definition of key terms within variable constraints established by a particular research design can be clearly demonstrated by the abundance of variable definitions for the same key term identified in the index of Dulbecco's *Encyclopedia of human biology* **(F39).** In science it is useful to be aware of the range of convenient use for any definition. It is essential to understand that all research about the same thing may not be comparable. For this reason, a reference source that identifies different operational definitions of the same term has great value when the literature of a scientific subject is approached. Scholars with training in the humanities gravitate easily to absolutes, place a high value on absolute consistency, and often have difficulty with the transition to the more pragmatic approaches of scientific reporting.

Valuative retrospective reviews of the literature often identify key articles that define the boundaries of a paradigm and can provide a base from which to initiate a citation search strategy. They are often presented as a "History of . . .," and in the context of citation indexes they can provide candidates to serve as a basis for literature searches of a specialized scientific interest.

For many of the traditional areas of subject focus in physical anthropology, a citation search can start with seminal articles identified in Spencer's bibliographic guide, *Ecce Homo* **(F21);** the subject index entry provided by Lasker's *Yearbook of physical anthropology* **(F80);** or by bibliographic citations identified in Wolfe's *Field primatology* **(F02),** Day's *A guide to fossil man* **(F01),** and Tattersall, Delson, and Van Couvering's *Encyclopedia of human evolution and prehistory* **(F70).**

All literature searches should be coordinated with the reference sources identified throughout *Fieldwork in the Library.* This chapter on physical anthropology and human biology has cross-references to eight entries described in chapter 3, "Archaeology and Material Culture." These entries cover reference works about such common interests as geological time and the analysis of human remains.

In investigations of population biology, medical anthropology, and growth, machine-readable databases from other disciplines can be effective. For this purpose consult the machine-readable databases described in chapter 2 and the reference sources described in chapter 1, "What Every Anthropologist Needs to Know." Approaches to these resources can be guided by the discussion there of the reference strategies signaled by headings such as "Searching for Current Materials" and "Retrospective Searches." The annual volumes of *Anthropological literature* **(A36)** supplement the classified subject entry to periodical articles that was discontinued in the Tozzer Library's *Catalogues* [microfiche] **(A26)** in 1982. The coverage of monographs by the Tozzer Library's *Catalogues* [microfiche] **(A26)** can be extended to the end of 1988 by the British Museum, Museum of Mankind Library, *Museum of Mankind Library catalogues* [microfiche] **(A25),** which like Tozzer has a worldwide classified subject entry into monographs for aspects of anthropology from the beginning of that discipline. For a more selective entry to books and periodical articles, and a much more detailed classified subject entry, consult the printed index published by the Human relations area file's *HRAF source bibliography* **(D16).** Most research libraries will have in hard copy many of the periodical articles and books cited in this resource, and some will have all or part of the Human Relations Area Files's *Human relations area files* [microfiche] **(D69).** When anthropology is included, entry is available in detail for each area as subdivisions for indigenous peoples.

In the indexing terms used in Meiklejohn and Rokala's *The native peoples of Canada: An annotated bibliography of population biology, health, and illness* **(F61),** find an example of terms from other disciplines used to collect citations for a project dedicated to the conviction that research in physical anthropology could be designed to integrate all branches of anthropology. The terms used in this resource are uniquely sensitive to machine-readable databases.

Searching Bibliographic Guides

Most of the resources listed in Auckland's "Getting into the literature" **(A01)** cover all aspects of anthropology, including physical and biological anthropology.

Bibliographic Guides

Because anthropologists work across so many highly elaborated subspecialties, rapid but competent entry into a wide range of sharply focused research holds is essential. Consult Wyatt's *Information sources in the life sciences* **(F78),** which is arranged in a classification system that identifies specific journals and monographic series that consolidate research findings into systematic reviews. It is a splendid resource that deserves frequent consultation. For guidance in the selection of indexing terms in physical anthropology, inspect Meiklejohn and Rokala's *The native peoples of Canada: An annotated bibliography of population biology, health, and illness* **(F61)** for its extensive inventory of indexing terms. It is a model of excellence for the sensible selection of terms that propel a successful entry through the controlled vocabularies of machine-readable databases from other disciplines. Descriptions of several controlled vocabularies are included as part of the descriptive annotations for entries in chapter 2 of *Fieldwork in the Library.* Inspect especially the books described in the annotations to *BIOSIS previews* [computer file] **(B12),** *Life sciences collection* [computer file] **(B24),** *Medline* [computer file] **(B26),** and *EMbase plus* [computer file] **(B15).**

F01

Day, Michael H. *A guide to fossil man: A handbook of human paleontology.* 4th ed. Chicago: Univ. of Chicago Pr., 1986. 432p.

Treats forty-nine sites that are regarded as pivotal. Organized by geographic region and then by site. Documentation of fossils at each locality includes: details of discovery, site location, morphological descriptions, taxonomic affinity, cultural and faunal associations, location of original specimens, cast availability. Bibliographies on each fossil site are extensive and provide access to the published research. Glossary of technical terms.

F02

Wolfe, Linda D. *Field primatology: A guide to research.* New York: Garland, 1987. 288p. (Garland reference library of social science, v.356)

General studies followed by chapters on prosimians, New World monkeys, Old World monkeys, and apes. Subject index. Primate/genus index. Appendix supplies primate taxonomy. Long annotations with many cross-references.

Lists many of the bibliographies published in *Primates* **(F12),** which can also be consulted for its continuing interest in bibliographic control.

Searching for Current Materials

For special current awareness features of scholarly journals, inspect first the Royal Anthropological Institute's *Reference list of current periodicals* **(A14),** arranged by culture and by discipline thereunder; and, for more general articles, by discipline alone. Covers research as it is published in all scholarly languages. The listings in any issue will identify a select list of articles from journals relevant to a specialized topic in a particular culture area. A large number of newsgroups available on Internet [computer network] can be identified in "Announcements of new Internet services with Usenet." Some of special interest to physical anthropologists can be listed here to provide a sample. "Evolution especially molecular," bionet.molbio.evolution; "Human Genome Program issues," bionet.molbio.genome-program; "Population biology, especially theory," bionet.population-bio; "Anthropology discussion," sci.anthropology. Many computer sites support some sort of public access to archives of data such as "Paleoclimatology," ngdcl.ngdc.noaa.gov (USA) which can be accessed by e-mail, by anonymous FTP, and sometimes by public Telnet: "Evolution," evolution.genetics.washington.edu; "Usenet repository," rtfn.mit.edu (MA USA). Scholars without full Internet access can consult P. Kaminski, "Public dialup Internet access list (PDIAL)" on Usenet alt.internet.access. Read carefully the annotation to Krol, *The whole Internet* **(B04).**

Select Reviews in Scholarly Journals

F03

American journal of human genetics. v.1– , 1949– . Chicago: Univ. of Chicago Pr. for American Society of Human Genetics. Monthly.

Focuses on genetic principles applied to medicine and the social sciences. Five to ten book reviews per issue. Bibliographic information for additional titles. Organizational information about programs, meetings, workshops, and grants. Annual subject and author index.

F04

American journal of physical anthropology. v.1– , 1918– . New York: Alan R. Liss, Inc. Monthly.

An organ of the American Association of Physical Anthropology since 1929. In the discipline of anthropology, only the *International journal of anthropology* **(F10)** requires comparable typesetting and copy editing sophistication. Two or three substantive articles an issue. Brief book reviews in each issue with some coverage of English-language materials. The department "Publications received" can be used to survey current output in the disciplines. Some of the irregular special features are more detailed. For example, to achieve an overview of the range of interest of American physical anthropologists, consult: "Abstracts of papers to be presented at the fifty-seventh annual meeting of the American Association of Physical Anthropologists, Kansas City, Missouri, March 24–26, 1988," *American journal of physical anthropology* 75 (2) (1988): 197–290, "Program of the fifty-eighth annual meeting of the American Association of Physical Anthropologists, San Diego, California, April 4–8, 1989, Abstracts," *American journal of physical anthropology* 78 (Feb. 1989): 137–330 **(F05).** This annual feature includes departments for "Notice of meetings" and "Membership list." For a retrospective review of the range of coverage by this journal, inspect Morton H. Levine's *A topical guide to vols. 1–21 (new series) of the American journal of physical anthropology* (Philadelphia: Wistar Institute Pr., 1971 [132p.]) **(F06).**

F07

Homo. v.1– , 1948– . Göttingen: Muster-Schmidt Verlag. Quarterly.

Probably the most complete journal of review for physical anthropology in all of its aspects: "Neues schrifttum," "Allgemeine anthropologie" (classified thereunder "Morphologische anthropologie"), "Psychologische anthropologie," "Historische anthropologie," "Prähistorische anthropologie," and "Geographic anthropologie." A continuing focus in all of these sections is the theme of human adaptation to the environment.

F08

Human biology. v.1– , 1929– . Detroit: Wayne State Univ. Pr. Quarterly.

Between five and ten book reviews in an issue. Focus is on the underlying environmental and genetic causes of biological variation. Interested in the relationship of biological and social or cultural variations with a special interest in variations in disease and health between populations. Each issue reflects Gabriel W. Lasker's strong sense of bibliographic responsibility to the reader.

F09

Human evolution: An international journal. v.1– , 1986– . Florence, Italy: Editrice "Il Sedicesimo." 6/yr.

Institutional subscription is $145 a year. The *Journal of human evolution* was edited by Professor B. Chiarelli from 1971 until the end of 1985, when his editorial relationship with Academic Press was interrupted. In cooperation with leading scholars, Professor Chiarelli founded this new journal to provide a forum for articles dealing with the science of humanity from a naturalistic perspective. The "Lead review" often runs to ten pages with an extensive bibliography, and is followed by other signed book reviews about one page long. "Current events" offers an agenda for the announcement of new discoveries. Provides a forum for all aspects of human evolution, including articles and book reviews on fossil remains, evidence of hunting and gathering activities, and primate behavior.

F10

International journal of anthropology. v.1– , 1986– . Florence, Italy: Editrice "Il Sedicesimo" for the Assn. of European Anthropologists. Quarterly.

Subscriptions are $100 a year for institutions, $50 for associates and students. Signed book reviews including some reference works. Heavily weighted toward physical anthropology, human biology, paleoecology, human paleontology, primatology, and primate ethnology. A recent issue covered premature tooth loss among aborigines, scaling the social relationship of baboons, the incidence of Chinese technology in the fillings of teeth in sixteenth-century Europe, dietary and demographic transitions, estimates of the aboriginal populations of North America, and serum protein in Slovakia. This publication is extravagant in its use of tables, graphs, photographs, and mathematical formulas.

F11

Paleobiology. v.1– , 1975– . Ithaca, N.Y.: Paleontological Society. Quarterly.

A single book review section can run to 2,500 words. The focus of this journal is on processes and patterns in biology and their relation to historical analysis.

F12

Primates: Journal of primatology. v.1– , 1957– . Inuyama, Aichi, Japan: Japan Monkey Center. Quarterly.

Often includes definitive bibliographic reviews. One department lists newly available films. Many of the bibliographies of field studies of specific species first published in this journal can be identified in *Field primatology* **(F02).** For additional coverage, consult (1) Daniel Dow and Frank E. Poirier, "Bibliographic review of research on Cebus monkeys," *Primates: Journal of primatology* 18: 3 (1977): 731–46 **(F13),** which lists 169 items alphabetically and numbered consecutively. Subject access via a subject cross reference table based on keyword analysis. And (2) Gerald R. Stoffer and Judith E. Stoffer, "Stress and aversive behavior in non-human primates: A retrospective bibliography (1914–1974) indexed by type of primate, aversive event, and topical area," *Primates: Journal of primatology* 17: 4 (1976): 547–78. Cites 582 articles and includes coverage of collected papers, dissertations, and reports of the National Technical Information Service (NTIS), with each entry numbered consecutively for use with the subject index (p.574–78). Foreign-language article titles are given in English translation only. *Dissertation Abstracts* order number given for those unpublished dissertations available from University Microfilms.

F14

Social biology. v.1– , 1954– . Madison, Wis.: Society for the Study of Social Biology. Quarterly.

Title varies. Tends to focus on population studies. Signed book reviews usually run less than 600 words but can run to 2,000 words. Long, detailed articles often achieve a critical synthesis. Upholds a tradition of readability.

F15

Zeitschrift für morphologie und anthropologie. v.1– , 1899– . Stuttgart: E. Schweizerbarthsche Verlagsbuchhandlung. 3/yr.

Under "Bücherbesprechungen," three to six signed book reviews per issue. Wide-ranging interest in paleodemography, biological adaptation, population, paleo-epidemiology, fossil man, the quaternary, and dating techniques.

Selective Lists of Scholarly Journals

For a select list of serials in "biological anthropology," consult p.159–60 in Frantz's *A student anthropologist's handbook* **(A15),** listed in chapter 1, "What Every Anthropologist Needs to Know." The number of physical anthropologists working in European institutions encourages the newsletters of European anthropological associations to provide extensive coverage of physical anthropology including departments that regularly reproduce the current contents of journals. Consult British Museum, Museum of Mankind

Library, *Museum of Mankind Library catalogues* [microfiche] **(A25).**

Retrospective Searches

The published Tozzer Library's *Author and subject catalogues of the Tozzer Library* [microfiche] **(A26)** and the Peabody Museum Library's *Catalogue: Subjects* **(A29)** provide classified subject and author entry to periodical articles and monographs through 1982, and monographs only thereafter. The British Museum, Museum of Mankind Library, *Museum of Mankind Library catalogues* **(A25)** provides author and classified subject entry to monographs covering all aspects of anthropology.

Retrospective Bibliographies—Bibliographies of Bibliographies

F16

Gerlach, Gudrun, and Rolf Hachmann. *Verzeichnis vor ünd frühgeschichtlicher bibliographien.* Berlin: De Gruyter, 1971. 269p.

Bibliography of bibliographies on prehistory. An entry into problems of dating fossil remains. Consult also the consolidation of recent information in John Bower and David Lubell's *Prehistoric cultures and environments in the late Quaternary of Africa* (Oxford, England: B.A.R., 1988 [235p.]) (Cambridge monographs in African archaeology, v.25; BAR International series, v.405) **(F17).** For a sample of the range of contributions modern physical anthropologists can make to the discipline of archaeology, inspect the sophisticated *Investigations of ancient human tissue: Chemical analysis in anthropology,* ed. by Mary K. Sandford (Amsterdam: Gordon and Breach Science Publishers, 1993 [431p.]) **(F18),** with its discussion of the biogenic-digenetic continuum, isotopic analysis of paleodiets, the analysis of human hair and culture, and health and chemistry illustrated by case studies. This resource can be supplemented by other resources such as Allen's *Archaeological chemistry 4* **(C53)** and Bradley's *Quaternary paleoclimatology* **(C57).** The latter has an extensive index and a massive bibliography which lead archaeologists to entries that answer questions about the increasingly wide span of dating techniques and methods in climatic reconstruction.

F19

Smith, Margo. "Biological anthropology." In *Anthropological bibliographies: A selected guide.* Library-Anthropology Resources Group. South Salem, N.Y.: Redgrave, 1981. 307p.

Seventy-seven items, including many continuing series in paleontology. Especially strong in the identification of summary resources in metric anthropology such as: Finnegan, Michael, and M. A. Faust, *Bibliography of human and nonhuman nonmetric variation* (Amherst: Department of Anthropology, Univ. of Massachusetts, 1974 [133p.]) (Research reports, 14); Garrett, John William, and Kenneth W. Kennedy, *A collation of anthropometry* (Wright-Patterson Air Force Base, Ohio: Aerospace Medical Research Laboratory, Aerospace Medical Division, 1971. [2v.]): v.1, A–H; v.2, I–Z, plus index. See also Wilton Marion Krogman's *A bibliography of human morphology, 1914–1939* (Chicago: Univ. of Chicago Pr., 1941 [385p.]) **(F20).** And consult United States, Wright Air Development Division, Human Engineering Division, *Bibliography of research reports and publications issued by the Human Engineering Division, April 1946–December 1970,* edited by Sandra A. Stevenson (Wright-Patterson Air Force Base, Ohio: Aerospace Medical Research Laboratory, 1972 [184p.]), which is also available in microfiche.

Retrospective Bibliographies—Broad Scope

Physical and biological anthropology finds a double blessing in the collections at the Peabody Museum, Tozzer Library's *Author and subject catalogues of the Tozzer Library* [microfiche] **(A26)** and the British Museum, Museum of Mankind Library's *Museum of Mankind Library catalogues* [microfiche] **(A25).** Both of these libraries have published catalogs which classify holdings from the very beginning of anthropology as a discipline. They cover all aspects of physical and biological anthropology worldwide.

F21

Spencer, Frank, comp. *Ecce homo: An annotated bibliographic history of physical anthropology.* New York: Greenwood, 1986. 495p.

Organized by time period. The earlier periods can offer entry into some aspects of metrical anthropology. The twentieth century provides valuative entry into most of the scientific paradigms of current interest. Subject index includes site and species entries. *Ecce homo* provides starter bibliographies. Adequate guidance to reference sources for research in the history of anthropological disciplines would require a carefully discursive chapter about historical methodology, which is not attempted here. Skillful research into the history of the disciplines is everywhere in evidence.

Retrospective Bibliographies—Biographical Bibliographies

F22

Duroux, Paul Émile. *Dictionnaire des anthropologistes.* Paris: Éditions universitaires, 1975. 339p.

This alphabetic list of biographies includes a bibliography of publications for each scholar listed.

Retrospective Bibliographies—Continuing Bibliographies

F23

American Geological Institute. *Bibliography and index of geology.* v.1– , 1935– . Washington, D.C.: Geological Society of America. Available online from DIALOG. Available in part on CD-ROM from SilverPlatter with SilverPlatter software.

Title varies. This annotation is intended to support the idea that new users explore their subject in the printed index to get a better understanding of the carefully expanded and extensive controlled vocabulary developed for this resource. Inspect the annual cumulated volumes, which are divided into two parts: pt.1, *Cumulative bibliography;* pt.2, *Cumulative index.* Last inspected the printed index in 1989: under BIBLIOGRAPHY QUARTENARY, five items, including one for China and one for Kenya; under FOSSIL MAN—BIOCHEMISTRY, one item; under FOSSIL—BIOLOGICAL EVOLUTION, eight items subdivided by four subheadings; under FOSSIL MAN—FAUNAL STUDIES, seven items under four subheadings. These are only a sample of the findings under FOSSIL MAN. Items are entered into the indexing arrangement only once, and searches under variable terms are rewarded. For example, instead of FOSSIL MAN a search for AFRICA—PALEONTOLOGY—FOSSIL MAN yields one item; but AFRICA—MAMMALIA yields seven items on early man, including book reviews of monographs. Again, PALEOBOTANY yields fifteen items, including a review of Bruce H. Tiffney's "Paleobotany," *Geotimes* 34 (2) (1989): 42–43. Venturing to PALEOECOLOGY—QUATERNARY—AFRICA yields six items, and PALEONTOLOGY—DATA PROCESSING yields seven items, including one on a program to help identify fossils.

F24

Biological abstracts. v.1– , 1926– . Philadelphia: BioSciences Information Service. Bimonthly.

Author indexes. Broad subject indexes. Keyword indexes. Excellent for topical entry. Portions are available as *BIOSIS previews* [computer file] **(B12).**

F25

Current primate references. v.1– , 1966– . Seattle: Primate Information Center, Univ. of Washington. Monthly.

Does not cover hominids. The center publishes extensive special bibliographies, which are reported in this periodical. Includes book reviews. Lists books, articles in collections, and doctoral dissertations. The center has a machine-readable database and offers custom bibliographies for a small fee. "Primate behavior" is the section in the classed arrangement most likely to interest a broad audience. Indexes book reviews.

F26

The zoological record. v.1– , 1864– . Philadelphia: BioSciences Information Service; London: Zoological Society of London. Annual.

Portions of this printed index can be found in *The zoological record* [computer file] **(B39).**

V.1–6 entitled *Record of zoological literature: A comprehensive index to worldwide serials literature in systematic zoology.* Now published in twenty sections. Each section consists of five indexes: author, subject, geographical, palaeontological, and systematic. Full bibliographical information is given in the author index. The remaining indexes refer to the numbers assigned to the author entries. Indispensable.

Retrospective Bibliographies—Topical

Many of the technical skills needed for work in physical anthropology are shared with archaeology. This is especially true of problems of dating and of identifying fauna and flora associated with sites. A review of some selections from chapter 3, "Archaeology and Material Culture," in *Fieldwork in the Library* might include Ellis's *Laboratory techniques in archaeology* **(C28),** which is international in scope in all languages and indexed by method of analysis and type of material; Polach's *Radiocarbon dating literature* **(C29),** in which the reader finds guidance from the detailed annotations; Allen's *Archaeological chemistry 4* **(C53);** and Bradley's *Quaternary paleoclimatology* **(C57),** which is supported by an extensive index and a massive bibliography which lead archaeologists to entries that answer questions about the increasingly wide span of dating techniques and methods in climatic reconstruction. Dating methods here include radiocarbon, potassium-argon, uranium-series, thermoluminescence, obsidian hydration, tephrochronology, lichenometry, and dendrochronology—all with a review discussion of research topics and a list of primary references. In the *World archaeology* series **(C50),** find 7 (2) *Dating* and 8 (2) *Climate change.* For expansion of a literature search, consult Driesch's *Guide to the measurement of animal bones from archaeological sites* **(C64)** and Hillson's *Teeth* **(C73),** with nineteen plates, 110 drawings, and thirty-eight tables, which facilitate the identification of teeth from more than 150 genera. Covers tooth forms, dental microstructure, teeth and age, size and shape, and dental diseases. Summary information on the importance of teeth in identification of genera. The extensive bibliography (p.341–67) establishes this resource as a thorough review of the evidence provided by teeth in the investigations of archaeology and physical anthropology; Wheeler and Jones's *Fishes* **(C89),** which has illustrations by Rosalind Wheeler, consolidates research that establishes the reciprocal relationships between archaeology, paleontology, and ichthyology.

F27

Dingwall, William Orr. *Language and the brain: A bibliography and guide.* New York: Garland, 1981. 2v. (Garland reference library of social sciences, v.73)

Lists 5,746 items arranged alphabetically by author in each of nine topics, including neurolinguistics, hemispheric specialization, and evolution. Contains bibliographies and lists of relevant societies and journals. Topic index. Author index.

F28

Davis, Elisabeth B. *Using the biological literature: A practical guide.* New York: Dekker, 1981. 286p. (Books in library and information science, v.35)

See especially discussions of BIOSIS subject headings, and sections on genetics, general biology, biochemistry, zoology, biophysics, and molecular biology.

F29

Jack, J. L. "A bibliography on howler monkeys." *Primates: Journal of primatology* 8: 3 (1967): 271–90.

Lists reports dealing with howler monkeys since 1900. Includes references taken from T. C. Ruch's *Bibliographia Primatologica* (Springfield, Ill.: C. C. Thomas, 1941) **(F30)** and papers dealing more extensively with *Alouatta.*

F31

Mavalwala, Jamshed. *Dermatoglyphics: An international bibliography.* The Hague: Mouton, 1977. 306p.

All material in which dermatoglyphics are studied, except for information used by law enforcement agencies. Includes material published since the late nineteenth century.

F32

Nikitiuk, B. A. "Soviet medical anthropology over the last 70 years." *Arkhiv anatomii, gistologii i embriologii* 93, no.11 (1987): 27–36.

In Russian. Use of this material would require some conceptual sophistication; however, the reported results are clearly in the Western tradition. Yet the task is not entirely different from the intellectual challenge of other studies in comparative science with an emphasis on medicine for which Helaine Selin's *Science across cultures: An annotated bibliography of books on non-Western sciences, technology, and medicine* (New York: Garland, 1992 [431p.]) **(F33),** benefits from rich annotations to the 839 entries of English-language monographs.

F34

Sanderson, Lilian Passmore. *Female genital mutilation: Excision and infibulation: A bibliography.* London: The Anti-Slavery Society for the Protection of Human Rights, 1986. 72p.

Three sections: Anthropological, sociological, and philanthropic. Lists 1,150 books, articles, government documents, newspaper accounts.

F35

Scott, Richard G. "Dental anthropology." In v.2, *Encyclopedia of human biology,* p.789–804. Ed. by Renato Dulbecco. San Diego: Academic, 1991. 879p.

Starts with a glossary. Covers human dentition, dental phenetics and phylogeny, environmental interface, dental indicators of environmental stress. The bibliography is sensitive to a scholar's need for guidance into the most recent compendiums and review articles.

F36

Wulff, Lois Yvonne, comp. *Physiological factors relating to terrestrial altitudes: A bibliography.* Columbus: Ohio State Univ. Libraries, 1968. (Ohio State University Libraries publications, no.3)

Lists 4,000 items.

Informational Reference Searches

For American directory information on American physical anthropologists, consult first *AAA guide* **(A53).** For any narrow specialty in a more general field of science, expect to find directories that provide a survey of recent published output from the scholars and institutions listed in indexing services such as the American Geological Institute's *Bibliography and index of geology* **(F23).**

Directories

F37

American Association of Physical Anthropologists. "Membership list." *American journal of physical anthropology* 74 (1987) (4): 565–84.

An alphabetic list with current addresses. A regular feature last inspected in the 1987 issue. More specialized directories of scholars abound and are quickly dated. A recent scan of the American Geological Institute's *Bibliography and index of geology* **(F23)** identified the following items: (1) "I.P.I. directory: A reference tool for paleontologists," *Fossils quarterly* 7 (2) (1988): 29–30, and *Directory of sea-level research 1984,* comp. by Ian Shennan and Paolo Pirazzooli (Durham, U.K.: University of Durham, Department of Geology, 1987) (I.G.C.P project no.200). Serves many scholars who are interested in late quaternary sea-level changes: measurement, correlation, and future applications.

F38

Wisconsin Regional Primate Center. *International directory of primatology.* Madison: Univ. of Wisconsin Pr., 1992. 157p.

An excellent example of the trend in directories to become virtually guides to the discipline. Organizations are listed geographically under broad topical headings. Population management groups and studbook keepers are listed with addresses and phone numbers. Information for each entry includes mission, affiliation, research programs, key personnel, publications, field sites, and training opportunities. The section on field studies includes information on location, species, study dates, personnel, and addresses. It includes information on Primate Center bibliographies and newsletters with addresses. These features are supported with excellent indexing, thus making this resource an indispensable desk reference for anyone working with students or professionals in this specialty.

Encyclopedias, Dictionaries, and Manuals

F39

Dulbecco, Renato, ed. *Encyclopedia of human biology.* San Diego: Academic, 1991. 8v.

Can be used as a dictionary in a thoroughly scientific way. Each article starts with a brief glossary that provides a definition—as the term is used in the paradigm under discussion—in that article. From the main index, the definition of the term may have several entries, each to a glossary with the specialized definition specific to the scientific paradigm discussed in the article. Thus each item is defined in a range of convenient use as established in a particular body of theory and method. Does not attempt an inappropriate ideal definition.

Hundreds of experts contribute signed articles with brief bibliographies. Each article starts with a glossary. In the main index the word "defined" under a term follows references to these glossaries. The subject index is adequate, with many well-defined expansions on fundamental terms. Bibliographies tend to lead the user into the literature. For example, the bibliography to the article "Development, psychobiology" identifies a 1991 collection of essays and a 1988 handbook. Most useful as an entry into the "cutting-edge" technologies of the biological sciences.

F40

Falkner, Frank T., and James M. Tanner, eds. *Human growth: A comprehensive treatise.* 2d ed. New York and London: Plenum, 1986– . 3v.

Published to date: v.1, *Developmental biology;* v.2, *Prenatal growth;* v.3, *Methodology, ecological, genetic.* All contributions are written in a homogeneous style, with extensive bibliographies. Specialists deal with topics like the difference between regeneration and cell differentiation.

Also useful are the twenty-six review articles in Robert L. Monroe and Beatrice B. Whiting, eds., *Handbook of cross-cultural human development* (New York: Garland, 1981 [888p.]) **(F41).**

F42

Gershowitz, Henry, Donald L. Rucknagel, and Richard L. E. Tashian. *Evolutionary perspectives and the new genetics.* New York: Alan R. Liss, 1986. 192p. (Progress in clinical and biological research, v.218)

Uses the application of DNA technology to improve macro-evolutionary theories of speciation and evolutionary mode and tempo and for a discussion of structural changes in DNA in the context of natural selection and genetic variants. For a dictionary to guide the reader of this report use the index of *Dulbecco's Encyclopedia of human biology* **(F39)** and Riomar Reiger, A. Michaelis, and M. M. Green's *Glossary of genetics,* 5th ed. (Springer-Verlag, 1991 [553p.] **(F43)** which covers terms of classical, evolutionary, population, and molecular genetics. References are given for each entry and abundant cross-references guide the reader. Consult also T. Strachan's *The human genome* (Philadelphia: Bioservices, 1992. [160p]) **(F44)** for a detailed analysis of human genetics at the cytological and molecular levels from genome organization to expression. Covers DNA structure, nuclear and mitochondrial genomes, chromosome structure, coding versus noncoding DNA, transcription and translation, multigene families and repetitive DNA. The discussion of evolution and polymorphism considers gene duplication and divergence, exon duplication and shuffling, sequence and point mutation variation, gene conversion, recombination, and other variation-generation mechanisms.

F45

International Primatological Society. 10th Congress. 1984. Nairobi, Kenya. *Primate evolution.* Selected proceedings of the Tenth Congress of the International Primatological Society. Ed. by James G. Else and Phyllis C. Lee. Cambridge, England, and New York: Cambridge Univ. Pr., 1986. 3v.

V.1, *Primate evolution;* v.2, *Primate ecology and conservation;* v.3, *Primate ontology, cognition and social behavior.* Attempts to synthesize information on dating and other issues, including functional anatomy and evolutionary genetics. Can be used as a companion to Robert L. Carroll's *Vertebrate paleontology and evolution* (New York: Freeman, 1988 [698p.]) **(F46),** with its clear exposition of modern systematic methodology. Also useful for its review of recent interpretations of vertebrates in systematic and temporal sequence. Final chapter discusses evolutionary topics such as gradualism, macroevolution, adaptive radiation, and extinction. Encyclopedic. A similar quality of synthesis can be found in John F. Eisenberg's *The mammalian radiations: An analysis of trends in evolution, adaptation, and behavior* (Chicago: Univ. of Chicago Pr., 1983 [610p.]) **(F47)** and Ernest P. Walker, *Walker's mammals of the world,* ed. Ronald M. Mowak, 5th ed. (Baltimore: Johns Hopkins Univ. Pr., 1991 [2v.]) **(F48),** a rev. ed. of the 4th ed., 1983.

F49

Isaac, Glynn L. "The archaeology of human origins: Studies of the lower Pleistocene in East Africa, 1971–1981." *Advances in world archaeology* 3 (1984): 1–87.

Those sites dated between 0.7 and 2.5 million years old are covered with about 240 references. Includes some tables of interest and illustrations. Useful resources for the study of this time period in Africa are numerous and can be identified in Scheven's *Bibliographies for African studies* **(G24).**

F50

Johnson, Thomas M., and Carolyn F. Sargent. *Medical anthropology: A handbook of theory and method.* New York: Greenwood, 1990. 479p.

State-of-the-art survey organized into clusters: (1) Perspectives of the therapeutic process, political economy, rituals and routines of discipline and dissent, psychoanalytic perspectives, and clinically applied anthropology; (2) Medical systems with articles on ethnomedicine, ethnopsychiatry, ethnopharmacology, biological and behavioral perspectives of indigenous medicine, bioscience as a cultural system, nursing, and anthropology; (3) Health issues in human populations with articles on disease, reproduction, drug studies, culture, stress, and disease; (4) Methods in medical anthropology with articles on field methods, epidemiology, and demography; and (5) Policy and advocacy with articles on professionalization of indigenous healers.

For a continuing review, consult the journal *Human organization* **(D08),** which has long maintained an interest in the cultural determinant in medical care. Smith's "Biological anthropology" **(F19)** identifies earlier bibliographies. Harrison and Cosminsky's *Traditional medicine* **(D25)** and its *Supplement* **(D26)** provide expanded bibliographic entry into the behavioral and cultural aspects of medical anthropology. For a more technical dictionary, consult Clarence Wilbur Taber's *Cyclopedic medical dictionary* (Philadelphia: F. A. Davis, 1993 [2,590p.]) **(F51),** for the burden (and benefit) that comes from the use of detailed technical jargon.

F52

Keller, Evelyn Fox, ed. *Keywords in evolutionary biology.* Cambridge, Mass.: Harvard Univ. Pr., 1992. 414p.

There are fifty-one brief essays by forty-seven historians, biologists, and philosophers of science, with copious citations in the fifty pages of bibliography. The shifts in meaning of keywords are carefully examined. A useful source for the identification of seminal articles is placed in a context of comparisons that identify shifts in definition for different research approaches or objectives. The twenty-page subject and name index makes it possible to identify coverage of even the most subtle variations in approach.

A useful companion might be the concise summary of the history of geologic time, *Establishment of a geologic framework for paleoanthropology,* ed. by Léo Laporte (Boulder, Colo.: Geological Society of America, 1990) (Special paper, Geological Society of America, 242) **(F53).** In most American research libraries that hold copies of this monograph, its location can be identified in the library catalog only through the series title. *Terrestrial ecosystems through time: Evolutionary paleoecology of terrestrial plants and animals,* ed. by Anna K. Behrensmeyer et al. (Chicago: Univ. of Chicago Pr., 1992 [568p.]) **(F54)** applies paleogeography to study the continuing rejuxtaposition of habitats and changing climatic patterns. Attempts a synthesis of biota and environments in a survey of all life on earth.

F55

Lee, Phyllis C., Jane Thornback, and Elizabeth L. Bennett. *Threatened primates of Africa: The IUCN red data book.* Compiled by the IUCN Conservation Monitoring Centre, Cambridge, U.K. Gland, Switzerland: International Union for Conservation of Nature and Natural Resources, 1988. 153p.

Describes sixty species of endangered primates with information on how many still exist. Extensive bibliography on each species.

F56

Smith, Stephen J. *The atlas of Africa's principal mammals.* San Antonio: Natural History Books, 1985. 241p.

Distribution maps locate the range of 120 mammals. This establishes a base for ethnozoological studies. Index of species.

F57

Lohman, Timothy G., Alex F. Roche, and Reynaldo Martorell, eds. *Anthropometric standardization reference manual.* Champaign, Ill.: Human Kinetics Books, 1988. 177p.

Detailed review of measurements in the study of anthropometry, body composition, nutritional assessment, human growth, population surveys, human variation, sports medicine, etc. Bibliographies are rich in practical scientific technique. Author index. Detailed subject index. Appendix provides a list of equipment and supplies, and where to get them.

F58

McFarland, David, ed. *The Oxford companion to animal behavior.* Foreword by Niko Tinbergen. Rev. and enl. ed. with corrections and a new index. Oxford, England: Oxford Univ. Pr., 1987. 685p.

Concise signed articles by specialists on the concepts used to advance studies of animal behavior, with reference to 146 bibliographic entries. Terms are sometimes easier to locate in Klaus Immelmann and Colin Beer's *A dictionary of ethology* (Cambridge, Mass.: Harvard Univ. Pr., 1989 [336p.]) **(F59).** This translation from the German edition is organized into a series of encyclopedic entries of a page or less, with many cross-references and no index.

F60

McKusick, Victor. *Mendelian inheritance in man: Catalogs of autosomal dominant, autosomal recessive, and x-linked phenotypes.* Baltimore, Md.: Johns Hopkins Univ. Pr., 1992. 2v.

An encyclopedia of human chromosomes and phenotypes, with extensive bibliographies. Especially useful for chromosome abnormalities and medical genetics.

F61

Meiklejohn, Christopher, and D. A. Rokala. *The native peoples of Canada: An annotated bibliography of population biology, health, and illness.* Ottawa: National Museums of Canada, 1986. 564p. (Mercury series. Archaeological survey of Canada. Paper. No.134)

The range of topical coverage in the index suggests its use as a sample of productive terms for searches in machine-readable databases in investigations of other populations. This published product of a computerized search includes 2,100 entries, of which 80 percent are annotated. Includes prehistoric, historic, and contemporary native populations within the geopolitical boundaries of Canada. An alphabetic list. Author index includes all cited authors. The subject index (p.541–63) expands topic entry with many subheadings, e.g., TUBERCULOSIS is subdivided by 22 terms. Geographic terms are not subdivided by topic. Regularly updated in the *Manitoba masterfile (PBHD)* [computer file] (University of Manitoba, Winnipeg, Manitoba R3T 2N2) **(F62),** which currently contains 6,000 entries and includes in its geographic range of coverage much of North America.

F63

Rightmire, G. Philip. *The evolution of* Homo erectus: *Comparative studies on an extinct human species.* Cambridge, England, and New York: Cambridge Univ. Pr., 1990. 260p.

Descriptions, measurements, photographs, drawings, and comparisons of the anatomy of *Homo erectus* specimens from Asia and Africa. An important reference work for all scholars interested in human evolution.

F64

Seminar on Personal Identification in Mass Disasters, Smithsonian Institution, 1968. Personal report of a seminar held in Washington, D.C., 9–11 December 1968. *Personal identification in mass disasters.* Ed. by Thomas D. Steward. Washington, D.C.: Museum of Natural History, Smithsonian Institution, 1970. 158p.

The methodology reported in this volume is closely related to that used in forensic anthropology for which Thomas D. Steward's *Essentials of forensic anthropology, especially as developed in the United States* (Springfield, Ill.: Thomas, 1979) **(F65)** can be consulted for its summary coverage and extensive bibliography. As with any topic that is currently "in fashion," literature searches on topics relevant to this area of study can be supported by continuing bibliographies and state-of-the-art reviews found in chapter 1, "What Every Anthropologist Needs to Know," in *Fieldwork in the Library.*

F66

Spencer, Frank, ed. *History of American physical anthropology, 1930–1980.* New York: Academic, 1982. 495p.

Eighteen topics are given encyclopedic coverage with extensive bibliographies. Each section executed by an acknowledged expert. Author index. Subject index.

F67

Stevenson, Joan C. *Dictionary of concepts in physical anthropology.* New York: Greenwood, 1991. 432p. (Reference sources for the social sciences and humanities, 10)

Each of seventy-four terms is given a definition and a review of the literature to trace the development of the concept. For each concept, the reader is referred to a solid list of references for the broad topic entries with detailed entry through a subject and name index.

Consult also Keith E. Roe and Richard G. Frederick's *Dictionary of theoretical concepts in biology* (Metuchen, N.J.: Scarecrow, 1981 [267p.]) **(F68),** an alphabetical list of terms with a brief list of sources that discuss the theoretical concept. A remarkable piece of work. Cross-references help guide the reader. Can be expanded by reference to Judith A. Overmier's *The history of biology: A selected annotated bibliography* (New York: Garland, 1989 [157p.]) (Garland reference library of the humanities, v.419) **(F69).** The highly selective development of this work might exclude it from a science reference collection, but as a guide to articles that consolidate a body of knowledge, it can be used to increase the utility of citation searches through the 619 entries compiled to provide entry into a larger body of literature. These summary reviews are identified in thirty-six subject areas, including anatomy, animal research, evolution, and taxonomy. All entries are annotated. Subject index. Index for authors, editors, compilers, translators.

F70

Tattersall, Ian, Eric Delson, and John Van Couvering, eds. *Encyclopedia of human evolution and prehistory.* New York: Garland, 1988. 603p. (Garland reference library of the humanities, v.768)

Arranged alphabetically to include a wide range of topics, including fossil and extant primates, evolutionary theory, genetics, methodology, paleolithic archaeology, and sites. Current references to longer articles. All articles are signed by at least one of fifty experts. Many cross-references. Title correctly reflects coverage. Includes not only archaeology, paleontology, and evolutionary biology but also historical, geographical, and technical approaches to the study of prehistory. For encyclopedic survey of the application of evolutionary theory to modern peoples, consult Steve Jones, Robert Martin, and David Pilbeam's *Cambridge encyclopedia of human evolution* (London: Cambridge Univ. Pr., 1992 [512p.]) **(F71).**

Consult also *Palaeobiology: A synthesis,* ed. by Derek E. G. Briggs and Peter R. Crowther (Oxford, England: Blackwell for the Palaeontological Assn., 1990) **(F72),** and *Anthroquest: L. S. B. Leakey Foundation news,* v.1– , 1975– . (Pasadena, Calif.: L. S. B. Leakey Foundation) **(F73),** a quarterly which publishes on all topics related to human and other primate origins.

F74

Ubelaker, Douglas H. *Human skeletal remains: Excavation, analysis, interpretation.* 2d ed. Washington, D.C.: Taraxacum, 1989. 172p. (Manuals on archaeology, v.2)

Contains chapters on skeletal recovery; sex, stature, and age; cultural and pathological alterations; race, identity, and time since death; and prehistoric population dynamics. Has an appendix that provides tables for such variables as height by sex; formations of permanent mandibular canines.

State-of-the-Art Reviews

F75

Cold Spring Harbor Symposia on Quantitative Biology. v.1– , 1933– . Cold Springs Harbor, Long Island N.Y.: Cold Springs Harbor. Annual.

Each symposium focuses on a topic in biology and is encyclopedic for that topic. Indispensable resource. The span of coverage for the volumes in this series continues to be broad and deep. Every effort attracts contributions from top scholars in the discipline.

F76

Evolutionary biology. v.1– , 1967– . New York: Plenum.

Specializes in long reviews of controversial subjects. Includes all aspects of evolutionary biology (classical and modern), including many aspects of genetics and sociobiology.

F77

Journal of social and biological structures. v.1– , 1978– . New York: Academic. Quarterly.

Issues often have a guest editor for contributions on a single topic intended to display the cutting edge of a specialized approach. Examples of topics covered in a single issue: *Studies in human social biology; The punctuated equilibrium debate: scientific issues and implications.*

F78

Wyatt, Harold, ed. *Information sources in the life sciences.* 3d ed. London: Butterworths, 1987. 191p.

This guide is listed under state-of-the-art reviews because it identifies either a major monographic compendium or a reviewing series in each subfield of science. It includes these lists in a format designed to provide adequate treatment of each major subject area such as biochemistry, biotechnology, genetics, zoology, and ecology. Also includes an evaluative review of the literature extending even to historic and classic works in the field. It often identifies important specialized dictionaries and handbooks, and a core list of relevant journals devoted to the substantive issues.

F79

Yearbook of physical anthropology. v.23– , 1980– . New York: published by Alan R. Liss, Inc., for the American Assn. of Physical Anthropology.

Beginning with v.24 (1981), this work will be issued as a supplement to *American journal of physical anthropology,* v.1– , 1918– **(F04),** and included in the cost of that subscription.

Volume twenty-three functions as an annual review not of the discipline as a whole, but certainly of selected topics in which current published results seem to justify a survey of the research. When some new focus of interest approaches maturity, a review of developments can usually be found in this resource. The new publication arrangement has made this valuable reference less erratic in its publication schedule. Indexing entry into v.1–8 (1945–52) is provided by *Yearbook of physical anthropology: Bibliographies and proceedings,* by Gabriel Ward Lasker (Ann Arbor, Mich.: University Microfilms, 1976 [350p.]) **(F80).**

Consult also the bibliographic reviews of many specialized contributions of physical anthropology cited by *Fieldwork in the Library* including *Advances in world archaeology* **(C42)** and the *Annual review of anthropology* **(A57).**

Searching Graphic Materials

For a continuing record of films of primate behavior, consult issues of *Primates* **(F12).** For visual images of anatomy, consult:

F81

McMinn, Robert M. H., and R. T. Hutchings. *Color atlas of human anatomy.* 2d ed. Chicago: Year Book Medical Publishers, 1988. 358p.

Body specimens include head, neck, brain, vertebral column and spinal medulla, upper limb, thorax, abdomen and pelvis, and lower limbs as they actually exist in their natural size.

Color plates with clear numerical indicators for reference to the text. In contrast to the artificial clarity of drawings, Netter and Colacino's *Atlas of human anatomy* **(F82)** uses photography to prepare the scholar for the real thing.

F82

Netter, Frank H., and Sharon Colacino, eds. *Atlas of human anatomy.* Summit, N.J.: CIBA-GEIGY, 1989. 36p. 514p. of plates.

Five hundred fourteen color plates of human anatomy. Exquisitely detailed drawings notable for their balance between complexity and simplicity. Identifications made here can be contrasted to the life-size and real photographs found in McMinn and Hutchings's *Color atlas of human anatomy* **(F81).** The plates are available as slides.

See also Frank H. J. Figge and Johannes Sobotta's *Atlas of human anatomy,* 9th English ed. (New York: Hafner, 1974 [3v.]) **(F83),** for more detailed coverage.

Searching Unpublished Materials

Searches for unpublished materials often benefit from an inspection of the National Anthropological Archives, *Catalog to manuscripts at the National Anthropological Archives. Department of Anthropology. National Museum of Natural History. Smithsonian Institution* **(A69).**

Dissertations

Dissertations are often included in topical bibliographies. This is especially true of bibliographies published as articles in *Current primate references* **(F25)** and *Primates* **(F12),** which regularly identifies current dissertations. German-language material can be identified in *Abstracts in German anthropology* **(A33).** Some entry for English- and French-language dissertations can be achieved through access to the machine-readable databases described as *Dissertations abstracts ondisc* [computer file] **(B14)** and *Francis bulletin signalétique* [computer file] described in the annotation to *FRANCIS* **(B19).**

Monographic Series

In the organization of controls for the literature of the sciences, many useful sources are published in monographic series, and individual monographs of these monographic series can in many libraries be identified in the card catalogs only through a series entry. This method of processing library holdings creates great economies. In a contradiction of this method for controlling the literature to achieve economy, monographs from series published in foreign countries can often be identified only by the author and title entries from the British national database. For example:

F84

Occasional papers (International Association of Human Biologists). v.1– , 1982– . (Newcastle upon Tyne, Great Britain: International Assn. of Human Biologists)

Each volume covers the history of anthropology in a single country, supported by exhaustive bibliographies. There is no record in the Library of Congress that this series has been processed in the United States. It is possible that these publications may have been treated as pamphlets since they are less than fifty pages in length. Given the sponsorship, there is little question that these resources are being acquired in the United States. Cataloging practices make them difficult to identify in a specific collection. If these resources do not show up in a research library catalog, ask the librarians for help. They may be in the collection but subject to special handling. Correspondence with the publisher reveals that the following titles are available: v.1, no.1, Joseph Weiner, *History of physical anthropology in Great Britain* (1982 [33p.]); v.1, no.2, André A. Leguebe, *History of physical anthropology in Belgium* (1983 [35p.]); v.1, no.3, Trinette S. Constanda Westermann, *History of physical anthropology in the Netherlands* (1983 [35p.]); v.1, no.4, P. Smith and Bonné-Tamir Batsheva, *History of human biology in Israel* (1984 [32p.]); v.1, no.5, Robert L. Kirk, *History of physical anthropology in Australia* (1985 (34p.]); v.1, no.6, Tadeusz Bielicki, Tudeusz

Krupínski, and J. Strzalko, *History of physical anthropology in Poland* (1985 [45p.]); Denise Ferembach, *History of human biology in France: v.2, no.1 and no.2, The early years* (1987 [2v.]) and no.3 (1988); (v.2 and 3 were issued with alternate title, *History of biological anthropology in France*); v.2, no.4, O. G. Eiben, *History of human biology in Hungary* (1988 [73p.]); v.2, no.5, no.6, V. Correnti and G. F. de Stefano, *Forerunners in biological anthropology in Italy* (1988 [2v.]) in which v.2 was issued under the title *Anthropology in Italy;* v.3, no.1, Francisco M. Salzano, *History of human biology in Brazil* (1990).

Part Two

Access by Area Studies: With an Emphasis on Empirical Investigations

7

Africa South of the Sahara

Many useful reference sources for Africa listed in Scheven's *Bibliographies for African studies* **(G24),** Gosebrink's "Bibliography and sources for African studies" **(G02),** or McIlwaine's *Africa* **(G96)** are not duplicated. This chapter concentrates on resources with features that assist in searches defined by ethnic or site terms. Only a few resources are repeated here if they were listed in Scheven's *Bibliographies for African studies* **(G24).** But even for ethnic group bibliographies, most entries listed were published after Scheven. Earlier bibliographies are included only when they are needed to advance an argument or discussion in *Fieldwork in the Library* about how to use African reference sources.

Reference works listing in either Portuguese, German, Italian or English-language sources tend to be strongly dominant in any single bibliography. This concentration reflects variations between scholarly traditions in work completed in each of these languages. For archaeology, Robertshaw's *A history of African archaeology* **(G84)** provides full documentation for an argument that the variable scholarly traditions prevail in different parts of Africa (south, east, west, central). He examines the impact of different scholarly traditions on the study of Africa across a wide range of topical interests to demonstrate the immense variation in theoretical and technological traditions in the current study of African archaeology. See also the annotated survey of Shaw's "African archaeology" **(G07),** which can provide the reader a selective guide to this literature. In ethnography, the contrast in academic tradition between Yves Bonnefoy's *Mythologies* **(D36)** and the tradition of English-language research identified in Ofori *Black African traditional religions and philosophy* **(G61)** invites a comparison of two different approaches to the investigation of religious and philosophical knowledge. Other sources that contribute to an understanding of the variable academic traditions would include Jürgen Zwernemann's *Culture history and African anthropology: A century of research in Germany and Austria* (Uppsala, Sweden: Universitet, 1983 [170p.]) and Wim M. J. van Blinsbergen's *Dutch anthropology of Sub-Saharan Africa in the 1970's* (Leiden, Netherlands: African Studies Centre, 1982 [40p.]) (Rijksuniversiteit Leiden Afrika Studiecentrum, no.1982/16).

In searching bibliographic guides, consult first Duignan's *Guide to research and reference works on Sub-Saharan Africa* **(G12).** This indispensable work can be brought up to date by consulting two recent companion works: McIlwaine's *Africa* **(G96)** for informational reference works and Scheven's *Bibliographies for African studies* **(G24)** for bibliographies. As a companion guide to French-language reference sources, consult first Biebuyck's *The arts of central Africa* **(G01),** which is especially sensitive to ethnic-group studies.

To master a strategy for searching for African material in *Fieldwork in the Library,* start with the headnote to chapter 1, "What Every Anthropologist Needs to Know," and move across chapters into the guides cited in chapter 3, "Archaeology and Material Culture," chapter 4, "Ethnology and Cultural Anthropology," chapter 5, "Linguistics," and chapter 6, "Physical and Biological Anthropology."

The reference works covered under the chapters organized by discipline free us to concentrate on descriptions of ethnic-group behavior and on informational reference sources specific to African anthropology. With this narrow interest, the value of the basic resources could be described as follows: use Scheven's *Bibliographies for African studies* **(G24)** for bibliographies of bibliographies of ethnic groups. Use McIlwaine's *Africa* **(G96)** to identify ethnic-group maps and detailed gazetteers, and more general handbooks.

In searching bibliographic guides to Africa, Biebuyck's *The arts of central Africa* **(G01)** provides the best entry into French-language bibliographies and Gosebrink's "Bibliography and sources for African studies" **(G02)** provides a concise introduction organized by form into English-language indexes and informational reference sources. Stanley's "Documenting material culture" **(G03)** provides an essential guide for the identification of tribal name entry into studies of material culture.

For current awareness, consult the select list of scholarly journals described in entries **(G04)** through **(G12).** Additionally, anthropologists with a vigorous interest in current ethnographic and archaeological reports will almost always find something interesting in Stanley's *The arts of Africa* **(G36).** The quarterly issues of *Anthropological index* **(A35)** provide a resource for scanning published titles in scholarly journals under culture area headings.

In retrospective searches, Gibson's masterly "A bibliography of anthropological bibliographies" **(G23)** is basic. This list is not expanded in the Library-Anthropology Resource Group's *Anthropological bibliographies* **(A21),** which brings coverage to 1980. In any search for African reference materials, consult, once again, Scheven's *Bibliographies for African studies* **(G24).**

The most comprehensive retrospective indexing of articles in periodical publications is found in the Library of Congress's *Index to periodical literature* **(G21),** which has ethnic-group, geographic, and topical entries. For retrospective depth in monographs, consult the School of Oriental and African Studies, *Library catalogue* **(G17).** For tribal or ethnic-group entry to monographs, consult the Frankfurt Municipal and University Library's *Subject catalog* **(G14).**

Find additional retrospective subject entry in the annual bibliographies, **(G26)** through **(G30).** Again, consult also companion resources described only in chapters 1–6 under the appropriate search headings.

In approaching "Retrospective Bibliographies —Topical," we can concentrate on ethnic-group entry to resources published either before or after Scheven. Listed under "Art," find entries **(G31)** through **(G36);** under "Linguistics," find entries **(G37)** through **(G41);** and under "Other Topics," find entries **(G42)** through **(G73).** No search for select bibliographies with ethnic entry, however, can safely ignore Scheven's *Bibliographies for African studies* **(G24)** and Porgès's *Sources d'information sur l'Afrique noire francophone et Madagascar* **(G75).**

In informational searches using directories, consult first Porgès's *Sources d'information sur l'Afrique noire francophone et Madagascar* **(G75),** the International African Institute's *International guide to African studies research* **(G74),** and the many directories listed in chapters 1–6.

Under the subheading "Encyclopedias, Compendiums, Handbooks," inspect the entries **(G76)** through **(G87).** State-of-the-art reviews are listed between entries **(G88)** and **(G92),** and can be profitably supported by consulting resources listed in chapter 1.

Searching graphic materials can start with examination of entries listed from **(G93)** through **(G101),** and searching unpublished materials will find resources in the entries described between **(G102)** and **(G109),** and under "Dissertations," **(G110)** through **(G114).**

Searching Bibliographic Guides

In a search for anthropological literature, all bibliographic guides listed in this chapter should be treated as supplementary to the resources listed in Auckland's "Getting into the literature" **(A01).**

Bibliographic Guides to African Studies

For more recent identification of ethnic-group bibliographies for an expanded entry into the literature of material culture, consult Stanley's "Documenting material culture" **(G03),** which has a range far beyond the scope of its title; Scheven's *Bibliographies for African studies* **(G24);** and the following:

G01

Biebuyck, Daniel P. *The arts of central Africa: An annotated bibliography.* Boston: Hall, 1987. 300p. (Reference publications in art history)

Best available guide for ethnographic, archaeological, and linguistics searches that focus on the French-speaking area of Africa. Includes a well-constructed guide to general references, government publications, newspapers and periodicals, all classes of bibliography, theses and dissertations, Human Relation Area Files, and film and museum collections. Lists in appropriate subsections many French-language attempts to summarize knowledge about an ethnic group. These resources were prepared and published as an exhaustive review and supported by extensive bibliographic coverage. Many of these entries reflect what at the time was an international effort to prepare a base from which the United Nations would assume responsibility for bibliographic control of anthropological literature on an international scale. Examples would include Biebuyck's description of the ethnographic content in Jean Claude Willame and Benoît Verhaegen, *Les provinces du Congo: Structure et fonctionnement,* v.1– , 1964– (Leopòldville: Université Lovanium) contains ethnographic studies of some of the indigenous ethnic groups of the Congo. (1) *Kwilu, Luluabourg, Nord Katanga, Ubangi,* 1964 [184p.]), which includes short ethnographic summaries of work on groups in southern and northwestern Zaire. (2) *Lomani-Kivu central,* 1964 [198p.], with its succinct ethnographic syntheses on groups in the Lomami and central Kivu regions. (3) *Moyen Congo-Sankuru,* 1965 [145p.], with its short ethnographic syntheses for the Mbuja, Ngombe, Tetela-Hamba, and Riverain groups. (4) *Nord Kivu, Làc Léopold II,* 1964 [172p.], which can be consulted for its brief ethnographic study on peoples in the Maindombe and northern Kivu regions.

G02

Gosebrink, Jean E. Meeh. "Bibliography and sources for African studies." In *Africa,* ed. by Phyllis M. Martin and Patrick O'Meara, p.381–439. 2d ed. London: Macmillan, 1987. 456p.

Well constructed as a guide into eighteen broad topical interests, (e.g., history, sociology, etc.), with discussions of (1) bibliographies, (2) continuing sources, (3) the major journals in the field, and (4) selective reading lists (600 items) with many annotations. Includes Marxist contributions. This work does not supersede an earlier guide to African literature prepared for a 1977 edition of collected essays with the same editors under the same title, *Africa* (Bloomington: Indiana Univ. Pr., 1977 [482p.]). Anthropologists will find here useful special features such as a list of titles on Africa issued in the monographic series, case studies in cultural anthropology, and a list of reference sources for ethnographic films. The indexes are professionally structured.

For a recent and masterly guide to research in Africa in all scholarly languages, consult Porgès's *Sources d'information sur l'Afrique noire francophone et Madagascar* **(G75).** For any literature search about Africa, consult Scheven's *Bibliographies for African studies* **(G24).** For more recent examples of more specialized guides, consult (1) Janet Stanley's "Documenting material culture," in *African resources and collections: Three decades of development and achievement: A festschrift in honor of Hans Panofsky,* p.118–50, ed. by Julian W. Witherell (Metuchen, N.J.: Scarecrow, 1989 [257p.]) **(G03),** especially valuable for its long, detailed analyses of the most valuable reference sources.

Searching for Current Materials

Anthropologists with a vigorous interest in current ethnographic and archaeological reports will almost always find something interesting in the continuing bibliography, Stanley's *The arts of Africa* **(G36).** The quarterly issues of *Anthropological index* **(A35)** capture recently published titles in scholarly journals under culture area headings. At a more general level, research published in African academic journals and reflecting the concerns of African scholars can be identified in *Index of African social science periodical articles* (Dakar: Council for the Development of Economic and Social Research in Africa [CODESRIA]). It has indexed twenty-four periodicals published in Africa in English and French descriptors.

For special current awareness features of scholarly journals, inspect first the Royal Anthropological Institute's *Reference list of current periodicals* **(A14),** which arranges listings in any issue by culture area to identify a select list of articles from journals on a specialized topic in a particular culture area.

Select Sources of Review in Scholarly Publications

For an understanding of the recent elaboration in book reviews on Africa, inspect the extensive annotated bibliography of sources for book reviews on Africa in *African book publishing record* (Oxford, England: Hans Zell) 6(3)(4) (1980), p.183–88, in a special issue titled *Publishing in Africa in the eighties.* For additional select lists of scholarly journals with specialized topical coverage, consult once more Scheven's *Bibliographies for African studies* **(G24),** Gosebrink's "Bibliography and sources for African studies" **(G02),** and Duignan's *Guide to research and reference works on Sub-Saharan Africa* **(G12).**

G04

Africa: Journal of the International Institute of African Languages and Cultures. v.1– , 1928– . London: International African Institute. Quarterly.

Title varies. Longer reviews are published under the heading "Review articles." The section "Review of books" usually has eight to ten reviews, with coverage reflecting the substantive interests of this journal, including a focus on technological change, religion and ritual, social organization, kinship groups, customs of social life, trade activities, and fossils. The editorials command respect as a regular forum for a literate discussion of current research issues. This journal maintains a high standard of readability even on the most technical issues.

G05

African affairs: Journal of the Royal African Society. v.1– , 1901– . London: Oxford Univ. Pr. for the Royal African Society. Quarterly.

Official journal of the society and a long-standing forum for discussion of African problems. Features book reviews and a current but select international bibliography by the librarian of the Royal Commonwealth Society. Especially valuable for its contemporary focus on urban anthropology. See also *African urban studies,* v.1– , 1966– (East Lansing: African Studies Center, Michigan State University). 3/yr.

G06

The African archaeological review. v.1– , 1983– . Cambridge, England: Cambridge Univ. Pr. Annual.

Includes reports of research in progress, abstracts of theses, and lists of publications received for archaeology of Africa and neighboring islands. Covers all aspects of archaeological reporting and provides a forum for theoretical and methodological discussion. Excludes works on human biology and North African civilizations. Many definitive reviews such as Thurstan Shaw's "African archaeology: Looking back and looking forward" 7 (1989):3–31 **(G07)** remarkable for its short English and French résumés, which the author calls "histograms of important works," described here to illustrate the kind of selective review that often appears in the substantive content of this journal.

G08

"African notes and news." In *African research and documentation: The Journal of the African Studies Association of the UK and the Standing Conference on Library Materials on Africa (London), ASAUK and SCOLMA.* v.1– , 1973– . London: The African Studies Association. 3/yr.

A regular feature in all issues covers current activities of the society and other institutions. Each issue has either bibliographic essays or book reviews, and some issues could stand alone as reference works. A continuing source for coverage of theses in English on Africa in U.K. universities. Some issues are monographic in scope. Inspect v.55, *Nigeria in archives,* especially for the work of T. A. Barringer's "The Royal Commonwealth Society" 55 (1991): 21–22 **(G09).**

G10

ASA news. v.1– , 1981– . Los Angeles: African Studies Association. Quarterly.

Former title: *African studies newsletter* (1976–80). Reports association activities, grants, awards, meetings, and information about foreign research institutions. One department lists publications received, and another identifies new reference sources.

G11

Studies in African linguistics. v.1– , 1970– . Los Angeles: Department of Linguistics and the African Studies Center, UCLA. Quarterly.

In addition to its coverage of substantive scholarship, this journal publishes summaries of important symposia and conferences. There are brief descriptive summaries of books, serial publications, and proceedings. Indexed by language in the third issue of each volume.

Selective Lists of Scholarly Journals

Appropriate titles can be identified in "A list of abstracting services together with full titles of each publication," in Library of Congress, Reference Department, *Africa south of the Sahara,* p.ix–xxxvii **(G21),** and the following volumes:

G12

Duignan, Peter, ed. *Guide to research and reference works on Sub-Saharan Africa.* Stanford, Calif.: Hoover Institution Pr., Stanford Univ., 1971. 1,102p. (Stanford University. Hoover Institution on War, Revolution, and Peace. Bibliographical series, v.46)

Almost without exception, each of the many subsections in this work lists continuing sources. Provides excellent annotations with accurate descriptions of scholarly journals and reference sources in a classed arrangement displayed in a table of contents. This feature can be updated by consulting "Continuing sources" at the end of each classified section in Scheven's *Bibliographies for African studies* **(G24).**

Also useful, especially for its indexing and for its lengthy annotations, is the Library of Congress's *Sub-Saharan Africa: A guide to serials* (Washington, D.C.: Library of Congress, 1970 [409p.]). In the subject index, ANTHROPOLOGY has thirty-three items; ARCHAEOLOGY eleven items; LINGUISTICS twenty-eight items; PALEONTOLOGY two items. The index to publications by sponsoring organization identifies institutional concentration on African studies that includes a publishing tradition.

Retrospective Searches

The published Tozzer Library's *Author and subject catalogues of the Tozzer Library* [microfiche] **(A26),** the Peabody Library's *Catalogue: Subjects* **(A17),** and the British Museum, Museum of Mankind Library's *Museum of Mankind Library catalogues* [microfiche] **(A25)** provide author and classified subject entry into all aspects of anthropology and are described in chapter 1. Human Relations Area Files, *HRAF source bibliography* **(D16)** and the UNESCO

International bibliography of social and cultural anthropology **(D20)** provide some author and classified subject entry into all aspects of anthropology but are listed in chapter 4, where they can most powerfully support a search strategy in "Ethnology/Cultural Anthropology."

Retrospective Bibliographies

For the years beyond the cutoff date of Scheven's *Bibliographies for African studies* **(G24),** the continuing bibliography of bibliographies "African reference works" **(G22)** and *ASA news* **(G10)** can be usefully consulted. Consult also the heading "Continuing sources" at the end of each classified section in Scheven's *Bibliographies for African studies* **(G24).** Both the Frankfurt Municipal and University Library's *Subject catalog: Africa* **(G14)** and the retrospective volumes of the annual published bibliographies of the Musée de l'Afrique Centrale (formerly Musée Royal du Congo Belge), *Bibliographie ethnographique du congo belge et des regions avoisinantes* **(G15),** are indispensable ethnographic reference sources for all of east, west, and central Africa. Consult resources listed in chapter 1, "What Every Anthropologist Needs to Know." If the name of one investigator of importance has been identified, for author entries to 1987 and for monographs and periodical articles to 1983, consult Harvard University, Tozzer Library (formerly Harvard University, Peabody Museum of Archaeology and Ethnology, Library) **(A26).**

Consult the tribal entries in Museum of Mankind's "Tribal index" **(D13).** Consult also the retrospective volumes of such continuing services as *Abstracts in German anthropology* **(A33),** *Anthropological literature* **(A36),** *Anthropological index* **(A35),** *Francis bulletin signalétique* **(A34),** and the *MLA international bibliography of books and articles on the modern languages and literatures* **(A37).**

For ethnic-group entry, some of the most useful resources are described in chapter 4, "Ethnology/Cultural Anthropology." For continuing coverage of the intentional periodical output, consult *Anthropological literature* **(A36),** *Anthropological index* **(A35),** and *Abstracts in anthropology* **(A32).** See also the British Museum, Museum of Mankind Library's *Museum of Mankind Library catalogues* [microfiche] **(A25)** and the *HRAF source bibliography* **(D16).** For subject entry, these resources can be used as companions to additional references listed in chapter 3, "Archaeology and Material Culture," and chapter 4, "Anthropological Linguistics."

In any search of resources on Africa listed in *Fieldwork in the Library,* consult the many recent entries in Scheven's *Bibliographies for African studies* **(G24)** or Porgès's *Sources d'information sur l'Afrique noire francophone et Madagascar* **(G75)** which are not repeated here. Listed here are a number of resources published either after the cutoff date for entries or before the starting date of coverage by Scheven.

G13

Deutsches Übersee Institut. Hamburg. *Läederkatalog Afrika der Übersee. Dokumentation Hamburg, 1971–1984.* Munich: K. G. Saur, 1986. 231 microfiche.

Lists 59,500 titles with 250,000 entry words. Monographs, periodical articles, and book chapters are covered. Periodicals and book chapters make up 60 percent of the entries. The library continues the acquisition and cataloging policies that created this basic set. Supplements are technically possible.

The following sources are described here because they provide ethnic-group entry.

G14

Frankfurt Municipal and University Library. *Subject catalog: Africa.* New York and Munich: K. G. Saur; dist. by Gale, 1975–81.

Sometimes entered in the catalog files of research libraries under parallel author/title as Stadt- und Universitätsbibliothek. Frankfurt am Main. *Fachkatalog Afrika.* Reproduction of catalog cards of the Africa collection of the Frankfurt Municipal and University Library. Introduction in English, German, and French. V. 4, *Kulturanthropologie (Völkerkunde, kulturgeschichte, religion, kunst, afrikanische völker) = Social and cultural anthropology* (1980) has entries for 7,000 works in all languages on the ethnology, religion, cultural history, art, and peoples of Africa south of the Sahara. Includes many doctoral dissertations. There is an ethnic names index which exploits the fact that the library's holdings are coded for ethnic groups. A second list intersperses English and German keywords used in the classification of material in the collection. Also of interest: v.6, *Sprachen, linguistik* (1981). These volumes can be supplemented by reference to Otto H. Spohr and M. R. Poller's *German Africana: German publications on south and southwest Africa* (Pretoria: State Library, 1968 [332p.]), which includes an author listing with subject index.

G15

Musée Royal du Congo Belge. *Bibliographie ethnographique du Congo Belge et des regions avoisinantes.* 14v. Tervuren, Belgium: Musée Royal du Congo Belge, 1925/30–50.

Books and articles published 1925–46; alphabetically arranged and annotated with topical and ethnic indexes. Followed by Musée Royal du Congo Belge, *Bibliographie ethnographique du Congo Belge et des regions avoisinantes* (Tervuren, Belgium: Musée Royal du Congo Belge, 1952–59 [10 vols.]), an annotated bibliography organized to cover the years 1947 through 1957 and indexed for ethnic groups, topical entries, authors' names, and cross-references. Followed by Musée Royal de l'Afrique Centrale's *Bibliographie ethnographique de l'Afrique sud-saharienne* (Tervuren: Musée Royal de l'Afrique Centrale, 1962–81 [18v.]) **(G16)** followed by additions for the years 1960 through 1977 under the new title *Bibliographie de l'Afrique sud-saharienne, sciences humaines et sociales* **(G26),** which corresponds to its expansion of bibliographic coverage to include all areas south of Saharan Africa, excluding only Ethiopia, Somalia, and the Malagasy Republic. The format, beginning with the 1967 bibliography, presents each title alphabetically as an index card. A general index lists topics, countries, regions, and ethnic groups in annual editions.

G17

University of London. School of Oriental and African Studies. *Library catalogue.* Boston: Hall, 1963. 28v. With hardcover supplements 1–3, 1968–79. 51v.

British Africa covered in great depth. Classified arrangement by country, subdivided by subject, with ethnic-group indexes that have exceptional value for both anthropological linguistics and cultural anthropology.

G18

University of London. School of Oriental and African Studies. *Library catalogue: The fourth supplement, 1978–1984.* Zug, Switzerland: IDC, 1985. Microfiche edition.

This supplement of 430,000 cards includes the compete SOAS manuscript catalog. Main entry with author and subject catalogs.

Retrospective Searches for Periodical Articles

G19

Asamani, J. O. *Index Africanus.* Stanford, Calif.: Hoover Institution Pr., 1975. 659p. (Stanford Univ. Hoover Institution on War, Revolution, and Peace. Bibliographical series, v.53)

Covers 1885–1965. Significant articles from 200 journals, twenty memorial volumes, and sixty-eight proceedings of conferences organized by geographical area and further subdivided by subject. Lists 24,600 entries covering even such remote areas as the islands of Tristan da Cunha and Mauritius. Omits articles dealing with Islamic civilization. Compiled at School of Oriental and African Studies, University of London. Author index but no subject index. For ethnic-group entry into monographic works in this library's collection, consult the School of Oriental and African Studies, *Library catalogue* **(G17)** and **(G18).**

G20

International African Institute. Library. *Cumulative bibliography of African studies.* Boston: Hall, 1973. 5v.

Uses a divided author and subject catalog. Provides access to articles published on Africa from 1920 to 1970, and in the International African Bibliography for 1971 and 1972. Classified arrangement. The absence of running heads makes this reference source difficult to use. Organized by country and then by district and ethnic group thereunder. Provides a cumulative subject entry to most of the quarterly issues of *African abstracts,* v.1–23, 1950–1972 (London: International African Institute), consolidating many of that publication's achievements in ethnic-group indexing. Each volume has general, ethnic, and author indexes. Ceased publication with v.23 (1972).

G21

Library of Congress. African Section. General Reference and Bibliography Division. Reference Department. *Africa south of the Sahara: Index to periodical literature, 1900–1970.* Boston: Hall, 1971. 4v. With supplements. Available on microfilm, also from Hall.

A reference source of the first importance. Most effectively used as a part of a companion to more recent ethnic-group reference works identified in Scheven's *Bibliographies for African studies* **(G24)** which are not repeated in *Fieldwork in the Library.* It is a working file generously shared with the scholarly community. It is not user-friendly in all ways; the effort required to use it accurately, however, will reward the student of scholarly work if ethnic-group entries are needed. For example: in many cases, the heading card (photographed) includes a reference to the relevant chapter or item in Murdock's *Africa* **(G81)** and a citation, in abbreviated form, to the approximate volume of the several series of Forde's *Ethnographic survey of Africa* **(G80).** To illustrate, find under SENEGAL, ANTHROPOLOGY AND ETHNOLOGY, a subdivision for WOLOF (OUOLOF) with the notations Murdock–34:12 and Esw 14 (v.3:601). These citations refer respectively to chapter 34, item 12, of Murdock's *Africa* **(G81)** and Forde's *Ethnographic survey of Africa* **(G80).** This working file offers an international cumulated entry that can be found nowhere else. Some people have been critical of coding, which makes it difficult to use, and of the nonstandardized format. When research libraries hold this publication, Murdock's *Africa* **(G81)** is often nowhere to be found in the reference collection and missing in the stacks. It is difficult to believe that this resource is being effectively used.

First supplement (1973) covers items added from January 1971 to June 1972. In the "Introduction" to volume 1 of the *First supplement,* there is a list of the abbreviations used by the major abstracting services, together with the full title of each publication (p.ix–xxxvii). This is a working file constructed with cutouts from several abstracting services. The abbreviation for a specific journal may vary between entries because the cutouts can be extracted from different indexing or abstracting services that use different abbreviations. It also contains an alphabetical list of personal authors. The list of ethnic groups has cross-references to variant names and to the discussion of each ethnic group in Murdock's *Africa* **(G81).** A *Second supplement* providing coverage through 1976 in three volumes was published in 1982. A *Third supplement* abandons the working file format in a costly effort to cover the one year 1977. After a nine-year time lag, it was published in 1985 as African Section, African and Middle Eastern Division, *Africa south of the Sahara: Index to periodical literature,* 3d supplement (Washington, D.C.: Library of Congress, 1985 [306p.]), and has not been continued. In response to a call for higher standards, the economics of using a working file were abandoned and the scholarly community now has nothing. However, this unit of LC has returned to a working-file card catalog that provides entry to the contents of 3,000 journals with a gap of several years in its coverage, and some effort is being made to reconstruct the period when it was discontinued. It is available at the site.

The basic arrangement is by area (region and country), with subheadings of ANTHROPOLOGY AND ETHNOLOGY and LANGUAGE AND LINGUISTICS. These terms are expanded to provide entry by ethnic group. The original indexing of journals received by the Library of Congress did not start until 1960. As discussed above, a working file with great variation in entries can confuse a casual user. Nevertheless, many journals covered here are not adequately indexed in other sources, and the inclusion of Russian- and French-language bibliographic services beginning in 1960 greatly expanded the range of its retrospective coverage.

A recent effort supplements this resource with monographic titles: U.S. Library of Congress, Research Services, *U.S. imprints on Sub-Saharan Africa: A guide to publications catalogued at the Library of Congress;* 652 titles in the first issue, arranged by main entry with title and subject indexes. The LC policy of detailing bibliographies in the notes gives this resource added depth since it can sometimes be used to locate bibliographies of a subject so specialized in a monograph.

Retrospective Bibliographies—Bibliographies of Bibliographies

G22

"African reference works." *African book publishing record.* 1975– . Oxford, England: Hans Zell. Annual.

Since 1987, this special feature has organized concise annotations of select items into the following classified arrangement: Guides to bibliographies, review essays, bibliographies by subject and by region, directories, dictionaries, encyclopedias, geographical sources, handbooks and manuals, bibliographies, and guides to archival sources. This department places a strong emphasis on English-language sources and excludes from comprehensive coverage both north and south Africa.

G23

Gibson, Gordon D. "A bibliography of anthropological bibliographies: Africa." *Current anthropology* 10 (1969): 527–66.

A research aid of exceptional importance. A thorough list of 872 bibliographies published prior to 1969. As used here, anthropology comprises ethnography and ethnology, culture history, historic archaeology, prehistory, folklore, linguistics, race, and ancient humanity. Rules governing exclusion are explicitly and carefully stated. Brief but carefully written annotations for each entry pinpoint specialized topics and areas, and itemize the number of entries in each listed bibliography. Techniques for facilitating access to this bibliography include: Geographical arrangement supplemented by an index of subjects, authors, and, when necessary, the names of periodicals. This work establishes a bibliographic base that could be updated by the *International bibliography of social and cultural anthropology* **(D20)** and the Library-Anthropology Resource Group's *Anthropological bibliographies* **(A21).** Since nearly all of the entries in Gibson's list are repeated in Duignan's *Guide to research and reference works on Sub-Saharan Africa* **(G12),** Duignan's classified arrangement can be said to provide an alternate subject entry into Gibson's list. For recent bibliographies of bibliographies, consult Scheven's *Bibliographies for African studies* **(G24),** *ASA news* **(G10),** and "African reference works" **(G22).**

G24

Scheven, Yvette. *Bibliographies for African studies, 1970–1986.* London and New York: Hans Zell, 1988. 815p.

A reference source of the first importance in any serious literature search for African materials. Benefits from superb organization and critical annotations of exceptional insight and relevance to the materials. Organization provides both topical and geographic arrangement, with continuing bibliographies cited at the end of each section. The detailed author, title, and subject indexes (p.557–615) are a model of excellence. Gives the term DISSERTATION subdivision by fifty-six terms. ETHNIC GROUPS as a general term refers to a chapter with fifty-four entries. The index then expands for thirteen additional entries divided by geographic terms. Most chapter headings in this work lead to an entry that identifies some published bibliography touching on anthropological topics. Each bibliography is entered only once. Searches can profitably be expanded through several levels of generality and through alternative topical concepts. An illustration of the value that can accrue from multiple entries for materials of anthropological importance follows.

Listed in Scheven's *Bibliographies for African studies* **(G24),** under "Nigeria," find a listing for Ita's *Bibliography of Nigeria* **(G54).** Notice that this entry does not appear in Scheven's chapter on anthropology, even though it has an ethnic-group index to 5,411 richly annotated items and includes anthropologically significant Islamic materials.

Retrospective Bibliographies—Biographical Directories

In ethnic group searches only a limited number of scholars have produced ethnographic and linguistic studies of individual ethnic groups.

Therefore, when an author is identified as relevant to a particular ethnic group, it is often useful to look for more complete bibliographies of research by that author.

To start a comprehensive author search, go to chapter 1, "What Every Anthropologist Needs to Know," and consult Winters and the Library-Anthropology Resource Group's *International directory of anthropology* **(A22)** and Mann and the Library-Anthropology Resource Group's *Biographical directory of anthropologists born before 1920* **(A23).** For many individuals, a comprehensive published bibliography will be published in the obituaries that are cited. In the same chapter, consult also the author entry to Tozzer Library's *Catalogues* **(A26);** and the British Museum, Museum of Mankind Library's *Museum of Mankind Library catalogues* [microfiche] **(A25).** Because of its strong African collection and its comprehensive coverage of German-language works, the Frankfurt Municipal and University Library's *Subject catalog* **(G14)** can be useful in expanding entries in a list of some authors' published work. Since only a few trained scholars work with each tribe, this can be an important method of identifying additional studies about an ethnic group.

G25

Hodder-Williams, Richard, ed. *A directory of Africanists in Britain.* Bristol, England: Published on behalf of the Royal African Society by the Univ. of Bristol, 1991. 141p.

Lists 512 scholars. Biographical information for each entry includes a list of publications and a statement of research interests. Indexed by discipline and country of interest.

Retrospective Bibliographies—Continuing Bibliographies

Consult chapter 1, "What Every Anthropologist Needs to Know," especially Tozzer Library's *Catalogues* [microfiche] **(A26)** and the continuing services *Abstracts in German anthropology* **(A33),** *Anthropological literature* **(A36),** *Anthropological index* **(A35),** *Francis bulletin signalétique* **(A34),** and the Modern Language Association's *MLA international bibliography of books and articles on the modern languages and literatures* **(A37).** For subject entry these resources should find additional support in the references listed in chapter 3, "Archaeology and Material Culture," and chapter 5, "Anthropological Linguistics."

To expand the basic inventory of indexing services listed here, consult Gibson's "A bibliography of anthropological bibliographies" **(G23),** which, in "Periodical," identifies seventeen continuing sources to use in searches for the anthropological literature of Africa. He includes Islamic materials.

G26

Bibliographie de l'Afrique sud-saharienne, sciences humaines et sociales: Périodiques. Tervuren, Belgium: Musée Royal de l'Afrique Centrale, 1932– . Annual supplement.

Title 1925–59: *Bibliographie ethnographique du Congo Belge et regions avoisinantes.* Most items are annotated. Beginning in 1986 (for the volume covering 1981–83 publications), indexes only journal articles. These issues are international in coverage of an area that extends to all of the regions south of the Sahara, except for the area around the Horn of Africa. Can be supplemented with *Bulletin bibliographique: List d'acquisitions,* v.1– , 1985– (Brussels: Centre d'Étude et de Documentation), a semiannual with separate sections for monographs, theses, articles and papers, and government documents, which is now edited by Marcel d'Hertefelt and Anne-Marie Bouttiaux-Ndiaye.

G27

Blackhurst, Hector, comp. *Africa bibliography.* v.1– , 1984– . Manchester, England: Manchester Univ. Pr. in cooperation with the International African Institute.

Articles, books, and essays in edited volumes. Classified arrangement. A general section is followed by topical sections. Next a geographical arrangement is subdivided by topic. Only fiction and poetry are excluded. There is an anthropological perspective even in the selection of material from related disciplines. English-language sources are heavily favored over French- and German-language contributions. The first volume was sometimes cataloged as a monograph. Author and subject indexes.

G28

"Information bibliographiques." *Journal de la Société des Africanistes.* v.1– , 1931– . Paris: Musée de l'Homme for the Société des africanistes. Semiannual.

Includes a bibliography of bibliographies, separate bibliographies, and other information on published and ongoing research. Emphasizes archaeology, prehistory, anthropology, ethnography, linguistics, and sociology. Includes some items from history and geography. See also *Bibliographie des travaux en langue française sur l'Afrique au sud du sahara: Sciences humaines et sociales,* v.1– , 1977– (Paris: Centre d'analyse et du Recherche Documentaires pour l'Afrique noire (CARDAN), École des hautes études en sciences sociales, Centre d'études africaines). For many years CARDAN was integrated into the indexing of the Library of Congress, Reference Department, *Africa south of the Sahara* **(G21).** For some regions, the ethnic group name authority files for CARDAN can be identified in McIlwaine's *Africa* **(G96).**

G29

International African bibliography: Current books, articles and papers in African studies. v.1– , 1971– . London: Mansell. Quarterly.

Also available in a microform edition. Previously appeared as "Bibliography of current publications" in *Africa* **(G04)** for the years 1928–70. Sections: "Africa (general subdivided by topics) history"; "Ethnography"; "Anthropology and sociology"; "Religion and philosophy"; "Languages and literature"; "Economics and development"; "Politics and law"; "Education"; and regional coverage of "North Africa (excluding Egypt)," "Northeast Africa," "West Africa," "West central Africa," "East Africa," "Southeast central Africa," and "Southern Africa." Entries state price and description. Annual area and subject indexes.

G30

U.S. Library of Congress. African Section. African and Middle Eastern Division, Research Services. *U.S. imprints on Sub-Saharan Africa: A guide to publications cataloged at the Library of Congress.* v.1– , 1986– . Washington, D.C.: Library of Congress. Biennial.

Around 650 monographs a year are listed alphabetically by author and then by title. Includes a directory of publishers with address information. Planned as a continuing series. For retrospective ethnic-group entry to monographs, consult the Frankfurt Municipal and University Library's *Subject catalog* **(G14)** and the University of London, School of Oriental and African Studies, *Library catalogue* **(G17)** and **(G18).**

Retrospective Bibliographies—Topical

The section is constructed on the assumption that all sources itemized in Scheven's *Bibliographies for African studies* **(G24)** have been exhausted. In that work every ethnic-group bibliography for the period covered (1970–86) can be found in the index under the more contemporary term ETHNIC. Also useful is Gibson's "A bibliography of anthropological bibliographies: Africa" **(G23)** and the superb guide issued in 1988 by Porgès, *Sources d'information sur l'Afrique noire francophone et Madagascar* **(G75).**

Retrospective Bibliographies—Art Bibliographies

Among the topical bibliographies, the African art guides and bibliographies often have an ethnic and ethnic-group perspective that gives them special value far beyond the limits of their stated purpose. For example, inspect the works in Stanley's "Documenting material culture" **(G03)** and Stanley's *Arts of Africa* **(G36).** Biebuyck's *The arts of central Africa* **(G01)** can be used as an introduction to the continuing sources that access French contributions beyond the geographic scope of the title. In chapter 4, "Ethnology/Cultural Anthropology," art dissertations in Burt's *Ethnoart* **(D82)** can be useful in searches for ethnic-group material, as is Burt's indispensable *Bibliography of ethnoarts bibliographies* **(D11).** Consult also:

G31

Africa bibliography series B (London). v.1– , 1965– . London. International African Institute. Irregular.

Includes L. J. P. Gaskin's *A bibliography of African art* (London: International African Institute,

1965, [120p.], organized alphabetically under some general rubrics but mainly according to regions, with subdivisions such as figurines and masks, buildings and furniture, clothing and adornment. Includes a list of periodicals consulted and indexes of authors, subjects, places, and ethnic groups. See also the International African Institute's *A select bibliography of music in Africa* (London: International African Institute, 1965 [83p.]), which lists 3,370 titles with sections on music, musical instruments, dance, and general works. Entries are organized by country and by type of musical instrument.

G32

De Lerma, Dominique-René. *Bibliography of black music.* Westport, Conn.: Greenwood, 1981–84. 4v.

V.3, *Geographical studies,* has a section on Africa with 2,389 items; arranged by country and indexed by author/editor, and African culture group. In other volumes of the set, there are subsections for instruments, melody and tuning, harmony and counterpoint, dance, literature, and language.

G33

Görög, Veronika. *Littérature orale d'Afrique noire: Bibliographie analytique.* Paris: Maisonneuve, 1981. 394p.

Annotates 2,883 titles in an alphabetic arrangement, with detailed indexes by ethnic and linguistic groups and by genres. Includes entries for ethnic groups south of the Sahara. Also helpful for ethnic group entry, Harold Scheub's *African oral narratives, proverbs, riddles, poetry and song* (Boston: Hall, 1971 [160p.]) **(G34),** provides another culture index to the 2,373 bibliographic entries. Elaborating on this bibliographic base, Scheub in his "A review of African oral traditions and literature," *African studies review* 28 (2/3)(1985): 1–71, references 57–72 **(G35),** guides the reader through the available primary source material so important to anthropologists. The article stresses those links between oral and written literature so important to studies of culture at a distance.

G36

Stanley, Janet, comp. *The arts of Africa: An annotated bibliography: 1986 and 1987.* v.1– , 1990– . Waltham, Mass.: Crossroads Press for the African Studies Assn. Biennial.

The first issue organizes 949 items into a classified arrangement. Future years will include the years mentioned in the title and any works newly identified from earlier years. A section with broad general subject coverage precedes a topical arrangement that includes personal adornment, textiles, metals and metalwork, rock paintings, and engravings. The regional studies are subdivided by country. Descriptive annotations for all entries. Rich with cross-references. Subject index provides access to objects, concepts, ethnic groups, museums, and individuals. Author index includes personal and corporate authors, editors, photographers, and illustrators. Also includes a special list of items recommended for purchase to strengthen a basic academic collection. OCLC numbers are given for serials cited in the bibliography.

Retrospective Bibliographies—Linguistics Bibliographies

This section should use DeMiller's *Linguistics* **(E01)** as a starting point. Many resources cited there are not repeated here. The listings in McIlwaine's *Africa* **(G96)** are helpful, although the exclusion of bibliographic guides in the case of linguistics may place some of his arguments in context.

G37

Dwyer, David J. *Resource handbook for African languages: A listing of the institutional, human, and material resources for teaching and learning of the eighty-two highest priority African languages.* East Lansing: African Studies Center, Michigan State Univ., 1986. 596p. (Eric document ED280 274)

Provides information on classification, distribution, number of speakers, learning materials, and individuals and institutions teaching the language. Evaluates available teaching materials. Index provides cross entry by country to language and by language to country.

For a less tightly structured list of 1,266 dictionaries, grammars, and teaching materials, consult: University of Virginia, Library, *African languages: A guide to the library collection of the University of Virginia* (Charlottesville: Collection Development Department, Univ. of Virginia Library, 1986 [169p.]) **(G38).**

For a select list of works in the great literary languages of Hausa and Swahili that is annotated and divided under topical classifications like society and culture, history, social change, and contemporary literature, consult "African language publications," comp. by Ahmad Getso et al., in v.2, *The African experience,* p.55–80, ed. by John N. Paden and Edward W. Soja (Evanston, Ill.: Northwestern Univ. Pr., 1970). See also Nicholas Awde's "A Hausa language and linguistic bibliography 1976–86 (including supplementary materials from other years)," in *Studies in Hausa language and linguistics in honour of F. W. Parsons,* p.252–78, ed. by Graham Furniss and Philip J. Jaggar (London and New York: Kegan Paul in association with the International African Institute, 1988 [282p.]).

G39

Mann, Michael, et al. *A thesaurus of African languages: A classified and annotated inventory of the spoken languages of Africa with an appendix on their written representation.* London: Hans Zell for the International African Institute, 1987. 325p.

Lists 2,550 languages. The conventions used (p.8–9) must be fully understood to effectively utilize this resource. Expanded index of 12,000 terms. Table 1.2, a collation of Fivaz Derek and Patricia E. Scott's *African languages: A genetic and decimalized classification for bibliographic and general reference* (Boston: Hall, 1977 [332p.]) **(G40),** attempts to integrate results of earlier studies. Inspect chapter 1 for coverage of the spoken languages in classified order; chapter 3 for arrangement by political units; chapter 4 for research and debates within the field and including a phonological analysis of approximately twenty African languages; chapter 5 for a bibliography; and chapter 6 for a six-language index.

G41

Meier, Wilma, ed. *Bibliography of African languages (Bibliographie afrikanischer sprachen).* Wiesbaden: Otto Harrassowitz, 1984. 888p.

Includes approximately 14,000 entries for monographs and articles from anthologies, journals, monographs, and congresses published prior to 1980. Includes a "Bibliography of bibliographies." The classification schedule is described in the front matter (p.li–lix). A list of periodicals from which articles have been taken appears on pages lxi–lxxi. Emphasis is on publications since 1960. Main list with full bibliographic citations is arranged alphabetically by author and then chronologically thereunder (p.2–563); includes sources on more than 2,000 languages. Cites more than 4,000 authors. The rest of the book concerns special features designed to guide the reader. There is an index arranged alphabetically by language with the authors of relevant works listed under each language entry (p.574–714). Index by language and with appropriate research itemized chronologically under each language (p.714–888).

Retrospective Bibliographies—Other Topics

Several select bibliographies that are useful in the investigation of anthropological resources about Africa are described in chapter 11, "Islamic Influence and Israel."

G42

Anafulu, Joseph C. *The Ibo-speaking peoples of southern Nigeria: A selected annotated list of writings, 1627–1970.* Munich: Kraus, 1981. 321p.

Includes Islamic material. Classified arrangement: General, then biography, exploration, history, ecology, populating and settlement, medicine and health, economy, education and rural development, culture contact and social change, archaeology, art and crafts, music, theater and dance, linguistics, literature (including folklore and works in the Ibo language), politics and government (including traditional political organization), religion (including Christian missions and traditional religions), and unpublished government reports. Author index. Subject index.

G43

Bullwinkle, Davis. *African women: A general bibliography, 1976–1985.* New York: Greenwood, 1989. 335p. (African bibliography series, 11)

An elaborate table of contents. Includes a general section followed by geographic sections subdivided by subjects including arts, cultural roles, family life, history, marital relations, religion, sexual mutilation. Includes an author index but no annotations. In expansions of the subject matter in this volume, there are two titles with the same arrangement and by the same author: *Women of northern, western and central Africa: A bibliography, 1976–1985* (New York: Greenwood, 1989 [603p.]) (African special bibliography series, v.10); and *Women in eastern and southern Africa: A bibliography 1976–1985* (New York: Greenwood, 1989 [546p.]) (African special bibliographic series, v.11).

G44

Cooperative Africana Microform Project (U.S.) *CAMP Catalog,* 1985 cumulative edition. Chicago: Cooperative Africana Microform Project and the Center for Research Libraries, 1985. 642p.

A great wealth of rare materials. Especially valuable for the identification of holdings of government monographic series. A better understanding of the scope of this project can be reached by consulting D. L. Easterbrook's "The Archives Committee and the Cooperative African Microfilm Project: A brief history," in *African resources and collections: Three decades of development and achievement: A festschrift in honor of Hans Panofsky,* p.318–88, ed. by Julian W. Witherell (Metuchen, N.J.: Scarecrow, 1989 [257p.]) **(G45),** for a lucid and concise survey of the activities of this organization.

G46

Essomba, Joseph-Marie. *Bibliographie critique de l'archéologie camerounaise.* Yaoundé, Cameroon: Librarie Universitaire, Université Yaiybdé, 1986. 132p.

Bibliographical essay followed by author list of 120 titles. For other recent archaeological bibliographies of Africa with regional coverage, consult Scheven's *Bibliographies for African studies* **(G24).**

G47

European sources for Sub-Saharan Africa before 1900: Uses and abuses. Special issue of *Paideuma* 33 (1987): 1–230.

Identifies the problems of early contact literature and some excellent sources such as Ernst van den Boogaart's "Books on black Africa: The Dutch publications and their owners in the seventeenth and eighteenth centuries" (p.114–26). Also useful is Adam Jones's *Raw, medium, well done: A critical review of editorial and quasi-editorial work on pre-1885 European sources for Sub-Saharan Africa, 1960–1986* (Madison: African Studies Program, Univ. of Wisconsin, 1987 [154p.]) (Studies in African sources, no.1) **(G48).** This work includes 100 analytic works on individual authors, and seventeen analytic works on groups of texts. Indexed by geographic region and by author. Within the context of these studies, resources of interest to anthropologists can be identified in *Sources orales de l'histoire de l'Afrique,* ed. by Claude-Hélène Perrot, Gilbert Gonnin, and Ferdinand Nahimana (Paris: Editions du Centre National de la Recherche scientifique, 1989 [228p.]).

G49

Fage, J. D. *A guide to original sources for precolonial western Africa published in European languages.* Madison: African Studies Program, Univ. of Wisconsin, 1987. 192p.

Identifies sources for early contact observations published before 1884. Attempts comprehensive coverage of the published monographs of explorers, civil servants, and missionaries. Especially valuable for its inclusion of recorded legends. Organized chronologically. Includes geographic guide to major areas. Indexed by author, editor, and translator.

G50

Gray, John. *'Ashé, traditional religion and healing in Sub-Saharan Africa and the diaspora: A classified international bibliography.* New York: Greenwood, 1989. 518p. (Bibliographies and indexes in Afro-American and African studies, no.24)

Includes books, dissertations, unpublished papers, periodical articles, films, and videotapes in seven languages. General, regional, and country coverage subdivided for ethnic groups. The appendixes provide a guide to the literature with lists of reference works, archives, and research centers. Adequately indexed by ethnic group, by subject, and by author. Consult also Harrison and Cosminsky's *Traditional medicine* **(D25)** and **(D26).** The African section of this work is subdivided by subject.

G51

Hertefelt, Marcel d', and Danielle de Lame. *Société, culture et histoire du Rwanda: Encyclopédie bibliographique 1863–1987.* Tervuren, Belgium: Musée Royale de l'Afrique Centrale, 1987. 2v. (Annales. Séries in Sciences humaines, v.124, pts.1 & 2)

Lists 5,550 monographs, collective works, and articles in alphabetic order with a subject index. Entries are annotated and the location of consulted work (including libraries) indicated.

G52

Hertefelt, Marcel d'. *African governmental systems in static and changing conditions: A bibliographic contribution to political anthropology.* Tervuren, Belgium: Musée Royal de l'Afrique Centrale, 1968. 178p.

Arranged by author with index to peoples and severely limited subject entry. Includes only the post-colonial experience.

G53

Holland, Killian. *A selected bibliography of the Masai of Kenya and Tanzania.* Montreal: East African Pastoral Systems Project. Department of Anthropology. McGill University, 1989. 28p.

This update adds 280 titles to the 1965 bibliography of the Masai by Alan Jacobs which appeared in the *African studies bulletin* 8 (3): 40–60.

G54

Ita, Nduntuei O. *Bibliography of Nigeria: A survey of anthropological and linguistic writings from the earliest times to 1966.* London: Cass, 1971. 271p.

Classified arrangement with a general section followed by a second section arranged by ethnic groups. Includes Islamic materials. Author and ethnic indexes.

G55

Jones, Ruth, ed. *Africa bibliography series A: Ethnography, sociology, linguistics, and related subjects.* v.1– , 1958– . London: The International African Institute.

Four volumes to date, with the first appearing in 1961. Each volume of these bibliographies, compiled by Ruth Jones with the assistance of a panel of consultants, integrates ethnic-group reports into an arrangement by regions which are then subdivided for contemporary political units. Volumes to date: *West Africa: General, ethnography, sociology, linguistics* (London: Royal Anthropological Institute, 1958 [116p.]); *Northeast Africa: General, ethnology, sociology, linguistics* (London: Royal Anthropological Institute, 1959 [51p.]); *East Africa: General, ethnography, sociology, linguistics* (London: Royal Anthropological Institute, 1960 [61p.]); *Southeast central Africa and Madagascar: General, ethnography/sociology, linguistics* (London: Royal Anthropological Institute, 1961 [53p.]). Each volume attempts to cover all significant work to date of publication in an arrangement that is subdivided for geographic location, then for subject. Indexes by author and ethnic and linguistic groups. Bibliographic monographs from an equivalent series that covers French-speaking Africa have been issued as Musée Royal de L'Afrique Centrale, Bureau de Documentation Ethnographic, *Publications, Serié 1: Bibliographies,* v.1– , 1932– (Tervuren, Belgium: Musée Royal de l'Afrique Centrale) **(G56).** This series was not cataloged as a series by the U.S. Library of Congress; therefore, in many American libraries these volumes have been cataloged only as separate monographs.

G57

Liniger-Goumaz, Max. *Guinea equatorial: Bibliografia general.* V.5, *Recapitulative* (References 1–8125). Genéve: Les Editions du Temps, 1986. 264p.

Bibliographies by ethnic groups, place subjects, personal names, names of organizations, and political parties or movements.

G58

Mangulu, Motingea. *Eléments de grammaire Lingombe avec une bibliographie exhaustive.* Mbandaka, Zaire: Centre Aequatoria, 1988. 88p.

Lists 56 published works and 36 unpublished works on the Ngombe people and the Lingombe language.

G59

Milkias, Paulos. *Ethiopia: A comprehensive bibliography.* Boston: Hall, 1989. 694p.

Covers almost all material on Ethiopia in English, Amharic, Tigrinya, Oromo, German, Italian, French, and Russian from the first century A.D. to 1988. Arranges 19,286 items by subject. Author index.

G60

Molnos, Angela, comp. *Cultural source materials for population planning in east Africa.* Nairobi: East African Publishing House, 1972–1973. 4v.

Includes ethnic-group bibliographies which are selective for the most scholarly resources available to the date of publication. Covers Kenya, Tanzania, and Uganda. Includes ethnic and subject indexes.

G61

Ofori, Patrick E. *Black African traditional religions and philosophy: A select bibliographic survey of the sources from the earliest times to 1974.* Nendeln, Liechtenstein: Kraus-Thompson, 1975. 421p.

Books, dissertations, and periodical articles in a classified arrangement. Regional sections are first subdivided by country, then by ethnic group, then again by ethnic group subdivided by subject. Includes traditional medicine. Consult Scheven's *Bibliographies for African studies* **(G24)** and Robert C. Mitchell and Harold W. Turner's *A comprehensive bibliography of modern African religious movements* (Evanston, Ill.: Northwestern Univ. Pr., 1966 [H32]). Supplements appeared in the *Journal of religion in Africa* 1 (3) (1968): 173–211 and 3 (3) (1969): 161–208.

G62

Owomoyela, Oyekan. *A K'i i: Yor'uba proscriptive and prescriptive proverbs.* Lanham, Md.: Univ. Pr. of America, 1988. 388p.

Simplifies 875 idiomatic expressions and proverbs to make the Yoruba language easily understood. Integrates meaning into Yoruba history and culture.

G63

Roese, P. M., and A. R. Rees. "A bibliography of Benin: A commentary on published and unpublished sources written in German." *African research and documentation* 45 (1987): 15–26; 46 (1988): 31–39; 48 (1990): 23–36.

Lists 183 annotated references. Indexes to personal names, museums, and galleries.

G64

Salamone, Frank A., and James A. McCain. *The Hausa people: A bibliography.* New Haven, Conn.: Human Relations Area Files, 1983. 2v. (HRAFlex books, MS12–001. Bibliography series)

Bibliographic essay refers to bibliography containing 1,271 items, mostly English-language. Cited materials are arranged in a classified scheme under the headings basic data, origins and subgroups, travel and history, geography and customs, religion, language, life cycle, social structure, education, the arts, government, and technology. There follows an alphabetic (by author) list (p.48–237). The data quality control codes (p.238–40) follow the system developed by Naroll and give the highest rating to field-workers who stayed in the field for several years and learned the local language. There follow extensive charts into the second volume which use this coded system to measure the quality of the work in each cited resource.

G65

Spande, Dennis. *A historical perspective on metallurgy in Africa: A bibliography.* Waltham, Mass.: Crossroads Press for the African Studies Assn., Brandeis University, 1977. 68p. (The archival and bibliographic series)

Bibliography organized in a classified arrangement. After a section on iron technology, references to iron in Africa are organized by the regions: Maghreb, northeast Africa, west Africa, west central Africa, east Africa, southern Africa. There are chapters on iron as currency and on the use of radiocarbon dating methods on iron artifacts. For a recent consolidation of research results, consult Shaw et al., *The archaeology of Africa* **(G83).**

G66

Ugochukwu, Françoise. "Contes Igbos, 1900–1987." *Journal des africanistes* 58 (1) (1988): 133–43.

A bibliography of about 185 bibliographies, monographs, theses, articles, and archives. This brief coverage exhausts the published reports on this small group, and illustrates the need in ethnic-group searches to consult, for the years beyond the cutoff date of Scheven's *Bibliographies for African studies, 1970–1986* **(G24),** the continuing bibliography of bibliographies "African reference works" **(G22)** and *ASA news* **(G10).**

G67

UNESCO. Population Information Network for Africa (POPIN-AFRICA). *Population in Africa. Country bibliography series.* v.1– , 1986– . Addis Ababa: UNESCO. Population Information Network for Africa (POPIN-AFRICA).

V.1, *Kenya population: Annotated bibliography 1975–1985* (1986 [158p.]); v.2, *La population de la région du sahel: Bibliographie annotée 1960–86* (1987 [210p.]). Uniform organization for all volumes eases comparative analysis. Subject headings include population by sex, age, and ethnic group. Other subject headings include: household and family, social organization, culture, education and information, fertility, and migration. Indexed by author, title, series, subject, and geography.

G68

Van Warmelo, Nicholas J., comp. *Anthropology of southern Africa in periodicals to 1950: An analysis and index.* Johannesburg: Witwatersrand Univ. Pr., 1977. 1,484p.

Magnificent indexes by linguistic group, place, name, and author. The linguistic group index is further subdivided by subject, ethnic group, and person.

Consult McIlwaine's *Africa* **(G96).** In recognition of the wealth of research materials developed for the south African region, McIlwaine describes and annotates seven general guides to the reference sources by R. Musiker, including the most recent R. Musiker, *South African reference works and bibliographies of 1979–83* (Johannesburg: Witwatersrand University Library, 1983 [100p.]).

Retrospective entry for ethnic groups in southern Africa can be found in Isaac Schapera's *Select bibliography of south African native life and problems* (London: Oxford Univ. Pr., 1941 [249p.]) **(G69),** with the first three supplements published by the University of Capetown School of Librarianship, Capetown, 1958–64 and available in reprint: Schapera, *Select bibliography of south African native life and problems: Modern status and conditions: Supplements 1–3, 1939–1963* (New York: Kraus Reprint, 1969 [187p.]). An additional work, the fourth supplement, *Modern status and conditions, 1964–70,* comp. by Stephanie Alman (Capetown: Univ. of Cape Town Libraries, 1974 [39p.]) (University of Cape Town, School of Librarianship. Bibliographical series) **(G70),** was based on the collections of London libraries only and omits government publications and periodical articles. To some extent this elaborate series of bibliographic supplements can be kept up to date by consulting issues of *African studies,* v.1– , 1942– (Johannesburg: Witwatersrand Univ. Pr.) **(G71),** a quarterly that includes a regular ethnographic bibliography.

G72

Webster, John B., et al. *A bibliography on Kenya.* Syracuse, N.Y.: Syracuse University for Program of Eastern African Studies, 1967. 461p. (Syracuse University. Eastern African bibliographical series, no.2)

Lists 7,210 numbered entries. Included here for its coverage of archaeology and ancient history. Includes monographs and periodical articles. Indexed by author, subject, and keyword.

G73

Wold, Haile Meskel G. *Cushitic studies: A select bibliography on ethnology, anthropology and linguistics.* Addis Ababa: World Institute of Arabic Studies, 1986. 63p.

Lists 528 books, theses, manuscripts, conference papers, microfilms. Organized by subject subdivided for geographic area. Author index.

Informational Reference Searches

Fieldwork in the Library duplicates only nine resources cited in McIlwaine's *Africa* **(G96).** This duplication of only nine entries from a list of more than 1,400 handbooks, encyclopedias, maps, and gazetteers dramatically illustrates the need to consult this bibliographic base upon which this section proceeds.

For American anthropology, consult first the *AAA guide* **(A53)** for directory information. The best international directory is still the "International directory of anthropological institutions" **(A56),** which could usefully be reissued in a new edition.

Handbooks and census reports published by the governments of the United States and Great Britain are listed under the countries they cover in McIlwaine's *Africa* **(G96)** and are not repeated here.

Again McIlwaine's *Africa* **(G96)** lists and indexes the individual volumes of the *African historical dictionaries* **(G77).** The volume editors of this series are always expert. There is a frequent but not mandatory repetition of the same general format. Each volume provides a general introduction and chronology; tables are useful to consolidate numeric information, alphabetic listing of topics, organizations, and people. The bibliographies nearly always come to half of the volume. Many of these monographs were prepared by anthropologists. For some countries covered, a quality bibliography of any size is difficult to identify. While most volumes rely heavily on English-language sources, entries in other European languages are added when that is necessary for adequate coverage. The series shows unusually loose editorial control. Quality is uneven but frequently marked by a sensitivity to anthropological resources. A serious effort is being made by the publisher to bring out new editions of these sources before they become completely out of date. A lapse of ten years does not seem unreasonable.

McIlwaine's *Africa* **(G96)** describes the individual volumes in each of the subsets of Forde's *Ethnographic survey of Africa* **(G80).** In this resource, the series and all of the subsets (but not the described individual volumes) are indexed.

Great care must be exercised in the use of other ethnic-group lists such as those in Joyce Moss and George Wilson's *Peoples of the world: Africans south of the Sahara: The culture, geographical setting, and historical background of 34 African peoples* **(G76),** when so many excellent and expanded resources are available.

Directories

A special feature of the U.S. Library of Congress's annual *U.S. imprints on Sub-Saharan Africa* **(G30)** identifies the place of publication of all listed entries. This is also a special feature of the several excellent accessions lists of the Library of Congress's acquisitions programs in Third World countries.

Directory sources listed in Scheven's *Bibliographies for African studies* **(G24),** or Porgès's *Sources d'information sur l'Afrique noire francophone et Madagascar* **(G75)** are not systematically repeated in *Fieldwork in the Library.*

G74

International African Institute. *International guide to African studies research (Études africaines: Guide international recherches).* Comp. by Philip Baker. 2d rev. and exp. ed. New York and Paris: Hans Zell for the International African Institute, 1987. 264p.

Lists 1,100 institutions. For each institution listed, provides information on the structure, aims, teaching and research staff, programs offered, degrees granted, library collections, and publications. Personnel index gives institutional affiliation of scholars and staff members. "Index of publications" inventories communication from institutions. See also the "Organization index" (p.385–409). Arranged alphabetically by country. Countries are additionally subdivided by topics such as folklore, linguistics, sociology, anthropology, and ethnology. Under these topics each organization is listed alphabetically. Indexed for ethnic group and language names. Thematic and personal name indexes.

G75

Porgès, Laurence. *Sources d'information sur l'Afrique noire francophone et Madagascar: Institutions, répertoires, bibliographies: Collection analyse des sources d'information.* Paris: Ministère de la coopération la Documentation Française, 1988. 389p.

Chapter 1 (nearly half of the book) focuses first on Africa in general and then on the identification of institutions, universities, societies, associations, archives, centers for documentation, official publications, periodicals, theses, general bibliographies, and special bibliographies. Chapter 2 (the second half of the book) identifies sources by country and provides listings organized by these geographical units of universities, archives, scientific associations, centers for documentation, official journals, general bibliographies, special bibliographies, atlases, linguistic maps, ethnologies, and societies. Richly annotated in French. Indexed for periodicals cited, databases, authors cited, and institutions listed.

Encyclopedias, Compendiums, Handbooks

The resources that are listed under the classed arrangement devised by McIlwaine's *Africa* **(G96)** are especially rich when the search is for factual material, such as authority files for ethnic group names. For example, the term LANGUAGE in the index is subdivided for countries. It identifies the indigenous name files of CARDAN in Paris, a standardization of ethnic nomenclature of Liberian and other ethnic groups. Again we rely on McIlwaine's *Africa* **(G96)** for a complete list of the individual volumes in each of the subsets of Forde's *Ethnographic survey of Africa* **(G80).** In *Fieldwork in the Library* the series and all of the subsets—but not the individual volumes—are described and indexed.

In scholarly investigations, great care must be exercised in the use of limited ethnic-group lists such as those of Joyce Moss and George Wilson's *Peoples of the world: Africans south of the Sahara. The culture, geographical setting, and historical background of 34 African peoples* (Detroit: Gale, 1991 [443p.]) **(G76).** Expanded resources are available. For example, inspect the tribal list of UNESCO's *Thematic list of descriptors: Anthropology* **(D56).**

Handbooks and census reports published by the governments of the United States and Great Britain are listed under the countries they cover in McIlwaine's *Africa* **(G96),** and are not repeated here. McIlwaine's *Africa* **(G96)** also lists and indexes the individual volumes of the *African historical dictionaries,* no.1– , 1974– (Metuchen, N.J.: Scarecrow Pr.) **(G77).** The volume editors of this series are always expert. Each volume provides a general introduction and chronology, tables to consolidate numeric information, alphabetical listing of topics, and information on organizations and people. The bibliographies usually amount to half of the volume. Many of these monographs were prepared by anthropologists.

G78

Baumann, Hermann, ed. *Völker afrikas und ihre traditionallen kulturen.* Wiesbaden: Franz Steiner, 1975–79. 2v.

A revision of Baumann's *Völkerkunde von Afrika* (Esserner, 1940 [665p.]). In this later edition, v.1 covers eight cultural provinces in southern Africa and includes twenty-five maps, and v.2 covers fourteen cultural provinces in east, west, and north Africa and includes twenty-five maps. Each section is supported by a bibliography. The section on African linguistics is followed by a list of language groups with references to a bibliography (p.345–73). The list of names refers to this bibliography. Thus the resource provides some entry into an extensive literature by ethnic-group name. The ethnic-group list developed here has been used as an authority file by the Museum of Mankind, which has maintained the most comprehensive ethnic-group indexing for monographic works in its holdings, which are strong for African ethnography. For encyclopedic coverage, these two volumes are matched only by Forde's *Ethnographic survey of Africa = Monographies ethnologiques africaines* **(G80),** which is published in several series of many volumes.

Baumann's "Register of African ethnic groups" **(G82)** indexes indigenous language words to the text. As a source of survey information on African indigenous people, Baumann's *Völker afrikas und ihre traditionallen kulturen* **(G78)** in a two-volume set matches the many-volume coverage found in Forde's *Ethnographic survey of Africa* **(G80).**

The authority list for ethnic-group names used in the British Museum, Museum of Mankind Library's *Museum of Mankind Library catlogues* [microfiche] **(A25)** can be found in Baumann's "Register of African ethnic groups" **(G82).** Variant spellings of ethnic-group names are a continuing problem in literature searches. There is a completely different authority list for ethnic-group names that is much influenced by French spelling to be found in UNESCO's *Thematic list of descriptors* **(D56).** Other standards for spelling ethnic-group names continue to be used. Murdock's *Africa* **(G81)** includes a list of ethnic groups that was used as an authority file by the Library of Congress's *Africa south of the Sahara* **(G21).** From this discussion, it clearly follows that in searching ethnic groups or languages in the literature on Africa, the standard of spelling used in each reference source needs to be identified. This information is often included in introductions.

G79

Fage, J. D. and Roland Oliver, eds. *The Cambridge history of Africa.* London and New York: Cambridge Univ. Pr., 1975–1985. 8v.

V.1, Clark, J. Desmond, ed., *From the earliest times to c. 500 B.C.;* v.2, Fage, J. D., ed., *From c. 500 B.C. to A.D. 1050;* v.3, Oliver, Roland, ed., *From c. 1050 to c. 1600;* v.4, Gray, Richard, ed., *From c. 1600 to c. 1790;* v.5, Flint, John E., ed., *From c. 1790 to c. 1870;* v.6, Oliver, R., and G. N. Sanderson, eds., *From 1870 to 1905;* v.7, Roberts, Andrew D., ed., *From 1920 to 1942;* v.8, Crowder, Mitchell, ed., *From c. 1940 to c. 1975.*

G80

Forde, Cyril Daryll, ed. *Ethnographic survey of Africa (Monographies ethnologiques africaines).* v.1– , 1958. London: International African Institute.

Subsets include individual series for each of the following areas: western Africa in English language (17v.), western Africa in French language (10v.), Madagascar (1v.), northeastern Africa (3v.), west central Africa (4v.), southern Africa (4v.), east central Africa (18v.). Belgian Congo, later Congo, later Zaire (5v.), which was also published in the series *Annales de Musée Royal du Congo Belge, Sciences de l'homme, Monographies ethnographiques* (no.2, 3, 4, 5). The western Africa French-language volumes were published solely by Presses Universitaires de France.

For descriptions of the individual volumes in each of these groups, consult first McIlwaine's *Africa* **(G96),** which lists each subseries in a geographically classed system of organization and identifies other related handbooks, including many of ethnographic importance.

This monographic series attempts a summary coverage for much of Africa. Purpose of the survey is a concise, accurate account of present knowledge of ethnic groups. Each monograph is prepared by an expert and devoted to a particular people or cluster of peoples and is supported with a bibliography that is often annotated and always comprehensive to the date of publication. All volumes follow a common format that includes a summary review of culture areas followed by an extensive bibliography that is often exhaustive for scholarly anthropological research to the date of publication. Some volumes in this series (but not the series for southern Africa or French Africa) are indexed by ethnic group, found in Jones's *Africa bibliography series A* **(G55).** The list of "International African Institute publications" identifies the volumes covered by Jones. For these entries, ethnic-group entry can be reached through indexing in the Library of Congress's *Africa south of the Sahara* **(G21).**

Widely held in American research libraries, these volumes can sometimes be identified in cataloging files only by individual volumes and not by series entry. The Library of Congress sets a standard that is widely followed, and it has had an erratic policy in the cataloging of foreign monographic series and sets, which are often cataloged without series or set entry.

G81

Murdock, George Peter. *Africa: Its people and their culture history.* New York: McGraw-Hill, 1959. 456p. Map (1 fold in pocket).

The ethnographic map is useful. Index leads to brief descriptions of 5,000 ethnic groups. Used as an authority file by Library of Congress's *Africa south of the Sahara* **(G21).** The Library of Congress uses the page numbers of Murdock's descriptions as the only ethnic group identifications in subject headings. While this is the most comprehensive English-language survey of African peoples, it fails to match the German-language consolidation achieved in Baumann's *Völker afrikas und ihre tradition-*

allen kulturen **(G78).** It is important to note that this German-language historical and ethnographic survey of Africa contains the authority list for ethnic-group names used in the British Museum, Museum of Mankind Library's *Museum of Mankind Library catalogues* [microfiche] **(A25)** and in most of the published resources based on German library collections. Consult Hermann Baumann's "Register of African ethnic groups" in Hermann Baumann, ed., *Völker Afrikas und ihre traditionallen kulturen* 2: 621–734 (Wiesbaden: Franz Steiner, 1975–79 [2v.]) **(G82).**

G83

Shaw, Thurstan, et al. *Archaeology of Africa: Food, metals, and towns.* London and New York: Routledge, 1993. 857p.

Contributions to African archaeology from a distinguished group of scholars, many in residence in African universities. There are eleven articles on pre-colonial iron making, for which see also Spande's *A historical perspective on metallurgy in Africa* **(G65).** The last inspected issue had one article on urbanization, four articles on food production, two consolidations of research in a culture area, and one study of period transaction. These articles can be usefully pondered in a framework provided by *A history of African archaeology,* ed. by Peter Robertshaw (Portsmouth, N.H.: J. Currey, 1989. [320p.]) **(G84)** and by the analysis of the differences between regional approaches and studies structured on a particular period. Consult also "A recent and comprehensive review of the difficult time sequences in Africa," which is cited in chapter 3, "Archaeology," in Parkinton's "Changing views of the late Stone Age of South Africa" **(C43).** An introduction to thirty northern Cape prehistoric sites can be found in Peter B. Beaumont and David Morris's *Guide to archaeological sites in the northern Cape* (Kimberley, South Africa: McGregor Museum, 1992 [334p.]) **(G85).**

For a more general and concise coverage of African prehistory, consult D. W. Phillipson's *African archaeology* (Cambridge, England, and New York: Cambridge Univ. Pr., 1985 [234p.]) **(G86),** supported by a list of selected references. For regional bibliographies, consult Scheven's *Bibliographies for African studies* **(G24).** Current literature of prehistory can be searched in *Historical abstracts* [computer file] **(B22),** and in resources identified in chapter 1, "What Every Anthropologist Needs to Know," and chapter 3, "Archaeology and Material Culture."

G87

Tobias, Phillip. *Olduvai Gorge.* v.7, *The skulls, endocasts and teeth of* Homo habilis. Cambridge, England: Cambridge Univ. Pr., 1991. 2v.

A treasury of data on early hominids from south and east Africa.

State-of-the-Art Reviews

Several earlier reviews invite special mention. Consult Richard P. Webner's "The Manchester School in south central Africa," *Annual review of anthropology* 13 (1984): 157–85 **(G88),** which includes 190 references to work on Gluckman's interest in social process and conflict resolution, and Keith Hart's "The social anthropology of west Africa," *Annual review of anthropology* 14 (1985): 243–72 **(G89),** which identifies 226 titles that represent the work of the last four decades.

For comparative evaluation of recent work, see the African Studies Association's *A.S.A. review of books,* v.1–6, 1975–80 (Waltham, Mass.: African Studies Assn.). Annual. In 1981, this publication, following the same format, was absorbed by *African studies review,* v.13– , April 1970– **(G90).** Many review articles and reviews grouped by theme are used to establish some critical comparisons between scholarly productions. Detailed table of contents guides the reader.

Since 1986, "African reference works" **(G22)** has included a regular feature devoted to a list of recently published review essays. In the first issue of this annual bibliography, the most frequently cited sources came from the *African studies review* **(G90)** and *Advances in world archaeology* **(C42).**

G90

African studies review. v.1– , 1967– . Waltham, Mass.: African Studies Assn. Quarterly.

Earlier title: *African studies bulletin* (1958–67). Also incorporates the older but seldom retained *Africana newsletter. A.S.A. review of books* appears as the fourth quarterly number. Strong interdisciplinary focus on developing social and political institutions. Coverage includes social customs, sex roles, minorities, and patterns of subsistence and settlement. Some of these reviews introduce highly innovative approaches. For example, consult Paul Riesman's "The person and the life cycle in African social life and thought," *African studies review* 29 (2) (1986): 71–138 **(G91),** which uses sources from several disciplines to reinterpret data relevant to an understanding of how Africans experience the activities of a person in different life cycles.

G92

Africana annual. v.15– , 1985. New York: Africana. Annual.

Published quarterly as *Africana library journal* (1970–73) and as *Africana journal* (1974–84). Includes book reviews and original bibliographies, with specialized subject and geographic coverage.

Searching Graphic Materials

Searchers for nonprint materials should consult American Geographical Society of New York, Map Department, *Index to maps in books and periodicals* **(A59)** and Heider's *Films for anthropological teaching* **(A63).**

Maps and Atlases

G93

Ajayi, J. F. Ade, and Michael Crowder. *Historical atlas of Africa.* Cambridge, England: Cambridge Univ. Pr., 1985. 167p.

Includes seventy-two full pages of maps in full color, depicting event, process, and quantitative maps. Text contributed by fifty-seven prominent historians. Index of more than 4,000 names (people, places, groups, concepts).

G94

Boone, Olga. *Carte ethnique de la Republique du Zaire: Quart sud-ouest.* Tervuren, Belgium: Musée Royal de l'Afrique Centrale, 1973. 406p.

Inventory of names (and variants), location (with maps), and published and archival sources for thirty-six ethnic clusters and groups in southwestern Zaire. A seminal work.

G95

Dalby, David. *Language map of Africa and the adjacent islands,* Prov. ed., rev. ed. London: International African Institute, 1977. 63p. 1 map on four sheets.

Compiled at the School of Oriental and African Studies, University of London. Accompanied by text and index [63p.] and including diagrammatic key to classified list of languages and dialects.

G96

McIlwaine, John. *Africa: A guide to reference materials.* London: Hans Zell, 1993. 452p. (Regional reference guides, no.1)

No other resource so completely identifies valuable maps and gazetteers for Africa. Arranged by region and by nation state thereunder. Under each national heading there is coverage of handbooks, yearbooks, statistics, and atlases and gazetteers. The subseries of Forde's *Ethnographic survey of Africa* **(G80),** for example, are spread across these headings to guide the reader in the use of this complex series.

The most useful entries for the anthropologist are those under the heading "Atlases and Gazetteers." The sources listed under handbooks can often be useful. See especially "Handbooks—Special subjects—Ethnography," starting with bibliographic entry number 51 (p.19). The appendix: "Annual reports on the British possession in Africa," compiled by I. C. McIlwaine, is a contribution to the scholarly control of valuable primary source materials. In the French language, a comparable group of materials can be found in the semiofficial publications of influential nongovernmental committees. These are included in Gloria D. Westfall's *French colonial Africa: A guide to official sources* (London: Hans Zell, 1992 [226p.]) **(G97),** which is organized into five chapters to cover guides and bibliographies, French colonial archives, publications of the Central Administration, semiofficial publications, and publications of the Colonial Government.

Difficult-to-identify, separately published authority lists for ethnic-group names are carefully described, identified, and entered into the classed arrangement. In attempting to use an ethnic-group name across reference books and across libraries, these resources can be used as companions to Freda E. Otchere's *African studies thesaurus: Subject headings for library users* (Westport, Conn.: Greenwood, 1992 [435p.]) (Bibliographies and indexes in Afro-American and African studies) **(G98),** which pulls together language and ethnic names and adds cross-references to link each name to a language family or a geographic area. She has not added terms that have not already appeared in the Library of Congress system. Her contributions rest in the construction of a system of relationships within that vocabulary which eases the test of ethnic-group identification. There is a useful discussion of the use of geographic subdivision with subject headings.

To illustrate the importance of consulting McIlwaine's *Africa* **(G96),** we list below every duplication of listed entries from that resource in *Fieldwork in the Library:*

Hodder-Williams's *A directory of Africanists in Britain* **(G25);** Mann et al., *A thesaurus of African languages* **(G39);** Derek and Scott's *African languages* **(G40);** the International African Institute's *International guide to African studies research* **(G74)** as most useful of the many directories listed by McIlwaine's *Africa* **(G96);** Baumann's *Völker afrikas und ihre traditionallen kulturen* **(G78)** as the best of many surveys listed by McIlwaine's *Africa* **(G96);** Forde's *Ethnographic survey of Africa (Monographies ethnologiques africaines)* **(G80)** as best English- or French-language survey (McIlwaine's *Africa* **(G96)** describes all volumes and spreads the subsets of this important series across a geographical arrangement, which must be used with caution since his geographical labels do not correspond to the enthnographically defined regions used by Forde); Murdock's *Africa* **(G81),** which is used as an authority file in one useful Library of Congress periodical file; Ajayi and Crowder's *Historical atlas of Africa* **(G93)** as the best of many listed in McIlwaine; Dalby's *Language map of Africa and the adjacent islands* **(G95),** because its identification codes are used by other reference sources to identify and locate ethnic groups; and *African historical dictionaries* **(G77)** because McIlwaine spreads descriptions of individual volumes across a geographical classification system and because the bibliographies of these resources are sometimes of great value to anthropologists.

Photographs and films

G99

Ballantyne, James, and Andrew Roberts. *Africa: A handbook of film and video resources.* London: British Universities Film and Video Council, 1986. 120p.

Supplementary lists are irregularly issued. Published in two parts: part 1 provides brief descriptions of the principal British collections, and part 2 lists the films in a classified arrangement (History, ethnographies, . . .). Separate indexes for titles and themes subdivided by countries. Selective bibliography (p.114–20).

G100

Roberts, Andrew, ed. *Photographs as sources for African history: Papers presented at a workshop held at the School of Oriental and African Studies, London, May 12–13, 1988.* London: School of Oriental and African Studies, 1988. 168p.

From among the fifteen papers published here, inspect especially Andrew Roberts's "A bibliography on African archival material" (p.159–69). Other contributions include discussions of the archives at the University of Durham (Sudan Archive), Oxford University, the Pitt Rivers Museum, the Basel Archives, and Port Jesus Museum.

G101

Sonuga, Gbenga, ed. *Lagos State: Life and culture.* Ikeja, Lagos, Nigeria: Ministry of Information and Culture. Government of Lagos, State of Nigeria, 1987. 197p.

Emphasis is on traditional cultures. Includes sections on chiefs and citizens, traditional occupations, arts and crafts, festivals, masks and masquerades, and the life cycle of the Yoruba.

Searching Unpublished Materials

Searches for unpublished materials often benefit from an inspection of the National Anthropological Archives **(A69).**

At Oxford University the Colonial Records Project in the Commonwealth section of the Bodleian Library at Rhodes House collects and prepares for use by scholars privately held papers of value to research about the British colonial period. The collection includes diaries, correspondence, reports, and unpublished reminiscences. Accession lists are available. See also Barringer's "The Royal Commonwealth Society" **(G09),** Easterbrook's "The Archives Committee and the Cooperative African Microfilm Project" **(G45),** and Roberts's *Photographs as sources for African history* **(G100),** which includes Roberts's "A bibliography on African archival material" (p.159–69) and discussions of archives at the University of Durham (Sudan Archive), Oxford University, the Pitt Rivers Museum, the Basel Archives, and Port Jesus Museum.

G102

Biebuyck, Daniel P., J. Dufour, and Y. Kennes. *Bibliographie sur la tenure des terres et les problèmes fonciers.* Léopoldville: Commission Pour l'Ètude de problème foncier, 1957. 156p.

Organized by province, district, and territory. Lists unpublished ethnographic studies available in Zaire government archives.

G103

Guide to nonfederal archives and manuscripts in the United States relating to Africa. London: Hans Zell, 1988. 2v.

Both textual and nontextual materials.

G104

Haas, Waltraud, and Paul Jenkins. *Guide to the Basel Mission Cameroon archive.* Basel, Switzerland: Basel Mission, 1988. 159p.

Includes a section for materials on Cameroonian languages. Covers 1884–1950. Most of the sources are in the German language.

G105

Pearson, James D., and Ruth Jones, eds. "Bibliographic control of African manuscripts and archives collections." In *The bibliography of Africa: Proceedings and papers of the International Conference on African Bibliography.* Nairobi, 4–8 December 1967. New York: Africana, 1970. 362p.

A pioneering study that identifies many sources of anthropological importance.

G106

Simpson, Donald H., ed. "Africa." In the Royal Commonwealth Society. *The manuscript catalogue of the Library,* p.77–129. London: Mansell, 1975. 193p.

Records of colonial period observations (voyages and travel), with many cross-references. The annotations are always alert to published material and can be rigorously critical. Includes notes on character of each item. Index of personal names, subjects, and organizations. Consult also Barringer's "The Royal Commonwealth Society" **(G09).**

G107

Syracuse University. Libraries. *Africana microfilms at the E. S. Bird Library, Syracuse University: An annotated guide.* Comp. by David L. Easterbrook and Kenneth P. Lohrentz. Syracuse, N.Y.: Program of Eastern African Studies, Syracuse University, 1974. 72p.

Includes guidance to the vast resources of the National Archives of Kenya, which are available on microform at this American university. Four million pages on 2,000 rolls of microfilm. Includes many reports and observations from highly educated colonial administrators, who were sensitive to topics of anthropological interest. The African viewpoint can be found in the Musila Museum's "The University of Syracuse microfilms project," in Musila Musembi's *Archives management: The Kenyan experience* (Nairobi: Africa Book Services, 1985 [116p.]) **(G108).**

G109

Vandewoude, Emile. *Documents pour servir à la connaissance des populations du Congo Belge: Aperçu historique (1886–1933) de l'étude des populations autochtones, par les fonctionnaires et agents du Service territorial, suivi de l'inventaire des études historiques ethnographiques et linguistiques conservées aux Archives du Congo Belge.* Léopoldville: Archives du Congo Belge, Section documentation, 1958. 246 leaves.

Topically and geographically organized, this archival list identifies many unpublished historical, ethnographic, and linguistic documents in the archives of the former Belgian Congo. Indexes of author, place, and ethnic group.

Dissertations

Scheven's *Bibliographies for African studies, 1970–1986* **(G24)** is the first-choice guide for any African literature search that includes dissertations. A list that includes only some of the more recent publications and one that was published before the date of coverage in her work. Work completed in African universities is becoming more accessible through bibliographies that record dissertations completed in African universities. Consult Scheven **(G24).**

G110

Becker, Charles, and Mamadou Diouf. "Histoire de la Sénégambie: Une bibliographie des travaux universitaires." *Journal des africanistes* 58 (2) (1966): 163–209.

Lists 706 memoirs, diplomas, theses, and dissertations completed before 1988. Verifies by inspection 516 of these entries. Lists another 109 unverified entries. Tables illustrate distribution by time period studied, by themes, and by country, area, or ethnic group studied.

G111

Dinstel, Marion, comp. *List of French doctoral dissertations on Africa, 1884–1961.* Boston: Hall, 1966. 336p.

Arranged by country studied and alphabetically thereunder, with area index and subject index. For example, ANTHROPOLOGY—CAMEROON has seven entries. ARCHAEOLOGY—ETHIOPIA has two. Based on holdings of the Boston University Libraries of French-language dissertations on Africa.

G112

Lauer, Joseph J., Alfred Kagan, and Gregory Larkin Lauer, comp. *American and Canadian doctoral dissertations and master's theses on Africa, 1974–1987.* Atlanta: Crossroads Pr., Emory University, 1989. 356p.

Lists 8,500 entries. Arranged by country and region. Indexed by subject and author. This work continues the earlier work by Michael Sims and Alfred Kagan, *American and Canadian doctoral dissertations and master's theses on Africa, 1886–1974* (Waltham, Mass.: Brandeis University, African Studies Association, 1976) **(G113),** with 6,070 entries. Arranged by country and geographic area, subdivided by discipline, and listed alphabetically by author thereunder. New American dissertations are listed as granted in a regular department of the *ASA news* **(G10).**

G114

Standing Conference on Library Materials on Africa. *Theses on Africa, 1976–1988, accepted by universities in the United Kingdom and Ireland.* Cambridge, England: W. Heffer, 1964. 64p.

As an example of the strength of ethnic-group indexing, there are thirteen works itemized under YORUBA. Updated irregularly. The original index was arranged by topic and country, with a separate author index. Supplemented by Standing Conference on Library Materials, *Theses on Africa 1963–1975, accepted by universities in the United Kingdom and Ireland* (London: Mansell, 1978 [123p.]) **(G115).** Geographic with broad subject divisions thereunder. Author index. Updated by *African research and documentation* **(G08).**

Monographic Series

As always in anthropological investigations, the identification of one useful series of monographs invites an inspection of all volumes in the series. In actual practice the difference between a monographic series and a set is not as clear to other editors and scholars as it is to editors and scholars with library training. In truth it may not be clear even to librarians. Witness the variable approach by librarians even to such a massive project as the cataloging of the records of the Pacific Manuscript Bureau.

One recent innovation that attempts to consolidate the expansion of ethnographic reports has been the development of monographic series devoted to a particular culture area. For example, a series devoted to recording research developed as a result of activities by the Berlin Sudan Research Project has been announced. The first volume, Fritz W. Kramer and Bernhard Streck, eds., *Sudanesische marginalien—ein ethnographisches programm* (Munich: Trickster, 1991 [132p.]) **(G116),** has articles that introduce the program—articles by authors whose monographs will appear in later volumes in the series. The product of this effort promises to consolidate what is known about the ethnic groups of the Sudan.

8

The Americas

This chapter assumes that the reader has exhausted Balay's *Guide to reference books* **(B02),** especially for more general sources. In this chapter, reference works which cover both North and South America are located under the more general heading, "The Americas." This group of reference works is identified by the prefix "H."

Coverage of the Americas in anthropological reference works usually starts by dividing them into two groups. One group comprises northern Mexico, the United States, and Canada. The other is southern Mexico, Central and South America, and the Caribbean.

The reference sources covering the North American Indian exclusively provide a dense network. The internal culture areas of the North American Indian are well defined by major reference sources such as Sturtevant's *Handbook of North American Indians* **(I122)** and *Native North Americans on disc* **(I17).**

The populations south of the United States (excepting those Indians of Mexico classed in Southwestern culture areas) are usually covered in reference works identified by a general heading "Latin America and the Caribbean." This group of reference works is identified here by the prefix "J." For an example of this coverage, inspect Covington's *Latin America and the Caribbean* **(J02).** Find entries with the prefix "KA" under the heading "Mesoamerica and the Caribbean" and the prefix "KB" for "South America and the Caribbean" for entries that cover only part of the "Americas."

For a literature search in Latin America and the Caribbean, find subdivisions for "Mesoamerica and the Caribbean" and "South America." Anthropological reference works tend to divide the Latin American and Caribbean cultures between Mesoamerican/Caribbean cultures and South American/Caribbean cultures. Each of these subdivisions of cultural material has important reference sources in all forms devoted exclusively and independently to the subdivisions.

Mesoamerica is defined by such resources as Bernal's *Bibliografía de arqueología y etnografía: Mesoamérica y Norte de México, 1514–1960* **(KA15)** or Parra and Moreno's *Bibliografía indigenista de México y Centroamérica (1850–1950)* **(KA17).**

The organization of the section on the Caribbean is less clear-cut. In anthropology, the cultures of the Lowlands of northern South America are closely related to the cultures of the Caribbean. Some of the best resources for the study of the Caribs can be identified in bibliographies of Venezuela. The general reference works covering both Central America and the Caribbean are included because most modern ethnographic studies of the Caribbean do not include indigenous populations. Most indigenous populations were exterminated centuries ago.

For the South American culture areas, O'Leary's *Ethnographic bibliography of South America* **(KB01)** provides the latest attempt at consolidating the anthropological results for the whole continent. Among resources of the first importance, only *Handbook of Latin American studies* **(J26)** has maintained an organization that is sensitive to anthropological needs in all of its South American entries. Since the recent volumes of this resource have been converted into a machine-readable database, there should be, in the next ten years, a flood of bibliographies organized by the culture areas of South America.

Until current culture area bibliographies of South America become available, the organization of Block's "Anthropology" **(J01)** by nation states can be useful and should be consulted before proceeding with the development in *Fieldwork in the Library.* Successful searches will probably move quickly to the *Handbook of Latin American studies* **(J26)** and the resources listed in chapters 1 and 4.

These arrangements are admittedly imperfect. But the distortions are not as gross as the distortions that result from organizing anthropological reference sources for this region solely on the basis of nation states. Inspect the differences between this arrangement and the arrangement in Block's excellent guide, "Anthropology" **(J01).** Block's arrangement by nation state suitably supports work by historians and other social science disciplines but obscures many of the relationships between those anthropological reference sources best designed to cover this culture area.

For many disciplines in the humanities and the social sciences, the boundaries of current nation states are an adequate description for population groups. The point of departure in anthropological studies of the New World is the distribution of American Indians at the time of European contact. Even when the reference point becomes the modern distribution of indigenous ethnic groups, this distribution often spreads across two or more national boundaries.

Since Block's "Anthropology" **(J01)** is recent and comprehensive, it is possible here to identify only those clusters of reference sources that work well together at the sacrifice of completeness of coverage for each and every part of South America. For literature searches of South American anthropological materials, *Fieldwork in the Library* should be used as a supplement to Block **(J01).** Without the base of information available in Block **(J01)** this chapter might have been organized on the basis of nation states. This is particularly true when searching for studies of urban anthropology. See also the resources described between **(H01)** and **(H12).**

As a final note, the interest anthropology has shown in the modern populations of America suggest a strategic search that includes an inspection of the more general resources in chapter 2 of *Fieldwork in the Library.*

Searching Bibliographic Guides

Collectively the guides to all chapters form the bibliographic base upon which *Fieldwork in the Library* is constructed. Guides listed in chapters devoted to "Access by discipline" are indispensable to many searches. Consult first the resources listed in Auckland's "Getting into the literature" **(A01).**

H01

Gibson, Gordon D. "A bibliography of anthropological bibliographies: The Americas." *Current anthropology* 1 (1960):61–75.

This bibliography of bibliographies is still the best published guide to the anthropological literature on the Americas. When this work was undertaken, UNESCO had announced plans to publish the *International bibliography of social and cultural anthropology* **(D20)** as an annual index to anthropological research beginning in 1954. Gibson's work can be seen as part of an informal but international attempt to establish a firm base from which this new and continuing control of the literature could proceed. By concentrating on anthropological bibliographies published separately or in journals before 1955, Gibson forges a major link in the chain of control over an earlier body of material. It arranges 290 bibliographies geographically by an index of subjects, authors, and, when necessary, the names of periodicals. Many bibliographies listed here identify what even today is the majority of available information. With the addition of 54 entries and brief subject descriptions to the 290 entries in Gibson's "A bibliography of anthropological bibliographies," and LC numbers and brief subject descriptions to all 344 citations, James R. Jaquith's "Bibliography of anthropological bibliographies of the Americas," *America indígena* 20 (1970): 419–69 **(H02),** brings this coverage through 1969. Coverage can be further expanded by reference to *Anthropological bibliographies* **(A21),** which brings coverage forward through the 1970s.

Searching for Current Materials

European anthropologists tend to treat the whole of the Americas as a culture area and to extend to both North and South America coverage in the same reference sources. For special current awareness features in scholarly journals, inspect first the Royal Anthropological Institute's *Reference list of current periodicals* **(A14),** which is arranged so that listings in any issue will identify a select list of articles from journals in a particular culture area. The following journals can be inspected for special features that support searches for current awareness.

H03

Indiana. v.1– , 1973– . Berlin: Ibero-Amerika Nisches Institut, Preussischer Kulturbesitz.

Three to five book reviews per issue. Includes a department devoted to the publication of professional news. Coverage includes contributions to ethnology, linguistics, archaeology, and physical anthropology.

Retrospective Searches

The detailed indexing of Wolf and Folk's *Indians of North and South America* **(H04)** reaches at least one source on almost any topic. The annual volumes of the continuing indexing identified in chapters 1 and 2 of *Fieldwork in the Library* bring the coverage of this resource into the present. Consult especially *Anthropological literature* **(A36).** Consult also *Latin American studies* [computer file] **(J27).** Other resources of special interest listed in chapter 1 include Tozzer Library, *Catalogues* [microfiche] **(A26)** for its indexing of books, periodical articles, and the internal contents of books, and the British Museum, Museum of Mankind Library, *Museum of Mankind Library catalogues* [microfiche] **(A25),** for indexing with the Bliss classification system, including entry by names of indigenous peoples.

Retrospective Bibliographies—Broad Scope

H04

Wolf, Carolyn E., and Karen R. Folk. *Indians of North and South America.* Metuchen, N.J.: Scarecrow, 1977. 576p.

The *Supplement,* 1988 (654 p.), with 3,542 entries, has a cutoff date of May 1987. Both volumes have the same organization. The extensive subject indexing makes this the first place to look for almost any topic. Formats include books, periodical articles, essays or chapters in collected works, doctoral dissertations, and major collections of native American documents on microfilm. The two volumes have nearly 8,000 entries. Author and subject indexes.

Retrospective Bibliographies—Continuing Bibliographies

H05

"Bibliographie américaniste." *Journal de la Société des Américanistes.* ns. v.11– , 1895– . Paris: Société des Américanistes de Paris. Annual.

Text in English, French, German, Portuguese, and Spanish. Covers the Americas, including the Caribbean. A long tradition of bibliographic responsibility to the reader. Since 1985 this department has been compiled by Susana Monzon. The journal has included sections titled "Linguistique Améridienne" and "Archéologie et Préhistoire, Anthropologie et Ethnohistoire." Occasionally, find here publications of submitted bibliographic reviews such as Olinda Celestino's "Maria Rostworowski y la antropología histórica en el Perú" 71 (1985): 210–16. The magazine's consolidation of French bibliographic work on North and South America has been cumulated and separately published. Indexing of these bibliographies has usually included subject entry which itself includes names of indigenous populations, a geographic index, and an author index. Consult Mireille Guyot's *Bibliographie américaniste: Archéologie et préhistoire, anthropologie et ethnohistoire* (Paris: Musée de l'Homme, 1967–), and Michel Lambert's *Bibliographie latino-américaniste: France 1959–1972* (México City: Institut Française d' Amérique Latine, 1973 [159p.]) **(H06),** which provides a thematic index to 1,500 titles published in French.

Retrospective Searches—Topical

H07

Alcina Franch, José. *Bibliografía básica de arqueología americana.* Madrid: Ediciones Cultura Hispánica, Instituto de Cooperación Iberoamericana, 1985. 475p.

Of the first importance. Without annotation, this numbered bibliography provides extensive coverage of all aspects of American archaeology. Broad topics are given detailed subdivision in each chapter. For example, in "2. Arqueología americana. Generalidades," find such subdivisions as "2.1 Obras generales," "2.2 Bibliografías," and "2.3 Historia de la arqueología americana." It attempts to identify the best and most recent survey texts in each area. Includes books, journal articles, and proceedings of congresses. The subject index by cultural and geographical names is detailed, including many names for which there is a single reference such as AKAPANA and AKE, and names with extensive references such as ALASKA, with sixty-four items without expansion. A subject index includes the term BIBLIOGRAPHY and such concepts as AGRICULTURE, which has 163 entries, plus sixty-four entries scattered across the classed arrangement (in which studies of a localized system are entered). Provides detailed entry into highly technical concepts such as ALTARES and ANALISIS FACTORIAL and ARITMETICA MAYA. Author, place name, concept, and culture index. Detailed table of contents (in the Spanish publishing tradition, it is placed after the indexes at the very end of the monograph).

H08

Szwed, John F., and Abrahams, Roger D. *Afro-American folk culture: An annotated bibliography of materials from North, Central and South America, and the West Indies.* Philadelphia: Institute for the Study of Human Issues, 1978. 2v. (American Folklore Society, Bibliographical and special series, v.31–32)

Coverage includes first North America and then the West Indies, Central America, and South America. The geographical arrangement is indexed by subject and specific locale. See also Block's "Anthropology: Bibliography" **(J01),** which has reference sources for both folklore and black subcultures in Latin America. These have been organized (very appropriately for a study of the traditions of these peoples) under names of nation states.

Informational Reference Searches

For directory information about American anthropologists, consult first the *AAA guide* **(A53).** The best international directory is still the "International directory of anthropological institutions" **(A56),** which could usefully be reissued in a new edition. The most frequent attempts to summarize information about the entirety of the Americas come from the archaeologists.

Encyclopedias, Handbooks, Manuals

H09

Haberland, Wolfgang. *Amerikanische archäologie: Geschichte, theorie, kulturentwicklung.*

Darmstadt: Wissenschaftliche Buchgesellschaft, 1991. 269p.

Uses a temporal rather than a geographic perspective to show the differential evolution in many culture areas of North, Meso-, and South America. Deals in part 1 with the techniques, dating methods, and classification of American archaeology. Phases are defined as Paleo-Indian (to 8000 B.C.), Sedentariness (8000–2000 B.C.), the rise and art and cult (2000–200 B.C.), states and cities (200 B.C. to A.D. 800), the eve of conquest (800–1550).

H10

Willey, Gordon R. *An introduction to American archaeology.* Englewood Cliffs, N.J.: Prentice-Hall, 1966–71. 2v.

V.1, *North and Middle America* (1966 [540p.]), with bibliography (p.485–516); v.2, *South America* (1971 [573 p.]), with bibliography (p.513–47). Encyclopedic summary of North, Central, and South American prehistory. This work can be supplemented by R. E. Taylor and Clement W. Meigham's *Chronologies in New World archaeology* (New York: Academic, 1978 [587p.]) **(H11).** Also useful is a more recent series of essays by Richard M. Leventhal and Alan L. Kolata, eds., *Civilization in the ancient Americas: Essays in honor of Gordon R. Willey* (Albuquerque: Univ. of New Mexico Pr.; Cambridge, Mass.: Peabody Museum of Archaeology and Ethnology, Harvard University, 1983 [487p.]), which concentrates on Mayan topics but reflects the broad span of this scholar's activities in all areas of American archaeology.

Searching Graphic Materials

Searches for graphic materials should first consult American Geographical Society of New York, Map Department, *Index to maps in books and periodicals* **(A59).** Ethnographic resources in this index are often identified under the heading "Linguistic maps"; and since the internal contents of books and journals are cited, the identified resources often have ethnographic significance to match their graphics. For a select list of widely held ethnographic films, consult Heider's *Films for anthropological teaching* **(A63).**

Maps and Atlases

H12

Coe, Michael, Dean Snow, and Elizabeth Benson. *Atlas of ancient America.* New York: Facts on File, 1986. 240p.

Divided into six parts. Pt.3, "North America"; pt.4, "Mesoamerica"; pt.5, "South America." Excellent and accurate distribution maps of indigenous ethnic groups, and summary descriptions of precontact cultures, with detailed coverage of the major archaeological sites. Pt.6, "The living heritage," attempts to summarize present-day cultures. The bibliography is selective. The list of illlustrations is helpful and the detailed gazetteer includes archaeological sites identified on maps and in the text. The detailed subject-index expansions help to transform an excellent atlas into an indispensable reference source. For example, CROPS is expanded (or subdivided) into ARROWROOT and thirty-five other fruits and vegetables, and DIET is subdivided into ten culture areas.

THE AMERICAN INDIAN FROM NORTHERN MEXICO TO THE ARCTIC

Coverage of the populations included in this section follows the organization of major anthropological reference sources, such as Sturtevant's *Handbook of North American Indians* **(I122)** and *Native North Americans on disc* **(I17).** Study also the entries for resources covering both North and South America described between **(H01)** and **(H12).**

The importance of bibliographic series and informational sets to the study of the North American Indian cannot be overstated. In this chapter, many of the most important resources are clustered under series titles. This is done in the interest of economy of spacing. Every volume in these series deserves serious attention and should be consulted first when it provides related coverage. For examples of this treatment, inspect Sturtevant's *Handbook of North*

American Indians **(I122)** and *Bibliographical series* (Bloomington) **(I72).**

Under the heading "Searching Bibliographic Guides," find a dynamic discussion of reference sources organized by strategic heading. Organization of reference sources by form can be found in Haas's *Indians of North America* **(I02).** For the sub-Arctic and other culture areas located to the north of the United States, consult the additional resources of Canadian centers identified in Corley's *Resources for native peoples studies* **(I01).** If the focus of interest in a literature search is topical or local, consult Hirschfelder, Byler, and Dorris's *Guide to research on North American Indians* **(I05).** If the focus centers on indigenous ethnic groups in the context of cultures areas, consult Hoxie and Markowitz's *Native Americans* **(I06).**

In "Searching for Current Materials" about a culture area, inspect entries **(I08)** through **(I16)** for samples of special features available in the journals devoted to the culture areas of North America. Entries listed under "Selective Lists of Scholarly Journals" encourage a search for special features in scholarly journals.

Under "Retrospective Searches," see the subheading "Retrospective Bibliographies—Broad Scope," under which find listed *Native North Americans on disc* **(I17),** which excludes government documents. For a discussion of how to enter these government documents, consult O'Leary's "General discussion" **(I07).** When a search has a subject focus, move the search to the sources listed under "Retrospective Bibliographies—Topical" and select from the entries listed between **(I18)** and **(I67).** Other retrospective sources can be identified in the guides that define this chapter: Corley's *Resources for native peoples studies* **(I01)** and Haas's *Indians of North America* **(I02).**

In a search for "Informational Sources," strong bibliographic reviews are identified in the annotations to the *Bibliographical series* (Bloomington) **(I72).** Encyclopedic information on ethnic groups (defined to include indigenous ethnic groups) can be found in Thernstrom's *Harvard encyclopedia of American ethnic groups* **(I125)** and in the coverage of indigenous Indians in Sturtevant's *Handbook of North American Indians* **(I122).** In "Searching Graphic Materials," rich selections can be identified in the sources cited between **(I130)** and **(I148).** "Searching Unpublished Material" can start with entries **(I161)** to **(I188).**

The distribution of indigenous peoples at the time of contact with Western Europe can be established by inspecting maps in *Native North Americans on disc* **(I17).** The distribution of archaeological cultures can be established by inspecting the maps (p.45–50) found in Coe, Snow, and Benson's *Atlas of ancient America* **(H12),** which includes details of site distributions of Hopewellian (p.51), Caddoan Mississippian, Middle Mississippian, Plaquemine Mississippian, and South Appalachian Mississippian (p.54), and for Fremont, Hohokam, and Mogollon (p.69).

Searching Bibliographic Guides

Consult first the resources listed in Auckland's "Getting into the literature"**(A01).**

Bibliographic Guides

I01

Corley, Nora T. *Resources for native peoples studies.* Ottawa: Resources Survey Division, Collection Development Branch, National Library of Canada, 1984. 341p. (Research collections in Canadian libraries. Special studies, v.9)

Based on a survey of forty-three libraries, this resource includes a guide to eighty-eight reference sources, including bibliographies, directories, and union lists. A thorough review of 600 periodicals by or about native peoples and published in Canada, with holdings records for Canadian libraries. The main body is organized by province, then by city. Each section includes an overview, native peoples population, indigenous ethnic groups, and geographic locations. The "Sources of information" cites references used to develop this book and can serve as a bibliography of bibliographies for Canadian anthropology. Control of the literature of anthropology in Canada is fast shifting to computer files, which are not fully discussed in any of these resources. For example, the *Boreal Northern titles (BNT)* [computer file], 1970– (Edmonton, Alberta: Boreal Institute for Northern Studies, University of Alberta), is available online (QL Systems) and provides information from multidisciplinary sources, including archaeology, history, and current conditions of native peoples. The larger file, *Native Research Information System Database* [computer file], 1972– (Edmonton, Alberta: University of Alberta), is available online (Computing Department, University of Alberta) and covers books, articles, reports, conferences, films, and microfilms on the Alberta native peoples. It excludes land claims, which are included in the *Boreal Library Catalogue* [computer file], 1977– (Edmonton, Alberta: University Computing Center, University of Alberta for Boreal Institute for Northern Studies). Available online (CAN/OLE, SPIRES, BITNRT) to provide access to extensive coverage of much of western Canada, Alaska, Greenland, Iceland, and Scandinavia.

The two-year lag in issuing the annual publication, *Abstracts of native studies,* v.1– , 1984– (Brandon, Manitoba: Abstracts of native studies), is justified by its range of coverage and by its detailed entries. The fact that it is not widely held in the United States suggests the possibility that Canadian journals of review can provide the only information about bibliographic developments in that country.

Any archival search should start with the Grimshaw's *Images of the other* **(I167),** which concisely organizes entry to widely available resources.

I02

Haas, Marilyn L. *Indians of North America: Methods and sources for library research.* Hamden, Conn.: Library Professional Publications, 1983. 163p.

This useful guide includes under separate heading an indigenous North American Indian bibliography of 229 items. Ethnic groups are listed by Library of Congress name, with cross-references for popular names. In other sections, entries are annotated and arranged alphabetically by author under topical headings such as "Library catalogs," "Indexes," "Abstracts," "Handbooks, encyclopedias, dictionaries," and "Directories." Earlier but still useful bibliographies can be excluded here because they have already been described in Haas. She also provides rich guidance concerning the best use of many resources relevant to the investigation of Indian claims. This work covers the use of government documents, ERIC, indexing and abstracting services, encyclopedias, theses and dissertations, manuscripts and archives, nonprint material, and maps. For entry into maps, consult also O'Leary's "General discussion" **(I07).** Haas exercises a uniquely lucid understanding of the relationship between the basic reference resources of anthropology and the indexing and abstracting services developed for use in other related disciplines. Many of these are now available in the machine-readable databases described in chapter 2. They were selected for inclusion in *Fieldwork in the Library* on the basis of the reference experience concentrated into the Haas article "Anthropology" **(B01).** It is in this same article that Haas discusses several valuable but hidden sources for specialized topics. For example, the antecedent work of Harry Dee's "Basic bibliography for Native American law," *Law library journal* (Law Library Assn.) 69 (1979): 78–89 **(I03),** and of Michael L. Tate's "Studying the American Indian through government documents and the National Archives," *Government publications review: An international journal* 5 (1978): 285–94 **(I04),** which is remarkable for its profound understanding of the scholarly use of these resources and which can be used to supplement O'Leary's "General discussion" **(I07).**

I05

Hirschfelder, Arlene B., Mary Byler, and Michael A. Dorris. *Guide to research on North American Indians.* Chicago: American Library Assn., 1983. 330p.

This work can be used as a companion to Hoxie and Markowitz's *Native Americans* **(I06).** It abandons the traditional culture area organization favored in most anthropological sources and organizes the literature by topic. Excludes ethnographic monographs for which Hoxie and Markowitz's *Native Americans* **(I06)** can be consulted. However, does include published bibliographies of some tribal and indigenous ethnic groups. Research on the Native American Indian has become so vast that its bulk has become an obstacle to scholarly work. "From this mass of material, approximately 1,100 (English language) books, articles, government documents, and other written materials in twenty-seven fields of study have been selected and annotated for this guide" (p.ix). Encyclopedic monographs are boldly and helpfully integrated into lists that cover standard reference sources. A serious effort that identifies and selects only the most important and comprehensive works on Canada, Mexico, and the United States. The table of contents leads to bibliographic essays at the beginning of each section. A segregated list of bibliographic entries listed by author is entered at the end of each section. A ten-page subject index and an author-title index guide the reader. Students of the American Indian will be richly rewarded for a thorough study of any section of this guide that touches any aspect of a topical search. Most anthropologists would suggest that a selection of material about this "topic" be limited to one culture area or indigenous ethnic group at a time. This would encourage careful isolation of comparable reports and make it possible to define the topic in terms of the whole cultural complex under investigation.

This guide can be informally updated by reference to the machine-readable databases, *America: History and life* [computer file] **(B07)** and *Historical abstracts* [computer file] **(B22).**

I06

Hoxie, Frederick E., and Harvey Markowitz. *Native Americans: An annotated bibliography.* Pasadena, Calif.: Salem Pr., 1991. 325p.

Can be used as a complementary guide to Hirschfelder, Byler, and Dorris's *Guide to research on North American Indians* **(I05).** Excellent annotations to more than 1,000 books are organized under four main sections: "General studies and references," "History," "Culture areas," and "Contemporary life." Most of the book is devoted to "Culture areas" and is organized under eight subdivisions that reflect the traditional culture areas of North America. Each of these subdivisions is then divided into topical subdivisions such as "Archaeology," "Tribal life," and "Family and society." The author has created a "browsable" introduction to the literature with an organization that makes it possible to scan titles within a framework influenced by anthropological thinking. Topics are subordinated to the culture area. Given this understanding of anthropological investigations, the author wisely omits subject entry as an organizational feature. Even the most unsophisticated user is encouraged by the organization of this resource to identify information in its cultural context. Author index.

I07

O'Leary, Timothy J. "General discussion." In Murdock, George Peter, and Timothy J. O'Leary. *Ethnographic bibliography of North America.* V.1, *Central North America,* xii–xxxvi. 4th ed. New Haven, Conn.: Human Relations Area Files Pr., 1975. 454p. (Behavior sciences bibliographies)

In this discussion, O'Leary makes many useful suggestions about how a scholar can use printed indexes to expand *Native North Americans on disc* **(I17)** with continuing reference sources. Scholarly, detailed, readable. Provides useful guidance for searches of U.S. government documents. In a more recent development, the machine-readable databases like the *GPO monthly catalog* [computer file] **(B21)** can be used to identify often-elusive works published by government agencies. Identification of any agency responsible for the production of even a single work makes it possible to scan the monthly catalog for other resources on the American Indian produced by that agency. These works can be substantial. For example, consider the following recent publications on the Pueblo Indians: (1) Gardiner F. Dalley, *The Little Man archaeological sites: Excavations on the Virgin River near Hurricane, Utah* (Salt Lake City: Bureau of Land Management, Utah State Office, 1988 [328p.]); (2) David A. Breternitz, *Delores archaeological program: Final synthetic report* (Denver: U.S. Department of the Interior, Bureau of Reclamation, Engineering and Research Center; Springfield, Va.:

National Technical Information Service, Operations Division, 1987 [900p.]); (3) Bureau of Land Management, Utah State Office, *Excavations at Quail Creek* (Salt Lake City: Bureau of Land Management, Utah State Office, 1986 [498p.]); (4) U.S. Dept. of the Interior, Bureau of Reclamation, Engineering and Research Center, *Archaeological program: Anasazi communities at Dolores: Early Anasazi sites in the Sagehen Flats area* (Denver; Springfield, Va.: National Technical Information Service, 1986 [985p.]); (5) Nancy J. Akins, *A bio-cultural approach to human burials from Chaco Canyon, N.M.* (Santa Fe: Branch of Cultural Research, U.S. Department of Interior, National Park Service, 1985 [215p.]); (6) Peter J. McKenna, *Small site architecture of Chaco Canyon, New Mexico* (Santa Fe: National Park Service, U.S. Department of the Interior, GPO, 1986 [508p.]); (7) *Dolores Archaeological Program: Studies in environmental archaeology* (Denver: U.S. Department of the Interior, Bureau of Reclamation, Engineering and Research Center; Springfield, Va.: National Technical Information Service, 1985 [277p.]), with a fifteen-page bibliography; (8) *Recent research on Chaco prehistory* (Albuquerque: Division of Cultural Research, U.S. Department of Interior, National Park Service, 1984 [279p.]); (9) Peter J. McKenna, *The architecture and material culture of 29SJ1360* (Chaco Canyon, N.M., and Albuquerque: Division of Cultural Research, U.S. Department of the Interior, National Park Service, 1984 [532p.]); (10) Marjorie Baer, *Pueblo of Laguna: A project report* (Washington, D.C.: U.S. Department of the Interior, National Park Service, Historic American Buildings Survey, Historic American Engineering Record, 1984 [78p.]); (11) U.S. Office of the Assistant Secretary of the Army [Civil Works], *Fountain Creek, Pueblo, Colorado phase; General design memorandum: Communication from the Assistant Secretary of the Army (Civil Works) transmitting a letter from the Chief of Engineers, Department of the Army, dated December 23, 1981, submitting a report....* (Washington, D.C.: GPO, 1984 [695p.]); (12) *Excavation of two Anasazi sites in southern Utah* (Salt Lake City: Utah State Office, Bureau of Land Management, 1981 [2v.]).

Searching for Current Materials

For special current awareness features of scholarly journals, inspect first the Royal Anthropological Institute's *Reference list of current periodicals* **(A14),** which is arranged so that listings in any issue will identify a select list of articles from journals relevant to a particular culture area. Identified journals should then be inspected for special features that support current awareness.

Select Sources of Review in Scholarly Publications

I08

American Indian culture and research journal. v.1– , 1974– . Los Angeles: American Indian Studies Center, UCLA. Quarterly.

Often contains more than a dozen reviews and frequently includes review articles of bibliographic importance. Usually contains around ten substantive articles from all areas of anthropological interest, including mythology, linguistics, social customs, and subsistence patterns.

I09

American Indian quarterly, v.1– , 1974– . Berkeley: Native American Studies, Univ. of California. Quarterly.

See especially the department, "Bibliography, research and news." There are other bibliographic features, including the best recent list of contributions to ethnomedicine. The journal itself has as many as fifteen book reviews in an issue and maintains a sharp focus on the contemporary life of American Indians, including reports on urbanization, indigenous ethnic group relations, social life and customs, occupational roles, and folktales.

JOURNALS WITH A CULTURE AREA OR OTHER SPECIALIZED FOCUS

This list is presented as a representative sample that can be expanded by searching lists of periodicals described below under the heading "Selective Lists of Scholarly Journals."

Journals that concentrate on a regional interest are especially useful for their specialized book reviews and news about ongoing research, and for an overview of the kinds of research currently most favored for publication. Any entry in the list could easily have been replaced by *Man in the Northeast,* v.1– , 1971– (Albany: SUNY-Albany), or *Kiva,* v.1– , 1935– (Tucson: Arizona Archaeological and Historical Society, Arizona State Museum, University of Arizona), a quarterly with signed book reviews as long as four pages.

I10

Arctic. v.1– , 1948– . Calgary, Alberta: University of Calgary. Quarterly.

V.36, no.1 (1983), *Cumulative subject index 1948–1982,* by author, geographic term, and subject. Six or seven signed reviews of books are in each issue. Multidisciplinary, with articles of interest to ethnologists and archaeologists. Also useful, *Arctic anthropology* (Madison: Univ. of Wisconsin Pr.), a semiannual specializing in lengthy articles.

I11

El palacio. v.1– , 1913– . Santa Fe: Museum of New Mexico Pr. Monthly.

Book reviews and "News and notes" about the museum's activities are valued features. Articles on the archaeology and cultural anthropology of the Southwest include research developed with a historical methodology.

I12

The journal of California and Great Basin anthropology. v.1– , 1974– . Riverside: Malki Museum, University of California, Riverside. Semiannual.

Each issue contains several signed book reviews. Coverage includes ethnology, ethnohistory, languages, and art forms, and extends to site analysis and descriptions of artifacts. Focus is on California and the Great Basin area.

I13

Northwest anthropological research notes. v.1– , 1967– . Moscow, Idaho: University of Idaho. Semiannual.

Includes abstracts of papers presented at the Northwest Anthropological Conference. Devoted to the anthropology of the Pacific Northwest to include both historic and prehistoric periods. Covers site analysis, ethnology, religion, folklore, ethno-botany, and social organization.

I14

Plains anthropologist. v.1– , 1954– . Iowa City: Univ. of Iowa Pr. Quarterly.

"Announcements" include information about conferences, news about special programs, requests for papers, current information on grants. Devoted to the historic and prehistoric anthropology of the Plains and contiguous areas. Each issue has between five and seven book reviews.

I15

Southern Indian studies, v.1– , 1949– . Chapel Hill: Univ. of North Carolina Pr. 3/yr.

Always a few signed book reviews. Strong coverage of historic and prehistoric Indian life in terms of archaeology, linguistics, ethnology, and history. Topics of interest range from pottery and dance to social customs and settlement patterns. Sponsored by the Archaeological Society of North Carolina; coverage extends to the entire southern United States.

Selective Lists of Scholarly Journals

For current addresses of various periodicals, consult Klein's *Reference encyclopedia of the American Indian* **(I70).** See also the "List of Indian related periodicals," *Index to literature on the American Indian* (San Francisco: Indian Historian Pr.), 2 (1971): 191–230). Additional useful descriptions of sometimes neglected resources can be found in John A. Price's "U.S. and Canadian Indian periodicals," *Canadian review of sociology and anthropology* 9 (2) (1986): 150–62 **(I16).**

Retrospective Searches

In constructing a retrospective search pattern, consult the headnote of chapter 1, "What Every Anthropologist Needs to Know," in *Fieldwork in the Library* and consult especially *Abstracts in German anthropology* **(A33)** and *Anthropological literature* **(A36).** For a longer time span, consult Harvard University, Tozzer Library, *Catalogues* [microfiche] **(A26),** for its indexing of books, periodical articles and the contents of books, and the British Museum, Museum of Mankind Library's *Museum of Mankind Library catalogues* [microfiche] **(A25)** for indexing with the Bliss classification system, including entry by names of indigenous peoples. For bibliographies of indigenous groups consult *Bibliographic index* [computer file] **(B11)** and the Library-Anthropology Resource Group's *Anthropological bibliographies* **(A21)** under the name of each indigenous group.

Retrospective Bibliographies—Bibliographies of Bibliographies

Use of the resources entered in chapter 1, "What Every Anthropologist Needs to Know," is of critical importance. Consult also bibliographies of bibliographies such as Dempsey's *Bibliography of the Blackfoot* **(I48),** which has usefulness beyond the coverage indicated by its title. Gibson's classic "A bibliography of anthropological bibliographies" **(H01)** retains value even though it is fifty years old.

Retrospective Bibliographies—Broad Scope

I17

Native North Americans on disc [computer file]. 1600–present. New Haven, Conn.: Human Relations Area Files. Available on CD-ROM (ABC-CLIO)

An annual that corresponds in part to George Peter Murdock and Timothy O'Leary's *Ethnographic bibliography of North America,* 4th ed. (New Haven, Conn.: Human Relations Area Files Pr., 1975 [5v.]). The basic hardcover set includes v.1, *General North America;* v.2, *Arctic and Sub-Arctic;* v.3, *Far west and Pacific coast;* v.4, *Eastern United States;* v.5, *Plains and southwest.* Lists 40,000 entries for books and articles on indigenous ethnic groups of North America.

Even with the use of keyword searches in the machine-readable database, this resource is difficult to use for entry by name of indigenous peoples. Nevertheless, it is of the first importance for its classed arrangement by culture area of indigenous North American Indians. Since the early 1970s, it has covered the North American Indian as an ethnic group. Its coverage is a monumental effort of comprehensiveness for the printed forms it covers.

The supplements for the printed edition are available for coverage through 1990 (3v.), with the latest compiled by Marlene M. Martin and Timothy J. O'Leary. Coverage brings into the Southwest culture area the indigenous populations of the north of Mexico. Includes coverage of contemporary issues such as the relationship of the governments of Canada and the United States to the Indians, pan-Indianism, urban Indians, and Canadian Indians as ethnic groups. Does not include nonprint materials, which can be searched in U.S. government archives and documents (including maps), for which consult O'Leary **(I07).** Consult also *ERIC* [computer file] **(B16).**

Despite the mass of this bibliography, many valuable resources are excluded. For identifying these excluded materials, there is no better guide to other reference sources than the introductory remarks found in O'Leary's "General discussion" **(I07).**

Retrospective Bibliographies—Topical

In subject searches, consult Haywood's *A bibliography of North American folklore and folksong* **(I20)** and Hirschfelder, Byler, and Dorris's *Guide to research on North American Indians* **(I05)** as mutually complementary reference guides to subject entry. For selective subject entry into the monographic material, consult Hoxie and Markowitz's *Native Americans* **(I06)** and Szwed and Abrahams's *Afro-American folk culture* **(H08).** Because of its detailed subject entry, Wolf and Folk's *Indians of North and South America* **(H04)** is often neglected. On the shelf, the volumes do not look very impressive, but the indexing often identifies a source when all other searches have failed. The thematic and tribal index of Lambert's *Bibliographie latino-américaniste* **(H06)** can be useful. In archaeology, consult the subject index by cultural and geographic names found in Alcina's *Bibliografía básica de arqueología americana* **(H07).**

FOLKLORE

I18

Fowke, Edith F., and Carole Henderson Carpenter. *A bibliography of Canadian folklore in English.* Toronto: Univ. of Toronto Pr., 1981. 272p.

Organized by genre, subdivided for ethnic group. Sections for films, recordings, and dissertations. Author index. A more useful source for many anthropological purposes is Edith Fowke's earlier *Folklore of Canada* (Toronto: McClelland and Stewart, 1976 [349p.]) **(I19),** arranged by indigenous peoples with an extensive bibliography and elaborate indexing.

I20

Haywood, Charles. *A bibliography of North American folklore and folksong.* New York: Dover, 1961. 2v.

An extensive bibliography of more than 40,000 books, articles, sets, and recordings. V.1, *American people north of Mexico,* organized by geographic, indigenous ethnic group, and occupation subject headings; v.2, *American Indians north of Mexico including the Eskimos,* arranged by culture areas and subdivided alphabetically by ethnic group. Printed and recorded forms of music are treated as important forms of folksong. Especially important for coverage of those American ethnic groups excluded from *Native North Americans on disc* **(I17).** The detailed index strengthens this work.

More specialized guidance can be found in Richard M. Dorson's *Handbook of American folklore* (Bloomington: Indiana Univ. Pr., 1983 [584p.]), which has a classified arrangement of the 5,000 entries in its bibliography (p.541–63), which includes some unpublished works and informed guidance to other reference sources. The discussion of research is divided into four sections: (1) Topics, (2) Interpretation, (3) Methods, (4) Presentation. See especially R. Bauman, "The field study of folklore in context" (p.362–68).

Few scholars attempt the kind of broad scope found in Haywood. For an exception, inspect R. E. Walls's *Bibliography of Washington State folklore and folklife: Selected and partially annotated* (Seattle: Washington Folklore Council by the Univ. of Washington Pr., 1988 [301p.]), **(I21)** with 2,100 entries. Includes the cultures of both North American Indians and later immigrants. There is a list of periodicals, "A selected discography of Washington and northwest sound recordings," and a subject index.

More recent sources can be found in Cathleen C. Flanagan and John T. Flanagan's *American folklore: A bibliography, 1950–1974* **(I23).**

I22

Clements, William M., and Frances M. Malpezzi. *Native American folklore, 1879–1979: An annotated bibliography.* Athens, Ohio: Swallow, 1984. 247p.

Entries are arranged by indigenous peoples within sections for cultural areas. Indexes of subjects and authors, of editors, and of translators. Lists 5,550 entries.

I23

Flanagan, Cathleen C., and John T. Flanagan. *American folklore: A bibliography, 1950–1974.* Metuchen, N.J.: Scarecrow, 1977. 406p.

Arranges 3,600 items into broad general topics. The section "Bibliography, dictionaries, archives" is especially valuable. Author index.

LEGAL AND CONTEMPORARY

For elaboration of this section, consult Corley's *Resources for native peoples studies* **(I01);** Haas's *Indians of the North America* **(I02);** Hirschfelder, Byler, and Dorris's *Guide to research on North American Indians* **(I05);** Hoxie and Markowitz's *Native Americans* **(I06);** Dee's "Basic bibliography for Native American law" **(I03);** Abler's *A Canadian Indian bibliography* **(I39);** and from the *Bibliographical series* [Bloomington] **(I72)** Surtees's *Canadian Indian policy* **(I96)** and Prucha's *United States Indian policy* **(I102).** For entry into relevant United States government documents and archives, study O'Leary's "General discussion" **(I07).** Only the more important resources with value beyond their coverage of legal issues are mentioned below.

I24

Hodge, William H. *A bibliography of contemporary North American Indians: Selected and partially annotated with study guides.* New York: Interland, 1976. 310p.

Arranges 2,600 items under classified headings, with an excellent index providing entry by indigenous ethnic group, state, area, and regional grouping. Invaluable for its coverage of contemporary issues and subjects not available in other sources. Addresses such subjects as city living and migration patterns. There is an excellent section on music and dance (citations 1661–1715). Can be used as a companion to the more current and beautifully documented Hirschfelder and Kreipe de Montaño's *The Native American almanac.*

I25

Johnson, Steven L. *Guide to American Indian documents in the Congressional serial set: 1817–1899.* New York: Clearwater, 1977. 503p. (The Library of American Indian affairs)

Indexing is based on examination of every document in the series set. An enormous undertaking, professionally executed.

I26

U.S. Dept. of the Interior. Library. *Dictionary catalog of the Department Library.* Boston: Hall, 1967. 37v.

Four supplements to date. Includes archival material, periodical articles, and many books on government relations with the American Indian, and American Indian constitutions. Especially valuable as a source for biographical material.

I27

U.S. Dept. of the Interior. *Kappler's Indian affairs: Laws and treaties.* Washington, D.C.: U.S. Dept. of the Interior, 1979. 7v.

Volumes 6 and 7 include the index and "[revise and extend] Kappler's compilation to include all treaties, laws, executive orders, relating to Indian affairs in force on Sept. 1, 1967," commonly known as The Kappler Report. Originally published and widely available as *Indian affairs: Laws and treaties.* Compiled between 1904 and 1941, and published as: 57th Congress, 1st session. Senate. *Document 452;* 62nd Congress, 2nd session. Senate. *Document 719;* 70th Congress, 1st session. Senate. *Document 453;* 76th Congress, 3d session. Senate. *Document 194.* Supplement published by U.S. Dept. of the Interior under title: *Kappler Indian affairs,* 1975 (160p.). Consult also *Index to literature on the American Indian,* v.1–4, 1970–73. (San Francisco: Indian Historian Pr.) for reports on civil rights, hunting and fishing, and law, and Harry Dee's "Basic bibliography for Native American law" **(I03).**

LINGUISTICS

Comprehensive current bibliographic control for research in North American Indian linguistics is maintained in newsletters. Consult especially *SSILA newsletter,* v.1– , 1981– (Arcata, Calif.: Society for the Study of the Indigenous Languages of America. Department of Ethnic Studies. Humboldt State University) in which bibliographic entries extend to books, articles in periodicals and collections, and dissertations. See also *Algonquian and Iroquoian linguistics,* v.1– , 1985– (Winnipeg, Manitoba, R3T 2N2: Department of Native Studies, University of Manitoba); *Sioux and Caddoan linguistics,* v.1– , 1985– (Boulder: Department of Linguistics, University of Colorado).

This section is developed on the assumption that readers with a linguistic interest will consult first DeMiller's *Linguistics* **(E01)** for more specialized coverage, including annotated entry to Richard T. Parr's *A bibliography of the Athapaskan languages* (Ottawa: National Museums of Canada, 1974 [333p.]) (Paper ethnology division, no.14) for its arrangement by indigenous ethnic group, and to David H. Pentland and H. Christoph Wolfart's *Bibliography of Algonquian linguistics* (Winnipeg: Univ. of Manitoba Pr., 1982 [333p.], with its index by language.

I28

Bright, William. *Bibliography of the languages of native California including closely related languages of adjacent areas.* Metuchen, N.J.: Scarecrow, 1982. 220p. (Native American bibliography series, no.4)

An alphabetic listing by author of 1,077 entries. Includes all Yuman-speaking peoples. Index lists languages, language groupings, kinship terms, loanwords, numerals, place names, and songs. To establish a more complex view of native American languages, consult Herbert Landar's "Tribes and languages of North America: A checklist," in v.2, *Linguistics in North*

America, p.207–400 (The Hague: Mouton, 1973 [1,624p.]). Although the basic volume serves as a compendium with articles by experts on each of the major language groups of North, Central, and South America, it includes several general articles, such as Harry Hoijer's "History of American Indian linguistics."

I29

Evans, G. Edward. *Bibliography of language arts materials for native North Americans: Bilingual, English as a second language and native language materials 1975–1976 with supplemental entries for 1965–1974.* Los Angeles: American Indian Studies Center, UCLA, 1979. 120p. (American Indian bibliographic series, no.2)

Includes a directory of courses in American Indian languages (p.xii–xvi). Full addresses of publishing projects. The annotated entries are organized by language, subdivided between bilingual and monolingual, with alphabetic lists by author under these subject headings. Includes dictionaries, grammars, orthographies, primers, and readers. Author/title index. For descriptions of earlier editions of this work extending back to 1890, and other early linguistic material, consult Haas's *Indians of North America* **(I02)** and Hirschfelder, Byler, and Dorris's *Guide to research on North American Indians* **(I05).**

I30

Marken, Jack W., comp. *The American Indian language and literature.* Arlington Heights, Ill.: AHM, 1978. 204p. (Goldentree bibliographies in language and literature)

Classed organization with fifteen sections. The four general sections, which include bibliography, autobiography, general literature, and general language, are followed by geographic divisions, each of which has a general language subdivision subdivided by indigenous ethnic group. Lists 3,700 entries.

MATERIAL CULTURE

I31

Anderson, Frank G. *Southwestern archaeology: A bibliography.* New York: Garland, 1982. 539p. (Garland reference library of social science, v.69)

Alphabetic by author. Chronologic list of articles and books under each author. Covers Utah, New Mexico, western and southern Colorado, southeastern Nevada and California, Chihuahua, and Sonora and Trans-Pecos, Texas. Subject indexes by regional and by cultural and topical classification. Citations in the index list the author and date of publication.

I32

Fitting, James E., ed. *The development of North American archaeology: Essays in the development of regional traditions.* Garden City, N.Y.: Anchor, 1973. 309p.

Entered here especially because the selective bibliographies that appear at the end of each of the chapters summarize the history of ideas for nine regional traditions in North American archaeology. The seminal works that established these traditions can be used as the basis of searches with citation indexes as discussed in chapter 2 of *Fieldwork in the Library.*

I33

Milisauskas, Sarunas, Frances Pickin, and Charles Clark. *A selected bibliography of North American archaeological sites.* New Haven, Conn.: Human Relations Area Files, 1981. 2v.

Arranged alphabetically by author under states as subject headings. Indexed by author, cultural period, and site name.

I34

Osterreich, Shelley Anne, comp. *The American Indian ghost dance: 1870 and 1890: An annotated bibliography.* Westport, Conn.: Greenwood, 1991. 96p. (Bibliographies and indexes in American history, no.19)

The long, descriptive annotations provide enough detail to identify exactly the focus and scope of each of the 110 books, journal articles, and dissertations cited. Author, journal, and subject indexes.

I35

Oppelt, Norman T. *Southwestern pottery: An annotated bibliography and list of types and wares.* 2d. ed. rev. and exp. Metuchen, N.J.: Scarecrow, 1988. 325p.

Describes 955 numbered items with detailed annotations. List of Southwestern pottery types and wares (p.238), arranged alphabetically with references to the bibliography.

I36

Parezo, Nancy J., Ruth M. Perry, and Rebecca S. Allen. *Southwest Native American arts and material culture: A guide to research.* New York: Garland, 1991. 2v. (Studies in ethnic art, v.1)

Covers 8,363 books, journals, pamphlets, dissertations and theses, directories, and government documents. Entries are by author. Precontact-period archaeology reports are only sparingly cited. The introduction of more than forty pages defines the keywords and culture areas that are used as indexing terms. This organization, nearly 200 pages of it, makes this resource useful for many purposes beyond the range of its title. For each culture group in the index, there are subheadings for topics such as musical instruments and toys. There is a subject index.

I37

Porter, Frank W. *Native American basketry: An annotated bibliography.* Westport, Conn.: Greenwood, 1988. 249p. (Art reference collection, no.10)

An introductory essay provides an overview of research in Native American basketry. The supporting bibliography lists 1,100 annotated entries for books, journals, newspaper articles, and dissertations about North American Indian basketry.

I38

Storck, Peter L. *A preliminary bibliography of early man in eastern North America, 1839–1973.* Toronto: Royal Ontario Museum, 1975. 110p. (Archaeology monograph, 4)

Lists 1,242 journal articles, reviews, monographs, and books dealing in whole or in part with the subject of early man in eastern North America. Includes Canadian provinces east of Manitoba and those states in the United States east of the Mississippi. Geographic, subject, and site indexes.

INDIGENOUS ETHNIC GROUP AND REGIONAL BIBLIOGRAPHIC ORGANIZATION

Selective bibliographies of indigenous peoples can be found in the *Bibliographical series* [Bloomington] **(I72)** and in Sturtevant's *Handbook of North American Indians* **(I122).** Extensive bibliographies of indigenous ethnic groups can be found in *Native North Americans on disc* **(I17).** Both Haas's *Indians of North America* **(I02)** and Hirschfelder, Byler, and Dorris's *Guide to research on North American Indians* **(I05)** in their selective lists are sensitive to bibliographies of indigenous ethnic groups. In chapter 1, "What Every Anthropologist Needs to Know," the index to Weeks's *Introduction to library research in anthropology* **(A71)** identifies some rarely held ethnic-group bibliographies that are not listed here.

I39

Abler, Thomas S. *A Canadian Indian bibliography, 1960–1970.* Toronto: Univ. of Toronto Pr., 1974. 732p.

Lists 3,038 entries. Pt.1, Topical arrangement of books, periodicals, theses, and unpublished reports. Pt. 2, "Case law digest," which brings together all case law related to Indian questions in Canada since July 1, 1867. Consult also Evelyn J. Peters's *Aboriginal self-government in Canada: A bibliography* (Kingston, Ontario: Institute of Intergovernmental Relations, Queen's University, 1986 [112p.]) (Aboriginal peoples and constitutional reform) **(I40),** which is organized by broad topics with many subdivisions in which references are listed alphabetically by author with an author index. Supplemented with Evelyn J. Peters's *Aboriginal self-government in Canada: A bibliography, 1987–90* (Kingston, Ontario: Institute of Intergovernmental Relations, Queen's University, 1991 [58p.]) **(I41),** which adds 140 entries. The study of Indian languages in Canada can be updated by reference to the *Canadian journal of linguistics,* v.1– , 1954– (Toronto: Canadian Linguistic Society, University of Toronto), a semiannual publication that contains book reviews and announcements as well as substantive articles. Annual bibliographies and supplements for previous years are entitled *Linguistics Canadian.* For an informal update of ethnographic material, consult *Anthropologica* (Ontario) **(I129),** a semiannual journal concerned mainly with the physical anthropology and cultural anthropology and linguistics of the native peoples of Canada. Each issue has three or four signed critical book reviews and an annotated bibliography of other works newly available. For entry into research results published after 1980, consult either *Native Research Information System Database (NRIS)* by *Alberta Manpower* [computer archive], which is available online from University of Alberta, Department of Computing, for citations to book, articles, journals, reports, conferences, films, and microfilms on sociodemographic issues related to the Alberta native peoples (excluding material on land-claim issues), or the *Yukon Bibliography (YKB)* [computer archive], produced by the Boreal Institute for Northern Studies and available online from QL Systems, for its inclusion of the archaeology and ethnology of native peoples.

I42

Anderson, Eugene N., Jr. *A revised, annotated bibliography of the Chumash and their predecessors.* Socorro, N.M.: Ballena Pr. 88p. (Ballena Press anthropological papers, no.11)

The bibliographic entries are arranged alphabetically by author under the subject headings "Archaeology," "Ethnology," "History," "Linguistics," and "Physical anthropology."

I43

Arctic Institute of North America, Library. *Catalogue of the Library of the Arctic Institute of North America, Montreal.* Boston: Hall, 1971.

Three supplements to date. Beginning with the second supplement, coverage of social science material reflects special efforts to strengthen holdings on northern peoples. The library provides analytics for journal articles (4,500 in the 1968 volume). Includes nonpolar journals which are excluded from the Arctic Institute of North America's annual *Arctic bibliography,* v.1– , 1953– (Washington, D.C.: GPO). Consult also *Boreal northern titles* [computer file] (Boreal Institute for Northern Studies) **(I44).** This machine-readable database makes available online through QL Systems a database of more than 100,000 citations to native newspapers and northern newsletters, journal articles, and government documents in a coverage of the arctic region that includes Iceland and Siberia, with an emphasis on the northern North American regions.

I45

Burch, Ernst S., Jr. "The ethnography of northern North America: A guide to recent research." *Arctic anthropology* 16: 62–146.

An introductory section provides an evaluative review in a classified arrangement. Identifies major research institutes and lists useful bibliographies and reference works. Can be complemented by Albert A. Dekin's *Arctic archaeology: A bibliography and history* (New York: Garland, 1978 [279p.]) ([Garland reference library of science and technology, no.1]). The sections on "Explorers and ethnographers," "Chronologists and prehistorians," and "Archaeologists and anthropologists" reflect the impact of social science theory on archaeology. A brief list of important libraries and museums with collections of Arctic materials is included. A more selective list of sources useful in the study of this region can be identified in June Helm's sixty-four-page bibliography, *Sub-Arctic* (Washington, D.C.: Smithsonian Institution, 1981 [837p.]) (Handbook of North American Indians, v.6) **(I46),** an encyclopedic summary of available knowledge on this region by a group of distinguished scholars. Includes thirteen general articles, twenty-one articles on the Subarctic Shield and the Mackenzie borderlands, fourteen articles on the Subarctic Cordillera, eight articles on the Alaska Plateau, two articles on the South of Alaska range, six articles on native settlements, and two articles on special topics. There is besides the bibliography an extensive index in which the term *Eskimos and Indian words* is subdivided to identify thirty-five ethnic groups.

I47

Cashman, Marc, and Barry Klein. *Bibliography of American ethnology.* Bicentennial 1st ed. Rye, N.Y.: Todd, 1990. 1,078p.

The elaborate classified arrangement guides a reader into a select list with an emphasis on ethnic materials. For example, the major topic "General ethnology" has subdivisions including ethnic literature, ethnicity and education, ethnicity and employment, ethnicity and language, ethnicity and politics, race and religion, and race and racism. AMERICAN INDIANS is expanded for topical terms and ethnic-group names. JEWISH AMERICANS is expanded for topical terms. Most North American ethnic groups are given some treatment. Canadian material is included for the first time in this edition. Biographical section with current addresses and telephone information. The bibliography of this edition has been greatly expanded to 4,500 titles.

I48

Dempsey, Hugh Aylmer. *Bibliography of the Blackfoot.* Metuchen, N.J.: Scarecrow, 1989. 245p. (Native American bibliography series, no.13)

Lists 1,828 numbered entries arranged alphabetically by author under twenty-three topical subject headings without annotation. A helpful bibliography of bibliographies can be found (numbers 33–43) and a list of journals (numbers 44–66). There is a brief topical index at the end of the book.

I49

Herisson, Michel R. P. *An evaluative ethnohistorical bibliography of the Malecite Indians.* Ottawa: National Museum of Canada, 1974. 260p. (Mercury series. National Museum of Man. Ethnology Division. Paper no.16)

Published works are listed alphabetically by author, with extensive annotation (p.7–141). Manuscripts are described (p.142–228).

I50

Hirschfelder, Arlene, and Martha Kreipe de Montaño. "Bibliography." *The Native American almanac: A portrait of Native America today.* p.315–27. New York: Prentice Hall, 1993. 341p.

Includes the most recent sources of information about contemporary North American Indians including topics such as fishing treaties, tribal government, education and religion. Concise update of Hodge's *Bibliography of contemporary North American Indians* **(I24).**

I51

Hoyt, Anne Kelley. *Bibliography of the Chickasaw.* Metuchen, N.J.: Scarecrow, 1987. 212p. (Native American bibliography series, v.11)

Lists 1,636 numbered entries for books, journals, and government documents. There is a list of journals cited and archival material available. In the subject index, there are forty-five entries under CLAIMS with no terms for expansion, and there are ninety-four entries under COAL AND ASPHALT with no expansion terms.

I52

Johnson, Bryan R. *The bibliography of the Blackfeet: An annotated bibliography.* New York: Garland, 1988. 231p. (Garland reference library of the social science, 441)

Annotations and brief notes guide the reader. Citations for books, articles, phonograph records, filmstrips, motion pictures, dissertations, U.S. government documents (but not Canadian government documents), and manuscript entries arranged alphabetically by author. Includes all scholarly languages. Excludes reference works and essays in monographs. Author/subject index.

I53

Laird, W. David. *Hopi bibliography: Comprehensive and annotated.* Tucson: Univ. of Arizona Pr., 1977. 735p.

Describes 2,935 entries accurately with annotations. Arranged by author. There are extensive cross-references and author and subject indexes. Excludes book reviews, letters to the editor, photographs without text, newspaper articles.

I54

Marken, Jack Walter, and Herbert T. Hoover. *Bibliography of the Sioux.* Metuchen, N.J.: Scarecrow, 1980. 370p. (Native American bibliography series, no.1)

Topical arrangement of 3,367 books, articles, and government documents. Of special interest are the entries under the headings "Dissertations" and "Journals, newspapers and special reports." Subject index. Author index.

I55

Native American bibliography series, v.1– , 1981– . Metuchen, N.J.: Scarecrow. Irregular.

A continuing series of carefully delineated bibliographies. Consult especially no.1, Jack Walter Marken and Herbert T. Hoover's *Bibliography of the Sioux,* 1980 [370p.] **(I54);** no.2, Littlefield and Parins's *A bio-bibliography of Native American writers, 1772–1924* **(I158);**

no.4, Bright's *Bibliography of the languages of native California including closely related languages of adjacent areas* **(I28)**; no.5, Littlefield and Parins's *A bio-bibliography of Native American writers, 1772–1924* **(I159)**; no.6, Terry P. Wilson's *Bibliography of the Osage* (1985 [162p.]) **(I56),** with 722 annotated entries for books and articles in a classification arrangement; no.7, Kutsche's *Guide to Cherokee documents in the northeastern United States* **(I177)**; no.8, Frank W. Porter's *In pursuit of the past: An anthropological and bibliographic guide to Maryland and Delaware* (1986 [258p.]) **(I57)**; no.9, Michael L. Tate's *The Indians of Texas* (1986 [514p.]) **(I58):** book 1, Indigenous ethnic group arrangement, and book 2, Chronological arrangement; no.10, Thomas J. Blumer's *Bibliography of the Catawba* (1987 [547p.]) **(I59)**; no.11, Anne K. Hoyt's *Bibliography of the Chickasaw* **(I51)**; no.12, David R. Edmunds's *Kinsmen through time: An annotated bibliography of Potawatomi history* (1987 [217p.]) **(I60)**; no.13, Dempsey's *Bibliography of the Blackfoot* **(I48)**; no.14, Michael L. Tate's *The upstream people: An annotated bibliography of the Omaha tribe* (1991 [504p.]) **(I61),** which divides entries to categories with an author and subject index; no.15, Karen Booker's *Languages of the aboriginal Southeast: An annotated bibliography* (1991 [241p.]) **(I62)**; no.16, Trafzer's *Yakima, Palouse, Cayuse, Umatilla, Walla Walla, and Wanapam Indians* **(I66).**

I63

Olsen, Stanley J. *Mammal remains from archaeological sites: Southeastern and southwestern United States.* Cambridge, Mass.: Peabody Museum, Harvard University, 1980. 162p.

A standard handbook for the identification of deer, opossums, rats, dogs, wolves, foxes, pigs, sheep, cows, and bears.

I64

Salzmann, Z. *The Arapaho Indians: A research guide and bibliography.* New York: Greenwood, 1988. 113p. (Bibliographies and indexes in anthropology, no.4)

A brief historical and ethnographic sketch followed by 702 entries. Relevant topical categories for each entry are identified from thirty-two subject headings. Includes books, articles, archival materials, and government documents with detailed entry to all relevant items in the *Congressional serial set* and the *United States statutes at large.* An index by broad topic.

I65

Smith, Dwight La Vern. *Indians of the United States and Canada: A bibliography.* Santa Barbara, Calif.: ABC-Clio, 1974–83. 2v.

The section on the history (1492–1900) of indigenous ethnic groups is subdivided chronologically by culture area and ethnic group. Other broad topics include pre-Columbian history and the twentieth century. Table of contents guides the reader. In the index, an asterisk (*) indicates biography, and quotation marks (″) indicate autobiography. BIBLIOGRAPHY is an indexing term. Indexes by author, geographical area, and subject.

I66

Trafzer, Clifford E. *Yakima, Palouse, Cayuse, Umatilla, Walla Walla and Wanapam Indians: An historical bibliography.* Metuchen, N.J.: Scarecrow, 1992. 253p. (Native American bibliography series, 166)

Classifies 950 annotated entries in ten topical chapters with an author and subject index. Includes information on important repositories for these indigenous groups.

I67

Weist, Katherine, et al. *An annotated bibliography of northern Plains ethnohistory.* Missoula: Department of Anthropology, University of Montana, 1985. 299p. (Contributions to anthropology, no.8)

Arranges 718 entries in a detailed classification system. There is a combined personal-name, indigenous ethnic-group, and subject index, and a listing of forty-five bibliographies.

Informational Reference Searches

For directory information on American anthropologists, consult first the *AAA guide* **(A53)** for directory information. The best international directory is still the "International directory of anthropological institutions" **(A56),** which could usefully be reissued in a new edition. For an encyclopedic summary of current research, consult first the *Annual review of anthropology* **(A57),** which has frequent bibliographic reviews of all aspects of anthropology as the discipline develops worldwide.

Directories

I68

Furtaw, Julia C. *Native American information directory: A guide to organizations, agencies, institutions, programs, publications, services, and other resources concerned with the indigenous peoples of the United States and Canada, including: American Indians, Alaska natives, native Hawaiians, aboriginal Canadians.* Detroit: Gale, 1993. 371p.

Entries include name of organization, collection, publisher, address, telephone number, fax number, and contact person. Even the 4,500 entries in this work do not completely cover directory needs for these groups. To supplement this resource, consult Klein's *Reference encyclopedia of the American Indian* **(I70),** resources identified in Corley's *Resources for native peoples studies* **(I01),** a directory of American Indian language courses in Evans's *Bibliography of language arts materials for native North Americans* **(I29),** the list of directories in Haas's *Indians of North America* **(I02),** "U.S. and Canadian Indian periodicals" **(I16),** and directories listed in Parezo, Perry, and Allen's *Southwest Native American arts and material culture* **(I36).**

Relevant recent directories can often be identified in the machine-readable database described as *GPO monthly catalogue* [computer file] **(B21).** Examples include (1) *Major Indian health facilities in the United States* (Rockville, Md.: Indian Health Service, 1987 [4p.]); and (2) United States, Indian Health Service, *Directory of field offices, field installations and headquarters* (Rockville, Md.: U.S. Department of Health and Human Services, Public Health Services, Health Resources and Services Administration, 1985 [16p.]). "Arts and crafts" in *The American Indian index,* p.204–320 (Denver: Arrowstar, 1985 [320p.]) **(I69),** an alphabetic list of shops, trading posts, associations, and museums that sell Indian arts and crafts.

I70

Klein, Barry T. *Reference encyclopedia of the American Indian.* 4th ed. New York: Todd Publications, 1986. 2v.

V.1 contains directories of "Magazines and periodicals" (p.303–38) and to government agencies, reservations, American Indian councils, other Indian groups, federally recognized bands and groups, Canadian bands and reserves, national associations, state and regional associations, museums, monuments and parks, libraries, Native American centers, Indian health services, Indian schools, college courses, communications, audiovisual aids. There is an alphabetized list of all entries, a subject bibliography, and a publications index. V.2 is a far from comprehensive biographical directory. For biographies of the Southeastern woodlands Indians, consult Norman Heard's more complete *Handbook of the American frontier* **(I111).**

Encyclopedias and Handbooks

I71

American Indian civil rights handbook. 2d ed. Washington, D.C.: U.S. GPO for the U.S. Commission on Civil Rights, 1980. 71p.

Topics include "Fair treatment by the police," "When you are questioned," "Fair treatment in the courts," "Custody of children," "Civil and due process," "Right to vote," "Right to equal employment opportunities," "Where to find a lawyer," "Indian student rights," and "Complaints about violations of rights." There is a useful directory of agencies (p.51–57).

I72

Bibliographical series. [Bloomington] Newberry Library Center for the History of the American Indian. v.1– , 1976– . Bloomington: published for the Newberry Library by Indiana Univ. Pr.

The *Bibliographical series* provides an almost encyclopedic coverage of the North American Indian. When searching for these titles in a culture area context, readers will find that most of the volumes are distributed to appropriate culture areas by full descriptions and detailed annotations by Hoxie and Markowitz's *Native Americans* **(I06).** While cataloging practices for unnumbered series usually scatter these works throughout the collection of a research library, the achievement of Hoxie and Markowitz that places each volume in the context of related efforts has made it possible for us to concentrate attention on the encyclopedic value of this series. All volumes start with a bibliographic essay followed by numbered bibliographic entries. Directly preceding the bibliography is a list that identifies the five most basic works. Usually less than 100 pages in length, they are especially valuable for the selective identification of the most useful sources about a region, an indigenous ethnic group, or a topic. Titles to date include:

Titles that cover culture areas: William E. Unrau, *The emigrant Indians of Kansas* (1979 [80p.]) **(I73),** lists 187 bibliographic entries; Robert F. Heizer, *Indians of California* (1976 [68p.]) **(I74);** Frank W. Porter, *Indians in Maryland and Delaware* (1979 [107p.]) **(I75),** lists 230 bibliographic entries; Omer C. Stewart, *The Indians of the Great Basin* (1982 [138p.]) **(I76),** lists 364 bibliographic entries; Neal Salisbury, *The Indians of New England* (1982 [109p.]) **(I77),** lists 237 bibliographic entries; Elizabeth Tooker, *The Indians of the Northeast* (1978 [77p.]) **(I78);** Henry F. Dobyns and Robert C. Euler, *Indians of the Southwest* (1980 [153p.]) **(I79),** lists 434 bibliographic entries; June Helm, *The Indians of the Subarctic* (1976 [91p.]) **(I80);** Robert S. Grumet, *Native Americans of the northwest coast* (1979 [108p.]) **(I81);** Adamson Hoebel, *The Plains Indian* (1977 [75p.]) **(I82);** James Howlett O'Donnell, *Southeastern frontiers: Europeans, Africans, and American Indians, 1513–1840* (1982 [118p.]) **(I83),** lists 337 bibliographic entries.

Titles that introduce individual indigenous ethnic groups: Michael E. Melody, *The Apaches* (1977 [86p.]) **(I84);** Raymond D. Fogelson, *Cherokees* (1978 [98p.]) **(I85);** Peter J. Powell, *Cheyennes, Ma?heo?o'a* (1980 [123p.]) **(I86),** lists 241 bibliographic entries; Clara Sue Kidwell and Charles Roberts, *Choctaws* (1980 [110p.]) **(I87),** lists 234 bibliographic entries; Michael D. Green, *The Creeks* (1979 [114p.]) **(I88),** lists 215 bibliographic entries; Clinton Alfred Weslager, *The Delawares* (1978 [84p.]) **(I89);** Peter Iverson, *The Navajos* (1976 [64p.]) **(I90);** Helen Hornbeck Tanner, *The Ojibwas* (1976 [78p.]) **(I91);** Martha Royce Blaine, *The Pawnees* (1980 [109p.]) **(I92),** lists 274 bibliographic entries; Harry A. Kersey, Jr., *The Seminole and Miccosukee ethnic groups* (1987 [102p.]) **(I93),** lists 249 bibliographic entries; Herbert T. Hoover, *The Sioux* (1979 [79p.]) **(I94),** lists 213 bibliographic entries; Helen H. Schuster, *The Yakimas* (1982 [152p.]) **(I95),** lists 292 bibliographic entries.

Titles that introduce topical issues: Robert J. Surtees, *Canadian Indian policy* (1982 [107p.]) **(I96),** lists 293 bibliographic entries. The essay is divided between a discussion of the French period, the English period, and the Canadian period. James P. Ronda and James Axtell, *Indian missions* (1978 [85p.]) **(I97);** Henry F. Dobyns, *Native American historical demography* (1975 [95p.]) **(I98);** Rayna Green, *Native American women: A contextual bibliography* (1983 [120p.]) **(I99),** with a date index and a subject index; Russell Thornton and Mary K. Grasmick, *Sociology of the American Indians* (1980 [113p.]) **(I100),** Dean R. Snow, *Native American prehistory* (1979 [75p.]) **(I101);** Francis Paul Prucha, *United States Indian policy* (1977 [54p.]) **(I102);** Russell Thornton, Gary D. Sandefur, and Mary K. Grasmick, *The urbanization of American Indians* (1982 [87p.]) **(I103).** In a departure from the format of earlier volumes, W. R. Swagerty's *Scholars and the Indian experience: Critical reviews of recent writing in the social sciences,* ed. by W. R. Swagerty (1984 [296p.]) **(I104),** identifies sources and provides references that support a particular point of view.

I105

Damas, David, ed. *The Arctic.* 1984. Washington, D.C.: Smithsonian, 1984. 829p. (Handbook of North American Indians, v.5)

In a classified arrangement, nine articles on the Arctic as a whole, twenty-one articles on the Western Arctic (including the bands Nunivak, Asiatic Eskimo, Siberian, Saint Lawrence Island, Bering Strait, Kotzebue Sound, North Alaska coast, interior Alaska, and Mackenzie Delta), eleven articles on the Canadian Arctic (including the Central Copper, Netsilik, Iglulik, Caribou, Baffinland, and Inuit). The 1950–80 period is given coverage with nine articles on the contemporary situation. The maps, illustrations, seventy-seven-page bibliography, and index all meet the high standards of this series. In the index, the term ESKIMO AND INDIAN WORDS is subdivided to identify about twenty-six ethnic groups.

I106

D'Azevedo, Warren L., ed. *The Great Basin.* 1986. Washington, D.C.: Smithsonian, 1986. 852p. (Handbook of North American Indians, v.11)

Seven articles on the culture area as a whole, fourteen articles on prehistory, nine articles on ethnology, seven articles on history, and eight articles on special topics, including studies of kinship and mythology. There is an indigenous ethnic group coverage for Western Shoshone, Northern Shoshone and Bannock, Eastern Shoshone, Ute, Paiute, Owens Valley Paiute, and Washoe. Strong bibliography. Excellent indexing. In the index, the term INDIAN WORDS is subdivided to identify about 70 ethnic groups.

I107

Erichsen-Brown, Charlotte. *Medical and other uses of plants for the last 500 years.* Aurora, Ontario, Canada: Breezy Creeks Pr., 1979. 512p.

Develops the history of use of North American plants, especially by eastern indigenous ethnic groups. Organized under the chapter headings "Evergreen trees," "Deciduous trees," "Scrubs and vines," "Wet open places," "Woods and thickets," and "Dry open places." There is a glossary, a list of sources cited, a general index, and a botanical index. Consult also Daniel E. Moerman's *American medical ethnobotany: A reference dictionary* (New York: Garland, 1977 [527p.]) (Garland reference library of social science, v.34) in which 4,869 entries are listed under fifty-five indications or uses. Identifies 1,288 plant species for 530 genera for 118 families. The same information is available in Virgil J. Vogel's better organized and less costly *American Indian medicine* (Norman: Univ. of Oklahoma Pr., 1970 [583p.]) (Civilization of the American Indian series, v.95]) **(I108).** The appendix (p.148) lists by common names those botanical drugs used by the North American Indians, and cites the literature in which reports on this use can be documented. This study is closely related to studies of Native American medical practices, which can be informed by reference to Dianne R. Kelso and Carolyn L. Attneave's *Bibliography of North American Indian mental health* (Westport, Conn.: Greenwood, 1981 [411p.]) **(I109),** which organizes 1,363 bibliographic entries, including unpublished research reports and government documents. Covers nature healing practices, suicide, and witchcraft and includes belief systems. There are author, culture area, and indigenous ethnic group indexes and a descriptor index rich in terms such as ARCTIC HYSTERIA, WINDIGO PSYCHOSIS, WITCHCRAFT, and GHOST SICKNESS, but with as many as 100 items without subdivision. The entries for this printed bibliography are the product of printouts from the machine-readable database *(WIRS) White Cloud Information Center* [computer archive] (Gaines Hall, UOHSC, 840 S.W. Gaines Rd., Portland, OR 97201), from which lists of more recent material can be custom-prepared for interested scholars about any topic or indigenous ethnic group that is the focus of an individual inquiry.

I110

Gill, Sam D., and Irene F. Sullivan. *Dictionary of Native American mythology.* Santa Barbara, Calif.: ABC-Clio, 1992. 425p.

Organized to propel the user into the literature. Rich in entries that identify stories, characters, themes, symbols, and motifs of Native American culture, this has 1,300 entries and many cross-references as well as citations to the reference section in the back of the book. Eleven maps delineate culture areas and encourage controlled comparison in the use of the indigenous ethnic group index, which is also keyed to sources in the reference section.

I111

Heard, J. Norman. *Handbook of the American frontier: Four centuries of Indian-White relationships.* Metuchen, N.J.: Scarecrow, 1987. 5v. (planned) (Native American resources series, 1)

V.1, *The Southeastern woodlands* (1987 [487p.]). An achievement based on the traditions of historical scholarship, this dictionary of indigenous ethnic groups includes individual Indians, Blacks, and captives of note. There are entries for missionaries, frontier families, and events from the first White settlements to the end of the Indian wars. Each entry includes cross-references to related materials, and citations to sources used. Four additional volumes are planned, including an index in the last volume.

I112

Heizer, Robert F., ed. *California.* Washington, D.C.: Smithsonian, 1978. 800p. (Handbook of North American Indians, v.8)

There is a key to indigenous ethnic group territories and articles covering forty-six North American Indian ethnic groups. Topical issues are covered with twenty-five articles. The excellence of the illustrations and the detailed structure of the index meet the high standards of this series. Under the index term INDIAN WORDS, find subdivisions for sixty-nine ethnic groups.

I113

Hirschfelder, Arlene, and Paulette Molin. *The encyclopedia of Native American religions: An introduction.* New York: Facts on File, 1992. 367p.

Brief entries on belief, ceremonies, missionaries, movements, and court cases are arranged alphabetically. The structure, as the title suggests, invites its use as a specialized dictionary with compact statements of accurate fact, but because of its bibliographic limitations it fails to establish a basis for additional investigation. However, because of the close relationship between American Indian mythology and American Indian religion, this can be used as a companion volume to Gill and Sullivan's *Dictionary of Native American mythology* **(I110).**

I114

Hodge, Frederick Webb. *Handbook of American Indians north of Mexico.* Washington, D.C.: GPO, 1907–10. 2v. (Smithsonian Institution. Bureau of American Ethnology. Bulletin 30)

Reprint (Grosse Pointe, Mich.: Scholarly Pr. [1968]) provides an extensive compilation of authoritative information, arranged alphabetically, with a large number of cross-references. Aims to give a brief description of every linguistic group, confederacy, or indigenous ethnic group division, and settlement. Includes information concerning indigenous ethnic relations, history, languages, manners and customs, arts, and industries. Each entry includes the origin and derivation of the name treated, as well as a record of variant forms of the name, with references in each case to the authority used. These "synonyms" are assembled, in alphabetic order, in volume 2 as cross-references. All cited sources are listed in an extensive bibliography in volume 2. Many articles have illustrations. There are additionally regional handbooks of merit, such as Robert H. Ruby and John A. Brown's *A guide to the Indian tribes of the Pacific Northwest* (Norman: Univ. of Oklahoma Pr., 1986 [289p.]) (Civilization of the American Indian series, v.173) **(I115),** which describes histories, personalities, and cultures of 150 native indigenous ethnic groups in an encyclopedic format with many cross-references and suggested readings. There has been a recent reprint of Muriel H. Wright's 1951 *A guide to the Indian tribes of Oklahoma* (Norman: Univ. of Oklahoma Pr., 1987 [300p.]) **(I116),** in which the sixty-seven indigenous ethnic groups described are arranged in alphabetic order.

I117

Jenness, Diamond. *The Indians of Canada.* Toronto: Univ. of Toronto Pr., 1977. 432p.

Originally published in 1932 as National Museum of Canada, Anthropological series, no. 15. Still the standard source of information on Canadian Indians. Pt.1, Indian life under such topical headings as economic conditions, dwellings, social and political organizations, religion, art and music. Pt.2, Indigenous ethnic groups individually arranged by regional area, including Eastern Woodlands, Plains, Pacific Coast, Cordillera, Mackenzie and Yukon river basins, and Eskimos. Contains many quotes from the writings of early explorers. Since this work is carefully documented, the general index can be used to identify primary source material of early contacts. For a more contemporary compendium, inspect Hope MacLean's *Indians, Inuit, and Métis of Canada* (Toronto: Gage, 1982

[134p.]), with a bibliography that can be used in conjunction with John W. Freisen and Terry Lusty's *The Métis of Canada: An annotated bibliography* (Toronto: OISE Pr. for Ontario Institute for Studies in Education, 1980 [99p.]), with resources identified in Abler's *A Canadian Indian bibliography* **(I39)** and, more recently, Lokky Sai's *Native peoples of Canada in contemporary society: A demographic and socioeconomic bibliography* (London, Ontario: Population Studies Centre, University of Western Ontario, 1989 [82p.]) **(I118),** which includes books, articles, dissertations, working papers, and government publications.

I119

O'Leary, Timothy, and David Levinson, eds. *North America.* V.1, *Encyclopedia of world cultures.* Boston: Hall, 1991. 425p.

Makes available in conventional form the information previously available through resources described in chapter 4, "Ethnology and Cultural Anthropology," such as Murdock's *Ethnographic atlas* **(D73)** and the Human Relations Area Files, *HRAF source bibliography* **(D16).** The bibliography to the introduction includes a list of references, including directories and recent monographs that summarize what is known about the American Indian. In this volume, eighty-two authorities contribute signed articles on the "lifeways" of indigenous ethnic groups according to a format of cultural variables. Arranged A to Z by indigenous ethnic group name. An excellent ready-reference source when the most basic information is needed. Absolutely accurate. Extremely limited bibliographies often do not identify separately published indigenous ethnic group bibliographies even when comprehensive sources are available. A bibliographic volume for the set is promised.

I120

Ortiz, Alfonso, ed. *Southwest.* Washington, D.C.: Smithsonian, 1979. 701p. (Handbook of the North American Indians, v.9)

Covers the Pueblo (Hopi and Zuni) Indians and the Tewa for prehistory, history. Includes articles on individual pueblos and topical articles on such issues as worldview, mythology, fine arts, and the economy. Excellent bibliographic support to contents. Under the indexing term INDIAN WORDS, find subdivisions for twenty-four ethnic groups.

I121

Ortiz, Alfonso, ed. *Southwest.* Washington, D.C.: Smithsonian, 1983. 868p. (Handbook of North American Indians, v.10)

Covers historic southwestern groups other than the Pueblo. A consolidation of the complex literature dealing with the Apache, Navajo, Via, Papagos, Yumans, Havasupai, Mohave, Quechan, Tepehuan, and other groups in north central and northwest Mexico but excluding Baja. Excellent illustrations. A massive bibliography. Professionally structured indexing. Under the term INDIAN WORDS, find subdivisions for sixty-nine indigenous ethnic groups.

I122

Sturtevant, William C., ed. *Handbook of North American Indians.* v.1– , 1978– . Washington, D.C.: Smithsonian. 20v.

For sale by the Supt. of Documents, Govt. Print. Office. To be twenty volumes when completed. Each volume in this set has extensive bibliographic coverage to support the text. Approaches based on a familiarity with full set will be rewarded. Usually available in reference sections of research libraries as a set that brings information about all of North American Indian groups into a shared format. It is this structure that makes comparisons more reliable. No serious literature search about the American Indian can avoid the appropriate volumes since each volume provides a seasoned compendium of established results in the topics and North American Indian ethnic groups covered. Published to date: v.4, *History of Indian-white relations* **(I127);** v.5, *Arctic* **(I105);** v.6, *Sub-Arctic* **(I46);** v.7, *Northwest coast* **(I124);** v.8, *California* **(I112);** v.9, *Southwest* **(I120);** v.10, *Southwest* **(I121);** v.11, *Great Basin* **(I106);** v.15, *Northeast* **(I126).** Topics of the other volumes are v.1, *Introduction,* devoted to general descriptions of anthropological and historical methods, and sources and summaries for the whole continent on social and political organization, religion, and the performing arts; v.2, *Indians and Eskimos in contemporary society;*

v.3, *Environment, origins, and population* (physical anthropology); v.13, the *Plains;* v.14, the *Southeast;* v.16, *Technology and visual arts;* v.17, *Languages;* v.18 and v.19, *Bibliographical dictionary;* and v.20, *Index.*

The unrelenting excellence of each volume marks an editorial achievement of the first importance. The series continues a tradition of anthropological scholarship in which reports are consolidated and published in a style that any educated person can understand. The bibliographies are extensive and the illustrations valuable and profuse. In each volume, the indexing term ESKIMO AND INDIAN WORDS has been subdivided for all ethnic groups discussed in that volume. This handbook will be the standard source for years to come.

Hoxie and Markowitz's *Native Americans* **(I06)** has an arrangement that makes it possible to identify select related monographs for these summaries of culture area results. Additional encyclopedic surveys of indigenous ethnic units can be made through the somewhat less scholarly but highly accurate and ruthlessly contemporary *North American Indian series* (Phoenix: Indian Tribal Series Pubs.) **(I123),** which provides handbooks to the contemporary North American Indian. Edited in a contemporary tradition that binds the past to the present and predicts something of the future. These thin volumes usually include a portrait of the present North American Indian chairman. Readable and inexpensive. All authors have carried out some fresh research on the reservations since the 1930s. Some of the North American Indians included are the Oto-Missouria, Seneca, Kickapoos, Havasupai, Hopi, Paiute, Crow, Osage, Papago, Yakima, Mescalero Apache, Creek, Seminole, Kalispel, Cherokee, Chickasaw, Oneida, Cocopah, Comanche, Southern Ute, Kenaitze, Chitimacha, Quapaw, Narragansett, Ponca, Kaw, Minnesota Chippewa, Walapai, Pawnee, Coushatta, Modoc, Wichita, Potawatomi, and Eskimo.

I124

Suttles, Wayne, ed. *Northwest coast.* Washington, D.C.: Smithsonian, 1990. 777p. (Handbook of North American Indians, v.7)

Contributions include five general articles, six articles on the history of research in the area, six articles on the history of contact. There are thirty-eight articles on the native peoples and three topical articles. Consolidates the anthropological record of this culture area. Excellent illustrations and an excellent bibliography meet the high standards of this monographic set. The index is professionally structured. For example, under the term INDIAN WORDS, subdivisions identify the location in text of coverage for seventy-one ethnic groups.

I125

Thernstrom, Stephan, Ann Orlov, and Oscar Handlin, eds. *Harvard encyclopedia of American ethnic groups.* Cambridge, Mass.: Belnap Pr. of Harvard Univ., 1980. 1,076p.

A dictionary arrangement. Signed articles by hundreds of contributors. Twenty-eight thematic essays and hundreds of brief entries. An abundance of maps and tables are scattered to support the running text. There are extensive bibliographies even for the briefest entries. A sample of maps provides an illustration of the geographic origin of these groups: Afghanistan (p.3); Africa (p.7); Albania (p.24); Alsace and Lorraine (p.30); American Indian tribes, ca. 1600 (p.60). Primary locations of 173 American Indian groups, 1970 (p.61).

I126

Trager, Bruce G., ed. *Northeast.* Washington, D.C.: Smithsonian, 1978. 924p. (Handbook of North American Indians, v.15)

After a section on prehistory with nineteen articles, there is coverage of the St. Lawrence lowland with twenty-four articles, and of the Great Lakes with twenty-four articles. Excellent illustrations. Comprehensive consolidation of research in this culture area. Extensive bibliography. Excellent index in which INDIAN WORDS is subdivided for eighty-one ethnic groups.

I127

Washburn, Wilcomb E., ed. *History of Indian-White relations.* Washington, D.C.: Smithsonian, 1988. 838p. (Handbook of North American Indians, v.4)

Twelve articles on the national policies, three articles on the military situation, thirteen articles on political relations, eleven articles on economic relations, and eight articles on religious relations are followed by nine articles on conceptual relations. Excellent bibliography. Detailed index.

State-of-the-Art Reviews

I128

American Indian culture and research journal. v.1– , 1974– . Los Angeles: American Indian Studies Center, UCLA. Quarterly.

Issues frequently focus on a research topic. Often includes review articles which provide a number of views on some important topic of current interest. As many as ten book reviews, sometimes five pages each in length. Covers ethnology, social anthropology, and linguistics. Includes articles on mythology, religion and ritual, art forms, and social customs.

I129

Anthropologica. v.1– , 1955– . Ontario, Canada: Laurentian University. Semiannual.

Articles in an issue may focus on a single topic. Publishes longer review articles in the book review section which frequently contain bibliographical information on a dozen or more titles. Coverage includes contemporary life, social class, acculturation, myth, ideology, art forms, and discussions of theory and method.

Searching Graphic Materials

Searches for nonprint materials sometimes neglect American Geographical Society of New York, Map Department, *Index to maps in books and periodicals* **(A59).** Ethnographic resources in this index are often identified under the heading LINGUISTIC MAPS; and since the internal contents of books and journals are cited, the identified resources often have ethnographic significance to match their graphics value. For a select list of widely held ethnographic films, see Heider's *Films for anthropological teaching* **(A63).**

Maps and Atlases

I130

Driver, Harold E. *Indian tribes of North America.* Baltimore, Md.: Waverly, 1953. 30p.

Consists essentially of a map with explanatory notes, a bibliography of sources, and an index of North American Indian names. It is the third attempt to provide a continental map assigning definite North American Indian territories to 238 North American Indian ethnic groups. In an earlier and still valuable effort, seven maps were included in Alfred Louis Kroeber's *Cultural and natural areas of native North America* (Berkeley: Univ. of California Pr., 1953 [240p.]) (California University, Publications in American archaeology and ethnology, v.38) **(I131).** Consult also *Native North Americans on disc* **(I17).**

The maps of the distribution of American Indian languages can be used to display spatial relationships among North American Indian ethnic groups. See Charles F. Voegelin and E. W. Voegelin's *Map of North American Indian languages* (New York: American Ethnological Society in collaboration with Indiana Univ., 1944; dist. by J. J. Augustin, New York [97×90cm.], publication no.20) **(I132).** For one especially useful source for early maps, consult Laura E. Kelsay, comp., *List of cartographic records of the Bureau of Indian Affairs* (Washington, D.C.: General Services Administration, National Archives and Records Service, 1975 [187p.]) (Special list, National Archives and Records Service, no.13]) **(I133).** Describes in detail the maps of the Bureau of Indian Affairs. Covers exploration routes, North American Indian lands, and reservations. Subject index. See also National Anthropological Archives *Catalog to manuscripts at the National Anthropological Archives* **(A69).**

I134

Ferguson, T. J., and E. Richard Hart. *A Zuni atlas.* Norman: Univ. of Oklahoma Pr., 1985. 154p. (Civilization of the American Indian series, v.172)

Forty-four maps, including a number of water-related maps; climatic data; archaeological sites; sixteenth-century village locations;

"traditional" use areas for hunting, gathering, grazing, and agriculture; religious, nineteenth-century maps from various sources; and reservation maps showing changes over time. The text that accompanies each map is illustrated with line drawings and black-and-white photographs. Thorough documentation.

I135

Krauss, Michael E. *Native peoples and languages of Alaska.* Fairbanks: Alaska Native Language Center, University of Alaska, 1982. 79×118cm.

Color coding identifies range of twenty Alaskan native languages. "Table of language groups" shows language groups, and the number of speakers for each language.

I136

Prucha, Francis Paul. *Atlas of American Indian affairs.* Lincoln: Univ. of Nebraska Pr., 1990. 191p.

Large-scale maps graphically translate information about populations, land cessions, reservations, the army, and the Indian frontier. There are twelve sets of maps, and each set has an introduction with detailed information essential to the use of this atlas. Basically, this source is meant to inform studies of frontier policy.

I137

Tanner, Helen Hornbeck. *Atlas of Great Lakes Indian history.* Norman: Univ. of Oklahoma Pr., 1987. 224p. (Civilization of the American Indian series, v.174)

Thirty-three maps cover period 1640–1871. At the end of the text for each map there is a list of sources used. There is a twenty-one-page bibliography. Coordinate labels at the margins of the maps without a grid structure allow the introduction of densely compact information.

I138

Waldman, Carl. *Atlas of the North American Indian.* New York: Facts on File, 1985. 276p.

Combines maps, line drawings, and text in a presentation of seven broad topics: "Ancient Indians," "Ancient civilizations," "Indian lifeways," "Indians and explorers," "Indian wars," "Indian land cessions," and "Contemporary Indians." More than 100 maps. Includes ancient Mesoamerican area and discusses the distributions of agriculture from that center. Appendixes include an eleven-page chronology of native American history, twenty-one pages on North American Indians and their reservations, sixteen pages on native place names, six pages on museums and historical societies. There is a brief bibliography and an eight-page index.

Additional narrative support for this excellent volume can be found in Carl Waldman's *Encyclopedia of Native American tribes* (New York: Facts on File, 1988 [293p.]) **(I139),** with its brief coverage of 150 North American Indian ethnic groups of the United States, Canada, and Mexico, organized alphabetically by ethnic group. Each essay is packed with concise information on language families, means of subsistence, houses, art, legends, rituals, and other facets of indigenous ethnic lifeways. The list of references concentrates on popular titles. Three hundred color illustrations increase the reference value of this work for public libraries. See also O'Leary and Levinson's more scholarly *North America* **(I119).**

Photographs, Films, and Line Drawings

An inviting selection of ethnographic films can be identified as a special feature of O'Leary and Levinson's *North America* **(I119).** In the use of photography for scholarly communication, one standard of excellence was established by the publication of Oliver La Farge's *A pictorial history of the American Indian* (New York: Crown, 1956 [272p.]) **(I140),** which provides a vivid summary for the specialist and an introduction for the general reader. The coming of humans to the New World is followed by chapters on cultural areas and a chapter on the Indian in the modern world. Its emphasis is on arts, crafts, and the Indian way of life. Examples are well chosen from early drawings, museum artifacts, and elsewhere. The text is clear and concise. Also useful is *Indians: The great photographs that reveal North American Indian life, 1847–1929, from the unique collection of the Smithsonian Institution,* ed. by Joanna Cohan Scherer and Jean Burton Walker (New York: Crown, 1973 [189p.]) **(I141).**

Three regional groups are portrayed by Leonard McCombe's *Navaho means people,* with text by Evon Z. Vogt and Clyde Kluckhohn (Cambridge, Mass.: Harvard Univ. Pr., 1951 [159p.]) **(I142);** Emma L. Fundaburk's *Southeastern Indians: Life portraits, a catalog of pictures, 1564–1860* (Metuchen, N.J.: Scarecrow, 1969 [reprint of 1958 ed., 135p.]) **(I143);** and Emma L. Fundaburk and Mary D. Foreman's *Sun circles and human hands: The Southeastern Indians—Arts and industries* (Luverne, Ala.: Anchor, 1957 [232p.]) **(I144).** Recently, more and more of the rich holdings in photography preserved in museums are becoming accessible because of a remarkable increase in the publication of finding lists, which are often a byproduct of the new technologies used in the cataloging of modern preservation efforts.

I145

Bataille, Gretchen M., and Charles L. P. Silet. *Images of American Indians on film: An annotated bibliography.* New York: Garland, 1985. 216p. (Garland reference library of social science, v.307)

Arranges 364 items in three sections for period 1910–83: (1) General approaches as seen by dominant white culture, (2) Studies of Native Americans in film, (3) Individual reviews and essays about a single film. The appendix provides detailed descriptions of films which include Native Americans as subjects, giving date of film, running time, black-and-white or color, director, and primary actors. Index to essays, book titles, authors, film titles, major actors, directors, and other individuals connected with the film.

I146

Frazier, Patrick. *Portrait index of North American Indians in published collections.* Washington, D.C.: U.S. Government Printing Office for the Library of Congress, 1992. 1,422p.

An alphabetic list of 75 sources is followed first by an index of indigenous ethnic groups (with individuals thereunder) and then an index of Indian individual names. Many full-page illustrations reproduce selected portraits. Also useful is Lewis Barbara Burger's *Guide to the holdings of the still pictures branch of the National Archives,* Washington, D.C.: National Archives and Records Administration, 1990 [166p.]) **(I147),** which has not only an excellent name and subject index but also an arrangement that reflects the various agencies that created the records. Bibliographies devoted to individual North American Indian ethnic groups often identify the location of archival material. For example, Wilson's *Bibliography of the Osage* **(I56)** includes a description of the holdings of the Federal Records Center, a regional branch of the National Archives located at Ft. Worth, Texas, which houses the Osage Agency Records.

I148

Justice, Noel D. *Stone Age spear and arrow points of the midcontinental and eastern United States: A modern survey and reference.* Bloomington: Indiana Univ. Pr., 1987. 288p.

Descriptions arranged in chronological order. Each cluster includes line drawings to scale and a geographic distribution map. Eight color plates are placed at the front of the book. A text identifies sites and published references. A bibliography provides full descriptions of all sources mentioned in the text. Index.

Searching Published Source Material

The historical method is so widely applied to studies of the North American Indian that critical masses of bibliographic guides to published primary source materials are available. These ease entry into newspapers, contact-period travel accounts, and reproductions of documents and unpublished research reports. A more detailed guide to the use of the historical method with these resources would be helpful. Find here a representative sample of available materials. Since resources from other disciplines in *Fieldwork in the Library* have been concentrated largely into chapter 2, a careful inspection of that chapter can identify important materials that are the result of historical research into American Indian life.

I149

Danky, James Philip, Maureen E. Hady, and Ann Bowles. *Native American periodicals and newspapers, 1829–1982: Bibliography, publishing record, and holdings.* Westport, Conn.:

Greenwood, 1984. 532p. (Historical guide to the world's periodicals and newspapers)

The most comprehensive bibliography on the topic. Bibliographic descriptions of 1,164 serial titles with a short description of subject focus and library location and holding information. The entries have twenty-two elements and include OCLC number, LC number, and RLIN control number. Tells where entries are indexed, and records the availability of microfilm. Subject, editor, publisher, geographic, catchword, subtitle and chronological indexes greatly increase the reference value of this work.

I150

ERIC: Research in education. v.1– , 1966– . Washington, D.C.: GPO. Monthly.

An abstracting and indexing service. All indexed documents are available in microcopy from a basic set, *ERIC documents (1953–1963),* with annual additions thereafter as described above. Also available as a machine-readable database as described in *ERIC* [computer file] **(B16).** Can be useful in searches for unpublished material about the contemporary North American Indian. The rules of inclusion seem to be anything an educator might find useful. For example, Rudolph C. Troike's *Bibliography of bibliographies of the languages of the world, volume 1: General and Indo-European languages of Europe* (Philadelphia: John Benjamins, 1990 [473p.]) (Amsterdam studies in the theory and history of linguistic science, series 5, Library and information sources in linguistics, v.19) **(I151),** is devoted to languages so marginal to anthropological concerns as to be listed here only as an example of published work by an established scholar that may be less immediately valuable than some of his other papers available here in archival copy. Rudolph C. Troike's *Bibliographies of American Indian languages,* 1979 [180p.]) **(I152),** available only in microfiche in ERIC databases, contains twelve bibliographic lists of publications on twelve linguistic groups. Many of these entries have been collected into ERIC's *American Indian education: A selected bibliography,* v.1– , 1969– (Las Cruces, N.M.: ERIC Clearinghouse in Rural Education and Small Schools, New Mexico State University) **(I153).** The publisher varies. Most recently by the National Educational Laboratory Publishers, Inc., 813 Airport Blvd., Austin, TX 78702. *Supplement* no. 1, 1970 [124p.]; *Supplement* no. 2, 1971 [286p.]; *Supplement* no. 3, 1973 [437p.]; *Supplement* no. 5, 1975 [396p.]; *Supplement* no. 6, 1976 [242p.]; *Supplement* no. 7, 1976 [278p.]. Long, detailed abstracts.

I154

Evans, Karen, comp. *Masinahikan: Native language imprints in the archives and libraries of the Anglican Church of Canada.* Toronto: Anglican Book Centre, 1985. 357p.

Lists 746 works in forty-four native North American languages. Arranged first by language and then alphabetically by main entry. Indexed by author, translator, editor, printer, publisher, nonroman orthographic, native language title, and subject heading.

I155

Fay, George Emory. *Charters, constitutions, and by-laws of Indian tribes of North America.* Greeley: Colorado State College Museum of Anthropology, Colorado State College, 1967–80. 16 parts. (Ethnology series, 1–188)

Reproductions of the charters and other legal instruments governing present-day North American Indian organizations are arranged by cultural and geographic areas. v.1, *The Sioux tribes of South Dakota;* v.9, *The Northwest and Alaska.* An important contribution. Also consult Lester Hargrett's *A bibliography of the constitutions and laws of the American Indians* (Cambridge, Mass.: Harvard Univ. Pr., 1947 [124p.]) **(I156),** which records all published Indian legal instruments prior to the reorganization of North American Indian groups following the Act of 1934. Arranged by North American Indian group. Locates copies in fifty libraries, public and private.

I157

Littlefield, Daniel F., and James W. Parins. *American Indian and Alaskan native newspapers and periodicals.* Westport, Conn.: Greenwood, 1984. 3v. (Historical guides to the world's periodicals and newspapers)

V.1, *1825–1924;* v.2, *1925–1970;* v.3, *1971–1985.* Excludes Canadian and Mexican titles. Bibliographic description of each title is supported with a list of "information sources" about that title in other books. Seven of the fifty holdings sources are commercial firms. There is extensive descriptive information for each title (up to eight pages for one entry) and a twenty-page introductory essay in volume 1.

I158

Littlefield, Daniel F., Jr., and James W. Parins. *A bio-bibliography of Native American writers, 1772–1924.* Metuchen, N.J.: Scarecrow, 1981. 343p. (Native American bibliography series, no.2)

Pt.1, Author list with bibliographies; pt.2, Brief biographies of the authors. The author list includes 4,371 published letters, political essays and addresses, satirical works in dialect, poetry, fiction, myths, legends, historical works, and reminiscences written in English by Native Americans. There is an indigenous ethnic group affiliation index and a subject index.

I159

Littlefield, Daniel F., and James W. Parins. *A bio-bibliography of Native American writers, 1772–1924. A supplement.* Metuchen, N.J.: Scarecrow, 1985. 339p. (Native American bibliography series, v.5)

More primary source materials for the investigation of life cycles, cultural participation, religious rituals, and other topical interests of anthropologists. Continues the scope and arrangement of Littlefield and Parins's *A bio-bibliography of Native American writers, 1772–1924* **(I158).**

I160

National Museum of Canada. *Books in native languages in the Rare Book Collections of the National Library of Canada (Livres en langues autochtones dans les collections de livres rares de la Bibliothèque Nationale du Canada).* Joyce M. Banks, comp. Rev. and enl. ed. Ottawa: National Library of Canada, 1985. 190p. Lists 500 titles in fifty-eight languages.

Searching Unpublished Material

Any archival search should start with Polly Grimshaw's *Images of the other* **(I167).** Many topical bibliographies include dissertations in their coverage: Johnson's *The bibliography of the Blackfeet* **(I52),** Porter's *Native American basketry* **(I37),** Fowke and Carpenter's *A bibliography of Canadian folklore in English* **(I18).** Recent German-language dissertations can be identified in chapter 1, "What Every Anthropologist Needs to Know," from *Abstracts in German anthropology* **(A33).** Some entry into English- and French-language material can be achieved by the use of the machine-readable databases described in *Dissertations abstracts ondisc* [computer file] **(B14)** and *Francis bulletin signalétique* [computer file] described as a subfile of *FRANCIS* [computer file] **(B19).** The following bibliographies are devoted entirely to lists of dissertations and include research on the American Indian.

Searches for unpublished materials often benefit from an inspection of the National Anthropological Archives, *Catalog to manuscripts at the National Anthropological Archives* **(A69).** The unpublished material contained in archival collections of either the professional papers of anthropologists or the field notes of contact period observers is sometimes available in microform.

Archives

I161

Anderson, William L., and James A. Lewis. *A guide to Cherokee documents in foreign archives.* Metuchen, N.J., Scarecrow, 1983. 751p. (Native American bibliography series, no.4)

Describes 8,000 items in twenty-five archives in Europe, Canada, and Mexico. Arranged by country, archive, and then date. Thirty-four pages of index.

I162

Bean, Lowell John. *California Indians: Primary resources: A guide to manuscripts, artifacts, documents, serials, music, and illustrations.*

Ramono, Calif.: Ballena Pr., 1977. 227p. (Ballena Press anthropological papers, no.7)

Detailed descriptions of all collections of site reports, artifacts, photographs, and music held in the listed institutions. Arranged first under "California" in an alphabetic list of counties, subdivided by city. The second part covers the United States other than California, organized by state and subdivided by city. The last section is for "Other countries"—alphabetic and subdivided by city. A final section lists publications and references. In this resource, consult Joan Berman's "The literature search on Californian Indians" (p.15–21), which discusses bibliographies, books, and online databases. For an illustration of how little is known about most North American Indian ethnic groups in California, consult the detailed annotations provided for each entry in Mary La Lone's comprehensive *Gabrielino Indians of Southern California: An annotated ethnohistoric bibliography* (Los Angeles: Institute for Archaeology, UCLA, 1980 [72p.]) (Occasional paper, Institute of Archaeology, no.6) **(I163).**

I164

Chepesiuk, Ronald, and Arnold Shankman, comps. *American Indian archival material: A guide to holdings in the Southeast.* Westport, Conn.: Greenwood, 1982. 325p.

Arranged alphabetically by state and then by city. Lists repositories reporting no holdings. Name, place, and subject indexes.

I165

DeWitt, Donald, ed. *American Indian resource materials in the Western History Collections, University of Oklahoma.* Norman: Univ. of Oklahoma Pr., 1990. 272p.

Organizes 1,056 entries under topical terms such as "Primary documentation," "Photograph collections," "Oral histories," "Library collections of microform including publications of the National Archives," "Commercial microform collections," "Newspapers and periodicals." The index has adequate expansions. For example, under indigenous ethnic group names, BIBLIOGRAPHY leads to unpublished indigenous ethnic group bibliographies.

I166

Freeman, John F., and Murphy D. Smith. *A guide to manuscripts relating to the American Indian in the American Philosophical Society.* Philadelphia: The Society, 1966. 2v.

Pt.1, a description of 294 manuscript collections. Pt.2, arranged alphabetically by indigenous ethnic group and subdivided for ethnology and linguistics, with relevant manuscripts described under these categories. Can be supplemented by reference to Van Keuren's *"The proper study of mankind": An annotated bibliography of manuscript sources on anthropology and archaeology in the Library of the American Philosophical Society* **(D78).** Find here a discussion of the relationship between the American Philosophical Society and the early development of American archaeology and ethnology, and a user's guide to the bibliographic entries.

I167

Grimshaw, Polly. *Images of the other: A guide to microform manuscripts on Indian-White relations.* Champaign: Univ. of Illinois Pr., 1991. 117p.

Truly a guide to resources. Greatly eases entry into the holdings of 65 microform collections. The appendix lists other guides to American Indian primary research materials. Describes the history, content, editorial practices, printed guides, and finding aids to each of the described microform sets, which include government agency reports, missionary letters, Indian tribal documents. Gives location of original manuscripts. After each description there is a list of readings on the subject of that collection. The index has adequate expansion. Additional comments can be found for 20 microform sets in Richard N. Ellis's "Published source materials on Native Americans," *Western historical quarterly* 7(1976): 187–92 **(I168).**

I169

Harrington, John Peabody. *The papers of John Peabody Harrington in the Smithsonian Institution, 1907–1957: A guide to the field notes.* Ed. by Elaine L. Mills. Millwood, N.Y.: Kraus, 1981–88. 7v.

V.1, *Native American history, language, and culture of Alaska/Northwest coast;* v.2, *Native American history, language, and culture of northern and central California;* v.3, *Native American history, language, and culture of southern California Basin;* v.4, *Native American history, language, and culture of the Southwest;* v.5, *Native American history, language, and culture of the Plains;* v.6, *Native American history, language, and culture of the Northeast/Southeast;* v.7, *Native American history, language, and culture of Mexico/Central America/South America.*

I170

Hill, Edward E. *The Office of Indian Affairs, 1824–1880: Historical sketches.* New York: Clearwater, 1974. 246p.

The National Archives and Records Service sells 962 reels in a set of microfilmed correspondence received between 1824 and 1880 at the Bureau of Indian Affairs. The set can be purchased in single reels, groups of reels, or as a complete set, and the guide opens up the entire collection to scholars. The introduction identifies the variety of entries under which data may be found. A jurisdictional index identifies agencies. The indigenous ethnic group index provides the official list of indigenous ethnic groups from the point of view of the United States government.

I171

Hill, Edward E. *Guide to records in the National Archives of the United States relating to American Indians.* Washington, D.C.: National Archives and Records Service, General Services Administration, 1981. 467p.

"Much of this guide was developed from papers prepared for the National Archives Conference on Research in the History of Indian-White Relations, held in the National Archives Building, June 15–16, 1972" (p.4). Records are described according to the record groups to which they are allocated. First records from the period before the federal government was established; then records of the U.S. Government (chiefly treaties); next records of Bureau of Indian Affairs, then of Office of the Secretary of the Interior and agencies of that department; then records of the War Department. After that the guide follows federal hierarchy, with records of Congress and legislative agencies, the court records, records of presidential agencies, and records of executive departments.

I172

Jennings, Francis, William N. Fenton, and Mary A. Druke, eds. *Iroquois Indians [microform]: A documentary history of the diplomacy of the six nations and their league: Guide to the microfilm collection.* Woodbridge, Conn.: Research Publications, 1985. 50 microfilm rolls.

Filmed from the holdings of the Newberry Library of archives in English, Dutch, and French, with some bibliographical references. Extensive documentation of government relations, including copies of treaties and other primary source material.

I173

Keeling, Richard. *A guide to early field recordings (1900–1949) at the Lowie Museum of Anthropology.* Berkeley: Univ. of California Pr., 1991. 487p.

The front matter traces the history of the ethnographic survey of California Indians and validates the extensive documentation of the context of the recordings. Additionally it identifies other sources for California Indian recordings and recommends access through the "24 catalogue" numbers assigned at the time the cylinders were copied onto preservation tapes. The main body of the work consists of an item-level description of the contents of 113 series of recordings. The appendixes summarize the recording series and a bibliography. Both the index by indigenous ethnic groups and the index by collectors provide cylinder series, disc series, and tape number identifications. Also accessible are the recordings described in Dorothy Sara Lee's *Native North American music and oral data: A catalogue of sound recordings, 1893–1976* (Indiana Univ. Pr., 1979 [463p.]) **(I174),** and Anthony Seeger and Louise S. Spear's *Early field recordings: A catalogue of cylinder collections at Indiana University Archives of Traditional Music* (Indiana Univ. Pr., 1987 [198p.]) **(I175)** and the *Federal Cylinder Project catalog: A guide to cylinder collections in* *federal agencies,* v.1– , 1984– (Washington, D.C.: GPO) **(I176).** Eight volumes to date. To identify early field workers in indigenous languages, consult Voegelin and Harris's *Index to the Franz Boas collection of materials for American linguistics* **(E99).**

I177

Kutsche, Paul. *A guide to Cherokee documents in the northeastern United States.* Metuchen, N.J.: Scarecrow, 1986. 258p. (Native American bibliography, v.8)

Description of 6,257 documents held in twenty-one libraries listed alphabetically under each institution. Each entry has a brief but careful annotation. Index by name (including individuals, authors, and indigenous ethnic groups) with a very few subject entries interspersed into the name alphabet.

I178

Quinn, David Beers. *Sources for the ethnohistory of northeastern North America to 1611.* Ottawa: National Museums of Canada, 1981. 93p. (Paper, Canadian Ethnology Service, no.76)

Organized by date of reported contact between the Indians and presettlement Westerners as recorded in fifty-eight published sources and manuscripts. Each source is summarized in detail for ethnographic content.

I179

Roberts, Sharman E. "Cultural resources management bibliography." *CRM bulletin* 10 (1987) (4): 8.

Reports on a computerized bibliography that makes available thousands of reports from the national parks. *Cultural resources bibliography* (CRBIB) is being converted to dBase III Plus. Some of the reports cited are available on fiche. Additional help in identifying anthropological material can be found in the section on the National Park Service in *Directory of federal historical programs and activities,* v.1– , 1981– . (Washington, D.C.: American Historical Association, Society for History in the Federal Government, National Coordinating Committee for Promotion of History, 1988 [84p.]) **(I180).** Provides an alphabetical listing of all employees, with telephone numbers, a program section organized by agency which lists scope of historical activity, and relevant address information. An appendix lists societies active in federal history and documentary projects related to federal history, including archaeological records.

I181

Seaburg, William R. *Guide to Pacific Northwest Native American materials in the Melville Jacobs Collection and in other archival collections in the University of Washington Libraries.* Seattle: University of Washington Libraries, 1982. 113p. (Communications in librarianship, no.2)

Divided into two parts: pt.1, Melville Jacobs Collection of linguistic and ethnographic papers and sound recordings; pt.2, Anthropological collections of Mary Edel, V. E. Garfield, E. Gunther, R. Olsen, and R. Ransom. Indexes to sound recordings by language and dialect, to informants, to collectors of sound recordings, and to Jacobs linguistic and ethnographic papers.

I182

Washburn, Wilcomb E. *The American Indian and the United States: A documentary history.* New York: Random, 1973. 4v.

Reproduces twenty documents covering the period 1763–1970. Presented chronologically under broad subject headings such as reports of the Commissioner of Indian Affairs, congressional debates, judicial decisions, treaties, and acts of Congress.

I183

Wheelwright Museum of the American Indian. *Guide to the microfilm edition of the Washington Matthews papers: ten rolls.* Albuquerque: Univ. of New Mexico Pr., 1985. 109p.

Divided into three parts: pt.1, Biography of Matthews and biographical references; pt.2, bibliography of published works by Matthews; pt.3, descriptive inventory of papers, including correspondence, notes, notebooks, notes on readings, photos, sketches, followed by a list of items retained at the University of California at

Berkeley, the National Archives, the archives of the Southwest Museum, Los Angeles, and documents from miscellaneous sources. The roll list can also be entered through indexes by selected names and subjects.

Dissertations

I184

Dockstader, Frederick J., comp. *The American Indian in graduate studies: A bibliography of theses and dissertations.* New York: Museum of the American Indian. Heye Foundation, 1973–74. 2v. (Contributions from the Museum of the American Indian. Heye Foundation, v.25)

V.1, 2d ed. of 1957, covers 1890–1955; v.2, F. J. Dockstader and A. W. Dockstader, comps., covers 1955–70. Edition by same title published in two volumes as *Contributions from the Museum of the American Indian, Heye Foundation,* no.15. The bibliography does not attempt to be critical, but about half the entries have brief, informative annotations. Arrangement is alphabetic by author, with the degree, date, institution, title, and pages for each entry and reference to the published version (if any). Indexed for topics, indigenous ethnic groups, archaeological sites, geographical names. Covers 7,446 dissertations from 1890 to 1970. See also Gifford S. Nickerson's *Native North Americans in doctoral dissertations, 1971–1975: Classified and indexed research bibliography* (Monticello, Ill.: Council of Planning Librarians, 1977 [77p.]) (Council of Planning Librarians, Exchange bibliography, no.1232]) **(I185),** which adds 500 dissertations. Planned as a supplement to Dockstader; however, limited to United States and Canada and includes only items listed in *Comprehensive dissertation index,* described as item 2 in the annotation to Haas, "Anthropology" **(B01).**

I186

Kerst, Catherine Hiebert. *Ethnic folklife dissertations from the United States and Canada, 1960–1980: A selected annotated bibliography.* Washington, D.C.: American Folklife Center, Library of Congress, 1986. 69p. (Publications of the American Folklife Center, no.12)

A list arranged alphabetically by author with a list of eight bibliographic sources and an index by ethnic groups.

I187

Manson, Spero M., comp. *Psychosocial research on American Indian and Alaska native youth: An indexed guide to recent dissertations.* Westport, Conn.: Greenwood, 1984. 228p. (Bibliographies and indexes in psychology, no.1)

Table of contents includes the following topics: childbearing, personality development, mental health, bilingualism, intelligence, cognition, perceptual processes, social perceptions, self-imagery, achievement, school environment, educational policy, interventions. There is a glossary and description of index terms to assist entry from an expanded topical vocabulary.

MESOAMERICA, THE CARIBBEAN, AND SOUTH AMERICA

The development of this chapter on the Americas assumes that the reader has exhausted Balay's *Guide to reference books* **(B02).** As a class, reference resources covering both North and South America are often useful in Latin American studies. For example, in this section consult page 16 of Coe's *Atlas of ancient America* **(H12)** for maps that illustrate the differences between the areas of distribution for culture areas. The reference works cited below are often organized by culture area, and the geographical boundaries of culture areas are pragmatically used in *Fieldwork in the Library* by the organization of available resources. In some areas, like Mesoamerica, the leading bibliographic resources are organized without regard to national boundaries. In other areas, like Brazil, the national boundary has come to dominate the organization of reference sources. When this is true, anthropological resources tend to cover the national territory and "contiguous regions" so that culture areas are more or less retained as units of organization. Thus published reference books about a geographic area, rather than political subdivisions, define the geographic coverage of each section of *Fieldwork in the Library.* And the coverage of the bibliographic guides selected to head each chapter defines the geographic range of that chapter. Search strategies are defined in terms of these available resources.

For the detailed subject indexing of a powerful (but far from comprehensive) collection, consult first Wolf and Folk's *Indians of North and South America* **(H04).** For the more European perspective, consult other entries in the section between **(H01)** and **(H12).** For detailed, country-by-country entry, consult Block's "Anthropology" **(J01),** which greatly reduces the need for elaboration in this chapter.

For an introduction to reference works organized by form, consult both the general bibliography section in Covington's *Latin America and the Caribbean* **(J02)** and the list of reference works introduced in McNeil and Valk's *Latin American studies* **(J03).** For subject entry in related disciplines, the anthropologist can turn in confidence to the various chapters in Covington's *Latin America and the Caribbean* **(J02).** An annual bibliography of bibliographies compiled in recent years under Loroña's "Anthropology" **(J11)** can identify new reference books. Entry by names of indigenous peoples has been greatly eased by the publication of Welch's *The Indians of South America* **(J21).**

Recently, directories of anthropologists published in Latin American countries have been elaborated to provide detailed entry into contemporary scholarly efforts. Examples would include *MesoAmérica: Directorio y bibliografía, 1950–1980* **(KA14)** and Friedemann and Arocha's *Bibliografía anotada y directorio de antropólogos colombianos* **(KB64).** The indexing service HAPI **(J28)** corresponds in part to a subfile of *Latin American studies* [computer file] **(J27)** and provides subject entry into 250 scholarly journals. The more nearly comprehensive bibliographic control of monographs with some selective entries into a very wide range of periodicals can be found in the indispensable *Handbook of Latin American studies* **(J26)** and in the bibliographies supporting reviews in the *Latin American research review* **(J56).** There have been recent consolidations of bibliographies under very broad topical entries, which are described at entries **(J29)** through **(J34).** Steward's *Handbook of South American Indians* **(J43)** is the basic encyclopedic resource for South American Indians, including the circum-caribbean area. Elaborating on the consolidation of research results, regional handbooks are now being published to integrate more recent knowledge. Examples include Wauchope's *Handbook of Middle American Indians* **(KA62)** and more recently Moñtano Arágon's *Guía etnográfica lingüística de Bolivia* **(KB30)** and Ribeiro's *Suma etnológica brasileira* **(KB51).**

Searching Bibliographic Guides

Consult Auckland "Getting into the literature" **(A01)** and in *Fieldwork in the Library* see listed guides to the subdisciplines of anthropology. Inspect Covington's *Latin America and the Caribbean* **(J02),** Block's "Anthropology" **(J01),** and McNeil and Valk's *Latin American studies* **(J03).** Entry to published monographs by names of indigenous peoples has been greatly eased by Welch's *The Indians of South America* **(J21).**

Bibliographic Guides

J01

Block, David. "Anthropology: Bibliography." In Paula H. Covington, ed. *Latin America and the Caribbean: A critical guide to research sources,* p.57–98. Westport, Conn.: Greenwood, 1992. 924p.

Of the first importance. Extensive coverage of ethnology, social anthropology, archaeology, linguistics, and folklore. This work greatly reduces need for coverage here in the topical areas of archaeology, anthropological linguistics, and indigenous narrative. For linguistics, the Block list, with its rich annotations and nation-state arrangement, can be expanded for South American materials. Use, for this expansion, the indexing by language available in Tovar and Tovar's comprehensive *Catálogo de las lenguas de América del Sur* **(J34)** and the bibliographic elaborations identified in Ruhlen's *A guide to the world's languages* **(E73),** with its list of sources for language classification (p.ix and xiii) and the chapter on "North and South America" organized under Eskimo-Aleut, Na-Dene, and Amerind language families.

For archaeology, Block's "Anthropology" **(J01)** provides a select list with lucid annotations and a nation-state arrangement that can be expanded by consulting Alcina Franch's *Bibliografía básica de arqueología americana* **(H07),** which provides not only comprehensive coverage of bibliographies but also a knowledgeable selection of survey texts. For Latin American folklore and indigenous narrative, consult Block's "Anthropology" **(J01),** which can be usefully supplemented for South America by reference to Niles's *South American Indian narrative, theoretical and analytical approaches* **(KB02).** Consult indigenous peoples (p.166–74) and subject (p.175–83). Consult both Block's "Anthropology" **(J01)** and issues of *Latin American Indian literatures* **(J52)** to identify bibliographic reviews of indigenous religious traditions.

Block's identification of archival resources shows strength and can be expanded by reference to the more general sources listed in other chapters of Covington's *Latin America and the Caribbean* **(J02),** including a chapter on sociology for definitive coverage of the subcultures of the Negro and other nonindigenous ethnic groups in Latin America. This is an excellent source for entry into the bibliographic achievement of historians in their studies of ethnic groups. Such studies include Humberto Rodríguez Pastor et al., *Chinos culíes: Bibliografía y fuentes, documentos y ensayos* (Lima, Peru: Instituto de Apoyo Agrario e Instituto de Historia Rural Andina, 1984 [212p.]).

Block organized his contribution in a classified arrangement in which a general section is followed by coverage under the broad topics "Anthropological linguistics," "Archaeology," "Ethnohistory," and "Social anthropology." Each of these topics is subdivided by country, and under each country further subdivided by form. Within this elaborate organization, Block includes an extensive list of bibliographies, dictionaries, encyclopedias, and directories. An especially useful feature is the inclusion, under countries, of published descriptions of collections in important museums. Block includes more general sources such as volumes of the *World bibliographical series* **(B43),** which often provide select entry into anthropological monographs, with an emphasis on English-language materials. From this series, we cite in this chapter Biggins's *Argentina* **(KB84).**

Depth of coverage is strengthened by the bold and knowledgeable inclusion of summary texts such as Milcíades Chaves Chamorro's *Trayectoría de la antropología colombiana: De la Revolución en Marcha al Frente Nacional* (Bogotá, Colombia: Editorial Guadalupe; published for COLCIENCIAS, 1986 [220p.]), with its analysis of the history of anthropology in Colombia, and of many one-volume surveys of single countries such as Luis Ferrero's *Costa Rica precolumbian: Arqueología, etnología, arte,* 4th ed. (San José, Costa Rica: Editorial Costa Rica, 1981 [491p.]), which provides a synthesis of knowledge to 1980.

J02

Covington, Paula, ed. *Latin America and the Caribbean: A critical guide to research sources.* Westport, Conn.: Greenwood, 1992. 924p. (Bibliographies and indexes in Latin American and Caribbean studies, no.2)

The topical presentation of this work complements the presentation by form found in McNeil and Valk's *Latin American studies* **(J03).** The scope of the chapter written by Covington, "General bibliography," is indicated by the classification system: "Guides" (items 1–10), "Acronyms" (11–19), "Bibliographies" subdivided by country (items 20–152), "Bibliographies, national and trade," "Biography" (items 343–517), "Book reviews" (items 518–23), "Dictionaries, handbooks, yearbooks" (items 524–91), "Directories" (items 587–621), "Dissertations" (items 622–37), "Latin American studies—Guides" (items 638–45), "Library catalogues" subdivided by country (items 663–83), "Periodicals" (items 684–721), "Guides to resources" (items 656–62). Within this framework, Covington identifies many general reference sources useful in anthropological searches.

There follow additional chapters by experts on "Anthropology," "Art and architecture," "Data bases," "Economics," "Education," and "Geography." History is subdivided into chapters titled "General," "Colonial," "Middle," "Modern," and "Brazil." Coverage of literature can be found in chapters titled "Spanish America," "Caribbean," and "Brazil"; the performing arts have chapters titled "Dance," "Film," "Music," and "Theater." There are additional chapters on "Philosophy," "Politics," "Religion," "Sociology," and "Women's studies."

Every topical chapter of this work has two sections: (1) an essay reviewing current trends in ongoing research by a specialist in the field and (2) a bibliography. Nearly every chapter identifies resources with value for some aspect of anthropological literature searches. The recent reference sources in "Women's studies" often lead into work on indigenous patterns of kinship and marriage. "Sociology" includes traditional medicine, demography, marriage, and family, and identifies several journals with anthropological relevance. The inclusion here of urbanization (a major focus of contemporary anthropological research in this culture area) reduces our need to provide coverage on this topic. The bibliography for the chapter on "Geography" includes itemization of the editions of the *Area handbook series* (Washington, D.C.: U.S. Library of Congress). The chapter on geography identifies handbook coverage for *Commonwealth Caribbean* (1989), *Cuba* (1987), and *Paraguay* (1990). These works consistently provide basic factual information about the country covered and are indexed for author, title, and subject.

J03

McNeil, Robert A., and Barbara G. Valk, eds. *Latin American studies: A basic guide to sources.* 2d ed. rev. & enlarged. Metuchen, N.J., and London: Scarecrow, 1990. 458p.

Provides up-to-date entry into the difficult and complex literature of Latin American government documents. Provides a recent topical coverage of Mexican-American ethnic groups in the United States which is not duplicated in *Fieldwork in the Library.* A selection of key reference materials is organized under form, and entry is eased by a lucid table of contents and an innovative and useful reference source index. Libraries in the United States and Europe with exceptional strength in Latin American anthropology are discussed. The published catalogs are embedded in an essay on the use of classification schemes and on the problems of conducting searches for Latin American names. There is useful coverage of general bibliographies, special bibliographies, and encyclopedias. This resource also provides bibliographic essays on specialized subjects and carefully structured guidance through the problems encountered in the identification of dissertations. The chapters on visual materials and on maps are structured to encourage searches in clearly identified reference sources. The discussion of societies and associations in Europe and the Americas is useful for its selectivity.

Searching for Current Materials

In linguistics, *Latin American Indian literatures* **(J52)** has several current awareness features. For developments in archaeology, consult the department "Current research" in *American antiquity* **(C04),** which in the first issue each year summarizes any Latin American archaeological research that can be identified in reports, publications, and announcements of intentions to work in the field. Consult resources under this heading in chapter 1 and in the chapters devoted to the subdisciplines of anthropology.

Spanish-Language Machine-Readable Databases

The faculties of universities throughout Mexico have access to literature searches that access online data through the Universidad Nacional Autónoma de México (National Autonomous University of Mexico), Centro de Información Cientifica y Humanística (CICH). The center indexes journals in all subjects of interest to the Mexican university community. Searches and document delivery are available from the Department of Information, Center for Scientific and Humanistic Information, telex 1774523 (UNAMME), and the electric mail address on SCIENCEnet of CICH.MEXICO. Produces the online database *Clase* [computer file], 1978– (Mexico City: CICH) **(J04).** Available online and in a CD-ROM, which includes the social sciences indexes of 800 Latin American journals, *Bibliografía latino-americana,* and articles about Latin America or by Latin Americans from 8,000 journals published in other scholarly languages. Contains 250,000 citations, including the social sciences. This is the basic collection of resources from which the CD-ROM *Serie información bibliográfica latinoamericana* [computer file], v.1– , 1989– (México: Multiconsult), annual **(J05),** is constructed. This resource is sometimes described under the alternate title *Latin American bibliography on CD-ROM* [computer file]. The first (1989) disc included 62,700 records drawn from *Clase* [computer file] (1978–1987), 544,000 citations from *Periodica* [computer file] (1979–87), 52,000 citations from *Biblat* [computer file] (1978–87).

For a detailed discussion of these resources in a context that includes other machine-readable databases, consult Covington's *Latin America and the Caribbean* **(J02).** It would be difficult to anticipate every database of anthropological value. For example, researchers searching for the latitudinal and longitudinal coordinates for each of 200,000 geographic names might first consult the hardcover edition of Hanson's *Index to map of Hispanic America, 1:1,000,000* **(J59)** on the American Geographical Society's "Map of Hispanic America on the scale of 1:1,000,000." This information would make it possible to order the records of satellite observations of a village or an archaeological site in the Amazon from the United States Geological Survey EROS Data Center at Sioux Falls, South Dakota. Since enhancement techniques make it possible to bring out features hidden by underbrush and trees, anthropologists might want to investigate the *Remote sensing on-line retrieval system (RESORS)* (Ottawa, Ontario: Canadian Centre for Remote Sensing) **(J06),** which cites 84,000 documents and 8,000 35mm slides on instrumentation techniques and applications of remote sensing.

Access to resources listed in major English-language indexing services on Latin American research is available through *Latin American studies* [computer file] **(J27).** To identify computer files from other disciplines, inspect chapter 2 of *Fieldwork in the Library.*

Select Sources of Review in Scholarly Publications

J07

"Inter-American news." In *The Americas: A quarterly review of inter-American cultural history.* v.1– , 1944– . Washington, D.C.: Catholic University of America. Quarterly.

A regular department responsible for communicating current information on new publications, museum programs, conferences, symposia, and fellowships. A department titled "Documents" describes important collections of primary source material. "Book reviews" usually has more than a dozen reviews. Most of the articles focus on Latin America and describe social customs, art, ethnicity, religion, myth, and cultural remains.

J08

Revista española de antropología americana. v.4– , 1969– . Madrid: Departmento de Antropología y Étnología de América, Facultad de Filosofía y Letras, Universidad de Madrid. Annual.

Five to eight book reviews per issue on topics ranging from prehistoric America to contemporary issues reflect the range of substantive articles in this serial. Last issue seen was 1986, with articles on development, kinship, the grammar of an indigenous language, a feminine institution during the Inca period, and levels of abstraction in the study of incest.

Selective Lists of Scholarly Journals

In chapter 1, "What Every Anthropologist Needs to Know," consult p.178 of Frantz's *A student anthropologist's handbook* **(A15)** for a select international list of anthropological journals for Latin America and the Caribbean. More general guidance can be found in:

J09

Covington, Paula. *Indexed journals: A guide to Latin American serials.* Madison: Seminar on the Acquisition of Latin American Library Materials (SALALM) Secretariat, Memorial Library, University of Wisconsin-Madison, 1983. 458p. (Seminar on the Acquisition of Latin American Library Materials Bibliography Series, no.8)

Lists 1,500 periodicals in the social sciences and humanities by title, subject, and country of publication. Indicates sources that index and/or abstract the journals. Describes more than 100 indexing and abstracting services that include Latin America in their coverage. Pt.1, Annotated list of indexes and abstracts by subject. A paragraph at the end of each subject section includes a comparative valuation of the effectiveness of these resources for literature searches in that subject. Pt.2, Journals by broad topic and by country. Irene Zimmerman's *Current Latin American periodicals: Humanities and social sciences* (Gainesville, Fla.: Kallman, 1961 [357p.]) **(J10)** is still useful for its long, descriptive annotations of the established scholarly journals. Organized under broad subject topics, including anthropology, it is supported by a chronological list and a title list of cited serial publications.

Retrospective Searches

Block's "Anthropology" **(J01)** is organized by names of modern political units and provides dense entry into the retrospective bibliographies of this vast literature. McNeil and Valk's *Latin American studies* **(J03)** is organized by form and includes a discussion of general and special bibliographies. These two resources make it possible here to concentrate on the most vitally important sources for anthropologists.

The Columbus Memorial Library's *Index to Latin American periodical literature, 1929–1960* **(J16)** indexes in a single alphabet periodical articles from 1929 to 1968. The *Indice general* **(J16)** updates the Columbus Library catalog to 1970 and includes Instituto Nacional de Antropología y Historia (INAH) publications. *HAPI* **(J28)** can be used to partly update the *Indice general.* In chapter 1, "What Every Anthropologist Needs to Know," both the *Anthropological index* **(A35)** and *Anthropological literature* **(A36)** provide quarterly indexing for an international array of anthropological periodicals. At a more general level of resources with anthropological coverage, material in all scholarly languages can be identified in the databases *Social scisearch* [computer file] **(B37)** and *Humanities index* [computer file] **(B23).** Consult also the databases discussed in Covington's *Latin America and the Caribbean* **(J02).**

Retrospective Bibliographies—Bibliographies of Bibliographies

Consult also Gibson's superb "A bibliography of anthropological bibliographies" **(H01)** and the valuable Library-Anthropology Resource Group's *Anthropological bibliographies* **(A21).**

J11

Loroña, Lionel, ed. "Anthropology." In *Bibliography of Latin American and Caribbean bibliographies: Annual report.* v.1– , 1984–85. Albuquerque: SALAM Secretariat, University of New Mexico. Annual. (Seminar on the Acquisition of Latin American Library Materials)

This source regularly identifies recently published bibliographies of theses completed in Latin American universities, and bibliographic reviews with a topical focus. These special features can be approached through the subject index. Related resources can be placed in the context of preceding volumes by consulting bibliography of bibliographies identified in the "General bibliography" in Covington's *Latin*

America and the Caribbean **(J02),** with special attention to her discussion of the remarkable base constructed by Arthur Eric Gropp's *Bibliography of Latin American bibliographies* (Metuchen, N.J.: Scarecrow, 1976 [2v.]) **(J12),** with supplements. In a triumph of common sense over the main entry forms followed by the Library of Congress, Biggins in *Argentina* **(KB84)** provides what is perhaps the most understandable descriptive bibliography of this group of resources in the annotation to his entry for Gropp's basic work. The Library of Congress uses the main entry "Seminar on the acquisition of Latin American library materials" for the series listed here under the name of the editor. This Library of Congress form will be used by most American research libraries and should be used in most catalog searches to verify local holdings.

Regardless of the descriptive entry, the topical arrangement of these working papers greatly reduces the difficulty of staying current on specialized reference sources for Latin American studies. The issue last inspected was *Bibliography and reference series, 27.* Now in its eighth year, this excellent annual bibliography of bibliographies includes both "Anthropology" and "Archaeology." Maintenance of these subject headings was consistent in all issues inspected (1989–90, 1988–89, 1987–88, 1986–87, and 1984–85). When all volumes are described as a series, each volume has a different but not consecutive series number. Some entries listed in this work, such as Miguel Chase-Sardi's recent *Guía bibliográfica temática de la antropología paraguaya* (Asunción: Universidad Católica de Nuestra Señora de la Asunción, 1988 [253p.]), cannot be located through OCLC and were not in the cataloged collections of either the University of Texas, the University of California, or the Florida university libraries. Again, see *Teses de antropologia defendidas no Brasil* **(KB56),** which is held by the Museum of Mankind Library (London) but cannot be found on OCLC and has not been cataloged by the Benson Collection at the University of Texas. Holdings statements for each entry might be a useful feature for this list, which identifies so many recent but rarely held materials.

These annual volumes are part of a larger project and are compiled into five-year cumulations under the editorship of Lionel Loroña and published by Scarecrow Press. Inspect especially Loroña, Lionel, ed., *A bibliography of Latin American bibliographies, 1980–1984: Social sciences and humanities* (Metuchen, N.J.: Scarecrow, 1987 [225p.]) **(J13),** which cited 9,715 bibliographies from periodicals arranged by discipline and subdivided by country with author and subject indexes.

Retrospective Bibliographies—Biographical Directories

J14

Díaz Polanco, Héctor. *Directorio de antropólogos latinoamericanos, México.* Mexico City: Instituto Panamericano de Geografía e Historia, 1985. 191p. (In progress)

First of a three-volume series. Covers anthropologists who live in Latin America and whose research is about Latin America. Biographical information and a list of publications are provided for each entry. Indexed by educational degree, subject specialty, research by topic, geographic location, and historical time period.

J15

Harman, Inge María, ed. *National directory of Latin Americanists: Biographies of 4,915 specialists.* 3d ed. Washington, D.C.: Hispanic Division, Library of Congress; dist. by GPO, Washington, D.C., 1985. 1,011p.

One index lists specialists by field and subfield, another by country or region. Main entries are alphabetic and are followed by not more than three substantial works in each bibliography. Taylor Publishing has promised a new edition in 1993. There is a more limited coverage with less emphasis on indigenous ethnic group indexing in *HAPI* **(J28),** corresponding to a subfile of *Latin American studies* [computer file] **(J27).**

Retrospective Bibliographies—Broad Scope

Some of the entries below refer to the published catalogs of libraries with distinguished holdings of Latin American materials. These resources often provide classified subject cataloging. Other entries listed here refer to published bibliographies based on a single collection but with subject arrangements of special value to anthropologists. We will describe only the indispensable. Consult also McNeil and Valk's *Latin American studies* **(J03),** which provides excellent guidance in the use of the many published library catalogs used in Latin American studies.

FOR ARTICLES

J16

Columbus Memorial Library. *Index to Latin American periodical literature, 1929–1960.* Boston: Hall, 1962. 8v.

Index to 3,000 periodical articles. Includes indexing for indigenous ethnic groups. Two supplements extend the coverage to 1970. The absence of running heads makes this resource difficult to use. Supplemented to 1970 by Columbus Memorial Library, Pan American Union, *Indice general de publicaciones periódicas latin americanas: Humanidades y ciencias sociales (Index to Latin American periodicals: Humanities and social sciences),* v.1–10, 1961–70 (Metuchen, N.J.: Scarecrow) **(J17),** with each volume in quarterly segments. Volumes 1 and 2 have subject, author, and title entries listed in a dictionary arrangement. Beginning with volume 3, quarterly issues are grouped under subject headings, with cross-references and an annual author index. For complementary indexing of monographs held by the Columbus Memorial Library, consult Welch's *Indians of South America* **(J21),** which includes detailed indexing for indigenous ethnic groups. Covers 10,000 volumes.

FOR BOOKS

For German-language contributions, consult the Ibero-Amerikanisches Institut (Berlin), *Schlagwortkatalog des Ibero-Amerikanischen Instituts: Preussischer Kulturbesitz in Berlin (Subject catalog of the Ibero-American Institute, Prussian Heritage Foundation, Berlin),* v.1– , 1977– (Boston: Hall) **(J18),** with thirty volumes providing a classified arrangement by subject to monographs and articles from 2,000 periodicals with German subject headings. Spanish and English equivalency terms appear in the index and refer to the German term. For materials relating to Brazil and the Caribbean, special strength can be found in the Florida University Libraries, *Catalog of the Latin-American collection* (Boston: Hall, 1973 [13v.]) **(J19),** with a *First supplement* (1979 [7v.]) and regular publication of accessions lists.

J20

University of Texas at Austin. Library. Latin American Collection. *Catalog of the Latin American collection.* Boston: Hall, 1969. 31v. Available on CD-ROM (NISC).

Now named the Nellie Lee Benson Latin American Collection. Available on CD-ROM as a subfile of *Latin American studies* [computer file] **(J27).** Both editions are organized as a dictionary catalog of one of the premier Latin American collections in the world. The original base set included about 175,000 printed books, pamphlets, periodicals, microfilms, and newspapers, particularly those published before 1890. Supplements of five volumes (1971), three volumes (1973), and eight volumes (1975) have brought the bibliography up into the 1970s. Can be updated by the *Bibliographic guide to Latin American studies* **(J25).**

The most common mistake in entering this database is to choose too broad a subject heading. The use of the name of an individual state as an entry (subdivided perhaps by ANTIQUITIES) can often lead to the identification of material that would be identified under no other entry.

J21

Welch, Thomas L. *The Indians of South America: A bibliography.* Washington, D.C.: Columbus Memorial Library, Organization of American States, 1987. 594p. (Hipólito Unínue bibliographic series, v.2)

Contains regional, general, and topical chapters, each subdivided to provide detailed access to 9,161 monographs. It is the abundance of entries for indigenous ethnic groups that makes this an indispensable source. Based on the strong collection at the Columbus Memorial Library, the major subdivisions are (1) Indians of South America, general works; (2) Topical works; (3) Specific regions; (4) Specific peoples; and (5) Specific languages and dialects.

Topical and author/title indexes. A comparable monographic list that clearly dramatizes the strength of the collection at Columbus Memorial Library can be found in Richard A. Hand's *A bookman's guide to the Indians of the Americas: A compilation of over 10,000 catalogue entries with prices and annotations, both bibliographical and descriptive* (Metuchen, N.J.: Scarecrow, 1989 [750p.]) **(J22).** For complementary coverage of articles cataloged by this library, consult the Pan American Union's *Index to Latin American periodical literature* **(J16)** and the Ibero-Amerikanesches Institut's *Schlagwortkatalog des Ibero-Amerikanischen Instituts* **(J18).**

Retrospective Bibliographies—Continuing Bibliographies

Covington's *Indexed journals* **(J09)** identifies more than 100 periodical indexes with some Latin American coverage. Also useful is "Periodicals" in McNeil and Valk's *Latin American studies* **(J03),** which provides a detailed survey of materials, including the following indispensable resources.

J23

"Bibliografía de antropología américana." In *Boletín de antropología américana.* v.1– , 1980– . México [City]: Instituto Panamericano de Geografía e Historia. Semiannual.

A recurring feature. The title of this journal varies. Continues *Boletín bibliográfico de antropología americana* (v.1–41, 1937–79). Apart from the publication of this regular bibliography, the journal maintains a comprehensive worldwide overview of anthropological developments in the Americas, with a running account of research and organizational activity. For a country-by-country record over a period of time, this is the first-choice source both for work in progress and for scholarly publications. Includes obituaries and book reviews. Reviews contents of selected journals. Ethnographic, regional, ethnohistorical, linguistic, and archaeological bibliographies are regularly published. For example, inspect Robert V. Kemper's "Bibliografía comentada sobre la antropología urbana en américa latina" 33–34 (1971): 86–140 **(J24),** which provides an exhaustive listing of bibliographic entries related to his subject. It establishes a starting point on topics in urban research that are currently at the center of much of the active research activity in this culture area. An index volume covers the years 1937–67. In some libraries this serial is held only under the variant title *B.B.A.A: Boletín bibliográfico de antropología américana.* Publishes many topical bibliographies that are definitive to the date of publication. These can alert scholars to the achievement of a kind of critical mass in significant research that tends to attract additional study.

J25

Bibliographic guide to Latin American studies. v.1– , 1979– . Boston: Hall. Annual.

The title entry makes this resource especially valuable in establishing an exact description when an author's name is in question. Since the holdings of the Nellie Lee Benson Latin American Collection are entered semiannually into the CD-ROM *Latin American studies* [computer file] **(J27),** most of the coverage of this resource can be accessed from that resource. Subject, author, and title listings in one dictionary catalog sequence of recent acquisitions by the Benson Latin American Collection of the University of Texas at Austin are supplemented by titles from the Library of Congress in Washington, D.C. Early volumes include the holdings of the New York Public Library.

J26

Handbook of Latin American studies. v.1– , 1935– . Cambridge, Mass.: Harvard Univ. Pr., 1935–47; Gainesville: Univ. of Florida Pr., 1948–78; Austin: Univ. of Texas Pr., 1979– . Annual. Available on CD-ROM (NISC).

Publisher varies. Available in part on CD-ROM as a subfile of *Latin American studies* [computer file] **(J27)** from volume 50 forward. The principal annotated bibliography of books, articles, pamphlets, maps, dissertations, and documents relating to Latin America. Originally a listing of publications of the preceding year. Each volume since 1957 has included important older publications coming to the attention of the editors for the first time. Entries are classified by subtopic. Within each subtopic, the entries are arranged alphabetically. The subtopics are subordinated to topical chapter headings (culture areas which are again subdivided into academic disciplines for which subtopics like "General" and "Excavations and artifacts" are devised). Annotations, mostly in English, are critical as well as descriptive. Beginning in 1964, the handbook has been divided into two parts. Even years are devoted to the humanities, including ethnohistory and pre-Columbian arts and literature. The odd years are devoted to the social sciences, including anthropology and archaeology, subdivided by region and field. Each volume has an excellent subject index. Editorial attention to indexing is reflected in a laudable effort from year to year to expand indexing terms each time the literature grows in complexity and size. In 1968, Francisco José and María Elena Cardona compiled a cumulative author index for the 1936–66 issues of the *Handbook.* Each volume has an author index.

J27

Latin American studies: Volume 1: Multidisciplinary [computer file] (Baltimore, Md.: National Information Services Corporation) [computer file]. Annual. Available on CD-ROM (NISC).

Includes subfile corresponding to *HAPI: Hispanic American periodicals index,* v.1– , 1974– (Los Angeles: UCLA Latin American Center Publications, University of California) **(J28).** Published annually. Volumes for 1970–73 of the printed edition were added later. Available online. A subject and author index to 250 scholarly journals in the social sciences and humanities published worldwide. Book reviews are included. Some special strengths include the regular use of a section for bibliographies, the regular identification of entries for indigenous ethnic groups, and bibliographies of theses as they are published in periodicals. This resource reports bibliographic reviews published in journals like the *Latin American research review* **(J56)** and can be used to provide subject entry to these important sources. The hardcover edition of *HAPI* is dense with "see also" references.

Also useful for its subfile, which aptly corresponds to *Handbook of Latin American studies* **(J26),** for which printed volumes remain a preferred entry in many cases.

Provides partial entry into the Nellie Lee Benson Latin American Collection, described in University of Texas at Austin, Library, Latin American Collection, *Catalog of the Latin American collection* **(J20).**

Retrospective Bibliographies—Topical

Harrison and Cosminsky's *Traditional medicine* **(D25)** and **(D26)** provides entry into the study of ethnomedicine in Latin America. For a more elaborate entry, consult the coverage of sociology in Covington's *Latin America and the Caribbean* **(J02).**

J29

Boggs, Ralph Steele. *Bibliography of Latin American folklore.* New York: Wilson, 1940. 109p.

Reprinted by B. Ethridge-Books, Detroit, 1971. Covers entire region. Classed arrangement provides access to this best basic list. Since 1941, *Internationale volkskundliche bibliographie (International folklore bibliography) (Bibliographie internationale des arts et traditions populaires),* fully described at **(D21),** has issued every two years an index that includes folklore in the Spanish and Portuguese languages both in Europe and in the western hemisphere. It covers books, essays in collections, and articles from more than 1,000 journals worldwide. Organized in a classed system that is subdivided by linguistic group. Block's "Anthropology" **(J01)** provides significant coverage of Latin American folklore reference sources in a classified arrangement by nation state.

J30

Knaster, Meri. *Women in Spanish America: An annotated bibliography from preconquest to contemporary times.* Boston: Hall, 1977. 696p.

Annotates 2,435 items. A detailed subject arrangement is supported by forty-five pages of superb indexing. A companion essay can be found in the 1976 bibliographic review by Meri Knaster, "Women in Latin America: The state of the research," *Latin American research re-*

view 11:3–74, which covers topics of anthropological value beyond the scope of the title. These works in combination provide a useful reference source for anyone interested in family relationships in Latin America. They have a range of convenient use far beyond their topical titles and provide entry into materials of interest especially to cultural anthropologists.

J31

Marshall, Oliver. *European immigration and ethnicity in Latin America: A bibliography.* London: Institute of Latin American Studies, 1991. 165p.

List 1,468 entries in a classed arrangement. General studies are followed by a section that is subdivided by Latin American country. Each entry is capitalized by author under the heading provided by the classification system. There is a directory of migration studies centers (p.151–52). Author index.

J32

Paco, Delfina, and J. Carlos Aramayo. *Bibliografia comentada sobre educacion intercultural bilingue de Bolivia y America Latino (1952–1989).* La Paz: Centro Boliviano de Investigacion y Acción Educativas Area de Communicación y Documentación (ACD), 1989. 205p. (Cuadernos educativos, no.31)

Coverage for most of Bolivia, Mexico, Paraguay, and Peru. Lists 473 entries with long annotations and some material of ethnographic value. Author index.

J33

Standing Conference of National and University Librarians. Institute of Latin American Studies. *A guide to Latin American and Caribbean census material: A bibliography and union list.* London: Institute of Latin American Studies, 1990. 739p.

Includes records from the period of conquest and early colonization. Within the list the arrangement is chronological and by subject thereunder. The index is detailed by country, province, town, and subject. With the exception of the colonial period, it is confined to published censuses through 1979. Arranged alphabetically by country, with a short introduction and content list for each country.

J34

Tovar, Antonio, and Consuelo Larrucea de Tovar. *Catálogo de las lenguas de América del Sur: Con clasificaciones, indicaciones tipológicas, bibliografía y mapas.* Nueva ed. refundida. Madrid: Editorial Gredos, 1984. 632p.

Classed arrangement. A diversity of languages spreading from the southernmost part of South America upwards to Central America. Includes brief sections on bilingual education, "tipológicos," and linguistic maps. Author index. Indexed by languages and dialects. While Block's "Anthropology" **(J01)** does not cite this resource, it does provide excellent annotations for many of the entries that touch on Mesoamerican linguistics. DeMiller's *Linguistics* **(E01)** suggests that this work be used as a companion to Loukotka's *Ethnolinguistic distribution of South American Indians* **(KB07).**

Informational Reference Searches

McNeil and Valk's *Latin American studies* **(J03)** provides a detailed discussion of useful handbooks and of selected European and American societies and associations with an interest in Latin American studies. For American scholars, the American Anthropological Association's *AAA guide* **(A53)** usually provides the best current information about the institutional addresses and research interests of affiliated scholars.

Directories

J35

Cantrell, Karen, and Denise Wallen, eds. *Funding for research, study and travel: Latin America and the Caribbean.* Phoenix: Oryx Pr., 1987. 301p.

Arranges 393 sponsoring organizations alphabetically. Subject and sponsor indexes guide the reader. Samples of previously funded projects are included. Includes a useful bibliography of additional printed sources and online databases.

J36

Fenton, Thomas P., and Mary J. Heffron, eds. *Latin America and the Caribbean: A directory of resources.* Maryknoll, N.Y.: Orbis Bks.; London: Zed Bks., 1986. 142p.

Includes alternative and underground organizations as well as more conventional media and documentation centers. Indexed by organization, individual title of publication, geographic area, and subject.

J37

Macdonald, Roger, and Carole Travis. *Libraries and special collections on Latin America and the Caribbean: A directory of European resources.* 2d ed. London: Athlone Pr. for the Institute of Latin American Studies, University of London, 1988. 339p.

Directory information on printed material in 195 libraries in the United Kingdom and 272 collections in Europe. For a discussion that provides worldwide coverage of published catalogs useful in Latin American studies, consult not only McNeil and Valk's *Latin American studies* **(J03)** for its discussion of library collections but also the discussion of the anthropological value of the collections selected and described in the last section of Block's "Anthropology" **(J01).**

Encyclopedias, Compendiums, Handbooks, Manuals

J38

Collier, Simon, Thomas E. Skidmore, and Harold Blakemore. *Cambridge encyclopedia of Latin America and the Caribbean.* Cambridge: Cambridge Univ. Pr., 1992. 479p.

Signed articles by specialists. An excellent general desk reference book. Organized by broad topics with lengthy articles. With a focus on contemporary issues the topic "Physical environment" has an article titled "Tectonic history and structure." The topic "Economy" has an article "Trade and tourism." The topic "Peoples" has seven articles ranging from a survey of pre-Columbian settlement through current ethnic profiles and migration patterns. A name/subject index provides detailed entry.

J39

Lyons, Patricia J., ed. *Native South Americans: Ethnology of the least known continent.* Prospect Heights, Ill.: Waveland Pr., 1984. 433p.

Includes translations of important research by European and South American anthropologists. Adequately reveals the scope of current research on lowland South American Indians.

J40

Moss, J., and G. Wilson. *Peoples of the world: Latin Americans: The culture, the geographical setting and historical background of 42 Latin American people.* Detroit: Gale, 1989. 323p.

A useful ready reference source arranged in two sections. The first deals with the old cultures (Mayas, Aztecs, Incas). The second addresses cultures of today, devoting between five and ten pages to each group in an A–Z arrangement by indigenous ethnic group. Attempts for each group a compendium on culture, family structure, industry, religion, history, and physical geography. Brief bibliography. Subject index.

J41

Müller, Wolfgang. *Die Indianer lateinamerikas: Ein ethnostatistischer uberblick.* Berlin: D. Reimer, 1984. 179p.

Overview of indigenous Latin America. For each entry listed, information on group location, linguistic family, type of social structure, and approximate population.

J42

Olson, James Stuart. *The Indians of Central and South America: An ethnohistorical dictionary.* Westport, Conn.: Greenwood, 1991. 515p.

Again, a ready reference source with concise entries for Indian groups, with select bibliographies. There is a helpful list of living indigenous ethnic groups by country, and a substantial bibliography.

J43

Steward, Julian H., ed. *Handbook of South American Indians.* Washington, D.C.: U.S. Government Printing Office, 1946–59. 7v. (Smithsonian Institution. Bureau of American Ethnology Bulletin, no.143). Also reprint (New York: Cooper Square, 1963).

Comprehensive synthesis of knowledge about the aboriginal population of South America. Includes a discussion of the deficiencies in this knowledge and the need for future research. Centers attention on the culture of each Indian tribe at the time of its first contact with Europeans: v.1, *The marginal tribes;* v.2, *The Andean civilizations;* v.3, *The tropical forest tribes;* v.4, *The circum-Caribbean tribes;* v.5, *Comparative ethnology of South American Indians;* v.6, *Physical anthropology, linguistics and cultural geography of South American Indians;* v.7, *Index.* Each volume has a bibliography of all references cited in the text. There are many useful maps and photographs. Many of the findings discussed in this handbook have been consolidated in a widely available standard source, Julian Haynes Steward and Louis C. Faron's *Native peoples of South America* (New York: McGraw Hill, 1959 [481p.]) **(J44).**

State-of-the-Art Reviews

J45

América indígena. v.1– , 1941– . México [City]: Instituto Indigenista Interamericano. Quarterly.

Text in English and Spanish. Summaries in English. Often devotes an entire issue to a country, providing topical coverage of such areas as ethnohistory, contemporary culture and languages, theoretical reviews, and a bibliographic review of recent research. Inspect (1) *Panamá indígena* 32 (1972): 3–244 **(J46);** (2) *Paraguay indígena* 49 (1989): 405–605 **(J47);** (3) *Costa Rica* 43 (1983): 5–892 **(J48),** with strong coverage of social organization, religion, linguistics, ethnohistory, and physical anthropology; and *Honduras indígena* 44 (1984): 421–589 **(J49).** Publishes submitted bibliographies of indigenous ethnic groups such as Luis Eduardo Luna's "Bibliografía sobre el ayahuasca" 31 (1986): 235–45.

Additionally this journal maintains a continuing review which rotates around these topics: (1) Human rights and legislation; (2) Ethnic identity; (3) Education; (4) Traditional medicine; (5) Traditional technology; (6) Indian organizations. The volumes into which these topics have been distributed can be identified by consulting "Informe de actividades del Instituto Indigenista Interamericano 1977–1989," *Anuario indigenista* (México City: Instituto Indigenista Interamericano) 49 (1989): 57–160 **(J50).** This section also includes one five-year plan of action for the institute. For subject entry, consult *HAPI* **(J28),** also available as a subfile of *Latin American studies* [computer file] **(J27)** and *Amèricana indígena: 40 años: Índice general* (México City: Instituto Indigenista Interamericano, 1981 [3v.]) **(J51).** This annual is a regular source for bibliographic reviews.

J52

Latin American Indian literatures. v.1– , 1985– . Beaver Falls, Pa.: Geneva College. Semiannual.

Regularly publishes research on anthropological topics; a typical issue will contain at least one book review (sometimes in Spanish). Important for its Bibliography Department, which lists current publications of interest; most recently inspected were Eduardo Lozano's "Latin American Indian languages" 6 (2) (Fall 1990): 180–93, which is continued in 7 (1991). Regularly this journal has published submitted bibliographies and bibliographic essays. Some of these have values that are central to anthropological issues; examples include Eduardo Lozano's "Indian religion and mythology: Pt.1, Indians of Mexico: The Mayas and the Aztecs," 2 (2) (Fall 1986): 173–82 **(J53);** "Indian religion and mythology: Pt.2, Latin America (General), Central America and South America" 3 (1987): 109–25 **(J54);** and "Indian religion and mythology: Bibliography" 2 (Fall 1989): 84–94 **(J55)**—all of which collectively summarize the vast body of available material on the religious mythology of the indigenous people. See also Kazuyasu Ochiai's "Latin American Indian studies in Japan: Minimum information" 5(1989): 92–98, and his "Recent ethnohistorical publications by Japanese Latin Americanists" 7 (2) (Fall 1991): 215–19.

J56

Latin American research review. v.1– , 1965– . Albuquerque: Latin American Studies Assn. Quarterly.

State-of-the-art reviews of the highest quality, supported by bibliographies that are often definitive for scholarly resources. A recent survey of women's studies cited below includes ethnographic material from all of Latin America. But most anthropological reviews published in this journal concentrate narrowly on geographic areas that have traditionally drawn the attention of American scholars, such as John V. Murra, "Current research in Andean ethnohistory" 5 (1970): 3–36; Richard A. Diehl, "Current directions and perspectives in Mesoamerican cognitive archaeology" 19 (1984): 171–81; Frank Soloman, "Andean ethnology in the 1970's: A retrospective" 17 (1982): 75–128, a bibliographic review of a region undergoing a surge of anthropological activity; Grant D. Jones, "Recent ethnohistorical works on southeastern Mesoamerica" 22 (1987): 214–24; Prudence W. Rice, "Six recent works on the Maya" 21 (1986): 228–37; Daniel R. Gross, "Amazonia and the progress of ethnology" 22 (1985): 200–22 **(J57),** a recent bibliographic review of research in this area; Elizabeth M. Brumfiel's "Aztec religion and warfare: Past and present perspectives" 25 (2) (1990): 249–59; Robert S. Santley's "Recent works on Aztec history" 19 (1984): 261–69; Janis S. Alcorn's "Evaluating folk medicine: Stories of herbs, healing and healers" 25 (1990): 259–70.

Searching Graphic Materials

For sound recordings, consult McNeil and Valk's *Latin American studies* **(J03).** Consult Sable's *A guide to nonprint materials for Latin American studies* **(J58)** and Hanson's *Index to map of Hispanic America, 1:1,000,000* **(J59).**

Recorded Music, Photographs, Maps

J58

Sable, Martin H. *A guide to nonprint materials for Latin American studies.* Detroit: Blaine Ethridge, 1979. 141p.

Especially useful as a guide to illustrations. Establishes a bibliographic consolidation of earlier work. Includes an annotated bibliography of reference guides to Latin America. Extensive coverage of (1) visual, (2) audio recordings, and (3) paintings, sculpture, and crafts. Identifies forty sources for multimedia, sixty sources for maps and globes, seven sets of microforms, and eight museum collections. Especially strong in its coverage of music, which plays such an important role in daily life in Latin America. Author, title, and subject by genre indexes.

J59

Hanson, Earl Parker, ed. American Geographical Society. *Index to map of Hispanic America, 1:1,000,000.* Washington, D.C.: American Geographical Society, 1943–44. 12v. (American Geographic Society of New York. Map of Hispanic America Publication, no.5)

This is an index to the geographical names (200,000) on the American Geographical Society's "Map of Hispanic America on the scale of 1:1,000,000." Locations are alphabetically listed here by place name. Especially valuable because it identifies the latitudinal and longitudinal coordinates for each entry, and these must be established before it is possible to order aerial photographs from the U.S. Geological Survey, *EROS* [computer archive] (Sioux Falls, South Dakota, Data Center).

Searching Unpublished Materials

Consult both McNeil and Valk's *Latin American studies* **(J03)** for its coverage of sources on American and British doctoral theses, and also the resources cited under this strategic heading in chapter 1 and those chapters devoted to the subdisciplines of anthropology.

There is some inclusion of outstanding dissertations in *Handbook of Latin American studies* **(J26).** For recent German-language dissertations, consult *Abstracts in German anthropology* **(A33).** For some coverage of English- and French-language dissertations, consult descriptions of *Dissertations abstracts ondisc* [computer file] **(B14)** and *Francis bulletin signalétique* [computer file] **(A34).**

Dissertations

J60

Deal, Carl W. *Latin America and the Caribbean: A dissertation bibliography.* Ann Arbor, Mich.: University Microfilms International, 1978. 164p.

This basic volume lists 7,200 items in broad subject arrangement, divided by country.

J61

Miranda P., Jorge. "Tesis doctorales en antropología social y cultural." *América indígena* 27 (1967): 365–82.

List of 275 doctoral theses granted by U.S. universities in social and cultural anthropology which refer to Latin America. Indexed by country, indigenous group, nation, and topic.

J62

Román, Adelaida. *Repertorio de tesis europeas sobre América Latina: 1980–1990.* Madrid: 5th Centenario for Red Europea de Información y Docmentación sobre América Latina, 1992. 428p.

Lists 3,035 numbered entries in an arrangement classed by country and alphabetic by author thereunder. Author, title, date, and granting institution are provided in the description. Index by author, broad subject, geographic, and institutional names. There are more than 100 entries under ANTROPOLOGÍA without any expansion terms.

J63

Schechter, John M. "Doctoral dissertations in Latin American ethnomusicology, 1965–1984." In v.1, *Latin American masses and minorities: Their images and realities,* p.672–73. Ed. by Dan C. Hazen. Madison, Wis.: SALAM Secretariat, 1987. 2v.

In the same volume, consult John M. Schechter's "Selected bibliographic sources in Latin America" (p.664–72). Consult also Maria Elizabeth Lucas's "Directory of Latin American and Caribbean music theses and dissertations (1984–1988)," *Latin American music review (Revista de musica latinoamericanos)* 10 (1989): 148–76, and Gerard H. Behague's "Recent studies on music of Latin America," *Latin American research review* 20 (1985): 218–27. McNeil and Valk's *Latin American studies* **(J03)** discusses Latin American dissertations in a well-documented essay.

MESOAMERICA

Consult Coe, Snow, and Benson's *Atlas of ancient America* **(H12),** which has many maps identifying the distribution of the cultures (across time) and archaeological sites in this area. Examples include maps of the classic period (p.105), boundaries of the Hokaltecan (subdivided for two tribes), Otomanguean (seven tribes), Uto-Aztecan (two tribes), and Macromayan (seven tribes). Formative period sites: Early (p.91), Late (p.115).

Searching Bibliographic Guides

Consult Auckland's "Getting into the literature" **(A01)** and the guides to the subdisciplines of anthropology listed in *Fieldwork in the Library.* Inspect Covington's *Latin America and the Caribbean* **(J02),** Block's "Anthropology" **(J01),** and McNeil and Valk's *Latin American studies* **(J03).** Entry by names of indigenous peoples has been greatly eased by the publication of Welch's *The Indians of South America* **(J21).**

Bibliographic Guides

KA01

Garst, Rachel. *Bibliografía anotada de obras de referencia sobre Centroamérica y Panamá en el campo de las ciencias sociales.* San José, Costa Rica: Instituto de Investigaciones Sociales. Universidad de Costa Rica; Friends World College. Latin American Center, 1983. 2v. 662p.

Identifies sources on each country, subdivided by subject area in more than 1,400 citations. Author, subject, and title indexes. Discusses resource centers in each country.

KA02

Grieb, Kenneth J. *Central America in the nineteenth and twentieth centuries: An annotated bibliography.* Boston: Hall, 1988. 573p.

Annotates an enormous mass of scholarly material concisely and accurately. The index is professionally constructed. Example: under ETHNIC GROUPS GENERAL, three items, then subdivided by country: BELIZE, four items; COSTA RICA, four items; EL SALVADOR, two items; GUATEMALA, two items; PANAMA, one item. FOLKLORE has more than 100 items for which geographical location can be identified in the index because this resource numbers items as they are listed in a geographic arrangement.

KA03

Magee, Susan Fortson. *Mesoamerican archaeology: A guide to the literature and other information sources.* Austin: Institute of Latin American Studies, University of Texas at Austin, 1981. 72p. (Guides and bibliographies series, 12)

Outstanding coverage of the field. The appendix "Library of Congress classification schedule" for guidance in shelf browsing provides detailed descriptive terms and appropriate call numbers for such entries as INDIANS OF MEXICO, ANTIQUITIES, which is subdivided for "Codices" and sixteen ancient tribal names. The descriptive terms TRIBES, A–Z subdivided for two terms, for LOCAL, A–Z subdivided for one term, and for TOPICAL, A–Z subdivided, e.g., for one term. The term GUATEMALA, ANTIQUITIES (ANCIENT AND MODERN) is subdivided for "General works" with subdivisions for two terms. The term *Local, A–Z* is subdivided for three geographic terms. The term TRIBES, A–Z is subdivided for eleven names.

The introduction to Magee discusses the related fields of ethnohistory, pre-Columbian art, and architecture and establishes both the defining characteristics of the culture area and the extent of its geographic range. The bibliography proper has a classed arrangement under topics such as guides to the literature (p.9–11), retrospective bibliographies (p.10–13), current bibliographies (p.14), and periodicals, including directories and indexes. Other sections are devoted to reviews, news forms, theses and dissertations, associations and societies, grants and research centers, international agencies and bodies, government agencies, special collections, museums, atlases and maps, specialists, academic institutions, and field schools and nonprint materials. There is a list of references. Indexes by authors, institutions, and organizations.

Searching for Current Materials

In linguistics, *Latin American Indian literatures* **(J52)** has several current awareness features. For developments in archaeology, consult the department "Current research" in *American antiquity* **(C04)** which in the first issue each year summarizes any Latin American archaeological research that can be identified in reports, publications, and announcements of intentions to work in the field. Consult resources under this heading in *Fieldwork in the Library* and in the chapters devoted to the subdisciplines of anthropology.

Select Sources of Review in Scholarly Publications

KA04

Anales de antropología. v.1– , 1964– . México [City], D.F.: Instituto de Investigaciones Históricas, Universidad Nacional Autónoma de México. Annual.

Covers the ethnohistory, ethnology, and archaeology of indigenous groups of Mexico. Book reviews are a regular feature. Juan Comas's *Indices generales de Anales de antropología, Vols. 1–12, Años 1964–1974* (Mexico [City], D.F.: Instituto de Investigaciones Antropológicas de la Universidad Nacional Autónoma de México, 1975) **(KA05),** cumulates the years covered into a single list by author with a subject index.

KA06

Boletín del consejo de arqueología [computer file]. 1984– . México [City], D.F.: Instituto Nacional de Antropología y Historia.

Brief annual synopsis of current projects, including names of participants, key results, and bibliography of publications derived from projects.

KA07

Estudios de cultura maya. v.1– , 1961– . Mexico [City], D.F.: Universidad Nacional Autónoma de México, Dirección General de Publicaciones. Annual.

Publishes scholarship from an international community, with an emphasis on the historic period. A typical issue has about ten articles in Spanish and three articles in English and includes studies of a wide range of topics, including settlement patterns, transport systems, Mayan beliefs, Mayan linguistics, and reports on recent archaeological surveys. Usually includes a list of publications. Most recently inspected: Enrique Viloria Viazcán's "Publicaciones de reciente ingreso a la Biblioteca del Centro de Estudios Mayas" 17 (1988): 475–85. Other sources of information about scholarly studies of the Maya have become increasingly specialized, and the task of bibliographic control finds support in specialized newsletters like *Cerámica de cultura maya,* v.1– , 1976– (Philadelphia: Department of Anthropology, Temple University) **(KA08),** with its mandate to act as an informal medium of exchange of information concerning prehistoric and ethnographic Middle American culture, with a primary focus on the description and classification of ceramic materials from the Maya area; and specialized journals like *Belizean studies,* v.1– , 1967– (Belize City: Belize Institute of Social Research and Action) **(KA09),** which in three issues a year includes reports on current archaeological activity in Belize. The *Journal of Mayan linguistics,* v.1– , 1984– (Iowa City: Department of Anthropology, University of Iowa; dist. by Geoscience Publications). The Nettie Lee Benson Latin American Collection at the University of Texas at Austin frequently publishes excellent bibliographies with a sharply specialized focus on Mayan studies such as David Pardue's recent "Approaches to contemporary Mayan cultures: Personal histories, dreams, folk-tales," *Biblionoticias: Benson Latin American Collection* 49 (1989): 1–7 **(KA10),** an annotated bibliography of personal histories listed first under geographic headings for Guatemala and Mexico. Topics such as dreams and folktales are divided for Guatemala and Mexico. The basis for comprehensive searches can be established by consulting Valle's *Bibliografía maya* **(KA47).**

KA11

Estudios de cultura náhuatl. v.1– , 1959– . México [City], D.F.: Instituto de Historia, Universidad Nacional Autónoma de México. Annual.

Includes brief notes of recent work in archaeology, ethnology, sociology, linguistics, and literature. There is a bibliography of everything published worldwide on the Nahuatl, with book reviews for selected items most recently by Ascensión H. de León-Portilla, "Publicaciones recientes sobre lengua y literatura nahuas" 20 (1990): 371–418.

KA12

Estudios sociales centroamericanos. v.1– , 1972– . San José, Costa Rica: Programa Centroamericano de Ciencias Sociales. 3/yr.

Includes coverage of anthropology in the entire Central American area. Arranged in four sections: "Articles and essays," "Theoretical and methodological problems," "Bibliography and documentation," "Informational notes and reports."

Selective Lists of Scholarly Journals

Consult both "Periodicals" in Magee's *Mesoamerican archaeology* (p.14–24) **(KA03),** especially for the list of periodicals of outstanding value indexed in *HAPI* **(J28)** in the book review section to identify additional journals in which reviews are a regular feature.

Retrospective Searches

Block's "Anthropology" **(J01)** provides dense nation-state entry into the retrospective bibliographies of this vast literature. McNeil and Valk's *Latin American studies* **(J03)** includes a discussion of general and special bibliographies, which makes it possible here to direct attention only to the most vitally important sources of special value to anthropologists. The Columbus

Memorial Library's *Index to Latin American periodical literature, 1929–1960* **(J16)** indexes, in a single alphabet, periodical articles. The *Indice general* **(J17)** updates the Columbus Memorial Library catalog to 1970 and includes Instituto Nacional de Antropología e Historia (INAH) publications. The file corresponding to *HAPI* **(J28),** a subfile of *Latin American studies* [computer file] **(J27),** updates the *Indice general.* In chapter 1, "What Every Anthropologist Needs to Know," both the *Anthropological index* **(A35)** and *Anthropological literature* **(A36)** provide quarterly indexing for an international array of anthropological periodicals. At a more general level of resources with anthropological coverage, material in all scholarly languages can be identified in the databases *Social scisearch* [computer file] **(B37)** and *Humanities index* [computer file] **(B23).** Consult also the databases discussed in Covington's *Latin America and the Caribbean* **(J02).**

Retrospective Searches—Biographical Directories

KA13

Brunhouse, Robert Levere. *Pursuit of the ancient Maya: Some archaeologists of yesterday.* Albuquerque: Univ. of New Mexico Pr., 1975. 252p.

Biographies placed in the context of a detailed bibliography of the significant research published by listed scholars (p.221–43).

KA14

Méndez-Domínguez, Alfredo, ed. *MesoAmérica: Directorio y bibliografía, 1950–1980.* 1st ed. Guatemala City: Universidad del Valle de Guatemala, 1982. 313p.

The directory establishes the research interests and current addresses of several hundred scholars, thus providing some guidance into a bibliography arranged alphabetically by author, with 5,000 entries to their contributions to archaeology, cultural and social anthropology, folklore, linguistics, and physical anthropology. There is no subject index; however, once the names of scholars working on particular problems are identified, these bibliographies can greatly ease the search for recent work by that scholar on the problem under investigation.

Retrospective Bibliographies—Broad Scope

KA15

Bernal, Ignacio. *Bibliografía de arqueología y etnografía: Mesoamérica y Norte de México, 1514–1960.* México [City], D.F.: Instituto Nacional de Antropología e Historia, 1962. 634p. (Inst. Nacional de Antropología e Historia. Memorias, 7)

A list of 13,990 numbered entries is classed by region and then by subject. Covers monographic and serial publications. Entries are arranged by geographic and cultural areas. Areal groupings are divided further by general subject headings. The invaluable table of contents is located at the back of the book. For some works, citations to book reviews and translations are noted. Two folding maps define the geographic range of the coverage. Author index. For English-language sources this work can be supplemented by reference to Kendall's *The art and archaeology of precolumbian middle America* **(KA33),** which can be used as a resource for a range of subjects far beyond the scope of its title.

KA16

Comas, Juan. *Bibliografía selectiva de las culturas indígenas de América.* México [City], D.F.: Instituto Panamericano de Geografía e Historia, 1953. 292p. (Instituto Panamericano de Geografía e Historia. Comisión de Historia. Publicación num. 166. Bibliografías, v.1)

Classed arrangement with five maps of ethnic distribution. Index to indigenous groups makes this a preferred bibliographic resource. The preponderance of English-language titles in this source can be corrected by consulting the 6,445 entries identified in Manuel Germán Parra and Wigberto Jiménez Moreno's *Bibliografía indigenista de México y Centroamérica (1850–1950)* (México [City], D.F.: Inst. Nacional Indígenista, 1954 [342p.]) (Memorias del Inst. Nacional Indigenista, v.4) **(KA17),** which can also be used as a base for the construction of bibliographies of indigenous ethnic groups. These works can be informally brought current by UNESCO's *International bibliography of social and cultural anthropology* **(D20).** For more recent research, consult Méndez-Domínguez's *MesoAmérica* **(KA14).**

KA18

Mexico. National Library of Anthropology and History. *Catálogo de la Biblioteca Nacional de Antropología e Historia.* Boston: Hall, 1972. 10v.

One of the great Mesoamerican collections. Preface in English and Spanish guides the reader. Uses LC subject headings. Entries are often best approached through the names of states subdivided for subjects. Under the Farmington Plan, Tulane University's *Catalog of the Latin American Library of the Tulane University Library* (Boston: Hall, 1970 [9v.]) **(KA19),** with supplements to 1978, was responsible in the United States for collecting Central American materials, excluding Costa Rica but including Mexico.

Retrospective Bibliographies—Continuing

The *Handbook of Latin American studies* **(J26)** is indispensable. In chapter 1, "What Every Anthropologist Needs to Know," the table of contents of *Abstracts in anthropology* **(A32)** directs the user to a section, "Archaeology: Mesoamerica." The database *Francis bulletin signalétique* [computer file] described in the annotation to *FRANCIS* **(B19),** includes the controlled vocabulary entry, "Amérique et Régions Arctiques: Mexique et Amérique Centrale," and is indexed for cultures, geographic regions, sites in regions and "des matières."

KA20

Mexicon: Aktuelle informationen und studien zu Mesoamerika. v.1– , 1979– . Berlin: Karl-Friedrich von Flemming. 6/yr.

Consult especially department "News and studies on Mesoamerican anthropology" and its bibliography of recent publications about Mesoamerica, annotated in German. Most articles published in this journal focus on Maya archaeology, epigraphy, and ethnohistory.

Retrospective Bibliographies—Topical

Consult additionally Block's "Anthropology" **(J01),** especially for linguistics and folklore. For linguistics, additional resources can be identified in DeMiller's *Linguistics* **(E01).**

KA21

Aramoni Calderón, Delores. *Fuentes para el estudio de Chiapas.* Tuxtla Gutiérrez, Chiapas, México: Área de Humanidades de la Universidad Autónoma de Chiapas, 1978. 166p.

This list of 1,600 entries can guide an investigator to resources for the study of this state. These are organized in a classed arrangement under categories such as bibliographies, ethnology and social anthropology, ethnohistory, linguistics, ethnography, art, and religion. There is an author index. For anthropologists, a useful summary review can be found in "La Civilización indígena de Chiapas," *América indígena* 42 (1982): 5–147 **(KA22).**

KA23

Bastarrachea Manzano, Juan Ramón. *Bibliografía antropológica de Yucatán.* México [City], D.F.: Centro Regional del Sureste, Instituto Nacional de Antropología e Historia, 1984. 648p.

A state bibliography includes anthropological and related materials. Indexed by broad topics such as "Antropología" (p.25–30); "Antropología física" (p.30–31); "Etnología y antropología social" (p.197–228); "Maya" (p.475–508) "Mesoamérica" (p.526–28).

KA24

Berlo, Janet Catherine. *The art of prehispanic Mesoamerica: An annotated bibliography.* Boston: Hall, 1985. 272p.

Introductory bibliographic essay (p.1–33) and a subject index refer to 1,500 numbered items about pre-Columbian art in all Western languages. Bibliography is arranged alphabetically by author, with a subject index.

KA25

Cline, Howard. "Mexican community studies." *Hispanic American historical review* 32 (1952).

The entire second issue is devoted to a bibliographic review, with an annotated bibliography of 81 entries. Includes community studies, marginal community studies, and some related works from the period 1923–52, when this research focus was dominant in the anthropological studies of this area.

KA26

Contreras García, Irma. *Bibliografía sobre la castellanización de los grupos indígenas de la República Mexicana: Siglos XVI al XX.* México [City], D.F.: Universidad Nacional Autónoma de México. Instituto de Investigaciones Bibliográficas, 1985–86. 2v. (1,275p.)

In the preliminary section, an introduction is followed by a discussion of legal provisions, native alphabets, and native languages. There follows definitive descriptions of indigenous ethnic groups, each with as many as fourteen contributing experts. These sections are arranged alphabetically to include the Amuzgo, Azteca, Cakchiquel, Comanche, Concho, Cora, Chañabal, Chatino, Chiapaneco, Chichimeca-Pame, Chinantec, Chocho, Chol O Mopan, Chuchona, Cuicateco, Español O Castellano, Huasteco O Huaxteco, Huave, Huichol, Lacandon, Mame, Matlaltzinca, Mayo O Yucateca, Mayo, Mazahua, Mazateco, Mixi O Mije, Mixteco, Nahoa, Nahuatl, Otomi, Pai-Pai, Popoloco, Popoluca, Quiché, Seri O Ceri, Tarahumara, Tarasco, Tepeguan O Tepehuan, Tepehua, Tlapaneco, Totonaco, Trique, Tzelal, Tzotzil, Yaqui, Zapoteco, and Zoque. This is followed by a bibliography (p.324–1,119). One section (p.166–247) is devoted to records left by early missionaries. There is an additional list of reference sources used and an author/title index.

KA27

Florescano, Enrique, and Alejandra Moreno Toscano. *Bibliografía general del maíz en México.* 3d ed. México [City], D.F.: Instituto Nacional de Antropología e Historia, 1987. 251p.

Organizes the enormous documentation on the origin, diffusion, and distribution of this food, including a complete record of the documentation of the vast technical literature that informs these questions.

KA28

González, Rubia, Nancy Linarez, and Emillo Arriechi. *Introducción a una bibliografía indígena régional: 1041 etnia guajira.* Darachabo: Centro de Estudios Zulianos, Secretaria de Cultura, Biblioteca Pública del Estado, 1982. 120p.

Bibliographic entries are arranged alphabetically by author.

KA29

Gutiérrez Solana, Nelly, and Daniel G. Schávelzon. *Corpus bibliográfico de la cultura Olmeca.* México [City], D.F.: Universidad Nacional Autónoma de México, 1980. 136p.

A list of more than 900 entries relating to Olmec art and archaeology. After the introduction, there is a four-page comment on this bibliography and a five-page discussion of systems of classification, followed by six pages of thematic classification for the entries in the bibliography. The bibliography is listed alphabetically by author.

KA30

Guzmán, Virginia, comp. *Bibliografía de códices, mapas y lienzos del México prehispánico y colonial.* México [City], D.F.: Instituto Nacional de Antropología e Historia, 1979. 2v. (Colección científica, v.79)

Identifies 2,500 references to Mexican codices and lienzos. Entries are arranged chronologically under the name of the 600 codices or lienzos to which they relate. Author index. For codices alone, selective entry can be found in Michael Hironymous's "Mesoamerican codices," *Biblio-noticias: Benson Latin American Collection* 59 (1991): 1–9 **(KA31),** a rarely held annotated bibliography of bibliographies and codices. For detailed information on codices, consult also Glass's "Census of Native American pictorial manuscripts" **(KA63).**

KA32

Howard-Requindin, Pamela, and Ann E. Smith. *Author index to the publications of the Middle American Research Institute, Tulane University, 1926–1985.* New Orleans: Middle American Research Institute, Tulane University, 1985. 33p.

Provides entry into publications of one center of learning that specializes in this area.

KA33

Kendall, Aubyn. *The art and archaeology of precolumbian middle America: An annotated bibliography of works in English.* Boston: Hall, 1977. 324p. (Reference publications in Latin American studies)

An appendix contains a sample of recent dissertations. Limited to English-language sources. Lists 2,147 books and journal articles. The subject index includes site names. For a ninety-page overview of pre-Columbian art, consult the *Encyclopedia of world art* **(C35),** s.v. "Middle American protohistory." For a large number of quality resources available for this area, consult the monographic series *Studies in precolumbian art and archaeology,* v.1– , 1966– (Washington, D.C.: Harvard University, Dumbarton Oaks Research Library and Collections) **(KA34).**

KA35

Krusé, David Samuel, and Richard Swedberg. *El Salvador bibliography and research guide.* Cambridge, Mass.: Central America Information Office, 1982. 233p.

Table of contents guides the reader through an elaborate classified arrangement. A guide to political activity, including entry into the influential Marxist literature (p.137–55).

KA36

Ladrón de Guevara, Sara, and Otto Schöndube. *Bibliografía arqueológica del occidente de México.* Guadalajara, Jalisco: Editorial Universidad de Guadalajara, 1990. 197p.

An alphabetic list of 1,222 numbered articles, books, and theses. Especially useful for the segregation (p.161–95) of ethnohistorical material and for the site index. Indexed by state, by archaeological site, and by subject.

KA37

Marino Flores, Anselmo, Juan Carlos Catalán Blanco, and Roberto Cervantes-Delgado, comps. *Bibliografía antropológica del estado de Guerrero.* Chilpancingo, Guerrero: Instituto Guerrerense de la Cultura, Gobierno del Estado de Guerrero, 1987. 328p. (Serie Fuentes Chilpancingo, México, no.3)

"Antropología" (p.49–98); "Arqueología, prehistoria y arte" (p.99–160); "Etnohistoria" (p.161–216); "Lingüística" (p.217–42); "Folklore y narrativa indígena" (p.243–76); "Antropología física" (p.283–318).

KA38

Ochoa, Lorenzo. *100 años de investigaciones en antropología e historia prehispánica de Tabasco.* Villahermosa, México: Gobierno del Estado de Tabasco, 1988. 54p.

A bibliographic review divided into sections on "Linguistics, ethnography and other anthropological subjects" (p.13–19); "Historical sources" (p.19–23); and "Prehistory" (p.23–33). Includes bibliography (p.27–54).

KA39

Parodi, Claudia. *La investigación lingüística en México, 1970–1980.* México [City]: Universdad Nacional Autónoma de México, 1981. 205p. (Cuadernos del Instituto de Investigaciones Filológicas)

Surveys linguistic projects and institutions and provides a detailed bibliography of work done by Mexicans or published by Mexican institutions (1970–80). Especially useful for the eighty-page essay which precedes the bibliography and which provides a survey of this extensive work completed between 1970 and 1980 on Mexican Indian languages. Continues the bibliographic base established by Anselmo Marino Flores's *La investigacion linguistica de la República Mexicana* (Mexico City: Pólogo de Manuel Gamio, Instituto Indigenista Interamericano, 1957 [95p.]) **(KA40),** which arranges the extensive bibliography under forty indigenous languages.

KA41

Ramírez, Axel. *Bibliografía comentada de la medicina tradicional mexicana, 1900–1978.* México [City], D.F.: IMEPLAM, 1978. 147p. (Monografías científicas, no.3)

An alphabetic list of more than 500 entries by main entry. International coverage includes Mexican periodical publications. There is an author index, a geographical index, and a subject index.

KA42

Reyes Mazzoni, Roberto Ramón. *Bibliografía arqueológica de Honduras.* Tegucigalpa: Edition Nuevo Continente, 1976. 88p.

A list of nearly 600 references to monographic and serial publications from the United States, Mexico, and Honduras through 1975. This is volume 2 of the author's *Introducción a la arqueología de Honduras.* For this reason, the text in volume 1 identifies citations in a subject context and serves as an index to the bibliography. Most of the references are to Mayan areas since very little work has been done in other culture areas in Honduras.

KA43

Seele, Enno. *Puebla-Tlaxcala, México: Bibliografía; Bibliographie.* Vechta, Germany: Vechaer Druckerei und Verlag, 1988. 184p. (Vechtaer Arbeiten zur Geographie und Regionalwissenschaft, 7)

Pt.1 includes a directory of authors and coauthors and a section devoted to publications in series. Pt.2 includes a discussion of background information and a directory of pioneers, followed by a discussion of recent archaeological research with a supporting bibliography arranged alphabetically by author. This resource illustrates the need to enter library catalogs under the state names of Mexico in anthropological searches.

KA44

Sisson, Edward B., and Modeena Stultz. *Post Classic central Mexico: A preliminary bibliography.* Oxford: Univ. of Mississippi Pr., 1982. 143p.

A list of nearly 1,100 references to Post Classic sites, artifacts, excavations. Covers the Federal District and the states of Hidalgo, México, Tlaxcala, Morelos, Puebla, Oaxaca, and central Veracruz. Includes the many ethnohistorical references needed for knowledgeable interpretation of archaeological sites in this region. No subject index.

KA45

Topete, María de la Luz. *Bibliografía antropológica del estado de Oaxaca, 1974–1979.* México [City]: Instituto Nacional de Antropología e Historia, Centro Regional de Oaxaca, 1980. 168p. (Estudios de antropología e historia, 22)

Pt.1, "Social anthropology and ethnology," is subdivided by indigenous ethnic groups. Pt.2, "Physical anthropology," is divided by prehistoric and contemporary. Pt.3, "Archaeology," is divided by site. Pt.4, "History and ethnohistory," has a general section followed by sections for indigenous ethnic groups, followed by eighteenth- and nineteenth-century history. Pt.5, "Linguistics," has a general section and is subdivided by linguistic groups. There are sections for botany and ethnobotany, geology, art, folktales, and music. Includes local theses and research papers. There is a name index.

KA46

Universidad de San Carlos de Guatemala, Facultad de Humanidades, Escuela de Bibliotecología. *Bibliografía del folklore de Guatemala, 1892–1980.* Guatemala [City]: Dirección General de Antropología e Historia, 1980. 174p. (Colección Antropología e Historia)

Organized in an elaborate classified system which is identified in the table of contents. The first section deals with folk material culture in twenty-two categories, including "Cerámica," "Guitarras," "Instrumentos de Caza." The second section deals with social folklore in eighteen categories, including markets and holidays such as "Fiestas," "Fiestas en general," "Semana santa," "Carnaval," "La quema del diablo." The next section deals with literary folklore in twenty-seven categories, including "Textos folklóricos," "Discos música," "Medicina folklórica," and "Ceremonias." Subsequent sections cover the theory of folklore, a list of folklore activities, the influence of folklore on literature and music, and applied folklore. Indexes by author and title.

KA47

Valle, Rafael Heliodoro. *Bibliografía Maya.* New York: B. Franklin, 1971. 404p. (Burt Franklin bibliography and reference series, 435. Selected essays in history, economics, and social sciences, 306)

A reprint. At head of title: Instituto Panamericano de Geografía e Historia. Issued in parts as appendix to *Boletín bibliográfico de antropología américana,* v.1–5, 1937–41. Bibliography of materials about Mayan culture in various languages, covering all periods.

KA48

Welch, Thomas L., and Rene L. Gutierrez. *The Aztecs: A bibliography of books and periodical articles.* Washington, D.C.: Columbus Memorial Library. Organization of American States, 1987. 169p. (Hipólito Unánue bibliographic series, 3)

An author list with title and subject indexes. Includes a useful list of periodicals appearing in the bibliography.

Informational Reference Searches

McNeil and Valk's *Latin American studies* **(J03)** provides a detailed discussion of useful handbooks and of selected European and American societies and associations with an interest in Latin American studies. For American scholars, the American Anthropological Association's *AAA guide* **(A53)** usually provides the best current information about the institutional addresses and research interests of affiliated scholars.

Directories

KA49

McGlynn, Eileen A. *Middle American anthropology: Directory, bibliography, and guide to the UCLA Library collections.* Los Angeles: Latin American Center, UCLA, 1975. 131p. (Latin American collections in the UCLA Library: guides, ser.B, no.1)

The sources included are not restricted to holdings in the collections of UCLA. The first section identifies international directories of individuals and institutions. The second, a bibliography of reference books and serials, is still the best available guide to anthropological resources in this area. Designed for sophisticated library users, this resource covers journals, series, and proceedings in great detail and selectively identifies important books, monographs, and rare nonbook materials. The author/title index covers the entire work. The geographic and chronological index includes only the selective list of books and monographs. Consult also Méndez-Domínguez's *Mesoamérica* **(KA14)** and the directory of resource centers in Garst's *Bibliografía anotada de obras de referencia sobre Centroamérica y Panamá en el campo de las ciencias sociales* **(KA01).**

KA50

Oliphant, Dave, ed. *Nahuatl to Rayuela: The Latin American collection at Texas.* Austin: University of Texas, Harry Ransom Humanities Research Center, 1992. 155p.

Essays by seven authorities on various holdings in this strong collection.

Encyclopedias, Handbooks, Compendiums

Consult Block's "Anthropology" **(J01),** especially for sources of information about the laws protecting archaeological remains in Mexico and Central America, and for encyclopedias and handbooks of folklore.

KA51

Adams, Richard E. W. *Prehistoric Mesoamerica.* Boston: Little, 1977. 370p.

Encyclopedic synthesis of Mesoamerican prehistory that is in full command of the newest techniques of analysis, drawing on everything known about agriculture or cultures in the area. This seminal example sets a standard for the consolidation of area research in archaeology. A more recent synthesis of the diverse cultures of pre-Columbian Mesoamerica can be found in Muriel Porter Weaver's *The Aztecs, Maya, and their predecessors: Archaeology of Mesoamerica,* 2d ed. (New York: Academic, 1981) **(KA52).**

KA53

Alvarez, José Rogelio, ed. *Enciclopedia de México.* México [City]: Instituto de la Enciclopedia de México. Secretaría de Educación Pública, 1987–88. 14v.

Dictionary arrangement. Classified name index and subject index.

KA54

"Coloquio de antropología física Juan Comas, 4th, México, 1986." Rafael Ramos Galván and Rosa María Ramos Rodríguez, eds. *Estudios de antropología biológica.* México [City], D.F.: UNAM, Instituto de Investigaciones Antropológicas, 1986. 746p. (Serie antropológica, 10)

This series sets an international standard of excellence for the consolidation of research results in physical anthropology. Thirty-seven papers, with several contributions for Europe. Eight on the skeletal biology of early populations. Nine papers on growth and adaptability. Six papers on genetics. Many graphs, maps, and tables are used to visually consolidate information. The table of contents guides the reader.

KA55

Lange, Frederick W., and Doris Z. Stone, eds. *The archaeology of lower Central America.* 1st ed. Albuquerque: Univ. of New Mexico Pr., 1984. 476p. (School of American Research advanced seminar series)

A state-of-the-art survey by a group of recognized experts. Covers the northern edge of the Central American core of the southern frontier. The introduction includes surveys of the history and cultural geography of the area. Pt.2, seven articles with surveys of the work on archaeology in El Salvador, Honduras, Costa Rica, and Panama. Ten appendixes for radiocarbon samples. A fifty-page list for references (p.407–57). Summary by Gordon Willey. Indexed for author, subject, geographical place, and title.

KA56

Latin American historical dictionaries [Central America]. v.1– , 1967– . Metuchen, N.J.: Scarecrow, 1967–77. 6v.

Creedman, Theodore S., *Historical dictionary of Costa Rica,* 1977; Flemion, Philip F., *Historical dictionary of El Salvador,* 1972; Moore, Richard E., *Historical dictionary of Guatemala,* 1973; Meyer, Harvey K., *Historical dictionary of Honduras,* 1976; Meyer, Harvey K., *Historical dictionary of Nicaragua,* 1972; Hedrick, Basil C., and Anne K. Hedrick, *Historical dictionary of Panama,* 1970. While the quality of volumes varies, each is ethnographically sensitive. Can be supplemented by reference to handbooks from the U.S. Government Printing Office, such as *Guatemala: A country study,* by Richard F. Nyrop, 2d ed. (Washington, D.C.: GPO, 1983 [261p.]).

KA57

Macazaga Ordōno, César. *Diccionario de antropología mesoamericana.* Mexico [City]: Editorial Innovación, 1985. 2v.

V.1, *Aatlatl-joyeros;* v.2, *Juana-zutuhil.* Concise information on Indians of Mexico and Central America. Especially valuable for its entries on archaeological sites, its bibliographic detail, and its discussion of languages and cultures. Reliable chronological information.

KA58

Robelo, Cecilio Agustín. *Diccionario de mitología nahuatl.* México [City], D.F.: Editorial Innovación, 1980. 2v.

Concise information about Nahuatl cosmology, pantheon, and religious practices. Includes articles on historical figures and toponyms. Several excellent dictionaries for localized archaeology in Central America are listed under the headings by country in Block's "Anthropology" **(J01).**

KA59

Suárez, J. A. *The Mesoamerican Indian languages.* Cambridge, England, and New York: Cambridge Univ. Pr., 1983. 206p.

Traditional overview strongest in the final chapter dealing with contemporary languages. Must be supplemented for historic languages by such valuable compendiums of work applying linguistic methods and data to decipherment, such as John S. Justeson and Lyle Campbell, eds., *Phoneticism in Mayan hieroglyphic writing* (Albany, N.Y.: SUNY, Institute for Mesoamerican Studies, 1984 [388p.]) (Publication Institute of Mesoamerican Studies, State University at Albany, no.9) **(KA60);** and Robert M. Carmack and Francisco Morales Santos, eds., *Nuevas perspectivas sobre el Popol Vuh* (Guatemala [City]: Editorial Piedra Santa, 1983 [428p.]) **(KA61),** which contains twenty-nine papers (conference held at Santa Cruz del Quiche, 1979).

KA62

Wauchope, Robert, ed. *Handbook of Middle American Indians.* Austin: Univ. of Texas Pr., 1964–76. 16v.

The bibliographies are incidental to the development of the text and are not intended to be comprehensive. At the end of chapters, citations are incomplete. Only the bibliography at the end of the volume provides full bibliographic descriptions. There are brief signed articles on all topics that have interested anthropologists in this area. Contents: v.1, *Natural environment and early cultures;* v.2–3, *Archaeology of southern Mesoamerica;* v.4, *Archaeological frontiers and external connections;* v.5, *Linguistics;* v.6, *Social anthropology;* v.7–8, *Ethnology;* v.9, *Physical anthropology;* v.10–11, *Archaeology of northern Mesoamerica;* v.12–15, *Guide to ethnohistorical sources.* References are given and the bibliography to the citations is cumulated in v.15 and v.16. Bibliographically, take note of John B. Glass's "A census of Native American pictorial manuscripts," *Guide to ethnohistorical sources* 14 (1976): 81–252 **(KA63),** with its brief description of each codex, *lienzo,* and map produced in the native traditions of the region.

KA64

Wauchope, Robert, ed. *Supplement. Handbook of Middle American Indians.* v.1– , 1981– . Austin: Univ. of Texas Pr. Irregular.

The supplements to date include: v.1, *Archaeology,* which reprints readings from the *Scientific American;* v.2, *Linguistics;* and v.3, *Literatures,* which is especially useful as a handbook of native narratives.

In a different but related publication, edited by Charles C. Griffin, *Latin America: A guide to the historical literature* (Austin: Univ. of Texas Pr., 1971 [700p.]) **(KA65),** find by Robert Wauchope evaluative annotations to a select list of international publications on the archaeology of this region. Books and journal articles are classed in an informative bibliography. The cutoff date for inclusion was 1966.

State-of-the-Art Reviews

Examples cited in the annotation to the *Latin American research review* **(J56)** illustrate the consistency with which this publication solicits bibliographic reviews to consolidate research in this culture area.

For the Central American countries, consult the annotation for *América indígena* **(J45)** for identification of issues devoted to the consolidation of research results relevant to Costa Rica, Honduras, and Panama. The review of Panama is especially useful since Panama is outside the culture area of Mesoamerica but often included in reference books that are geographically defined as Central American. A useful summary of recent research in this area can be found in Carol A. Smith's "Central America since 1979, Part 1," *Annual review of anthropology* 16: 197–221 **(KA66),** and her "Central America since 1979, Part 2," *Annual review of anthropology* 17: 331–64 **(KA67),** which provide current bibliographic reviews with citation lists by author describing the research discussed. Especially valuable for its inclusion of materials from related disciplines relevant to anthropological thinking.

Searching Graphic Materials

For sound recordings, consult McNeil and Valk's *Latin American studies* **(J03).** For sources of maps, consult Sable's *A guide to nonprint materials for Latin American studies* **(J58).** For maps, consult Hanson's *Index to maps of Hispanic America, 1:1,000,000* **(J59).**

Atlases and Maps

KA68

Atlas cultural de México. México [City]: Secretaría de Educación Pública, Instituto Nacional de Antropología e Historia, Grupo Editorial Planeta, 1987. 9v.

A consistent geographical orientation is applied to numerous themes. Volumes of interest to anthropologists would include archaeology, museums, and handicrafts. Especially valuable is *Atlas cultural de México: Departamento de Lingüística del Instituto Nacional de Antropología e Historia Lingüística* (Mexico City:

Secretaría de Educación Pública, Instituto Nacional de Antropología e Historia, Grupo Editorial Planeta, 1988 [184p.]) **(KA69)** for its color-coded linguistic maps (p.141–68), with excellent subject index; it shares with all volumes entry by geographical name index. Still useful is Instituto Nacional de Antropología e Historia, *Atlas arqueológico de la República Méxicana* (Mexico [City]: Instituto Panamericano de Geografía e Historia, 1939) **(KA70),** with black-and-white fold-out maps that locate archaeological sites in each state. Under each state the sites are arranged alphabetically. Some bibliographical references are given. Attempts to show location of nearest town and to show how to get to the site. For archaeological maps of Campeche, consult México, Departamento de Monumentos Prehispánicos, *Atlas arqueológico de la República Méxicana* (Mexico [City]: Instituto Nacional de Antropología e Historia, 1959) **(KA71).**

KA72

Garza Tarazona de González, Silvia. *Atlas arqueológico del estado de Yucatán.* Mexico [City]: SEP, INAH, Centro Regional del Sureste, 1980. 2v.

V.1, [249p.]; v.2, [plates]. Catalog of archaeological sites surveyed and recorded by the Instituto Nacional de Antropología e Historia. In v.1, techniques in mapmaking include a directory of locations for map archives. There is a section devoted to such structures as pyramids, causeways, platforms, etc. Another section is devoted to forms of settlement, and a section is devoted to methods of analysis for patterns of settlement such as cultural, economic, and social change. Atlas displays locations of the nineteen cataloged sites. Alphabetic indexes by site with bibliography for each site, by author. There is a general bibliography (p.227–49). This work includes eighteen plates and a useful index to sites.

KA73

Johnson, Frederick. "The linguistic map of Mexico and Central America." In *The Maya and their neighbors,* p.88–114. New York: Appleton-Century, 1941.

Can be used to elaborate on information found in Coe, Snow, and Benson's *Atlas of ancient America* **(H12).**

KA74

Millon, René. *Urbanization at Teotihuacán, Mexico.* Austin: Univ. of Texas Pr., 1973. 2 parts.

Pt.1 includes the base map and its grid system, the fieldwork procedures used in the project, and the architectural reconstructions used in the maps. Included are the survey and the photographs of the city. Pt.2 comprises 147 map sheets, each with overlays. Each map has been photogrammetrically constructed from aerial photographs. For a thorough discussion of the rationale of this project, consult David M. Pendergast's "The Teotihuacan map: A review article," *Archaeology* (New York) 288 (3): 164–70 **(KA75).**

Photographs and Drawings

KA76

Anawalt, Patricia Rieff. *Indian clothing before Cortés: Mesoamerican costumes from the Codices.* Norman: Univ. of Oklahoma Pr., 1981. 232p.

There is a discussion of the data and the methodology used in this study. This is followed by the parallel coverage for draped, slip-on, open-sewn, closed-sewn, and limb-encasing garments for the Aztecs of central Mexico, the Tlaxcalans of central Mexico, the Tarascans, the Mixtecs, the Borgia, the lowland Mayas of Yucatán. There follows a comparative analysis of the six costume repertoires. Included here for the many illustrations. Indexed by subject, title of codices, scholars, and individuals.

Searching Unpublished Materials

Consult McNeil and Valk's *Latin American studies* **(J03)** for its coverage of sources on American and British doctoral theses, the resources cited under this strategic heading in chapter 1, and the chapters devoted to the subdisciplines of anthropology.

There is some inclusion of outstanding dissertations in *Handbook of Latin American studies* **(J26).** For recent German-language dissertations, consult *Abstracts in German anthropology* **(A33).** For some coverage of English- and French-language dissertations, consult descriptions of *Dissertation abstracts ondisc* [computer file] **(B14)** and *Francis bulletin signalétique* [computer file] discussed in the annotation to *FRANCIS* **(B19).**

Archives

Consult items 907–15 in Block's "Anthropology" **(J01)** for extensive coverage of guides to archival records in this culture area. For a number of archival guides designed for ethnohistorical investigations, see Vanderbilt University's monograph series *Publications in anthropology,* v.1– , 1972– (Nashville: Vanderbilt University Pr.) **(KA77).** Especially useful: v.13, v.17, and v.34.

KA78

Catálogo del Ramo Misiones. México [City]: Archivo General de la Nación, 1977. 166p. (Serie guías y catálogos, 16)

Entries refer to bound volumes of documents for which there is a document title identification of date and place of writing and some indication of the subject of its contents. Includes missionary accounts and reports. Geographic, personal name, and thematic indexes.

KA79

Grieb, Kenneth J., et al., eds. *Research guide to Central America and the Caribbean.* Madison: Univ. of Wisconsin Pr., 1985. 431p.

A directory to the many sources of the archival resources so valuable to the ethnohistory and archaeology of this area.

KA80

Indice del archivo Técnico de la Dirección de Monumentos Prehispánicos del INAH. México [City]: Dirección de Monumentos Prehispánicos, Instituto Nacional de Antropología e Historia, 1982. 304p. (Colección científica, 120)

Catalog of archaeological site surveys and field reports. Classified arrangement based on the library's classification system and list of subject headings. Topical, site, and personal name indexes.

KA81

Pérez Martínez, Hector. *Yucatán: An annotated bibliography of documents and manuscripts on the archaeology and history of Yucatán in archives & libraries of Mexico, North America and Europe (Catálogo de documentos para la historia de Yucatán y Campeche que se hallan en diversos archivos y bibliotecas de México y del extranjero).* Salisbury, N.C.: Documentary Publications, 1980. 133p.

Reprint. Originally published as *Catálogo de documentos para la historia de Yucatán y Campeche que se hallan en diversos archivos y bibliotecas de México y del extranjero* (Campeche: Museo Arquelológico Historico y Etnográfico de Campeche, 1943 [133p.]), providing sources for the study of Campeche (State) and Yucatán (State). Accurate descriptions of collections and libraries in France, Mexico, Spain, and Texas, with documents of value in the study of the Yucatán.

KA82

Tozzer Library. *Middle American Indians: A guide to the manuscript collection at Tozzer Library, Harvard University.* Edited by John M. Weeks. New York: Garland, 1985. 244p. (Garland reference library of social science, v.332)

Lists 856 entries alphabetically by author, with detailed descriptions. Identifies published versions, including many translations of research first published in German. Reproductions of manuscripts held at Tozzer are listed and arranged by the archive in which the originals can be found. Indexed by personal name, place name, and subject. See also John M. Weeks's *Maya ethnohistory: A guide to Spanish colonial documents at Tozzer Library, Harvard University* (Nashville: Vanderbilt University Pr., 1987 [121p.]) (Vanderbilt University publications in anthropology, no.34)

Alphabetic list with careful descriptions. Excellent descriptive bibliography.

KA83

University of Texas at Arlington. Library. *Catálogo de las fotocopias de los documentos y periódicos yucatecos en la Biblioteca de la Universidad de Texas en Arlington (Catalogue of Yucatán documents and newspapers on microfilm in the University of Texas at Arlington Library).* Ed. by Maritza Arrigunaga Coello. Arlington: Univ. of Texas at Arlington Pr., 1983. 211p.

Reproductions of the *archivo de la mitra* (1782–1897), distributed into eighteen groups; the *archivo general del estado* (the section "Documentos Coloniales, 1683–1824" includes eighteen groups); and the *archivo notarial del estado,* has a chronological index. There is, in contrast, a working document at the University of Texas, Austin: *Research microform collections at the Benson Latin American Collection* (Austin: Nellie Lee Benson Latin American Collection, n.d. [53p.]) **(KA84),** an alphabetic list of that much larger resource, with only title entries and no annotation to guide the user.

Dissertations

KA85

Montemayor, Felipe. *28 [i.e., Veintiocho] años de antropología: Tesis de la Escuela Nacional de Antropología e Historia, 1944–1971.* México [City]: Instituto Nacional de Antropología e Historia, 1971. 615p.

Subtitle "Catálogo . . . de las tesis de antropología presentadas en la Escuela." Chronological listing with detailed abstracts and subject, place, and author indexes.

Monographic Series

KA86

Harvard University. Peabody Museum of Archaeology and Ethnology. *Memoirs.* v.1– , 1986– . Cambridge, Mass.: Peabody Museum of Archaeology and Ethnology, Harvard University.

The emphasis of this series has traditionally been on contributions to Mesoamerican scholarship.

KA87

Tropical Science Center. *Occasional paper.* v.1– , 1965– . San José, Costa Rica: The Institute.

All bibliographies in this series are by author without subject index. Issued to date: Shook, Edwin M., Jorge A. Lines, [and] Michael D. Olien, *Anthropological bibliography of aboriginal Panama (Bibliografía antropológica aborigen de Panamá),* prov. ed. (1965 [79p.]) (Occasional paper, no.2) **(KA88);** Lines, Jorge A., Edwin M. Shook, and Michael D. Olien, *Anthropological bibliography of aboriginal Nicaragua (Bibliografía antropológica aborigen de Nicaragua),* prov. ed. (1965 [98p.]) (Occasional paper, no.3) **(KA89);** Lines, Jorge A., Edwin M. Shook, and Michael D. Olien, *Anthropological bibliography of aboriginal El Salvador (Bibliografía antropológica aborigen de El Salvador),* prov. ed. (1965 [114p.]) (Occasional paper, no.4) **(KA90);** Lines, Jorge A., Edwin M. Shook, Michael D. Olien, *Anthropological bibliography of aboriginal Honduras (Bibliografía antropológica aborigen de Honduras),* prov. ed. (1966 [190p.]) (Occasional paper, no.5) **(KA91);** Lines, Jorge A., *Anthropological bibliography of aboriginal Guatemala, British Honduras (Bibliografía antropológica aborigen de Guatemala, Belice),* prov. ed. (1967 [309p.]) (Occasional paper, no.6) **(KA92);** Lines, Jorge A., *Anthropological bibliography of aboriginal Costa Rica (Bibliografía antropológica aborigen de Costa Rica),* prov. ed. (1967 [196p.]) (Occasional paper, no.7) **(KA93).**

The volume on Costa Rica was preceded by an earlier work: Jorge A. Lines's *Bibliografía antropológica aborigen de Costa Rica: Incluye especialmente: Arqueología, cartografía, etnología, geografía, historia y lingüística* (San José, Costa Rica, 1943 [263p.]) **(KA94).** Consult item 962 in Block's "Anthropology" **(J01)** for a description of the publications that update the Lines volumes to 1986.

THE CARIBBEAN

Consult Coe, Snow, and Benson's *Atlas of ancient America* (p.161) **(H12)** for a map of the circum-Caribbean areas, including Hispaniola, the Greater Antilles, the Lesser Antilles, and the coastal lowlands of northern South America and Panama. Within this geographic area the distributions of indigenous ethnic groups such as the Arawak, Carib, and Ciboney are outlined and archaeological sites located. All searches for Caribbean material should start with the reference sources identified in pt.1, "Access by Disciplines." Refer to the discussion there of the reference strategies signaled by the headings "Current Awareness" and "Retrospective Searches," which do not change from chapter to chapter. A discussion of the system of primary, secondary, and tertiary entries that define the structure of the internal contents of entries under headings can be found in the introduction.

Searching Bibliographic Guides

Consult Auckland's "Getting into the literature" **(A01)** and the guides to the subdisciplines of anthropology listed in "Access by Discipline and Subdiscipline." See also Covington's *Latin America and the Caribbean* **(J02),** Block's "Anthropology" **(J01),** and McNeil and Valk's *Latin American studies* **(J03).** Entry by names of indigenous peoples has been greatly eased by the publication of Welch's *The Indians of South America* **(J21).**

Bibliographic Guides

Julian H. Steward's *Handbook of South American Indians,* v.4, *The circum-Caribbean tribes* **(J43),** offers a compendium on the indigenous ethnic groups of Central America which share Carib traditions.

KA95

Comitas, Lambros. *The complete Caribbeana, 1900–1975: A bibliographic guide to the scholarly literature.* Milwood, N.Y.: KTO Pr., 1977. 4v.

Excludes Cuba, Hispaniola, and Puerto Rico. The Amerindian groups in the Caribbean areas (including Belize and the Guianas) are included in v.1, *People.* Author and geographical indexes.

KA96

Koulen, Ingrid, and Gert Oostindie. *The Netherlands Antilles and Aruba: A research guide.* Dordrecht, Holland: Foris Publications, 1987. 162p. (Koninklijk Insituut Voor Taal,-Land-en Volkenkunde. Caribbean series, no.7)

Chapter 2 is an extensive bibliographic essay on social science studies, 1967–86, in which the extensive anthropological materials are identified. Chapter 3, Dutch Caribbean studies. Chapter notes to all chapters (p.107–13) and a bibliography of 550 items increase the reference value of this work. This can be informally updated by consulting *Caribbean abstracts,* v.1– , 1990– (Leiden: Department of Caribbean Studies, Royal Institute of Linguistics and Anthropology).

KA97

Laguerre, Michel S. *The complete Haitiana: A bibliographic guide to the scholarly literature 1900–1980.* Millwood, N.Y.: Kraus, 1982. 2v.

From the sixty-five chapters, those most useful for anthropology are chapter 4, "Population"; chapter 5, "Culture"; and chapter 6, "Structure of Haitian society."

Searching for Current Materials

In linguistics, *Latin American Indian literatures* **(J52)** has several current awareness features. For developments in archaeology, consult the department "Current research" in *American antiquity* **(C04)** which in the first issue each year summarizes any Latin American archaeological research that can be identified in reports, publications, and announcements of intentions to work in the field. Consult resources under this heading in chapter 1 and in the chapters devoted to the subdisciplines of anthropology.

Select Sources of Review in Scholarly Publications

KA98

Current bibliography. In *Caribbean studies.* v.1– , 1961– . Rio Pedras, Puerto Rico: University of Puerto Rico. Institute of Caribbean Studies. 6/yr.

Reports new publications. Includes books, pamphlets, and articles. The geographic coverage extends to the contiguous areas of Central and South America. Multidisciplinary, with many anthropological contributions.

KA99

Museo del Hombre Dominicano. *Boletín.* v.1– , 1972– . Santo Domingo: Cultural Dominicana, S.A. Instituto de Cultura Dominicana. Semiannual.

Articles on archaeology, ethnology, and ethnohistory of the Caribbean area. There is material of anthropological interest in Lozano Wilfredo, Nelson Ramírez, and Bernardo Vega's *Ciencias sociales en la Republica Dominicana: Sociologia, demografía, economia: Evolución y bibliografía* (Santo Domingo: Rundacion Friedrich Erbert, 1989 [296p.]) **(KA100)**

Retrospective Searches

Block's "Anthropology" **(J01)** provides dense nation-state entry into the retrospective bibliographies of this vast literature. McNeil and Valk's *Latin American studies* **(J03)** includes a discussion of general and special bibliographies which makes it possible here to direct attention only to the most vitally important sources with special value to anthropologists. The Columbus Memorial Library's *Index to Latin American periodical literature, 1929–1960* **(J16)** indexes in a single alphabet. The *Indice general* **(J17)** updates the Columbus Memorial Library catalog to 1970 and includes Instituto Nacional de Antropología e Historia (INAH) publications. The file corresponding to *HAPI* **(J28),** a subfile of *Latin American studies* [computer file] **(J27),** updates the *Indice general.* In chapter 1, "What Every Anthropologist Needs to Know," both the *Anthropological index* **(A35)** and *Anthropological literature* **(A36)** provide quarterly indexing for an international array of anthropological periodicals. At a more general level of resources with anthropological coverage, material in all scholarly languages can be identified in the databases *Social scisearch* [computer file] **(B37)** and *Humanities index* [computer file] **(B23).** Consult also the databases discussed in Covington's *Latin America and the Caribbean* **(J02).**

Retrospective Bibliographies—Bibliographies of Bibliographies

KA101

Jordan, Alma, and Barbara Comissiong. *The English speaking Caribbean: A bibliography of bibliographies.* Boston: Hall, 1984. 411p.

Classified arrangement. Anthropology (510–16), Archives (517–20), Ethnic groups (660–70), Ethnography (660–70), Ethnology (676–98), Ethnomusicology (699–705), Folklore (178–224).

Retrospective Bibliographies—Topical

KA102

Cordero, J. F., "Bibliografía sobre indigenismo en Cuba." *Revista de la Biblioteca Nacional* 1 (1949): 113–204.

Can be supplemented by reference to Louis A. Pérez's *Cuba: An annotated bibliography* (Westport, Conn.: Greenwood, 1988 [301p.]) (Bibliographies and indexes in world history, no.10) **(KA103),** which organizes 1,120 annotated entries into forty-five major headings, including many Spanish-language works with an analytical index of authors, topics, and titles. Since Cuba is excluded from Comitas, another important source of retrospective coverage is the Library, University of Miami, Coral Gables, *Catalog of the Cuban and Caribbean Library* (Boston: Hall, 1977 [6v.]) **(KA104)** and the great Florida University Libraries, *Catalog of the Latin-American collection* **(J19),** with its published supplements.

KA105

Myers, Robert A. *Amerindians of the Lesser Antilles: A bibliography.* New Haven, Conn.: Human Relations Area Files. HRAFlex Books, 1981. 158 leaves (HRAF books ST 1–001. Bibliography series)

About 1,300 references to archaeological, historical, and linguistic research on the Ciboney, Arawak, and Carib peoples of the eastern Caribbean. Geographical and author indexes. This resource can be usefully supplemented by consulting Richard Price's *The historical and bibliographical introduction* (Baltimore: Johns Hopkins Univ. Pr., 1976 [184p.]) **(KA106),** with excellent indexing and documentation so dense that the work can be used as a bibliographic review. This resource can also be consulted to consolidate an understanding of the coastal region of South America as part of the Caribbean culture area.

KA107

Myers, Robert A. *A resource guide to Dominica 1493–1986.* New Haven, Conn.: Human Relations Area Files, 1987. 649 leaves (HRAFlex books, ST 4–001. Bibliography series)

An outline history of Dominica introduces a bibliography divided into twenty-five segments. There is a location guide to documents in Europe and the United States, and in West Indian archives. Sixty-nine pages of name and subject index.

KA108

Sued Badillo, Jalil. *Bibliografía antropológica para el estudio de los pueblos indígenas en el Caribe.* Santo Domingo: Fundacíon García Arévalo, 1977. 579p. (Serie investigaciones, N.8)

Under broad subject and geographic headings, entries are listed alphabetically by author. Includes monographs and journal articles. Covers insular Caribbean with Bahamas, Cuba, Jamaica, Haiti, Puerto Rico, the Antilles. Includes Central America and the Caribe in Colombia. No annotations.

KA109

Vivó, Paquita, ed. *The Puerto Ricans: An annotated bibliography.* New York: Bowker, 1973. 299p.

Comprehensive to date of publication. Most listed items are annotated. Excellent subject, author, and title indexes. Consult also "Puerto Rican studies: Resources in the United States and Puerto Rico," in v.2, *Latin American masses and minorities: Their images and realities* (Madison: Univ. of Wisconsin Pr. for SALALM Secretariat, 1987 [2v.], 2: 549–55) **(KA110),** a concise bibliographic introduction to reference sources for this region which can be expanded by reference to María de los Angeles Castro's "The historical archives of Puerto Rico," *Latin American masses and minorities: Their images and realities* (Madison: Univ. of Wisconsin Pr. for SALALM Secretariat, 1987 [2v.], 2: 573–79) **(KA111).**

KA112

West India Reference Library [Jamaica]. *The catalogue of the West India Reference Library.* Millwood, N.Y.: Kraus, 1980. 2v. in 6.

Attempts to be comprehensive for Jamaica and the English-speaking Caribbean.

Searching Unpublished Materials

Dissertations

KA113

Commonwealth Caribbean Resource Centre. *Theses on the Commonwealth Caribbean, 1891–1973.* London, Ontario, Canada: Office of International Education. University of Western Ontario, 1975. 139p.

An author list, indexed by country where theses were submitted and by countries studied.

SOUTH AMERICA

Block's "Anthropology" **(J01)** provides dense nation-state entry into the retrospective bibliographies of this vast literature. McNeil and Valk's *Latin American studies* **(J03)** includes a discussion of general and special bibliographies, which makes it possible here to direct attention only to the most vitally important sources of special value to anthropologists. The Columbus Memorial Library's *Index to Latin American periodical literature, 1929–1960* **(J16)** indexes in a single alphabet. The *Indice general* **(J17)** updates the Columbus Memorial Library catalog to 1970. The file corresponding to *HAPI* **(J28),** a subfile of *Latin American studies* [computer file] **(J27),** updates the *Indice general.* In chapter 1, "What Every Anthropologist Needs to Know," both the *Anthropological index* **(A35)** and *Anthropological literature* **(A36)** provide quarterly indexing for an international array of anthropological periodicals. At a more general level of resources with anthropological coverage, material in all scholarly languages can be identified in the databases *Social scisearch* [computer file] **(B37)** and *Humanities index* [computer file] **(B23).** Consult also the databases discussed in Covington's *Latin America and the Caribbean* **(J02).**

Retrospective Searches

Retrospective Bibliography—Broad Scope

KB01

O'Leary, Timothy J. *Ethnographic bibliography of South America.* New Haven, Conn.: Human Relations Area Files Pr., 1963. 387p.

Important for its access by indigenous ethnic group to research on South American anthropology. Lists 24,000 items (including articles from 650 journals) covering ethnography; pre-Columbian, colonial, and present-day Indians; social anthropology; archaeology; linguistics; physical anthropology; and sociology. It is organized by cultural areas and within each area by indigenous ethnic group. Can be brought up to date for monographs by consulting Welch's *Indians of South America* **(J21)** and for periodicals by Columbus Memorial Library's *Index to Latin American periodical literature, 1929–1960* **(J16).** Can be updated by consulting *International bibliography of social and cultural anthropology* **(D20).** The cultures of Panama are closely related to those of South America, but O'Leary does not include Panama, which is also often excluded from Mesoamerican reference sources. For that country, consult *América indígena* **(J45)** to identify issues devoted to a single country.

Retrospective Bibliography—Topical

KB02

Niles, Susan A. *South American Indian narrative, theoretical and analytical approaches: An annotated bibliography.* New York: Garland, 1981. 183p. (Garland folklore bibliographies, v.1) (Garland reference library of the humanities, v.276)

Lists 651 sources for South American Indian narrative folklore. Arranged by author. Indigenous ethnic group (p.166–74) and subject (p.175–83) indexes. Can be updated by the section "Bibliography," a regular feature in *Latin American Indian literatures* **(J52).** For comparative Mesoamerican folklore and literature, consult the supplementary v.3, *Literatures,* in Wauchope's *Handbook of Middle American Indians, Supplement* **(KA64).** Consult also Block's "Anthropology" **(J01).**

Consult also Tovar and Tovar, *Catálogo de las lenguas de América del Sur: Con clasificaciones, indicaciones tipológicas, bibliografía y mapas* **(J34),** which is indexed by languages and dialects. While Block's "Anthropology" **(J01)** does not cite this resource, it does provide excellent annotations for many of the entries that touch on Mesoamerican linguistics. DeMiller's *Linguistics* **(E01)** suggests that this work be used as a companion to Loukotka's *Classification of South American Indian languages* **(KB08)** and Loukotka's *Ethnolinguistic distribution of South American Indians* **(KB07).** See also Key's *The grouping of South American Indian languages* **(KB04).**

Informational Reference Searches

McNeil and Valk's *Latin American studies* **(J03)** provides a detailed discussion of useful handbooks and of selected European and American societies and associations with an interest in Latin American studies. For American scholars, the American Anthropological Association's *AAA guide* **(A53)** usually provides the best current information about the institutional addresses and research interests of affiliated scholars.

Directories

KB03

Dent, David W. "Major research centers and institutes in Latin America and the Caribbean." In *Handbook of political science research on Latin America: Trends from the 1960s to the 1990s,* p.393–411. Westport, Conn.: Greenwood, 1990.

Classed arrangement by country with addresses and some indication of research focus.

Handbooks

KB04

Key, Mary Ritchie. *The grouping of South American Indian languages.* Tübingen, Germany: Gunter Narr Verlag, 1979. 170p.

A sourcebook for work done on South American languages to date of publication. Focus in on phonology rather than grammatical comparisons. Strongest coverage of Andean-equatorial languages. Can be complemented by reference to Harriet E. Marelis Klein and Louisa R. Stark, ed., *South American Indian languages: Retrospect and prospect* (Austin: Univ. of Texas Pr., 1985 [863p.]) **(KB05),** with its descriptive summary in the tradition of Boasian anthropology. Twenty-two papers in three sections: Lowlands, Andes, Eastern South America. Concerned with basic issues such as locations, number of speakers, prospects for survival. Each article includes a survey of the literature and an attempt to deal with genetic classification. Detailed language index makes this resource especially valuable for anthropologists. For Amazonian languages, consult also Derbyshire and Pullum's *Handbook of Amazonian languages* **(KB50).**

KB06

Murdock, George P. "South American culture areas." *Southwestern journal of anthropology* 7(1951): 415–36.

Detailed explication of the distribution of indigenous ethnic groups. This work can be used in conjunction with Loukotka's *Classification of South American Indian languages* **(KB08)** and Loukotka's *Ethnolinguistic distribution of South American Indians* **(KB07).** See also Key's *The grouping of South American Indian languages* **(KB04).**

Searching Graphic Materials

KB07

Loukotka, Cestmir. *Ethnolinguistic distribution of South American Indians.* Washington, D.C.: Association of American Geographers, 1967. (Association of American Geographers. Map supplement, no.8)

Issued with *Annals of the American Association of Geographers,* 57 (2): 1967. Fully described in the *American geographers annals* 57(1967): 437–38. This work is used in conjunction with Cestmir Loukotka's *Classification of South American Indian languages,* ed. by Johannes Wilbert (Los Angeles: Latin American Center, UCLA 1968 [436p.]) (Latin American Center, UCLA, Reference series, v.7) **(KB08),** which groups 117 language stocks into these main categories. There is an ethnolinguistic index for the names of indigenous ethnic groups used as synonyms, and an index by author. Use in conjunction with Tovar and Tovar's *Catálogo de las lenguas de América del Sur* **(J34).**

THE ANDES

In an ethnological sense, Colombia, Ecuador, and Venezuela are not strictly Andean but have cultures of recognizable Andean origin in the region from Sierra de Mate to the Paria Peninsula.

Searching for Current Materials

In linguistics, *Latin American Indian literatures* **(J52)** has several current awareness features. For developments in archaeology, consult the department "Current research" in *American antiquity* **(C04).** Consult in *Fieldwork in the Library* resources under this heading in chapter 1 and in the chapters devoted to the subdisciplines of anthropology.

Selective Sources of Review in Scholarly Publications

KB09

Gaceta arqueológica andina. v.1– , 1982– . Lima, Perú: Instituto Andino de Estudios Arqueológicos. Bimonthly.

Summarizes ongoing or recently completed projects conducted by North American as well as Latin American archaeologists in Andean countries. This journal publishes the newest research results from Venezuela, Colombia,

Ecuador, Peru, Bolivia, Chile, and Argentina. For more general but recent coverage, consult Carmen Checa de Silva's *Gaceta bibliotecaria del Peru, 1963–1987: Indice analitico* (Lima: Gaceta bibliotecaria del Perú, 1991 [142p.]).

KB10

Nawpa pacha. Berkeley, Calif.: Institute of Andean Studies, 1963– . Annual.

Archaeology, art, and ethnohistory of the Andean region of South America. Includes "New publications of interest to our readers." Consult also *Bulletin de l'Institut français d'études andines,* v.1– , 1972– (Lima: Institut français d'études andines), a quarterly with international bibliographic coverage.

Retrospective Searches

Block's "Anthropology" **(J01)** provides dense nation-state entry into the retrospective bibliographies of this vast literature. McNeil and Valk's *Latin American studies* **(J03)** includes a discussion of general and special bibliographies, which makes it possible here to direct attention only to the most vitally important sources of special value to anthropologists. The Columbus Memorial Library's *Index to Latin American periodical literature, 1929–1960* **(J16)** indexes in a single alphabet. The *Indice general* **(J17)** updates the Columbus Memorial Library catalog to 1970. The file corresponding to *HAPI* **(J28),** a subfile of *Latin American studies* [computer file] **(J27),** updates the *Indice general.* In chapter 1, "What Every Anthropologist Needs to Know," both the *Anthropological index* **(A35)** and *Anthropological literature* **(A36)** provide quarterly indexing for an international array of anthropological periodicals. At a more general level of resources with anthropological coverage, material in all scholarly languages can be identified in the databases *Social scisearch* [computer file] **(B37)** and *Humanities index* [computer file] **(B23).** Consult also the databases discussed in Covington's *Latin America and the Caribbean* **(J02).** A useful start for entry by names of contiguous peoples can always be made with O'Leary's *Ethnographic bibliography of South America* **(KB01),** and with Welch's *Indians of South America* **(J21).**

Retrospective Bibliographies—Broad Scope

KB11

Barnadas, Josep. *Manual de bibliografía: Introducción a los estudios bolivianos contemporáneos, 1960–1984.* Casco, Peru: Centre de estudios rurales andinas, 1987. 514p.

The extensive bibliography of bibliographies (p.1–28) is classified with the general section containing many references to doctoral lists. Anthropologists can find in the arrangement of the main body of this work, with its 6,109 entries, coverage under the headings "Archaeology," "Ethnology," and "Cultural anthropology." Can be supplemented in searches for material on indigenous ethnic groups by the richly indexed Centro de Documentación Antropológica (Bolivia), *Catálogo—Materiales del Instituto Lingüístico de Verano sobre grupos étnicos de Bolivia, 1955–1980,* ed. by Luis Oporto (La Paz: Instituto Boliviano de Cultura, Instituto Nacional de Antropología, Centro de Documentación Antropológica, 1981 [47p.]) (Serie Bibliografía antropológica, 1) **(KB12),** for a resource with an arrangement by indigenous ethnic group and ethnographic as well as linguistic material.

Retrospective Bibliographies—Topical

Many of the bibliographies for this area cited in Gibson's "Bibliography of anthropological bibliographies" **(H01)** are still useful.

KB13

Convenio Andrés Bello. *Bibliografía sobre medicina tradicional del área andina.* La Paz: Instituto Internacional de Integración, 1987. 178p.

Lists 2,600 entries for books, articles, documents, and conference proceedings. Each entry is coded for broad subjects. Covers Callahuaya and Aymara Indians. The list lacks indexing or table of contents.

KB14

Berg, Hans van den. *Material bibliográfico para el estudio de los Aymaras, Callawayas, Chipayas, Urus.* Cochabamba, Bolivia: Facultad de Filosofía y Ciencias Religiosas, Universidad Católica Boliviana, 1980–88. 5v.

An annotated bibliography on the Bolivian and Peruvian ethnic groups named in the title. Alphabetical by author list of 7,000 items. The final volume contains an index by ethnic group, subject, and author. There is an index by subject which is then subdivided for ethnic groups. Volume 1 was published in 1980. Second supplement was published in 1988.

KB15

Giacama, Mariana, Patricia Sanzana, Carlos Zapata, comps. *Campesinado chileno: Bibliografía.* Santiago: Grupo de Investigaciones Agrarias, Academia de Humanismo Cristiano, 1987. 141p.

Even though land reform is the central issue, the bibliography integrates nearly 1,000 scholarly studies of land use by the peasantry in a context of their social organization. Arranged by author with chronological breakdown. Most of the early fieldwork in the region can be captured in the bibliographies listed in Gibson's "Bibliography of anthropological bibliographies" **(H01),** which identifies (1) three bibliographic reviews completed in 1941 by Donald D. Brand which have some emphasis on Araucanian studies; (2) Richard E. Latch, comp., "Bibliografía chilena de las ciencias antropológicas," *Revista de bibliografía chilena y extranjera* (Santiago) 3 (1915): 148–95, 229–661, which has 1,172 items; (3) the 250 entries with elaborate annotations found in Philip A. Mean's *Biblioteca andina,* pt.1, The chroniclers . . . of the sixteenth and seventeenth century who treated . . . the prehispanic history and culture of the Andean countries. Connecticut Academy of Arts and Sciences, *Transactions.* 29 (1928): 276–525. Much of this early work is integrated into later bibliographies of indigenous ethnic groups such as O'Leary's bibliography **(KB01)** and more recently Héctor Zumaeta Zúñiga's *Bibliografía selectiva sobre la cultura mapuche* (Temuco: Pontificia Universidad Católica de Chile, Sede Regional Temuco, 1976 [154p.]) **(KB16),** which includes works under broad topics such as sociocultural anthropology, linguistics, physical anthropology, archaeology, art, religion, history, documents, education, literature, and law.

KB17

Instituto Nacional de Cultura. *Tradicion oral peruana: Hemerografía (1896–1976).* Lima: Instituto Nacional de Cultura, 1978. 133p.

Annotates in Spanish 731 entries to journal articles and books. The subject index is a classification system referring to the numbered entries, which have been entered alphabetically. Can informally supplement the Pan American Institute of Geography and History, Commission on History, Committee on Folklore, *Bibliografía del folklore peruano* (Mexico [City]: Pan American Institute of Geography and History, 1960 [186p.]) (Publicación 92) **(KB18),** which arranges 1,809 entries by broad subject category with detailed subject index. Author index.

KB19

Key, Harold H., and Mary Key. *Bolivian Indian tribes: Classification, bibliography, and map of present language distribution.* Norman: Summer Institute of Linguistics of the University of Oklahoma, 1967. 128p. (Summer Institute of Linguistics. Publications in linguistics and related fields, no.15).

Describes 624 bibliographies for linguistics, ethnology, and archaeological reports. Includes useful general bibliographies. Covers all languages of Bolivia except Aymara and Quechua. Especially valuable for indexes of language groups. The linguistic material can be brought to the early 1980s by reference to Mary Ritchie Key's "Lenguas de las tierras bajas de Bolivia," *América Indígena* 43 (1983): 877–92 **(KB20),** with a useful map that shows the present location of thirty-two languages in twelve families, and six languages listed as unclassified. Can be supplemented by Paul Rivet and Georges de Créqui-Montfort's *Bibliographies des langues aymará et kicua* (Paris: Institut de l'ethnologie, 1954–56 [4v.]) (Travaux et mémoires de l'Institut de l'ethnologie, v.51) **(KB21).** The ethnographic coverage can be expanded by reference to Dwight B. Heath's *Historical* *dictionary of Bolivia* (Metuchen, N.J.: Scarecrow, 1972 [324p.]) (Latin American Historical Dictionaries, no.4). Nearly one-fifth of Heath's work is devoted to a bibliographic essay that reflects his anthropological training.

KB22

Martínez, Héctor. *Migraciones internas en el Perú: Aproximación crítica y bibliografía.* Lima, Perú: Instituto de Estudios Peruanos, 1980. 188p. (Guías bibliográs, 3)

Lists 700 annotated entries. Population movements to cities and mining centers. Traces movement from mountains to coast and to eastern lowlands.

KB23

Martínez, Héctor, Miguel Cameo C., and Jesús Ramírez S. *Bibliografía indígena andina peruana, 1900–1968.* Lima: Ministerio de Trabajo y Comunidades. Instituto Indigenista Peruano, 1968. 2v. 651p.

A classified list with 1,700 entries. A general section is followed by sections for the northern, central, and southern areas of Peru, each with geographical and topical subdivisions. Includes citations to work in regional journals. Separate indexes by author, subject, and place. Some of the literature about these indigenous peoples as an ethnic group can be found in Margarita Salas Sánchez's *Bibliografía sobre identidad cultural en el Perú* (Lima: Instituto Indigenista Peruano, Centro Interamericano de Administración del Trabajo, 1982 [126p.] (Serie bibliográfica [Instituto Indigenista Peruano], no.2) **(KB24),** which introduces the literature relevant to the relationship between the government and ethnic groups. Provides access to recent research about indigenous ethnic groups. Entries are ordered by a classification system under broad topics such as "Language" and "Folklore."

KB25

Summer Institute of Linguistics. *Bibliografía del Instituto Lingüístico de Verano en el Perú, suplemento: Enero de 1977 a agosto de 1981.* Recopilación de Mary Ruth Wise y Ann Shanks. Lima: Instituto Lingüístico de Verano, 1981. 56p.

Author listing with subject index.

KB26

Vega Centeno, Imelda, Daniel Rodríguez, and Blanca Cerpa. *Bibliografía Aguaruna-Huambita.* Lima: Centro de Investigación y Promoción Amazónica, 1986. 100p. (Documento, 8)

Classified arrangement with entries under history, geography, natural resources, anthropological studies (p.35–48), education, health, language. Author index.

KB27

Welch, Thomas L., and Rene L. Gutiérrez. *The Incas: A bibliography of books and periodicals.* Washington, D.C.: Columbus Memorial Library, Organization of American States, 1987. 145p. (Hipólito Unánue bibliographic series, no.1)

Alphabetic list by author of 401 periodical articles and 715 books. The subject index is by broad topic such as QUIPU (912 items); WAR AND WARFARE (31 items); BIBLIOGRAPHY (4 items).

Informational Reference Searches

McNeil and Valk's *Latin American studies* **(J03)** provides a detailed discussion of useful handbooks and of selected European and American societies and associations with an interest in Latin American studies. For American scholars the American Anthropological Association's *AAA guide* **(A53)** usually provides the best current information about the institutional addresses and research interests of affiliated scholars.

Encyclopedias, Compendiums, Handbooks, Manuals

A synopsis of the laws governing archaeology in Peru is included in the recent bibliographic essay by Rogger Ravines, *Introducción a una bibliografía general de la arqueología del Perú, 1860–1988* (Lima: Editorial los Pinos, 1989 [296p.]) **(KB28).**

KB29

Masuda, Shozo, Izumi Shimada, and Craig Morris, eds. *Andean ecology and civilization: An interdisciplinary perspective on*

Andean ecological complementarity. Tokyo: Univ. of Tokyo Pr., 1985. 550p. (Papers from Wenner-Gren Foundation for Anthropological Research, Symposium no.91)

Twenty-one Andeanists from Chile, Great Britain, Japan, Peru, and the United States examine the "Vertical archipelago model" for archaeological, ethnohistoric, ecological, economic, social, and temporal perspectives. The breadth of insight into the complementarity between vertical and horizontal organizations makes it possible for this volume to consolidate a great deal of what is known in this area.

KB30

Montaño Aragón, Mario. *Guía etnográfica lingüística de Bolivia: Tribus de la selva.* La Paz: Editorial Don Bosco, 1987– . 2v. to date.

Planned as a multivolume set to consolidate all contemporary research and bibliographic information on the indigenous peoples of Bolivia. The Introduction to the first volume establishes the topics to be developed and discusses the methodological and philosophical bases of social anthropology and linguistics. There follows for each of fifteen linguistics groups (1) Statistical data, (2) Historical review, (3) Current situation, (4) Sociocultural description, (5) Idiom, and (6) Linguistic studies with extensive notes and a bibliography. V.1, Indigenous ethnic groups including: Pano, Tacana, Chapacura, Tupi-Guarano, Yuki, Kuruguas o Kuraguas, Arawak (Mojeños), Apolistas (Arawak), Baure (Arawak), Chan (Arawak), Movima, Cayubaba, Canichana, Itonama. V.2 includes: Chimane, Bororo, Saravica, Paiconeca, Curaves, Curucaneca, Curuminacas, Tapii o Tapio, Otuke, Guato y Guasarapo, Chamacoco o Timinaha, Chiquito, Gorgotogui, Yuracare. As a useful desk reference, Jédu Antonio Sagárnaga Meneses's *Diccionario de etnoarqueología Boliviana* (La Paz: CIMA, 1990 [201p.]) **(KB31)** is arranged alphabetically with brief definitions and biographies of authors, including reference to their relevant works. There is a select bibliography of sources consulted.

KB32

Rodríguez Pastor, Humberto, compilador y anotaciones. Congreso Nacional de Investigaciones en Antropología (1st: 1985; Lima) *La antropología en el Perú.* Lima: Consejo Nacional de Ciencia y Tecnología, 1985. 285p.

Encyclopedic review. The first section, "History," includes articles on the origin, directions, and history of Peruvian anthropology (especially from 1940 to 1980). The next section, "Field accounts," includes bibliographic reviews of peasant communities, migratory movements, indigenous religions and transformations, and an overview of Amazonian anthropology and Andean myths. The third section is devoted to discussions of professional organizations of anthropologists in Peru. Bibliographies include books, journal articles, and dissertations. The last section is devoted to a listing of theses on Peruvian anthropology. Geographic and subject indexes.

State-of-the-Art Reviews

For Peruvian archaeology there has been a recent surge of bibliographic consolidation. Inspect the following: R. Schaedel's "Peruvian archaeology, 1946–80: An overview," *World archaeology* 13 (1982): 359–71; Richard L. Burger's "An overview of Peruvian archaeology (1976–1986)," *Annual review of anthropology* 18 (1989): 37–69 **(KB33);** Mario A. Rivera's "Acerca de la arqueología andina del norte de Chile," *Revista andina* 2 (1984): 283–98, and "La investigación arqueológica en el norte de Chile, 1984–1990," *Revista andina* 8 (2) (1990): 555–78. In the same issue, Ramiro Matos Mendieta's "Arqueología peruana (1970–1990): Algunos comentarios," *Revista andina* 8 (2) (1990): 507–53.

Consult articles in the *Latin American research review* **(J56),** especially James M. Wallace's "Urban anthropology in Lima: An overview" 19 (1984): 57–85.

KB34

Revista andina. v.1– , 1983– . Cusco, Peru: Centro de Estudios Rurales Andinas "Bartolomé de las Casas." Semiannual.

Last inspected: July 1990. Included articles on symbolism, on popular culture processes, on music, and on a Cochabamba archive. Each issue is divided into five sections: studies, notes and documents, bibliographies, reviews, and listings of periodicals publishing articles on the Andes. Reviews of books published in Spanish and English. Bibliographic reviews are regularly published. Recent examples: Rodolfo Merlino and Alicia Quereilhac's "Acerca de los estudios andinos en la Argentina" 1 (1984): 265–82; Italo Oberti R., "Cusco arqueológico y etnohistórico: Una introducción bibliográfica" 1 (1983): 443–74; Joseph W. Bastien's "Los Aymará: Notas bibliográficas" 1 (1983): 445–78, 545–78; Roswith Hartmann's "Medio siglo de estudios quechuas en la Universidad de Bonn" 4 (1986): 607–14; Henrique-Osvaldo Urbano's "Historia y etnohistoria andinas" 9 (1991): 123–63; and Margot Beyersdorff's "La tradición oral quechua vista desde la perspectiva de la literatura" 4 (1986): 213–36. Consult other bibliographic reviews from this journal as they have been embedded in the annotation given to Martínez, Cameo C., and Ramírez S.'s *Bibliografía indígena andina peruana, 1900–1968* **(KB23).**

Searching Unpublished Materials

Consult McNeil and Valk's *Latin American studies* **(J03)** for its coverage of sources on American and British doctoral theses, the resources cited under this strategic heading in chapter 1, and the chapters devoted to the subdisciplines of anthropology.

Some outstanding dissertations are included in *Handbook of Latin American studies* **(J26).** For recent German-language dissertations, consult *Abstracts in German anthropology* **(A33).** For some coverage of English- and French-language dissertations, consult descriptions of *Dissertation abstracts ondisc* [computer file] **(B14)** and *Francis bulletin signalétique* [computer file], discussed in the annotation to *FRANCIS* **(B19).**

Archives

KB35

Ravines, Rogger. *Inventario de monumentos arqueológicos del Perú: Primera aproximación.* v.1– , 1883– . Lima: Instituto Nacional de Cultura.

Two volumes to date. Places archaeological sites of Peru on maps of 1:200,000, making it possible to acquire aerial maps from the descriptions. Completed: The Ecuadorian frontier to Lima, and sites of metropolitan Lima. Consult also Deborah Wood's *Directed change in Peru: A guide to the Viscos collection* (Ithaca, N.Y.: [Cornell University, Olin Library] Department of Manuscripts and University Archives, 1975 [78p.]) **(KB36),** which describes the preservation in the Viscos Project of records of collected data, including field notes of participants in the Cornell Peru Project spanning the years 1946–72. For a history of the Viscos Project, consult Paul L. Doughty's "Review of *Directed culture change in Peru: A guide to the Viscos Collection,*" *American anthropologist* 79 (1977): 144–46 **(KB37).**

Dissertations

KB38

Muñoz de Linares, Elba Céspedes de Reynaga, and Alicia Céspedes de Reynaga. *Bibliografía de tesis peruanas sobre indigenismo y ciencias sociales.* Lima: Instituto Indigenista Peruano: Centro Interamericano de Administración del Trabajo, 1983. 2v. (733p.) (Serie bibliográfica, no.4)

Author listing under broad topics. "Anthropology" (p. 27–60), "Archaeology" (p. 61–70), "Linguistics" (p.289–94), "Medicine" (p.303–26), "Psychology" (p.327–32), "Sociology" (p.333–416). Indexes by author, subject, ethnic group, geography, and institution. Additional access to these materials can be found in the coverage of Rodríguez Pastor's *La antropología en el Perú* (p.183–274) **(KB32),** which is limited to anthropological theses and divided into three sections: (1) Peruvian universities, (2) North American universities, (3) French universities with geographic and subject indexes.

BRAZIL AND THE AMAZON

Searching Bibliographic Guides

Consult Auckland's "Getting into the literature"**(A01)** and the guides to the subdisciplines of anthropology listed in *Fieldwork in the Library,* Covington's *Latin America and the*

Caribbean **(J02),** Block's "Anthropology" **(J01),** and McNeil and Valk's *Latin American studies* **(J03).** Entry by names of indigenous peoples has been greatly eased by the publication of Welch *The Indians of South America* **(J21).**

Bibliographic Guides

KB39

Baldus, Herbert. *Bibliografía crítica da etnologia brasileira.* São Paulo: Comissão do IV Centenário da cidade de São Paulo, Serviço de Comemorações Culturais, 1954. 2v. (Volkerkundliche Abhandlungen, bd. 3, 4, 9)

V.3, a new work by Thekla Hartman, *Bibliografía crítica da etnologia brasileira* (Berlin: Reiner Verlag, 1984 [729p.]) **(KB40).** It extends the critical review of works published between 1967 and 1982, adding 1,883 entries that are thoroughly annotated with references to book reviews. Like the original volumes, it is indexed by author, subject, and place and names of indigenous ethnic groups. Volumes 1 and 2 were compiled by Herbert Baldus and first published in 1958–68. All volumes are arranged by author. Introduction in Portuguese, English, and German. Of first importance.

KB41

Hartness, Ann. *Brazil in reference books, 1965–1989: An annotated bibliography.* Metuchen, N.J.: Scarecrow, 1991. 351p.

Lists 1,669 entries with concise descriptive annotations. The classed arrangement includes a section on ethnic groups that will be especially useful to anthropologists. Identification of bibliographies for states can be useful when research is planned in a local setting. The index provides excellent entry to anthropological materials. Identifies, for example, seven bibliographies of women and one bibliography for the Yanomami.

Searching for Current Materials

In linguistics, *Latin American Indian literatures* **(J52)** has several current awareness features. For developments in archaeology, consult the department "Current research" in *American antiquity* **(C04),** which in the first issue each year summarizes any Latin American archaeological research that can be identified in reports, publications, and announcements of intentions to work in the field. Consult in *Fieldwork in the Library* resources under this heading in chapter 1 and in the chapters devoted to the subdisciplines of anthropology.

Select Sources of Review in Scholarly Publications

KB42

Revista de antropología (Brazil). v.1– , 1953– . São Paulo: Associação Brasileira de Antropología. Annual.

Five to eleven book reviews per issue. Includes a department with reports on Brazilian meetings, and reports on courses of study available. Publishes bibliographic studies such as Eduardo B. Viveiros de Castro's "Bibliografía etnológica básca tupi-guaraní" 27–28 (1984–85): 7–24.

Selective Lists of Scholarly Journals

KB43

"Union list of selected Brazilian periodicals in the humanities and social sciences." In Jackson, William Vernon, *Library guide for Brazilian studies* (Pittsburgh: Pittsburgh Book Center, 1964). Appendix. 197p.

Jackson rewards examination by students of Brazil who wish to exploit American library resources.

Retrospective Searches

Block's "Anthropology" **(J01)** provides dense nation-state entry into the retrospective bibliographies of this vast literature. McNeil and Valk's *Latin American studies* **(J03)** includes a discussion of general and special bibliographies which makes it possible here to direct attention only to the most vitally important sources with special value to anthropologists. The Columbus Memorial Library's *Index to Latin American periodical literature, 1929–1960* **(J16)** indexes, in a single alphabet, periodical articles. The *Indice general* **(J17)** updates the Columbus Memorial Library catalog to 1970. The file corresponding to *HAPI* **(J28),** a subfile of *Latin American studies* [computer file] **(J27),** updates the *Indice general.* In chapter 1, "What Every Anthropologist Needs to Know," both the *Anthropological index* **(A35)** and *Anthropological literature* **(A36)** provide quarterly indexing for an international array of anthropological periodicals. At a more general level of resources with anthropological coverage, material in all scholarly languages can be identified in the databases *Social scisearch* [computer file] **(B37)** and *Humanities index* [computer file] **(B23).** Consult also the databases discussed in Covington's *Latin America and the Caribbean* **(J02).** A useful start for entry by names of contiguous peoples can always be made with O'Leary's *Ethnographic bibliography of South America* **(KB01).**

Retrospective Bibliographies—Broad Scope

Consult *Catalog of the Latin American collection* **(J20),** with supplements for the strongest collection of Brazilian material in the United States, and the Hispanic and Luso Brazilian Councils, *Canning House Library, Hispanic Council, London, Author and subject catalogue* **(KB47),** in the United Kingdom for published records of library holdings on Brazil.

Retrospective Bibliographies—Continuing

KB44

Indice de ciências sociais. v.1– , 1979– . Rio de Janeiro: Instituto Universitário de Pesquisas do Rio de Janeiro (IUPERJ). 2/yr.

Bibliography for anthropology, sociology, and political science.

Retrospective Bibliographies—Topical

For detailed coverage of reference sources relevant to Brazilian folklore linguistics (dictionaries and bibliographies), consult Block's "Anthropology" **(J01).**

KB45

Domínguez, Camilo A. *Bibliografía de la Amazonia colombiana y áreas fronterizas amazónicas.* Bogotá: DAINCO Corporación Aracuara: published for COLCIENCIAS, 1985. 226p.

Covers articles and books on the northwestern Amazon, which includes anthropology, biology, and geography. The bibliography is an alphabetically ordered list (p.1–189), with a geographic key to scholarly institutions referred to in the text or in descriptions of their publishing efforts. There is an index of species by technical name, an index of plant species by technical name, an index of indigenous populations, a geographical index, and a thematic index. Regularly updated by the bibliographies and notes and comments found in *Amazonia colombiana Americanista,* v.1– , 1947– (Sibundoy, Colombia: Centro de Investigaciones Linguísticas y Etnográficas de la Amazonia Colombiana), an annual with about fifteen articles per issue.

KB46

Levine, Robert M. *Brazil since 1930: An annotated bibliography for social historians.* New York: Garland, 1980. 336p. (Garland reference library of social science, v.59)

A list of 1,673 entries selected for their interdisciplinary utility with strength in coverage of studies of cults and ethnic groups. Additional entry to the more general monographs of relevance to research in the social sciences can be achieved by consulting Hispanic and Luso Brazilian Councils, *Canning House Library, Hispanic Council, London, Author and subject catalogue* (Boston: Hall, 1967 [4v.]) **(KB47),** with *First supplement* (Boston: Hall, 1973 [627p.]).

KB48

Schwab, Federico. *Bibliografía etnológica de la Amazonia peruana, 1542–1942.* Lima: Compañía de impresiones y publicidad, 1942. 76p.

A list of 1,895 annotated items in alphabetical order by author, with introductory essay. Especially strong in coverage of ethnohistorical sources.

Informational Reference Searches

McNeil and Valk's *Latin American studies* **(J03)** provides a detailed discussion of useful handbooks and of selected European and American societies and associations with an interest in Latin American studies. For American scholars, the American Anthropological Association's *AAA guide* **(A53)** usually provides the best current information about the institutional addresses and research interests of affiliated scholars.

Directories

KB49

Muricy, Carman M. *The Brazilian Amazon: Institutions and publications.* Albuquerque: SALAM Secretariat, Central Library, University of New Mexico, 1990. 50p. (Seminar on the Acquisition of Latin American Library Materials. Bibliography and Reference series, 28)

Classed by regional institutions and by Brazilian institutions, with address information. For the 154 listed institutions, there is often a brief note of their interest in the Amazon and a list of their publications. Title index. Institution index.

Encyclopedias, Handbooks, Manuals

KB50

Derbyshire, Desmond C., and Geoffrey K. Pullum. *Handbook of Amazonian languages, Volume 1.* Berlin: Mouton de Gruyter, 1986. 642p.

The first in a planned series of three on languages of Amazonia. Records descriptive and interpretive material relating to their grammatical structure. Especially valuable for Mary Ruth Wise's "Grammatical characteristics of pre-Andean Arawakan languages of Peru" (p.567–642). Consult also Key's *The grouping of South American Indian languages* **(KB04).**

KB51

Ribeiro, Berta G., ed. *Suma etnológica brasileira.* Petrópolis: FINEP, 1986. 3v.

Organized by topics and culture areas, this set (seven volumes are planned) consolidates everything presently known about Brazilian Indians into a handbook. Signed articles by experts, with supporting bibliographies. V.1, *Etnobiología* (1986 [301p.]), has eleven articles by experts on ethnobotany and five articles on ethnozoology with a supporting bibliography. V.2, *Arte India* (1986 [297p.]), includes eleven articles by experts, including one by A. L. Kroeber. For archaeology there is a closely related effort in *Documents pour la préhistoire du Brésil méridional* (Paris: Mouton, 1973–) (Cahiers d'archéologie d'América, 2) **(KB52).** A multivolume set by state, with two volumes completed. Each volume provides summaries of the archaeology and precontact period cultures of one state and includes bibliographies and descriptions of museums and other institutions that support research.

State-of-the-Art Bibliographic Reviews

KB53

Amazonia peruana. v.1– , 1977– . Lima: Centro Amazónica de Antropología y Aplicación Práctica. Semiannual.

Largely devoted to descriptions of contemporary indigenous ethnic groups. Comprehensive bibliographies and bibliographic reviews are a regular feature. Recent examples would include Alonso Zarzar's "Bibliografía sobre etnicidad en la amazonia" 9 (1989): 153–61; María C. Chavarria Mendoza and José Cerna's "Fuentes para la investigación de la literatura oral de las étnias de la Amazonia peruana" 7 (1986): 161–75; Erwin H. Frank's "Bibliografía anotada de fuentes con interés para la etnología y etnohistoria de los Uni" 8 (1987): 151–60; Jean Pierre Goulard's "Elementos para una bibliografía de los Ticuna" 9 (1989): 185–206; J. P. Chaummeil's "Bibliografía Yagua II" 88 (1987): 161–64; Esther Espinoza and Alejandro Camino's "Bibliografía machiguenga" 6 (1985): 165–69; Juan Aguilar Zevallos's "Bibliografía de la medicina amazónica" 8 (1988): 137–52 **(KB54);** Esther Espinoza and Alejandro Camino's "Bibliografía machiguenga" 6 (1985): 159–82 **(KB55),** which is an author list exhaustive even to unpublished manuscripts. There is a venture into archaeology in Alejandro

Camino and Carlos Dávila's "Bibliografía de la arqueología de la amazonia peruana" 4(1983): 103–12, with 160 citations.

Searching Unpublished Materials

Consult McNeil and Valk's *Latin American studies* **(J03)** for its coverage of sources on American and British doctoral theses, and the resources cited under this strategic heading in chapter 1, and the chapters devoted to the subdisciplines of anthropology.

Some outstanding dissertations are included in *Handbook of Latin American studies* **(J26).** For recent German-language dissertations, consult *Abstracts in German anthropology* **(A33).** For some coverage of English- and French-language dissertations, consult descriptions of *Dissertation abstracts ondisc* [computer file] **(B14)** and *Francis bulletin signalétique* [computer file] discussed in the annotation to *FRANCIS* **(B19).**

Dissertations

KB56

Associação Brasileira de Antropología. *Teses de antropología defendidas no Brasil: 1945–1987.* São Paulo: Departamento de Ciéncias sociais. Universidade de São Paulo, 1988. 179p.

The description is by author, with an indication of where the work is held. There is a brief resumé of the contents of each entry. There are indexes by geographic area, indigenous ethnic group, and subject.

KB57

Valencia, Enrique Hugo Garcia. *Catalogo Latino Americano de tesis de antropología en antropología social.* Xalapa, Vera Cruz: Centro de Investigaciones y Estudios, 1990. 98p.

Serves also as a directory of Brazilian universities, with details of their graduate programs in anthropology (p. 7–17). The list of fifty-five theses is organized by granting university, then by date and by author alphabetically thereunder. There is an author index.

COLOMBIA, ECUADOR, AND VENEZUELA

Searching Bibliographic Guides

Consult Auckland's "Getting into the literature" **(A01)** and the guides to the subdisciplines of anthropology listed in the chapters "Access by disciplines." See also Covington's *Latin America and the Caribbean* **(J02),** Block's "Anthropology" **(J01),** and McNeil and Valk's *Latin American studies* **(J03).** Entry by names of indigenous peoples has been greatly eased by the publication of Welch's *The Indians of South America* **(J21).**

Bibliographic Guides

KB58

Bernal Villa, Segunda. *Guía bibliográfica de Colombia de interés para el antropólogo.* Bogotá: Ediciones Universidad de los Andes, 1969. 782p.

Classed arrangement with author index. Covers cultural anthropology, and work in linguistics and archaeology that is relevant to cultural anthropology.

KB59

Fuchs, Helmuth. *Bibliografía básica de etnología de Venezuela.* Seville, Spain: Universidad de Seville, 1964. 251p. (Universidad de Sevilla. Facultad de Filosofía y Letras. Publicaciones del Seminario de Antropología Americana, 5)

An alphabetic list of 2,413 bibliographic entries. The coverage extends to neighboring countries. The subject and ethnonymic index is by broad subject, with adequate expansions. Under BIBLIOGRAPHIES, there are thirty-six items. Under ARAWAK, identify fourteen subdivisions, with five items under SHAMAN. COLOMBIA has twelve subdivisions. Under ANTILLES the expansions include eight terms of subdivision.

KB60

Larrea, Carlos Manuel. *Bibliografía científica del Ecuador: Antropología, etnografía, ar-*

queología, prehistoria, lingüística. 3d ed. Quito: Corporación de Estudios y Publicaciones, 1968. 289p.

An author list of 1,598 entries. First edition appeared as v.3, Larrea, *Bibliografía científica del Ecuador* (Quito, 1948–53). Includes book and periodical materials with a subject index. Consult Holm's "Bibliografía antropológica ecuadoriana" **(KB67).** Also useful, the ethnic-group bibliography of Juan Carlos (Karus Watnik) Zanutto and Jan Botasso, *Bibliografía general de la nación jivaro* (Sucua [Morona Santigo], Ecuador: Editorial "Mundo Shuar" Centro de Documentación del Ecuador, 1983 [192p.]) (Serie H, no.1) **(KB61),** which is a main entry list (without indexing) of books, articles, government documents, missionary reports, and available descriptions of archival resources.

KB62

Watson, Gayle H. *Colombia, Ecuador and Venezuela: An annotated guide to reference materials in the humanities and social sciences.* Metuchen, N.J.: Scarecrow, 1971. 279p.

Lists 894 entries and includes government publications. Critical essays followed by bibliography. Arranged by subject, first subdivided into general works, humanities, and social sciences. Traditional disciplines are used as subdivisions under these broad categories. The extensive index (p.243–78) greatly enhances value for entry into general reference sources relevant to some anthropological issues.

Searching for Current Materials

In linguistics, *Latin American Indian literatures* **(J52)** has several current awareness features. For developments in archaeology, consult the department "Current research" in *American antiquity* **(C04),** which in the first issue each year summarizes any Latin American archaeological research that can be identified in reports, publications, and announcements of intentions to work in the field. Consult resources under this heading in chapter 1 and in the chapters devoted to the subdisciplines of anthropology.

Select Sources of Review in Scholarly Publications

KB63

Revista colombiana de antropología. v.1– , 1953– . Bogota: Instituto Colombiano de Antropología, Ministerio de Educación Nacional. Annual.

Last seen was volume 24 covering the years 1986–88, which included five signed book reviews of two to three pages. Articles included a bibliography of the work of Professor Jorge Morales Gómez, articles on kinship and on silversmithing, a description of a Paleolithic-era skull, a historical review of control of the indigenous labor force, and two ethnographic articles on individual indigenous ethnic groups.

Retrospective Searches

Block's "Anthropology" **(J01)** provides dense nation-state entry into the retrospective bibliographies of this vast literature. McNeil and Valk's *Latin American studies* **(J03)** includes a discussion of general and special bibliographies which makes it possible here to direct attention only to the most vitally important sources with special value to anthropologists. The Columbus Memorial Library's *Index to Latin American periodical literature, 1929–1960* **(J16)** indexes in a single alphabet periodical articles from 1929 to 1960. The *Indice general* **(J17)** updates the Columbus Memorial Library catalog to 1970. The file corresponding to *HAPI* **(J28),** a subfile of *Latin American studies* [computer file] **(J27),** updates the *Indice general.* In chapter 1, "What Every Anthropologist Needs to Know," both the *Anthropological index* **(A35)** and *Anthropological literature* **(A36)** provide quarterly indexing for an international array of anthropological periodicals. At a more general level of resources with anthropological coverage, material in all scholarly languages can be identified in the databases *Social scisearch* [computer file] **(B37)** and *Humanities index* [computer file] **(B23).** Consult also the databases discussed in Covington's *Latin America and the Caribbean* **(J02).** A useful start for entry by names of contiguous peoples can always be made with O'Leary's *Ethnographic bibliography of South America* **(KB01).**

Retrospective Bibliographies—Biographical Directories

KB64

Friedemann, Nina S. de, and Jaime Arocha. *Bibliografía anotada y directorio de antropólogos colombianos.* Bogotá: Sociedad Anthropológia de Colombia, 1979. 441p.

Directory section identifies educational background, affiliation, and addresses for 277 Colombian anthropologists. Their published works are then listed and coded for subdiscipline, subject, indigenous group or indigenous ethnic group, and geographic area. Each entry is annotated and indexed by these codified categories.

Retrospective Bibliographies—Continuing

KB65

Boletín indigenista venezolano. v.1– , 1953– . Caracas: Ministerio de Justicia. Comisión Indigenista. Semiannual.

Bibliographies of recent works are a regular feature. Useful for ethnographic and linguistic studies of contemporary indigenous ethnic groups.

KB66

Cuadernos de historia y arqueología. v.1– , 1951– . Guayaquil, Ecuador: Casa de la Cultura Ecuatoriana, Núcleo del Guayas. Annual.

Bibliographic department attempts ongoing coverage of all subdisciplines of anthropology.

KB67

Holm, Olaf. "Bibliografía antropológica ecuadoriana." In *Miscelánea antropológica ecuadoriana.* v.1– , 1981– . Cuenca, Ecuador: Museos del Banco Central del Ecuador.

This alphabetic list has been a regular feature by this author. Last inspected 5(1985): 219–37.

KB68

Wagner, Erika L., and Walter Coppens. "Novena bibliografía antropológica reciente sobre Venezuela." *Antropógica* 55 (1981): 73–92.

Titles and authors vary in six irregular supplements. Last inspected Erika L. Wagner and Mireya Viloria's "Décima sexta bibliografía antropológica reciente sobre Venezuela," *Antropógica* 70 (1988): 3,974. This excellent bibliography by these authors has been an important contribution to bibliographic control over the record of published research in and about the peoples of Venezuela and bordering countries.

Retrospective Bibliographies—Topical

KB69

Instituto Lingüístico de Verano en el Ecuador, 1990. Bibliografía de Instituto Lingüístico de Verano en el Ecuador. Lomalinda, Meta, Colombia: Instituto Lingüístico de Verano, 1990. 92p.

A continuing update to record efforts of this group. The place of publication and the editor for each issue vary. This production lists 1,305 entries first by indigenous ethnic group, with classified entries thereunder with such headings as "Bibliographies," "Ethnology," and "Native language writings in print." Subject and author index. Previous edition, with the same organization and supplement, includes Michael B. Maxwell's *Bibliografía de Instituto Lingüístico de Verano en el Ecuador, 1955–1980, Con suplemento, 1981–1985* [microfiche], 2d ed. (Quito, Ecuador: Instituto Lingüístico de Verano, División en el Ecuador, 1985 [67p.; 12 p.]), and a supplement, *Bibliografía de Instituto Lingüístico de Verano en el Ecuador, 1980–1982* [10p.] **(KB70),** which was issued in 1983 as an author list with subject index.

KB71

Itztein, Gertraud, and Heiko Prümers. *Einführende bibliographie zur archäologie ecuador: Bibliografía básica sobre la arquelogía del Ecuador.* Bonn: Seminar für Völkerkunde der Universität Bonn, 1981. 110p. (Bonner Amerikanistische Studien. Estudios americanistas de Bonn, v.8)

A list of 1,200 entries that identifies research published since 1900. Anything of archaeological interest from the ethnohistorical perspective is included.

KB72

Pachón, Consuelo de. *Bibliografía sobre grupos indígenas.* Bogotá: Ministerio de Gobierno, DIGIDEC, 1975. 91p.

Alphabetic list identifies groups covered in the classified arrangement of fifty bibliographies of indigenous ethnic groups.

KB73

Pollák-Eltz, Angelina. *Bibliografía antropológica venezolana.* Caracas: Instituto de Lenguas Indígenas y Centro de Estudios Comparados de Religión, Universidad Católica Andrés Bello [i.e., Bello], 1983. 66p.

Main entry by author list with content notes. Subject index.

KB74

Rivas, Rafael Angel. *Bibliografía sobre las lenguas indígenas de Venezuela.* Caracas: Instituto Autónoma Biblioteca Nacional y de Servicios de Bibliotecas: Instituto Universitario Pedagógico de Caracas, 1983. 162p.

A general section lists atlases and maps and provides a bibliographic review of anthropological linguistics. Included are specific studies with sections on texts for indigenous languages (p.115–20) and cultural problems (p.121–37). Language and dialect index.

Informational Reference Searches

McNeil and Valk's *Latin American studies* **(J03)** provides a detailed discussion of useful handbooks and of selected European and American societies and associations with an interest in Latin American studies. For American scholars, the American Anthropological Association's *AAA guide* **(A53)** usually provides the best current information about the institutional addresses and research interests of affiliated scholars.

Encyclopedias, Handbooks, Manuals

KB75

Coppens, Walter, and Bernarda Escalante, eds. *Los aborígenes de Venezuela.* Caracas: Fundación La Salle de Ciencias Naturales, Instituto Caribe de Antropología y Sociología, 1980–1988. 3v. (Monografía [Instituto Caribe de Antropología y Sociología]; no.26–)

V.1, *Etnología antigua,* achieves a historical reconstruction. V.2, *Etnología contemporánea,* and v.3, *Etnología contemporánea,* contain ethnographic articles. Encyclopedic summary of everything known about each indigenous ethnic group is included with excellent supporting bibliographies. Each volume has three indexes: subject, name (individual and indigenous ethnic groups), and geographic.

KB76

Telban, Blaz. *Grupos étnicos en Colombia: Etnografía e bibliografía.* Quito: Ediciones ABYA-YALA, 1988. 526p. (Colección 500 años)

The ethnographic sketches are brief. Includes brief bibliographic information on seventy contemporary groups. Consult Gerardo Reichel-Dolmatoff's more scholarly *Colombia* (New York: Praeger, 1965 [231p.]) **(KB77),** a survey of early Indian cultures in Colombia, with black-and-white drawings (including maps).

State-of-the-Art Reviews

KB78

Antropológica. v.1– , 1956– . Caracas: Editorial Sucre. 3/yr.

Issues tend to unite around a single theme and to collectively reflect the current status of research on the topic. Substantive interest in the surrounding regions.

Searching Graphic Materials

For sound recordings, consult McNeil and Valk's *Latin American studies* **(J03).** For sources of maps, consult Sable's *A guide to nonprint materials for Latin American studies* **(J58).** For maps, consult Hanson's *Index to map of Hispanic America, 1:1,000,000* **(J59).**

Maps

KB79

Arango Montoya, Francisco. *Colombia: Atlas indigenista.* Bogotá: Lito-grafía, 1977. 246p. 12 leaves.

Organized geographically by ecclesiastical jurisdiction. Combines maps, photographs, and text, which includes statistical tables and information on laws and legislation.

Photographs

KB80

Museo del Oro. *Museo del Oro. Colombia. Banco de la República.* Bogotá: Editions Delroisse, 1982. 238p.

Dense with photographs illustrating the technical aspects of pre-Columbian gold working.

Searching Unpublished Materials

Consult McNeil and Valk's *Latin American studies* **(J03)** for its coverage of sources on American and British doctoral theses, and the resources cited under this strategic heading in chapter 1, as well as those chapters devoted to the subdisciplines of anthropology.

Some outstanding dissertations are included in *Handbook of Latin American studies* **(J26).** For recent German-language dissertations consult *Abstracts in German anthropology* **(A33).** For some coverage of English- and French-language dissertations, consult descriptions of *Dissertations abstracts ondisc* [computer file] **(B14)** and *Francis bulletin signalétique* [computer file] discussed in the annotation to *FRANCIS* **(B19).**

Dissertations

KB81

Sullivan, William M. *Dissertations and theses on Venezuelan topics, 1900–1985.* Metuchen, N.J.: Scarecrow, 1988. 274p.

Consult "Anthropology, ethnology, paleontology, and limnology" (p.1–11) and "Sociology" (p.224–35). Coverage limited to Anglo-Saxon and French institutions. Indexes by author and subject.

A hint of vigorous completed research can be found in Paulina Ledergerber's "Tesis en antropología ecuadoriana aprobadas por universidades del Canadá o Estados Unidos," *Miscelánea antropológica ecuadoriana: Boletín de los Museos del Banco Central del Ecuador* 6 (1986): 189–211 **(KB82).**

SOUTHERN CONE

Consult Coe, Snow, and Benson's *Atlas of ancient America* **(H12)** for maps of this culture area that indicate distribution of the Eastern Highlands, the Gran Chaco, Pampas, and Tierra del Fuego. For a more detailed explication of distributions of individual ethnic groups, consult Enrique Palavecino's "Areas y capas culturales en el territorio argentino," *Gaea* (1948): 447–523 **(KB83).** The decision not to repeat volumes in *World bibliographical series* **(B43)** that could be identified in Balay's *Guide to reference books* **(B02)** was based in part on the more general nature of these resources and on their tendency to concentrate on English-language materials. Biggins's *Argentina* **(KB84)** includes in its coverage masterly annotations to many of the Spanish-language resources that are of the first importance to the anthropologist. This section assumes that the reader has consulted this valuable reference source.

Searching Bibliographic Guides

Consult Auckland's "Getting into the literature" **(A01),** the guides to the subdisciplines of anthropology listed in the chapters "Access by disciplines," guides listed in Covington's *Latin America and the Caribbean* **(J02)** and McNeil and Valk's *Latin American studies* **(J03).** Entry by names of indigenous peoples has been greatly eased by the publication of Welch's *The Indians of South America* **(J21).**

KB84

Biggins, Alan. *Argentina.* Santa Barbara, Calif.: ABC-Clio Pr., 1991. 461p. (World bibliographical series, v.130)

Especially valuable for the excellent annotations of all reference works of the first importance and for its select list of English and Spanish summary volumes that consolidate findings in a text or monograph. Entries under the broad topic "Bibliographies" include Rodolfo Geoghegan's fundamental *Bibliografía argentina, 1807–1970* (Buenos Aires, Casa Pardo, 1970 [130p.]), which lists 432 bibliographies. Find under "folklore" Augusto Raúl Cortázar's useful *Bibligrafía del folklore argentino* (Buenos Aires: Fondo Nacional de las artes, 1965–66 [2v.]) (Bibliografía Argentina de Artes y Letras, Compilaciones especiales, 21/22, 25/26), which lists 932 books and 1,504 articles.

Coverage of the indigenous populations is close to comprehensive for important Argentine reference sources. It clearly annotates the numerous English- and Spanish-language bibliographies of indigenous population groups and draws attention to Andrés Serbín's "Las organizaciones indígenas en la Argentina," *América indígena* 41 (3) (1981): 407–34, which provides a contemporary assessment of federations representing the largest groups of Argentina's Indians. This establishes a base for studies of contemporary conditions.

Clearly this work transcends the always-high standards of this series and will provide a basic guide to the literature of Argentina for the next decade. While meeting the expectation of reference librarians for rapid entry into English-language sources, Biggins has stretched the subjective constraints of the series to include English-language annotations to listed Spanish-language reference sources.

KB85

Albornoz, Dilma, and Miriam Legarreta. *Comunidades aborígenes de América.* Buenos Aires: Imprenta del Congreso de la Nación, 1987. 378p.

The section on Argentina has subdivisions for indigenous ethnic groups under the headings for anthropology, archaeology and linguistics. For culture area outside of Argentina, the lists are brief but always include some reference to resources that describe the actual situation of native populations today. Consult also Saugy de Kliauga's "Bibliography" **(KB89).**

Searching for Current Materials

In linguistics, *Latin American Indian literatures* **(J52)** has several current awareness features. For developments in archaeology, consult the department "Current research" in *American antiquity* **(C04),** which in the first issue each year summarizes any Latin American archaeological research that can be identified in reports, publications, and announcements of intentions to work in the field. Consult resources under this heading in chapter 1 and in the chapters devoted to the subdisciplines of anthropology.

Select Sources of Review in Scholarly Journals

KB86

LARDA informativa. v.1– , 1980– . La Plata: Universidad Nacional de La Plata. Laboratorio de análisis y registro de datos Antropológicos.

Maintains a record of ongoing archaeological and anthropological research and provides a forum for issues of methodology. Consult also *Scripta etnológica,* v.1– , 1978– (Buenos Aires: Centro Argentino de Etnología Americana) **(KB87),** an annual that includes regular publication of book reviews and professional news. The substantive contents of each issue concentrate on a specific area such as the Sirionó. It also publishes submitted bibliographic works such as Elsa Galeotti and María Davassee's "Aportes para un índice bibliográfico de antropología," *Scripta etnológica* 7 (1983): 85–142 **(KB88).**

Retrospective Searches

Block's "Anthropology" **(J01)** provides dense nation-state entry into the retrospective bibliographies of this vast literature. McNeil and Valk's *Latin American studies* **(J03)** includes a discussion of general and special bibliographies which makes it possible here to direct attention only to the most vitally important sources with special value to anthropologists. The Columbus

Memorial Library's *Index to Latin American periodical literature, 1929–1960* **(J16)** indexes in a single alphabet periodical articles from 1929 to 1960. The *Indice general* **(J17)** updates the Columbus Memorial Library catalog. The file corresponding to *HAPI* **(J28),** a subfile of *Latin American studies* [computer file] **(J27),** updates the *Indice general.* In chapter 1, "What Every Anthropologist Needs to Know," both the *Anthropological index* **(A35)** and *Anthropological literature* **(A36)** provide quarterly indexing for an international array of anthropological periodicals. At a more general level of resources with anthropological coverage, material in all scholarly languages can be identified in the databases *Social scisearch* [computer file] **(B37)** and *Humanities index* [computer file] **(B23).** Consult also the databases discussed in Covington's *Latin America and the Caribbean* **(J02).** A useful start for entry by names of contiguous peoples can always be made with O'Leary's *Ethnographic bibliography of South America* **(KB01).**

Retrospective Bibliographies—Bibliographies of Bibliographies

KB89

Saugy de Kliauga, Catilina. "Bibliography." In Saugy de Kliauga, Catilina. *Bibliografía antropológica argentina, 19–20.* Buenos Aires: Fundación José María Aragón, 1982, 1983. 35p. (Bibliográfica, 1)

Lists fourteen anthropological bibliographies of bibliographies for Argentina. This list consolidates contributions by Argentina to the UNESCO series *International bibliography of social and cultural anthropology* **(D20).** The basic volume in which this list appears was reissued as Catilina Saugy de Kliauga, "Bibliografía antropológica argentina, 1982," in *Bibliografía argentina de ciencias sociales* 83: 71–104. It has permanent value for the serious scholar. One section is a classed arrangement. Another section lists seventy-nine Argentine anthropological serial publications (p.11–14). Forty foreign serial publications with regular coverage of Argentine material (p.14–16). There is a list of thirty-three Argentine publishers of anthropological monographs (p.16–17), and one of seventeen regular Argentine congresses that enjoy the participation of anthropologists. Supplement appeared as Catilina Saugy de Kliauga, "Bibliografía antropológica argentina, 1983," *Bibliografía argentina de ciencias sociales* 84: 104–39, and continuing supplements have been promised. The basic bibliography consolidates previous work, including several regional bibliographies of anthropology such as Eduardo Mario Cigliano, Horacio A. Calandra, Néstor H. Palma, *Bibliografía antropológica de la provincia de Buenos Aires* (La Plata: Provincia de Buenos Aires, Comisión de Investigación Científica, 1964 [60p.]), an author list with no table of contents and no index. For other districts, see Arguello de Dorsch and Lina Elsa y Seisddos's "Bibliografía antropológica de la provincia de Córdoba," *Publicaciones del Instituto de Antropología* 3 (1981): 21–29, and Nélida Cuetos's "Bibliografía antropológica de Mendoza," *Anales de arqueología etnológica* 22 (1977), 23 (1978): 219–35; the bibliographic reviews cited in the annotation to *Revista andina* **(KB34).**

Retrospective Bibliographies—Broad Scope

KB90

Cooper, John. *Analytical and critical bibliography of the tribes of Tierra del Fuego and adjacent territory.* Washington, D.C.: Government Printing Office, 1917. 233p. (Smithsonian Institution. Bureau of American Ethnology, Bulletin no.63)

A list of 750 annotated items arranged alphabetically by author. Indexed by subject and tribe. For the adjacent territory, there is recent bibliographic work in *Patagonia documental,* no.7– , 1981 (Centro de Documentación Patagónica, Departmento de Humanidades, Universidad Nacional del Sur) **(KB91),** that includes such bibliographies as Nicolás Matijevic's "Bibliografía patagónica del Dr. Robert Lehman-Nitsche" 7 (1981): 47–56 **(KB92).** See also a compendium of research results in *Culturas indigenas de la Patagonia, Seminario sobre la sitación de la investigación de las culturas indígenas de la Patagonia, Madrid, 12–13 abril, 1984* (Madrid: Comisión Nacional para la Celebración del 5°

Centenario del Descubrimiento de América, Instituto de Cooperación Iberoamericana, 1984 [272p.]) **(KB93).** Consult also Meinrado Hux P., *Guía bibliográfica: El indio en la llanura del Plata* (La Plata: Provincia de Buenos Aires, Dirección General de Escuelas, Archivo Histórico 'Ricardo Levene', 1984 [262p.]) **(KB94).** For more general sources and with a chapter devoted to anthropology, consult David Lewis Jones's *Paraguay: A bibliography* (New York: Garland, 1979 [499p.]) **(KB95),** which includes a select list of Paraguayan periodicals (p.431–99).

KB96

Miller, Elmer S. *A critically annotated bibliography of the Gran Chaco Toba.* New Haven, Conn.: Human Relation Area Files, 1980. 2v. (257 leaves)

Alphabetic lists with detailed annotations identifying available information on the Tobas Indians of the Chaco. A topic index provides some entry under twenty-one broad subject headings without subdivision.

Informational Reference Searches

McNeil and Valk's *Latin American studies* **(J03)** provides a detailed discussion of useful handbooks and of selected European and American societies and associations with an interest in Latin American studies. For American scholars, the American Anthropological Association's *AAA guide* **(A53)** usually provides the best current information about the institutional addresses and research interests of affiliated scholars.

KB97

Susñik, Branislava. *El rol de los indígenas en la formación y en la vivencia del Paraguay.* Asunción, Paraguay: Instituto Paraguayo de Estudios, 1982. 2v.

Transcriptions of lectures in social anthropology prepared for the Paraguayan Institute for National Studies. Describes the original inhabitants, Guaraní and Chaco residents; enumeration of Guaraní subgroups; account of Spanish conquest and major mestizo groups.

KB98

Susñik, Branislava. *Los aborígenes del Paraguay.* Asunción, Paraguay: Museo Etnográfico Andrés Bárbaro, 1978–87. 7v.

Each volume provides a handbook with extensive coverage for individual indigenous ethnic groups and exhaustive documentation at the end of each volume. V.1, *Etnología del chaco boreal y sueriferia.* After a section on archaeology and early contact, there are summary discussions that include, among others, the Guapay, Arawak, Zamucos, Mbayá, Cochaboth, and Mataco. V.2, *Etnohistoria de los guaraníes: Epoca Colonial;* v.3, pt.1, *Etnohistoria de los chaqueños: 1650–1910,* has a topical presentation under such terms as SUBSISTENCE, HOUSING, IMPLEMENTS, BASKETS, AND CERAMICS; *Ciclo vital y estructura social* is divided between a section on life cycles, and one on occupations and social organizations; v.6, *Aproximación a las creencias de los indígenas,* is devoted to beliefs and mythology; v.7, *Tribus actualmente sobrevivientes: adaptación cultural,* deals with present-day cultural adaptation; v.8, pt.2, *La problemática sociolingüística. Reseña analítica de las fuentes bibliográficas* has been announced. An analytical review of bibliographical services is promised. Pt.1, *Lenguas chaqueñas,* discusses first the general characteristics of the Chaco languages. This is followed by an ethnolinguistic analysis of five Chaco languages with supporting bibliographies.

9

Asia and the Pacific

This chapter assumes that the reader has exhausted Balay's *Guide to reference books* **(B02).** Asia and the Pacific are treated in a unified manner by Günter Siemers's *Bibliographie Asien und Ozeanienbezogener Bibliographien (Bibliography of bibliographies on Asia and Oceania)* **(L01)** and, by broad-scope retrospective catalogs of area libraries like the *Subject catalogue of Commonwealth of Australia, Dominion of New Zealand, South Pacific, General voyages and travels, Arctic and Antarctic regions* **(L02)** and the University of London, School of Oriental and African Studies, *Library catalogue* **(G17)** and **(G18).** Consult Nunn's *Asia and Oceania: A guide to archival and manuscript sources in the United States* **(L05).** The reference sources in this chapter are best used as a supplement to the more fundamental resources identified in chapter 1, "What Every Anthropologist Needs to Know"; chapter 3, "Archaeology and Material Culture"; chapter 4, "Ethnology/Cultural Anthropology"; and chapter 5, "Anthropological Linguistics." Many of these resources are indispensable.

A discussion of the structured arrangement of entries clustered under subject headings can be found in the introduction.

Retrospective Searches

Find under this same heading in other chapters retrospective search resources for anthropology. Inspect especially chapters for subdisciplines of anthropology. In Chapter 1, consult first the Tozzer Library (formerly Peabody Museum of Archaeology and Ethnology), *Author and subject catalogues of the Tozzer Library* [microfiche] **(A26)** and the older hardcover edition of Peabody Museum Library (now Tozzer), *Catalogue* **(A29)** for author and classified subject entry to monographs, periodical articles, and the internal contents of books. This resource has a companion for coverage of monographs only in the published catalogs of the British Museum, Museum of Mankind Library, *Museum of Mankind Library catalogues* [microfiche] **(A25),** which includes a sustained classified subject index to monographic and pamphlet publications and a "Tribal index" **(D13),** which includes 17,000 entries by tribal names.

Retrospective Bibliographies—Bibliographies of Bibliographies

L01

Siemers, Günter. *Bibliographie Asien und Ozeanienbezogener bibliographien (Bibliography of bibliographies on Asia and Oceania).* Hamburg: Institut für Asienkunde, Dokumentations-Leitstelle Asien, 1979. 172p. (Dokumentationsdienst Asien. Reihe A, v.12)

Covers Oceania and Asia east of Pakistan. Lists 902 titles from the holdings of seventy libraries. Extensively indexed. Fully describes even some valuable pamphlets. For example, the many island bibliographies compiled by N. L. H. Krauss, which were privately published and are infrequently cataloged because they are often fewer than forty pages in length even though exhaustive for the islands they cover. They are listed here.

Retrospective Bibliographies—Broad Scope

L02

Lewin, Evans. *Commonwealth of Australia, Dominion of New Zealand, South Pacific, general voyages and travels, Arctic and Antarctic regions.* v.2, Royal Commonwealth Society. Library. *Subject catalogue of the Library of the Royal Empire Society.* Introduction by Donald H. Simpson. London: The Royal Empire Society, 1930–37. Reprint: London: Dawsons for the Royal Commonwealth Society, 1967. 4v.

A library of distinction has holdings with an interdisciplinary focus on scholarly research about the culture areas encompassed by the collection. The main set, which has a cutoff date in the 1930s, has been supplemented by Donald H. Simpson's *Biography catalog* (London: Royal Commonwealth Society, 1961 [511p.]). G. K. Hall (Boston) **(L03)** published an updated version on the *Subject catalog* in seven volumes in 1971 and followed up with a two-volume *First supplement* in 1977. Consult also the University of London, School of Oriental and African Studies, Library, *Library catalogue* **(G17)** and **(G18),** which also deals with the whole of Asia and Oceania. This catalog excludes only science, medicine, and technology. It is especially strong in history, anthropology, and law. It includes author, title, and subject access. It has strong cataloged holdings in the Chinese and Japanese languages. Manuscript holdings are described.

Informational Reference Searches

Each of the chapters devoted to the subdisciplines of anthropology in *Fieldwork in the Library* will identify useful sources relevant to this culture area. In anthropological linguistics, consult especially Sebeok's *Linguistics in East Asia and South East Asia* **(E76).** Across chapters, "Informational Reference Searches" introduces lists of reference books that answer an inquiry for summaries of anthropological results and for brief descriptions of institutions or address information for individuals. In chapter 1, inspect also listings under the subheading "State-of-the-Art Reviews." Find there the *Annual review of anthropology* **(A57),** with its summary coverage of recent research activity. Many searches that start in other chapters must return to chapter 1 for the directory information. *AAA guide* **(A53)** is listed for addresses and other information relevant to contemporary American anthropology.

L04

UNESCO. *Sociology and social anthropology in Asia and the Pacific.* Paris: Wiley Eastern, 1985. 524p.

Reviews the states of two disciplines in twelve countries in an attempt to identify who does what where in the social sciences in these countries. Covers Japan, People's Republic of China, Republic of Korea, Thailand, Indonesia, Philippines, Singapore, India, Pakistan, Bangladesh, Australia, and New Zealand. Includes bibliographic surveys. Name and subject indexes.

Searching Unpublished Materials

Many of the archival resources for this region are available on microfiche and held in numerous research libraries. When a manuscript is cited anywhere, there is a good chance that it is in one of these massive sets and series of microfiche. No other geographic region comes even close to the comprehensiveness of coverage available for the Pacific.

Archives

L05

Nunn, Godfrey Raymond. *Asia and Oceania: A guide to archival and manuscript sources in the United States.* London: Mansell; dist., New York: Wilson, 1985. 5v.

Five hundred fifty pages of index to 150,000 entries. Incomparable access to materials in 450 repositories. Coverage extends from Iran and Turkey in the west to Japan and the Pacific Islands, excluding Hawaii and Australia. Individual collections are annotated file by file and reel by reel. Includes, for example, the complete cataloging by the University of Hawaii of an enormous microfilm collection published as a series by the Pacific Manuscripts Bureau **(N23)** using the series entries of the University of Hawaii. This set is also held at the University of California, San Diego, where it is being slowly recataloged as a set. This means that scholars with access to MELVIL [computer file] will not find this set listed in the series subfile because it is being recataloged as a set and is available in the author-title subfile of the University of California, San Diego. More recently, Judith Boruchoff's *Register to the papers of William Louis Abbott* (Washington, D.C.: National Anthropological Archives, 1986 [22p.] (National Anthropological Archives) makes available field notes on Malaysia.

ASIA

Searching Bibliographic Guides

A move to entries listed under this heading in all of the chapters devoted to the subdisciplines of anthropology will be productive. All searches should start with the resources identified in Auckland's "Getting into the literature" **(A01).**

Bibliographic Guides

L06

Nunn, Godfrey Raymond. *Asia: Reference works: A select annotated guide.* London: Mansell, 1980. 365p.

Superb bibliographic control with 1,567 entries. Chapters are given letters A through T, and each entry is assigned a unique letter and number. Coverage is organized by geographic units subdivided by form and then by subject. There are sections for Asia as a whole, Southeast Asia, south and southern Asia, and the nations of Asia. Particularly comprehensive in its coverage of bibliographies, encyclopedias, handbooks, yearbooks, directories, atlases, theses, and dissertations. Though always accurate, the annotations are brief and cannot, for example, include the information that "Social anthropology" is a subject division in *Asian social science bibliography,* ed. by N. K. Goil, v.1– , 1952– (Delhi: Institute of Economic Growth) (Documentation series), an annual **(L07).**

L08

Reynolds, Frank E., John Holt, and John Strong, eds. *Guide to Buddhist religion.* Art section by Bardwell Smith with Hollis Waldo and Jonathan Clyde Glass. Boston: Hall, 1981. 415p.

Annotated entries in classed arrangement that covers historical development in all countries between India and Japan, religious thought (general, then by the three major schools, then by topic, including a list of thirteen "Buddhist periodicals" (p.87) in European languages). Includes "Buddhism in relation to national culture and society" and "Buddhism and the social order" (p.215–39), lists many anthropological works with annotations, and identifies monographs on the establishment, historical and present-day structure of the Buddhist kingdoms in central, south, and southeastern Asia. There are additional sections on religious rituals, ideal beings, mythology, sacred places, soteriological experiences and processes, paths, and goals. For anthropological entry, the subject index must be approached adventurously to identify entries such as VILLAGE LIFE, which identifies fifteen works, or PSYCHOLOGY, which identifies fifteen published works. Inspect especially the section on popular beliefs for entries such as John F. Embree's *Suye Mura: A Japanese village* (Chicago: Univ. of Chicago Pr., 1964 [354p.]) (Phoenix book, p.173) **(L09),** a classic sociological study, and Christoph von Furer-Haimendorf's *Morals and merit: A study of values and social controls in south Asian societies* (Chicago: Univ. of Chicago Pr., 1967 [239p.]) **(L10),** which deals with the relationship between Hindu, Buddhist, and popular elements of religion.

Searching for Current Materials

For this kind of search the resources cited in chapter 1 under this heading will be useful for entry into this area. Consult also under this heading the entries selected for chapters on the subdisciplines of anthropology.

Select Sources of Review in Scholarly Publications

L11

Asian folklore studies. v.1– , 1963– . Nagoya: Anthropological Institute. Annual.

Devoted to myths, rituals, folktales, ethnography, religion, social organization, kinship groups, class, and caste. About ten book reviews in each issue, including reviews of new serial publications. Also publishes notices of meetings and workshops.

L12

Asian studies newsletter. v.1– , 1971– . Ann Arbor, Mich.: Association for Asian Studies. Quarterly.

Especially valuable for its regular notification of grants available, conferences planned, exhibitions available, and special study programs established.

Retrospective Searches

Retrospective catalogs of area libraries like the *Subject catalogue of the Library of the Royal Empire Society* **(L02);** the University of London, School of Oriental and African Studies, *Library catalogue* **(G17)** and **(G18);** and Nunn's *Asia and Oceania: A guide to archival and manuscript sources in the United States* **(L05).** The reference sources in this chapter are best used as a supplement to the more fundamental resources identified in chapter 1, "What Every Anthropologist Needs to Know"; chapter 3, "Archaeology and Material Culture"; chapter 4, "Ethnology/Cultural Anthropology"; and chapter 5, "Anthropological Linguistics." Many of these resources are indispensable.

A discussion of the structured arrangement of entries clustered under subject headings can be found in the introduction.

Retrospective Bibliographies—Bibliographies of Bibliographies

L13

Drews, Lucy B., and Paul Hockings. "Asia bibliographies." In Library-Anthropology Resource Group. *Anthropological bibliographies: A selected guide,* ed. by Margo L. Smith and Yvonne M. Damien, p.89–141. South Salem, N.Y.: Redgrave, 1981. 307p.

Drews and Hockings provide a select and informed bibliography of bibliographies. Under the term RELIGION in the index, there are thirty-six items in the item number sequence for Asia. Because the numbered sequence reflects the geographic arrangement, RELIGION has an implicit subdivision for EAST ASIA, GENERAL (identified from running heads in the text which pinpoints the range of numbers used to span that geographic region)—Japan has 2 items. Deserves careful study and a detailed exploration for topical entries because it is much too rich to justify a casual approach. This bibliographic list, while admirable, cannot be comprehensive. This work clearly demonstrates the need to carefully consult antecedent resources described in a bibliography of bibliographies. Although the authors identify indexes to serial publications such as Sibadas Chaudhuri's *Journal of the Buddhist Text Society of India (1893–1899)* and the *Proceedings and transactions* of twenty-two sessions of the *All India Oriental Conferences,* they do not include Sibadas Chaudhuri's *Index to the publications of the Asiatic Society, 1788–1953* (Calcutta: Asiatic Society, 1965 [3d ser., extra numbers v.22 (1956), v.23 (1957)]) **(L14),** which has by the same author a supplement that extends coverage to 1968. Again, Drews and Hockings do not include Edwin Capers Kirkland's *Bibliography of South Asian folklore* (Bloomington: Indiana University. Research Center in Anthropology, Folklore, Linguistics, 1966 [291p.]) (Indiana University folklore series, no.21: Asian folklore monographs, no.4), with its 7,000-item bibliography in all languages covering India, Pakistan, Nepal, Bhutan, Sikkim, and Ceylon. Also missing from the Drews and Hockings list is Aralinda Basu's "Physical anthropological research in south India: A bibliographical review," *Journal of the Indian Anthropological Society* 13 (1978): 196–213p.] **(L15),** which clearly establishes the special focus and vigorous activity of Indian anthropologists in this subdiscipline.

Retrospective Bibliographies—Broad Scope

L16

Harvard Yenching Library. *Catalogues of the Harvard-Yenching Library.* New York, N.Y.: Garland, 1986. 72v.

The Chinese and Japanese catalogs of the Harvard-Yenching Library. A reproduction of catalog cards. Contents: Chinese catalogue, v.1–28; Japanese catalogue: v.1–22.

Records holding through March 1986 with cross-references to variant titles. The largest university collection of oriental books in the world.

Retrospective Bibliographies—Continuing

L17

Bibliography of Asian studies. v.1– , 1956– . Ann Arbor, Mich.: Association for Asian Studies. Annual.

Title, frequency, and scope of this excellent source vary. As now structured, the *Bibliography of Asian studies* makes available a listing of significant books and articles in European languages concerning countries of the Far East, Southeast Asia, and South Asia. Coverage includes the disciplines of philosophy, religion, history, economics, social science, education, language and literature, and political science. This list dates from the American Council of Learned Societies's lists of periodical articles on Chinese subjects, which originated in 1934. Expanded mimeographed lists appeared from 1936 through 1940. Stable publication dates from 1941, when *Far Eastern Quarterly* began publishing the list in each issue. It became an annual in v.9 (1949–50). The present title dates from 1956 at the time that the *Quarterly* became the *Journal of Asian studies.* Lists more than 20,000 books, articles, and government reports a year. The range and growing significance of the service led to publication of the Association for Asian Studies *Cumulative bibliography of Asian studies, 1941–1965, Author bibliography* (Boston: Hall, 1965 [4v.]) **(L18);** the Association for Asian Studies *Cumulative bibliography of Asian studies, 1941–65, Subject bibliography* (Boston: Hall, 1970 [4v.]) **(L19);** and a later six-volume set covering the years 1966–70 and published in 1972–73. This series can be used as a companion to the series of Koyoto Imperial University, Research Institute for Humanistic Science, *Annual bibliography of oriental studies* **(L21),** which provides coverage of scholarly work published in the oriental languages.

L20

Kokogaku Nenpō. v.1– , 1951– . Tokyo: Seibundō Shinkōsa. Annual.

Yearbook/bibliography of Japanese antiquities and archaeology. Can be used as a companion volume to the *Annual bibliography of Indian archaeology* **(M22).**

L21

Kyoto Daigaku. Jinbun Kagaku Ruimoku (Kyoto Imperial University). Research Institute for Humanistic Science. *Toyogaku bunken ruimoku (Annual bibliography of oriental studies)* v.1– , 1934– . Kyoto: Kokysho Sankokai. Annual.

Can be used as a companion to the *Bibliography of Asian studies* **(L17).** It has a selective list of books and articles in Western and oriental languages pertaining to all countries of the Orient, except Japan. Organized in two sections subdivided for books and periodicals and then arranged by broad topics. Coverage extends to Russian Asia and the Middle East. Author index.

Informational Reference Searches

Each of the chapters devoted to the subdisciplines of anthropology will have resources of value for this culture area. Consult especially the *Annual review of anthropology* **(A57).**

Encyclopedias, Handbooks, Manuals

L22

Embree, Ainslie T., ed. *Encyclopedia of Asian history.* Prepared under the auspices of the Asia Society. New York: Scribner; London: Collier Macmillan, 1988. 4v.

More than 3,000 articles. Excludes countries west of Iran and peoples in the USSR. Hundreds of scholars have contributed signed articles with select bibliographies. Pinyin system is used in transliteration. An elaborate "Syntoptic outline" must be mastered to fully benefit from the organization of the volumes. Indexing is barely adequate. Can be usefully approached as a source of summary knowledge and for identification of seminal works. For example, the article on Chinese archaeology identifies one monograph that has been through several editions.

For an innovative attempt to reach a social science overview, consult Myron L. Cohen, ed., *Asia: Case studies in the social sciences: A guide for teaching* (Armonk, N.Y.: M.E. Sharpe, 1992 [626p.]) **(L23),** which is a product of the Columbia Project on Asia in the Core Curriculum. Arranged alphabetically by country. Under each country, there is a series of articles by experts in the field attempting to summarize knowledge of that country's social dynamics in terms of a social science framework. There is a table of contents by discipline and subdiscipline (pp.ix–xiv), and by country and discipline (p.xv–xx). Under a final subheading "Comparative/inter area," there is a discussion of comparative demography and a study of the problems of rapid modernization.

State-of-the-Art Review

L24

Hahn, Man-Youn, ed. "East Asian musics." *Yearbook for traditional music* 15 (1983): 1–213.

The title is a continuation since 1980 of the *Yearbook of the International Folk Music Council,* published under the auspices of UNESCO. A state-of-the-art issue with twelve articles by experts, three bibliographic reviews, and book reviews of recent monographs on Asian music in English, French, and German. Sponsored by the Korea Culture and Arts Foundation, Seoul.

Searching Unpublished Materials

Consult also National Anthropological Archives, *Catalog to manuscripts at the National Anthropological Archives* **(A69).** Consult Nunn's *Asia and Oceania: A guide to archival and manuscript sources in the United States* **(L05).** The chapters devoted to each of the subdisciplines of anthropology will list resources of value under this heading.

Dissertations

L25

Shulman, Frank Joseph, comp. *Doctoral dissertations on Asia: An annotated bibliographical journal of current international research.* v.1– , 1975– . Ann Arbor: Xerox University Microfilms for Association for Asian Studies. Secretariat. University of Michigan. Semiannual.

Title varies. Continues listing available for earlier years in the Association for Asian Studies *Newsletter* (1969–71) **(L12)** and *Asian studies professional review* (1971–74). Covers Afghanistan in the west to Japan in the east, Mongolia in the north to Indonesia and Sri

Lanka in the south. Classed arrangement by country. Includes names and addresses of many individuals. Items are entered once, and there is no subject index. The arrangement by region, subdivided by time period, makes it difficult to use for any anthropological topics, with the exception of archaeology. Far from comprehensive. Inspect the dissertation chapter in J. D. Pearson's *South Asian bibliography* **(M05)** for an understanding of the enormous body of unpublished research available from Asian countries with vigorous scholarly establishments.

EAST ASIA

Searching Bibliographic Guides

A move to entries listed under this heading in all of the chapters devoted to the subdisciplines of anthropology will be productive. All searches should start with the resources identified in Auckland's "Getting into the literature" **(A01).**

Bibliographic Guides

Consult first Nunn's *Asia: Reference works* **(L06),** with special attention to his chapter on East Asia for the description of handbooks and bibliographies.

Retrospective Searches

Retrospective catalogs of area libraries like the *Subject catalogue of the Library of the Royal Empire Society* **(L02);** the University of London, School of Oriental and African Studies, *Library catalogue* **(G17);** and Nunn's *Asia and Oceania: A guide to archival and manuscript sources in the United States* **(L05).** The reference sources in this chapter are best used as a supplement to the more fundamental resources identified in chapter 1, "What Every Anthropologist Needs to Know"; chapter 3, "Archaeology and Material Culture"; chapter 4, "Ethnology/Cultural Anthropology"; and chapter 5, "Anthropological Linguistics." Many of these resources are indispensable.

A discussion of the structured arrangement of entries clustered under subject headings can be found in the introduction.

Retrospective Bibliographies—Comprehensive

The catalogs of many of the great oriental collections have now been published. The University of Michigan, Asia Library, has produced the *Catalogs of the Asia Library* (Boston: Hall, 1978 [25v.]) **(L26),** which emphasizes China, Japan, and Korea. Consult also University of London, School of Oriental and African Studies, Library, *Library catalogue* (with *Supplement*) **(G18).** It includes author, title, and subject access along with a catalog of manuscripts and microfilms, a Chinese catalog, and a Japanese catalog. Three supplements of 16, 16, and 19 volumes respectively have been published by Hall between 1968 and 1979, bringing coverage up to 1978. Records in this library include descriptions of maps, recorded disks, and tapes.

Informational Reference Searches

Across chapters this heading introduces lists of reference books that answer a need for summaries of anthropological results and for brief descriptions of institutions or address information for individuals.

In chapter 1 inspect listings under the subheading "State-of-the-Art Reviews." Find there the *Annual review of anthropology* **(A57)** with its summary coverage of recent research activity. Many searches that start in other chapters must return to chapter 1 for the directory information. *AAA Guide* **(A53)** is listed for the address and other information relevant to contemporary American anthropology. Each of the chapters on the subdisciplines of anthropology in *Fieldwork in the Library* will have resources of value.

Directories

L27

Yang, Teresa Shu-yi Chin, Thomas C. Kuo, and Frank J. Shulman. *East Asian resources in American libraries.* New York: Paragon Book Gallery, 1977. 143p.

Includes T. S. Yang's valuable "American library resources on east Asia," T. C. Kuo's "East Asian collections in American libraries," and F. J. Shulman's "A bibliographical guide to East Asian resources in American libraries." "Millions of volumes, serials, and newspapers can be identified only in these local sources" (p.36).

CHINA

Searching Bibliographic Guides

A move to entries listed under this heading in all of the chapters of *Fieldwork in the Library* devoted to the subdisciplines of anthropology will be productive. All searches should start with the resources identified in Auckland's "Getting into the literature" **(A01).**

Bibliographic Guides

For a guide to the work of a generation of scholars sensitive to the events in the People's Republic of China between 1949 and 1980, consult the "Annotated bibliography" in Kaplan, Fredric M., Julian M. Sobin, and Stephen Andors, eds., *Encyclopedia of China today* (Fair Lawn, N.J.: Eurasia Pr., 1980 [336p.]) **(L28).** The 1980 bibliography provides accurate and concise annotations of reference sources in classified arrangement, with emphasis on English-language materials. See Kaplan, Fredric M., and Julian M. Sobin, *Encyclopedia of China today,* 3d rev. ed. (New York: Eurasia Pr., 1981 [446p.]) **(L29),** especially the bibliography (p.387–403), which does not include or repeat the bibliographic guide of the first edition. It does, however, have several appendixes that identify and explain the use of major publication sources, and a revised and updated but less useful bibliography. For an expansion of these basic sources, consult Nunn's *Asia* **(L06)** for his chapter (Q), "China," for encyclopedias, handbooks, and yearbooks in English, Japanese, and Chinese; for bibliographies of bibliographies and dictionaries and directories; for gazetteers and statistics; for official publications and maps; for dissertations and subject bibliographies of the social sciences, history, Chinese art, religion, and geography; for geographical dictionaries and atlases; and for Chinese- and Western-language bibliographies.

L30

Birch, Alan, Y. C. Jao, and Elizabeth Sinn, eds. *Research materials for Hong Kong studies.* Hong Kong: Centre of Asian Studies, University of Hong Kong, 1984. 339p.

Inspect especially Maria Chu's "Research materials for Hong Kong studies: Cartographic materials" (p.21–300) and C. P. Lu's "Remote sensing data for geographical research in Hong Kong" (p.244–85); the review article by Harold Traver, "Social research in Hong Kong: Past and present" (p.224–43); and H. A. Rydings's "Reference materials for Hong Kong studies" (p.3–14).

L31

Wolff, Ernst. *Chinese studies: A bibliographic manual.* San Francisco: Chinese Materials Center, 1981. 152p. (Bibliographic series: Chinese Materials Center, v.1)

Lists 606 entries, including fifteen general bibliographies, nineteen Western-language reference sources, and five Russian sources. Discusses fifty-three bibliographic aids in Chinese and 514 described in a classed arrangement by forms such as dictionaries, encyclopedias, and newspapers.

Retrospective Searches

Retrospective catalogs of area libraries like the *Subject catalogue of the Library of the Royal Empire Society* **(L02);** the University of London, School of Oriental and African Studies, *Library* *catalogue* **(G17)** and **(G18);** and Nunn's *Asia and Oceania: A guide to archival and manuscript sources in the United States* **(L05).** The reference sources in this chapter are best used as a supplement to the more fundamental resources identified in chapter 1, "What Every Anthropologist Needs to Know"; chapter 3, "Archaeology and Material Culture"; chapter 4, "Ethnology/Cultural Anthropology"; and chapter 5, "Anthropological Linguistics." Many of these resources are indispensable. A discussion of the structured arrangement of entries clustered under subject headings can be found in the introduction.

The study of China has produced a copious amount of material for a very long time. The best studies are not necessarily the most recent studies. Entry into the older literature can be eased by consulting the basic and still useful work of Henri Cordier, *Bibliotheca sinica: dictionnaire bibliographique des ouvrages relatifs à l'Empire Chinois,* 2d ed. (Paris: Guilmoto, 1904–1908 [4v.]) **(L32),** and extended by reference to John Lust's *Index sinicus: A catalogue of articles relating to China in periodicals and other collective publications, 1920–1955* (Cambridge, England: W. Heffer, 1964 [663p.]) **(L33),** which is well organized by subject with additional entry through a subject index. Authors and titles are also indexed. Entry provided by this resource can be given additional range by consulting Yüan T'ung-li's *China in Western literature: A continuation of Cordier's* Bibliotheca sinica (New Haven, Conn.: Far Eastern Publications, Yale University, 1958 [802p.]) **(L34),** which is limited to European-language books appearing between 1921 and 1957 and organized under broad subject headings with detailed breakdown.

Retrospective Bibliographies—Bibliographies of Bibliographies

L35

Tsien, Tsuen-hsuin. *China: An annotated bibliography of bibliographies.* Boston: Hall, 1978. 604p.

More than 2,500 bibliographies in Chinese, Japanese, English, and other Western languages published through 1970. Classified arrangement with author, title, and subject indexes.

Retrospective Bibliographies—Broad Scope

L36

Ching, Peter P. *Current books on China 1983–1988: An annotated bibliography.* New York: Garland, 1990. 268p.

Classed bibliography. Under "Society and social structure," thirty-seven entries. There are chapters on education, medicine, health, and law. Archaeology has three entries, including the masterful fourth edition of K. C. Chang's *The archaeology of ancient China* (New Haven, Conn.: Yale Univ. Pr., 1989 [544p.]), which covers the time periods from early humans and the Paleolithic cultures through the first agricultural settlements.

L37

Lust, John. *Western books published on China up to 1850 in the Library of the School of Oriental and African Studies, University of London: A descriptive catalogue.* London: Bamboo, 1987. 336p.

Classified listing of 1,283 books on China, east central Asia, Tibet, Manchuria, and Mongolia. Title-page descriptions with annotations and an indication of a major catalog where cited. These resources provide some observations of China when it had been less intensely modified by Western contact. Author and title indexes. "Supplementary subject index."

Retrospective Bibliographies—Topical

L38

Dessaint, Alain Y. *Minorities of southwest China: An introduction to the Yi (Lolo) and related peoples and an annotated bibliography.* New Haven, Conn.: HRAF Pr., 1980. 373p.

The annotations relate items to other works. An introduction to Yi studies. Excellent abstracts. Detailed indexes are carefully structured to serve the needs of anthropologists. See also LeBar and Appell's *Ethnic groups of mainland Southeast Asia* **(M101),** which includes the ethnic groups of southern China.

L39

Dien, Albert E., Jeffrey K. Rliegel, and Nancy T. Price, eds. *Chinese archaeological abstracts.*

Vols. 2, 3, 4. Los Angeles: Monumenta archaeologica, 1985. (Institute of Archaeology, UCLA, vols. 9, 10, 11) 3v.

Chinese archaeology (1972–81) abstracted from Chinese journals. V.2, *Prehistoric to western Zhou,* abstracts 110 articles; v.3, *Eastern Zhou to Han,* abstracts 130 articles; v.4, *Post Han,* abstracts 140 articles.

L40

Jacobs, J. Bruce, Jean Hagger, and Anne Sedgley, comps. *Taiwan: A comprehensive bibliography of English language publications.* Bundoora, Australia: The Borchardt Library, La Trobe University; New York: East Asian Institute of Columbia University, 1984. 214p. (Research Aids of the East Asian Institute. Columbia University)

Arranged alphabetically by category within eighteen categories. See especially "Bibliography and reference," "Society," "Culture," and "Prehistory and history to 1945." Author/title index. For Chinese-language materials in addition to works in Western languages, consult *Kuang fu i lai T'ai-wan ti ch'hu ch'u pan jen lei hseuh lun chu my lulc chu pien Huang Ying-kuei: pien chi hsiao tsu Hsieh Mei-chhuan, Huang Chih-hui, Li Te-jen; Chung-kuo min tsu hsueh hui, Han hshueh yen chiu tzu liao chi fu wu chung hsin pein yin* (T' ai-pei shih: Chung-kuo min tsu hshueh hui: Han hsueh yen chiu tzu liao chi fu wu chung hsin, min Kuo, 1983 [189p.]) **(L41).** Title on added t.p.: *Bibliography of anthropological works published in Taiwan, 1945–1982, in a classed arrangement.* Since research published in European languages is interfiled, this resource can be used by students with a minimal command of the Chinese language.

L42

Kim, Tai Whan, and Alekssandra K. Wawrzyszko. *A bibliographical guide to the study of Chinese language and linguistics.* Carbondale, Ill., and Edmonton, Canada: Linguistic Research, 1980. 88p. (Current inquiry into language and linguistics, 39)

Of the first importance. Pt.7, "Bibliographies" (p.73–82), annotates a list of reference sources useful to linguistics. The annotations are accurate, detailed, and a model of clarity. Other sections include pt.1, "Textbooks"; pt.2, "Dictionaries"; pt.3, resources for the study of "Mandarin Chinese"; pt.4, "General descriptions of Chinese"; pt.5, reference works in "Linguistics" under the subtopics (a) anthologies, (b) phonetics and phonology, and (c) grammar; pt.6, reference sources about "Writing systems." All entries are carefully annotated. Author index. Consult also DeMiller's *Linguistics* **(E01)** for detailed annotations to listed bibliographies of Chinese linguistics.

L43

Schwarz, Henry G. *The minorities of northern China: A survey.* Bellingham: Western Washington, 1989 [c1984]. 309p. (Western Washington University. Program on East Asian Studies. *Occasional papers.* Program on East Asian Studies, v.17)

Encyclopedic review of all groups, including (1) the Turkic group: Kazak, Kirgiz, Salar, Uzbek, Yuzur, and Tartar; (2) the Mongolian group: Tu, Daur, Bonan; (3) the Manchu-Tunugus group: Manchu, Sibe, Evenk, Oroqen, Hezhen; and (4) Others: Hui, Korean, Russian. Survey of each group includes information about size and location, history, language and literature, society, and recent developments. The bibliographies (p.233–309) include books and journal articles in English, French, German, Russian, Chinese, and the languages of minorities such as Uighur, Kazur and Kirgiz. This resource consolidates information into twelve tables. There are twenty-one maps showing the distribution of groups, and forty-eight illustrations. Another useful source by Henry G. Schwarz, *Bibliotheca Mongolica* (Bellingham: Western Washington, Center for East Asian Studies, 1978. [355p.]) (Studies on East Asia, v.12) **(L44),** can be consulted with confidence for regional coverage. Other sections of *Fieldwork in the Library,* with reference sources relevant to this area, include chapter 1, "What Every Anthropologist Needs to Know"; chapter 9, "Asia and the Pacific"; and chapter 11, "The Islamic Influence and Israel."

L45

Thompson, Laurence G., and Justine Pinto, comps. *Studies of Chinese religion: A comprehensive and classified bibliography of publications in English, French, and German through 1970.* Encino, Calif.: Dickenson, 1976. 190p.

A useful select bibliography for the study of the impact of the major religions on China. Classifies 5,000 entries for books and periodical articles into two major categories subdivided into more than forty headings. For additional material, consult P. Cohen's "A bibliography of the writings contributory to the study of Chinese folk religion," in the American Academy of Religion's *American Academy of Religion journal* 43 (2) (1975): 238–65 **(L46).**

Informational Reference Searches

Across chapters this heading introduces lists of reference books that answer a need for summaries of anthropological results and for brief descriptions of institutions or address information for individuals.

In chapter 1, inspect listings under the subheading "State-of-the-Art Reviews." Find there the *Annual review of anthropology* **(A57)** with its summary coverage of recent research activity. Many searches that start in other chapters must return to chapter 1 for the directory. *AAA Guide* **(A53)** is listed for addresses and other information relevant to contemporary American anthropology. Each of the chapters on the subdisciplines of anthropology will have resources of value.

Encyclopedias, Handbooks

L47

Mackerras, Colin, and Amanda Yorke. *Cambridge handbook of contemporary China.* New York: Cambridge Univ. Pr., 1991. 266p.

The contents of the eleven chapters include one devoted to "Reference sources," with an annotated bibliography and a gazetteer. Includes 70 tables. Covers China since the disintegration of the Communist Party in Russia.

L48

Twitchett, Denis, and John K. Fairbank, eds. *The Cambridge history of China.* Cambridge, England: Cambridge Univ. Pr., 1986– . In progress.

Many of these volumes have been translated into Chinese and published in the People's Republic. Contributions are signed by recognized scholars and supported by useful bibliographies.

L49

Wu, Yuan-li. *China: A handbook.* New York: Praeger, 1973. 915p.

Subject specialists contribute signed articles on thirty topics, including "Physical geography," "Official population data," "Overseas Chinese," "Chinese society; stratification, minorities, and the family," and "Sources of information: A brief survey." Provides some entry into the government documents of Communist China, and the statistical summaries can be used for valuable notations of sources. Still useful are the directories found under the topical headings "Research institutes of the Academy of Sciences," "Research institutes of the Chinese Academy of Agricultural Sciences" "Scientific research institutes and personnel in medical science and public health." There is a sixteen-page index that greatly adds to the value of this work.

Searching Graphic Materials

See Spencer and Johnson's *Atlas for anthropology* **(A65)** and Heider's *Films for anthropological teaching* **(A63).** Useful resources will be listed under this heading in all chapters devoted to the subdisciplines of anthropology.

Maps and Atlases

L50

Blunden, Caroline, and Mark Elvin. *Cultural atlas of China.* New York: Facts on File, 1983. 237p.

Fifty-eight maps. Covers space, time, and symbols and society. The section on symbols and society provides graphic representation of many topical interests such as language, the arts, medicine, and family life. Bibliography, index, and gazetteer at the end. Bibliography is in classed arrangement with annotations.

L51

Population Census Office of the State Council of the People's Republic of China and the Institute of Geography of the Chinese Academy of Sciences, eds. *Population atlas of China.* Oxford, England: Oxford Univ. Pr., 1987. 217p.

Based on China's 1982 census. One hundred thirty-seven maps with demographic indicators, physical and human background maps, and comparative population distribution maps. A monumental research atlas. Includes index to county-level administrative unit. Provides word list, in two sections: Pinyin to English and English to Pinyin.

JAPAN

Searching Bibliographic Guides

A move to entries listed under this heading in all of the chapters devoted to the subdisciplines of anthropology will be productive. All searches should start with the resources identified in Auckland's "Getting into the literature" **(A01).**

Bibliographic Guides

L52

Beardsley, Richard K., John B. Cornell, and Edward Norbeck. *Bibliographic materials in the Japanese language on Far Eastern archaeology and ethnology.* Ann Arbor: Univ. of Michigan Pr., 1950. 74p. (University of Michigan. Center for Japanese studies. Bibliographical series, no.3)

A compendium of classics from an earlier and founding period that established anthropology as an academic discipline in Japan. Long annotations. Intended for Western scholars working with the Japanese language. A classed arrangement. Pt.1, Journals and serials (sixty-four items); pt.2, Bibliographies (twenty-two items); pt.3, Glossaries (five items); pt.4, General anthropology (fourteen items); pt.5, Archaeology (191 items); pt.6, Japanese ethnology; pt.7, Ainu ethnology; pt.8, Ryukyu ethnology; pt.10, Micronesia; pt.11, Continental East Asia. Consult also Richard K. Beardsley and Takashi Nakano's *Japanese sociology and social anthropology: A guide to Japanese reference and research materials* (Ann Arbor: Univ. of Michigan Pr., 1970 [276p.]) **(L53),** a select list of 1,700 entries for periodical articles and books published 1946–66 with author and locality indexes.

L54

Kokusai Bunka Kaikan (Tokyo). Toshoshitsu. *A guide to reference books for Japanese studies (Nihon kenkyū no tame sankō tosho),* comp. by International House of Japan Library (Kokusai Bunka Kaikan Koksai Bunka Kaikan). Toshoshitsu henshu. Tokyo: International House of Japan Library, 1989. 156p.

Lists of English-language reference sources and Japanese-language reference sources are developed in separate sections. There is coverage of general reference sources by form, and of topical coverage by subject. Anthropologists will find the sections of folklore and sociology especially helpful. There is a list of English-language journals about Japan, with a section devoted to Japanese online and CD-ROM databases. For a scholarly select guide with strength in the historical perspective, consult John W. Dower's *Japanese history and culture from ancient to modern times: Seven basic bibliographies* (New York: Wiener, 1986 [232p.]) **(L55),** which places emphasis on English-language monographs, articles from scholarly collections, bibliographies, research guides, and serials. The section on bibliographies and research guides is useful, but this work is not directly focused on anthropology. An arrangement of reference sources by form can be found in Raymond Nunn's *Asia* **(L06)** for encyclopedias and handbooks (traditional, general, and by subject), yearbooks, dictionaries, atlases, geographical dictionaries, gazetteers, chronological tables, and chronology. Includes descriptions of the Imperial Library catalogs, National Diet Library catalogs, official publications, select Western-language (including Russian) bibliographies covering religion, history, the social sciences, linguistics, geography, and archaeology.

L56

Perren, Richard. *Japanese studies from prehistory to 1990: A bibliographical guide.* Manchester, England: Manchester Univ. Pr., 1992. 172p.

Organized under historical and thematic headings with few cross-references. Author index. The subject guidance here is sparse. This can be updated with what is both a more laborious and a more rewarding approach through Maruzen Kabushiki Kaisha's *Books on Japan and Asian countries in foreign languages published in Japan 1992–1993* (Tokyo: Maruzen, 1993 [214p.]) **(L57),** a bookseller's catalog with indexes in English and Japanese.

Retrospective Searches

Retrospective catalogs of area libraries like the *Subject catalogue of the Library of the Royal Empire Society* **(L02);** the University of London, School of Oriental and African Studies, *Library catalogue* **(G17);** and Nunn's *Asia and Oceania: A guide to archival and manuscript sources in the United States* **(L05).** The reference sources in this chapter are best used as a supplement to the more fundamental resources identified in chapter 1, "What Every Anthropologist Needs to Know"; chapter 3, "Archaeology and Material Culture"; chapter 4, "Ethnology/Cultural Anthropology"; and chapter 5, "Anthropological Linguistics." Many of these resources are indispensable.

A discussion of the structured arrangement of entries clustered under subject headings can be found in the introduction.

Retrospective Bibliographies—Broad Scope

L58

Borton, Hugh. *A selected list of books and articles on Japan in English, French and German.* Rev. and enl. ed. Cambridge, Mass.: Harvard Univ. Pr. for the Harvard-Yenching Inst., 1954. 272p.

A selective and critical bibliography of 1,781 works relating to the humanities and social sciences, published to 1952. Analytical index of authors, titles, and subjects. More recently, consult International Christian University Library (Kokusai Kirisutokyō Daigaku. Toshoshitsu), International House of Japan Library (Kokusai bunka kaikan toshoshitsu), *Books on Japan in English; Joint holding list of the International Christian University Library and the International House of Japan Library, September 1983* (Tokyo: International Christian University Library, 1984 [683p.]) **(L59),** which lists 6,000 titles with division by subject. Consult also Kokusai Kōryū Kikin's *Catalogue of books in English on Japan, 1945–1981 (Eigaku Ninon kankei hōbun tosha mokuroku 1945–1981)* (Tokyo: The Japan Foundation, 1986 [726p.]) **(L60),** which lists 9,000 titles including all books listed in the *Bibliography of Asian studies,* up to the 1979 edition, and Frank J. Shulman's *Japan* (Oxford, England: Clio Pr., 1989 [873p.]) (World bibliographical series) **(L61),** a select 1,600 English-language entries fully annotated and arranged by subject.

Retrospective Bibliographies—Topical

The inclusion of 420 reference books in the classed arrangement of Nichigai Associates' *Bunka jinruigaku kenkyū bunken yōran 1945–1974* **(L67)** helps identify topical entries of importance. The list also classifies 8,700 articles, and 2,300 monographs. There are author and subject indexes. Supplement this source with Asakura Haruhiko and Fukai Hitoshi's *Shoshi nenkan (Annual bibliography of bibliographies),* v.1– , 1982– (Tokyo: Nichigai Associates) **(L62)** in the section devoted to subject bibliographies.

J63

Huber, Kristina Ruth. *Women in Japanese society: An annotated bibliography of selected English language materials.* Westport, Conn.: Greenwood, 1992. 484p. (Bibliographies and indexes in women's studies, 16)

Covers books, chapters in books, and periodical articles. Annotations include reference to bibliographic and indexing features. Includes art, recreation, religion, and the home. As is usual, the bibliography on women touches on many aspects of interest to ethnologists. Indexes by author, title, translator, interviewee, title phrase, series, and subject.

L64

Japanese Society of Ethnology (Nihon minzokugakkai). *Ethnology in Japan; Historical review, 1968 (Nihon minzokugaku no kaiko to tenbō).* Tokyo: K. Shibusawa Memorial Foundation for Ethnology, 1968. 147p.

Bibliographic review in Japanese, followed by bibliography on p.95–147.

L65

Japanese Society of Ethnology, Tokyo. "Classified list of field works . . . in ethnology, sociology, linguistics, archaeology, physical anthropology and related sciences." *Minzokugaku-kenkyu (Japanese Journal of Ethnology)* 28 (1) (1964): 1–145.

A classified arrangement of nine regions of Japan, with entries by author thereunder, is followed by coverage of overseas areas, including Kuril Islands, Sakhalin, Korea, Mongolia, China, Formosa, Southeast Asia, Philippine Islands, Indonesia, Melanesia, Polynesia, Micronesia, India and adjacent areas, west Asia, Africa, Europe, and North and South America.

L66

Matsui, Masato, Tomoyoshi Kurokawa, and Minako I. Song. *Ryukyu: An annotated bibliography.* With an introduction by Mitsugu Sakihari. Based on a collection held by the Thomas Hale Hamilton Library. Honolulu: Center for Asian and Pacific Studies, 1981. 345p.

An introductory bibliographic essay (p.1–68) summarizes the research published in the bibliographic list, which describes 460 entries in a classed arrangement. Items 141–289 are entered under the term ANTHROPOLOGY.

L67

Nichigai Associates, Inc. *Bunka jinruigaku kenkyū bunken yōran 1945–1974 (Sengohen) (Subject guide to periodical literature 1945–1974: Cultural anthropology, custom).* Tokyo: Nichigai Associates, 1979. 326p. (20-seiki bunken yōran taikei, 7)

In Japanese. Classed arrangement of three lists. Pt.1, 420 reference works; pt.2, 8,700 articles from journals; pt.3, 2,300 book titles. Author and subject indexes. Updated with the same classed arrangement by *Nihon kenmei tosho mokuroku 77/84, 13: Minzoku, fūzoku (Subject guide to Japanese books, pt. 13: Customs and folklore, 1977/1984)* (Tokyo: Nichigai Associates, 1985 [516p.]) **(L68),** and by Nichigai Associates, Inc., *Bunka jinruigaku minzokugaku ni kansuru 10-nenkan no Zasshi Bunken Mokuroku: Showa 59-nen (Subject guide to periodical literature, 1975–1984: Cultural anthropology, custom)* (Tokyo: Nichigai Associates, 1987 [230p.]) **(L69),** which includes sections on daily life, marriage customs, annual rites, social and family cultures, dialects, and folk art. Subject index. For annual update, consult *Nihon kenmei tosho mokuroku (Subject guide to Japanese books),* v.1– , 1986– (Tokyo: Nichigai Associates) **(L70).**

L71

Nihon minzokugaku kankei zasshi ronbun sōmokuroku 1925–1959 (Bibliography of periodical articles in ethnology 1925–1959). Tokyo: Seibundō, 1961. 192p.

A bibliography of 6,000 journal articles covering early ethnological studies in Japan. Organized first under topical headings such as society, art, and psychology, then organized by geographical areas: Japan, Korea, and then other Asian countries.

Informational Reference Searches

Across chapters this heading introduces lists of reference books that answer an inquiry for summaries of anthropological results and for brief descriptions of institutions or address information for individuals.

In chapter 1 inspect listings under the subheading "State-of-the-Art Reviews." Find there the *Annual review of anthropology* **(A57),** with its summary coverage of recent research activity. Many searches that start in other chapters of

Fieldwork in the Library must return to chapter 1 for directory information. *AAA guide* **(A53)** is listed for the address and other information relevant to contemporary American anthropology. Each of the chapters on the subdisciplines of anthropology will have resources of value.

Encyclopedias

L72

Kodansha encyclopedia of Japan. Tokyo: Kodansha; dist., New York: Harper, 1983. 9v.

Covers 9,417 topics in thirty-seven categories of information. One hundred twenty-three major articles of more than 3,500 words each, 1,429 medium-length entries of 720 to 2,500 words, and 7,865 shorter entries of fifty to 500 words. In addition there are approximately 1,000 photographs, maps, and charts. Some 60 percent of the encyclopedia was originally written in English, with the remainder translated from Japanese.

L73

Minzokugakkai, Ōtsuka, ed. *Nihon minzoku jiten.* Tokyo: Kōbundō, 1972. 862p.

Encyclopedic dictionary of ethnology in Japanese. Nearly 100 contributing scholars in a classed arrangement first by topics like methodology, social traditions, religious beliefs, etc., then by geographic units. Also useful is *Nihon minzoku jiten* by Nihon minzokugaku Kyōkai (Tokyo: Meicho Fakyūkai, 1987 [1,280p.]) **(L74),** a dictionary of folklore oriented to ethnology. Arranged in Japanese equivalent to alphabetic order (a phonetic system). Also useful is Akira Matsumura's *A gazetteer of ethnology* (Tokyo: Maruzen-Kabushiki-Kaisha, 1908 [492p.]) **(L75),** with an alphabetic list in English, with a parallel column of Japanese. The appendix has a series of tables in which people are arranged by the political divisions of the world, followed by a list of works used in the preparation of these books. There is an index of names of races and peoples written in Kana, and an index of Chinese names for races and peoples. A series of maps illustrate the distribution of races and peoples.

L76

Perkins, Dorothy. *Encyclopedia of Japan: Japanese history and culture, from abacus to zori.* New York: Facts on File, 1991. 410p.

Alphabetically ordered entries, each with generous coverage. Compact enough to be a desk reference, this sturdy edition has many cross-references and a thirty-six-column index. For many, the use of English equivalents to Japanese words eases the reference search.

State-of-the-Art Reviews

L77

Kokusai Kōryū Kikin. *An introductory bibliography for Japanese studies.* v.1– , 1974– . Tokyo: The Japan Foundation.

Provides bibliographic reviews in English of Japanese work, with extensive bibliographies that cumulatively form a record of scholarly research. The social sciences and the humanities are covered in alternate years. Continues the information made available in Kokusai Bunka Shinkokai's *K.B.S. bibliography of standard reference books for Japanese studies, with descriptive notes,* v.1–10, 1959–70 (Tokyo: Society for International Cultural Relations) **(L78).**

L79

"Review of studies." *Minzokugaku-kenkyu (The Japanese journal of ethnology)* 54 (3) (1989): 360–437.

Bibliographic essays covering earliest scholarly efforts to present, with supporting bibliography. Divided by national source of contribution. Includes Robert Smith's "Japanese studies in the U.S.A." (p.360–73), Joy Henry's "Social anthropology of Japan in the U.K." (p.374–76), Josef Kreiner's "Ethnological studies of Japan in Europe" (p.377–80), Norbert R. Adami's "Soviet studies on Japanese ethnography and folklore" (p.381), Kilsong Ch'eg's "Anthropological studies of Japan in Korea" (p.382–83), Sung-hsing's "Anthropological studies of Japan in China," and analysis of contributions (p.350–437).

L80

Ramming, Martin. *Japan handbuch: Nachschlagewerk der Japankunde.* Berlin: Steiniger, 1941. 740p.

An alphabetic dictionary of things Japanese. A remarkable book. Covers almost all aspects of Japanese culture in brief paragraphs. No references. Alphabetic arrangement.

L81

Nihon Minzokugaku Kyōkai. *Nihon shakai minzoku jiten.* Tokyo: Seibundō Shinkosha, 1952–1960. 4v.

Broad entries with bibliographies make it possible to use this resource as a source for review of the study of Japanese folklore oriented to cultural anthropology. To bring the review current, consult Kokusai Kōryū Kikin's *An introductory bibliography for Japanese studies* **(L77).**

KOREA

Searching Bibliographic Guides

A move to entries listed under this heading in all of the chapters devoted to the subdisciplines of anthropology will be productive. All searches should start with the resources identified in Auckland's "Getting into the literature" **(A01).**

Bibliographic Guides

L82

Kim, Han-Kyo, and Hong Kyoo Park, eds. *Studies on Korea: A scholar's guide.* Honolulu: Univ. Pr. of Hawaii, 1980. 438p.

Largely English-language works of scholarly value. Classed arrangement with an author index. Professionally structured and executed. This can be supplemented by reference to Nunn's *Asia* **(L06)** for encyclopedias and handbooks, directories, dictionaries, gazetteers, atlases, chronological tables, statistical yearbooks, bibliographies of bibliography (including those in Korean), official publications, periodicals, theses and dissertations, films, and a subject bibliography on Buddhism, the social sciences, and history. Because so few scholarly journals specialize solely on this region, the cumulated indexes to these journals are of more than usual reference value. Consult, for example, "Index [Revue de corée: été 1969–été 1984]," *Revue de Corée* 16 (3) (1984): 85–120 **(L83),** which identifies research in French that is indexed fully nowhere else in anthropology.

Retrospective Searches

Consult the retrospective catalogs of area libraries like the *Subject catalogue of the Library of the Royal Empire Society* **(L02)** and the University of London, School of Oriental and African Studies, *Library catalogue* **(G17).**

RUSSIAN ASIA IN THE CIS

Retrospective Searches

Several reference works that have value for anthropological searches of the literature on this area can be found in *Fieldwork in the Library,* chapter 11, "The Islamic Influence and Israel." Allworth's *Soviet Asia* **(P46);** Lee's *An annotated bibliography on inner Asia* **(P49);** Sinor's *Introduction à l'étude de l'Eurasie centrale* **(P48);** and the "Bibliography of periodical literature" **(P11)** are especially recommended. Where there is an Islamic tradition for indigenous ethnic groups, White and Rossi's *Articles on the Middle East 1947–1971* **(P70)** provides extensive coverage. Consult also Nunn's *Asia* **(L06)** for handbooks, dictionaries, gazetteers, and bibliographies.

Retrospective Bibliographies

L84

Jakobson, Roman, Greta Hütti-Worth, and John Fred Beebe. *Paleosiberian peoples and languages: A bibliographical guide.* New Haven, Conn.: HRAF Pr., 1957. 222p. (Behavior science bibliographies)

Reprint by Greenwood Press, 1981. An extensive bibliography dealing with the peoples of northeast Asiatic Russia. The 1,898 entries include a large number of Russian titles (translated) as well as material in other Western languages. Two general chapters are followed by one devoted to each of the four groups. Some brief explanatory annotations. No index. Also useful is Robert Arthur Rupen's *Mongols of the twentieth century* (Bloomington: Indiana Univ. Pr., 1964 [2v.]) (Indiana University publications, Uralic and Altaic series, v.37) **(L85).**

L86

Wilson Library. *Mongolian publications at Western Washington University.* Schwarz, Henry G., comp. Bellingham: Center for East Asian Studies, Western Washington University, 1984. 371p. (East Asian research aids, v.1)

The 2,123 entries are arranged by author or title. The library's category codes are also given. The category codes, containing sixty-nine subjects from archaeology to zoology, are dominated by the humanities and social sciences.

Informational Reference Searches

Across chapters this heading introduces lists of reference books that answer a need for summaries of anthropological results and for brief descriptions of institutions or address information for individuals. A search that starts with an encyclopedia identified in chapter 1 could expand across chapters for an informational reference search in related encyclopedias and state-of-the-art reviews in other chapters. In chapter 1 inspect listings under the subheading "State-of-the-Art Reviews." Find there the *Annual review of anthropology* **(A57),** with its summary coverage of recent research activity. Many searches that start in other chapters must return to chapter 1 for the directory. *AAA guide* **(A53)** is listed for the address and other information relevant to contemporary American anthropology. Each of the chapters on the subdisciplines of anthropology found in *Fieldwork in the Library* will have resources of value.

Encyclopedias, Handbooks

L87

Academy of Sciences (MPR). *Information Mongolia: The comprehensive reference source of the People's Republic of Mongolia (MPR).* New York: Pergamon, 1990. 505p.

Encyclopedic coverage arranged alphabetically with most references in Russian or Mongolian. The forty-five plates and maps are useful. Surveys the land and its peoples.

L88

Sinor, Dennis, ed. *Cambridge history of early inner Asia.* Cambridge, England: Cambridge Univ. Pr., 1990. 518p.

Definitive work of reference. From prehistory to the eve of the founding of Genghis Khan's Mongol empire. Chapters on Hsiung-un, Huns, Avars, Uighurs, the coming of Islam to the Steppes; on Tibet; and on the Manchurian Kitans and Jurchens. Impressive group of collaborators. Consult also chapter 11, "The Islamic Influence and Israel," in *Fieldwork in the Library.*

SOUTH ASIA AND THE BUDDHIST KINGDOMS

The development of this section assumes that the reader has exhausted Balay's *Guide to reference books* **(B02),** especially for more recent general sources. Consult Nunn's *Asia* **(L06)** in its general chapter for theses and dissertations. The coverage of "India" extends from southern to southeastern Asia for bibliographies, encyclopedias, handbooks, yearbooks, dictionaries, directories, atlases, dissertations, gazetteers, statistical yearbooks, bibliographies of bibliographies, and current bibliographies. Nunn **(L06)** includes publications in Bengali, Hindi, Hindustani, Kannada, Malayalam, Marathi, Panjabi, Sanskrit, Pali, Prakrit, Tamil, and Telugu, and Russian-language sources. The chapter on Nepal is organized by form for handbooks, dictionaries, directories, censuses, gazetteers, official publications, newspapers and other periodicals, and dissertations. Subject bibliographies include the social sciences. The chapter on Sri Lanka lists reference sources by form, including encyclopedias, handbooks, yearbooks, dictionaries, atlases, gazetteers, censuses, statistics, and bibliography. The coverage of "Burma" includes encyclopedias, yearbooks, handbooks, dictionaries, directories, gazetteers, censuses, statistics, and bibliography. The chapter on Laos covers handbooks, dictionaries, gazetteers, statistics, and bibliography. For coverage of both "Burma" and "Laos," Nunn **(L06)** suggests that users first exhaust the more general chapter, "Southeast Asia," which covers bibliographies (in Western languages, Chinese, Japanese, and Russian) of dissertations and maps.

Reference sources of value to anthropologists working with Muslim populations in this area can also be found in chapter 11, *Fieldwork in the Library,* under the heading, "The Islamic Influence and Israel."

Searching Bibliographic Guides

The body of bibliographic guides used to define the chapters under "Searching Bibliographic Guides" serves as our base. Consult especially Auckland's "Getting into the literature" **(A01)** and the guides under this heading described in each of the chapters of *Fieldwork in the Library* devoted to the subdisciplines of anthropology.

Bibliographic Guides

For linguistics, consult also the extensive list of cumulative bibliographies in South Asian linguistics, including Indo-Iranian, Hindi, Sanskrit, Dravidian, Mon Khmer, Siamese-Chinese, Tibeto-Burman, Munda, Eranian, Gypsy, and the minor languages of India in DeMiller's *Linguistics* **(E01).** DeMiller provides detailed annotations that explain even complex structures like those of J. Sakuntala Sharma's *Classified bibliography of linguistic dissertations on Indian languages* (Mysore: Central Institute of Indian Languages, 1978 [288p.]) (CIIL occasional monographs series, no.14).

M01

Dewey, Clive. *The settlement literature of the Greater Punjab: A handbook.* New Delhi: Manohar, 1991. 107p.

Covers northwest India and Pakistan. After a section on reading the entries, there are chronological lists of assessment and settlement reports, district gazetteers, and codes of customary law produced between 1803 and 1947. After these have been given, there is a list of additional bibliographic materials and an author index that groups all contributions made by officials.

M02

Padmanabha, P. *India census and anthropological investigations.* Rev. and updated. New Delhi: Comptroller of Publications, 1983. 150p.

Pt.1, resources for anthropology, divided by preindependence and postindependence periods. Pt.2, a general discussion and bibliographic list followed by a number of sections titled after individual states and subdivided by census, with alphabetic bibliographies by author under each heading.

A general discussion that explains the organization of these materials can be found in Sashi Bhusan Chaudhuri's *History of the gazetteers of India* (New Delhi: Ministry of Education, Government of India, 1964 [230p.]) **(M03),** and note especially the appendixes (p.175–211). Both of these resources prepare the user for effective use of the detailed information, including descriptions of local groups contained in the elaborate *Imperial gazetteer of India,* rev. ed. (Oxford, England: Clarendon, 1907–31 [26v.]), and the *Imperial gazetteer of India (Provincial series)* (Calcutta: Supt. of Govt. Print., 1908–1909 [25v.]) **(M04);** reprint available from Today and Tomorrow's Printers and Publishers (New Delhi), 1972–73.

M05

Pearson, James D., ed. *South Asian bibliography: A handbook and guide.* South Asia Library Group, comp. Sussex, England: Harvester Pr.; Atlantic Highlands, N.J.: Humanities Pr., 1979. 381p.

Supersedes all previous guides to this area. Twenty-six British scholars have compiled this extensive handbook of bibliographies, finding aids, and reference works. Subject bibliographies include religion, anthropology, sociology, art and archaeology, music and dance, language and literature, history, law, economics, traditional sciences, and technology. Section that covers regions and countries is subdivided into subjects. The nearby regions of Afghanistan, "Burma," the Maldives, the Himalayas, and Tibet are also included. Each of the thirty-seven articles is professionally structured and maintains the model of excellence that makes this volume definitive for the area. G. Shaw's "Art and archaeology" in this widely distributed volume is still useful, but searches can be expanded in part by reference to Bernard Goldman's "Bibliographies," in *The ancient arts of western and central Asia: A guide to the literature* (Ames: Iowa State Univ. Pr., 1991 [305p.]) **(M06),** in which a reference key (p.13–54) is organized under broad topics with many expansions of terms. This key includes coverage to geographic and institutional names. For example, the term ITALIAN is expanded for archaeological terms and for a bibliography of journals relevant to Italian archaeology. PERSEPOLIS has fifteen indexing expansion terms. A superbly detailed guide.

Retrospective Searches

When retrospective searches include searches for descriptions of indigenous peoples, consult Human Relations Area Files, *HRAF source bibliography* **(D16),** and the Museum of Mankind Library's "Tribal index" [microfiche] **(D13).** For continuing coverage of the intentional periodical output consult *Anthropological literature* **(A36),** *Anthropological index* **(A35),** and *Abstracts in anthropology* **(A32).** The annual *International bibliography of social and cultural anthropology* **(D20)** succeeds in maintaining some ethnic-group entry in its indexing.

Retrospective Bibliographies—Bibliography of Bibliographies

M07

Ray, Shyamal. "Bibliography of bibliographies on anthropology of India." *Bulletin of the Anthropological Survey of India* 29 (1980): 98–119.

Lists 153 entries selected by the reference librarian at the Central Library of the Anthropological Survey of India. An illustrative sample of entries from this resource could include its description of India, Office of Registrar General, *Bibliography on scheduled castes, scheduled tribes and selected marginal communities* **(M32),** which provides a basic documentation for studies in indigenous ethnic group research. This work can be supplemented by Patel's *Bibliography on scheduled castes and scheduled tribes* **(M31).** Regional bibliographies of indigenous ethnic groups include Bishwa B. Chatterjee's "Literature on Bhotias of Kumaon-Garohals: A bibliography," *Italian anthropologist* 7: 2 (1977): 125–37 **(M08);** Sibadas Chaudhuri's *Selected bibliography on the north eastern frontier of India* (Calcutta: The Author, 1958 [64p.]) **(M09),** which contains 574 entries; Edward A. Gait's *Report on the progress of historical research in Assam Shillong* (Shillong, Assam: Secretariat Printing, 1897 [75p.]) **(M10),** which provides entry into archaeology, ethnology, mythology, and linguistics; A. M. Kurup's "Bibliography on Bhils," *Bulletin of the Tribal Research Institute* (Chindwar) 2 (1958): 3, 39–45 **(M11);** and *Bibliography of the Punjab,* ed. by Ganda Singh (Patiala: Punjab University, 1966 [246p.]) **(M12),** which provides author lists by language of report and covers published works in English, Persian, Urdu, Hindi, Marathi, Sanskrit, Gujarati, and Bengali.

Retrospective Bibliographies—Biographical Directories

M13

Ray, Shyamal. *Bibliographies of eminent Indian anthropologists with life-sketches.* Calcutta: Anthropological Survey of India, Government of India, 1974. 184p.

Contains extensive bibliographies of twelve pioneer anthropologists of India, including L. K. Ananthakrisna Iyer, Sarat Chandra Roy, Ramaprasad Chandra, Haran Chandra Chakdladar, Biraja Shankar Guha, K. P. Chattopadhyay, T. C. Das, N. K. Bose, Verrier Elwin, D. N. Majumdar, Irawati Karve, and S. S. Sarkar. Together with brief life sketches, it includes publications of these scholars in both English and vernacular languages.

Retrospective Bibliographies—Broad Scope

Some earlier sources remain valuable for their arrangement of bibliographic entries, such as the Calcutta National Library's *A bibliography of indology,* v.1, *Indian anthropology* (Calcutta: National Library, 1960 [290p.]) **(M14),** which contains 2,067 entries arranged by geographic region. Annotates 1,004 entries. Includes "Physical anthropology," "Anthropological Linguistics," and "Socio-cultural anthropology" relating to the subcontinent of India. Journal articles are included only when coverage cannot be achieved from monographic sources. Author and subject indexes. For older material, nothing has yet superseded David G. Mandelbaum's *Bibliography of the ethnology of India* (Berkeley: Univ. of California Dept. of Anthropology, 1949 [220p.]), a mimeographed publication still valuable for anthropological purposes because of its selectivity and organization around an anthropologically sensitive classification system.

M15

Ames Library of South Asia. *Catalog of the Ames Library of South Asia, University of Minnesota.* Boston: Hall, 1980. 16v.

Fine source for the identification of monographic material on India, Pakistan, Nepal, and Burma.

M16

Furer-Haimendorf, Elizabeth von. *An anthropological bibliography of South Asia, together with a directory of recent anthropological field work.* Paris: Mouton, 1958–70. 3v. (Le Monde d'outremer passé et present. 4. ser.: Bibliographies, 3–4, 8)

A valuable tool restricted in coverage to India, Pakistan, Nepal, Sikkim, Bhutan, and Ceylon. V.3, appendix on "Ethnology of India as depicted in literature 500 A.D. to 1750 A.D." No annotations. Author index.

The publication dates of this volume and Kanitkar's *An anthropological bibliography of South Asia* **(M19)** make it necessary to supplement these resources with a search for more recent contributions. Consider the following reference sources cited in Drews and Hockings's "Asia bibliographies" **(L13):** *The social system and culture of modern India: A research bibliography,* ed. by D. G. Cekki (New York: Garland, 1975 [843p.]) **(M17),** with 5,487 entries meticulously organized to include anthropology and social psychology. Also listed there: J. Troisi, *The Santals: A classified and annotated bibliography* (New Delhi: Manohar, 1976 [234p.]) **(M18).**

M19

Kanitkar, Helen A., comp. *An anthropological bibliography of South Asia.* The Hague: Mouton, 1976– .

Lists 2,757 items. Continuation of Furer-Haimendorf's *An anthropological bibliography of South Asia* **(M16),** with some changes in scope. Drops coverage of physical anthropology and prehistoric archaeology. Adds coverage of South Asians overseas, welfare of indigenous ethnic groups, urbanization, political sociology, and sociolinguistics. Continues the department "Ethnology of India in literature," providing coverage from 1750 to the present.

M20

Indian states bibliography series. v.1– , 1976– . Gurgaon, Haryana: Indian Documentation Service.

Issued to date in this format: No.1, Satyaprakash, *Andra Pradash: A select bibliography, 1962–1975* (1976 [175p.]); no.2, Satyaprakash, *Assam: A select bibliography, 1962–1975* (1976 [187p.]); no.3, Satyaprakash, *Bihar: A select bibliography, 1962–1975* (1976 [155p.]); no.4, Satyaprakash, *Gujarat: A select bibliography* (1976 [168p.]); no.8, Satyaprakash, *Karnataka: A select bibliography* (1978 [276p.]); no.9, Satyaprakash, *Kerala: A select bibliography* (1979 [205p.]); no.10, Satyaprakash, *Madhya Pradesh: A select bibliography* (1982 [175p.]).

One recent volume of this series by S. Y. Quraishi, *Harayana rediscovered: A bibliographical area study* (Gurgaon, Harayana: Indian Documentation Service, 1985 [2v.]) **(M21),** includes reference to book articles, government documents, and dissertations, with an emphasis on history, life, culture, language and literature, education, geography, urbanization, sociology, social welfare, politics, public administration, and laws and legislation. Each volume has a subject and an author index and a list of journals surveyed.

Retrospective Bibliographies—Continuing

M22

Annual bibliography of Indian archaeology. v.1–23, 1928–84. Leiden, Netherlands: Dordrichr for Instituut Kern.

Last issue carries the bibliography through 1972. Pt.1, "General works," includes a subdivision for bibliography which cites all relevant continuing series as well as bibliographies in books. Pt.2 covers reference to work published by or about India and the regions within its influence. Pt.3 covers entries that deal with the Indian subcontinent. Pt.4 covers regions within the sphere of Indian influence, including some of Southeast Asia (Burma, Cambodia, Laos, Malaya, Siam, and Indonesia, subdivided for Java and Bali) and southwestern Asia (Iran, Afghanistan). Because of its extensive coverage of contiguous territories to the east of India, this resource, with its emphasis on Western language forms, can be used as a companion to *Man and environment* **(M46).** The excellence of the annotations helps this resource retain permanent value.

M23

Asian social science bibliography with annotations and abstracts. v.1– , 1966– . Delhi: Institute of Economic Growth. Annual. (Documentation series)

"Social anthropology" is a subject division. Some coverage of all of Asia, but the real emphasis is on those areas that neighbor India.

Retrospective Bibliographies—Topical

M24

Agesthialingom, S., and S. Sakthivel. *A bibliography for the study of Nilagiri Hill tribes.* Annamalainagar, India: Annamalai University, 1973. 60p. (Publications; Annamalainagar University. Department of Linguistics, no.31)

Lists 623 entries. Ethnographic bibliography of the Nilagiri Hills, Tamil Nadu, with coverage of books, journal articles, and articles in monographs. A general section is followed by bibliographies for twenty-six indigenous ethnic groups. More useful for anthropologists is Paul Hockings's *A bibliography for the Nilagiri Hills of southern India* (New Haven, Conn.: Human Relations Area File, 1972 [172p.]) (HRAFlex books, Bibliography series AW16-001) **(M25),** with 1,563 entries without division for indigenous ethnic groups organized under broad topics, including ethnology. Author index.

M26

Barrier, Norman Gerald. *The Sikhs and their literature: A guide to books, tracts and periodicals 1849–1919.* Delhi: Menobar Book Service, 1970. 153p.

Includes an author list of publications (p.5–41). There is also a list of anonymous publications (p.47–58), a list of Sikh institutional publications (p.63–70), a list of Sikh periodicals (p.75–88), and a select bibliography (p.123–28). Subject/title index. General index of names.

M27

Karashima, N. "Bibliography of South Indian epigraphy." *Journal of Asian and African studies* 6 (1973): 151–63.

Alphabetic list by author.

M28

Kirkland, Edwin Capers. *A bibliography of South Asian folklore.* Bloomington: Indiana University Research Center in Anthropology, Folklore, and Linguistics, 1966. 291p. (Asian folklore studies monographs, no.4; Indiana University folklore series, no.21)

Lists 7,000 titles in all Western languages covering publications on folklore of India, Pakistan, Nepal, Bhutan, Sikkim, and Ceylon.

M29

Kulke, Hermann. *Orissa: A comprehensive and classified bibliography.* Balubazar Cuttack, India: Vidyapuri, 1981. 416p.

A table of contents guides the reader. Thorough execution. For example, under census of 1961, a list of tables on scheduled castes is enriched by a bibliography of eight village monographs. Topical arrangement under headings such as "Language and linguistics" (p.128–53). The section on "Social anthropology" (p.272–300) includes subdivisions for indigenous ethnic groups, with coverage of forty groups, including the BHUMIJ with 28 entries, the HO with 23 entries, the JUANG with 32 entries, the HANDH with 54 entries, the ORAON with 17 entries, and the SANTALS with 63 entries.

M30

Misra, P. K., ed. *Tribes of southern region: A select bibliography.* New Delhi: Inter-India Publications; dist., New York: Apt Books, 1986. 171p. (Tribal Studies of India Series, T-116)

Indigenous ethnic groups of the southern region. A section that briefly identifies the indigenous ethnic groups with their location and outstanding characteristics is followed by a bibliographic list arranged alphabetically by author. Includes states of Andhra Pradesh, Kornataka, Kesaln and Tamil Nadu. Laborious to use.

M31

Patel, A. A. *Bibliography on scheduled castes and scheduled tribes.* New Delhi: Social Studies Division. Office of the Registrar General, Ministry of Home Affairs, 1982. 561p. (*Occasional paper*) (Census of India, 1982–1)

V.1 (A–K) published in 1970, and volume 2 (L–Z) published in 1972. Organized alphabetically by indigenous ethnic group (*Abor . . . Zemi*), with entries under names of indigenous ethnic groups being listed alphabetically by author. Pt.1, bibliography of scholarly contributions to the study of scheduled castes and scheduled indigenous ethnic groups generally. This *Supplement* brings to 1980 the converge started in the earlier *Bibliography on scheduled castes, scheduled tribes and selected marginal communities* (New Delhi: Social Studies Division, Office of the Registrar General, Ministry of Home Affairs, 1968 [2v.]) **(M32).**

M33

Possehl, Gregory L. *Indian archaeology: A review guide to excavated sites, 1953–82.* Philadelphia: The University Museum of Archaeology/Anthropology, 1985. 100p.

Alphabetic by state and district. A list of sites with reference to published reports of excavation, with a brief description of the finds at the site in *Indian archaeology.* Available on 5-1/4″ diskette.

M34

Roy, Ashim Kumar, and N. N. Gidwani. *Indus valley civilization: A bibliographic essay.* New Delhi: Oxford and IBH, 1982. 264p.

Bibliographic essays are followed by a predominantly English-language bibliography, which includes articles, books, unpublished dissertations, and newspaper articles. There is an addendum bibliography of materials not mentioned in the review section. The discussions of all facets of the study of Harappan sites are authoritative to date of publication. No index.

M35

Sakala, Carol. *Women of South Asia: A guide to resources.* Millwood, N.Y.: Kraus, 1980. 517p.

Useful far beyond the range of its title as a guide to social life in India. Includes 4,700 books, articles, and dissertations for India, Pakistan, Bangladesh, Sri Lanka, and Nepal. Identifies some audiovisual materials. Less useful is Harshida Pandit's *Women of India: An annotated bibliography* (New York: Garland, 1985 [278p.]) (Garland reference library of social science, v.152) **(M36).**

M37

Sen, Sipra. *Arunachal Pradesh and the tribes: A select bibliography.* Delhi: Gian, 1986. 232p.

Lists 2,073 entries including scholarly work published in books, articles in journals and books, and newspapers in English, French, German, Hindi, Assamese, and Bengali. Pt.1 provides a brief description of districts and of indigenous ethnic groups (p.25–41). Pt.2 lists the bibliographic entries (p.42–179), arranged by author. Appendix A lists the 110 scheduled indigenous ethnic groups covered. Appendix B lists periodicals and newspapers consulted. Name index.

M38

Sen, Sipra. *Tribes of Meghalaya.* Delhi: Mittal, 1985. 170p.

Lists 1,597 descriptions and bibliographies of three indigenous ethnic groups: Garos, Hajongs, and Khasi. Author index.

M39

Sen, Sipra. *Tribes of Nagaland.* Delhi: Mittal, 1987. 283p.

Pt.1 provides brief descriptions of districts with statistical information and of fifteen main indigenous ethnic groups. Pt.2 lists bibliographic entries alphabetically by author (p.65–228). An appendix classifies the scheduled indigenous ethnic groups covered. For Nega (thirty-four indigenous ethnic groups); for non-Nega (four indigenous ethnic groups). There is a list of journals and newspapers consulted, and an author index. Entry by indigenous ethnic group.

M40

Sharma, Rajendra N., and Santosh Bakshi. *Tribes and tribal development: A select bibliography.* New Delhi: Uppal Publishing House, 1984. 489p.

There is an alphabetic list of scheduled indigenous ethnic groups (p.1–24) and a table of population of scheduled indigenous ethnic groups. There follows 4,431 entries listed alphabetically by author under the chapter headings, such as general studies, social system, organization and change, economic system, political system, religion, magic and witchcraft, art, folklore, language and literature, population, physical structure, health and medicine, crime, criminals and justice, welfare and development of indigenous ethnic groups, education, constitutional safeguards, and research methods. Bibliographies include such valuable works as Sankar Sen Gupta's "Bibliography of village studies," *Folklore* 8: 4 (April 1967) 131–39 **(M41),** which consolidates research based on this methodology for studying group behavior in a complex society.

M42

Sharma, H. D. "Dictionaries." Chapter in *Indian reference sources: An annotated guide to Indian reference material.* 2d ed. v.1, *Generalia and humanities,* p.65–124. Varanasi [Banaras], India: Indian Bibliographic Center, 1988. 250p.

Given the linguistic diversity of India, this annotated list of dictionaries can be useful. Many languages have not had a new dictionary since the turn of the century, and, except for this reference source, many of these entries are listed only by author in national bibliographies, making them difficult to identify.

M43

Sharma, R. K. (ed.) *Indian archaeology; New perspectives: Proceedings of the 11th Annual Congress of the Indian Archaeological Society, 1980.* Delhi: Agam Kala Prakashan, 1982. 319p. (Indian history and culture series. Centre of Advanced Studies in Indian History and Museology (Bhop, India). Prachya Nikaton 2)

Papers divided into four sections: Prehistory, protohistory, protohistoric chronology of central India, and general. Consult also Denise E. King's *A comprehensive bibliography of Pakistan archaeology* (East Lansing: Michigan State University, 1975 [95p.]) (Asian Studies Center. South Asia series. Occasional Paper no.24) **(M44)** and K. S. Pamachandram's *Neolithic cultures of India: An annotated bibliography* (Madras: Tamil Nadu State Department of Archaeology, 1980 [194p.]) **(M45).** For a record of recent advances in the Stone Age in south India, consult issues of *Man and environment,* v.1– , 1977– (Ahmadabad, India: Indian Society for Prehistoric and Quaternary Studies) **(M46),** an annual.

M47

Tribal studies of India. v.1– , 1984– . New Delhi: Inter-India Publications; New York: dist. by Apt Books.

There are nearly as many anthropologists in India as in the United States, and some recent ethnographic work from these researchers can be sampled through this series of monographic ethnographies, each with a bibliographic review of relevant literature. Some representative volumes are described below: T-112, Ajit Raizada's *Tribal development in Madhya Pradesh: A planning perspective* (1984 [220p. with 6p. of plates]); T-113, Pranab Kumar Das Gupta's *Life and culture of the matrilineal tribe of Meghalaya* (1984 [210p. with 19p. of plates]) **(M48);**

T-114, Rajat Kanti Das's *Manipur tribal scene: Studies in society and change* (1985 [106p. with 8p. of plates]); T-115, Onkar Prasad's *Santal music: A study in pattern and process of cultural persistence* (1986 [133p.]); T-116, P. K. Misra's *Tribes of southern region: A select bibliography* **(M30);** T-117, Krishna Kumar Upadhyaya's *Development problems and prospects of Mizoram* (1986 [64p.]); T-118, Alok Kumar's *Tribal culture and economy* (1986 [328p. with 12p. of plates]); T-119, Sachindra Narayan's *Dimensions of development in tribal Bihar* (1986 [89p.]); T-120, Buddhadeb Chaudhuri's *Tribal health: Sociocultural dimensions* (1986 [350p.]); T-121, Rama Shankar Singh's *Changing occupational structure of scheduled tribes* (1986 [291p.]); T-122, M. K. Sukumaran Nair's *Tribal economy in transition: A study of Meghalaya* (1987 [159p.]); T-123, Abraham George's *Lakshadweep, economy and society* (1987 [275p. with 8p. of plates]); T-124, Stephen Fuchs's *The Korkus of the Vindhya Hills* (1988 [443p. with 7 pages of plates]); T-125, Inuganti Murali Krishna Rao's *Marketing in tribal economy; A study with special reference to Shandies (periodic markets); A study in the tribal belt of Srikakulam District of Andhra Pradesh* (1988 [339p.]); T-126, Ponnada Venkata Rao's *Institutional framework for tribal development* (1988 [219p.]); T-128, Yanao Lungharnao Shimmi Roland's *Comparative history of the Nagas from ancient period till 1826* (1988 [206p. with 8p. of plates]); T-129, Kanti Rajat Das's *Tribal social structure; A study of the Maring society of Manipur* (1988 [222p.]); T-130, Sachindra Narayan's *Movements development; Police and judiciary in tribal world* (1988 [140p.]); T-131, Sachindra Narayan's *Tribe in transition* (1988 [167p.]); T-132, Jaganath Pathy's *Underdevelopment and destitution; Essays on Orissan society* (1988 [284p.]); T-133, Veena Bhasin's *Ecology, culture, and change; Tribals of Sikkim Himalayas* (1989 [407p.]); T-135, Madan Chandra Paul's *Dimensions of tribal movements in India: A study of Udayachal in Assam Valley* (1989 [89p.]); T-136, Sambhuti Ranjan Bhattacharjee's *Tribal insurgency in Tripura: A study in exploration of causes* (1989 [211p. with 88p. of plates]).

There are other tribal bibliographies such as Troisi's *Santals* **(M18),** which gives entries in English, Santali, and Italian for more than 500 books, articles, and government reports on the Santals of Bihar and Bengal.

M49

Van Willigen, John. *The Indian city: A bibliographic guide to the literature on urban India.* New Haven, Conn.: Human Relations Area Files, 1979. 2v. (HRAFlex books; AW1-001. Bibliography series)

Lists 3,800 books, articles, conference papers, theses, and dissertations.

Informational Reference Searches

Across chapters of *Fieldwork in the Library,* the above heading introduces lists of reference books that answer a need for summaries of anthropological results and for brief descriptions of institutions or address information for individuals. Any search of informational sources can at some point move from other chapters back to chapter 1 for an inspection of resources under the subheading "State-of-the-Art Reviews." Find there the *Annual review of anthropology* **(A57),** with its summary coverage of recent research activity.

Directories

M50

Bhattacharya, D. K., ed. *Anthropologists in India: Directory of professional anthropologists.* Delhi: Indian Anthropological Association, 1970. 305p.

The introduction provides a review of village studies, caste, power and leadership, religion, urban studies, and folklore (p.iii–xxiii). There follow lists of select publications (p.1–81) and complete bibliographies of listed scholars (p.82–292). Institutional index. Subject index.

M51

Rakshit, Hirendra K., ed. *Directory of anthropologists in India.* Calcutta: Anthropological

Survey of India, Government of India, 1981. 366p.

Very few academic anthropologists are included in this directory, which concentrates instead on anthropologists employed by government agencies. Many photographs of youthful scholars. Biographical information for 539 individuals, with information about research interests and descriptions of publications. Subject index for cultural and physical anthropology and for archaeology and prehistory. Institutional index.

Encyclopedias, Handbooks, Manuals

Consult Nunn's *Asia* **(L06)** for a list of those FASD Area handbooks which provide a frequently revised source of concise coverage for statistical and survey information, maps, and selective but general bibliographies. In addition, some historical dictionaries for the area, reflect the anthropological training of their authors and provide useful survey bibliographies. For example, see especially Mohammed Jamil Hanifi's *Historical and cultural dictionary of Afghanistan* (Metuchen, N.J.: Scarecrow, 1976 [141p.]) (Historical and cultural dictionaries of Asia, no.5) **(M52),** with its extensive and anthropologically sensitive bibliography.

M53

Gaur, Albertine, ed. *South Asian studies: Papers presented at a colloquium 24–26 April, 1985.* London: British Library, 1986. 327p. (British Library occasional papers, 7)

Describes holdings of the British Library and its divisions; the India Office Library; libraries of the Universities of Cambridge, Oxford, and London; the Royal Asiatic Society; the national libraries of India, of Pakistan, of Sri Lanka, and of Australia; the Nehru Memorial Library; and the Shastri IndoCanadian Institute. Contains detailed reports on bibliographical projects such as SAMP (the Library of Congress bibliographical, processing, and microfilming program on South Asia) and the multivolume catalog of topographical prints of South Asia, prepared by the India Office staff. Papers on Asian resources in Denmark, France, Germany, Italy, Netherlands, Poland, and Czechoslovakia. An indispensable handbook.

M54

Ghosh, A., ed. *An encyclopedia of Indian archaeology.* New Delhi: Munshiram Manoharlal Publishers, 1989. 2v.

V.1 contains twenty chapters with broad topical arrangement. Includes paleobotany, settlement patterns, skeletal remains, pottery, and other aspects of material culture. Each chapter is divided into subsections, and the bibliographies follow these subsections. The chapter on culture summarizes Indian cultures from the Paleolithic era through the twelfth century. V.2 provides a gazetteer with a 470-page alphabetic list of all known archaeological sites in India to 1980. Each of these entries includes a reference to a published report on that site.

M55

Hockings, Paul. *Encyclopedia of world cultures: Volume 3: South India.* New York: Hall, 379p.

Bangladesh, Bhutan, India, Maldives, Mauritius, Nepal, Pakistan, and Sri Lanka are included. There is a long introduction and cultural summaries by fifty-nine scholars. An alphabetic arrangement of concise factual material. There is a thirty-one-page appendix of additional castes, caste clusters, and indigenous ethnic groups, with cross-references to appropriate sections of the main text. Find also the filmography and ethnonym index.

M56

Roy, Ashim Kumar, and N. N. Gidwani. *A dictionary of indology.* New Delhi: Oxford and IBH Publishing, 1983–86. 4v.

Includes influence of India on Afghanistan, Central Asia, China, Indonesia, Japan, Korea, Malaysia, South Asia (Bangladesh, India, Nepal, Pakistan, Sri Lanka), Thailand, and Vietnam. Twenty-five hundred entries by established scholars for subjects such as Buddhist jataka tales, archaeology, language and linguistics, ichnography, mythology, and sociology.

M57

Saletore, Rajaram Narayam. *Encyclopaedia of Indian culture.* New Delhi: Sterling, 1981–85. 5v.

Entries arranged chronologically. Includes art, astronomy, erotica, folklore, geography, and religions. Based on original source material in Kannada, Sanskrit, Pali, and Prakrit. Detailed index.

More specialized topical dictionaries are useful in studies of complex cultural traditions. Nunn's *Asia* **(L06)** can be consulted to add many entries. Especially useful: Margaret Stutley and James Stutley's *Harper's dictionary of Hinduism: Its mythology, folklore, philosophy, literature, and history* (New York: Harper, 1977 [372p.]) **(M58),** with 2,500 entries providing historical, philosophical, and religious analysis. More than 1,000 references are used to support the explanatory statements of the entries.

THE BUDDHIST KINGDOMS

Exhaust first Balay's *Guide to reference books* **(B02).** See also the more general section of "Southeast Asia" in Nunn's *Asia* **(L06)** for additional reference sources on "Burma," Laos, and Thailand. Many of the reference works developed for South Asia include coverage of these countries, and for "Burma" the reference sources identified in the more general section on Southeast Asia are especially important. See also Graham Shaw's "The South Asia and Burma retrospective bibliography (SABREB)," in *South Asian studies: Papers presented at a colloquium 24–26 April, 1985,* p.135–44, ed. by Albertaine Gaur (London: British Library, 1986 [327p.]) (British Library occasional papers, 7) **(M59).**

Retrospective Searches

Consult this strategic search heading in the more general section of this chapter, in chapter 1, and in the chapters devoted to the subdisciplines of anthropology.

Retrospective Bibliographies—Broad Scope

M60

Chaudhuri, Sibadas. *Bibliography of Tibetan studies: Being a record of printed publications mainly in European languages.* Calcutta: Asiatic Society, 1971, 1973. 232p.

Arranges 2,000 entries in thirteen categories, including bibliography, anthropology, ethnology, archaeology, dance, and linguistics. Covers all Western languages and romanized Japanese. A classified subject index of sixty-four pages.

M61

Goonetileke, H. A. I. *A bibliography of Ceylon: A systematic guide to the literature on the land, people, history and culture published in Western languages from the sixteenth century to the present day.* Zug, Switzerland: Inter Documentation, 1970–73. (Bibliothica Asiatica, no.5, 14)

V.1 and v.2 were published in 1970; v.3 and 2d ed. were published in 1973. This general bibliography of Ceylon (Sri Lanka) has an organization that permits the identification of sections of interest to anthropologists such as those on physical anthropology and ethnology of racial and indigenous ethnic groups, on social organization, on cultural and social change, on religions, on folk religion and popular religious cults, on folklore, and on games, sports, and amusements.

M62

Hedrick, Basil C., comp. *A bibliography of Nepal.* Metuchen, N.J.: Scarecrow, 1973. 302p.

Lists 3,300 entries under subject categories, including "Anthropology," "Archaeology," and "Sociology." There is an author index, and the preface promises annotations in the next edition. Includes books, journal articles, and unpublished manuscripts. Author index.

Searching Graphic Materials

Consult Spencer and Johnson's *Atlas for anthropology* **(A65)** for monographic references tied to maps of culture area distribution, and Heider's *Films for anthropological teaching* **(A63)** for select entry into another massive body of material.

Maps

M63

Breton, Roland J. L. *Atlas géographique des langues et des ethnies de l'Indie et du subcontinent: Bangladesh, Pakistan, Sri Lanka, Népal, Bhoutan, Sikkim.* Québec: Presses de l'Université Laval, 1976. 648p. (Travaux du Centre International de Recherche sur le Bilinguisme, A-10)

An exhaustive coverage of the distribution of indigenous ethnic groups and languages in India and contiguous areas. After introducing the reader to the rationale of the study, the work is divided by geographic units. There is a discussion of the languages distributed in these units, a classification of languages (p.631–48), an index to the statistical tables (p.581–84) with the extensive tables (p.585–629) and an index by language (p.550). The bibliography has a classified arrangement (p.562–79).

M64

Schwartzberg, Joseph E., and Shiva G. Bajpai. *A historical atlas of South Asia.* Chicago: Univ. of Chicago Pr., 1978. 352p. (Association for Asian Studies. Reference series, no.2)

Cartographic record covering Afghanistan, Bangladesh, Bhutan, India, Nepal, Pakistan, Sri Lanka, and the Maldives from the Paleolithic period to the present.

Searching Unpublished Materials

Consult Nunn's *Asia* **(L06)** for coverage of dissertations. The most comprehensive coverage of the complex opportunities for entry into this complex body of materials is provided by Pearson's *South Asian bibliography* **(M05).** Increasingly, dissertations are included in topical bibliographies. Some regional bibliographies include unpublished materials. An example would be Hedrick's *A bibliography of Nepal* **(M62).** Less useful is the National Anthropological Archives, *Catalog to manuscripts at the National Anthropological Archives* **(A69).**

SOUTHEAST ASIA

This section assumes that the reader has exhausted Balay's *Guide to reference books* **(B02).** The most useful guides to the literature can be found in *Southeast Asian research tools* **(M65).** This resource warrants careful use. Each unit is organized to serve as a selection guide in collection building. Collectively they comprise the best available guide to reference sources in this important culture area. For selective retrospective searches into the scholarly periodical literature, consult Johnson's *Index to Southeast Asian journals* **(M73)** and **(M74).** For more comprehensive coverage that includes monographs and microforms, consult the Library of Congress's *Southeast Asia subject catalog* **(M76)** and the topical bibliographies **(M78)** through **(M100);** for valuative encyclopedic coverage consult the works compiled by Frank M. LeBar with George N. Appell described at **(M101).** For work on Muslim populations, entries of value can be found in Lim's *The Malay world of Southeast Asia* **(M92)** and chapter 11, "The Islamic Influence and Israel," including Lent and Mulliner's *Malaysian studies* **(P58).**

In the anthropological investigation of Southeast Asia, all searches can make a productive start with Nunn's *Asia* **(L06).** In that guide, consult especially chapter (G), "Southeast Asia," for directories, atlases, subject bibliographies in the social sciences, dissertations, maps, and bibliographies of materials in Russian, other Western languages, Chinese, and Japanese; chapter (H), "Burma," for encyclopedias, yearbooks, handbooks, dictionaries, directories, gazetteers, census materials, statistics, and bibliographies. See also chapter (O), "Vietnam," for handbooks, encyclopedias, dictionaries, directories, gazetteers, censuses, statistics, and bibliographies of official publications, periodicals, and dissertations as well as subject bibliographies of social sciences, languages, religions, and history. See chapter (N), "Thailand," for encyclopedias, handbooks, dictionaries, directories, gazetteers, censuses, statistics, and bibliographies in Thai and Western languages that cover the social sciences and history; chapter (K), "Laos," with reference sources as itemized in the section on South Asia; chapter (J), "Indonesia," for encyclopedias, handbooks, yearbooks, dictionaries, directories, atlases, gazetteers, censuses, statistics, bibliographies of bibliographies, official publications, subject bibliographies in the social sciences, and dissertations; chapter (L), "Malaysia" and "Singapore" for handbooks, yearbooks, dictionaries, directories, dissertations, atlases, gazetteers, censuses, periodicals, and subject bibliographies covering the social sciences, literature, history, and geography. Chapter (M), "Philippines," for encyclopedias, handbooks, yearbooks, dictionaries, directories, atlases, gazetteers, periodicals, dissertations, maps, and subject bibliographies covering the social sciences, languages, history, and geography.

Searching Bibliographic Guides

The body of bibliographic guides used to define the chapters under this heading serve as our bibliographic base. Consult especially Auckland's "Getting into the literature" **(A01)** and the guides under this heading in the chapters of *Fieldwork in the Library* devoted to the subdisciplines of anthropology.

Bibliographic Guides

M65

University of Hawaii at Manoa. Southeast Asian Studies Program. *Southeast Asian research tools.* Honolulu: Southeast Asian Studies, Asian Studies Program, University of Hawaii, 1979. 9v. (Southeast Asia paper; v.16 [parts 1–9])

Includes pt.1, Saito, S., *Summary and needs* [64p.]; pt.2, Char, L. H., *Indonesia* [189p.]; pt.3, Thwin, M. A., *Burma* [67p.]; pt.4, Roff, W. R., *Malaysia, Singapore, Brunei* [125p.]; pt.5, Baradi, E. R., *The Philippines* [304p.]; pt.6, Keyes, C. F., *Thailand* [188p.]; pt.7, Keyes, C. F., *Laos* [69p.]; pt.8, Keyes, C. F., *Cambodia* [70p.]; pt.9, Cotter, M. G., *Vietnam* [49p.]. This bibliography was sponsored by the Association for Asian Studies and developed primarily as an instrument for rationalizing collection development. It has value far beyond that narrow use. Often neglected as a reference source, it makes a major contribution to bibliographic control of the area's literature with its many guides to the reference sources (including publications in the vernacular languages). No section of these works can be neglected. The introductory and general bibliography sections in each of these works often yield sources of value in anthropological searches. Koninklijk Instituut voor Taal-, Land-en Volkenkunde, *Bibliographical survey of Thailand: Based on books in the library of the Royal Institute of Linguistics and Anthropology and on articles of the Journal of the Siam Society,* Gerald A. Nagelkerke, comp. (Leiden, Netherlands: Library, Royal Institute of Linguistics and Anthropology, 1974 [63p.]) **(M66)** is listed only in the "bibliography" section of the *Thailand* volume, even though multiple listings sometimes occur in this work. Again, under "Bibliographies: General" for the volume *Malaysia, Singapore, Brunei,* nothing indicates the anthropological value of the work by Karl Josef Pelzer, *West Malaysia and Singapore: A selected bibliography,* described under the subheading "Retrospective bibliographies—Topical bibliographies" **(M93),** even though its section "Man and culture" (p.130–231) is specific to the interests of ethnologists and may be definitive for scholarly contributions. Again, listed in the volume *Burma,* under "Bibliographies" without explication of its limitations, Trager's *Burma* **(M99)** was written as a survey but is still of considerable reference value if carefully used with its stated limitations fully understood. Excludes articles in the *Journal* of the Burma Research Society and works listed in Frank N. Trager's earlier *Furnivall of Burma; Annotated bibliography of the works of John S. Furnivall,* 1953, reprint (New Haven, Conn.: Yale Univ. Pr., 1963 [51p.]) (Southeast Asia studies bibliography series, no.8) **(M67),** with long annotations and excellent organization first as list and then in topically arranged sections.

Searching for Current Materials

An inspection for frequency of citation in each section of Johnson's *Index to Southeast Asian journals* **(M73)** and **(M74)** will quickly reveal the journals with an interest in each of the individual nation-states. These journals often include sections that also address current awareness issues such as a department for book reviews. This is especially true of journals sponsored by a society or by a professional association.

Selective Lists of Scholarly Journals

M68

United States. Library of Congress. *Southeast Asia: Western-language periodicals in the Library of Congress.* A. Kohar Rony, comp. Washington, D.C.: Southern Asia Section. Asia Division. Library of Congress, 1979. 201p.

For sale by the Superintendent of Documents of the U.S. Government Printing Office. For the identification of the several reference works that describe the serials in this area, consult Nunn's *Asia* **(L06).**

Retrospective Searches

When retrospective searches include searches for descriptions of indigenous peoples, consult the Human Relations Area Files's *HRAF source bibliography* **(D16)** and the Museum of Mankind Library's "Tribal index" [microfiche] **(D13).** For continuing coverage of the periodical output, consult *Anthropological literature* **(A36),** *Anthropological index* **(A35),** and *Abstracts in anthropology* **(A32).** The annual *International bibliography of social and cultural anthropology* **(D20)** succeeds in maintaining some ethnic-group entry in its indexing.

Retrospective Bibliographies—Bibliographies of Bibliographies

M69

Choo Ming, Ding. *A bibliography of bibliographies on Malaysia.* Petaling, Java: Hexagon Elite Publications, 1981. 184p.

Arranges 504 items under twenty-two categories with author index and title index. Long, descriptive annotations. The general bibliography contains many items of regional significance. For example, N. Blakiston's "Maps, plans and charts of Southeast Asia in the Pacific Records Office," *Southeast Asian archives* 2 (1969): 21–54 **(M70).** The social science section includes F. L. Dunn and A. V. Peacock's "Annotated bibliography of Malayan (West Malaysian) archaeology, 1962–1969," *Asian perspectives* 14 (1971): 43–48 **(M71),** which includes general review articles on Malaysia in the context of Southeast Asian prehistory.

Retrospective Bibliographies—Broad Scope

M72

Hill, Ronald David. *Index Indochinese: An English and French index to Revue Indochinoise, Extrême-Asie, Extrême-Asie—Revue Indochinoise and La Revue Indochinoise Juridique et Économique.* Hong Kong: Centre for Asian Studies, University of Hong Kong, 1983. 155 leaves. (Centre of Asian Studies. Bibliographies and research guides, no.22)

All of Asia was covered by these journals during the time period indexed. It is basic for the area of Southeast Asia covered. Especially useful for the identification of early contact materials and publications in French of the more recent work by scholars with anthropological training.

M73

Johnson, Donald Clay. *Index to Southeast Asian journals, 1960–1974: A guide to articles, book reviews, and composite works.* Boston: Hall, 1977. 811p.

M74

Johnson, Donald Clay. *Index to Southeast Asian journals, 1975–1979: A guide to articles, book reviews, and composite works.* Boston: Hall, 1982. 265p.

Limited to forty-one scholarly journals. Classified arrangement of articles, with second section for book reviews. For French-language materials, consult also Hill's *Index Indochinese* **(M72).**

M75

Lim, Huck-Tee, and D. E. K. Wijasuriya. "Index Malaysiana: An index to the *Journal* of the Malayan Branch of the Royal Asiatic

Society," *Journal of the Malayan Branch of the Royal Asiatic Society* 36: 4 (1970): 1–395.

Supplement 1964–73. Two sequences with full bibliographic descriptions, both by author and title and by Library of Congress classification. *See* and *see also* references are abundant. The cumulation of indexing has been an editorial policy of this journal since 1878. In its entirety this serial is probably the best single source for English-language material that is sensitive to the scope of anthropological research about Southeast Asia.

M76

United States. Library of Congress. Orientalia Division. *Southeast Asia subject catalog.* Boston: Hall, 1972. 6v.

Citations to books, journal articles, theses, and microforms in Western languages. Sections on each country are subdivided by subject, including "Anthropology" and "Archaeology." For the identification of reference works that describe the serial publications about this area, consult Nunn's *Asia* **(L06)** under the heading "Searching Bibliographic Guides."

Retrospective Bibliographies—Topical

M77

Bernot, Denise. *Bibliographie birmane, années 1950–1960.* Paris: Éditions du Centre National de la Recherche Scientifique, 1968. 231p. (Atlas ethnolinguistique. Troisieme série. bibliographies)

Compiled as a supplement on Burma in Embree and Dotson's *Bibliography of the peoples and cultures of mainland Southeast Asia* (1950) **(M104),** with classed arrangement. See also Trager's *Burma* **(M99),** Shulman's *Burma* **(M105),** and Cordier *Bibliotheca Indosinica* **(M80).**

M78

Boutin, Michael, and Alanna Boutin. *Indigenous groups of Sabah: An annotated bibliography of linguistics and anthropological sources.* Sabah, E. Malaysia: Institut Linguistik, SIL, 1984–86. 2v. (Sabah Museum monograph, no.1, no.2)

Extensive annotations arranged by author, with an ethnic group index and a topical index. A list of ethnic groups and a list of topics covered are provided.

M79

Boutin, Michael, and Alanna Boutin. *Indigenous groups of Sabah: An annotated bibliography of linguistic and anthropological sources; Supplement 1.* Kota Kinabalu, Malaysia: Summer Institute of Linguistics in cooperation with the Government of the State of Sabah, Malaysia, 1985. 328p. (Sabah Museum monograph, no.1 [pt.2])

An ethnographic and linguistic bibliography in a classed arrangement. Author index.

M80

Cordier, Henri. *Bibliotheca Indosinica: Dictionaire bibliographique des ouvrages relatifs à la Péninsule Indochinoise.* Paris: Imprimerie Nationale E. Leroux, 1912–15. 4v. (Publications de l'École Française d'Extrême Orient, v.15–18)

Lists 20,000 items in all European languages. Standard bibliography for Vietnam (Indo-China), Burma, and Malaya. Covers all fields of scholarly and scientific knowledge.

M81

Cotter, Michael. *Vietnam: A guide to reference sources.* Boston: Hall, 1977. 272p.

Some 1,400 reference sources divided into a section for general reference, followed by sections for the major disciplines. The introduction must be read for information on forms used, for abbreviations, and for the coding practices that support the index and serve as annotations. Funded in part by the Vietnam Studies Group of the Association for Asian Studies. See also Hill's *Index Indochinese* **(M72)** and the Library of Congress's *Southeast Asia: Western-language periodicals in the Library of Congress* **(M68).**

M82

Herbert, Patricia, and Anthony Milner. *South East Asia: Languages and literature: A select guide.* Honolulu: Univ. of Hawaii Pr., 1989. 182p.

Sponsored by the South East Asia Library Group to meet the needs of scholars who rely less and less on European-language source materials.

For each country there is coverage of background, dating systems, language and script, manuscripts, printing, and literature. Reference bibliography at end of each chapter. Consult also DeMiller's *Linguistics* **(E01)** for detailed annotations to the available cumulative bibliographies of the area, including Franklin E. Huffman's *Bibliography and index of mainland Southeast Asian languages and linguistics* (New Haven, Conn.: Yale Univ. Pr., 1986 [640p.]), which incorporates and brings up to date the two standard bibliographies of the field to provide a list of 10,000 entries.

M83

Higham, Charles. *The archaeology of mainland Southeast Asia from 10,000 B.C. to the fall of Angkor.* Cambridge, England: Cambridge Univ. Pr., 1989. 387p.

Geographic boundaries of the modern nation-state are strictly observed. Stresses importance of a sedentary lifestyle and domestication. Finds origins of civilization rooted in local change. Argues that any increase in population size and economic inequality is proof of political development. For a record of recent contributions to the study of the relationship between South China and Southeast Asia, consult issues of the *Journal of Hong Kong Archaeological Society,* v.1– , 1969– (Hong Kong: The Society) **(M84),** an annual.

M85

Huffman, Franklin E. *Bibliography and index of mainland Southeast Asian languages and linguistics.* New Haven, Conn.: Yale Univ. Pr., 1986. 640p. (Yale language series)

Lists 10,000 titles. Cross-references. Detailed subject index to long author list. English translations for titles in rarely spoken languages and for Asian languages. Includes Austroasiatic (including Khmer and Vietnamese), Tibeto-Burman, Tai-Kadai, Miao-Yao, and mainland Austronesian (Cham, but not Malay).

M86

Keyes, Charles F. "Ethnography and anthropological interpretation in the study of Thailand." In *The study of Thailand: Analyses of knowledge, approaches and prospects in anthropology, art history, economics, history, and political science.* Ed. by Eliezer B. Ayal. Athens: Ohio University, Center for International Studies. Southeast Asia Program, 1978. 257p. (Southeast Asia series, no.54)

Lists 197 entries. Twenty-nine entries are annotated. Consolidates and reviews important work in the area. See also Hill's *Index Indochinese* **(M72).**

M87

Koentjaraningrat. *Anthropology in Indonesia: A bibliographical review.* The Hague: Nijhoff, 1975. 343p. (Bibliographical series. Instituut voor Taal-, Land-en Volkenkunde, v.8)

A long, descriptive, and evaluative essay followed by an alphabetic list (by author) of references cited. A review of cultural anthropology for the area. Consult also Gerald A. Nagelkerke's *Bibliografisch overzicht uit periodieken over Indonesie 1930–1945 (Bibliographical survey based on periodicals on Indonesia)* (Leiden, Netherlands: Stationsplein 10: Bibliotheek Koninklijk Instituut voor Taal-, Land-en Volkenkunde, 1974 [232p.]) **(M88),** which lists 3,159 articles arranged geographically with a subject index. See also the older and most valuable Raymond Kennedy, Thomas W. Maretzki, and H. Th. Fischer, *Bibliography of Indonesia peoples and cultures,* 2d ed. (New Haven, Conn.: Human Relations Area Files, 1955 [2v.]) **(M89),** with its excellent arrangement by islands and then by peoples or indigenous ethnic groups. Items are in a helpful classed arrangement, but there is no index. More recently, David J. Stuart-Fox's *Bibliography of Bali: Publications from 1920 to 1990* (Detroit: Cellar Book Shop distributor for KITLV Pr., 1992 [708p.]) **(M90)** documents the flood of anthropological information included in the 8,000 entries divided into 109 subject categories. There are indexes of authors, of corporate authors, and subjects. Herman C. Kemp's *Annotated bibliography of bibliographies on Indonesia* **(M91)** is organized to identify bibliographies about a geographic area. In the case of Bali, he cites 29 bibliographies.

M92

Lim, Patricia Pui Huen. *The Malay world of Southeast Asia: A select cultural bibliography.* Singapore: Program on the Cultural Heritage of Southeast Asia. Institute of Southeast Asian Studies, 1986. 456p.

Lists 5,327 books, articles, and dissertations. Comprises Brunei, Indonesia, Singapore, Thailand, Malaysia, and the Philippines. Anthropology is subdivided by geographical area. Author index. Detailed coverage in a classed arrangement of related disciplines such as sociology and literature.

M93

Pelzer, Karl Joseph. *West Malaysia and Singapore.* New Haven, Conn.: Human Relations Area Files Pr., 1971. 394p.

Best works on anthropology are listed in "General" section.

M94

Rony, A. Kohar, comp. *Vietnamese holdings in the Library of Congress: A bibliography.* Washington, D.C.: Library of Congress; dist., Washington, D.C.: U.S. GPO, 1982. 236p.

Lists 2,902 monographic entries, 217 serial entries, and 27 newspapers. See also *Vietnam,* described in **(M65).**

M95

Saito, Shiro. *Philippine ethnography: A critically annotated and selected bibliography.* Honolulu: Univ. Pr. of Hawaii, 1972. 512p. (East-West bibliographic series)

Most comprehensive work to date. Includes books, journal articles, and official publications published in the major Western languages. Adequate subject and geographic entry. C. Richard Gieser has recently compiled the *Bibliography of the Summer Institute of Linguistics: Philippines 1953–1988* (Manila: Summer Institute of Linguistics, 1989 [206p.]) **(M96),** which shows sensitivity to ethnographic issues, with entry by name of indigenous ethnic group.

M97

Thailand: An annotated bibliography on local and regional development. Prepared in collaboration with the Library and Information Center. National Institute of Development Administration. Bangkok. Nagoya, Japan: United Nations Centre for Regional development, 1982. 168p. index. (Country bibliography series, no.6)

Covers regional problems with an emphasis on plan formulation and implementation, rural development, rural urban linkages, and similar topics. The first of the volume's two sections consists of a subject, author, and title index. The second section provides bibliographic citations and annotations for 388 publications. Addresses social science concerns relevant to the people who live in Thailand. Previous volumes in this series focused on Japan, India, the Philippines, and Pakistan. Annotated.

M98

Tiamson, Alfredo T. *Muslim Filipinos.* Manila: Filipinas Foundation, 1979. 388p.

Arranged alphabetically by author, with multiple entries for each author in a second list by date of publication. Detailed annotations in English. Includes theses and dissertations, book and journal articles. The introduction is a scholarly review of the literature. There is a valuable list of relevant scholarly journals. Subject index.

M99

Trager, Frank N. *Burma: A selected and annotated bibliography.* New Haven, Conn.: Human Relations Area Files Pr., 1973. 356p.

Excludes work of J. S. Furnivall and C. H. Luce. Excludes articles in the *Journal* of the Burma Research Society for which Johnson's *Index to Southeast Asian journals* **(M73)** and **(M74)** can be consulted. Can be supplemented by reference to Bernot's *Bibliographie birmane* **(M77)** and the more general reference sources for both South Asia and Southeast Asia. A companion piece deserves attention: New York University, Burma Research Project, *Japanese and Chinese language sources on Burma: An annotated bibliography,* ed. by F. N. Trager (New York: New York University, Burma Research Project, 1957 [122p.]) **(M100),** which has 229 entries. For a more recent bibliography, consult Shaw's "The South Asian and Burma retrospective bibliography" **(M59).**

Informational Reference Searches

Across chapters this heading introduces lists of reference books that answer an inquiry for summaries of anthropological results and for brief descriptions of institutions or address information for individuals. Any search of informational sources can at some point move from other chapters back to chapter 1 for an inspection of resources under the subheading "State-of-the-Art Reviews." Find there the *Annual review of anthropology* **(A57)** with its summary coverage of recent research activity. Many searches that start in other chapters can profitably return to chapter 1 of *Fieldwork in the Library.* For example, few directories scattered through this text are as up to date as *AAA guide* **(A53),** which provides address and other information relevant to contemporary American anthropology.

State-of-the-Art Reviews

M101

LeBar, Frank M., and George N. Appell. *Ethnic groups of mainland Southeast Asia.* New Haven, Conn.: Human Relations Area Files Pr., 1964. 288p.

Concise ethnographic descriptions in terms of major language stocks, with distinctions between lowland and upland groups. Provides selective bibliographies for 151 groups, including those of southern China, when they are culturally related. Ethnographic maps and ethnic indexes increase the reference value of this encyclopedic treatment.

M102

LeBar, Frank M. *Ethnic groups of insular Southeast Asia.* New Haven, Conn.: Human Relations Area Files Pr., 1972–75. 2v.

V.1, *Indonesia, Andaman Island, and Madagascar;* v.2, *Philippines and Formosa.* Descriptive summaries are evaluative and supported by bibliographies. Ethnic and terminological indexes with ethnolinguistic maps. Nineteen recognized scholars contributed to this work. A fuller, unedited manuscript is available as Frank M. LeBar, *Ethnic groups of insular Southeast Asia* (New Haven, Conn.: Human Relations Area Files Pr., 1976–77 [6v. in 4 sections]) **(M103).** An older source by John F. Embree and Lillian Ota Dotson, *Bibliography of the peoples and cultures of mainland Southeast Asia* (New York: Russell and Russell, 1972 (c1959) [821p.]) **(M104),** is an extensive arrangement of listed books and articles in English and European languages, first by general area, then by indigenous ethnic group, and finally by subject. Detailed table of contents, but no indexes. Still valuable for its organization and scope. Consult also Bernot's *Bibliographie birmane* **(M77).**

Searching Unpublished Materials

Consult Nunn's *Asia* **(L06)** for coverage of dissertations. The most comprehensive coverage of the complex opportunities for entry into this complex body of materials is provided by Pearson's *South Asian bibliography* **(M05).** Increasingly, dissertations are included in topical bibliographies. Less useful is the National Anthropological Archives's *Catalog to manuscripts at the National Anthropological Archives* **(A69).**

Dissertations

M105

Shulman, Frank Joseph. *Burma: An annotated bibliographical guide to international doctoral dissertation research 1898–1985.* Lanham, Md.: Univ. Pr. of America; Washington, D.C.: Wilson Center, 1986. 247p.

Lists 707 dissertations of which 285 are primarily about Burma, with the rest having Burma material in a regional study. Descriptive annotations for the bibliographic entries, which are arranged by broad subject. Indexes by author and institution, and a subject index that has an adequate expansion of terms.

M106

Stephens, Helen L. *Theses on South East Asia 1965–1985 accepted in the United Kingdom and Ireland.* Hull, England: Centre for South East Asian Studies. University of Hull, 1986. 74p. (Bibliography and literature series, no.1)

Table of contents with numerous subdivisions under geographic headings (includes Papua New Guinea). Indexes by subject and author/title.

SOUTHWEST ASIA

This section assumes that the reader has exhausted Balay's *Guide to reference books* **(B02).** A number of reference sources with value for the anthropological investigation of this region are described in chapter 11, "The Islamic Influence and Israel," including Wilber's *Annotated bibliography of Afghanistan* **(P52).** Consult also Hanifi's *Historical and cultural dictionary of Afghanistan* **(M52)** for the more general sources listed there.

Retrospective Searches

When retrospective searches include searches for descriptions of indigenous peoples, consult the Human Relations Area Files's *HRAF source bibliography* **(D16)** and the Museum of Mankind Library's "Tribal index" [microfiche] **(D13).** For continuing coverage of the periodical output, consult *Anthropological literature* **(A36),** *Anthropological index* **(A35),** and *Abstracts in anthropology* **(A32).** The annual *International bibliography of social and cultural anthropology* **(D20)** succeeds in maintaining some ethnic-group entry in its indexing.

Retrospective Bibliographies—Broad Scope

M107

Berghe, Louis vanden, B. de Wulf, and E. Haerinck. *Bibliographie analytique de l'archeologie de l'Iran ancien.* Leiden, Netherlands: Brill, 1979. 329p.

Alphabetic list of sites with bibliographic information for all published research relevant to that site. Detailed table of contents guides the reader.

M108

Field, Henry. *Bibliography on southwestern Asia.* Coral Gables, Fla.: Univ. of Miami Pr., 1953–62.

V.1, 1953 [106p.]; v.2, 1955 [126p.]; v.3, 1956 [230p.]; v.4, 1957 [464p.]; v.5, 1958 [275p.]; v.6, 1959 [328p.]; v.7, 1962 [305p.]. This work is supplemented by *Southwestern Asia: Supplement* (Coconut Grove, Fla.: Field Research Projects, 1968–72 [8v. in 7]): v.1, 1968 [92p.]; v.4, *Anthropology, maps, botany and zoology,* 1969 [78p.]; v.7, *Anthropogeography, botany, and zoology,* 1972 [68p.].

Comprehensive on anthropology and geography in all languages for the area that extends from Istanbul to the Hindu Kush on the north, and from Aden to the Makran coast on the south. Many works published by Field Research Projects, such as Rodman E. Snead's *Bibliography on the Makran regions of Iran and west Pakistan,* ed. by Henry Field (Coconut Grove, Fla.: Field Research Projects, 1970 [38p.]), evade the normal channels of bibliographic review and distribution. There is Edith W. Ware's *Subject index to bibliographies on southwestern Asia, 1–5 (1959–61), published in 19 parts.* Pt.1, *Anthropogeography* (Coconut Grove, Fla.: Field Research Projects, 1961 [157p.]) **(M109).**

M110

Nawabi, Y. M. *A bibliography of Iran: A catalogue of books and articles on Iranian subjects, mainly in European languages.* Tehran: Cultural Studies and Research Institute, 1987. 7v. to date.

V.7, *Linguistics,* has extensive coverage of Iranian languages and dialects, with an addendum on Persian languages and literatures. Inspect *Abstracts in German anthropology* **(A33)** for current English-language annotations to recent reports on the vigorous German activity in this region.

M111

Pearson, James Douglas. *A bibliography of pre-Islamic Persia.* London: Mansell, 1975. 288p. (Persians studies series, no.2)

Classed arrangement of 7,300 items under four major subject headings, with a detailed table of contents. Absolutely accurate.

Retrospective bibliography—Continuing

M112

Internationale Jahresbibliographie Südwesasien (International annual bibliography South

West Asia): SWA. Jahrg. 1, 1985– . Osnabrück: F. Dietriich.

The three-year lag between the end of coverage of research and publication does not seem to be excessive given the difficulty of coverage in this area. A classified arrangement of books, articles, book reviews, Festschriften, and conference proceedings. In recognition of the cultural cohesion, extends into Africa through the Sudan.

THE PACIFIC

Searching Bibliographic Guides

In chapter 1 anthropological reference sources provide important entry into Pacific materials. Consult Auckland's "Getting into the literature" **(A01)** for guidance. Consult also the guide to the literature in *Fieldwork in the Library* in each of the chapters on the subdisciplines of anthropology. Note also *HRAF source bibliography* **(D16),** with its printed index to printed materials held in research libraries. It is especially strong in its coverage of the Pacific region and provides entry into materials held in hard copy in the stacks of a research library collection.

Bibliographic Guides

N01

Jackson, Miles M., ed. *Pacific Island studies: A survey of the literature.* Westport, Conn.: Greenwood Pr., 1986. 244p. index. (Bibliographies and indexes in sociology, no.7)

Unannotated bibliographies limited to recent English-language work are used to support bibliographic essays by experts for all areas of native life in the Pacific. A second volume describing more advanced reference sources is promised. Taylor's *A Pacific bibliography* **(N10),** because its classed arrangement is sensitive to anthropological concerns and because of its comprehensive coverage, is the best guide to early sources. Most English-language bibliographies since Taylor have been local in coverage and are listed under appropriate regional sections in Gerald W. Fry's *Pacific basin and Oceania* (Oxford, England: Clio, 1987 [468p.]) (World bibliographical series, v.70) **(N02),** where lucid annotations encourage entry into a select group of resources (and a very few reference sources) listed in the classed arrangement that is usual for this series.

For Russian-language materials, consult O. O. Tumarkin's "Main trends in the USSR in the ethnographic study of Pacific Islands peoples, 1961–1988," *Pacific studies: A journal devoted to the study of the Pacific—Its islands and adjacent countries,* 11, no.2 (1988): 97–120 **(N03).** For serial bibliographies that continue the record of Russian publication, consult Ruble and Teeter's *A scholar's guide to humanities and the social sciences in the Soviet Union* **(A38).**

Searching for Current Materials

Any effort to keep current with the output and research activities of each of the special subdisciplines in anthropology will be rewarded by an inspection of the entries listed under this heading in the chapters devoted to the subdisciplines of anthropology. There is an Internet address for Pacific Rim archaeology: Pacarc-L @Wsuvmi through (Bitnet) Listserv@Wsuvm1 (Internet).

Select Sources of Review in Scholarly Journals

N04

Archaeology in Oceania. v.1– , 1966– . Sydney, Australia: University of Sydney. 3/yr.

Often six book reviews an issue. Previously titled *Archaeology and physical anthropology* (1960–80). Primarily archaeology and physical anthropology of the western Pacific Rim. Issues sometimes focus on a theme to provide a summary review of research on a topic to the date of publication.

N05

Oceania. v.1– , 1930– . Sydney: Oceania Publications, University of Sydney. Quarterly.

Each issue will review between five and twenty-five books primarily on anthropological and linguistic topics. Covers the indigenous peoples of Australia, Melanesia, Micronesia, and Polynesia. There is a department "Publications received." Because this resource has such a long history of leadership in the publication of results of anthropological research in the Pacific culture area, we mention for retrospective use *Oceania* 6 (1): 1–131, for author/title and keyword subject index to v.1–60.

Retrospective Searches

Find several sources that organize entry under geographically defined areas. Consult first the Tozzer Library's *Author and subject catalogues of the Tozzer Library* [microfiche] **(A26)** and the older hardcover edition of Peabody Museum Library's *Catalogue* [microfiche] **(A29)** for author and classified subject entry to monographs, periodical articles, and the internal contents of books. This resource has a companion for coverage of monographs in the British Museum, Museum of Mankind Library's *Museum of Mankind Library catalogues* [microfiche] **(A25)**, which includes a sustained classified subject index to monographic and pamphlet publications.

Retrospective Bibliographies—Bibliographies of Bibliographies

N06

Leeson, Ida. *A bibliography of bibliographies of the South Pacific.* Published under the auspices of the South Pacific Commission. London and New York: Oxford Univ. Pr., 1954. 61p.

General and subject bibliographies appearing in books and periodicals. Index. Can be informally updated for anthropological materials by consulting Library-Anthropology Resource Group's *Anthropological bibliographies* **(A21)**. For Melanesia, in which there is much current anthropological research interest, consult Colin Filer and Papiya Chakravarti's *A bibliography of Melnesian bibliographies* (Borokp, Papua New Guinea: University of Papua New Guinea, Department of Anthropology and Sociology, 1990 [42p.]) (Occasional paper, no.5).

N07

Thompson, Anne-Gabrielle. *Southwest Pacific: An annotated guide to bibliographies, indexes and collections in Australian libraries.* Canberra: Research School of Pacific Studies, The Australian National University in association with the Academy of Social Sciences in Australia, 1986. 126p. (Aids to research series [ANU.RSPS] no. A/6).

Lists 479 entries. A comprehensive and annotated bibliography of the area of the Pacific that has recently seen the most research activity. Listed under six geographic subject headings, with subdivisions for broad subject topics. Author and subject indexes.

Retrospective Bibliographies—Broad Scope

N08

Bernice P. Bishop Museum. Library. Honolulu. *Dictionary catalog of the Library of the Bernice P. Bishop Museum.* Boston: Hall, 1964. 9v.

First supplement [microform] (1967), *Second supplement* [microform] (1969). Lists 150,000 entries. Cataloging includes subject entries for internal contents of early exploration accounts. Useful for all areas of the Pacific.

N09

New South Wales. The Mitchell Library. *Dictionary catalog of printed books.* Boston: Hall, 1968–69. 38v.

The *First supplement* adds 17,500 entries to the 603,000 photolithographed cards of the basic set, which includes monographs, manuscripts, microfilms, pictures, and 220,000 printed maps. Coverage of the Pacific Islands includes rare holdings such as the early government documents of Tonga.

N10

Taylor, Clyde Romer Hughes. *A Pacific bibliography: Printed matter relating to the native peoples of Polynesia, Melanesia and Micronesia.* 2d ed. Oxford: Clarendon, 1965. 692p.

Arranged by island group and subdivided by topics that are useful to anthropologists. Superb control of books and periodical articles. Definitive within its scope.

Retrospective Bibliographies—Continuing Bibliographies

N11

"Bibliographie de l'Oceanie." *Journal de la Société des Oceanistes.* v.2– , 1946– . Paris: Musée de l'Homme. Annual.

This selective, classified bibliography covers Polynesia, Micronesia, Melanesia, and Australia (excludes the Philippines, Japan, and Indonesia). Emphasis is on anthropology, ethnology, acculturation, and linguistics but also has material on history and geography, economics, art, and literature. The 1,000–1,500 items per year include books, articles, society publications, documents, theses, and newspaper articles that are significant. No index or annotations.

N12

South Pacific periodicals index. v.6– , 1979– . Suva, Fiji: Pacific Information Center in association with University of South Pacific Library. Annual.

Previous title, *Bibliography of periodical articles relating to the South Pacific,* v.1–5, 1974–78. Classed index with coverage of all areas of Melanesia, Micronesia, and Polynesia in 200 journals.

Retrospective Bibliographies—Topical

N13

Goetzfredt, Nicholas J. *Indigenous navigation and voyaging in the Pacific: A reference guide.* Westport, Conn.: Greenwood Pr., 1992. 294p. (Bibliographies and indexes in anthropology, no.6)

Detailed annotations to 694 entries in which the issue of technology in a social context pervades the cited material. Consult also E. H. Bryan, Jr., "Native fishing in the Pacific: An annotated bibliography," in *The fishing cultures of the world: Studies in ethnology, cultural ecology, and folklore,* p.1,025–1,100, ed. by Bela Gunda (Budapest: Akadémiai Kiadó, 1984 [1,253p.]) **(N14),** in which the interrelationship of material culture and the technology of fishing in the Pacific are a dominant issue.

N15

Hanson, Louise, and F. Allan Hanson. *The art of Oceania: A bibliography.* Boston: Hall, 1984. 539p.

Includes monographs, books, journal articles, theses, and dissertations. Brief annotation of some items. Excellent indexes.

N16

Klieneberg, Hans L. *Bibliography of Oceanic linguistics.* London: Oxford Univ. Pr., 1957. 143p. (London Oriental bibliographies, v.1)

A useful bibliography of 2,100 references to books and periodical articles covering the whole of Oceania. Emphasizes linguistic works such as dictionaries, grammars, and individual and comparative studies, leaving aside the extensive literature published in many South Seas languages. Entries are arranged by region and subdivided by language. Some articles include references to reviews. Locates rare material. No annotations. Index of personal and corporate authors.

All branches of the Summer Institute of Linguistics regularly publish local classified bibliographies for this region. Consult Patrick's *Bibliography of the Summer Institute of Linguistics, Papua New Guinea Branch, 1956–1980* **(N75),** for entry by indigenous group into both ethnographic and linguistic materials.

N17

Rumney, Thomas. *Australia, New Zealand, and the Western Pacific: A selected bibliography of geography of the region.* Monticello, Ill.: Vance Bibliographies, 1989. 91p. (Public administration series no. 0198-78X)

Introduction includes a list of thirty-seven journals used as important sources. Arranged by broad topic and alphabetically by author thereunder. "Cultural/social geography" and "Physical/environmental" are especially useful as entry points for anthropological materials.

N18

Sherlock, K. A. *A bibliography of Timor including East (formerly Portuguese) Timor and West (formerly Dutch) Timor and the island of Roti.* Canberra: Research School of Pacific Studies, Australian National University,

1980. 292p. (Aids to research series. Research School of Pacific Studies, no.A-4)

Arranged under seventeen broad subject headings without subdivision. There is a list of periodicals published in Timor (p.274–80). Author index.

Informational Reference Searches

Across chapters this heading introduces lists of reference books that answer an inquiry for summaries of anthropological results and for brief descriptions of institutions or address information for individuals. Find in chapter 1 the *Annual review of anthropology* **(A57),** with its summary coverage of recent research activity. Find also the *AAA guide* **(A53),** which provides the most recent address and other information relevant to contemporary American anthropology.

Encyclopedias, Handbooks, Manuals

N19

Hays, Terence E., ed. V.2, *Oceania.* In *Encyclopedia of world cultures.* Ed. by David Levinson. Boston: Hall, 1991. 409p.

The "Ethnonym" index (p.407–9) guides the reader to names variantly used in alphabetic arrangement. Signed articles with brief bibliography provide for each culture information according to a standard format. The basic information found in the Human Relations Area Files codes is here converted to conventional form. Most articles are about three pages in length. There is a filmography (p.403–6) and six area maps. The "Subject and peoples" index identifies Douglas L. Oliver's *Oceania: The native cultures of Australia and the Pacific Islands* (Honolulu: Univ. of Hawaii Pr., 1989 [2v.]), a monograph that is an excellent descriptive survey of the peoples of the Pacific Islands as they were before the arrival of foreigners (Europeans). For a more comprehensive entry to anthropological data with detailed entry by indigenous ethnic group, see the Human Relations Area Files, *HRAF source bibliography* **(D16).**

State-of-the-Art Reviews

N20

Mankind. v.1– , 1931– . Sydney: Anthropological Society of New South Wales. 3/yr.

Each issue is on a thematic topic, with a guest editor. Can and often does serve as a continuing review of topics in which progress is being made in Australia and adjacent countries. Focus includes topics like sex roles, kinship patterns, settlement patterns, class roles, social organization, etc. Some issues contain thirty or more signed book reviews, many with additional titles cited (frequently enough to indicate editorial policy at work). Issues devoted to a summary review of a single topic are an occasional feature of *Archaeology in Oceania* **(N04).**

Searching Graphic Materials

Consult Spencer and Johnson's *Atlas for anthropology* **(A65)** for monographs about indigenous peoples that are keyed to culture area maps. Consult Heider's *Films for anthropological teaching* **(A63).**

Maps

N21

Wurm, Stephen Adolphe, and Shirô Hattori. *Language atlas of the Pacific area.* Canberra: Australian Academy of the Humanities in collaboration with the Japan Academy, 1981–1982. 2 parts in portfolio (Pacific linguistics series c, *Monographs,* no.66, 67) pt.1, New Guinea, Oceania, Australia. Maps (44 × 61 cm) are in a case.

Consult the Mitchell Library's *Dictionary catalog of printed books* **(N09)** for entry into 220,000 maps and many photographs. The photographs held by the South Pacific Archives are described in the Library of Congress's *Papers of Margaret Mead and the South Pacific Archives* **(N24).**

Searching Unpublished Materials

Consult the National Anthropological Archives's *Catalog to manuscripts at the National Anthropological Archives* **(A69)** and Nunn's *Asia and Oceania* **(L05)** for an elaborately detailed description of archival material, including microfiche sets and series held in the United States.

Archives

N22

National Library of Australia. *Australian joint copying project handbook.* Canberra: National Library of Australia and the Library of New South Wales, 1972–1980. 8v.

Lists the microfilms of primary source material in Great Britain concerning Australia and the Pacific Islands. Includes material from both public and private collections of archival material in Great Britain. A largely successful attempt to reproduce anything that might be of scholarly value.

N23

Pacific Manuscripts Bureau. *Short titles and index to microfilms PMB DOC 1-1000 (Manuscript series) /Pacific Manuscripts Bureau.* Canberra: The Bureau, 1980. 56p.

This index itemizes the enormous number of manuscript collections of Pacific material held in collections in the Pacific Islands but outside of Australia that have been microfilmed by the Pacific Manuscripts Bureau. Many first-contact reports. These titles are held in microform both by the University of Hawaii and the University of California, San Diego. They are cataloged at the University of Hawaii as a monographic series, and this is the entry used in most bibliographic resources, including the superior indexing found in Nunn's *Asia and Oceania* **(L05).** However, this resource is being slowly cataloged as a monographic set at the University of California, San Diego. Therefore, in searching the University of California MELVIL [computer file], the series entry will not be in the serials subfile but rather will be found under the title in author/title subfile. Entry by author or title of the individual items can be made in the University of Hawaii catalog but will work only for those titles that have been converted by original cataloging at the University of California, San Diego.

Resources on Pacific anthropology located in archives in the United States are less forthrightly, and less commonly, available. Field notes and photographs of several outstanding field anthropologists are included in the Library of Congress, Manuscript Division, *The papers of Margaret Mead and the South Pacific Archives* (Washington, D.C.: Library of Congress, 1989 [2v. of loose-leaf manuscript]) **(N24),** which includes the research materials for the Institute for Intercultural Studies and the South Pacific Ethnographic Archives (which contains field notes of Margaret Mead, Gregory Bateson, Jane Belo, Theodore Swartz, Leonora Swartz Foerstel, Lola Romanuici Swartz Ross, and others). Also included are the records of the now inactive Columbia University Research in Contemporary Cultures. Listed personal papers of Gregory Bateson, Jane Belo, Ruth Benedict, Edith M. Cobb, Margaret Lowenfield, and Martha Wolfenstein are briefly described. Motion-picture film, sound recordings, and maps were transferred to appropriate divisions of the Library of Congress. The photographic file, 1879–1978, contains 50,000 images and forms the bulk of the South Pacific Ethnographic Archives field data.

The list of Margaret Mead's publications (p.186–288) includes bibliography numbers referring to citations in *Margaret Mead: The complete bibliography 1925–1975,* ed. by Joan Gordan (The Hague, Paris: Mouton, 1976 [202p.]) **(N25).**

Dissertations

N26

Coppell, William G. *A bibliography of Pacific Island theses and dissertations.* Honolulu: Research School of Pacific Studies, Australian National University in conjunction with the Institute for Polynesian Studies, Brigham Young University. Hawaii campus, 1983. 520p.

Includes author, title, discipline from which degree was earned, and pagination. Detailed index of 144 pages. Excludes New Zealand and Hawaii.

AUSTRALIA

Searching Bibliographic Guides

In chapter 1 anthropological reference sources provide important entry into Pacific materials. Consult Auckland's "Getting into the literature" **(A01)** for guidance. Consult also the guide to the literature in each of the chapters on the subdisciplines of anthropology. Note especially *HRAF source bibliography* **(D16)** with its printed index to printed materials held in research libraries. It is especially strong in its coverage of the Pacific region.

N27

Swain, Tony. *Aboriginal religions in Australia: A bibliographical survey.* Westport, Conn.: Greenwood Pr., 1991. 336p. (Bibliographies and indexes in religious studies, 18).

Has a value far beyond the range of its title. Scholarly annotations give this resource considerable value. Certainly the best available guide to native life. Arranges more than 1,000 entries regionally, using the standard ten regions describing Aboriginal cultures. Under each region there are topical subdivisions such as women, death, and mythology. The first sixty pages are a survey of the religious significance of the cited works, and religion is shown to permeate all aspects of native life. There is an author/title index and a subject index.

Searching for Current Materials

Any effort to keep current about the output and research activities of each of the special subdisciplines in anthropology will be rewarded by an inspection of the entries listed under this heading in the chapters devoted to the subdisciplines of anthropology.

Sources of Review in Scholarly Publications

N28

Australian and Torres Straits aboriginal studies. v.1– , 1983– . Canberra: Australian Institute of Aboriginal Studies and Torres Straits Aboriginal Studies. 2/yr.

Replaces *Australian Institute of Aboriginal Studies newsletter,* v.1–19, 1963–82. Retains the communication and information functions of the newsletter. Signed book reviews cover all aspects of Aboriginal society from prehistoric to modern times, and this coverage reflects the range of coverage in articles accepted for scholarly publication.

Select Lists of Scholarly Journals

N29

Wesley-Smith, Terrence A., and Michael P. Hamnet. *A Melanesian bibliography: Selected references for Fiji, Papua New Guinea, Solomon Islands, New Caledonia and Irian Jaya.* Honolulu: Pacific Islands Development Program, East-West Center, 1984. 45p.

Includes a select guide to useful periodicals, developed by experienced professionals, which can be used with confidence to narrow the range of resources for which special features may identify sources of recurring review. It is followed by an unannotated bibliography that contains many ethnographies. Developed to support essays found in Jackson's *Pacific Island studies* **(N01).**

Retrospective Searches

Find several sources that organize entry under geographically defined areas. Consult first the Tozzer Library's *Author and subject catalogues of the Tozzer Library* [microfiche] **(A26)** and the older hardcover edition of Peabody Museum Library's *Catalogue* **(A29)** for author and classified subject entry to monographs, periodical articles, and the contents of books. This resource has a companion for coverage of monographs in the Museum of Mankind Library's *Museum of Mankind Library catalogues* [microfiche] **(A25),** which includes a sustained classified subject index to monographic and pamphlet publications.

Retrospective Bibliographies—Bibliographies of Bibliographies

N30

Thawley, J., and S. Gauci. *Bibliographies on the Australian aborigine: An annotated listing.* 2d ed. Bundoora, Victoria: The Burchardt Library, La Trobe University, 1987. 44p. (Library publication [La Trobe University. Library], no.32)

An alphabetic list by author of 163 entries. Subject and geographical index.

Retrospective Bibliographies—Broad Scope

N31

Australian Institute of Aboriginal Studies. *Bibliography series.* v.1– , 1966– . Sydney: Rushcutter Printing for Australian Institute of Aboriginal Studies. Irregular.

Each volume of this series includes a list of ethnic groups with a location map of indigenous ethnic groups and with excellent indexes by indigenous ethnic group and by subject. Especially valuable: no.2, *Cape York,* comp. by Beryl F. Craig (1967 [233p.]) **(N32);** no.3, *Kimberley region: An annotated bibliography,* comp. by Beryl F. Craig (1968 [209p.]) **(N33);** no.4, *A list of French naval records and illustrations relating to Australian and Tasmanian aborigines, 1771 to 1828,* comp. by Leslie R. Marchant (1969 [83p.]) **(N34);** no.5, *Central Australian and western desert regions: An annotated bibliography,* comp. by Beryl F. Craig (1969 [351p.]) **(N35);** no.8, *Arnhem Land peninsula region (including Bathurst and Melville Islands),* comp. by Beryl F. Craig (1966 [205p.]) **(N36).**

The volume published in this series as number 6 was published also as a subset of the institute's larger series and can be described as *North-west-central Queensland: An annotated bibliography,* comp. by Beryl F. Craig (Canberra: Australian Inst. of Aboriginal Studies, 1970 [137p.]) (Australian aboriginal studies, v.41; Bibliography series, no.6) **(N37).** See also *An annotated bibliography of the Tasmanian aborigines,* comp. by Norman James Brian Plomley (London: Royal Anthropological Institute, 1969 [143p.]) (Royal Anthropological Institute. Occasional paper, no.28) **(N38).**

N39

Greenway, John. *Bibliography of the Australian aborigines and the native peoples of Torres Strait to 1959.* Sydney: Angus and Robertson, 1963. 420p.

A thorough international bibliography of monographic and serial publications. Arranged alphabetically by author. Detailed subject index. No annotations but some citations to reviews of major books. Supplemented and kept current by Australian Institute of Aboriginal Studies, *Partial accessions list,* no.1– , 1961/62– (Canberra: Australian Inst. of Aboriginal Studies) **(N40);** semiannual. Title varies. Most recently *Annual bibliography,* 1975– . Lists books, articles, and parts of books on Australian aboriginal peoples; does not purport to be exhaustive. Each issue is divided into ten sections, ranging from social anthropology to prehistory and culture contact. Sections arranged alphabetically by author. No indexes. However, the library plans, following computerization of its catalogs, to provide more convenient access. Consult also *International bibliography of social and cultural anthropology* **(D20),** which continues to provide in its annual volumes a record of research from the 1959 cutoff date to current coverage.

For linguistics there is a companion volume in W. J. Oates and Lynette F. Oates's *A linguistic survey of Australia* (Canberra: Australian Institute of Aboriginal Studies, 1970 [282p.]) (Australian Institute of Aboriginal Studies, no.33, linguistic series, no.12) **(N41),** with excellent language maps as endpapers. Grammar and phonology, vocabulary, and text and tapes available are all covered to the date of publication. The classification system provides entry for each of the twelve traditional areas, and each area has supporting maps. There is a key to the map code for indigenous ethnic groups in each area (p.xii–xv). The introduction must be carefully studied to understand the coding system used in the entries, and to establish the limitations even of this extensive bibliographic base, which explicitly relies on previous coverage (also described in the introduction). The range of this source can be supplemented by consulting Else Jagst (comp.), *Bibliography of the Summer Institute of Linguistics, Australian Aborigines Branch up to August, 1981* (Darwin: Summer Institute of Linguistics, 1981 [43p.]) **(N42),** with one section devoted to lists of articles, monographs, and book reviews on linguistics and anthropology, while a second section is devoted to works in Aboriginal languages. A more systematic coverage can be established by referring in *Fieldwork in the Library* to entries listed under "Retrospective Bibliographies—Continuing" in chapter 5, "Anthropological Linguistics."

For human geography, see Sandi Kekoe-Forutan's *A bibliography of the Torres Strait Islands* (Brisbane: University of Queensland, 1987 [131p.]) **(N43),** organized under broad subject headings that include "Anthropology." Lists 1,217 entries to journal articles, books, and theses; subject index.

Retrospective Bibliographies—Topical

In the absence of a recent bibliography of bibliographies for this area, topical bibliographies should be consulted for this feature even when the search is not directed centrally to the subject coverage of these resources. In chapter 1, "What Every Anthropologist Needs to Know," consult entries under the heading "Retrospective Bibliographies—Bibliographies of Bibliographies."

N44

Lucas, Rodney. *Resources for aboriginal family history.* Canberra: Institute of Aboriginal Studies, 1986. 123p.

Includes reference to field notes. This reflects a growing use in the discipline of anthropology of field notes made available as archival material. Pt.1, Aboriginal genealogies register, includes 50 annotated entries classed under geographic area and in each area under indigenous ethnic group. Pt.2, Oral history, lists tapes alphabetically by investigator, with descriptive annotations indexed for persons and again for geographic regions subdivided for indigenous ethnic groups.

N45

Thomson, Neil, and Patricia Merrifield. *Aboriginal health: An annotated bibliography.* Canberra: Aboriginal Institute of Aboriginal Studies and Australian Institute of Health, 1988. 289p.

Designed to help health professionals with important material published since 1970. Significant for its use of resources from related disciplines and its command of technical vocabulary. Search terms identified here can be used to approach anthropological questions with the controlled vocabularies of related disciplines. When machine-readable databases are used, the identification of indexing terms that get results can be a difficult problem.

Informational Reference Searches

Across chapters this heading introduces lists of reference books that answer an inquiry for summaries of anthropological results and for brief descriptions of institutions or address information for individuals. Find in chapter 1 the *Annual review of anthropology* **(A57)** with its summary coverage of recent research activity. Find also another parallel subheading, "Directories," in the *AAA guide* **(A53),** which provides the most recent address and other information relevant to contemporary American anthropology.

Encyclopedias, Handbooks, Manuals

N46

Australian aborigines. V.2, in *The Australian people: An encyclopedia of the nation, its people and their origins.* Ed. by James Jupp. North Ryde, New South Wales: Angus and Robertson, 1988. 4v.

Signed articles by recognized experts. Bibliography in volume 4.

N47

Berndt, Ronald, and Catherine Berndt. *The world of the first Australians: Aboriginal traditional life past and present.* Revised with new foreword and added references. Canberra: Aboriginal Studies Pr., 1987. 634p.

An important contribution to the consolidation of anthropological knowledge. This encyclopedic text lists more than 800 entries in its bibliography, which supports the analysis achieved in this detailed and authoritative introduction to Aboriginal life past and present. Studies of the impact of the legal processes on contemporary Aboriginal populations can benefit from the annotated list of 1,500 sources (Royal Commissions, theses, books, letters, and articles from journals). Can be supplemented by Norman Burnett Tindale's classic *Aboriginal tribes of Australia: Their terrain, environmental controls, distribution, limits, and proper names* (Berkeley: Univ. of California Pr., 1974 [404p.]) **(N48).** An introductory statement includes detailed information on the communities' indigenous ethnic groups, their patterns of settlement, and the linguistics of names for indigenous ethnic groups. The catalog of indigenous ethnic groups provides geographical locations of groups and their variant names. Arrangement is geographical by Australian states, with an appendix by Rhys Jones which discusses indigenous ethnic groups of Tasmania. The bibliography is extensive and the maps and illustrations valuable.

N49

Handbook of Australian languages. Dixon, R. M. W., and Barry J. Blake, eds. Canberra: Australian National Univ. Pr., 1979– . 2v.

Three volumes planned. Makes available short grammatical sketches.

N50

McCorquodale, John. *Aborigines and the law: A digest.* Canberra: Aborigines Studies Pr., 1987. 528p.

A description of all relevant legislation (Imperial, Commonwealth, State, and Territory), with a bibliography that supports this analysis.

N51

Mills, Carol M. *A bibliography of the Northern Territory: Monographs.* Bruce, Canberra: College of Advanced Education Library, 1977–83. 4v. in 5 (Bibliography series no.3,5,6,10)

Includes entry by name of indigenous ethnic group to a case law digest prepared by Douglas E. Sanders with Paul C. Taylor. The coverage of the set includes books, journals, theses, unpublished papers, government documents, and "Author-Indian" publications. "Language and linguistics" are covered in no.5, pt.2, p.313–40. The culture and artifacts of the Aborigines are covered in no.10 (2v.).

MELANESIA

Searching Bibliographic Guides

In chapter 1 anthropological reference sources provide important entry into Pacific materials. Consult Auckland's "Getting into the literature" **(A01)** for guidance. Consult also the guide to the literature in each of the chapters in *Fieldwork in the Library* on the subdisciplines of anthropology. Note especially *HRAF source bibliography* **(D16)** with its printed index to printed materials held in research libraries. It is especially strong in its coverage of the Pacific region.

Bibliographic Guides

N52

Baal, Jan van, K. W. Galis, and R. M. Koentjaraningrat. *West Irian: A bibliography.* Dordrecht, Netherlands: Foris, 1984. 307p. (Bibliographical series. Koninklijk Instituut voor Taal-, Land-en Volkenkunde, v.15)

Conceived as a guide. Assumes that the user will trace the additional sources of information cited in the works listed. Well organized by subject, with regional and subdivisions by name of indigenous ethnic groups as needed. Includes books, journal articles, and unpublished materials in which much of the information on West Irian has been recorded. Thus, this work provides entry into the collection described in 1968 by P. Nienhuis in his manuscript *Inventaris van stukken afkomstig uit de archieven van de Algemene Secretarie en van andere Departmenten te Batavia betreffende Nieuw Guinea* (Den Haag, 1968 [103p.]) [manuscript] **(N53),** which is reproduced in *West Irian* as an appendix which identifies 921 documents covering well over 25,000 pages that have been microfilmed and made available for scholarly use.

N54

Cleverley, John, and Christabel Wescombe. *Papua New Guinea: Guide to sources in education.* Sydney: Sydney Univ. Pr., 1979. 150p.

More than 900 entries. Material up to 1978 published in organized form. A basic guide to the area includes directory information to major institutes and centers of learning. The bibliography of bibliographies is annotated with great skill. A guide to research in the area regardless of the discipline of interest. Includes reference to *New Guinea bibliography: A subject list of books published in the New Guinea area and books dealing wholly or partially with a New Guinea subject, published overseas,* v.1–14, 1967–80 (Port Moresby: University of Papua New Guinea Library) **(N55),** an annual with classed arrangement with author/title and subject indexes to 1971. From 1972 a dictionary catalog form is adopted. Includes all material received by the University of Papua New Guinea Library. Cleverley's *Papua New Guinea* **(N54)** discusses the relationship of *New Guinea bibliography* **(N55)** to the *Australian national bibliography,* v.1– , 1961– (Canberra: National Library of Australia), an annual. Superseded by *Papua New Guinea national bibliography,* v.1– , 1981– (Waigani: National Library Service of Papua New Guinea) **(N56),** an annual. Consult also Patrick's *Bibliography of the Summer Institute of Linguistics* **(N75)** for bibliography entries with ethnographic and linguistic relevance.

Searching for Current Materials

Any effort to keep current about the output and research activities of each of the special subdisciplines in anthropology will be rewarded by an inspection of the entries listed under this heading in the chapters devoted to the subdisciplines of anthropology.

Select Sources of Review in Scholarly Publications

N57

Research in Melanesia. v.1– , 1968– . Port Moresby: University of Papua New Guinea. Semiannual.

Titled *Man in New Guinea* to 1975. Signed book reviews together with correspondence from readers regarding previous book reviews. Acts as clearinghouse for research in Melanesia. Reports on regulations governing field activities. Includes reports about ongoing research. Ethnographic studies and site analyses of such broad questions as methodology and theory are within the range of this journal. Currently the primary focus of interest seems to be in political anthropology, prehistoric research, mental health, population problems, subsistence patterns, and gender and occupational roles. Definitive bibliographies that are narrowly focused continue to attract the interest of the editors. Inspect a recent example by D. Hutchinson, "A bibliography of anthropological and related writings on the province of New Ireland, Papua New Guinea" 7 (1983) (1–2): 35–87 **(N58),** which lists entries alphabetically by author, and D. D. Johnson's "A bibliography on women in Papua New Guinea" 6 (1–2) (1982): 33–54 **(N59),** again alphabetic by author.

Selective Lists of Scholarly Journals

N60

Lea, Mary Anne, and Eve Rannells. *Checklist of current Papua New Guinea periodicals.* Lae, Papua New Guinea: Matheson Library. Papua New Guinea University of Technology, 1985. 60p. (Matheson Library Occasional Bibliography, no.1)

Lists 400 entries describing the joint resources of the National Library Papua monograph collection and the Papua New Guinea University of Technology periodical collection. Listed alphabetically by title with the publishers' addresses and information about frequency and availability.

Retrospective Searches

Find several sources that organize entry under geographically defined areas. Consult first the Tozzer Library's *Author and subject catalogues of the Tozzer Library* [microfiche] **(A26)** and the older hardcover edition of the Peabody Museum Library's *Catalogue* **(A29)** for author and classified subject entry to monographs, periodical articles, and the contents of books. This resource has a companion for coverage of monographs only in the published catalogs of the British Museum, Museum of Mankind Library, *Museum of Mankind Library catalogues* [microfiche] **(A25),** which includes a sustained classified subject index to monographic and pamphlet publications.

Bibliographies of Bibliographies

N61

McConnell, Fraiser. "Bibliographies." Chapter in *Papua New Guinea,* items 834–65. Oxford, England: Clio, 1988. 378p. (World bibliographical series, v.90)

The bibliographies of Papua New Guinea are listed here with long descriptive and evaluative annotations. Listed in alphabetic order by author. Includes coverage of topics such as land tenure, population studies, a bibliography of *kuru,* human biology, land settlement, traditional art, and migration.

Retrospective Bibliographies—Continuing

N62

New Guinea periodical index. v.1–15, 1968–83. Waigini: University of Papua New Guinea.

Alphabetic by author and subject. Attempts worldwide coverage of articles published on any aspect of New Guinea. Detailed indexing. For verification of periodical titles, consult Brenda E. Moon's *Periodicals for South East Asian studies: A union catalogue of holdings in British and selected European libraries* (London: Mansell, 1979 [610p.]) **(N63),** with cross-references to variant titles. Periodicals published in or relating to Papua New Guinea, Melanesia, and Polynesia are included, but the emphasis is clearly on Melanesian materials.

Retrospective Bibliographies—Topical and Regional

N64

Australian National University (Canberra). Department of Anthropology and Sociology. *An ethnographic bibliography of New Guinea.* Canberra: Australian Univ. Pr., 1968. 3v.

Covers a century of Western-language books and articles from 1860 to 1964 on the present Territory of Papua, the trusteeship territory of New Guinea, and Indonesian Irian. The names index includes a comprehensive selection of physical features, languages, and social groups. Extensive analytical indexing in volumes 2 and 3. Indispensable as a record of ethnographic research in the area.

N65

Butler, Alan. *A New Guinea bibliography.* Waigani: Univ. of Papua New Guinea Pr., 1984– . 5v.

An attempt to include all separately published items. Does have entry by indigenous ethnic groups. Index.

N66

Galis, Klaas Wilhelm. *Bibliography of west New Guinea.* New Haven, Conn.: Yale Univ. Pr., 1956. 135p. (Yale University. Southeast Asia Studies. Bibliography ser.)

Lists 3,760 entries by author with no subject index. Many of the entries are Dutch-language materials from colonial period serial publications.

N67

Gourlay, Ken A., comp. *A bibliography of traditional music in Papua New Guinea.* Port Moresby, [Australia]: Institute of Papua New Guinea Studies, c1974, 1980. 176p.

Some coverage of neighboring Irian Jaya, the Solomon Islands, and the Torres Strait. Includes most published ethnographies of indigenous ethnic groups in the area. Alphabetic by author with detailed annotations. Eight subject indexes: ethnology, ceremonial, dance, musical instruments, musicology, mythology, ethnic groups, and geographical regions. Entry by names of indigenous ethnic groups.

N68

Hays, Terence E. *Anthropology in the New Guinea highlands: An annotated bibliography.* New York: Garland, 1976. 238p. (Garland reference library in social science, v.17)

Lists 1,800 entries under broad subject headings. Includes a general section of useful bibliographies and reports by observers who were not trained as anthropologists. Brief annotations. Covers doctoral dissertations, books, and journal articles through 1974 in broad coverage of all aspects of anthropology, with author and ethnolinguistic group indexes.

N69

Hornabrook, R. W., and G. H. F. Skeldon. *A bibliography of medicine and human biology of Papua New Guinea.* Faringdon, England: Classey for the Papua New Guinea Institute of Medical Research, 1977. 335p. (Monograph series: Papua New Guinea Institute of Medical Research, v.5)

Lists 3,913 citations plus 375 items in a supplement. Covers ethnology and anthropometry as well as the more traditional interests of public health. Includes Irian Jaya, Solomon Islands, and New Caledonia. Subject index includes ethnolinguistic and geographical names.

N70

Macintyre, Martha. *The Kula: A bibliography.* New York: Cambridge Univ. Pr., 1983. 90p.

Eight sections include government publications, anthropological material, archaeological material, Massim art, and films. Alphabetic by author in each section. Author index to the 625 entries. Includes descriptions of museum collections. Exceptional for its critically perceptive annotations.

N71

Oli, Eileen. *Motu-Koita bibliography.* Port Moresby: National Library Service of Papua New Guinea, 1987. 26p.

Lists 323 entries alphabetically by author with subject index.

N72

O'Reilly, Patrick. *Bibliographie méthodique analytique et critique de la Nouvelle-Calédonie.* Paris: Musée de l'Homme, 1955. 361p. (Société des Océanistes. Publication, no.4)

Includes 4,100 entries with a section on ethnography which lists native language texts. Continued by Georges Pisier's *Bibliographie méthodique, analytique et critique de la Nouvelle-Calédonie, 1955–1982* (Nouméa: Société d'Ètudes Historiques de la Nouvelle-Calédonie, 1983. [350p.]) (Publications no.34) **(N73),** a topical listing of 3,338 books, articles, theses, and book reviews. Name index.

N74

O'Reilly, Patrick. *Bibliographie méthodique analytique et critique des Nouvelles-Hebrides.* Paris: Musée de l'Homme, 1958. 304p. (Société des Océanistes. Publication, no.8)

Annotated bibliography of books and periodical articles.

N75

Patrick, Heather. *Bibliography of the Summer Institute of Linguistics, Papua New Guinea Branch, 1956–1980.* Ukarumpa, Papua New Guinea: Summer Institute of Linguistics, 1981. 2v.

List of all publications written by institute members or its associates in its first twenty-five years in the country. V.1, *Vernacular publications in scripture translations and related material, literacy materials* (180p.), cites 897 publications to support vernacular literacy programs. V.2, *English publications in linguistics and anthropology, literacy and community development, translation* (103p.), lists 610 items on cultural anthropology and general linguistics, arranged alphabetically by author in each of the topical areas. Indexes are provided by language, province, and author. Consult also Klieneberg's *Bibliography of Oceanic linguistics* **(N16).** Entry and use of these resources can be greatly eased by reference to Thomas Edward Dutton's *A checklist of languages and present-day villages of central and southeast mainland Papua* (Canberra: Australian National University. Research School of Pacific Studies. Department of

Linguistics, 1973 [80p.]) (Pacific linguistics, series B monographs, v.24) **(N76).**

N77

Sack, Peter. *German New Guinea: A bibliography.* Canberra: Department of Law Research School of Social Sciences. Australian National University, 1980. 298p.

More than 3,000 entries are discussed in a bibliographic essay on sources published in German and on German New Guinea between 1884 and 1914. Includes a list of periodicals (p.288–98). Excludes manuscripts.

Retrospective Bibliographies—Indigenous Ethnic Groups

The detailed indexing and wide extension of ethnographic interest in the work of O'Sullivan's *Tradition and law in Papua New Guinea* **(N79)** and Potter's *Traditional law in Papua New Guinea* **(N80)** make these sources the first choice for almost any entry into a literature search for materials on indigenous ethnic groups. See also the reference sources developed by Butler's *A New Guinea bibliography* **(N65)** and Hays's *Anthropology in the New Guinea highlands* **(N68)** and *Melanesian newsletter and accessions list* **(N84).**

N78

"Ethnic groups." Chapter in *Papua New Guinea,* p.87–136. Comp. by Fraiser McConnell (Oxford, England, and Santa Barbara, Calif.: Clio Pr. 1988. 378p. (World bibliographical series, v.90)

Includes 139 entries in a classed arrangement, with subject headings such as "General," "Papuan region," "Highlands," "Momase or north coast region," and "New Guinea islands region." Excellent annotations.

N79

O'Sullivan, Catherine. *Tradition and law in Papua New Guinea: An annotated and selected bibliography.* Canberra: Dept. of Law, Research School of Social Sciences, Australian National University, 1986. 118p.

Coverage includes almost all ethnographic categories. Lists 378 entries, alphabetic by author with annotations. Systematic and ethnolinguistic indexes. Updates Michelle Potter's *Traditional law in Papua New Guinea* **(N80).**

N80

Potter, Michelle. *Traditional law in Papua New Guinea: An annotated selected bibliography.* Canberra: Australian Natl. Univ. Dept. of Law, Research School of Social Sciences, 1973. 132p.

A range of coverage far beyond the scope of its title makes this a valuable place to start a search. Detailed index. Cutoff date is 1970. Indexed for indigenous ethnic groups. Updated by O'Sullivan's *Tradition and law in Papua New Guinea* **(N79).**

Informational Reference Searches

Across chapters this heading introduces lists of reference books that answer an inquiry for summaries of anthropological results and for brief descriptions of institutions or address information for individuals. Find in chapter 1 the *Annual review of anthropology* **(A57),** with its summary coverage of recent research activity. Find also another parallel subheading, "Directories," in the *AAA guide* **(A53),** which provides the most recent address and other information relevant to contemporary American anthropology.

Directories

N81

"Publishers and research institutions." In Fraiser McConnell, comp. *Papua New Guinea,* p.xxvi. Oxford: Clio Pr., 1988. 378p. (World bibliographical series, v.90)

Directory information with knowledgeable annotations. Reflects the years McConnell spent at the National Library of Papua New Guinea. Bibliographic entries in the bibliography itself are given long, accurate annotations. Adequate index.

Encyclopedias, Handbooks, Manuals

N82

Foley, William. *The Papuan languages of New Guinea.* London: Cambridge Univ. Pr., 1986. 305p.

Includes studies of language in social contexts and relevance to problems of prehistory. Discusses the comparative method and identifies technical features. Language and subject indexes.

N83

McKaughan, Howard, ed. *Anthropological studies in the eastern highlands of New Guinea.* Seattle: Univ. of Washington Pr., 1972– .

Planned as a nine-volume set. To date, volumes on languages, physical anthropology, prehistory, geography, and additional volumes on ethnography.

Searching Unpublished Materials

Dissertations

For the years 1965–85 theses accepted by universities in the United Kingdom and Ireland can be identified in Helen L. Stephens's *Theses on South East Asia* **(M106).** The table of contents is subdivided for Papua New Guinea and under that geographic unit has numerous subject subdivisions. This provides an extension to Coppell's *A bibliography of Pacific Island theses and dissertations* **(N26).**

Archives

N84

Melanesian newsletter and accessions list. no.8– , 1989– . La Jolla, Calif.: Melanesian Studies Resource Center and Melanesian Archive, University of California, San Diego. Annual.

Title varies. Has been *Accessions list of unpublished material.* An unannotated but numbered list with an index of ethnic groups and languages and a geographic index. Itemizes unpublished papers, manuscripts, and other written materials pertaining to the cultures and societies of Melanesia. Attempts acquisition worldwide of dissertations and even some honors papers for which the index provides entry. Includes reference to archival lists of papers of anthropologists and often makes these available on microfiche to all scholars. Lists and indexes copies of the patrol reports held at this library in microfilm, and the holdings of microfiche on Melanesia from *Archives et documents,* produced by the Musée de l'Homme (Paris) **(A67).**

MICRONESIA

Searching for Current Materials

Any effort to keep current about the output and research activities of each of the special subdisciplines in anthropology will be rewarded by an inspection of the entries listed under this heading in the chapters devoted to the subdisciplines of anthropology.

Select Sources of Review in Scholarly Publications

N85

Micronesia; Devoted to the natural sciences of Micronesia. v.1– , 1964– . Agana, Guam: University of Guam, Micronesian Area Research Center. 2/yr.

Two to three book reviews per issue. Physical anthropology and some ethnographic reporting in this natural science journal. Text in English, with summaries in foreign languages.

Retrospective Searches

Find several sources that organize entry under geographically defined areas. Consult first the Tozzer Library's *Author and subject catalogues of the Tozzer Library* [microfiche] **(A26)** and the older hardcover edition of the Peabody Museum Library's *Catalogue* **(A29)** for author and classified subject entry to monographs, periodical articles, and the contents of books. This resource has a companion for coverage of monographs only in the published catalogs of the British Museum, Museum of Mankind Library, *Museum of Mankind Library catalogues* [microfiche] **(A25),** which includes a sustained classified subject index to monographic and pamphlet publications.

Retrospective Bibliography—Broad Scope

N86

Goetzfridt, Nicholas J., and William L. Wuerch. *Micronesia, 1975–1987: A social science bibliography.* New York; Westport, Conn.; London: Greenwood, 1989. 194p. (Bibliographies and indexes in anthropology, no.5)

Lists 1,849 numbered items in an author list without annotations. Overwhelming emphasis on anthropological materials. Unannotated English-language books, government documents, articles, dissertations, and theses. Helpful list of place names (p.177–78). In the geographic index, entries under major subdivisions are subdivided by as many as twenty-nine terms listed on page xi. The subject index, on the other hand, divides these terms by geographic and ethnic-group names.

Arranged by authors A–Z. Covers Caroline, Mariana, and Marshall Islands; excludes the Gilberts. Includes books, periodical articles, articles in collections, unpublished papers, and doctoral dissertations. Geographical and topical indexes. A continuation of Fugio Uchinomi's *Bibliography of Micronesia* (Univ. of Hawaii Pr., 1950 [157p.]) **(N87)** and Mac Marshall, Mac, and James D. Nason's *Micronesia 1944–1974: A bibliography of anthropological and related materials concerning Micronesia since World War II* (New Haven, Conn.: HRAF Pr., 1976 [337p.]) **(N88),** this work adds 2,000 entries to the bibliographic control of the anthropological investigation of this area.

POLYNESIA

Searching Bibliographic Guides

The guides from chapter 1 and from the chapters devoted to the subdisciplines of anthropology can be used to establish a bibliographic base from which to proceed in this area. Consult especially the reference works listed in chapters 1 and 4. For a study of the indigenous populations of this region as they thrive in the modern nation states, consult first the resources developed in New Zealand, which maintains an interest in all of the Pacific Islands but which has special strength in Polynesian cultures.

N89

Graham, Theresa. *A finding aid to reference works in South Pacific studies.* Auckland: Auckland University Library, 1988. 48p. (Bibliographical bulletin. University of Auckland. Library, 15)

Especially useful for its coverage of bibliographies of bibliographies, atlases, and other informational reference sources.

Searching for Current Materials

Any effort to keep current about the output and research activities of each of the special subdisciplines in anthropology will be rewarded by an inspection of the entries listed under this heading in the chapters devoted to the subdisciplines of anthropology.

Select Sources of Review in Scholarly Publications

N90

Journal of the Polynesian Society. v.1– , 1892– . Auckland: University of Auckland for the Polynesian Society. Quarterly.

Around five book reviews and bibliographic information for additional titles. Focus on ethnology, physical anthropology, archaeology, and linguistics of the New Zealand Maori and other Pacific Island peoples. "Notes and news" has organizational information about meetings, research projects, symposia, and society publications.

Retrospective Searches

Find several sources that organize entry under geographically defined areas. Consult first the Tozzer Library's *Author and subject catalogues of the Tozzer Library* [microfiche] **(A26)** and the older hardcover edition of the Peabody Museum Library's *Catalogue* **(A29)** for author and classified subject entry to monographs, periodical articles, and the contents of books. This resource has a companion for coverage of monographs only in the published catalogs of the British Museum, Museum of Mankind Library, *Museum of Mankind Library catalogues* [microfiche] **(A25),** which includes a sustained classified subject index to monographic and pamphlet publications.

Retrospective Bibliographies—Topical

N91

Edridge, Sally. *Solomon Islands bibliography to 1980.* Suva, Fiji: Institute of Pacific Studies. University of the South Pacific, 1985. 476p.

Classed arrangement with complete entries. Long, useful annotations. See especially "Anthropology," p.72–163. A second and less satisfactory entry into the same material can be found in L. D. Holmes's *Samoan Islands bibliography* (Wichita, Kans.: Poly Concepts, 1984. [329p.]) **(N92),** which is divided into forty-four subject areas.

N93

Hanson, F. Allan, and P. O'Reilly, eds. *Bibliographie de Rapa: Polynésie française.* Paris: Museé de l'Homme, 1973. 257p. (Publications de la Société des Océanistes, no.32)

An author list of 259 entries with some annotations.

N94

Kittelson, David J. *The Hawaiians: An annotated bibliography.* Honolulu: Social Science Research Institute, University of Hawaii, 1985. 384p. index. (Hawaii series, no.7)

2,712 annotated items from journal articles, reports, theses, and monographs. Subject index should be expanded in next edition.

N95

O'Reilly, Patrick, and Edouard Reitman. *Bibliographie de Tahiti et de la Polynesie française.* Paris: Museé de l'Homme, 1967. 1,048p. (Société des Océanistes. Publication, no.14)

A classified and annotated bibliography of 10,501 items. "Ethnology" is a topic. There is an elaboration for Rapa published in Hanson and O'Reilly's *Bibliographie de Rapa* **(N93),** with 259 entries and some annotations illustrating a trend in which narrowly defined bibliographies expand highly specific sections of a base source.

N96

Snow, P. A. *A bibliography of Fiji, Tonga and Rotuma.* Canberra: Australian National Univ. Pr., 1969. 418p.

Classed arrangement of 10,000 entries. The section on Fiji has sixty-three sections.

N97

Taylor, Clyde Romer Hughes. *A bibliography of publications on the New Zealand Maori and the Moriori of the Chatham Islands.* Oxford, England: Clarendon, 1972. 161p.

Classed arrangement of 3,900 items. Author index provides abbreviated titles for authors with more than one item. Apart from the coverage in more general journals of Oceanic anthropology, the journals publishing research in the area are not numerous. For that reason, in this region to a greater extent than in most culture areas the cumulated indexes to a very few journals become essential resources in comprehensive searches for anthropological literature. Inspect the National Museum of New Zealand's *Publications of the Colonial Museum, 1865–1907, Dominion Museum, 1907–1973 and Museum of New Zealand, 1973–1981,* by J. C. Yaldwyn (Wellington: National Museum of New Zealand, 1982 [41p.]) (Miscellaneous series. National Museum of New Zealand, no.4) **(N98).** Once again the importance of newsletters in a bibliographic and historical resource has been validated by Louise Furey and Nigel Prickett's *Author, title and subject index of the New Zealand Archaeological Association Newsletter, volumes 1–30, 1957–87* (Auckland: New Zealand Archaeological Association, 1988

[149p.]) (New Zealand Archaeological Association monograph, no.16) **(N99).** An alphabetic list by author and by date thereunder. Subject index. Book review index.

N100

University of Hawaii. Sinclair Library. *Dictionary catalog of the Hawaiian collection.* Boston: Hall, 1963. 4v.

Includes 68,000 entries of which 42,000 are Hawaiiana. Covers monographs, Hawaiian government documents since 1915, and more than 1,500 Hawaiian serials.

Informational Reference Searches

Across chapters this heading introduces lists of reference books that answer an inquiry for summaries of anthropological results and for brief descriptions of institutions or address information for individuals. Find in chapter 1 the *Annual review of anthropology* **(A57)** with its summary coverage of recent research activity. Find also another parallel subheading, "Directories," in the *AAA guide* **(A53),** which provides the most recent address and other information relevant to contemporary American anthropology.

N101

l'Encyclopédie de la Polynésie. Ed. by B. Salvat [et.al.]. Papeete: Éditions de l'Allizé, 1985– . 9v.

More than 100 distinguished scholars contributed signed articles with brief bibliographies. Individual coverage for 110 islands. More than 4,000 color illustrations. For mythology an additional supplementary source can be found in Robert D. Craig's *Dictionary of Polynesian mythology* (Westport, Conn.: Greenwood, 1989 [409p.]) **(N102)** for an English-language resource with a concise dictionary presentation and an enormous amount of basic information. There is an appendix, "Categories of gods and goddesses."

Searching Unpublished Materials

Archives

N103

University of Auckland. Library. *A guide to manuscripts and archives collections on microtext at Auckland University Library.* Compiled by Angela Zivkovic. Auckland: Auckland University Library, 1981. 58p.

Rich in the microfiche reproduction of resources held internationally. Indispensable for early contact reports and for field notes of an unusually talented group of early anthropologists. The holdings of the University of Hawaii and other American libraries are of great importance. Consult especially the great coverage and indexing of these resources in Nunn's *Asia and Oceania* **(L05),** which can lead even to specific identification of many of these helpful resources.

10

CIS and Europe

The development of this chapter assumes that the reader has exhausted the sources identified in Balay's *Guide to reference books* **(B02),** especially for the more general sources which are elaborately developed for this geographic region.

The conventional guides, **(O01)** through **(O03),** often fail to provide an adequate and relevant entry into the abundance of ethnographic research on European populations. This is especially true of research completed since the early 1970s. The reader is advised to initiate a search via the following path: Consult first Rogers, Gilmore, and Clegg's *Directory of Europeanist anthropologists in North America* **(O18),** with its detailed index. Included in its bibliographic lists are seminal articles that can be used for citation searches in *Arts and humanities search* [computer file] **(B10),** *Scisearch* [computer file] **(B35),** and *Social scisearch* [computer file] **(B37).** Representative book reviews for European ethnography can be found in **(O04), (O05),** and **(O06),** and an effort to maintain current awareness can be supported by journals identified in the bibliography **(O07).** Retrospective searches are strongly supported by the bibliographies of bibliographies identified in the entries **(O12)** through **(O17).** Continuing bibliographies **(O19)** through **(O28)** should be extended to Eastern Europe through sources identified in the department "Anthropology" in *Bibliographische berichte* **(O12).** Topical bibliographies (including regional guides) are listed **(O29)** through **(O73).** An excellent dictionary and several encyclopedic handbooks are described in entries **(O74)** through **(O85),** providing accurate, concise information about a number of important concepts as they are applied to population groups. Consult also the state-of-the-art reviews in **(O86)** through **(O91).**

All searches should start with the reference sources identified in chapter 1 of *Fieldwork in the Library.* Refer to the discussion there of the reference strategies signaled by the headings "Searching for Current Materials" and "Retrospective Searches," which do not change from chapter to chapter. A discussion of the system of primary, secondary, and tertiary entries defining the structure of entries under headings can be found in the introduction.

Searching Bibliographic Guides

The development of this section assumes that the reader has consulted the resources in chapter 1 with the guidance of Auckland's "Getting into the literature" **(A01).** When a search is defined by one of the subdisciplines of anthropology, the guides to the chapters devoted to these subdisciplines should also be consulted and treated as companion guides to this chapter.

Bibliographic Guides

O01

Kuter, Lois. *The anthropology of Western Europe: A selected bibliography.* Bloomington: West European Studies. Indiana University, 1978. 133p. (West European studies. Indiana occasional papers, no.1)

Lists 1,112 numbered items: Section 1, list of journals by subject; Section 2, geographic topics with an alphabetic author listing under each area. Strong in English and French sources. There is an author index. The subject index has terms with as many as 150 entries and no subdivisions. Some unpublished dissertations are included. No annotations. Many ethnographic resources are cited.

O02

Theodoratus, Robert J. *Europe: A selected ethnographic bibliography.* (New Haven, Conn.: Human Relations Area Files, 1969. 544p. (Behavior science bibliographies)

No annotations for these massive lists of monographs deemed useful for the study of European ethnology. For the period covered, most of the available resources were produced by scholars without anthropological training. For this reason, its broad scope is more likely to overwhelm than to guide. The listed items are loosely organized in broad categories. A scholar could spend weeks in even a great library going through these lists without identifying any source that exactly meets some restricted but well-defined literature search with an anthropological objective.

In an interesting expansion that captures many of the more useful contemporary efforts, the work by authors identified in this bibliography but published after 1970 is listed in Weeks and Brogan's *Social anthropology of Western Europe* **(O03).** See also Rogers, Gilmore, and Clegg's *Directory of Europeanist anthropologists in North America* **(O18)** and the extensive coverage found in the *Anthropological index* to current periodicals in the Museum of Mankind Library **(A35).**

O03

Weeks, John M., and Martha L. Brogan. *Social anthropology of Western Europe: A selective bibliography of books in the humanities and social science libraries, University of Minnesota.* Minneapolis: Western European Studies Center, University of Minnesota, 1988. 124p. (Western European studies series, v.9)

Range of geographic coverage is limited to the twelve member countries of the European community as well as Austria, Finland, Norway, Sweden, Switzerland, and several coastal islands. Far from comprehensive for reference sources. Kuter's *The anthropology of Western Europe* **(O01),** published in 1978, is not included in this list of post-1970 publications. Authors whose recent titles were included in this list were identified by compiling a list of authors with work cited in either Cole's "Anthropology comes part-way home" **(O86);** Rogers, Gilmore, and Clegg's *Directory of Europeanist anthropologists in North America* **(O18);** or Theodoratus's *Europe* **(O02).** These names were then checked against the strong collection at the University of Minnesota at Minneapolis to identify more recent publications by these authors. The subject headings that had been assigned to cataloged books thus identified were then used to identify additional resources.

Weeks provides "Table 2, Subject headings related to the social anthropology of Western Europe" (pp.xv–xvii), which identifies the subject headings from the *Library of Congress subject headings,* 9th ed. (Washington, D.C.: Library of Congress, 1980 [2v.]). The more recent 14th edition (3v.) was not used for this expansion. It both illustrates the difficulties of using these subject headings for anthropological searches and alerts the reader to the modest expectations of elaboration this kind of effort can achieve.

The lists are alphabetically arranged by main entry under country headings. Reference works are interfiled with other works and can sometimes be identified by scanning. Among the resources identified in Weeks but not annotated here, find Rosa María Capel Martínez and Julio Iglesias de Ussel's *Mujer española y sociedad; Bibliografía (1900–1984)* (Madrid: Ministerio de Cultura, Instituto de la Mujer, 1984 [391p.]).

Searching for Current Materials

For special current awareness features of scholarly journals, inspect first the Royal Anthropological Institute's *Reference list of current periodicals* **(A14),** which is arranged so that listings in any issue will identify a select list of articles from journals relevant to a specialized topic in a particular culture area.

Select Sources of Review in Scholarly Publications

For a list of journals with substantive coverage of anthropological topics in English and French, consult Kuter's *The anthropology of Western Europe* **(O01).**

O04

Ethnologia Europaea: Journal of European ethnology. v.1– , 1967– . Göttingen: Ethnologia Europaea. Quarterly.

The journal offers an agenda for breaking the barriers that divide research on Europe from general ethnology and the barriers created by different national schools. Text in English, French, German. Book reviews reflect inclusion of these various traditions so that topical coverage extends past studies of kinship and class into agricultural production. The editorial offices are at the University of Copenhagen.

O05

Ethnologia Scandinavia. v.1– , 1971– . Bjarred, Sweden: Ethnologia Scandinavia. Annual.

Book reviews are a regular feature. Articles in English and German tend to apply contemporary theory to all aspects of Nordic social and material culture. Usually reviews monographic titles that have European populations as an object of study. These are becoming increasingly frequent.

O06

Folklife: Journal of ethnological studies. v.1– , 1963– . Cardiff, Wales: Society for Folk Life Studies. Annual.

Book reviews. Ethnological studies include a focus on agricultural life and technologies, crafts and industries, linguistics, costume, customs, and folklore.

Scanning More Narrowly Focused Scholarly Journals

Because of the European inclusion of geographic variables in ethnographic work, the Geographisch-Ethnographische Gesellschaft, Zurich, *Geographical helvetica,* v.1– , 1946– (Bern: Kümmerly and Frey) **(O07),** a quarterly with text and titles in French, German, and Italian, can be usefully consulted. It includes human geography in the European tradition with its ethnographic scope and extends into studies of the social function of sports and recreation.

For an emphasis on Eastern Europe, consult the list of international periodicals, series, monographic sets, and dictionaries of European and Oriental archaeology and ethnology in volume 9/10 (1978–79) (p.169–383) of *Acta praehistorica et archaeologica,* v.1– , 1970 (Berlin: Volker Spiess. Gesellschaft für Anthropologie, Ethnologie und Urgeschichte), an annual.

O08

Brogan, Martha L., Steve Alvin, and Charles Spetland. *Contemporary Western Europe: A selective bibliography of serials in the humanities/social sciences libraries, University of Minnesota.* Minneapolis: Western European Area Studies Center, University of Minnesota, 1988. 256p.

Based on a strong collection, this bibliography identifies 1,415 serials published in or about contemporary Western Europe. Monographic series and theoretical journals are omitted. Each entry provides corporate author, title, holdings, bibliographic notes, indexes or abstracts covering the title, country of publication, languages, subject headings, and ISSN and OCLC control numbers. Entries are listed alphabetically. The subject index is by broad topic and lists under each topic the brief title of relevant journals. For example, under ANTHROPOLOGY, five brief titles are listed; under BALTIC STUDIES, three brief titles are listed; under BIBLIOGRAPHY, seventeen brief titles are listed; under BOOK REVIEWS, five titles are listed; under CENTRAL EUROPE, three titles are listed; under DEMOGRAPHY, four brief titles are listed; under DOCUMENTATION, three titles are listed; under ETHNOLOGY, eight brief titles are listed; under GREECE, six brief titles are listed; and under ICELAND, five brief titles are listed. There is also a country of publication index and a language of publication index.

Directories

Rogers, Gilmore, and Clegg's *Directory of Europeanist anthropologists in North America* **(O18)** provides the best guide and the best retrospective entry to the anthropological literature of Europe. These features overshadow its value as a directory.

O09

McCall, Grant. "American anthropological interest and prospects in Basque studies." *Current anthropology* 14 (2) (1973): 73–82.

Biographical and address information on 100 individuals with a list of their publications.

O10

Veiter, Theodor. *Handbuch der institute, forschungsstellen und forschungsgesellschaften. . . .* Wien: Braumüller for the Internationales Institut für Nationalitänrecht und Regionalismus, 1988. 307p. (Ethnos, bd.33)

Directory of learned institutions and associations dealing with minorities in Europe. See also Gerhard Teich's *Topographie der Osteuropa-, Südosteuropaund, und DDR-Sammlungen.* (München and New York: Verlag Dokumentation, 1978 [388p.]) **(O11),** a companion to the specialist working in German libraries and archives because it describes for each institution the holdings on national minorities.

Retrospective Searches

The Tozzer Library's *Author and subject catalogues of the Tozzer Library* [microfiche] **(A26),** the Peabody Library's *Catalogue: Subject* **(A29),** and the Museum of Mankind Library's *Museum of Mankind Library catalogues* [microfiche] **(A25)** provide author and classified subject entry into all aspects of anthropology. The most useful printed index for identifying ethnographic material contained in the hardcover resources of research libraries can be found in the Human Relations Area Files, *HRAF source bibliography* **(D16).** For those who prefer to work with microfiche, consult the microfiche edition (when available) of the HRAF's *Human relations area files* **(D69).** The organization difficulties of entry into the printed Human Relations Area Files' *HRAF source bibliography* **(D16)** should not discourage its regular use by anthropologists. In fact the use of this bibliographic tool provides an excellent introduction to the use of the microfiche files when they are approached for research activities other than bibliographic searches for printed information. The *International bibliography of social and cultural anthropology* **(D20)** provides some author and classified subject entry into all aspects of anthropology but is listed in chapter 4, where it can most powerfully support a search strategy in "Ethnology/Cultural Anthropology."

When retrospective searches include searches for descriptions of indigenous peoples, consult also the Museum of Mankind Library's "Tribal index" [microfiche] **(D13).** For continuing coverage of the periodical output that can be cumulated into a retrospective search, consult *Anthropological literature* **(A36),** *Anthropological index* **(A35),** and *Abstracts in anthropology* **(A32).**

Retrospective Bibliographies—Bibliographies of Bibliographies

O12

"Anthropology." In *Bibliographische berichte.* Jahrg. 1–30, 1959–88. Frankfurt a. Main: Klostermann.

"Anthropology" appears as a topical section in every issue. Publisher, title, and frequency vary. Provides a classified listing of recent bibliographies in periodical articles and books as well as separate publications. Coverage is international, with a high percentage of German titles. Very strong in identification of Slavic folklore and linguistics, especially continuing sources. The index provides detailed subject expansions.

O13

Dickinson, Dennis, and Ruda Pempe, comps. "Europe bibliographies." In *Anthropological bibliographies: A selected guide,* p.143–63. South Salem, N.J.: Redgrave, 1981. 307p.

Classified arrangement with running heads to facilitate entry. Rich if not comprehensive coverage to 1980. Especially useful for its ability to isolate anthropologically significant materials from resources with a more general purpose.

O14

Institut etnografii imeni N. N. Miklukho-Maklaia. *Bibliography of Soviet ethnographical publications, 1977–1982.* Moscow: Institute of Ethnography, 1982. 86p.

Lists 514 entries alphabetically by author. No annotations. Covers bibliographies in English, French, Spanish, East European languages, and German. Geographical and subject/methodological indexes. Preceded by Zoia Dmitrievna Titova's *Etnografiia; Bibliografiia russkikh bibliografii po etnografii norodov SSSR (1851–1969)* (Moskva: "Kniga," 1970 [142p.]) **(O15),** which arranges and annotates 734 entries by geographic area, with author and subject indexes.

O16

Mann, Thomas L., comp. "U.S.S.R. bibliographies." In *Anthropological bibliographies: A selected guide,* p.211–24. South Salem, N.Y.: Redgrave, 1981. 307p.

A classed arrangement with running heads to facilitate entry. Rich if not comprehensive coverage to 1980. Especially useful for its ability to isolate anthropologically significant materials.

O17

Svanberg, Ingvar, and Eva-Charlotte Ekström. *People and cultures: A guide to bibliographies in cultural anthropology, ethnology and folklore.* Viborg: NEFA-Nordens dokumentationsudvalg, 1985. 69p. (NEFA dokumentation, no.7)

No annotations. The entries are arranged in a detailed classification system. Page 9 lists guides to anthropological, ethnological, and folkloristic literature. There are lists of European bibliographies (p.11–30) first under general, then by region and by country thereunder. Almost exclusively devoted to separately published items.

Retrospective Bibliographies—Biographical Directories

O18

Rogers, Susan Carol, David D. Gilmore, and Melissa Clegg, comps. *Directory of Europeanist anthropologists in North America.* Washington, D.C.: Society for the Anthropology of Europe by the American Anthropological Association, 1987. 106p.

This directory is placed here because its bibliographic functions might be missed if the entry were placed under the heading "Directories." It is a perfect example of the need for the category "Retrospective Bibliographies—Biographical Directories." Includes directory information on the 340 scholars listed. It provides such information as address, title, institutional affiliation, degree awarded, awarding institution, and date of award. Background information on each individual includes geographic specialty, field research sites, and topical specialties. All of this is valuable as networking information. But this directory has special features which transform a list of scholars specializing in European ethnology into an important resource for retrospective searches. Each listing is followed by a selected bibliography with up to four publications for geographic location identified on a series of maps showing approximate research sites. This is followed by a series of indexes to identify individuals or literature dealing with a particular geographic area or topic. The index for topical specialties has twenty-four subject headings that reflect a willingness to examine areas and problems in urbanized, post-industrial Europe. Multidisciplinary subject headings used here could usefully be extended in other searches by topical entry in such reference sources as annual bibliographic indexes.

At least 80 percent of the bibliography refers to monographs or to articles in collections published as monographs. This means they would not have been identified in quarterly issues of the *Anthropological index,* v.1– , 1963– **(A35),** with its classified arrangement for European ethnology which though highly selective still provides the best indexing entry to anthropological studies of European populations. Consult also the *International bibliography of social and cultural anthropology* **(D20).**

Retrospective Bibliographies—Continuing

O19

American bibliography of Slavic and East European studies. v.1– , 1967– . Palo Alto, Calif.: American Association for the Advancement of Slavic Studies. History Department. Stanford University. Annual.

Since 1973, compiled by the staff of the Slavic and Central European Division, U.S. Library of Congress. Arrangement by subject and provides entry for "Anthropology," "Archaeology," "Folklore," and "Language and linguistics." A complete record of North American publications in Slavic and East European studies. Consult also *European bibliography of Soviet, East European and Slavonic studies,* v.1– , 1975– (Birmingham, England: University of Birmingham) **(O20),** an annual covering French, German, and British publications on Eastern European minority groups. For some Russian ethnic groups, consult the "Bibliography of periodical literature" in the *Middle East journal* **(P11).** Consult also *Internationale volkskundliche bibliographie (International folklore bibliography) (Bibliographie internationale des arts et traditions populaires)* **(D21).**

O21

"Annual bibliographies." *Scottish studies.* v.1– , 1957– . Edinburgh: School of Scottish Studies. University of Edinburgh.

An author/title list of publications related to Scottish studies. Semiannual from 1957 to 1974.

O22

British archaeological abstracts. v.1– , 1968– . London: Council for British Archaeology. Semiannual.

Indexes periodicals, monographic series, and occasional papers. Provides full bibliographic information and covers Great Britain, Ireland, and Europe.

O23

Demos: Internationale ethnographische und folkloristische informationen. v.1– , 1958– . Berlin: Akademie Verlag. Quarterly.

A bulletin that classifies and fully annotates books, articles, and pamphlets in ethnography and folklore that originate in the cooperating countries. Prepared under the auspices of Institut fur Deutsche Volkskunde an der Deutschen Akademie der Wissenschaft zu Berlin in cooperation with learned societies and various ministries of culture in the Soviet Union, Czechoslovakia, Poland, Albania, Bulgaria, Romania, and Hungary. Author index.

O24

Industrial archaeology review. v.1– , 1976– . Oxford, England: Oxford Univ. Pr. 3/yr.

Six or seven articles and several book reviews are published in each issue. Excellent organizational information and studies of early industry and technology on surviving materials.

O25

Nordic archaeological abstracts. v.1– , 1975– . Viborg, Denmark: Nordic Archaeological Abstracts. Annual.

Includes periodical articles, serials, symposia, and collected works. Mostly in Scandinavian languages, with English-language abstracts. Covers prehistorical, medieval, and post-medieval archaeology in all of the Scandinavian countries.

O26

Osterreichische volkskundliche bibliographie. v.1/3– , 1965/67– . Wien: Verhand fur Volkskunde.

Provides a continuing international bibliography of Austrian folklore.

O27

Musikethnologische Jahresbibliographie Europas (Annual bibliography of European ethnomusicology). Bratislava: National Museum. International Folk Music Council. Annual.

Bibliography of European ethnomusicology with introductory and editorial notes in English.

O28

Polish archaeological abstracts. v.1– , 1972– . Pozman: Polish Academy of Sciences. Institute of the History of Material Culture. Annual.

Arranged by period from the Paleolithic to fifteenth century, by subject thereunder and then by author. Abstracts are in English. Covers periodicals, monographs, review articles, and excavation reports in Polish.

Retrospective Bibliographies—Topical

Consult Rolf Baumgarter, comp., *Bibliography of Irish linguistics and literature, 1942–71* (Dublin: Institute for Advanced Studies, 1986 [776p.]) **(O29),** a classed bibliography of studies of Irish traditions. The chapter "General" includes bibliography and serials; "Linguistics" includes psycholinguistics; "Society" contains items 7227–7583; "Prehistory and cultural history" contains items 8825–9312. Indexes are by words and proper names, by first line of verse, and by author/title. For a more generous coverage of Irish folklore as ethnography, consult Kevin Danahen's *A bibliography of Irish ethnology and folk tradition* (Dublin: Mercier Pr., 1978 [95p.]) **(O30).**

Consult any topical work edited or compiled by Hastings Donnan, who often brings to print the activities of a small but vigorous community of anthropologists living in Ireland. From this critical mass of scholars, a unified vision has formed of the most useful application of anthropology to Irish national concerns. This group seems to have a cohesion that is comparable to that of the small band of anthropological scholars who worked in the United States before World War II. Anthropology has established itself as an independent discipline in Ireland.

O31

Aldcroft, Derek Howard, and Richard Rodger. *Bibliography of European economic and social history.* Manchester, England: Manchester University, 1984. 243p.

Classed arrangement under headings for geographic regions such as "Europe," "Western Europe," "East central and south eastern Europe." The heading "Southern Europe" is subdivided for Italy, Spain, Turkey. "Scandinavia" is subdivided for general works: Norway, Sweden, Denmark, and Finland. The "Baltic states" heading is subdivided for general works and for Estonia, Latvia, and Lithuania. Each geographic unit is further subdivided for social science topics, including "Social structure and social conditions." Author index. Consult also G. Bentley Carter's *Ethnicity and nationality: A bibliographic guide* (Seattle: Univ. of Washington Pr., 1981 [455p.]) (School of International Studies. Publications on ethnicity and nationality, no.3) **(O32).** Annotates 308 entries listed alphabetically by author. An additional 2,030 numbered entries are not annotated and are listed in a second alphabetic order by author. The index by geographic area is useful and sometimes has expansion terms. Charts list each article under sixteen categories. Thus if the user follows a code label *four,* it is possible to identify all articles that relate to a specific academic field. *Four* (a) would identify all articles in the annotated list written by anthropologists (a total of 99 articles). The coding system would indicate an article by Barth surveying primary data for scholars with an interest in demography and questions of class and social mobility.

O33

Bibliography of Finnish sociology, 1960–1969. Helsinki: Academic Bookstore, 1973. 370p. (Westermarck Society. *Transactions,* v.20)

Supplemented by *Bibliography of Finnish sociology, 1970–1979,* comp. by Terttu Turunen-Noro (Helsinki: Academic Bookstore, 1973 [370p.]) (Westermarck Society. *Transactions,* v.19) **(O34),** and *Bibliography of Finnish sociology, 1980–1984,* comp. by Maria Forsman (Helsinki: Academic Bookstore, 1989 [151p.]) (Westermarck Society, n.21) **(O35).** A table of contents is given in English. Includes books, journal articles, dissertations, and research reports with some brief English-language annotations. Classed arrangement under topics, with some of special relevance to anthropology, including: "Social structure," "Culture" (p.28–40), "Sociology of the family age groups," "Bibliographies." Indexes by author and subject.

O36

Bonser, Wilfrid. *A bibliography of folklore: As contained in the first eighty years of the publications of the Folklore Society.* London: W. Glaisher, 1961. 126p. (Publications of the Folklore Society, 121, no.4)

A classic. Excellent organization. Limited only by the interests of the members. Supplemented by Wilfrid Bonser's *A bibliography of folklore for 1958–1967: Being a subject index to vols. 69–78 of the journal Folklore* (London: Folklore Society; distributed by W. Glaisher, 1969 [54p.]) (Publications of the Folklore Society, 130) **(O37).**

O38

Bonser, Wilfrid. *A prehistoric bibliography.* Ext. and ed. by June Troy. Oxford, England: Blackwell, 1976. 425p.

The sections on "Specific cities" and "Material finds" are arranged by the system of the Council of British Archaeologists to cover the British Isles. Indexes of authors and subjects.

O39

Buhociu, Octavian. "Folklore and ethnography in Rumania." *Current anthropology* 7 (3) (1966): 309–14.

Bibliographic review with supporting records listed alphabetically by main entry. Consult also Comité National Roumain D'Études du Sud-Est Européen, *Les études du sud-est Européennes en Roumanie: Guide de documentation* (Bucarest: Comité National Roumain d'Études du Sud-Est Européen, 1966 [265p.]) **(O40).** As a part of UNESCO effort in the mid-1960s to encourage the consolidation of what was known in preparation for an international indexing effort, this work provided a list of scientific organizations, a list of libraries and archives, and a classified, annotated list of reference sources covering both monographs and articles. Material on national minorities is listed under numerous subject headings requiring determined and multiple entry for an effective search.

O41

Falassi, Alessendro. *Italian folklore: An annotated bibliography.* New York: Garland, 1985. 438p. (Garland folklore bibliography, v.7)

Lists 3,000 entries with subject and name index for regional entry. FISHERMEN has two entries; ABRUZZI "life cycle" has three entries; ABRUZZI "Social life and customs" has four entries. A knowledgeable introduction greatly adds to the strength of this work, which is intended to add to the entries found in 100 bibliographies identified (which in turn provide access to more than 50,000 titles). Includes periodical articles and books. Lists dissertations that can be classed as reference works such as Ralf E. Carriuolo's *Materials for the study of Italian folk music* (Middletown, Conn.: Wesleyan University Ph.D dissertation, 1974 [425p.]) **(O42).** Other reference works interfiled in the alphabetic list include Alberto M. Cirese's "Folklore in Italy: A historical and systematic profile and bibliography," *Journal of the Folklore Institute* (1975): 7–79 **(O43),** which provides a bibliographic review with an extensive select bibliography, and Paolo Toschi's *Bibliografia delle tradizioni popolari d'Italia dal 1916 al 1940.* (Florence: Barbera, 1946 [144p.]) **(O44),** with 2,642 entries. This was planned as a three-volume work but volumes 2 and 3 were never published.

O45

Gobel, Peter. Museum für Völkerkunde zu Leipzig 1869–1969. "Bibliographie." Museum fur Volkerkunde *Jahrbuch* 26 (1969): 361–407.

Bibliography of publications edited by the Museum of Anthropology, Leipzig, 1869–1969. The best index to the full ethnographic content of a journal with extensive descriptions of the activities of European ethnic groups.

O46

González Ollé, Fernando. *Manual bibliográfico de estudios españoles.* Pamplona: Ediciones Universidad de Navarra, 1976. 1,375p.

A substantial work with twenty-two main categories, each being closely divided into an elaborate classification system. A detailed table of contents and author and subject indexes guide the reader.

O47

Halpern, Joel M., ed. *Bibliography of anthropological and sociological publications on Eastern Europe and the USSR (English language sources).* Los Angeles: University of California. Russian and East European Studies Center, 1961. 124p. (Russian and East European Study Center series, v.1, no.2)

A preliminary but extensive bibliography of the most available books and articles in English. Entries are arranged geographically and cover the Slavs in general, Eastern Europe, the Balkans, Albania, Bulgaria, Czechoslovakia, Hungary, Poland, Romania, Yugoslavia, and the CIS. Still valuable for its arrangement and for its identification of the seminal works. Entries for each area are classified by subject, such as archaeology and history, ethnology, geography, linguistics, religion, demography, and social change. Includes a supplement compiled by Raymond H. Fisher on Siberian travel accounts. No index.

O48

Horak, Stephan M. *Eastern European national minorities: 1919–1980: A handbook.* Littleton, Colo.: Libraries Unlimited, 1985. 353p.

A classified bibliographic guide with rich annotations to reference works in all scholarly languages. The chapters organize the ten major subject divisions. There is a general section with a historical summary followed by a detailed classified bibliography of general reference sources. There follows nine chapters devoted to the distribution of national minorities in each country. Within chapters devoted to specific minorities there is a historical summary followed by a bibliography subdivided for general reference works and other types of publications. There follows a section that lists the various national minorities, with appropriate specialized reference works listed in several subdivisions under the identified minority. There is an author/short-title index. Consult also *Les études balkaniques* (Sofia: Comité Bulgare des sciences. Comite National d'Études Balkaniques) **(O49),** which was developed as part of the effort by UNESCO to consolidate a base from which international indexing could proceed. It provides a list of scientific organizations, a list of libraries and archives, and a classified, annotated list of reference sources covering both monographs and articles. Material on national minorities is listed under numerous subject headings requiring determined and multiple entry for an effective search.

O50

Horak, Stephan M. *Russia, the USSR, and Eastern Europe: A bibliographic guide to English language publications, 1981–1985.* Littleton, Colo.: Libraries Unlimited, 1987. 273p.

The present volume is a supplement to earlier works in the same area covering the years 1964–74 and 1975–80. Divided into three parts: (1) General and interrelated themes; (2) Russian Empire prior to 1917 and USSR and CIS, non-Russian republics, Jews, and others; and (3) Eastern Europe. Each entry consists of a bibliographic citation plus a brief but informative abstract. Access to the entries is provided by a detailed table of contents, an author/title index, and a subject index. Citations to reviews in major journals are given.

O51

Johann Gottfried Herder-Institut. Marburg. Bibliothek. *Alphabetischer katalog.* Boston: Hall, 1964. 5v.

Entry to all aspects of cultural life of east central Europe. First supplement adds 38,500 cards.

O52

Krewson, Margrit B. *The German-speaking countries of Europe: A selective bibliography.* 2d ed. rev. and enl. Washington, D.C.: Library of Congress, 1989. 318p.

The five parts cover Austria, the Federal Republic of Germany, the German Democratic Republic, Liechtenstein, and Switzerland. Each of these parts, except that on Liechtenstein, is subdivided into seven sections: "Bibliographies and reference works," "Description and travel," "Economy," "Intellectual and cultural life," "Politics and government," "Religion," and "Society." Consult also Larry Richardson's *Introduction to library research in German studies: Language, literature, and civilization* (Boulder, Colo.: Westview Pr., 1984 [227p.]) **(O53).**

"Prehistory and folklore" (p.126–30) provides a useful introduction to reference sources, including oral folk narrative material.

O54

Leeds. University. Brotherton Library. *Catalogue of the Romany collection formed by D. U. McGrigor Phillips L.L.D. and presented to the University of Leeds.* Edinburgh: published by Nelson for the Brotherton Collection, 1962. 227p.

A classified bibliography of more than 1,200 books, pamphlets, manuscripts, music items, letters, playbills, pictures, and engravings relating to Gypsies in many countries. Author and title indexes. Inclusion of manuscript items increases its importance. See also Dennis Binns's *A Gypsy bibliography: A bibliography of all recent books, pamphlets, articles, broadsheets, theses and dissertations pertaining to the Gypsies and other travellers that the author is aware of at the time of printing* (Manchester, England: Dennis Binns pubs., 1982–88 [3v.]) **(O55)** and Pieter Hovens and Jeanne Hovens's *Zigeuners, woonwagenbewoners en reizenden: Een bibliografie* (Rijswijk, Ministerie van Cultuur, 1982 [120p.]) **(O56),** which lists 100 entries alphabetically by author with geographic and broad topic indexes. This can be informally updated by reference to "Bibliographical notes" in *Journal* of the Gypsy Lore Society, v.1– , 1988– (Coventry, England: The Gypsy Lore Society) **(O57).**

O58

Lovett, Clara Maria. *Contemporary Italy: A selective bibliography.* Washington, D.C.: Library of Congress, 1985. 106p.

Lists 1,300 books published between 1945 and 1983 with an emphasis on social science materials. A separate chapter segregates English-language materials. Author index and a professionally structured subject index.

O59

Marduel, Marie-Laure, and Michel Robert. *Les sociétés rurales françaises; Eléments de bibliographie.* Paris: Éditions du Centre National de la Recherche Scientifique, 1979. 262p. (Écrits et travaux du Groupe de Sociologie Rurale du CNRS, v.3)

Pt.1, "General studies," is subdivided into eleven headings. Entries under "Vie et institutions villageoises" (p.123–34) are most relevant to anthropological questions. Pt.2, subdivided for nine regions. The appendixes include A guide to the analysis of villages, Techniques of study, and A list of periodicals (annotated). There are indexes both by names of persons and by names of institutions. Consult also F. Lapadu-Hargues and D. Gluck's "Bibliographie d'ethnologie française, 1968," *Arts et traditions populaires* 7 (3/4) (1969): 306–89 **(O60).**

O61

McGreehan, Jean R., and Sarah Stephens. *Celtic serials: A guide to periodical indexes for Celtic studies and bibliography of Celtic serials in the Libraries of the University of Minnesota, Twin Cities, and the O'Shaughnessy Library at the College of Saint Thomas, St. Paul.* Minneapolis: Western European Studies Center. University of Minnesota, 1983. 66p. (Western European Studies Center series, no.6)

An innovative solution to the problem of dealing with the abundance of material in this area. There is a guide to relevant indexes and abstracts (p.13–17) under topical subheadings. There follows a list of relevant journals (many of which are indexed nowhere) with an indication of holdings and subject notations. Pt.4, a subject index to these serial publications with topics such as ARCHAEOLOGY (with 33 relevant journals listed), BIBLIOGRAPHY with 30 relevant journals listed), and FOLKLORE (with 14 journals listed).

O62

Meyer, Klaus. *Bibliographie zur osteuropäischen geschichte. Verzeichnis d. zwischen 1939 u. 1964 veröffentlichten literatur in west-europäischen sprachen zur osteuropäischen geschichte bis 1945.* Wiesbaden: Harrassowitz in Kommission, 1972. 649p. (Bibliographische Mitteilungen des Osteuropa-Instituts an der Freien Universität Berlin, 10)

More than 12,000 entries for books, periodical articles, and monographs published in the many languages of Eastern Europe, including the Baltic Republics, Finland, and Poland. There are subject headings for national minorities. For example, under POLAND entries 10529–10615. Arranged by topic. Author index.

O63

New York (City) Public Library. Research Libraries. Slavonic Division. *Dictionary catalog of the Slavonic collection.* 2d rev. ed. Boston: Hall, 1974. 44v.

Organized by subject. For example, see v.2, Anthropology and archaeology; v.13, Folklore. Updated by *Bibliographic guide to Soviet and East European studies,* v.1– , 1979– (Boston: Hall), an annual **(O64).** Lists material cataloged at New York Public Library and entries identified on MARC tapes.

O65

Niewiadomska, Maria. *Bibliografia etnografii polskiej zalata 1961–1969.* Wrocaw: Zakad Narodowy imienia Ossolinskich Wydawnictwo Polskiej Akademii Nauk, 1982–83. 2v. (Prace Komitetu Nauk Etnologicznych PAN, 3–4)

A supplement has been issued (1983 [1,059p.]) which extends coverage to 1974. Earlier periods were covered by Halina Bittner-Szewczykowa's "Materialy do bibliografi etnografi polskiejzalata 1945–54," which appeared as a supplement to *Lud* 43 (1958), and by Boleslaw Gawin's "Bibliografia etnografii polskiej 1955–60" with earlier issues carrying the department as *Lud* 44 (1960), 46 (1962), and 51 (1967). Covers works on the ethnography of Poland published in other countries. Indexed.

O66

O'Leary, Timothy J., and Joan Steffens. *Lapps ethnographic bibliography.* New Haven, Conn.: Human Relations Area Files, 1975. 2v.

Lists 1,421 entries covering books, periodical articles, and chapters from collected works. Indexed by author, subgroup, geographic location, field date, and bibliographic date. Codes for these indexed features are included with the bibliographic description of each entry.

O67

Ottó, Domonkos, and Péter Nagybákay. *Magyarország kézmuvesipartörtének váfája.* MTA Néprajzi Kutatóintézet, 1992. 461p.

Contains all of the documents relating to the constitutional, economic, social, legal, linguistic, and local history of handcraft, with special attention to its ethnographic significance.

O68

Pearson, Raymond. *Russian and Eastern Europe, 1789–1985: A bibliographic guide.* Manchester, England: Manchester Univ. Pr., 1989. 210p.

Annotated list of books and articles that are most important and useful. Chronological arrangement with thematic arrangement thereunder. The topic "Society" is subdivided for agrarian life, elites, everyday life, marriage and family, national character, women, and youth. Religion in the section on the CIS has a subdivision for Islam.

O69

Pereira, Benjamin Enes. *Bibliografía analítica de ethografía portuguesa.* Lisboa: Centro de Estudios de Etnologia Peninsular. Instituto de Alta Cultura, 1965. 670p.

Annotates 3,834 entries describing books and periodical articles on the ethnology of Portugal. Classified subject arrangement. Author index.

O70

Sanders, Irwin Taylor. *East European peasantries: Social relations: An annotated bibliography of periodical articles.* Boston: Hall, 1976. 179p.

A bibliography of a thirty-volume collection of periodical articles at the Mugar Library, Boston University. There is a geographical arrangement with no subject index. Conceptually it is a thorough reading list of periodical articles only. Fully annotated with coverage of the countries of communist East Europe and Greece.

O71

Veiter, Theodor. *Bibliographie zur südirolfrage, 1945–83.* Wien: Braumüller, 1984. 281p. (Ethnos [Vienna, Austria], bd.26)

Annotates 1,389 entries on Trentino-Alto Adige (Italy). Includes books, periodicals, and dissertations. Covers regionalism, ethnicity, and ethnic and linguistic groups. In the subject/name index, the heading BIBLIOGRAPHY leads to seventeen entries.

O72

Vlachos, Evan. *Modern Greek society: Continuity and change; An annotated classification of selected sources.* Fort Collins: Colorado State University Department of Sociology and Anthropology, 1969. 177p. (Colorado State University. Department of Sociology and Anthropology. Special monograph series, no.1)

Entries are arranged alphabetically under broad subject terms such as "Greek people," "Form and extent of groups in Greece," "Culture and personality," and "Nature and characteristics of Greek institutions." Long introductory sections with evaluative comments and bibliographic lists at the end of each section. Limited to work completed since 1950, with a bias toward work in English and Greek. Author index. For more recent monographs but with reduced coverage of Greek-language materials, consult Stephanie Boyé's *Modern Greece: A guide to recent works in Wilson Library* (Minneapolis: Western European Area Studies Center, University of Minnesota, 1985 [76p.]) **(O73),** a list with 500-plus entries to recent scholarship in modern Greek studies identified in a single strong collection. Arranged under broad topics, with GEOGRAPHY and SOCIAL AFFAIRS being relevant to anthropology. Limited to resources in a single library with a strong collection.

Informational Reference Searches

For American anthropology, consult first the *AAA guide* **(A53)** for directory information. The best international directory is still the "International directory of anthropological institutions" **(A56),** which could usefully be reissued in a new edition. Consult Sebeok's *Soviet and East European linguistics* **(E75)** and all chapters in Part 1, "Access by Discipline and Subdiscipline," of *Fieldwork in the Library.*

Dictionaries

O74

International dictionary of regional European ethnology and folklore. Copenhagen: Published by Rosenkilde and Bagger for the International Commission on Folk Arts and Folklore, 1960–65. 2v.

Best available dictionary for ethnographic concepts. Produced under a cooperative arrangement between the International Council for Philosophy and Humanistic Studies and UNESCO to provide definitions of general ethnological concepts. Languages include English, French, Spanish, German, and a Scandinavian language (usually Swedish). Provides citations to the use of a term in retrospective literature. V.1, a dictionary of ethnological concepts arranged by the English word. Definitions are contemporary to the date of publication, with historical depth and adequate bibliographic references. These definitions do not reflect the recent influence of linguistics on ethnographic concepts. For these innovations, consult *Fieldwork in the Library,* chapter 5, "Anthropological Linguistics," and chapter 4, "Ethnology/Cultural Anthropology." For many ethnographic purposes useful explication can be found in *Funk and Wagnalls standard dictionary of folklore, mythology and legend* **(D45),** which has a range of convenient use far beyond the scope of its title.

Encyclopedias, Handbooks, Manuals

O75

Bach, Adolf. *Deutsche volkskunde: Werke und organisation, probleme, system, methoden, ergebnisse und aufgaben, schriftum.* Heidelberg: Quelle & Heyer, 1960. 708p.

A detailed table of contents guides the reader. Extensive coverage of sociological and psychological facets of folk culture makes this source useful for European ethnography. For an English-language review of the influence of this anthropologist and the tradition in which, until recently, most ethnographic descriptions of Europe have been written, consult G. Cocchiara's *The history of folklore in Europe,* tr. by John N. McDaniel (Philadelphia: ISHI, 1981

[703p.]) **(O76).** For a bibliographic review of the powerful influence in Europe of Marxist theory, consult J. E. Limon's "Western Marxism and folklore," *Journal of American folklore* (1983) 96: 34–52 **(O77),** and J. E. Limon's "Western Marxism and folklore," *Journal of American folklore* (1984) 97: 337–44 **(O78).**

O79

Dow, James R., and Hannjost Lixfeld, eds. *German volkskunde: A decade of theoretical confrontation, debate, and reorientation (1967–1977).* Bloomington: Indiana Univ. Pr., 1986. 343p.

Contributions by twenty recognized experts. There is an acronym list (p.278) that identifies eleven most frequently cited journals in studies of ethnography of Germany. The bibliography of more than 800 entries is strengthened by interfiling items not mentioned in the running text but suggested by the twenty experts as most important or most frequently cited. For this reason this work can be used as a review of the literature, with 101 pages of bibliographic description.

O80

Katz, Zev, ed. *Handbook of major Soviet nationalities.* New York: Free Pr., 1975. 481p.

Divided into five parts: Slavs, Baltic, Transcaucasians, Central Asia, and other nationalities. All chapters are by recognized scholars, with selective bibliographies. A basic reference tool. Does not cover the religions of these groups. Each chapter deals with the territory, demography, language, and culture of seventeen of the Soviet nations. References are cited, and there is an appendix of comparative tables for all groups.

O81

Riedl, Franz Heironymus, and Theodor Veiter. *Féderalisme, régionalisme et droit des groupes ethniques en Europe (Föderalismus, regionalismus und volksgruppenrecht in Europa); Hommage á Guy Héraud: Festschrift für Guy Héraud.* Wein: W. Braumüller, 1989. 521p. (Ethnos, 30)

Contributions focus on the relationship between ethnic groups and regional and national development in Europe. Extensive bibliographies support the contributions. Forty-seven authorities summarize what is known about covered minorities and the relationship of minorities to regionalism and devolution. There are short biographies of contributors. Consult also Association International d'Études du Sud-est Europêen, *Acts du Premier Congres International des Études Balkanique et Sud-est Européennes* (Sophia: L'Académie Bulgares des Sciences et l'UNESCO, 1955–71 [7v.]) **(O82),** an effort sponsored by UNESCO to consolidate in the French language all social science information about the Balkans to the date of publication. See especially v.1, *Histoire de l'antiueité,* for the section on archaeology (p.185–643, and v.7, *Littérature, ethnographie, folklore* for the sections of folklore (p.653–933) and ethnography (p.383–639).

Recently, scholars with a sound background in the cultures of Africa and of the East are beginning to make contributions to the study of minority ethnic populations in Europe. For an outstanding example of a bibliography that offers a base for studies in controlled comparison, inspect Hans Werner Debrunner's *Presence and prestige: Africans in Europe: A history of Africans in Europe before 1981.* (Basel: Basler Afrika Bibliographien, 1979 [433p.]) (Communications from the Basel Africa bibliography, v.22) **(O83),** which brings together resources for the study of the very different integrative forces that dominated the relationship between the Third World and Europe in the days before the Great War revealed that the European confederacy could not sustain a world of lasting peace.

O84

Wiegelmann, Günter. *Theoretische konzepte der europäischen ethnologie: Diskussionen um regeln und modelle.* Münster: Lit Verlag, 1991. 293p.

Assembles papers written over a period of years and adds recent commentaries and revised positions. Deals with the theoretical problems of European ethnography, folk-culture, and its structure. Outlines the system-environment theory, and town-country relations. There is a discussion of regionalism in the German context and of the periodization of folk culture.

O85

Wixman, Ronald. *The peoples of the USSR: An ethnographic handbook.* Armonk, N.Y.: M. E. Sharpe, 1984. 246p.

Ethnic groups in alphabetic order with fifteen ethnographic maps. Invaluable dictionary of ethnography for this area. Can be supplemented by reference to *Guide to the study of Soviet nationalities,* ed. by S. M. Horak (Littleton, Colo.: Libraries Unlimited, 1982 [265p.]) and Weekes's *Muslim peoples* **(P18).**

State-of-the-Art Reviews

Consolidation of research in this area has benefited from many published reviews of recent research efforts. Consult John W. Cole's "Anthropology comes part-way home: Community studies in Europe," *Annual review of anthropology* 6 (1977): 349–78 **(O86);** David D. Gilmore's "Anthropology of the Mediterranean area," *Annual review of anthropology* 11 (1982): 175–205 **(O87);** Joel Martin Halpern and David A. Kideckel's "Anthropology of Eastern Europe," *Annual review of anthropology* 12 (1983): 277–402 **(O88);** Marianne Gullestad's "Small facts and large issues: The anthropology of contemporary Scandinavian society," *Annual review of anthropology* 18 (1989): 71–93 **(O89);** T. Douglas Price's "The Mesolithic of northern Europe" *Annual review of anthropology* 20 (1991): 211–33 **(O90);** Robert R. Sokal's "The continental population structure of Europe," *Annual review of anthropology* 20 (1991): 119–40 **(O91).** Each of these bibliographic reviews has reference lists that describe the sources of research cited in the review. This dense set of bibliographic reviews is an excellent illustration of the ability of the *Annual review of anthropology* to identify, clarify, and support a research interest that shows increasing vitality but that has not yet established a specialized publication apparatus.

Searching Graphic Materials

Ethnographic work on European populations is keyed to maps by Rogers, Gilmore, and Clegg's *Directory of Europeanist anthropologists in North America* **(O18).** For linguistic distributions, archaeological sites, and other specialized entries, consult American Geographical Society of New York, Map Department, *Index to maps in books and periodicals* **(A59).**

Searching Unpublished Materials

Searches for unpublished materials often benefit from an inspection of the National Anthropological Archives, *Catalog to manuscripts at the National Anthropological Archives* **(A69).** Some unpublished materials are cited in Kuter's *The anthropology of Western Europe* **(O01).**

Archives

O92

Grimsted, Patricia Kennedy. *A handbook for archival research in the USSR.* Princeton, N.J.: International Research and Exchanges Board; Kennan Institute for Advanced Russian Studies, 1989. 430p.

Lists major reference works, finding aids, directories, and bibliographies needed for archival research in specialized fields of study. Also discusses research in published materials in the major academic and state libraries in Moscow and Leningrad. Appendixes focus on archive and manuscript repositories in Moscow and Leningrad, and the state archives of the Union Republics that are not Russian.

11

The Islamic Influence and Israel

This chapter describes core reference sources for social studies conducted about the Islamic World and about Israel. The selection of entries for chapter 11 assumes that the reader has exhausted Balay's *Guide to reference books* **(B02),** especially for recent general sources such as the *Asian historical dictionaries,* v.1– , 1989– (Metuchen, N.J.: Scarecrow), and Fawzi Khoury and Rachel Simon's *National union catalog of Middle Eastern microforms* (Seattle: University of Washington Libraries, 1989 [77p.]).

Some important reference sources for Islamic studies such as Grimwood-Jones, Hopwood, and Pearson's *Arab-Islamic bibliography* **(P02);** *The encyclopedia of Islam* **(P13);** and the University of London, School of Oriental and African Studies, *The quarterly index Islamicus* **(P12),** exclude Israel. Yet other reference sources useful for Islamic studies also cover Israel. Despite the Islamic fiction that Israel does not exist, it is geographically placed in the center of the Islamic world and occupies a great deal of Islamic attention. Some reference sources about the Middle East are both powerful and rich in coverage of Israel. The best source for broad-based coverage is the University of London, School of Oriental and African Studies, *Library catalogue* **(G18).**

Harned's "Ancient Egypt" **(P80)** should be consulted as an example of the extensive reference sources that can develop around a specialized interest in archaeology. Because there is no comparable guide for Assyriology, the user is first introduced to the Oriental Institute's *Publications of the Oriental Institute* **(P115),** to Lloyd's highly readable *The archaeology of Mesopotamia, from the Old Stone Age to the Persian conquest* **(P116),** and Ebling and Meissner's scholarly *Reallexikon der assyriologie und vorderasiatischen archäeologie* **(P117).** Egyptology can be placed in the Islamic world (North Africa) and Assyriology can be placed in the Islamic world (Middle East), just as Mayan can be placed in the Americas (Mesoamerica).

For select bibliographies of localized groups with an Islamic tradition, consult Weekes's *Muslim peoples* **(P18).** However, even searches about anthropological studies of Islamic traditions should start with chapter 1 of *Fieldwork in the Library* for the reference sources identified there and for the discussion of the reference strategies signaled by the headings "Searching for Current Materials" and "Retrospective Searches." In the introduction find a discussion of the structure of internal organization of entries under subject headings.

Several more general machine-readable databases are available. Inspect recent directories of computer files to verify current availability of *Magreb* [computer file] (Provence, France: CRESM Centre de Recherche et d'Études sur les Sociétés Méditerranéennes). Utilizes the several printed publications of the Centre. Available online (SUNIST file Serveur Universitait National de l'Information Scientifique et Technique). Records 22,000 citations. Adds about 750 records a quarter. Citations and abstracts from social science publications on Algeria, Libya, Morocco, Tunisia. Covers monographs, theses, reports. Includes journal articles in Arabic, English, French, German, Italian, and Spanish. Also useful is *Middle East: Abstracts and index* [computer file] (Pittsburgh: Northumberland Corp.), which utilizes portions of the printed *Middle East: Abstracts and index* **(P72).** Available online (DIALOG file 248). Includes 30,000 records. Adds about 4,000 records a quarter. Includes citations to articles from 1,500 journals, books, book reviews, government documents, technical reports, conference proceedings, and dissertations. Covers archaeology, anthropology, Islam, language, religion, and psychology. A list of periodical articles scanned is available on request. A thesaurus of indexing terms can be purchased from Northumberland Press. The file most detailed for issues of anthropological interest is possibly the *MidEast file* [computer file] (Israel: Dayan Center, Shiloah Institute for Middle Eastern and African Studies), which utilizes portions of the printed *MEF,* v.1– , 1979 (Oxford, England: Learned Information). Available online (DIALOG). Records 70,000 citations. Includes books, reports, dissertations, book reviews, official gazettes, and 1,200 periodicals. Covers anthropology, demography, psychology, and sociology of Bahrain, Egypt, Iran, Iraq, Israel, Jordan, Kuwait, Lebanon, Libya, Oman, Qatar, Saudi Arabia, Sudan, Syria, Turkey, United Arab Emirates, and North and South Yemen.

Searching Bibliographic Guides

Consult Auckland's "Getting into the literature" **(A01)** and each of the defining guides identified in the chapters devoted to the subdisciplines of anthropology.

Bibliographic Guides

P01

Geddes, Charles L. *Guide to reference books for Islamic studies.* Denver, Colo.: American Institute of Islamic Studies, 1985. 429p.

A classified and annotated bibliography with 1,200 entries. Many reference works are included. Especially useful for its selective but thorough discussion of maps. The section on bibliographies is followed by a list of reference sources that identify specialized libraries and archives. Anthropologists will find most useful section K, "Geography," and section M, "Social sciences."

P02

Grimwood-Jones, Diana, Derek Hopwood, James D. Pearson, eds. *Arab-Islamic bibliography: The Middle East Library Committee guide: Based on Giuseppe Gabrieli's Manuale di bibliografia musulimana.* Hassocks, England: Harvester Press: Humanities, 1977. 292p.

A truly remarkable work with coverage of a large number of reference sources and in-depth studies of essential source materials for the study of Islam. It is not designed to reward a casual approach. For example, the user must infer from a table of contents entry that reads "Bibliographies II Islam in general. New and Middle East (with or without North Africa: general and subjects)" that bibliographies of histories will include works of primary value to anthropologists. Ibn Khaldun, for example, is listed in this category, and no fewer than four bibliographies of his life and work are included; but the absence of annotations means that the breadth of Ibn Khaldun's social thought and its impact on the Arab mentality go unremarked. Similarly, there is no notation to indicate the value of important editions or translations. Careful, detailed, thoughtful use is needed but will be richly rewarded. Includes a directory of institutions supporting Islamic studies. The bibliographic sections of this earlier work can be brought up to date by consulting the carefully annotated *Introductory guide to Middle Eastern and Islamic bibliography,* ed. by Paul Auchterlonie (Oxford, England: Middle East Library Committee, 1990 [84p.]) (Research guide, 5) **(P03).** Updated in part by Hopwood and Grimwood-Jones's *Middle East and Islam* **(P64),** Auchterlonie's *Middle East and Islam* **(P68),** and Grimwood-Jones's *Middle East and Islam* **(P69).** As a companion for entry into the periodical literature in all scholarly languages, Strijp's desk reference *Cultural anthropology of the Middle East* **(P10)** provides a classified arrangement of a broad selection of monographs and articles with different sections for works published by anthropologists and nonanthropologists.

Searching for Current Materials

For special current awareness features of scholarly journals, inspect first the Royal Anthropological Institute's *Reference list of current periodicals* **(A14),** which is arranged so that listings in any issue will identify a select list of articles from journals relevant to a specialized topic in a particular culture area.

The bibliographic data in the *Middle East Studies Association bulletin* **(P122)** have been a quarterly source of review of current publications in the area of its coverage since 1967. Centre de Recherches et d'Études sur les Sociétés Méditerranéennes, Bibliothéque, *Liste des nouvelles acquisitions,* v.1– , 1984– (Paris: Entre National de la Recherche Scientifíque) **(P04),** is useful for its coverage of French-language serial publications within its area of coverage. For a quarterly review of German-language scholarship, *Die Welt des Islam,* v.1– , 1913– (Leiden, Netherlands: E. J. Brill) **(P05),** has, in the new series that started in 1951, been the best single source for identifying new work in what continues to be a vigorous German tradition. While the *Muslim world,* v.1– , 1911– (Hartford, Conn.: Hartford Seminary Foundation) **(P06)** has a perspective of dialogue between Christians and Muslims, each issue contains a listing of articles that have recently appeared elsewhere, and these often correctly identify the favored themes of discussion in contemporary thinking about present-day Islamic social life.

Retrospective Searches

When retrospective searches include searches for descriptions of the social behavior of indigenous peoples, consult the Human Relations Area Files, *HRAF source bibliography* **(D16)** and the Museum of Mankind Library's "Tribal index" [microfiche] **(D13).** For continuing coverage of the periodical output, consult *Anthropological literature* **(A36),** *Anthropological index* **(A35),** and *Abstracts in anthropology* **(A32).** The annual *International bibliography of social and cultural anthropology* **(D20)** succeeds in maintaining some ethnic-group entry in its indexing.

Retrospective Bibliographies—Bibliographies of Bibliographies

P07

Berque, Jacques, and others. "Matériels de référence." Chapter in *Bibliographie de la culture arabe contemporaine,* p.53–78. [Paris]: Sindbad/Les Presses de l'UNESCO, 1981. 283p.

Scholarly annotations to 132 reference sources in European languages, including Russian, and in Arabic with a discussion of their value in the study of contemporary Arabs. This section includes not only encyclopedias and bibliographies but also a list of journals that can be used as a source of review and of scholarly compendiums. There are 1,507 additional entries with some annotations. Includes a valuable list of periodicals cited and a useful index with names and titles listed in Arabic.

Retrospective Bibliographies—Broad Scope

Entries under this subject heading in chapter 1 are useful and deserve to be used as companion resources to the following more specialized resources:

P08

Behn, Wolfgang H. *Index Islamicus, 1665–1905: A bibliography of articles on Islamic subjects in periodicals and other collective publications.* Millersville, Pa.: Ad-yok Publications, 1989. 869p.

Covers the years preceding University of London, *Index Islamicus 1906–1955* **(P09),** and its supplements (1971–), being cumulations of *The quarterly index Islamicus* **(P12),** a serial that is divided by subject and geographic area and that includes a list of sources and subject and author indexes.

P09

University of London. School of Oriental and African Studies. Library. *Index Islamicus, 1906–1955; A catalogue of articles on Islamic subjects in periodicals and other collective publications.* Comp. by James D. Pearson with the assistance of Julia F. Ashton. Cambridge, England: W. Heffner, 1958. 897p.

Reprinted by Mansell in London in 1972 with *Supplements* every five years thereafter and with quarterly updates in *The quarterly index Islamicus* **(P12).** Of the first importance for entry into the periodical literature on the Muslim world of North Africa, the Middle East, and east and central Asia. Includes law, geography, history, anthropology, demography, folklore, and education. The bibliography with its published supplements includes 21,000 entries in Western languages. No entry is placed twice in the classified structure of the organization. During most literature searches that use this resource, multiple subject entry is essential. A sensible classification (systematic, historical, geographical) that eases the difficulty of identifying an article on a particular subject of research completed by a particular discipline.

Periodical articles are structured into this detailed classified system on the basis of geographic headings. For anthropologists working with Middle Eastern materials, a great deal of this information can be more easily accessed from Ruud Strijp's *Cultural anthropology of the Middle East: A bibliography: Volume 1, 1965–1987* (Leiden, Netherlands: Brill, 1992 [565p.]) (Handbuch der Orientalistik, Erste abteilung, Der nahe und mittlere osten, 10) **(P10),** with entries—again without annotation—entered in a classed arrangement to provide a handy desk reference source. Publications in European languages divided into six sections: Anthropological monographs (451 references) and articles (2,780 references), relevant books (223), articles (340) by nonanthropologists, a subject index, and an author index. Annotations for many of the entries identified here can be identified in Littlefield's *The Islamic Near East and North Africa* **(P66).**

These resources dovetail neatly with the published catalog of the library of the London University School of Oriental and African Studies **(G17),** a library catalog that is especially strong in history and law, providing author, title, and subject access to its extensive resources. Attempts coverage of both historical scholarship and printed sources that reflect the more current concerns of the present-day Islamic world. For selective annotated descriptions of monographs, consult Hopwood and Grimwood-Jones's *Middle East and Islam* **(P64),** Grimwood-Jones, Hopwood, and Pearson's *Arab-Islamic bibliography* **(P02),** Auchterlonie's *Middle East and Islam* **(P68),** and Grimwood-Jones's *Middle East and Islam* **(P69).**

Retrospective Bibliography—Continuing

P11

"Bibliography of periodical literature." In *Middle East journal.* v.1– , 1947– . Washington, D.C.: Middle East Institute. Quarterly.

A regular feature covering the major journals in all languages. Lists about 1,500 references per year. Three hundred journals with an interest in the Middle East, Islamic studies, and related fields. Covers North Africa and Muslim Spain, the Arab world, Israel, Turkey, the Transcaucasian states of the Soviet Union, Iran, Afghanistan, Pakistan, and Turkestan. Entries are classified under broad categories, including geography, social conditions, religion, language, and book reviews. Inspect also Rossi and White's *Articles on the Middle East* **(P70)** for a cumulation of these entries.

P12

The quarterly index Islamicus. v.1– , 1977– . London: Mansell.

Arranged by region, country, or language and divided by subject. Personal name and subject indexes.

Informational Reference Searches

For American anthropology consult first the *AAA guide* **(A53)** for directory information. The best international directory is still the "International directory of anthropological institutions" **(A56),** which could usefully be reissued in a new edition.

Encyclopedias, Compendiums, Handbooks, Manuals

P13

The encyclopedia of Islam: A dictionary of the geography, ethnography and biography of the Muhammadan peoples. 1st ed. Leiden, Netherlands: E. J. Brill, 1913–36. 4v.

Supplement (1938). Each article provides a summary of what is known about the subject, plus an excellent selective bibliography. The stress is on history with some coverage of geography, literature, and Islamic thought. French, German, and Turkish versions contain articles not in the English-language edition. Uses a German-based romanization system. Articles are arranged according to vernacular terms. The basic reference for the serious student of Islam with an objective of consolidating all but the most recent historical research about this area. Does not consolidate the findings of the social sciences relevant to contemporary populations. A second edition prepared under the patronage of the International Union of Academies is in progress and has been completed through volume 5; *Encyclopedia of Islam* was prepared by a number of leading orientalists (Leiden, Netherlands: E. J. Brill; London: Luzac, 1960– [10v.]) **(P14).** Édition française *Encyclopédie de l'Islam* (Paris: Maisonneuve, 1960– [10v.]) **(P15).** This second edition contains a large number of proper names for persons and places. Includes technical terms and covers the basic concepts of linguistics, institutions, arts, philosophy, and religious thought. Again, this resource does not integrate the research results of studies of modern populations by investigators in the social sciences for which consult Weekes's *Muslim peoples* **(P18).** Includes coverage of Islam in Africa south of the Sahara and in Asia.

P16

Holt, P. M., Ann K. S. Lambton, and Bernard Lewis. *The Cambridge history of Islam.* Cambridge, England: Cambridge Univ. Pr., 1970. 2v.

Still especially useful for anthropologists. Intended for general reading about the history of Islam as a cultural whole. V.1, *Central Islamic lands;* v.2, *Further Islamic lands and Islamic society and civilization.* In both volumes the stress is on a political history of the Muslim lands of the Middle East.

P17

Schacht, Joseph, and C. E. Bosworth, eds. *The legacy of Islam.* 2d ed. Oxford, England: Clarendon Pr. 1974. 530p.

First published in 1931. Seventeen contributors to ten sections (each with footnotes and bibliographies): (1) The Western image and Western studies of Islam; (2) Islam in the Mediterranean world; (3) Islamic frontiers in Africa and Asia (Africa south of the Sahara, Central Asia, India, Indonesia); (4) Politics and war; (5) Economic developments; (6) Art and architecture; (7) Literature; (8) Philosophy, theology and mysticism; (9) Law and state (including Islamic political thought); and (10) Science (including music). Partly analytical index, p.506–530. An introduction guides the reader.

P18

Weekes, Richard V., ed. *Muslim peoples: A world ethnographic survey.* Westport, Conn., and London: Greenwood, 1984. 2v.

Seventy-one contributors. Life and culture of thirty major ethnic groups (each with a Muslim population in excess of 100,000), such as the "Somali" (tribe). Bibliographies include periodical articles and theses. There are maps showing the distribution of ethnic groups. Three valuable appendixes: (1) Muslim nationalities of the world, (2) Muslim ethnic groups within nations, (3) major Muslim ethnic groups. Bibliography of books. Analytical index.

State-of-the-Art Reviews

P19

Makdisi, J. "Islamic law bibliography." *Law library journal* 78 (1) (1986): 103–89.

The bibliographic review discusses basic sources of the law and the schools of legal doctrine in a brief treatment of the development of Islamic law. It surveys primary source material (in Arabic) and secondary sources (in English and French). Provides a list of 875 references. Note especially the reference to A.A.A. Fyzee in *Outlines of Muhammadan law,* 4th ed. (New Delhi: Oxford Univ. Pr., 1974 [520p.]) **(P20).** Use the detailed index of that work to cover topics which are densely supported by references to an extensive bibliography.

Searching Graphic Materials

Searches for nonprint materials should consult American Geographical Society of New York, Map Department, *Index to maps in books and periodicals* **(A59)** and Heider's *Films for anthropological teaching* **(A63).**

Searching Unpublished Materials

Searches for unpublished materials often benefit from an inspection of the National Anthropological Archives, *Catalog to manuscripts at the National Anthropological Archives* **(A69).** Consult for dissertations Selim's *American doctoral dissertations on the Arab world, 1883–1974* **(P43),** Lent and Mulliner's *Malaysian studies: Archaeology, historiography, geography, and bibliography* **(P58),** Andrews and Benninghaus's *Ethnic groups in the Republic of Turkey* **(P74);** see also machine-readable databases listed in chapter 2.

Dissertations

P21

Sluglett, Peter, comp. *Theses on Islam, the Middle East and Northwest Africa, 1880–1978: Accepted by universities in the United Kingdom and Ireland.* London: Mansell, 1983. 147p.

Classified arrangement with sections on Islamic and Christian studies, followed by geographic arrangements subdivided by subject. Social studies and language are included. For American contributions, consult D. Straley's *An annotated bibliography of American doctoral dissertations on Arabic language, literature and culture, 1967–1987* **(P44),** which can be informally updated by the *Middle East Studies Association bulletin* **(P122),** which lists new doctoral dissertations in each issue. For a detailed examination of recent French-language resources consult Association Française des Arabisants, *Dix ans de recherche universitaire française sur le monde arabe et islamique de 1968–69 á 1979* (Paris: Editions Recherche sur les Civilizations, 1983 [438p.]) **(P22),** which lists entries in a classed arrangement. There is an index to the scholars who directed theses and a discussion of research centers in France.

AFRICA

Searching Bibliographic Guides

A rich assortment of bibliographic guides is introduced in chapter 7, "Africa South of the Sahara." Consult especially Scheven's *Bibliographies for African studies* **(G24)** for entry into bibliographies covering Islamic subject matter.

Bibliographic Guides

P23

Adam, André. *Bibliographie critique de sociologie, d'ethnologie et de géographie humaine du Maroc: Travaux de langues anglaise, arabe, espagnole et française.* Algiers: Centre de recherches anthropologiques, prehistoriques, et ethnographiques, Alger, 1972. 353p. (Mémoires du Centre de Recherches anthropologiques. Préhistoriques et ethnographiques, 20)

Includes a valuable section devoted to bibliographies of bibliographies. Special features include a list of monographs most frequently cited and an extensive list of relevant journals. The bibliography proper is unnumbered and without annotations, but a detailed classified arrangement guides the reader and is supported by both an author and a topical index.

P24

Brenner, Louis. "Une orientation bibliographique sur l'Islam en Afrique." *Islam et sociétés au sud de Sahara (Paris)* 1 (1987): 123–43.

Lists 215 bibliographic entries under four themes: Sufism, the slave trade, east Africa, and techniques of healing. Issued by Programme Islam Tropical de la Maison des Sciences l'Homme.

Retrospective Searches

When retrospective searches include searches for descriptions of the social behavior of indigenous peoples, consult the Human Relations Area Files, *HRAF source bibliography* **(D16),** and the Museum of Mankind Library "Tribal index" [microfiche] **(D13).** For continuing coverage of the intentional periodical output, consult *Anthropological literature* **(A36),** *Anthropological index* **(A35),** and *Abstracts in anthropology* **(A32).** The annual *International bibliography of social and cultural anthropology* **(D20)** succeeds in maintaining some ethnic-group entry in its indexing.

Retrospective Searches—Bibliography of Bibliographies

The bibliographies of bibliographies in Berque's "Matérials de référence" **(P07)** is particularly strong for its inclusion of Arabic coverage and for the identification of German- and French-language reference sources. It annotates in French each of 132 reference entries published in Arabic and European languages.

Retrospective Searches—Topical Bibliographies

P25

Louis, André. *Bibliographie ethno-sociologique de la Tunisie.* Tunis: Institut des Belles Lettres Arabes, 1977. 393p. (Tunis. Publications de l'Institut des Belles Lettres Arabes, v.31)

Title does not reveal scope of coverage, which includes some materials on Tunisia, Algeria, and Morocco. Includes also basic works, sources of review literature, bibliographies, a list of works most often cited, a list of journals, and festschriften. The thematic arrangement is detailed (forty-seven subject headings). Ease of entry supported by author and subject indexes.

P26

Lubell, David, and Peter Sheppard. "Community in the Epipaleolithic of North Africa with emphasis on the Magreb." *Advances in world archaeology* 3 (1984): 143–91.

Bibliographic essay with about 100 items in its bibliography.

P27

Shinar, Pessah. *Essai de bibliographie sélective et annotée sur l'Islam magrébin contemporain: Maroc, Algérie, Tunisie, Libye: 1830–1978.* Paris: Éditions du Centre national de la recherche scientifique, 1983. 506p.

Annotates 2,025 bibliographic entries. Arranged by country with subdivisions such as ethnography, folklore, rituals. Indexed by author, subject, and place.

P28

Silverman, David A., and David Owusu-Ansah. "Islam among the Akan of Ghana." *History in Africa* 16 (1989): 325–39.

A bibliographic essay. The most useful entries can be found in pt.2, "Survey of Arabic sources"; pt.3, "Survey of European primary sources"; and pt.4, "Historical archaeological and art historical studies since 1940." The essay is supported by an extensive bibliography organized alphabetically by author.

P29

Sipe, Lynn F. *Western Sahara: A comprehensive bibliography.* New York: Garland, 1984.

418p. (Garland Reference Library of Social Science, v.178)

Spanish-language sources dominate this selection of 3,345 items. Brief annotations help the reader. Author/title index refers to entry numbers.

P30

Zoghby, Samir M., comp. *Islam in Sub-Saharan Africa: A partially annotated guide.* Washington, D.C.: Library of Congress, 1978. 318p.

Superb scholarship. Organizes 2,682 annotated entries by historical period, then by region, and then by subject. Covers material prior to December 1974. Provides a glossary, a list of periodicals, and an index. Consult also the Islamic items in Nduntuei O. Ita's *Bibliography of Nigeria* **(G54).**

THE ARABS

Searching Bibliographic Guides

Consult also Auckland "Getting into the literature" **(A01)** and the defining guides to each chapter devoted to a subdiscipline of anthropology.

P31

Berque, Jacques, and others. *Bibliographie de la culture arabe contemporaine.* [Paris]: Sinbad/Les Presses de l'UNESCO, 1981. 483p.

Lists 1,639 entries with some annotations in French. The coverage is international and includes all European language sources as well as Arabic sources. The focus is on the contemporary Arab world. There is a list of periodicals cited that can also encourage a systematic search for special features that might be useful in maintaining bibliographic control over the research output of a narrowly defined research interest. The indexes list names of authors and Arabic titles.

Retrospective Searches

When retrospective searches include searches for descriptions of the social behavior of indigenous peoples, consult the Human Relations Area Files, *HRAF source bibliography* **(D16)** and the Museum of Mankind Library's "Tribal index" [microfiche] **(D13).** For continuing coverage of the periodical output, consult *Anthropological literature* **(A36),** *Anthropological index* **(A35),** and *Abstracts in anthropology* **(A32).** The annual *International bibliography of social and cultural anthropology* **(D20)** succeeds in maintaining some ethnic-group entry in its indexing.

Retrospective Searches—Bibliographies of Bibliographies

The bibliographies of bibliographies in Berque's "Matérials de référence" **(P07)** are particularly strong for their inclusion of Arabic coverage and for the identification of German- and French-language reference sources. It annotates in French each of 132 reference entries published in Arabic and European languages.

Retrospective Bibliographies—Broad Scope

For lists of libraries with relevant collections, see Simon's *The modern Middle East* **(P65)** using the index terms "libraries—directories" and "library catalogs." Also useful is "Directory of library collections on the Middle East," *Middle East Studies Association bulletin* 17 (1974): 22–48 **(P125).** Listed in *Fieldwork in the Library* for its special value to librarians and scholars who do not work easily in Arabic, find below:

P32

University of Utah. Middle East Library. *Catalog of the Arabic collection Aziz S. Atiga Library for Middle East studies.* Salt Lake City: Univ. of Utah Pr., 1968. 841p. (Middle East Library. Catalogue series, v.1)

Supplement, 1971– . Includes transliterated author and title indexes of considerable value to librarians. For another special collection that is available as a published catalog, consult Hoover Institution on War, Revolution, and Peace, *The library catalogs of the Hoover Institution on War, Revolution, and Peace, Stanford Univer-*

sity: Catalog of the Arabic collection (Boston: Hall, 1969 [902p.]) **(P33).**

Retrospective Bibliographies—Continuing

P34

Abstracta Islamica; Supplément á la Revue des Études Islamiques (Paris). v.1– , 1927– . Annual.

Indispensable instrument for work in the periodical literature. Covers both classic and modern periods. There are contents notes to entries in a bibliographic section devoted to recent publications.

Retrospective Bibliographies—Topical

P35

Anderson, Margaret. *Arabic materials in English translation: A bibliography of works from the pre-Islamic period to 1977.* Boston: Hall, 1980. 249p. (A reference publication in Middle Eastern studies)

Arranged by subject classification and then alphabetically by author. The table of contents is useful. Sections of value in an anthropological search include "Geography" (p.117–39) and "Social science materials" (p.140–49). There is an author index in which "see references" are given for variant forms of proper names. The resources identified here can be most important in the kind of "studies at a distance" that Ruth Benedict made famous with her ethnography of the Japanese people. Ethnographers working in cultures with great literary and historical traditions rarely become completely comfortable until they gain some control over the basic works that support these traditions. For this reason the sections on "Islamic studies" (p.32–73), "Philosophy" (p.74–79), "History" (p.113–31), "Classical Arabic literature" (p.150–79), and "Modern Arabic literature" (p.180–207) in this resource are also useful.

P36

Bakalla, M. H. *Arabic linguistics: An introduction and bibliography.* 2d rev. ed. London: Mansell; dist., New York: Wilson, 1983. 741p.

Lists 5,500 entries written in Arabic, English, French, and more than a dozen other Oriental and Western languages. Includes books, articles, dissertations, theses, and other published materials in the field of Arabic linguistics. Divided into three parts. Coverage of bibliographies and other general references is followed by sections devoted to works written in the Occidental and Oriental languages, respectively. Bibliographic entries are ordered alphabetically under broad subject headings. There is a subject index.

P37

Bennett, Norman Robert. *The Arab state of Zanzibar: A bibliography.* Boston: Hall, 1984. 231p.

List 2,492 titles of books, articles, theses, and pamphlets published to 1982 and covering the period to 1964. Classed arrangement with author index and an index by person, place, and subject. Includes a valuable list of archival collections and published guides to these collections.

P38

Meghdessian, Samira Refidi. *The status of the Arab woman: A select bibliography.* London: Mansell, 1980. 176p.

Provides a separate section on each country. Subject and author indexes. A useful entry into the literature of kinship and family organization. Sponsored by the Institute for Women Studies in the Arab World.

P39

Universite Saint-Joseph (Beirut). Centre d'Études pour le Monde Arabe Moderne. *Arab culture and society in change: A partially annotated bibliography of books and articles in English, French, German and Italian.* Beirut, Lebanon: Dar el-Mashreq, 1973. 318p.

Integrates many periodicals not covered by the standard indexes. Fifteen sections, including "Acculturation" and "Islam in modern society." Index of references by region. This extensive bibliography of 4,950 entries covers Arab countries in Africa and the Near East from the First World War to the date of publication. There are separate sections for "Countrymen and nomads," "Condition of women," and "Marriage and family."

Informational Reference Searches

For lists of libraries with relevant collections, see Simon's *The modern Middle East* **(P65)** using the index terms "libraries—directories" and "library catalogs." Also useful is "Directory of library collections on the Middle East," *Middle East Studies Association bulletin* 17 (1974): 22–48 **(P125).** For American anthropology consult first the *AAA guide* **(A53)** for directory information. The best international directory is still the "International directory of anthropological institutions" **(A56),** which could usefully be reissued in a new edition.

Encyclopedias, Compendiums, Manuals

P40

Bibliographie der deutschsprachigen arabistik und islamkunde. Frankfurt am Main: Institut für Geschichte der arabisch-Islamischen Wessenschaften, 1990. 12v.

V.1 is especially useful for its listing of handbooks (p.3–10) and bibliographies (p.11–46). Each volume is organized around a topical coverage. V.6 covers culture and, like all volumes, has a detailed table of contents in German and Arabic.

P41

Hourani, Albert Habib. *A history of the Arab peoples.* Cambridge, Mass.: Belknap Pr. of Harvard Univ. Pr., 1991. 551p.

Covers fourteen centuries. The interpretative organization draws on Ibn Khaldun (1332–1406). Creates a coherent account of the contributions of other scholars from both the medieval and the modern periods. Maintains a balance between the Arab East (Mashriq) and the Arab West (Maghreb). Includes social developments such as urbanization, urban ties to the countryside, and the evolving role of women. Lucid and detailed discussion of the impact of Western ways on Arabic life.

P42

Ronart, Stephan, and Nandy Ronart. *Concise encyclopaedia of Arabic civilization.* New York: Praeger, 1960–66. 2v.

Subtitles: *The Arab East* (1960 [589p.]); *The Arab West (including Libya)* (1966 [410p.]). The volumes deal with self-contained articles on the cultural, social, economic, and political aspects of the Arab world. Coverage includes both historical and current issues. Contemporary ideas, places, events, political parties, sects, and organizations are placed in perspective by treatments of the people of its past, with concise statements of their achievements. Arranged as a dictionary with cross-references and maps. V.1 covers the Arab east, and v.2, the Arab west. Deals with contemporary issues. There is a selected bibliography but no index. Available in German-language translation.

Searching Unpublished Materials

Searches for unpublished materials often benefit from an inspection of the National Anthropological Archives, *Catalog to manuscripts at the National Anthropological Archives* **(A69).**

Dissertations

P43

Selim, George Dimitri, comp. *American doctoral dissertations on the Arab World, 1883–1974.* 2d ed. Washington, D.C.: Library of Congress, 1976. 173p.

Supplemented by *Dissertations on the Arab world accepted by U.S. and Canadian universities from the years 1975–1981* (1983 [200p.]) and *Supplement: 1981–1988.* For detailed annotations consult Donas Straley's *An annotated bibliography of American doctoral dissertations on Arabic language, literature and culture, 1967–1987* (Columbus, Ohio: American Association of Teachers of Arabic, 1989 [178p.]) (Al-Árabiyyat: AATA monographs in Arabic studies, 1) **(P44).** A more select and more international list can be found in Frank A. Clements's "Theses and dissertations on Saudi Arabia," chapter in *Saudi Arabia,* rev. and exp. ed. (Santa Barbara, Calif.: ABC-Clio Pr., 1988 [354p.]) (World bibliographical series, v.5) **(P45).** This select list can be expanded by

Abdullah N. al-Subaiy's *American and Canadian doctoral dissertations on the Kingdom of Saudi Arabia, 1935–1987* (Washington, D.C.: Saudi Arabian Educational Mission, 1987 [276p.]). Informally, these can be updated by the *Middle East Studies Association bulletin* **(P122),** which lists new doctoral dissertations in each issue.

EURASIA

In these areas, only in the Malay world has there been an elaboration of specialized Islamic reference sources. Of the more general sources, *The quarterly index Islamicus* **(P12)** will provide the most productive entry into these areas for the anthropologist. Many bibliographic problems related to the regions of Iran, Soviet Asia, Central Asia, and Pakistan can be solved by consulting the "Bibliography of periodical literature" **(P11).**

CENTRAL ASIA (INCLUDING SOVIET ASIA)

Searching Bibliographic Guides

Consult Auckland's "Getting into the literature" **(A01)** and the defining guides in chapters in *Fieldwork in the Library* devoted to the subdisciplines of anthropology.

Bibliographic Guides

P46

Allworth, Edward. *Soviet Asia, bibliographies; A compilation of social science and humanities sources on the Iranian, Mongolian and Turkic nationalities, with an essay on the Soviet-Asian controversy.* New York: Praeger, 1975. 686p. (Praeger special studies on international politics and government)

Lists 5,200 Russian and Soviet bibliographies published between 1850 and 1970. Arranged according to four major geographical regions, subdivided into Union republics, autonomous republics, and ethnic groups, and again subdivided by subjects, including anthropology and ethnography.

P47

Collins, David N. (comp.) *Siberia and Soviet far east.* Santa Barbara, Calif.: Clio, 1991. 217p. (World bibliography series, no.127)

English-language sources that fully reflect the cultural variety of this region are annotated. There is a list of ethnic groups with variant names. A general bibliography with some anthropological material. For the individual tribes, the continuing Islamic indexes identified in this chapter, the Russian resources identified in chapter 1, "What Every Anthropologist Needs to Know," and the ethnographic entry identified in chapter 4, "Ethnology/Cultural Anthropology," provide entry into an abundance of material published in other European languages. Author, title, and subject indexes.

P48

Sinor, Denis. *Introduction à l'étude de l'Eurasie centrale.* Wiesbaden: Harrassowitz, 1963. 371p.

Lists 4,003 numbered items in three parts. Consult especially pt.1, Les langues et les peuples (l'Ouralien l'Altiaique), and pt.3, Notes sur l'ethnographie. Brief commentary and short introductions to these sections; author and anonymous title index.

Retrospective Searches

When retrospective searches include searches for descriptions of the social behavior of indigenous peoples, consult the Human Relations Area Files, *HRAF source bibliography* **(D16)** and the Museum of Mankind Library's "Tribal index" [microfiche] **(D13).** For continuing coverage of the periodical output, consult *Anthropological literature* **(A36),** *Anthropological index* **(A35),** and *Abstracts in anthropology* **(A32).** The annual *International bibliography of social and cultural anthropology* **(D20)** succeeds in maintaining some ethnic-group entry in its indexing.

Retrospective Bibliographies—Topical Bibliographies

P49

Lee, Don Y. *An annotated bibliography on inner Asia: Pre-modern.* Bloomington, Ind.: Eastern Pr., 1983. 183p.

Includes index. Coverage is for the central Asian area. There is a companion volume by Don Y. Lee and Jane Workman, *An annotated archaeological bibliography of selected works on northern and central Asia* (Bloomington, Ind.: Eastern Pr., 1983 [94p.]) **(P50).**

P51

Loewenthal, Rudolf. *The Turkic languages and literatures of central Asia: A bibliography.* Gravenhage, Netherlands: Mouton, 1957. 212p. (Central Asiatic studies, 1)

Lists 2,093 numbered entries in four sections: (a) Bibliographies and biographies, general; (b) Old Turkic: Old and middle Uighur, Orkhon and Yenisei; (c) Middle Turkic; and (d) Modern.

P52

Wilber, Donald Newton. *Annotated bibliography of Afghanistan.* 4th ed. New Haven, Conn.: HRAF Pr., 1982. 454p. (Behavior science bibliographies)

Arranges entries under nine headings: "General sources of information," "reference books," "geography," "history," "social organization," "social evolution and institutions," "political and economic structure," "language and literature," "art and archaeology." Author index. Consult also *Afghan Studies,* v.1–5, 1978–82 (London: Society for Afghan Studies, British Institute of Afghan Studies) **(P53),** which is issued irregularly with coverage of history, antiquities, archaeology, ethnography, languages, literature, art, culture, customs, and natural history of Afghanistan.

Informational Reference Searches

For American anthropology, consult first the *AAA guide* **(A53)** for directory information. The best international directory is still the "International directory of anthropological institutions" **(A56),** which could usefully be reissued in a new edition.

Encyclopedias and Compendiums

P54

Gross, Jo-Ann, ed. *Muslims in central Asia: Expressions of identity and change.* Durham, N.C.: Duke University, 1992. 224p.

Five of the nine essays concern tribal groups. Two of the essays study the response of individuals to control by the agents of the Russian Empire.

SOUTH AND SOUTHEAST ASIA

Searching Bibliographic Guides

For a more general guide to the area, consult Godfrey Raymond Nunn's invaluable *Asia* **(L06)** for the chapter (B), "Bangladesh," with a listing of handbooks, yearbooks, dictionaries, gazetteers, statistics, and bibliographies. Consult chapter (E), "Pakistan," for handbooks, yearbooks, directories, dictionaries, gazetteers, census and statistics, official publications, periodicals and dissertations. For specialized subject bibliographies in the social sciences, history and geography, consult chapter (A), "Asia."

Also relevant are chapter (G), "Southeast Asia"; chapter (L), "Malaysia"; chapter (M), "Philippines"; and chapter (J), "Indonesia." In the anthropological investigation of the Islamic Malay cultures of Southeast Asia, essential best sources can be identified in the works compiled by LeBar and Appell, *Ethnic groups of mainland Southeast Asia* **(M101),** and LeBar's *Ethnic groups of insular Southeast Asia* **(M102).** Consult also an older source, Embree and Dotson's *Bibliography of the peoples and cultures of mainland Southeast Asia* **(M104),** for the arrangement first by general area, then by tribal groups, and finally by subject.

Bibliographic Guides

P55

Bhatty, K. M. *Annotated bibliography of social research in Pakistan.* Peshawar: Pakistan Academy for Rural Development, 1986. 141p.

Arranges 540 entries under eighteen annotated entries. Includes a few books, many typewritten research reports, articles, and government documents. Still useful for sources by European scholars is Eric W. Gustafson's *Pakistan and Bangladesh: Bibliographic essays in social science* (Islamabad: Univ. of Islamabad Pr., 1976 [364p.]) **(P56).**

This collection of bibliographical essays is a product of the National Seminar on Pakistan and Bangladesh, which has met at the Southern Asian Institute, Columbia University, since November 1970. Reasonably comprehensive bibliographic essays by recognized scholars on the subdisciplines of the social sciences, including anthropology. A supplementary bibliography divided into sixteen categories and valuable for its selectivity and for its clear and concise annotations can be found in George L. Abernethy, comp., *Pakistan: A selected, annotated bibliography,* 4th ed. (Davidson, N.C.: Davidson College Publications Office, 1974 [50p.]) **(P57).** Also valuable are Henry Field's *Bibliography on Southwestern Asia* (Coral Gables, Fla.: University of Miami, 1953–), with *Supplement* and subject index **(M108),** and the "Bibliography of periodical literature" **(P11).**

P58

Lent, John A., and Kent Mulliner, eds. *Malaysian studies: Archaeology, historiography, geography, and bibliography.* DeKalb: Northern Illinois University, Center for Southeast Asian Studies; dist., Detroit: Cellar Book Shop, 1986. (Monograph series on Southeast Asia. Occasional paper. Northern Illinois University, Center for Southeast Asian Studies, no.11)

Organized into a series of brief essays under topics like "Brunei" and "A survey and evaluation of Sarawak and Sabah history," each with extensive supporting bibliographies. All listed entries have detailed annotations. Includes articles, books, dissertations, and unpublished papers. There is a useful discussion of bibliographic activity in Singapore and Malaysia. See also Lim's *The Malay world of Southeast Asia* **(M92).**

P59

Salina-Ud-Din, Quraishi. *A survey of bibliographical works relating to Pakistan.* London: University College, London, 1974. 350p. Master's thesis.

About 1,000 unannotated entries in nine sections: (1) Bibliography of bibliographies; (2) International bibliographies; (3) Pakistan: General bibliographies (A. Pre-1947; B. 1947–1974; C. Select bibliographies); (4) Bibliographies relating to a part of Pakistan; (5) Bibliographies of books in Urdu, Panjabi, Sindhi, Pushtu, and Baluchi languages; (6) Bibliographies of government publications; (7) Publications of periodical literature; (8) Bibliographies of manuscripts; (9) Conclusion. No index. Detailed bibliographical essay precedes the classified bibliography.

P60

Satyaprakash. *Muslims in India: A bibliography of their religious, socioeconomic and political literature.* Gurgaon, India: Indian Documentation Service; dist. Columbia, Mo.: South Asia Books, 1985. 279p. (Subject bibliography series, 8)

More than 3,149 research papers, notes, news reports, and book reviews from 154 journals and daily newspapers. Separate sections list Indian books on Islam, periodicals indexed, and publishers. Consult also Tiamson's *The Muslim Filipinos* **(M98),** an alphabetic list by author without annotation. There is a broad term index.

SOUTHWEST ASIA

Consult chapter 9 under the heading "Southeast Asia" for more complete coverage of this region, which is too complex even to define. Some geographers and anthropologists even include Sudan in this geographic area. See *Internationale Jahresbibliographie Südwesasien (International annual bibliography South West Asia)* **(M112).**

Informational Reference Searches

Again consult Godfrey Raymond Nunn's invaluable *Asia* **(L06).**

Encyclopedias, Surveys, Handbooks, Manuals

P61

Yar-Shater, Ehsan, ed. *Encyclopaedia Iranica.* London and Boston; Routledge & Paul, 1982–88. 7v.

Detailed coverage of archaeology, geography, ethnography, history, religion, linguistics, and folklore of Iranian studies. Especially valuable for tribal entries.

THE MIDDLE EAST

Searching Bibliographic Guides

Consult Auckland's "Getting into the literature" **(A01)** and the defining guides in chapters of *Fieldwork in the Library* devoted to a subdiscipline of anthropology.

Bibliographic Guides

Consult Antoun's "Three approaches to the cultural anthropology of the Middle East" **(P123),** Gulick's *The Middle East* **(P63),** and Gulick's "The anthropology of the Middle East" **(P124)** for detailed guides to the ethnographic investigations of the Middle East that retain value because of their organization. Among these three resources, most of the early ethnographic and psychological literature reporting results of studies of modern Middle Eastern populations can be identified. For entry into more general reference materials with relevance for anthropology, the most useful source is Simon's *The modern Middle East* **(P65);** and for a select list of monographs on most topical issues, the guide by Littlefield **(P66)** can be helpful.

Many of the reference works compiled for this section exclude Israel, except for discussions of the Arab-Israeli war. Some reference sources make outstanding efforts to include Israel, including Sweet's *The central Middle East* **(P120).** See also Smooha, *Social research on Jewish ethnicity in Israel* **(P90).**

P62

Atiyeh, George Nicholas, comp. *The contemporary Middle East, 1948–1973: A selective and annotated bibliography.* Boston: Hall, 1975. 664p.

Focuses on social conditions and related subjects but excludes Israel except for the Arab-Israeli conflict. Arranged by geographical area. Brief annotations ease the identification of relevant entries. Dated but still valuable for its range of coverage.

P63

Gulick, John, *The Middle East: An anthropological perspective.* Pacific Palisades, Calif.: Goodyear, 1976. 244p.

Reprint, University Press of America, 1983. Organized around theoretical issues and richly annotated. Reflects masterly control over the anthropological value of research completed on modern populations. Consult also Antoun's "Three approaches to the cultural anthropology of the Middle East" **(P123)** and Gulick's "The anthropology of the Middle East" **(P124)** for guides to the ethnographic investigations of the Middle East that retain value because of their organization. Among these three resources, most of the early ethnographic and psychological literature reporting results of studies of modern Middle Eastern populations can be identified.

P64

Hopwood, Derek, and Diana Grimwood-Jones. *Middle East and Islam; A bibliographical introduction.* Foreword by J. D. Pearson. Zug,

Switzerland: Inter Documentation, 1972, 368p. (Bibliotheca Asiatica, no.9)

Selectively covers monographic scholarly material in all languages. Arranged by country and topics. Entries are selected by a panel of scholars. Covers North Africa, Turkey, and Iran. Of the five major sections, the one on reference materials and the anthropology subdivision of the section on subject bibliographies are the most helpful. Identifies out-of-print translations and includes a list of the most significant Islamic and Middle Eastern periodicals. Consult also Grimwood-Jones, Hopwood, and Pearson's *Arab-Islamic bibliography* **(P02),** Auchterlonie's *Middle East and Islam* **(P68),** and Grimwood-Jones's *Middle East and Islam* **(P69).** As a companion for entry into the periodical literature in all scholarly languages, the desk reference Strijp's, *Cultural anthropology of the Middle East* **(P10),** provides a classified arrangement of a broad selection of articles and monographs published in European languages and neatly divided into separate sections for work completed by anthropologists and nonanthropologists.

P65

Simon, Reeva S. *The modern Middle East: A guide to research tools in the social sciences.* Boulder, Colo.: Westview Pr., 1978. 283p. (Westview special studies on the Middle East, no.10)

Provides a most useful reference guide for the social scientist. The sections on "Specialized bibliography by countries" (p.53–89) and "Bibliographies of dissertations" (p.90–94) have exceptional value. Section 5, "Report literature," with Columbia University call numbers, begins on page 209 and includes published reports from such agencies as the American Universities Field Staff, Human Relations Area Files, Hudson Institute, Rand Corporation, and the U.S. Information Agency. Annotates 724 entries in Western and Middle Eastern languages covering Afghanistan, Iran, Iraq, Turkey, Syria, Jordan, Israel, Lebanon, Egypt, and the Sudan as well as the nations of the Arabian Peninsula and North Africa. In bibliographic descriptions, pagination of entries is not given and series information is sometimes missing. Extremely useful for its forthright format, range of coverage, and splendid organization. Subject/author/title index in a single alphabet includes geographic and topical subdivisions.

P66

Littlefield, David W. *The Islamic Near East and North Africa: An annotated guide to books in English for non-specialists.* Littleton, Colo.: Libraries Unlimited, 1977. 375p.

A list of monographs. Remarkable for its selectivity, for its useful annotations, and for the completeness of its bibliographic citations. Arranges 1,166 titles in a classification system. Completely indexed. Seems to include everything in English that is fundamentally important. As a companion for entry into the periodical literature in all scholarly languages, the desk reference, Strijp's *Cultural anthropology of the Middle East* **(P10),** provides a classified arrangement of a broad selection of articles.

Retrospective Searches

When retrospective searches include searches for descriptions of the social behavior of indigenous peoples, consult the Human Relations Area Files, *HRAF source bibliography* **(D16)** and the Museum of Mankind Library's "Tribal index" [microfiche] **(D13).** For continuing coverage of the periodical output, consult *Anthropological literature* **(A36),** *Anthropological index* **(A35),** and *Abstracts in anthropology* **(A32).** The annual *International bibliography of social and cultural anthropology* **(D20)** succeeds in maintaining some ethnic-group entry in its indexing.

Bibliography of Bibliographies

P67

Edelheit, Abraham J., and Hershel Edelheit. "Bibliographies and guides." Chapter in *The Jewish world in modern times: A select, annotated bibliography,* p.458–59. London: Mansell, 1988. 469p.

The bibliography of bibliographies annotates 21 entries. The rest of this work identifies 2,190 English-language publications. Especially useful for anthropology are the sections on "Social history," "Cultural trends," and all of part 2, "The Jewish community," with its geographic arrangement.

Retrospective Bibliographies—Broad Scope

P68

Auchterlonie, Paul, ed. *Middle East and Islam: A bibliographical introduction: Supplement, 1977–1983.* Zug, Switzerland: Inter Documentation, 1986. 244p. (Bibliotheca Asiatica, v.20)

Covers monographic scholarly material in all languages. Arranged by country and topics. Entries are selected by a panel of scholars. Identifies out-of-print translations and includes a list of the most significant Islamic and Middle Eastern periodicals. Consult also Grimwood-Jones, Hopwood, and Pearson's *Arab-Islamic bibliography* **(P02),** Grimwood-Jones's *Middle East and Islam* **(P69),** and Hopwood and Grimwood-Jones's *Middle East and Islam* **(P64).** As a companion for entry into the periodical literature in all scholarly languages, the desk reference, Strijp's *Cultural anthropology of the Middle East* **(P10),** provides a classified arrangement of a broad selection of articles.

P69

Grimwood-Jones, Diane, ed. *Middle East and Islam: A bibliographical introduction.* Rev. and enl. ed. Zug, Switzerland: Inter Documentation, 1979. 429p. (Bibliotheca Asiatica, v.15)

Covers monographic scholarly material in all languages. Arranged by country and topics. Entries are selected by a panel of scholars. Identifies out-of-print translations and includes a list of the most significant Islamic and Middle Eastern periodicals. Consult also Grimwood-Jones, Hopwood, and Pearson's *Arab-Islamic bibliography* **(P02),** Auchterlonie's *Middle East and Islam* **(P68),** and Hopwood and Grimwood-Jones's *Middle East and Islam* **(P64).** As a companion for entry into the periodical literature in all scholarly languages, Strijp's *Cultural anthropology of the Middle East* **(P10)** provides a classified arrangement of a broad selection of articles.

P70

Rossi, Peter M., and Wayne E. White, eds. *Articles on the Middle East 1947–1971: A cumulation of the bibliographies from the Middle East journal.* Ann Arbor, Mich.: Pierian, 1980. 4v. (Cumulated bibliography series, no.7)

Provides a reprint of these quarterly records, with cumulative index. Provides entry to book reviews under an "Author/main entry/reviewer" index, giving a comprehensive approach to more than 42,000 references. A "Subject index: Personal names" provides an approach to more than 9,200 references to the names of individuals treated as subjects in the cumulation. "Subject index: Categories" identifies by page number the location of the subject areas classified in each quarterly bibliography. A list of periodicals indexed over the years is provided. Indispensable for access to an important body of periodical literature. Updated by "Bibliography of periodical literature" **(P11).** Israel is excluded from coverage. Much of this material with anthropological relevance can be more easily identified in the desk reference, Strijp's *Cultural anthropology of the Middle East* **(P10),** which provides a single unified classified entry for a broad selection of articles.

Retrospective Bibliographies—Continuing

P71

Annual Egyptological bibliography (Bibliographie Egyptologique). v.1– , 1947– . Leiden, Netherlands: For International Association of Egyptologists by E. J. Brill. Annual.

Provides the best coverage of social science research by or about modern Egypt, with a three- or four-year delay.

P72

The Middle East: Abstracts and index. v.1– , 1978– . Pittsburgh: Northumberland Pr. Quarterly.

Abstracts about 2,000 items per issue. Divided into nineteen sections, with subarrangement by form so that dissertations or government documents, for example, can be searched by form. A topical and geographical index provides entry only to English-language publications. The term "Psychological and social studies" in the index provides a useful starting point for a literature search on anthropological topics.

Other sources for current bibliographic information could include "Bibliography of periodical literature" **(P11)** and the following databases based in part on published indexes and abstracting services: *Francis bulletin signalétiqe* [computer file], described in the annotation of *FRANCIS* **(B19).**

Retrospective Bibliographies—Topical

P73

Abd al-Rahman, Abd al-Jabbar. *A bibliography of Iraq: A classified list of printed materials on the land, people, history, economics and culture published in Western languages.* Baghdad: Al-Irshad Pr., 1977. 304p. (Centre for Arab Gulf publications, no.10)

Classed arrangement. Includes doctoral dissertations. Covers 1900–75. Author, title indexes. There is a more widely distributed source by the same author, entitled *Iraq* (Santa Barbara, Calif.: Clio Pr., 1984).

P74

Andrews, Peter Alford, and Rüdiger Benninghaus. *Ethnic groups in the Republic of Turkey.* Wiesbaden: Ludwig Reichert Verlag, 1989. 639p. (Beihefte zum Tübinger atlas des vorderen orients: Herausgegehen im Auftrag des Sonderforschungsbereichs, 19) (Reihe B, Geisteswissenschaften, 60)

Following a scholarly introduction which acts as a review of research and a guide to the arrangement of the text, there follows a catalog of ethnic groups in forty-seven sections in which ethnic groups are listed by villages in administrative districts. This in turn is followed by a survey of selected tribes and ethnic groups by various authors with extensive bibliography divided for published and unpublished sources, and alphabetic by author under this division.

P75

Antoun, Richard, and Iliya Harik. *Rural politics and social change in the Middle East.* Bloomington: Indiana Univ. Pr., 1972. 498p. (International Development Research Center. Studies in development, no.5)

Includes specialized critique by H. Rosenfeld (p.45–74), which reviews the work of ethnographers and social anthropologists.

P76

Banuazizi, Ali. *Social stratification in the Middle East and North Africa: A bibliographic essay.* London: Mansell, 1984. 248p.

Arranged by country. Lists 2,000 entries with subject and author indexes. The subject index is by broad topic, sometimes subdivided by country. For example, RURAL COMMUNITIES subdivided by country with relevant authors listed alphabetically under each country; MINORITIES, ETHNIC/LINGUISTIC subdivided by country with relevant authors listed alphabetically under each country as follows: "Afghanistan," twenty-nine works listed alphabetically by author; "Algeria," seven works listed alphabetically by author; "Egypt," three works listed alphabetically by author; "Gulf States," one work; "Iran," seventeen works; "Israel," 115 works; "Lebanon," five works; "Libya," one work; "Middle East/North Africa," twelve works; "Morocco," twenty-one works; "Palestine—Mandate," one work; "Sudan," one work; "Syria," one work; "Tunisia," one work; "Turkey," four works; "Yemens," one work.

P77

Coult, Lyman H., and Karim Durzi. *An annotated research bibliography of studies in Arabic, English and French, of the Fellah of the Egyptian Nile, 1798–1955.* Coral Gables, Fla.: Univ. of Miami Pr., 1958. 144p.

P78

Cutter, Charles, and Micha Falk Oppenheim. *Jewish reference sources: A selective, annotated bibliographic guide.* New York: Garland, 1982. 180p. (Garland reference library of social science, v.126)

General references include entries for bibliographies, encyclopedias, yearbooks, directories, periodicals. Subject references include art, Israel, and Judaism. Author index. Title index.

P79

Garsse, Yvan van. *Ethnological and anthropological literature on the three southern Sudan provinces: Upper Nile, Bahr el Ghazal, Equatoria.* Wien: Published for the Institute for Völkerkunde. University of Wien by Engelbert Stiglmayr, 1972. 88p. (Acta ethnologica et linguistica, no.29. Series Africana, no.7)

Arranges 1,072 entries by author, with subject index.

P80

Harned, Robert L. "Ancient Egypt." *RSR: Reference services review* 12 (Fall); 115–22.

Detailed annotations to bibliographic entries organized in the following categories: (1) Guides to the literature; (2) Bibliographies; (3) Periodical indexes; (4) Dictionaries and encyclopedias; (5) Biographical sources; (6) Directories; (7) Atlases; (8) Periodicals and serials.

P81

Harrison, Gail G. *Food and nutrition in the Middle East, 1970–1986: An annotated bibliography.* Westport, Conn.: Greenwood, 1988. 258p.

Includes agriculture, food technology, and medical therapy. Citations are arranged alphabetically by main entry under country headings with access by subject and author indexes.

P82

Leupen, A. H. A. *Bibliographie des populations touaregues: Sahara et Soudan centraux.* Leyden, Netherlands: Afrika-Studiecentrum, 1978. 240p.

A substantial work. Annotates 1,415 items, which are arranged by topic with some topical subdivisions. Author and subject index. The folding map of Tuareg lands illustrates their range over the Sahara. Also useful is Richard I. Lawless's *Algerian bibliography: English language publications, 1830–1973* (London: Bowker for the Centre for Middle Eastern and Islamic studies of the Univ. of Durham, 1976 [114p.] [Centre for Middle Eastern and Islamic Studies, publication no.4]) **(P83),** which arranges 1,490 entries topically with cross-references. Excludes publications by United Nations agencies.

P84

Moorey, P. R. S. *A century of biblical archaeology.* London: Westminster - J. Knox, 1992. 189p.

Covers the first excavations in Palestine in the nineteenth century and discusses the changes in methods of excavation and interpretation. Discusses the controversy between those who would use archaeology to prove the Bible as a historical document and those who think the Bible has no historical value. There is a glossary of technical terms. Discusses significant archaeological finds from other Near Eastern countries. For more technical coverage of this topic, consult the reference sources described in chapter 3, "Archaeology and Material Culture," of *Fieldwork in the Library.*

P85

Qazzaz, Ayad. *Frauenfragen in Modernen Orient: Eine auswahlbibliographie (Women in the Middle East and North Africa: A selected bibliography).* Hamburg: Deutsches Orient-Institut, Dokumentations-Leitstelle Moderner Orient, 1982. 247p. (Documentationsdienst moderner orient. Reihe A. Middle East documentation service. Series A; v.12)

Classified arrangement with thirty-eight pages of index. Covers both Western and Arabic languages with 1,242 entries. Consult also John Gulick's *An annotated bibliography of sources concerned with women in the modern Muslim Middle East.* Princeton, N.J.: Princeton University, Program in Near Eastern Studies, 1974 [26p.]) (Princeton Near East papers, no.17) **(P86).** Extremely sensitive to the anthropological focus. Classed arrangement under heading most relevant to anthropological searches. Consult also Antoun's "Three approaches to the cultural anthropology of the Middle East" **(P123)** and Gulick's "The anthropology of the Middle East" **(P124);** both in the 1970s published detailed guides to the ethnographic investigations of the Middle East and still retain value because of their organization. Among these three resources, most of the early ethnographic and psychological literature reporting results of studies of modern Middle Eastern populations can be identified.

P87

Saliba, Maurice. *Index Libanicus: Analytical index of publications in European languages on Lebanon.* Antélias, Lebanon: Saliba, 1979–82. 2v.

Nearly 10,000 entries arranged alphabetically by author. Analytical index of descriptors.

P88

Scheffler, Thomas. *Ethnisch-religöse konflikte und gesellschaftliche integration im vorderen und Mittleren Orient.* Berlin: Free University, 1990. 251p. (Ethizität und Gesellschaft. Occasional papers, 11)

See especially the bibliographic review of ethnicity (p.17–33) and of social structure (p.44–46). Lists 3,500 entries alphabetically by author.

P89

Shur, Shimon. *The kibbutz: A bibliography of scientific and professional publications in English.* Darby, Pa.: Norwood Editions, 1983. 103p. (Kibbutz studies book series, no.4)

Entries are listed alphabetically by author. The subject index is by broad topic, such as BIBLIOGRAPHIES (nine items) and CHILDREARING (ninety-one items).

P90

Smooha, Sammy. *Social research on Jewish ethnicity in Israel, 1948–1986.* Haifa: Haifa Univ. Pr., 1987. 277p.

Annotates and describes more than 600 entries to published works that address the conflicts between Askenazi and Oriental Jews in Israel. Includes research completed in the fields of anthropology, psychology, and sociology. Includes an essay "Three approaches to the sociology of ethnic relations in Israel" and a "Directory of active researchers" in the field with addresses, affiliations, and a subject index.

P91

Thomsen, Peter. *Die pälastina-literatur: Eine internationale bibliographie in systematischer ordnung mit autoren und sachregister. . . .* Leipzig: J. C. Hinrich, 1911–1972.

Two series: The first series includes v.1–6 and covers 1895–1945; the second series (1957–) covers an earlier period (v.1, 1878–94 [1960]). Publisher varies.

Informational Reference Searches

For American anthropology consult first the *AAA guide* **(A53)** for directory information. The best international directory is still the "International directory of anthropological institutions" **(A56),** which could usefully be reissued in a new edition.

Directories

P92

British Society for Middle Eastern Studies. *Directory of BriSMES members, 1989.* Oxford: British Society for Middle Eastern Studies, 1989. 145p.

Publishes addresses, teaching specializations, and research interests in British universities. For French institutions, consult Association Française de Arabisants, *Dix ans de recherche universitaire française sur la monde arabe et islamique de 1968–69 á 1979* **(P22);** includes a directory of French institutions with Islamic interests. For a country-by-country review of Islamic influences, inspect Farzana Shaikh's *Islam and Islamic groups; A worldwide reference guide* (Harlow, Essex: CIRCA Research and Reference Information Limited, 1992 [316p.]) **(P93)** in which Islamic organizations are listed alphabetically under geographic headings. Directory of research institutions. Inspect *The Middle East and North Africa 1984–85,* p.148–63, 31st ed. (London: Europa Publications; dist. Detroit: Gale, 1984 [801p.]) **(P94),** which lists research institutes and associations studying the Middle East and North Africa. Organized by name of organization under an alphabetic list of countries. For each entry, this resource provides information on address, library holdings, and names of principal associates as well as a brief discussion of research focus. Many centers of Arabic and Islamic studies can also be identified in the subject index to *Commonwealth universities yearbook* (London: The Assn. of Commonwealth Universities, 1989 [4v.]) **(P95)** of this basic set, which benefits from continuing revisions. Find also Bacharach's "Scholarly organizations concerned with Middle East topics" **(P126).**

Encyclopedias, Compendiums, Handbooks, Manuals

P96

American University. Foreign Area Studies Division. *Area handbooks.* v.1– , 1961– . Washington, D.C.: American Univ. Pr.

The Foreign Area Studies Division of the Special Operations Research Office (SORO) serves as a research contractor for the Dept. of the Army. Most volumes in this unnumbered sequence appear as U.S. Department of the Army pamphlets; more recently they appear as *Handbook* series under the sponsorship of the Library of Congress. FASD has been prolific, producing important and influential social science research. Funded by the military, however, the work is affected by unresolved problems between the management of social science and the management of government. Examples of FASD work are the area handbooks, all distributed from Washington by the Government Printing Office and now cataloged by the Library of Congress under the name of the principal author. Recently the Library of Congress has taken over editorial responsibility for the series. These handbooks can provide basic social science information for whole regions and share a common format. Sections on the people and on social organization are most useful to anthropological searches. Each volume attempts to be factual, with as little interpretation as possible, and each volume follows the common format to supply current information on population, government, and the economy. For the Middle East, see the following guides by Richard F. Nyrop: *Area handbook for the Yemens* (1977 [266p.]) **(P97);** *Area handbook for the Republic of Turkey* (1973 [415p.]) **(P98);** *Area handbook for Syria* (1971 [357p.]) **(P99);** *Area handbook for Saudi Arabia,* 3d ed. (1977 [389p.]) **(P100);** *Area handbook for the Persian Gulf states* (1977 [488p.]) **(P101);** *Area handbook for Morocco* (1972 [403p.]) **(P102);** *Area handbook for Libya,* 2d ed. (1973 [317p.]) **(P103);** *Area handbook for the Hashemite Kingdom of Jordan,* 2d ed. (1974 [280p.]) **(P104);** *Area handbook for Egypt,* 3d ed. (1976 [454p.]) **(P105);** *Area handbook for Algeria,* 2d revision (1972 [401p.]) **(P106).** See also Howard C. Reese's *Area handbook for the Republic of Tunisia* (1970 [415p.]) **(P107);** Harvey Henry Smith's *Area handbook for Lebanon* (1974 [354p.]) **(P108);** Smith's *Area handbook for Israel* (1979 [456p.]) **(P109);** his *Area handbook for Iraq* (1971 [413p.]) **(P110);** and the Stanford Research Institute's (SRI) *Area handbook for the peripheral states of the Arabian peninsula* (1971 [201p.]) **(P111).** Collectively this list provides coverage of the Middle East, but the coverage of the series is nearly worldwide in range. For additional sources or more general but anthropologically informed information, consult the *Asian Historical Dictionaries,* v.1– , 1989– (Metuchen, N.J.: Scarecrow) **(P112).**

P113

Bacharach, Jere L. *A Middle East studies handbook.* Seattle: Univ. of Washington Pr., 1984. 160p.

Historical in perspective. Covers medieval times to the present. The glossary, gazetteer, and indexes are useful features. A second printing with corrections, 1986.

P114

Briggs, R. D. *The Assyrian dictionary of the Oriental Institute of the University of Chicago (CAD).* Chicago: University of Chicago, 1956– .

Of a proposed set of twenty-one volumes, nineteen have been completed. To access the vast coverage of this resource, a user can review the Oriental Institute's *Publications of the Oriental Institute, 1906–1991* (Chicago: Oriental Institute of the University of Chicago, 1992 [126p.]) (Oriental Institute Communications, no.26) **(P115),** for a detailed description of these volumes for the individual titles in the twelve series they publish and for related volumes that are published outside the series. For a scholarly compendium written in a style that any educated reader can follow, consult Seton Lloyd's *The archaeology of Mesopotamia, from the Old Stone Age to the Persian conquest* (London: Thames and Hudson, 1984 [251p.]) **(P116),** which is organized into ten chapters, the last being "Babylon: The last Mesopotamian monarchy." Notes on text, pages 232–37. Bibliography, p.238–43. Index, p.245–52.

P117

Ebling, Erich, and Bruno Meissner. *Reallexikon der assyriologie und vorderasiatischen archäeologie.* Berlin: de Gruyter, 1928– . v.1– .

Working in the enormously specialized vocabulary developed by scholars of this tradition, the editors have completed volumes 1–4 and 6. Intended to be encyclopedic for Assyriology and the archaeology of the Near East. Much of the contemporary work in the broader area of the Near East is carried in the journal *Syro-Mesopotamian studies,* v.1– , 1977– (Malibu, Calif.: Undena Publications) **(P118),** an annual serving as a forum for archaeological, linguistic, and historical analysis of Iran and Syria from prehistory to the first millennium B.C.; and *Levant,* v.1– , 1950– (London: British School of Archaeology in Jerusalem) **(P119),** a quarterly that includes document analysis, faunal evidence, art, and ritual.

P120

Sweet, Louise E., ed. *The central Middle East: A handbook of anthropology and published research on the Nile valley, the Arab levant, southern Mesopotamia, the Arabian peninsula, and Israel.* New Haven, Conn.: HRAF Pr., 1971. 323p.

Originally published in 1968 as an HRAFlex book. Now available in durable copy. Especially valuable for its inclusion of Israel. Each of the five chapters provides a survey of a region, including religion and culture, with a lengthy, critical annotated bibliography. Dated but still a valuable first source.

P121

Trigger, Bruce G. *Ancient Egypt: A social history.* Cambridge, England, and New York: Cambridge Univ. Pr., 1983. 450p.

Verso of the title page indicated that "Chapters 1, 2, and 3 . . . were previously published in *The Cambridge history of Africa, vol. 1.*" Includes index for volume. Expanded range of this work reflects an effort to include ethnographic inferences in the tradition of the new archaeology. Bibliography: p.365–427.

State-of-the-Art Reviews

P122

Middle East Studies Association of North America. *Middle East Studies Association bulletin.* v.1– , 1967– . New York: New York University for the Middle East Studies Association of North America. Biennial.

State-of-the-art reviews for subject disciplines. Each issue lists doctoral dissertations completed. Publishes submitted bibliographic reviews of the anthropological literature such as the 1971 contribution of Richard T. Antoun, "Three approaches to the cultural anthropology of the Middle East" 5:24–53 **(P123),** which develops a syllabus and a 336-item bibliography, and John Gulick's "The anthropology of the Middle East" 3 (1069): 1–14 **(P124),** which provides a bibliographic review of early reports, child rearing, community studies, and social organization. Of more general value is its recent description of research libraries in the United States and Canada, "Directory of library collections on the Middle East" 17 (1974): 22–48 **(P125).** Since the catalogs of so many Arabic collections have not been published, the student may need to plan visits to several libraries. A more recent effort to provide directory information for the members of this organization can be found in J. L. Bacharach's "Scholarly organizations concerned with Middle East topics" 24 (1990): 29–35 **(P126).**

TITLE INDEX

Note: Initial articles such as *a, the, an, les,* and *la* have been dropped from the titles in this index. In several instances the same work appears under different strategic headings requiring different annotations. In these cases, the bibliographic entry is fully described twice and the index instructs the reader to look in two places to achieve a full understanding of the value of the work.

AUTHOR AND ABBREVIATED TITLE INDEX